CW00923979

Romantic Moods

Romantic Moods

Paranoia, Trauma, and Melancholy, 1790–1840

Thomas Pfau

The Johns Hopkins University Press
Baltimore

Printed in the United States of America on acid-free paper
9 8 7 6 5 4 3 2 1

The Johns Hopkins University Press
2715 North Charles Street
Baltimore, Maryland 21218-4363
www.press.jhu.edu

Library of Congress Cataloging-in-Publication Data
Pfau, Thomas, 1960–
Romantic moods: paranoia, trauma, and melancholy, 1790–1840 / Thomas Pfau.
p. cm.
Includes bibliographical references and index.
ISBN 0-8018-8197-8 (alk. paper)
1. English literature—19th century—History and criticism. 2. Romanticism—Great Britain. 3. German literature—19th century—History and criticism. 4. Literature, Comparative—English and German. 5. Literature, Comparative—German and English. 6. Psychic trauma in literature. 7. Melancholy in literature. 8. Paranoia in literature. 9. Emotions in literature. 10. Romanticism—Germany. 1. Title.
PR457 .P48 2005
820.9′145—dc22 2004028273

A catalog record for this book is available from the British Library.

List of Figures

Introduction

> This deep commotion
> And turmoil in me, I would speak
> Its name, find words for this emotion—
> Through the whole world my soul and senses seek
> The loftiest words for it: this flame
> That burns in me, it must have a name!
> And so I say: eternal, endless, endless—why,
> You devil, do you call all that a lie?
>
> — GOETHE, *Faust,* PART I, TRANS. DAVID LUKE

> Every art form is defined by the metaphysical dissonance of life which it accepts and organizes as the basis of a totality complete in itself; the mood of the resulting world, and the atmosphere in which the persons and events thus created have their being, are determined by the danger which arises from this incompletely resolved dissonance and which therefore threatens the form.
>
> — GEORG LUKÁCS, *Theory of the Novel*

Let me begin by providing a first rationale for the tripartite structure of this book, whose interconnected chapters on paranoia, trauma, and melancholy aim to map a psychohistorical narrative of European romanticism in three successive stages. The objective is—through patient consideration of the period's formal-aesthetic, epistemological, and discursive profile—to trace the evolution of romantic interiority, a concept "always-already" embedded in collective histories and often faltering or untrustworthy languages seeking to articulate the import of these histories. Seen against the backdrop of legal, political, feudal, and early capitalist structures pressured to the point of disintegration, first by the divisive impact of the French Revolution, next by seemingly interminable postrevolutionary warfare, and finally by a post-Napoleonic European Restoration that appeared to defy all progressive conceptions of historical time, romanticism's models of subjectivity exhibit a persistent dialectic between vaunted claims for spiritual renewal, political justice, and cultural innovation, on the one hand, and a continual sense of affective and epistemological bewilderment, on the other. Responding to a persistent and emotionally charged sense that concepts of intentionality, causation, memory, rhetorical, moral, and aesthetic purity have become acutely unreliable, even void, English and German writers of the period thus shift toward experimentation with "virtual" (aesthetic) solutions to experiences often "felt" to be wholly intractable. If what Jacques Lacan calls "the Real" was being experienced, materially and affectively, as both volatile and inscrutable, romanticism's quest for solutions in the mediated, imaginary sphere of aesthetic productivity also reflects the period's conclusion that the languages by which the Augustans and the Enlightenment had sought to make uneven sense of their experiential worlds were no longer reliable or even trustworthy. For the most part, the romantics' attempts to trace political, economic, and spiritual history back to its manifestation as emotional experience can only be unfolded in the chapters that follow. Yet before doing so, it is necessary to adumbrate a number of basic, interconnected propositions from which this study proceeds. In unfolding them at the beginning, I do not mean to deny that each remains eminently debatable and in need of much fine-tuning, most of which is to take place in the individual sections of this book. Still, some preliminary remarks on the key concept of mood are in order, specifically as that concept relates dialectically to aesthetic form, which in turn is viewed as part of broader, evolving patterns of discourse in which history becomes prima facie legible.

The status of emotions, long understood to have played a foundational role for the aesthetic and poetic theories of romantics like Kant, Schiller, Novalis, Hölderlin, Wordsworth, Coleridge, William Godwin, Mary Hays, and Joanna Baillie, among many others, has recently made a strong reappearance in literary theory. Following Cathy Caruth's more specialized, though highly influential, study of how literary and psychoanalytic representation intersect in traumatic experiences, several recent studies, employing often diverse methodologies and reaching quite disparate conclusions, have explored the broad spectrum of emotions, feeling, affect, passion, and other Proustian "upheavals of thought." Aside from Martha Nussbaum's eponymous study, work by Adela Pinch, William Reddy, Philip Fisher, Paul Redding, Julie Ellison, and Rei Terada stands out. Notwithstanding their often dissimilar approaches, these projects all posit emotion as a kind of quasi-knowledge rather than as the (unreflexive) other of cognition. Instead of viewing emotion as psychological miscellany or a mere dress rehearsal for the eventual, and supposedly more desirable, acuity of conceptual, analytic thought, the emotions are credited with establishing a holistic, tacitly evaluative relation to the world. Such a view, as Adela Pinch has argued, gained noticeable momentum around the middle of the eighteenth century, particularly in the work of Hume and Smith. With its frequent reference to "contagious" feelings and "correspondent movements in every human creature" (Hume, 576), Hume's *Treatise of Human Nature* (1740) uncovered a paradoxical situation where "individuals . . . can rely on the authenticity of their own emotional responsiveness" even as "feelings are trans-subjective entities that pass between persons" and hence "are always really someone else's."[1]

Without mentioning Hume by name, Jean-Luc Nancy likewise remarks on how " 'the unleashing of passions' is not the free doing of a subjectivity" but, instead, "is of the order of what Bataille himself often designated as 'contagion,' another name for communication." Yet what is communicated—a point of critical importance to Kant, as we shall see—is, according to Nancy "the *passion* of singularity as such. The singular being, because it is singular, is in the passion . . . of sharing its singularity. The presence of the other does not constitute a boundary that would limit the unleashing of 'my' passions: on the contrary, only exposition to the other unleashes my passions. Whereas the individual can know another individual, juxtaposed to him both as identical to him and as a thing . . . the singular being does not know, but rather experiences his *like* [*son* semblable] . . . This is the passion. Singularity is the passion of being" (Nancy, 32–33). "Community" thus involves the individual's coming up against the feeling of his or her own "originary or ontological sociality" (ibid., 28). While community can never be claimed as a definitive fact or product, it is "an infinite task at the heart of finitude" (ibid., 35). It is the pathos or passion that unfolds in every address to another, every attempt at instantiating community as the communication between two finite, distinct, yet interimplicated individuals. As such, Nancy remarks, finitude "is nothing. It is neither a ground, nor an essence, nor a substance. But it appears, it presents itself, it exposes itself, and thus it *exists* as communication. . . . Finite being always presents itself 'together,' hence severally; for finitude always presents itself in being-in-common and as this being itself" (ibid., 28). Revealing a very similar insight into the vicarious sociability of the individual's passions Adam Smith's *Theory of Moral Sentiments* (1759) introduced "sympathy" as the master trope through which every discrete feeling and passion must be filtered so as to evaluate its utility and propriety. As an obliquely juridical faculty charged with evaluating "the pitch [of a given passion] which the spectator can go along with," sympathy operates primarily as a discursive, often narrowly lexical, principle; overcoming bodily cravings is "*properly called* temperance," and a lover downplaying his private passions "with raillery and ridicule" has justly hit upon "the only style in which we are disposed to talk of [love]" (Adam Smith 1984, 27, 28, 32; emphasis added).

Despite its constant stress on the ductility of "sympathy" as a kind of metalingual regulatory agency for the passions, Adam Smith's melioristic account in the *Theory of Moral Sentiments* ultimately could not overcome what had so bewildered Hume; namely, that something as ostensibly private and inward as a feeling should be imbued with so much social energy. Mobilizing the concept of "sympathy" so as to achieve a kind of homeostasis between self and other ultimately led to the incessant labor of fortifying the language of benevolence against the specter of an Enlightenment subjectivity whose underlying emotive strata no longer bear any no stable and readily discernible relation to reason. John Mullan's *Sentiment and Sociability* (1988) makes the representative point when approaching Richardson, Sterne, and Hume as "writers committed to the resources of a language of feeling for the purpose of representing necessary social bonds; all discover in their writings a sociability which is dependent upon the communication of passions and sentiments. . . . For all three, sociability depends upon the traffic not only of opinions, but of harmoniously organized feelings" (Mullan, 2, 7). For Mullan, it is no coincidence that the choreography of emotion should have primarily devolved upon "literature" in the emergent modern sense of "imaginative writing" and thus shifted away from the discipline of epistemology and its default genre, the treatise. For "philosophy cannot finally generalize a natural sociability when in doing so it removes itself from society—when it can find no embracing society of readers to address" (ibid., 13). The increasingly speculative turn of romantic philosophy, particularly in Germany, would appear to bear out Mullan's hypothesis of a disciplinary dead end. Yet beginning with the Jena romantics, the apparent failure of pre-Kantian epistemology to articulate the essential social force of preconceptual emotive strata (variously and in partially overlapping ways identified as passion, sensibility, sentiment, or feeling) was dialectically reformulated as a unique and enabling point of departure for a sweeping aesthetic program. Prior to Kant's transcendental conception of aesthetic "feeling" (*Gefühl*) and its subsequent, radical reappraisal by the Jena romantics, theorizing about the emotions' apparent lack of rational, discursive accountability used empirical expedients that are basically lexical. This Augustan strategy of containment, recently revived in Philip Fisher's *The Vehement Passions*, is repeatedly resorted to in Smith's *Theory of Moral Sentiments* and in his subsequent *Lectures on Rhetoric and Belles Lettres* (1762–63). Thus feelings would be assigned "proper" lexical names that putatively signified their content and also classified these emotional phenomena (e.g., feelings, affections, passions, sentiments, anxiety, anger, mourning) depending on their perceived volatility or durability. In current philosophical parlance, emotions were being classified based on whether they were being experienced (in curiously unexamined, a priori fashion) as ephemeral "states" or settled "dispositions."[2]

What in Hume had surfaced as a threat to the possibility of reason would by the time of Edmund Burke's *Reflections on the Revolution in France* (1790) be indicted as Jacobinism's' "riotous farce" of political, socioeconomic, moral, and sexual enthusiasms, feelings so entirely self-authorizing and irresistibly communicative as to be widely embraced as "truth." Samuel Johnson's decision to exclude the "fugitive cant" of the rapidly expanding class of upwardly mobile professional and entrepreneurial Britons from his 1755 *Dictionary* already hinted that the fluctuating psychology and moral constitution of these new "middling" classes was being perceived as intimately entwined with shifts in the fabric of language. By the latter half of the century, psychological and, by extension, class-specific developments appeared prima facie legible *in* and *as* language. Hence, it seemed only logical that efforts to contain the middle class's volatile sociopolitical energy should take the form of instituting a durable lexical nomenclature for those self-authorizing and self-interested passions that had propelled it into economic and cultural prominence. While already perceived as subtending all social relations and as determining (however obliquely) the ostensibly private, self-conscious individual's mode of being, emotion came to be treated in a topical, lexical, and objectively indexical language. The kind of policing of semantic nuance in polite speech, poetry, and rhetorical theory as we see it unfold in writings by George Campbell, William Enfield, John Newbery, Adam Smith, or Hugh Blair appears an increasingly desperate attempt to remedy the inherent ambivalence and waywardness of emotions—a predicament that in Hume's text already takes on the hue of an ineluctable, as it were, "transcendental," condition. Fisher's *The Vehement Passions* thus deals with "the occasioned, dramatic, experiential moments of the passions, not with . . . underlying dispositional or inclinational facts." For Fisher, it is this conspicuousness and vehemence that identifies the passions as a "template for inner life" and as the "internal material of the self." Once routed through literature as their privileged, indeed their only, medium of reflection—offering "moments of experience, rather than summary, generalization, or long perspectives of time"—the passions as they emerge from Fisher's study also appear immune against all historical contingency. "Fear, anger, grief, and shame have been the states least shaped by the waves of culture and the passage of time." Seen as "among the least culturally constructed materials we have . . . their stability argues for a certain core of what Hume called, in the title of his book, human nature" (Fisher, 14–15, 21, 22–23).

However edifying, Fisher's attempt to recover "human nature" in the shape of timeless passions in the postmodern age seems rather unconcerned with the nervous, often fitful vigilance with which the Scottish rhetoricians and economic theorists of the later eighteenth century sought to police the passions by empirical, specifically rhetorical means. Hume's *Treatise* and Smith's *Theory of Moral Sentiments* already acknowledge the social and historical determinacy of the passions, that "men in the different professions and states of life" will invariably be in the grip of "very different passions." In the face of emotion as differentiated according to socioeconomic criteria that are themselves in constant flux, any empirical theory of manners and conduct can ultimately only marshal the rhetoric of melioration and open-ended self-regulation. Hence, "as in all species of things, we are particularly pleased with the middle conformation" (Adam Smith 1984, 201). At the same time, Smith's recognition of passion as subject to socioeconomic—and that means, historically fluctuating—determinants actually holds a promising methodological implication. For it hints that history manifests itself as a fundamental psychological climate, which in turn has been encrypted in a distinctive *structure of discourse* rather than being openly divulged in local, contingent, and variously stylized expressive acts. As Julie Ellison puts it, "sensibility is a transaction, not a character type" (98). In finding its proper focus in the study of *langue* rather than *parole,* the conception of emotion as "mood"—and, in a mediate sense, the study of romanticism as a distinctive historical period—moves away from construing emotion as passion, that is, as a conspicuous type of expression whose degree of sincerity or performativity remains, in any event, unverifiable.[3] In what follows, my aim is to distinguish and trace a distinctive "mood" as it subtends larger patterns of rhetorical behavior, both in imaginative and discursive writing. Approaching emotion via the concept of "mood"—an approach that Chapter 1 seeks to justify on both historical and theoretical grounds—is a more rewarding (and also more cautious) strategy for identifying romanticism as a distinctive historical epoch with its own differentiated formal organization.

Once lifted out of the topical or lexical taxonomies by means of which Scottish Enlightenment philosophers and rhetoricians had so anxiously sought to contain it, emotion begins to reveal itself as a holistic and historically distinctive component in the unfolding story of modernity.[4] When approached as a latent principle bestowing enigmatic coherence on all social and discursive practice at a given moment, "mood" opens up a new type of historical understanding: no longer referential, thematic, or accumulatively contextual. Rather, in its rhetorical and formal-aesthetic sedimentation, mood speaks—if only circumstantially—to the deep-structural situatedness of individuals within history as something never actually intelligible to them in fully coherent, timely, and definitive form. However "contemptible," it is "details" that "make part of a history . . . [and] the turn of most lives is hardly to be accounted for without them. They are continually entering with cumulative force into a mood until it gets the mass and momentum of a theory or a motive," George Eliot observed in 1876 (228). Arguably, a decisive methodological step toward such a conception of mood (to whose influential Heideggerian articulation we shall shortly turn) arises at the very threshold of romanticism in the form of Kant's transcendental reformulation of the problem of representation. In uncharacteristically succinct and colloquial terms, Kant's brief essay entitled "What Does It Mean to Orient Oneself in Thinking?" restates what his first *Critique* had unfolded in more rigorous, if enigmatic form as the "transcendental synthesis of apperception." The self-awareness of thought *as thought* rests on the logical premise of an inherently alien stratum of "feeling," Kant asserts. What is more, in finding its tenuous "ground" in some oblique affective substratum that is not (at least not *yet*) thought, conscious representation "feels" driven to slay its own shadowy progenitor. It aims to overcome an ontological and seemingly unshakeable feeling of disorientation that appears to linger as the very *causa materialis* and *causa finalis* of thought itself, an opacity in response to which thought springs into existence and from which it derives its mission. At first glance, though, Kant's epistemological sketch does not spotlight such Oedipal slings and arrows; in fact, his account appears at first quite orderly and comforting:

> Properly speaking, to *orient* oneself means to use a given direction (our horizon being divided into four of them) in order to find the others—literally, to find the *sunrise.* When I perceive the sun in the sky and so know it to be midday, I am able to determine south, west, north, and east. Yet to do so I also need a *feeling of a difference* in my own subject, namely, the difference between my right and left hands. I call this a *feeling* because intuitively these two sides do not differ from one another. . . . Now I can extend this geographical concept of the procedure of orienting myself, and understand it by orienting myself in any given space in general, which is to say, by orienting oneself in strictly mathematical form. I may orient myself in a dark room familiar to me if I take hold of even one single object whose position I remember. Clearly, in this process I am aided by nothing except the faculty for determining position according to a *subjective* ground of differentiation: for I do not see any of the objects whose place I am to find; and if, as a practical joke, some other person were to have rearranged all the objects in that room, such that what was previously on the right now was on the left, I would be altogether at a loss to find anything in a room whose outer walls were otherwise wholly identical.[5]

This preternatural, strictly "subjective" "feeling" of difference per se—that is, the subject's witnessing the operation of difference prima facie as an emotive value suddenly apparent, rather than as logical tool purposely sought out—constitutes for Kant the (fundamentally irrational) linchpin of all rational thought. Oddly enough, the transformation of a mere "feeling" of difference into a logical principle is possible only if the world that is to be "known" remains constant. Perhaps Kant's image of good domestic order, of rooms whose furniture remains predictably inert, required no more than the good offices of a competent maid.[6] More seriously, though, Kant's example appears to gravitate toward the unpalatable choice between a wholly chaotic and a wholly predictable world, with either scenario bound to give rise to a profound feeling of disorientation. For chaos would lead to disorientation for a subject engulfed by differences that could never be conceptualized and directed toward definite purposes. The obverse scenario, particularly relevant to my exploration of melancholy in late romantic writing, would regard all purposes and objectives to be always already fixed in advance, such that a subject's capacity for "feeling" difference would soon atrophy for sheer lack of application within a claustrophobic, overdetermined reality. Precisely because thought appears so eager to get on with its local, discursive business as "representation" (*Vorstellung*), its emotive substratum—that enigmatic Kantian "feeling of difference"—never actually reaches or crosses the threshold of conscious awareness. The predicament of "feeling" as a structural mood subtending the business of representation is to be not only operative but also forgotten a priori. This implication of Kant's transcendental notion of "mood" (*Stimmung*) is substantially extended by Heidegger, who remarks that—unlike this or that particular thing or feeling as it happens to be at hand—*Dasein* necessarily implies a capacity for obliviousness, for "not being there" (*Wegseinkönnen* [1983, 95 / English: 1995, 61]).

At the same time, Heidegger views Kant's transcendental method as offering an insufficient account of what he calls *Dasein*, that is, the ontological nexus of purposes and identifications (*Zeugzusammenhang*) already in play for all quotidian practice and theoretical reflection.[7] Thus in the above passage from Kant, the "feeling" of a difference turned out to be already premised on "remembering" a particular piece of furniture as the Archimedian point of reference. Kant thus does not fully acknowledge the way in which his own transcendental method presupposes "world" as something already "given," an anterior and holistic "disposition" (*Befindlichkeit*) of which the Kantian "feeling of difference" is only a specific manifestation. World, for Heidegger, constitutes that into which transcendental apperception itself has always already been "thrust." What Heidegger means by such "having-been-thrust" (*Geworfenheit dieses Seienden in sein Da* [1979, 135]) thus amounts to a dispositional relation to the world logically prior to any sustained cognitive engagement or incidental affective experience.

Building on Kant's transcendental reflection, in which "feeling" is explicitly contrasted with occasional and empirically locatable sensations, sentiments, or passions (*Empfindung, Leidenschaft*), Heidegger's conception of "mood" (which I shall retain over McNeill and Walker's recent translation of *Stimmung* as "attunement") thus names "not a particular being [but] . . . a fundamental manner, the *fundamental way in which Dasein is as Dasein.*" It is "that which gives Dasein *subsistence and possibility* in its very foundations." While occasional emotions or sentiments will by their very nature expire, their eventual absence, Heidegger cautions, must not be construed to mean that during such intervals we are ever "out of attunement." Hence, "*Dasein* as *Dasein* is always already attuned in its very grounds. There is only ever a change of attunement," and provisionally speaking "moods are the 'presupposition' for, and 'medium' of thinking and acting" (1995, 67–68). It is readily apparent, then, that "mood" in Heidegger operates at an level analogical to (though not identical with) Kant's "transcendental conditions of possibility." It is the horizon wherein all conscious practice—including the whole spectrum from hyperrational pursuits to vehement passions—is being transacted, a horizon that therefore can never come into view as such. As the presupposition for maintaining *any* cognitive or, for that matter, emotive relationship to the world whatsoever, "mood" is ontologically anterior to the realm of what may be logically verified and discursively represented as knowledge. It is in the nature of "mood" not to be reflexively aware but, as the substratum of conscious awareness and representation, to resist discernment, particularly where attempts are made to positively, consciously fix it in representational form. Form, then, functions like the symptom in post-Freudian psychoanalysis by simultaneously indexing and concealing a pervasive disequilibrium that simultaneously organizes and vexes historical communities. As Lukács puts it, "the creation of forms is the most profound confirmation of the existence of a dissonance."[8]

It is this inaccessibility of Heidegger's "mood" to conventional forms of demonstration that accounts for why philosophical inquiry must submit to a fundamental methodological reorientation. Heidegger responds to that exigency with the figural language of "awakening" (*Wecken*) a "mood" rather than positively knowing it. "What," he asks, "does it mean to awaken a mood," and "how are we to relate toward man himself if we wish to awaken a mood" (1995, 63; trans. modified)?

> Moods [*Stimmung*] are something that cannot be straightforwardly ascertained in a universally valid way, like a fact that we could lead everyone to see. Not only can mood not be ascertained, it ought not to be ascertained, even if it were possible to do so. For all ascertaining means bringing to consciousness. With respect to mood, all making conscious means destroying, altering in each case, whereas in awakening a mood we are concerned to let this mood be as it is, as this mood. Awakening means letting a mood be, one that, prior to this, has evidently been sleeping, if we may employ this image.[9]

Heidegger's Blakean metaphoric play on sleep and rousing, his delicate balancing act of awakening *Dasein* to its own ontological situatedness without fixing the latter in outright positivistic terms is crucial for several reasons. First and foremost, Heidegger's shift toward an overtly metaphoric register hints that, methodologically speaking, the desired awakening can only ever be realized in the figural, virtual domain of the aesthetic. Secondly, Heidegger's account effectively claims that, far from being the deficient other of conscious awareness, sleep constitutes an integral part of *Dasein.* For the trope of sleep also tells us how *Dasein* has always already been thrust into a historical moment and consequently can never arrive at a positive and verifiable representation of its disposition (*Befindlichkeit*); or, as Alfonso Lingis summarizes the case: "All mood is bewilderment" (152). In its very mode of historical being, *Dasein* thus continually enacts the essential obliquity of the Kantian sublime. Finally, any awakening of *Dasein* to its latent disposition as such requires that we understand mood not as an occasional or even transcendental feeling but, rather, as the horizon encompassing both, the "being-there" and apparent "not-being-there" of quotidian no less than philosophical consciousness. "It is fundamentally misleading," Heidegger notes, "to say that a mood is there, for in such a case we take mood as something like one existing property that appears amongst others" (1995, 65 / 1983, 97–98; translation modified).

As a methodological challenge, Heidegger's "awakening" will be of concern throughout this study. At the same time, I argue that romanticism itself confronted the task of awakening to its own historicity during the massive upheavals brought about by Napoleon's drastic transformation of Europe's political, legal, and economic landscape between 1800 and 1815. As my middle chapters argue, it is a central purpose of romantic lyricism to facilitate the transition of romantic communities to the drastically altered world into which they had so abruptly been thrust as a result of these changes. With its simultaneous searching, if cryptic, tropes, lyric form in particular aims to awaken romantic subjectivity *from* its dormant state and *to* its perilous historical situatedness, all the while sheltering (at least partially) the subject of such awakening from the traumatic impact of the knowledge so produced in the cocoon of aesthetic form.

What more recent studies, in particular Rei Terada's lucid account in *Feeling in Theory* and also, if less consistently, Martha Nussbaum's *Upheavals of Thought* share with Heidegger's analysis of "mood" as a deep-structural "disposition" (*Befindlichkeit*) is the view that, by virtue of its nonintentional character, mood opens up a deeper understanding of *Dasein* as irreducibly historical. If, as even Philip Fisher's very differently oriented study notes, the eighteenth century saw a gradual "shift from a vocabulary of passions to one of feelings, emotions, or moods" (Fisher, 6), I hope to show that this transformation comes into its own in the theoretical and literary writings of European romanticism. Hence, throughout this study, my use of "emotion" departs from the Kantian notion of "feeling" (*Gefühl*) as it is explored in Chapter 1. In addition, my discussion there also traces how, because of what Kant had shown to be the essentially nonpropositional status of feeling—itself the condition of representation (*Vorstellung*) "in general"— his successors, particularly Johann Gottlieb Fichte (1762–1814), Novalis (the nom de plume of Friedrich von Hardenberg [1772–1801]), and Friedrich Hölderlin (1770–1843), progressively conceived "mood" as an aesthetic phenomenon, something that can be laid bare only in the modality of virtual, figural constructions. In departing from Heidegger's conception of "mood" (*Stimmung* or *Grundstimmung*), my focus on a dispositional rather than situational understanding of "emotion" in no way means to deny that romanticism, like earlier elective or repressive regimes, also and regularly sought to curtail the more vehement passions. Other more empirical kinds of inquiry, such as exploring "how and when it became productive to know feelings as difficult and wayward" (Pinch, 15), remain without doubt just as valuable and necessary. Yet inasmuch as the latter type of investigation posits feeling as holding discrete empirical contents that it deems susceptible of objective reconstruction, it is not the kind of inquiry that this study means to undertake. Rather, I hope to explore the broader implications for European romanticism of the conception of feeling first articulated in Kant's transcendental writings. Instead of bemoaning, expressing alarm at, or hoping to remedy the emotions' alleged lack of conceptual distinctness and clarity (to recall Leibniz's criteria), post-Kantian philosophical and, above all, literary writing approaches feeling as mood, and hence as operating at a level logically anterior to the business of discrete reference, object-representation, and analytic, discrete knowledge.

Building on, though also departing from, Martha Nussbaum's recent study of the emotions, Chapter 1 argues that in feeling or emotion, (terms that both Nussbaum and the romantics tend to use interchangeably) individuals and, ultimately, communities establish a sustained, quasi-intentional and tacitly evaluative relation to their experiential world. Far from constituting psychological miscellany, mood establishes a quasi-cognitive relation to the world in the specific modality of *emotion,* that is, as an intrinsically evaluative experience. This does not disengage emotive experience from analytic behavior, especially since, as Kant was the first to argue, it is precisely in feeling that the underpinnings of "cognition in general" and its subsequent objectification and circulation as propositional language are to be found. The aesthetic overall, and literature and poetry more particularly, reconstitute the at once emotive and

For Sandra

. . . a sé mi fece atteso
con l'armonia che temperi

. . . you drew me
with the harmony you temper

— DANTE, *Divine Comedy, Paradiso* 1.77–78

Contents

evaluative foundation of the Kantian subject inasmuch as they are *not* geared toward discrete, analytical object-knowledge but instead draw attention to a holistic and evaluative a priori "mood" on which discrete intellectual acts and articulations inadvertently rest. The "voice" (*Stimme*) of such an ontological mood (*Stimmung*) takes the temperature of conscious historical existence; Heidegger calls it the "mood of thought." In qualifying emotion as "*quasi*-intentional" and "*quasi*-cognitive," I also imply that a comprehensively determined, holistic disposition vis-à-vis the world such as transpires *in* and *as* emotion will not be transparent to individuals or communities; it cannot be experienced in the same ways as ordinary propositional object knowledge. Approaching the matter from a slightly different angle, Julie Ellison also notes how "sensibility and a host of other conditions were *always* sophisticated, reflective, and complex." As "the *admitted* connection between speculation, mood, and power . . . sensibility is consciously bound up with the social management of sympathetic knowledge" (Ellison, 6–7). To be sure, a condition does not attain reflective awareness *as such;* or, as Novalis, perhaps romanticism's most analytical thinker on the subject of emotion, puts it so succinctly: "feeling cannot feel itself." Yet such an observation does not so much indict "feeling" as a condition of blindness as ascribe to it a holistic function that cannot be fulfilled—indeed, would be forestalled by—self-awareness. In other words, behind Novalis's gnomic statement there lurks the important insight that emotions are not "owned" by the solitary individual. Rather, in curious ways, they prove antecedent to and foundational for the constitution and self-awareness of the individual subject. The emotions' apparent lack of reflexivity thus does not so much constitute a shortcoming as point to their categorically different phenomenological status and, consequently, to a different role of emotions in the overall architecture of human affairs. Emotions in the foundational and abiding sense in which this entire study aims to explore them are not experienced "as such" but constitute a latent evaluative grid for all possible experience, as well as for all discursive and expressive behavior.

As Novalis and most of the romantics in Germany and England clearly understood, the project of bringing emotions into focus for a belated, "critical" intelligence requires that we trace them in the formal and structural operations of romantic writing. That such a method of reading should oddly resemble the conspiratorial, even paranoid, mode of social understanding on which the first two chapters of this book are focused amounts to a hermeneutic circularity, which I hope to address at various junctures of the book. For the time being, suffice it to say that romantic studies—both as developed in this book and in earlier, perhaps more orthodox, deconstructionist, materialist, and historicist forms over the past three decades—cannot contain its object of study within some autonomous methodological program. Rather, its aim ought to be to elucidate the contiguity of contemporary critical and theoretical models with European romanticism. Hence, if anything like a theory *of* romanticism is to emerge from what follows, it will be so in the double sense in which romanticism can become an object of knowledge only if, at every turn of the analysis, the intellectual and aesthetic heritage of the romantic era is recognized as both the driving motivation and the abiding conceptual framework shaping the critical results. As Hans-Georg Gadamer put it long ago, the challenge of understanding lies not in evading the hermeneutic circle but in determining how properly to enter into it.

It should thus come as no surprise that the first articulations of the ontological role of feeling can already be found in the theoretical writings of the early romantic era, in particular in texts of Rousseau, Godwin, Wordsworth, Kant, Novalis, and Hölderlin. Kant above all was the first, perhaps the only, writer to succeed in articulating a socially and aesthetically purposive role for the "specious good" (in Lionel Trilling's apt phrase) of "pleasure." I explore in some detail here what allows feeling to hold such a pivotal role in the aesthetic theories of Kant and early romantics such as Novalis, Hölderlin, and Wordsworth. For feeling, less in spite than because of its imperviousness to conceptual thinking is intrinsically oriented toward social life and communal values and purposes. Indeed, its holistic cognition mandates an equally holistic mode of articulation—"literature"—that presents these purposes in condensed or encrypted, rather than propositional, form. Kant locates the archetypal form of this feeling of pleasure in a simultaneously formal and evaluative act called "aesthetic-reflective judgment." To the extent that it acquires phenomenal distinctness as a feeling "voiced" *for others,* Kant's aesthetic judgment instantiates an imagined community. In the language of the *Critique of Judgment,* it "imputes assent" to the other. In extension of Adam Smith's *Theory of Moral Sentiments,* which explores "sympathy" as the master trope for the implicit connectivity of all subjective behavior, Kant's feeling of pleasure *qua* (aesthetic) judgment demarcates the individual's holistic and evaluative awareness of its socially embedded existence; hence Kant's claim that the "feeling of pleasure" at once instantiates and performatively reinforces a *sensus communis.* What motivates a voice to introduce a value, in the expressive modality of a judgment of taste, into public, discursive circulation is the premise of the fundamental connectedness of all individuals. It is a premise intrinsic to feeling itself, though also one to be continually reaffirmed with each new judgment of taste.

For Novalis and Hölderlin, the originally Kantian projection of feeling, not simply *into* the public arena but prima facie as that virtual, imaginary public sphere itself, mandates a new, radically constructivist aesthetic. Literature no longer functions as the incidental embodiment of normative moral or contingent and fleeting affective states. Rather, romanticism conceives of literature as a unique heuristic medium that allows individuals to objectify their "felt" connectedness by reconstituting and objectively preserving such holistic experience in the virtual reality of imaginative writing. Seen in this protomodernist perspective, the radical aesthetics of early romanticism also realize a quasi-evolutionist objective of self-prolongation, a core motive equally intrinsic to "feeling" and to civilization *tout court.* Faust's ardent plea at the moment of absorbed contemplation of his beloved's image—"Linger yet! Thou art so beautiful!" (Verweile doch! Du bist so schön)—echoes Rousseau's capturing of pleasure in autobiographical writing, one where the medium of the text reconstitutes pleasure to the extent that it succeeds in suspending the flow of empirical time. Rousseau's fifth *Reverie* meanwhile resonates in Kant's remarks about how we "linger" over the feeling of the beautiful and "seek to prolong it." Thus the mythically significant blips on the radar screen of the individual psyche—that is, a holistic and overdetermined social knowledge encrypted as a "feeling"—seek to acquire *durée* in the malleable and objective medium of aesthetic construction. The literary work forgets its "work character" (as labor and objective otherness) to the extent that it successfully reconstitutes pleasure in a formal simulacrum whose aesthetic experience is, in turn, to mirror and thus prolong that very pleasure.

As the readings of Kant and Novalis in Chapter 1 argue, early romanticism conceives of emotion as kind of intelligential longing. Indeed, for the writers in question, emotion constitutes the archetypal experience of intelligence *as* longing for an ultimately elusive closure. This conception of emotion as a searching for its own cause remains valid for the entire study and, I would argue, remains theoretically relevant to this day. Following through on the romantics' intuition that emotive complexions are best explored in virtual, imaginary constructions (poems, novels, etc.), this study traces its key romantic moods—paranoia, trauma, and melancholy—through their speculative embodiment *in* and *as* literary form. It is this malleable objectivity of literary form, freed from the pragmatism of quotidian thought (what Schleiermacher called "das geschäftliche Denken"), that allows its subjects—authors and readers alike—to close in on an understanding of what Heidegger was to analyze as the structure of *Dasein* ("being-in-the- world"). Philosophy has always found itself most forcefully drawn to the literary when struggling to justify its hypothesis of a "negative" universal, a motoric, precognitive, and hence inscrutable agency said to circumscribe all possible historical and material experience, whether thought of as a Kantian *Ding an sich,* Schopenhauer's *Wille,* Freud's unconscious, or Heidegger's *Dasein.* Beyond introducing and legitimating the romantic master tropes as a theoretical exigency, however, philosophy after Kant still had to account for them in phenomenological terms. In each case, the need to connect a transcendental or ontological postulate to a welter of empirical experience (now held to be untrustworthy because premised on ineluctable conditions) prompts the writers to introduce a concept closely related to what the present study designates as emotion. Thus Kant speaks of *Gefühl and* Heidegger of *Stimmung,* while Freud routinely focuses on an "affective charge" that, although not transparent to the speaking subject, ties the latter's representations in symptomatic form to what Freud's metapsychological writings (1911–15) designate as the universal "system Unconscious." In each case, the emotion's persistent, albeit prediscursive gravitational pull—its characteristically "symptomatic" mode of appearance—draws attention to the myriad ways in which individuals and communities are always embedded in antagonistic ideological and discursive networks that they can neither transcend nor comprehend in systematic form.

Throughout this study I argue that romantic literature is impelled by an agenda remarkably similar to that of the thinkers just named. Yet if romantic literature broaches fundamental ontological questions, it does so not in discursive or propositional form but, rather, in formal-aesthetic constructs whose very design aims to mediate an abiding "mood" or *Stimmung.* The role of the aesthetic thus becomes to trace how individuals and communities are at once embedded in and estranged from their experiential, historical reality. With its focus on "anxiety" (*Angst*) as the quintessential "mood" of *Dasein,* Heidegger's *Being and Time* largely recaptures what romanticism had already come upon in its own figural mode: namely, that the prevailing "mood" of anxiety constitutes the ontological echo of man as a strictly *historical* phenomenon, a "being-in-the-world" that knows of its utter lack of any transcendent point of reference or "ground." For that reason, whatever its generic filiations and thematic surface concerns, romantic literature's true *sujet* can never be reduced either to a mere aggregate of discrete historical information or a sum total of antagonistic aims, purposes, hopes, fears, or longings. Rather, it explores how experience in the aggregate molds the emotional fabric of its subject—namely, as a persistent and unsettling "feeling" of the irreducible tenuousness and volatility of being, a quality to be mirrored in lyric and narrative forms whose interpretive complexity proves just as palpable and irreducible.

From what has been said thus far, it follows that the concept most commonly associated with romanticism and with emotions, "expression," will not have a central role in this inquiry. While "expression" has certainly proven itself "the dominant trope of thought about emotion" (Terada, 11), the moods here proposed as a paradigmatic, loosely chronological sequence for British and German romanticism—paranoia (1789–1800), trauma (1800–1815), and melancholy (1815–1840)—yield little if approached through the expressive hypothesis. The reasons for that dilemma (if it is one) will be considered shortly; suffice it to say for the moment that in the cases of paranoia and melancholy, the mood in question, however essential to the constitution of its subjects, can only be inferred and traced through its vivid rhetorical effects. Neither state can be secured through its supposed expressive manifestations, for both the paranoid and the melancholy subject themselves appear to be consumed by the acquisition, manipulation, and citation-like display of expressive techniques and conventions. The exception, trauma, refuses assimilation to the expressive hypothesis for more or less obverse reasons; thus one of its constitutive features involves a nearly complete lack of affect, and whatever emotional charge may be seething beneath the faltering, quasi-catatonic locutions of its subject puzzles the reader-observer with its seeming lack of intensity and content. Yet even here inwardness seizes upon socially sanctioned models of expressive behavior, such as ballads and folk songs said to have been serendipitously reclaimed from the brink of extinction from memory. Their expressive pathos—now stylized as a literature offering itself as the ideal medium and repository for a nation's collective identity—is once again shaped by the very specter against which it defends romantic reading audiences in Britain and Germany alike: the traumatic shock of economic, political, and cultural modernity itself.

The first chapter establishes a theoretical framework for what might easily be objected to as an anachronistic Heideggerian and Freudian conceptual armature. In revisiting seminal texts by Kant, Novalis, and Hegel—punctuated by brief forays into Rousseau, Fichte, Wordsworth, and Hölderlin—I aim to trace the concept of "mood" (*Stimmung*) back to a contiguous nomenclature as it prevails in early romanticism and German idealism. The term "mood" is itself already in play, especially in Kant, yet it is framed by a number of related concepts—some decidedly bequests of Enlightenment thought ("feeling," "pleasure," and "sentiment"), others presaging nineteenth-century advances in psychology and evolutionary theory ("intuition," "drive," and "instinct"). Whichever of these terms happens to be developed by one of the above writers, it tends to be invested with a transcendental function. The purpose of organizing this opening, theoretical exploration of "mood" in romantic writing as a sequence of readings in Kant, Novalis, and Hegel, is to isolate and work through three theoretical problems within this key concept itself as they came to be addressed after 1790. First, there is the Kantian problem of how the dual structure of "pleasure" (in the beautiful and the sublime respectively) reflects back on his late-Enlightenment conception of rationality. "Feeling" (*Gefühl*) in Kant, not only guarantees the mutual "attunement" of the faculties and so facilitates "cognition in general"; it also attests to the subject's fundamental disposition to a constructive engagement with the world as a nexus of social and moral relations that needs to be continually fashioned anew. Next, in his brilliant critique of Fichte's early *Science of Knowledge,* Novalis demonstrates that any distinction between a primal "feeling" and a self-conscious agency to be deduced from it is theoretically indefensible and indemonstrable. Given the dramatic collapse of any systematic and rational nexus between "feeling" and self-awareness, Novalis is among the first to argue that the prereflexive identity of "feeling" or "mood" (*Gefühl, Stimmung*) demands, not objective and systematic "grounding," but aesthetic mediation. What is called for is not philosophy but art, not a logician's *ultima ratio* but a skillfully and ironically wrought supplemental order of symbols, themselves arranged as highly complex and continually evolving structures (e.g., Hölderlin's triadic hymns or the developmental novel [*Bildungsroman*]). This transmutation of an epistemological impasse into the very premise of aesthetic production finally brings us to the last question, one crystallized in Hegel's *Aesthetics* and obviously still pressing today. What is the aim of a critical engagement with art? Is the discernment of some complex (though historically quite specific) "mood" encrypted in artworks to result in a conceptual gain? Does Hegel's historical-systematic discussion of the "lyric," which will be our focal point, seek to contain and sublate the complex "mood" that had given rise to that particular genre? Or does the project of Hegel's *Aesthetics* recognize its own narrative and systematic argumentation to be dialectically conditioned, that is, to have become possible only *through* its engagement with the nonsystematic "mood" of the literary?

Chapters 2 and 3 take up the first of the three paradigms, paranoia, as the mood underlying and formally organizing political and literary writing in Britain during the 1790s. To employ the technical, even clinical, term "paranoia" again would appear to risk imposing an alien conceptual structure on the textual phenomena in question. The potential risks of such an approach are mitigated, however, by the fact that both for Freud and for the romantics, mood is fundamentally something dynamic, a process whose symptomatic character involves the dialectical, functional interaction of pathological *and* remedial features. Both Freud and the romantics, to whom, as he never tired stressing, he was greatly indebted, thus conceive of emotion as an intelligential operation obsessively concerned with ascertaining its own cause. To that end, emotion continually strives to embody itself in objective forms whose role is at once expressive *and* heuristic, burdensome *and* (potentially) recuperative. As I argue in Chapter 3, Freud's attempt at establishing a universally valid model for the "mechanism of paranoia" ultimately succumbs to the same predicament as bedeviled the crown's attorney general during his ill-fated 1794 attempt at securing convictions of members of the London Corresponding Society charged with the "imaginary" or "unconsummated" crime of high treason. Both for Freud and Attorney General John Scott, the analytical master narrative that aims to expose and so resolve conspiratorial anxiety effectively instantiates the very conspiracy against which it professes to defend the constitution by imputing it as a malicious intent to the defendants. Paranoia thus emerges as a constitutive feature of political, legal, sociological, and eventually psychoanalytic narrative: the form of narration and of analytic discovery is perilously cued by the logic of the symptom against which such a narrative seeks to defend its producers. In the end, the legal narrative of the crown, like that yielded by Freud's 1911 reading of Dr. Daniel Paul Schreber's autobiographical account of paranoia, *Memoirs of My Nervous Illness (1903)*, formally mirrors and reinforces the disorderly emotion against which it had been conceived as a defense mechanism.

The treason trials of 1794 highlight in particularly succinct form a pattern of retroactive, anxious cognition that can also be observed in a number of prominent texts of the early 1790s. Chapter 2 briefly explores some of those, such as Burke's *Reflections*, Paine's *Rights of Man*, Wollstonecraft's 1792 *Vindication*, Blake's early prophecies, and Kant's first *Critique*. The objective in these short forays is strictly limited to highlighting a shared argumentative structure that points back to an underlying, all-encompassing anxiety of the modern. The chapter then proceeds to a more thorough analysis of paranoid emotion as it crystallizes into a radical concept of retroactivity in Godwin's *Political Justice*. The result of that book's rigorous inquiry into the structure of consciousness and its elusive, indeed chaotic, a priori sources (impulses, emotions, anxieties, cryptic memories, etc.) renders anarchy less a political objective than the epistemological default. *Political Justice* thus confronts Godwin with an entropic psychosocial world from which the concept of causation has materially disappeared except as an all-consuming, retroactive fantasy about the hidden coherence of acts and outcomes. In response, Godwin's *Things as They Are, or, The Adventures of Caleb Williams* (1794) turns to the imaginary world of romance so as to explore political and communal relations whose subterranean operational logic, like the Kantian noumenon, seems tantalizingly inaccessible. Kant's "transcendental apperception" and Godwin's eponymous protagonist in *Caleb Williams* dramatize how early romantic history (1789–98) is experienced as an unrelenting condition of anxious hyperlucidity or paranoia. As encountered in theoretical and fictional narratives of the 1790s, social and political knowledge proves inextricably entwined with its emotional phenomenology—namely, as a feeling of lucid, all-encompassing vigilance or "agitation" (a key concept for Blake, as Steven Goldsmith has shown) whose axiomatic, nonfalsifiable principle could be formulated thus: *the experience of the real hinges on one's constant preparedness to distrust the reality of experience and to expose the latter as so many ideological frames conspiring against our genuine access to the real.*

The middle chapters (4 and 5) of this book, focused on trauma, explore what happens when those symbolic frames for defending against a subterranean and incipient catastrophic change (a.k.a. the sublime) are about to disintegrate. Beginning with the Napoleonic era, one of unremitting warfare and unprecedented political, legal, and cultural change compressed into twenty-two tumultuous years (1793–1815), the dilemma of early romanticism seems almost reversed. The challenge suddenly becomes, not how to change a recalcitrant ancien régime, but how to assimilate rapid and pervasive changes that confound the explanatory reach of available political, economic, and cultural languages. With Wordsworth and the German romantic Joseph von

Eichendorff serving as the principal and representative figures, the emotive and historical scenario of romanticism seems utterly changed from that of the 1790s. Characteristic of trauma is the nearly total absence of any affective or emotive disturbance, an interpretive conundrum that requires particularly attentive reading of catastrophic meanings typically lurking beneath the stoic, marked impersonality of balladic and pastoral writing. Not surprisingly, the era in question witnesses the temporary displacement of drama by the cryptic depth of lyric poetry. Chapters 4 and 5 explore how the seemingly stoic "composure" and "tranquility" of lyric or pastoral writing reveals itself as a phantasmagoria painstakingly elaborated so as to shelter its speakers from the impinging knowledge of their complicity in a historical world so entropic and volatile as to preclude its timely comprehension. In its very concision, made apparent by its fixation on seemingly autonomous images (e.g., the sheepfold in "Michael"), lyric writing of the period between 1800 and 1815 presents itself as the generic and rhetorical outgrowth of a traumatic, which is to say, comprehensive and overwhelming, disturbance of the subject. As I argue, at the heart of that disturbance lies the recognition that no one, however peripheral to the economic and geopolitical upheavals of the Napoleonic and early capitalist era, can escape being implicated in this inchoate and threatening welter of modernity.

As Proust, Freud, and Benjamin have pointed out, the epistemological form corresponding to trauma is that of an involuntary, yet also inescapable, sudden memory. Hence, just as the paranoid narratives examined in Chapters 2 and 3 appear equivocally poised between the symptomatically defensive and the inadvertently lucid, high romantic lyricism also precipitates its subject's awakening to the very modernity against which the lyric form itself was meant to furnish symbolic shelter. To clinch these larger implications, the second chapter in each of this book's three parts aims to expand our focus beyond the basic configuration between emotion, genre, and history to include the broader ideological effects that are an inadvertent result of lyric writing and reading. Here in particular it emerges how thinking about emotion in transindividual and structural-discursive (rather than thematic, topical) ways "is one of the best arguments that we have for cultural memory" (Fisher, 7). In the case of Joseph von Eichendorff, such effects include a significant advance in the conception of romantic allegory and, on the level of political discourse, the emergence of a new language (romantic conservatism) that turns out to presage postmodern theories of fantasy. Suffice it to say for now that romantic *Altkonservatismus*—

a fusion of classical Stoicism and post-Enlightenment theory—not only differs sharply from the politics of post-1819 *Reaktion* with which it is often confused; it also stands far apart from what conservatism denotes today, especially in the United States: rapacious economic practices pursued on a *global* scale by any means necessary, in callous indifference to human dignity and a sustainable environment alike, and sold, with scant rhetorical effort (usually ex post facto) as "our national interest" to a politically illiterate and apathetic electorate.

If the traumatic period 1798–1815 unfolds as the progressive awakening of romantic subjects and communities to a world whose economic, legal, and spiritual bearings had been decisively altered, indeed rendered almost unrecognizably alien and disconcerting, the period following the defeat of Napoleon and the Congress of Vienna presents a nearly obverse scenario. In approaching post-Napoleonic culture and writing in England and Germany under the umbrella concept of melancholy, however, I do not aim to align myself with already well-established historicist efforts at reconstructing the covert though insistent political thrust of the writings of Keats, Shelley, the Leigh Hunt circle, Cobbett, and other radicals, something exhaustively documented by Jeffrey Cox, James Chandler, Nicholas Roe, William Keach, Leonora Nattrass, and Ian McCalmain, among others. Rather than scanning romantic "literary" writing for political meanings that historicism is prepared to acknowledge only in propositional, "nonliterary" form, my concluding chapters locate the historical significance of late romantic lyric writing precisely in its vexed relation to the public value (or fetish) of "literariness." Unfolding in each case as a minority literature with startlingly modernist overtones of social, ethnic, and spiritual abjection, the writings of Keats and Heine throw into relief the perceived exhaustion of "literature" in its by then well established self-presentation as visionary, transcendent, and permanent.

As I first argue in my reading of Keats's early style, melancholy is not so much a thematic preoccupation in literature as homologous with the notion of literariness itself. So as to revive literature's intrinsic potential and salvage it from its impending fate as canonical heritage or tradition, both Keats and Heine strategically amalgamate literary genres and their basic rhetorical figures with overtly nonliterary and supposedly "impure" techniques of writing and speech. This takes the form of blurring the boundaries between lyric description and sentiment with the serial monotony of journalistic writing, or of importing dialect features and references—derived from Cockney and

German-Jewish culture, respectively—into the "literary work" so as to unmask its claims to autonomy and exemplarity as a class-specific fraud.

Beyond its ostensibly satiric effect, such a hybridization of literature also reveals a deeper and intrinsically melancholic insight, one already located by Renaissance humanism in the troubling enjambment of spirit and matter in print culture and book learning. Namely, melancholy bespeaks the deep-structural fatigue of a culture that has grown oppressively familiar with itself and hence begins to despair over the apparent inefficacy of its generic and rhetorical means. Born of an excess of knowledge and, it would seem, terminally mired in the lucid inertia of the saturnine individual, the late romantic writings of Keats and Heine thus reconstitute in objective, textual form the correspondingly abject mood of their historical audiences. In suspending high romantic sentiment, feeling, or emotion between genuine experience and mere literary citation, their writings not only raise fundamental questions about the expressive limits of canonical literary writing but, simultaneously, expose the atrophied inwardness of reading audiences who continued to subscribe unconditionally to the very concept of literariness as a "pure" and timeless value. This stylistic insurrection of literature against the formal characteristics and narrow ideological purposes of "literariness" also accounts for the uncommonly divisive reception with which Keats's and Heine's poetry met. As my opening discussion of Heine's early lyric oeuvre, his *Buch der Lieder* of 1827, seeks to establish via Nietzsche and Freud, a reading of late romantic lyricism must remain especially attentive to the persistent affiliation of melancholy and ressentiment. Such a correlation is borne out by the particularly volatile history of Keats's and Heine's receptions with their continuing (indeed, in Heine's case steadily intensifying) outbursts of class-based and anti-Semitic prejudice, respectively.

As I develop it in the closing chapters of this book, romantic melancholy is distinguished from the earlier paradigms of emotion (paranoia, trauma) by its apparent proximity to what Hegel calls self-consciousness. Because romantic melancholy seems an emotion born of a comprehensive awareness of its historical moment as massively overdetermined, our critical task should not be to redeem this mood by means of a belated hyperlucid method (historicism, deconstruction) but descriptively to capture the full scope of the emotive awareness that was romantic melancholy. As a result, the readings of Keats and Heine must recover a particularly expansive frame of theoretical and historical reference in which they knew their writings to be inescapably embedded or ensnared. In the case of Heine, this means reconstructing his remarkably supple and complex relationship to the normative conception of High German, as both a vernacular and a "literary" language. Responding to the subaltern roles that German and "Germanness" were being assigned in the cultural, legal, and ethno-political retrenchment of the post-Napoleonic Restoration, Heine's writings subject the idea of literature to linguistic and referential hybridization by injecting into it fragments of gossip, sexual innuendo, Yiddish expressions, and fragmentary tokens of high literary pathos that appear disconcertingly manufactured and staged. Given the fact that Heinrich Heine and, even more so, Joseph von Eichendorff are not as familiar as they might be to contemporary nineteenth-century literary and cultural studies—which, its interdisciplinary pretensions notwithstanding, remains overwhelmingly anglophone and monolingual—it will be appropriate to offer a somewhat richer historical picture. Still, in keeping with my central thesis—namely, that the (re-)construction of emotion as an aesthetic form, a "voice," is a more reliable mode of access to history than the garden-variety methods of associative or contextual rumination—my individual chapters postpone historical sketches, such as of romantic conservatism or German-Jewish cultural and linguistic relations in the early nineteenth century, until the formal-aesthetic drama and intellectual plot has been firmly established through focused literary interpretation.

It goes without saying that, notwithstanding its area-studies and interdisciplinary orientation (or perhaps because of it), this book does not purport to offer sequential and uninterrupted historical accounts of British and German romantic cultural and literary life. To be sure, historical facts, events, and practices—censorship, territorial changes, demographic and economic shifts, fledgling constitutional debates—are addressed at various turns in my argument, though only inasmuch as they accentuate a formal and hence ideological dynamic also apparent in the literature under discussion. This restriction should not be construed as a reactionary call on my part for identification with the transcendent gestures that can be found at various turns in the writings of some (though surely not all) of the authors under discussion. At the same time, it would be unwise to dismiss such transhistorical claims in Eichendorff or Wordsworth outright. The transcendent orientation of literature should not preemptively be collapsed back into a historical matrix against which—successfully or not—it had sought to establish itself; nor can it ever be understood without consideration of the historical antagonisms that prima facie motivated and shaped its articulate emergence *as* literature. Rather, in dissenting from the vexing determinacy of history as it reproduces itself in often rigid and irrational languages and beliefs, literature does not simply imagine some dreamworld but aims to recover a knowledge occluded by the specious, indeed irrational, fixity and coherence of so-called actual history.[10] From Kant, Godwin, Wordsworth, Schopenhauer, and Nietzsche to Freud and Lacan, the basic interpretive figure at issue here posits that all empirical experience and culture broadly speaking acquires its formal consistency and social significance at the expense of another (transcendental, unconscious) experience—the real, or "history"—that has necessarily been "missed." This study's exploration of paranoia, trauma and, to a certain extent, melancholy rests on the fundamental validity of that explanatory model. Inasmuch as, at its most genuine, all literature unfolds as an attempt to imagine and articulate values, it involves a strong counterfactual dissenting strain. For a value, properly so called, can come into focus only *ex negativo* and a posteriori, that is, as something belatedly found to have been occluded or repressed by the Lacanian symbolic broadly speaking—that is, by historical tradition, present necessity, accepted morality, or aesthetic decorum, and the like. Hence the language of literature tends to be oriented toward an as yet unknown, perhaps unpresentable "openness"—which, in an expression anterior to the distinction between literal and figurative speech, Hölderlin calls "das Offene."

Another desired implication of this project for the future of romantic studies has to do with its attempt to reclaim a broader European focus for a field thus far sadly unresponsive to a geographical and interdisciplinary widening of its critical lenses. At a time when university administrators frequently hijack the language of interdisciplinarity as a rationale for undermining the institutional autonomy of traditional departments and downsizing faculty and associated costs, it seems especially important to articulate the intellectual potential of broadly synthesizing forms of argumentation. All too long, the teaching and study of romanticism has been unduly constrained by its historically unjustifiable subspecialization as "British romantic studies," premised, as it happens, on a typically unexamined concept of nationhood and on equally dubious notions of canonical tradition and curricular order as its entailments. For romanticism no less than for modernism, national boundaries—like the monolithic idea of a "national literature" itself—ultimately always prove artificial and vexing—not a location, certainly not a home, but most typically a noble word for social, intellectual, and aesthetic constraints. The Cockney

John Keats, the German-Jewish Heinrich Heine, and the *altkonservativ* Catholic Joseph von Eichendorff all "felt" themselves to be political, cultural, and linguistic exiles, and Heine was also a geographic exile (one of the some 60,000 German expatriates in Paris in the Metternich era).

All these vectors converge and become legible in especially powerful ways in the melancholic texture of Keats's and Heine's writings, an anti-literature revelatory of an acutely dissociated linguistic, aesthetic, and political sensibility. There, melancholy and its conceptual next of kin, ressentiment, arise from a deeply felt alienation and aversion to the emergent hegemony of the nation—an imagined community of middle-class, professionally trained, gentile subjects justifying and reinforcing its specious coherence by worshipping the *imago* of a national literature. Rather than falling back on the questionable genre-based coherence of old-style "comparative literature" models, however, this study advocates that romantic studies henceforth attempt to trace the experience of history through its epistemological, discursive, and ideological effects across a broader spectrum of European culture. Such an "area-studies" model, to which romanticism as a field ought to look in the interest of its continued and broad relevance, has already gained firm footing in some parts of the European university system; and there are signs that it may finally have begun to establish communications among an excessively large number of subspecializations and disciplines (British, American, and foreign-language literary studies, critical theory, the "new musicology," nonquantitative political science, and cultural anthropology) that have lived institutional parallel lives far too long.

CHAPTER ONE

Feeling, Self-Awareness, and Aesthetic Formalization after Kant

> Man seeks to articulate his purpose both in an overly subjective and in an overly objective state. . . . Yet this purpose can be attained only in a sacred, divine feeling, one that is beautiful because it is neither simply agreeable and fortunate, neither simply sublime and strong, nor simply unified and tranquil, but which is all of these simultaneously—a feeling which is transcendental and where a pure, formal mood has been distilled from it that encompasses life in its entirety.
>
> — HÖLDERLIN, *"Über Die Verfahrungsweise Des Poëtischen Geistes" (On the Process of the Poetic Mind)*, TRANS. THOMAS PFAU

> Is it possible to grasp this structural whole of the everydayness of being (*Dasein*) in its entirety? — HEIDEGGER, *Being and Time*

It is a commonplace that romanticism seems unusually preoccupied with concepts of "feeling," with emotional states to which, in ways that "critical" or analytical sensibilities often find unpalatable or spurious, broad human significance is being ascribed. Yet from Wordsworth's ever-ready shorthand definition of poetry as the "spontaneous overflow of powerful feelings" to T. S. Eliot's definition of it as the representation of "complex emotions," the concept of feeling—and those peripherally grouped around it: pleasure, affect, agitation, emotion—has curiously resisted its absorption into critical knowledge; for that it has proven at once too enigmatic and too complex. Indeed, in breaking down the concept of feeling into three distinctive and, for the romantic period, representative types—paranoia, trauma, melancholy—the present study also acknowledges the opacity of some holistic "mood" to critical understanding. This predicament should, however, prompt further sustained reflection on alternative ways of thinking about emotion. To that end, this chapter considers how, in the work of Kant, Novalis, and, to some extent, even Hegel emotion constitutes neither the antithesis of critical knowledge nor its anticipation in a lesser key. Rather, it amounts to a qualitatively different form of awareness whose relation to critical, analytic knowledge is one of complementarity. T. S. Eliot's suggestion that "emotion in . . . poetry will be a very complex thing," and that it is "a concentration, and a new thing resulting from the concentration, of a very great number of experiences which to the practical and active person would not seem to be experiences at all" (Eliot, 10) points us in the right direction. Indeed, one may simplify his assertion further by noting that the phrase "complex emotions" is something of a redundancy, since complexity is precisely what causes certain kinds of awareness to be experienced and conveyed *as* emotions. Still, the complexity of emotional life, even if postulated as a constitutive feature, hardly guarantees the cogency of one's awareness of "feeling" this way or that. On the contrary, in charting one's own affective dispositions or surmising about those of someone else, the language employed typically characterizes the mental life under scrutiny as insufficiently focused or disciplined. Such a dialectical conception of feeling as "not-yet-knowledge" may date back as far as Aristotle. Certainly, beginning with Freud (and arguably earlier than that), it has caused feeling to be viewed as a phenomenon begging the *caritas* of critical discernment.[1] Indeed, theoretical innovations of the early-twentieth-century humanities (e.g., psychoanalysis and phenomenology) stake their disciplinary and institutional authority on their ability to hold ephemeral psychological states and dispositions conceptually accountable.

A different view, albeit one less certain to purchase critical authority, approaches emotion as a categorically different type of awareness, one complementary rather than inferior to speculative or psychoanalytic epistemologies. To suggest that a complementary kind of cognition takes place in emotional life or, more accurately, in a type of representation that focuses both on a complex reality and the emotive charge that accompanies its perception proves rather more difficult. For it runs counter to a rich philosophical tradition, one that could list Descartes, Leibniz, Hegel, and Freud among others, in which feeling is repeatedly posited as an embryonic anticipation of reflective knowledge, a hapless *singularium* or Leibnizian monad "as yet" unaware of its systematic purpose and conceptual destiny, and, once aware of it, no longer a "feeling." To counter speculative and psychoanalytic arguments in which feeling serves a strictly transitional and anticipatory function on the road to conceptual and systematic self-possession appears an almost willfully capricious undertaking, with the prospects of intellectual yield dim at best. To begin with, if we are to accord emotion a quasi truth-value, some distinction (however problematic) would have to be drawn between emotions so contingent, ephemeral, and personal as to elude even the attentiveness of the individual who supposedly holds them and more fundamental "structures of feeling" (Raymond Williams's useful term) that show a subject uneasily embedded within its historical moment.

In her recent work on emotions, Martha Nussbaum does just that when she proposes a distinction between "background and situational" emotions, a more cautious variant of Richard Wollheim's earlier categorical antithesis between "states and dispositions" (Nussbaum, 69n). It is the latter kind, an abiding emotive state signaling what it is like to be structurally embedded in a complex world that, for Nussbaum, comes into view when, at certain points, it erupts into a Proustian "upheaval of thought." Clearly, Nussbaum's "background" emotion comprises cognitive and evaluative thoughts of such complexity as to render the upheaval—whereby the background becomes phenomenally distinct—"part of the experience of what it is like to have those thoughts" (ibid., 62).[2] In an apparent echo of Kant's third *Critique,* which identifies feeling as the phenomenon that accompanies and announces the basic intellectual operation of judgment—and thereby renders judgment both reflective *and* aesthetic—Nussbaum identifies the following constitutive features of emotional experience: "emotions are appraisals or value judgments, which ascribe to things or persons outside the person's own control great importance for that person's own flourishing. It thus contains three salient ideas: the idea of a *cognitive appraisal* or *evaluation;* the idea of *one's own flourishing* or *one's important goals and projects;* and the idea of the *salience of external objects as elements in one's own scheme of goals*" (ibid., 4). Underlying all three aspects of emotional experience is the premise that emotion instantiates an enduring, quasi-intentional relation to the world; in other words, "emotions are not *about* their objects" but rather involve a holistic, though still highly differentiated perceptual relation to the world. "Their aboutness is more internal, and embodies a way of seeing" (ibid., 27). Though she soon compromises several aspects of her key hypothesis, Nussbaum begins with a persuasive description of the quasi-intentional steadiness that can be observed in emotional dispositions, as well as their capacious evaluative relationship to one's goals. As she would have it, emotions proper are neither ephemeral nor partial. Yet because Nussbaum's neo-Stoic account is so invested in articulating the epistemological saliency of human emotions, it also ascribes to them a tranquil, settled quality that ultimately contradicts the ordinary evidence for how emotions announce themselves *as such,* namely, as a sudden and conspicuous affective discharge or, on the other hand, as a palpable absence of any emoting whatsoever (e.g., post-traumatic catatonia).

While acknowledging that her perspective on the emotions makes it "difficult to account for their urgency and heat," Nussbaum nonetheless stays the course, arguing that emotions per se are devoid of content until "an inspection of thought discriminates" between their possible valences. Yet to argue that "it seems necessary to put the thought into the definition of the emotion itself" (ibid., 27–30) is to reinstate the traditional, rigid assumption of a categorical divide between the acuity of reflective thought and the amorphous quality of emotion. In a familiar, perhaps inevitable, Hegelian turn, this view will sooner or later assert that conscious thought not only "corrects" or "purifies" emotions but, in so doing, utterly emancipates thought itself from the taint of emotive contingency; reflection yields something durable, universal and, thus, ultimately "good," whereas emotion proves transient, oblique, hopelessly particular and, thus, ultimately "bad." For in tying the reality and cognitive value of emotions to their eventual "inspection" by consciousness, Nussbaum effectively abandons her earlier hypothesis that emotions are themselves a form of cognition, that they "embody not simply ways of seeing an object, but beliefs—often very complex—about the object" (ibid., 28). Retaining the latter view, I shall argue that it is precisely the complex and holistic reality—what Wilhelm Dilthey long ago termed "an experiential complexion" (*Erlebniszusammenhang*)—that we find encrypted as a preconscious "mood" that circumscribes and defines individuals and communities. To speak of emotion or feeling is thus not to lament the persistence of phenomena not yet broken down into analytic components and concepts; rather, it is to encounter—in the symptomatic form of persistent affective charges—the antagonistic totality that Heidegger calls *Dasein* and that Lacan refers to as "the Real." True to their representational origins in Attic tragedy and hence anything but amorphous and ephemeral, emotions involve the onset of an overwhelming, holistic clarity. Their comprehensive lucidity, well beyond the scope of conceptual, analytic knowledge, also renders them communally relevant. Echoing Nietzsche's contention that "the subject, the individual who wills can be considered only the adversary and not the origin of art" (Nietzsche 1993, 32), T. S. Eliot declares that "the emotion of art is impersonal, [and] . . . the poet has, not a 'personality' to express, but a particular medium, which is only a medium and not a personality, in which impressions and experiences combine in peculiar and unexpected ways" (Eliot, 11, 9). As we shall see in the case of paranoia in the 1790s, this impersonality is not only a constitutive feature of that particular emotion but also accounts for its charged, all-encompassing anxious quality; for the subject cannot locate itself as the origin or "owner" of the emotion but, characteristically, appears wholly in its grip. Let us summarize some of the characteristics of emotion that guide the following inquiry:

- As a dynamic and holistic, cognitive event (*Ereignis*), emotion does not isolate a representational object. Rather, it constitutes an evaluative response to an experiential complexion before the latter is broken down into its isolated parts by analytic and discursive understanding.
- Because of its holistic and event-like character, emotion can never become an object for individual consciousness. Its subjects—who, as Rei Terada has argued, are not to be thought of as reified "subjects" at all *to the extent that they have emotions*—cannot grasp the foundational role of emotion as it shapes their analytic and representational commerce with a world forever experienced as an aggregate of discrete "things" and "issues."
- Emotions thus are not "owned" by an individual as some discrete representation but, instead, are experienced as a dynamic or mood by which the quotidian practice of representation and cognition is suffused.
- In suspending—latently or as a sudden "upheaval"—the Cartesian axiom of a conscious and autonomous self, the "event" of emotion alerts the subject to its having been implicated all along in a seemingly uncontainable network of antagonistic historical forces. The holistic, nonintentional perspicacity captured in Kant's and Heidegger's notion of "mood" (*Stimmung*) stages the confrontation of subjectivity with historical forces that the subject can neither anticipate nor transcend.
- Rather than accessing reality in propositional form, mood necessarily involves mediation via inherently aesthetic forms of representation. Even where "mood" discharges itself as conspicuous emotion, it can do so only by formal, discursive, or expressive means of whose regulatory impact the individual subject remains largely unaware. Consequently, the task of reconstructing the "mood of (romantic) history" must locate its prima facie evidence in distinctive formal patterns of representation rather than in the urgent topicality of subjective expression.

- In attaining intersubjective reality and validity only by being embodied in "a more finely perfected medium" (Eliot, 7), emotion becomes the focal point for a "constructionist" aesthetic that often presages high modernism. Yet given the impossibility of a complete break from social conventions of expression, romantic "mood" (*Stimmung*) also experiences its transposition into "voice" (*Stimme*) as intrinsically alienating. It is here, too, that we can locate the origins of romanticism's often vehement reaction against inauthentic or contrived (i.e., purely "literary") emotions.

In positing historical experience as a subject's inexorable, if belated, awakening to a traumatic (missed) event, contemporary theory fundamentally revives Kant's and the early romantics' theory of the sublime. For the latter had first argued that all cognition effectively amounts to a tracing of an antecedent, noumenal event of which a distinctive mood (*Stimmung*) is the only trace. Dilthey's term for the holistic knowledge realized in literature—an "experiential complexion" (*Erlebniszusammenhang*)—later reappears as a theory of fate in Walter Benjamin, who defines fate as "the nexus of guilt among the living" (*Schuldzusammenhang des Lebendigen*).[3] As we shall see, romantic emotion becomes particularly conspicuous where the subject confronts history as an oblique, "hidden," and at best belatedly intelligible determinant. The specter of historicity as "fate," and the consequent, often frantic, attempts of romantic writing to recover some type of individual agency, manifests itself in paranoid and traumatic "structures of feeling," particularly between 1789 and 1815.

Most romantic writers seem well aware of the duplicitous status of emotion—that is, as a foundational and holistic "mood" of thought that can be captured only in the alien modality of aesthetic (textual) construction. Yet this very awareness itself can no longer be remedied in the way that one may "correct" a false or incomplete thought process. For the "mood" in question proves logically anterior to all reflection. Mood appears terminally resistant to conceptual analysis, including that proffered by dialectical thinking that views instances of material or conceptual opacity as nothing but "semblance" (*Schein*), and hence as the very fuel that keeps the dialectical machine running. Mood proves resistant to any dialectical recovery, because it has never staked out any claim to an object in the first place. Since it does not belong to the order of signs and reference, it appears to fall outside the Hegelian logic of "semblance" (*Schein*) that seeks to assimilate all otherness as an "as yet" insufficiently determined meaning. In contrast, mood constitutes an overdetermined, intuitive recognition of the inadequacy of available conceptual models for explaining the myriad antagonisms that define the subject's historicity. For the time being, we shall view emotions as signals traceable in the fabric of literary and aesthetic form and indicating the persistence of factors or qualities that resist outright assimilation to rationalist or dialectical models of discursive thinking. Indeed, it is just this persistence of emotion that indicates a rupture within the purposive logic of rational, discursive thinking—a momentous tear in the fabric of quotidian knowledge on the order of the Kantian sublime. Inasmuch as the breakdown of traditional modes of cognition produces the "feeling of the sublime," it would obviously be circular to try and enlist those very modes of rational thought once again for the comprehension of that very feeling.

Stimme/Stimmung: Tuning into Thought in Kant's *Critique of Judgment*

So much just by way of preamble. What remains for now is to articulate in more fundamental theoretical terms: (1) the structural nexus between romantic "interiority" and the *aesthetic;* (2) the dynamic between reflection and feeling; and (3) the curious reciprocity between the indeterminacy of emotional life and that of the aesthetic, between a holistic perception that announces itself as the enigma of emotion and the complex task of mediating such emotion as aesthetic work. Few periods in Western culture offer more ample material for the exploration of such issues than the period spanning from the late 1780s to the late 1830s, both in Britain and on the Continent.[4] Throughout this introduction, as indeed throughout the entire book, as it explores the commerce between an inwardness defined by its emotional complexity and aesthetic, particularly literary form, "interiority" denotes subjectivity or inwardness as an *effect* (not an origin or source) produced by the subtle interaction of historical-material and formal-aesthetic forces. The latter are those conventionally associated with the period's broad (preponderantly middle-class) notion of "art" and the disciplinary institutions of criticism seeking to articulate the deeper epistemological and historical implications of aesthetic experience.[5] Three decades of "poststructuralist" and neo-Marxist historicist critique have variously insisted that what appears in a text to be the central, coordinating agency, or "voice," is theoretically and ideologically suspect—perhaps nowhere more so than in key texts of European romanticism where such a voice seems to arrogate to itself an inalienable expressive authority, both as source of socially relevant experience and as the expressive medium for its collective revelation. Against that programmatic assertion, readers have found themselves experiencing that curiously self-focused voice—preponderantly, though not exclusively, in lyric writing—as a self-authorizing, self-privileging articulate structure eager to solicit a complex interpretive aesthetic response, albeit unified and hence communicable in its effects. This the voice of romantic texts does, even as it also purports to be itself a response to or resuscitation of some anterior literary model and its perceived social effects. Fundamentally, the aesthetic response to romantic writing suggests that what we call voice is the specific form required by the balancing of individual against universal values.

Both historically and conceptually, Kant's *Critique of Judgment* (1790) is the key text for any attempt to map the coordinates for these basic questions. As Kant argues in that text, the larger significance of aesthetic judgment inheres in its overall application to what he calls "cognition in general," as well as in its performativity as a distinctive type of utterance. By contrast, the propositional specificity and force of aesthetic judgments appears slight at best. For "in the judgment of taste nothing is postulated but . . . a *universal voice* [*allgemeine Stimme*], in respect of the satisfaction without the intervention of concepts, and thus the *possibility* of an aesthetic judgment that can . . . be regarded as valid for everyone" (§ 8, 50). The "pleasure" that is bound up with aesthetic judgment is not the *cause* of it (for as such it would be purely sensual enjoyment). Rather, it is a pleasure growing out of the subject's reflexive understanding that its own "subjective condition" at the moment of aesthetic experience amounts to something "universally communicable" (*allgemein mitteilungsfähig*). The "proportionate accord" (*proportionierte Stimmung*) of the faculties of cognition, Kant argues, constitutes both the cause and the substance of the aesthetic-reflective judgment (§ 9, 54). At its most general, all cognition (*Erkenntnis*) can thus be characterized as a way of being "attuned" to discrete phenomena, such that their contemplation will gradually "determine" (*bestimmen*) the subject via its affective experience of a "concord" (*Übereinstimmung*) or "conformity" (*Zusammenstimmung*) that connects an (empirical) appearance to the (transcendental) form in which the subject's sensory and discursive faculties relate to one another: "The subjective universal communicability of the mode of representation in a judgment of taste . . . can refer to nothing else than the state of mind [*Gemützustand*] in the free play of the imagination and the understanding (so far as they agree with each other [*zusammen stimmen*], as is requisite for cognition in general" (*CrJ* § 9, 52 / German: Kant 1968, 10: 132). Kant identifies "pleasure" as the manifestation of cognitive potentialities at the level of affect; as Andrew Bowie formulates it, "the very possibility of judgment is therefore grounded in the pleasure of grasping and articulating a world" (58). Reminiscent of Leibniz's "monads," the aesthetic is conceived as an encryption of the very intelligence that will constitute itself through its interpretive discernment. Or, as Rei Terada puts—appropriately routing her discussion of Derrida through a brief revisitation of *Gefühl* in Kant: "The object of emotion . . . is not the loss of something cognition sacrifices or subordinates; it is the struggle of cognition itself" (Terada, 31).

Pleasure in Kantian judgment, then, is no mere private affect; rather, it announces the emergence of a capable social agency in the virtual modality of the aesthetic—what Kant's eighteenth-century precursor Alexander Baumgarten had already defined as the *analogon rationis.* "Feeling" here has a content, though none that is to be grasped and conveyed in conceptual form. Rather, what is *felt* by the subject is his or her own capacity for agency per se—the possibility of creating or transforming a community through the discursive work of critique. Kantian judgment does not simply constitute a subjective act or experience. Rather, it constitutes the affective template for social praxis—with "praxis" carrying certainly discursive and likely political overtones. The practice of judgment announces the individual's fundamental and vital engagement with the other, a will toward communication and social, intersubjective relations. In the words of Hans Graubner, Kant's "disinterested judgments . . . can yet realize a deferred interest [*ein nachträgliches Interesse*] in the object of pleasure. Such is the case in all moral judgments. What I declare necessarily good, I must also want to produce."[6] For this "disinterestedness signifies the possibility of a very particular kind of intersubjectivity." As Graubner summarizes the case, "aesthetic pleasure is a pleasure derived from the intersubjectivity of feeling" (Graubner, 56–59; my translation). Kant's *Critique of Judgment* draws out the startlingly social conception of feeling that had already taken shape in Adam Smith's *Theory of Moral Sentiments,* where "sympathy" arises as an assessment of the "situation which excites [passion]" in someone else—and hence as an act of imaginative transference and substitution of one agent for another: "We sometimes feel for another, a passion of which he himself seems to be altogether incapable; because, when we put ourselves in his case, that passion arises in our breast from the imagination, though it does not in his from the reality. We blush from the impudence and rudeness of another, though he himself appears to have no sense of the impropriety of his own behavior; because we cannot help feeling with what confusion we ourselves should be covered, had we behaved in so absurd a manner" (Smith 1984, 12). Beyond all propositional language, the affect of sympathy attests to a deep-seated intersubjective logic at work within a given individual and indeed constitutive of his or her humanity. What feeling instantiates in the individual is the *fact* of its social connectedness—Coleridge metaphorizes it as an "electric force" (Coleridge 1983, 1: 199)—as well as an ethical obligation that is also intrinsic to such "feeling": namely, to extend the social *potentiality* experienced in the aesthetic feeling of "communicability" into a livable *reality.*

Far from being a merely contingent and ephemeral sympathy for someone else, feeling here unfolds as an inherently transferential process, a feeling of otherness within one's own self. Hence it is misleading to conceive of Kant's aesthetic-reflective judgment has having merely indirect freedom (i.e., the absence of some determinate concept or a specific idea of a moral good). For the freedom of the faculties of cognition, whose very harmonious interplay (*Übereinstimmung*) is reflexively understood to be the source of aesthetic pleasure, always looks forward. "It aspires toward an objective knowledge wherein the faculties of cognition could effectively retain their freedom. We are looking as it were at a mission anchored in the empirical experience of aesthetic pleasure, namely, the mission of an intersubjective utopia" (Graubner, 67). The emancipation of the faculties from their strictly empirical and interested application also liberates the subject that, until now, had appeared little more than a derivative or effect of the smooth synthetic operation of knowledge. Kantian "feeling" demarcates the onset of a truly free, truly capable agency—unfettered by interests, fixed perceptions, moral norms, and, for that matter, untrammeled by any monolithic sense of self. Far from the "subjective turn" that Gadamer had so peremptorily ascribed to Kant (and which has dutifully been radicalized by subsequent criticism bent on revealing the supposed elitism and social indifference of Kant's aesthetic theories), "feeling" in the third *Critique* persistently draws our attention to the inherent sociality of all subjective existence. As a fundamentally open, disinterested engagement with one's own intrinsic otherness—an imaginative exploration of the possibility of relating to the other—"feeling" in Kant constitutes such a genuinely social and epistemological act. Speaking of "sociality" as a "sharing," Jean-Luc Nancy similarly understands community as the "articulation of 'particularities,'" and hence not as "founded in any autonomous essence that would subsist by itself and that would reabsorb or assume singular beings into itself" (Nancy, 75). Consumed by the objective of radical "communicability," Kant's account identifies the aesthetic as the *conditio sine qua non* of community, that is, as the domain where the individual experiences the inherently ethical challenge of existence.[7]

And yet, Kant insists on the strict heterogeneity of the two faculties (viz., imagination and understanding) that are said to circumscribe any knowledge whatsoever, including all knowledge of self. Consequently, their contingent relation can never be objectified by consciousness as such, and the *Critique of Judgment* appears to surrender the transcendental, formal dynamic of "feeling" (*Gefühl*) to an inherently empirical and material vocabulary of "sensation" (*Empfindung*). The "subjective unity of relation can only make itself known by means of sensation," Kant now remarks (*CrJ* § 9, 53).[8] This metonymic slippage from "feeling" to "sensation" imperils the entire transcendental structure of the third *Critique* and, not surprisingly, some readers have suggested that Kant's argument (particularly his digression on music) exposes itself to an "intru[sion of] bodily pleasure into the space reserved for thought."[9] At the very least, we have been alerted to the presence of a contingent empirical quality and, consequently, to the overall precarious balance of the "analytic of the beautiful." Other evidence (as we have already noticed) involves the text's critical reliance on various cognates of "voice" (*Stimme*).[10] This shift from "feeling" to "sensation" is inescapable, because all "pleasure," if it is to appear *for* the consciousness whose formal and social authority it underwrites, demands the materiality of "sensation." Speaking about a related conceptual crisis that besets Kant's account of the sublime, Paul de Man conceives of Kant's transcendental discourse as a purely "tropological system" in which conceptual advances of any kind are "conceivable only within the limits of such a system." When "translated back, so to speak, from language into cognition, from formal description into philosophical argument, [such insight] loses all inherent coherence and dissolves in the aporias of intellectual and sensory appearance" (de Man, 78). Surprisingly, de Man never troubles himself to inquire whether his conspicuously generalized account of Kant's (tropological) strategy of generalization might also pertain to the latter's "Analytic of the Beautiful."[11] Needless to say, the above passage from that section suggests a pervasive debt of Kant's transcendental argumentation to contingent empirical sensation. For inasmuch as the "Analytic of the Beautiful" purports to secure the grounds for a unique "feeling of pleasure," which, in turn, is to ensure the coherence of Kant's overall critical project, such pleasure will have to *prolong itself.* Put simply, such a realm of (supposedly) pure affect cannot just be claimed as a theoretical fact, since the overall coherence of transcendental thought stands or falls with the hypothesis of "feeling," and that always means its potential detour through the social and material netherworld of appearance and representation. In short, pleasure will have to manifest itself as an appearance at once philosophically pure and materially authentic. That is, it must become art, for as Rousseau had so eloquently explored it in his fifth *Reverie,* all pleasure demands empirical mediation:

> I would go sit in some hidden nook along the beach at the edge of the lake. There, the noise of the waves and the tossing of the water, captivating my senses and chasing all other disturbance from my soul, plunged it into a delightful reverie in which night would often surprise me without my having noticed it. The ebb and flow of this water and its noise, continual but magnified at intervals, striking my ears and eyes without respite, took the place of the internal movements which reverie extinguished within me and was enough to make me feel my existence with pleasure.[12]

Having fled the stoning of his house at Môtiers, Rousseau not only "embarks" on a private sojourn on the lake (famously echoed in book 1 of Wordsworth's *Prelude*), but also confirms inwardness as the site, not of self-possession, but of self-recovery in the intrinsically alienated condition of reflexive writing. One cannot miss in this passage the recuperative pathos of the written text, of signs obviously constructed *after* and *against* the fact of a self dispossessed. In their artificial and remedial modality as written *récit,* the *Reveries* posit "voice" as imbued with intuitive self-presence and political efficacy only by continually ruminating its phenomenal disappearance or loss.[13] The plenitude of a socially integrated voice is posited in vivid, albeit strictly retroactive, terms as a point of absolute anteriority and presence, the Lacanian "Imaginary" that precedes all, not only Rousseau's escape from nocturnal rioting and public notoriety, but also the publication of his *Confessions,* even the spectacular transgressions tabulated by that book. As the quintessential dialectical solicitation of inwardness as the locus of expressive and political exile, Rousseau's *Reveries* position voice strictly as the effect, no longer the origin, of a radically speculative and reflexive writing that no longer promises an integral and fully socialized self but merely the ever-increasing awareness of the latter's impossibility. What Jacques Derrida long ago worked out as the logic of *différance* emerges in the late work of Rousseau as an instance of self-reflection that no longer allows for the reintegration of its constitutive parts (past / present; self / other; intuition / cognition). As the principle of nonclosure sensu stricto, the written word simultaneously reflects back on its hypostatized precursor ("voice") and grasps its reflexive present as an inescapably alienated condition ("exile").[14]

Just as Rousseau contrasts "short moments of delirium and passion" with "a simple and permanent state . . . whose duration increases its charm to the point that I finally find supreme felicity in it" (Rousseau, 68), Kant's third *Critique* aims to configure the *punctum* of empirical sensation with the *durée* of an interior "feeling." The result of this negotiation is a subject "attuned" to "knowledge in general" or experiencing what Rousseau famously calls *le sentiment de l'existence*—a state said to be both, phenomenally distinct *and* transcendentally pure. Not surprisingly, Rousseau's often-quoted formulation recurs verbatim in Kant's third *Critique,* which asserts that the onset of an aesthetic reflective judgment and its implicit "communicability" of "knowledge in general" constitutes a *Lebensgefühl,* a vivid sense of being and its limitless possibilities (freedom).[15] It is important here to note how the language that asserts the contingency of sentiment and pleasure on "a uniform and moderate movement which has neither shocks nor pauses" itself contributes to and prolongs the experience in question. Or, in Kant's words, "'pure' in a simple mode of sensation means that its uniformity is neither troubled nor interrupted by any foreign sensation, and it belongs merely to the form" (§ 14, *CrJ* 60; translation modified). Such uniformity, Margery Sabin observes, manifests itself in "Rousseau's evident satisfaction with his own language of analysis" (113). A similar striving for immanent argumentation arguably prevails throughout Kant's critical philosophy and informs his claim that the language of cognition itself prolongs a pleasure that it had previously introduced as its critical object. The virtual beauty of "harmony" and "proportion" said to prevail between the intellect's discrete faculties must become vocal, audible, and lasting, and the reflexive operations of critical writing are at least one way of achieving that outcome. For the transcendental "disposition" (*Stimmung*) of our intellectual temper always strives to objectify itself through the formal-material continuity of a "voice" (*Stimme*). In a late fragment, Novalis appears to take up the hint, remarking how "the word *Stimmung* hints at the inherently musical constitution of the soul. The acoustics of our soul is as yet an obscure terrain, though probably one of vital importance" (Das Wort Stimmung deutet auf musicalische Seelenverhältnisse—Acoustik der Seele ist noch ein dunkles, vielleicht aber sehr wichtiges Feld [*WTB*, 2: 715]).

What renders the trope of the voice so pivotal for Kant is its potential for establishing communication between two otherwise opposed spheres, the contingent world of phenomena and their sensory experience, on the one hand, and the rational claims of formal-intellectual processes, on the other. With these concerns on his mind, Kant now invests "voice" with the further hypothesis that aesthetic experience, far from being something ephemeral, is in essence "contemplative" and therefore invested in its own prolongation:

> [T]he pleasure in aesthetical judgments . . . is merely contemplative and does not bring about an interest in the object. . . . The consciousness of the mere formal purposiveness in the play of the subject's cognition . . . is the pleasure itself, because it contains a determining ground of the activity of the subject in respect of the excitement of its cognitive powers, and therefore an inner causality. . . . This pleasure [of the aesthetic reflective judgment] is in no way practical, neither like that arising from the pathological ground of pleasantness, nor that from the intellectual ground of the presented good. But yet it involves causality, viz. of *maintaining* without further design the state of the representation itself and the occupation of the cognitive powers. We *linger* over the contemplation of the beautiful because this contemplation strengthens and reproduces itself." (*CrJ* §12, 57–8; emphases in the original / German: Kant 1968, 10: 137–38)

So as to accommodate the instinctual desire of "pleasure" for self-perpetuation, "contemplation" seeks to recover from the spatiotemporal sphere of empirical *sensation* precisely those formal conditions that support Kant's basic transcendental argument about "cognition in general" (viz., as resting on the proportionate interplay of the faculties). A few years later, Novalis was to state the matter most succinctly: "Perpetuating is itself a drive . . . namely the drive to be an 'I'" (Ein Fortsetzen in sich selbst ist ein Trieb . . . und zwar der Trieb ein Ich zu seyn [*WTB*, 2: 39]). What Kant ultimately requires (as would subsequent generations of aestheticians and critics) is the seeming paradox of a pure form that is to become phenomenally distinct as empirical sensation: a "voice" untainted by the contingencies of interest, signification, and context.[16] To the extent that the critical significance of pleasure requires its temporal extension, the "voice" that gave rise to such pleasure will seek its own formalization. Put differently, the prolongation of pleasure, as well as its sustained reflexive experience, is best realized through forms characterized by a high degree of internal differentiation and, consequently, by their susceptibility to complex formal development. For if articulate intuition is postulated to be the foundation for all further critical activity, aesthetic form effectively consolidates a measure of rationality that is already postulated by the individual voice but also seems imperiled by the contingent manifestation of that voice as material sensation.

Formalization, however, implies transfiguring "feeling" into a fundamentally different order (*metabasis allo genos*), less an "event" than its aesthetic simulation by a mind anxious to ensure the continuity of its own internal functioning. Commenting on Derrida, Rei Terada reaches essentially the same conclusion: "In Derrida's texts emotions are 'quasi' in that they respond not just to mental representations but to their perceived representationality as such. Unlike the expressive hypothesis of emotional response, this account is normatively aesthetic: it has no difficulty fitting aesthetics because aesthetics fits it. There is no reason to guard mental life against theatricality [as Rousseau appears to do in his *Lettre à d'Alembert*], to guard emotion against representation, or to worry that layers of mediation diminish emotional intensity as copies degrade" (Terada, 40). To elucidate this still contested view, we should briefly recall the Kantian sublime, where "the mind feels itself *moved* in the representation of the sublime . . . while in aesthetical judgments about the beautiful it is in *restful* contemplation" (*CrJ* 97). Such a distinction exemplifies Kant's lifelong investment in a symmetrical philosophical architecture, comforting in its accurate juxtaposition of dynamism and stasis, conflict and harmony, war and peace. Yet the symmetry cracks once we recall that only the beautiful affirms the integrity of the Enlightenment project positively—that is, through the purposive and pleasurable accord between imagination and understanding.[17] By contrast, the sublime can reinforce reason's prospects only negatively. For in it, imagination *and reason* "bring about a feeling that we possess pure self-subsistent reason, or a faculty . . . whose superiority can be made intuitively evident only by the inadequacy of that faculty [imagination] which is itself unbounded in the presentation of magnitudes (of sensible) objects" (*CrJ* 97).

On that count, rationality constitutes itself as a self-authorizing and self-generating fantasy ("respect for our own destination, which, *by a certain subreption*, we attribute to an object of nature" [*CrJ* 96]). The professed content of that feeling, that is, "our supersensible destination" (*Bestimmung*), really cannot be felt at all, properly speaking, since the substance of feeling the sublime involves the experience of a "conflict," not a formal accord, between the faculties. The content of sublime feeling is, if anything, a negative one—a feeling that should routinely occur suddenly fails to do so and, in response to that traumatic rupture, the subject "affects" the notion of reason *as* a (quasi-) "feeling" of its own "supersensible destination." In short, the Kantian sublime constitutes no feeling per se but, rather, a reaction to the fact that "feeling" (the expected accord of the faculties that defines the beautiful) did *not* occur. Considered as a "feeling" properly speaking, the sublime can be experienced only as an absence ("the want of accordance" [*CrJ* 96]), a void ("an abyss in which [the imagination] fears to lose itself" [*CrJ* 97]) or, simply, the nothingness that takes the place of the accustomed formalism of "cognition in general" as it is momentarily suspended.[18]

In response to this disintegration of the formally purposive relation between its discrete faculties—and hence of its own constitution—the subject projects the simulacrum of a feeling, "respect" (*Achtung*). It "affects" a feeling precisely where nothing at all can be felt. This simulation of feeling constitutes, properly speaking, the birth of reason. Or, more precisely, it marks the moment when the Kantian subject positively gives birth to reason, rather than being itself cradled in the protorational womb of the "beautiful," whose harmonies could never properly be known but only surmised, by a reflection upon a vexingly contentless "feeling" of the beautiful. Meanwhile, this birth of reason out of the spirit of the sublime not only proves traumatic as, perhaps, any birth must, but also comes at a steep price. For what is surrendered in exchange for the subject's defensive affirmation of its supersensible, rational destiny is nothing less than the integrity of "feeling" itself. Notwithstanding its identical nomenclature, the "feeling" of the sublime is nothing like that of the beautiful; or, rather, it throws into relief the strictly "virtual" character of all feeling, including that of the beautiful, to begin with. For in the Kantian sublime, pleasure—which, after all, was what had been "felt" in the judgment of the beautiful— "arises only indirectly; viz. . . . is produced by the feeling of a momentary checking of the vital powers and a consequent stronger outflow of them" (*CrJ* 83). In a curious and revealing turn of phrase, Kant hints that the "feeling" of the sublime lacks autonomy, and that its experience only "*seems* to be regarded as emotion" (*CrJ* 83; emphasis added). He names it a "negative pleasure," a notion roughly akin to what Slavoj Žižek defines as "fantasy."[19] For if the sublime revolves around the subject experiencing its own interiority as an ineffable locus, a void or "abyss" for which no commensurate representation can ever be found, its experience does not constitute an experience at all, properly speaking. Rather, its event-character belongs to the order of a "missed experience" substantially identical with the Freudian conception of trauma, to which we shall return later. Without doubt, Kant's theory of the sublime relates suggestively (albeit only by implication) to the experience of history as a chaotic and forceful disruption of inherited and proven models of cognition. If "the feeling of the sublime may appear . . . to do violence to the imagination" (*CrJ* 83), this means, above all, that the routes of communication between feeling and cognition, interiority and representation, are themselves severed. In short, what is called "feeling" in the Kantian sublime originates in the subject's incapacity to witness the traumatic breakdown of all "accord" between its formal (transcendental) and perceptual (empirical) faculties. In response to this cognitive and emotive catastrophe, the subject rededicates itself to the project of Reason by professing to "feel" its supersensible destination in the affective simulacrum of "respect." Such "direction by indirection," as Polonius might say, transforms the entire conception of "feeling" from an inward and authentic event into something essentially notional and figural in kind. Or, as de Man puts it, "the sublime . . . posits itself by claiming to exist by dint of the impossibility of its own existence."[20]

The later pages of the *Critique of Judgment* effectively expand the fantasy character of the sublime—its simulation of feeling as formal-aesthetic construction—by telling us how the crisis of the sublime, which is to say the crisis of representation, of giving a "voice" (*Stimme*) to a subjective "accord" (*Übereinstimmung*) effectively lies at the origin of all "aesthetic" ideas. Far more than the "remainders of hallucinatory formations" that Kant had refuted along with Swedenborgianism, such ideas constitute "the fantasmatic frame of our access to reality" (Žižek, 1993, 90). With Kant's shift from an aesthetics of reception (§§ 1–38) to one of production (§§ 39–60), his previously vital antithesis between the beautiful and the sublime suddenly loses all interest. In what may well be the most idealist passage in Kant's entire oeuvre, we learn that "spirit" (*Geist*) constitutes the properly "animating principle of the mind" and "that this principle is no other than the faculty of presenting *aesthetical ideas.*"

> And by an aesthetical idea I understand that representation of the imagination which occasions much thought, without however any definite thought, i.e., any *concept*, being capable of being adequate to it; it consequently cannot be com-

pletely compassed and made intelligible by language. We easily see that it is the counterpart (pendant) of a *rational idea,* which conversely is a concept to which no *intuition* (ore representation of the imagination) can be adequate. The imagination (as a productive faculty of cognition) is very powerful in creating another nature, as it were, out of the material that actual nature gives it. We entertain ourselves with it when experience becomes too commonplace. (*CrJ* 157 / German: Kant 1968, 10: 257–58)

Kant here proclaims an exact homology between the operative structure of the sublime and that of the aesthetic idea. Both "strive after something which lies beyond the bounds of experience and so seek to approximate to a presentation of concepts of reason (intellectual ideas)" (ibid.), Reason itself constitutes less the framework for Kant's inquiry into aesthetic experience than its vicarious and formally tenuous offspring. In the case of the sublime, reason *is* an aesthetic idea imaginatively fashioned out of the affective and formal debris of an experience that had yielded nothingness ("negative pleasure"). Kant conceives of the aesthetic idea as a simulacrum or supplement, wrought by the imagination, that "is very powerful in creating another nature." Responding to the sublime's traumatic ineffability, the aesthetic idea "animates" (Kant's motional trope is *Schwung*) the subject to emancipate itself from the monotonous realm of nature and its predictable causality—in other words, from "experience" as a mere "commonplace."

Here lie the origins of the radical theory of *Darstellung* that the Jena romantics would soon seize upon as their intellectual point of departure. In § 59 of *The Critique of Judgment,* the aesthetic thus becomes *hypotyposis,* a "symbolical mode of presentation" at once estranged from its implicit center (reason) and, in its compositional structure, clearly moving beyond the scope of Kant's transcendental logic. Whereas in the case of the sublime, reason could be attained only in conjectural form, namely, as an artificial "feeling of respect" (*Achtung*), the aesthetic idea, with literature as its preferred medium, simulates the operational coherence of reason through a performative staging of the subject's development (*Bildung*). Both at the level of production and reception, literature as symbolic practice (*Darstellung*) continually enlists and mobilizes the subject's intelligence or "spirit" (*Geist*) for a fundamentally open-ended progression of thought: "such a representation, therefore, adds to a concept much ineffable thought, the feeling of which quickens the cognitive faculties, and with language, which is the mere letter, binds up the spirit also" (*CrJ* 160). At the same time, it is the letter itself that will destabilize the traditional opposition of letter and spirit and, in so doing, redefine literature as constitutively ironic. More than anything else, it was this ironic tension (uncontainable by any systematic argument) that would be seized upon by the Jena romantics and that would persist in the oeuvre of Keats and Heine. That it also links the Jena project with that of twentieth-century deconstruction can be sampled, among many other places, in Rei Terada's *Feeling in Theory;* as she remarks on Derrida's 1967 *Of Grammatology,* and it might as well be Keats in 1817, "not only is there a *conceptual* gain when phenomena are converted into signs; there is an *emotive* gain when we see those signs *as* signs. As signs, they 'penetrate' better, they really move us now."[21]

The faculties, as indeed the work of epistemology or "cognition in general," are quickened in their operative, formal relationship rather than at the level of content. In positing aesthetic form as an (ironic) expression of the unattainability of its underlying rational motive—namely, the aesthetic idea—Kant profoundly alters the essential bond between interiority and expression, feeling and text, to which the movements of sentimentalism and *Sturm und Drang* had been so attached. The epistemological crisis of the sublime replicates itself in the self-deconstructing form (*Darstellung*) taken by the aesthetic idea: in both, feeling is experienced as "negative pleasure," as the nothing that takes the place of the disinterested pleasure of cognition that should have been. This crisis threatens not only the account of the sublime but the totality of the *Critique of Judgment,* inasmuch as its entire conceptual architecture is predicated on the a priori continuity of reason. In response, aesthetic, and particularly literary, form forges an (ironically self-qualifying) passage from the dream of the subject as the originator of its own rational constitution to the harsher reality of the subject as the Sisyphus-like producer of symbols. Such a subject no longer "feels" itself cradled by the formal accord of its own faculties but has been consigned to the tenuous realm of simulacra that may "affect" rationality as a necessary, albeit necessarily "inadequate," presentation.

Reflection, Feeling, and the Text: Novalis Reads the *Science of Knowledge*

Oddly, Kant's *Critique of Judgment* did not have the same impact as his first two *Critiques* for the generation of romantics and idealist thinkers immediately succeeding him (with Schelling and Goethe as the notable exceptions

here). Eager to unify what he perceived as the overly scholastic and compartmentalized presentation of Kant's philosophy, Fichte in particular set out to rethink the foundational role of *Gefühl* for the development of the individual and philosophy itself. Yet even then, his focus lies primarily with the *Critique of Pure Reason* and the *Critique of Practical Reason,* and there is little to suggest that Fichte gave much thought to the role of aesthetics (as work and as a heuristic object of judgment) in establishing continuity between the polarities of intuition and concept. At the same time, that seminal connection is being worked out most insistently by the Jena romantics, and specifically so by way of formulating a critique of Fichte's early drafts of his *Science of Knowledge* as they appeared between 1794 and 1797. Novalis in particular deserves close attention, because his response to Fichte and the entire project of a systematic philosophical determination of the modern subject brings about a crucial bifurcation in German intellectual history around 1800. With Jena as its ground zero, the split between a philosophical idealism premised on an axiomatic bond between self-consciousness and formal logic (Fichte, Schelling, Hegel) and the development of a poetics predicated on open-ended reflexive development (Hölderlin) or on the unending reversals (*Parekbase*) of irony (Novalis, Schlegel) is intriguing for multiple reasons.[22] To appreciate the significance of Novalis's critique of Fichte (subsequently echoed, for once quite independently, by Coleridge), one must briefly recall the fundamental paradox of Fichte's early theory of knowledge as expressed in his 1794 *Foundation of the Science of Knowledge.* Only then does it become possible to gauge the significance of Novalis's critical reading of Fichte, in particular the former's intricate filiation of "feeling" and "image"—two terms of obvious centrality to romantic poetry and poetics. In wading through the discontinuous prose of the *Fichte-Studien,* one is tempted to seize on the suddenly pivotal concepts of image and feeling as evidence of a profound epistemological crisis.[23]

Yet what seems most significant is Novalis's radical inflection of Kant's late theoretical bequest, namely, that the representation (and "representability") of "feeling" constitute the (admittedly hypothetical, or virtual) foundation for all conscious and reflexive subjectivity. Novalis's fragments and notes on Fichte's *Wissenschaftslehre* yield what may well be romanticism's most incisive conception of feeling—far less schematic than Fichte's or, for that matter, Kant's notion of *Gefühl.* For in Novalis's early fragments, "feeling" is the other that continually haunts reflective consciousness, at once the inalienable precondition of the subject's forever partial and etiolated cogitations and, for that very reason, persistently inaccessible to these. Already around 1795, that is, "feeling" is being conceived of in a prototypically Freudian manner, inasmuch as its mere presupposition triggers the development of a (poetic) theory eager to bridge the chasm that forever separates self-awareness from its affective sources. Novalis's poetics of *erdenken* startlingly foreshadow Freud's tracing of the unconscious through its displaced manifestations. Contrary to Fichte, who had sought to "ground" the self in one unchanging, all-encompassing, and transparent principle, Novalis conceives of literature as a type of speculative thinking aimed no longer aimed at closure in an ultimate "ground" but rather at gauging what is left once it has been acknowledged that reflection can only ever acquire its objects (including feeling) in alienated and essentially inverse, untrue form. If "the boundaries of feeling are those of philosophy" (Die Grenzen des Gefühls sind die Grenzen der Filosofie [*WTB*, 2: 18]), feeling identifies the threshold separating philosophy—itself purposive, teleological, and committed to integrating reflective consciousness with any conceivable object, including its own self—from a very different, intrinsically poetic thinking that seeks to delimit the scope and authority of philosophical reflection.[24] Such a poetics of *erdenken* parts company with systematic philosophy inasmuch as the latter predicates its claims on a reflective relationship of mind to its perceptual data (or to itself), thereby reifying a fundamentally dynamic experience. For Novalis, such cognition-by-reflection allows "objects" to become intelligible only in inverse relation to their very essence (what he terms *inverso ordine*): "Semblance in all our knowledge arises from the elevation of a half to the whole—or from halving what is indivisible" (Der Schein in unserer Erkenntnis entsteht aus dem Erheben des Halben zum Ganzen—oder aus dem Halbiren des Untheilbaren [*WTB*, 2: 88]). Novalis's theoretical speculations thus bear a curious resemblance to Blake's paranoid rereading of Genesis as the disastrous imposition of finitude on the wide expanses of pre-Urizenic being ("Eternity roll'd wide apart / Wide asunder . . . / Leaving ruinous fragments of life" (*CPP*, 73).[25]

Fichte's 1794 *Wissenschaftslehre* had responded to the fact that Kant's first *Critique,* while relying on the rational and seemingly reflexive agency of "transcendental apperception," had never analyzed that subjectivity as a principle but merely presupposed it as a necessary correlate of all representation. Specifically in the "transcendental deduction of the pure categories of the understanding," Kant's efforts at consolidating the rationality of all representation through the abiding correlate of a "transcendental apperception" appeared to run into trouble. In attempting to identify the conditions of possible experience—that is, both our receptivity to external phenomena and our ability to convert them into knowledge *for* ourselves—Kant finds that the subject cannot simply be thought of as a monolithic "entity," "personality," or "self."[26] On the contrary, the subject's internal constitution involves an intricate synthetic relation between our *sensibility* and our *understanding.* Because knowledge cannot originate without the continuous interplay of sensory reception and conceptual spontaneity, both of these faculties prove themselves less "in" than actualized "by" experience. They must already have achieved a synthesis in order for there to be something called "experience" and for us to be able to represent it *as our* experience. Kant remains vexed, however, by the question concerning the actual nature of that "inside" said to determine or construct the conditions under which we are to have experience in the first place. That subjective agency, Kant realizes, must be more than a mere synthetic *relation* between our sensibility and our understanding. It must govern or transcend that relation, for otherwise it might fashion representations of the outside world, to be sure, but it could never come to *know* them as "its" world. Hence, inasmuch as knowledge remains bound up with representation, the latter must yet be accompanied by a *consciousness* so as to convert its mere occurrence to meaning, representation into knowledge, fact into value, and so on.

As is well known, Fichte conceives of self-consciousness as a primordial phenomenon that, because of its very foundational nature, cannot "know" its own ground. Self-awareness, he argues, cannot originate in reflection—that is, an operation that institutes a comparative relation between the knowing subject and its objective self-image. For to ground self-awareness in reflection would presuppose the capacity of the reflecting self both to recognize the *unity* of the knower and the known and to reclaim that knowledge for itself *as its own identity.* Hence, as Dieter Henrich has shown, Fichte shifts the conception of self-knowledge from one of relation to one of production, with "the act of production . . . taken to be a real activity, while the product is taken to be the knowledge of this act."[27] Novalis was to significantly extend and intensify Fichte's strictures on the scope and reach of reflection, which can never lay foundations but only clarify appearances a posteriori. Fichte's performative model of self-consciousness as the supposed center and circumference of all philosophical knowledge had already run into difficulties. For the possibility of converting the production of a self (*Setzung*) into a knowledge of the product (self-consciousness) as the self-same clearly demands the self-transparency of the act of positing itself. As Fichte puts it, "the self is to posit itself, not merely for some intelligence outside it, but simply *for itself;* it is to posit itself *as* posited by itself. Hence, as surely as it is a self, it must have the principle of life and consciousness solely within itself" (*SK,* 241).[28] As Helmut Müller-Sievers puts it in his fine account of the ascendancy of "epigenetic" over "preformationist" models of theory: "To the Kantian fallacy of a preformed I that can never get at its own origin Fichte thus opposes the reciprocal structure of an intellectual intuition in which the totality of the I is given while its constituent parts are still distinguishable" (68).[29] And yet, even within the seemingly closed economy of Fichte's brazenly self-privileging mode of theorizing (what Benjamin calls Fichte's "confining and fixing [of] reflection in the absolute thesis" [1996, 130]), the progressive determination of the "I" as self still entails an element of difference, and Müller-Sievers remarks on the "distinguishable parts" within Fichte's intellectual intuition. Even an epigenetic "I" conceived of as capable of generating from within itself the distinct qualities of intuition and reflection, as well as its own knowledge of them, presupposes a certain awareness of its own unity by the positing "I," or, in Fichte's words, premises all "determination" (*Bestimmung*) on a certain "feeling of determinability" (*Gefühl von Bestimmbarkeit*). For the formal unity of the self's performative self-generation must itself be mediated, that is, *re*cognized and *re*claimed by the resulting subject *as its own* identity. For Fichte, the ground wherein the intuition and concept, content and form, substance and accident all converge in one subjective *identity* is known as "intellectual intuition."

The *identity* of the Fichtean "I"—that is, the predication of the individual on an absolute foundation, of contingent self-awareness on humanity as a shared condition and destiny—requires that that "I" recognize the formal *unity* of its constitutive materials (namely, intuition and concept) as the very foundation of its own being and so recognize itself as part of the greater plot of rationality in its unfolding. This experience of its own "determinability" (*Bestimmbarkeit*), according to Fichte, manifests itself at first in affective form. That is, what philosophy calls an "intellectual intuition" attains phenomenal distinctness only in the subject's "feeling" of its own potential determinability. Novalis puts it most succinctly: "Philosophy is originally a feeling" (Die Filosofie ist ursprünglich ein Gefühl [Novalis 1997, 96 / *WTB,* 2: 18]). Aside from having anchored the subject in an "immediate" and seemingly indisputable ground—of transcendental function in Fichte's system, though strikingly reminiscent of empiricist models of "sensation"—not much has been accomplished. For the "feeling" of determinability must itself once again be recognized by the "I" *as its own* foundation or identity, and yet as Novalis so laconically remarks: "Feeling cannot feel itself" (Das Gefühl kann sich nicht selbst fühlen [Novalis 1997, 96 / *WTB*, 2: 18]). It is a crucial, albeit to Fichte most unwelcome, qualification, whereby "feeling" succumbs to the vagaries of representation, figurative expression, and interpretive contingency. Involuntarily, Fichte here finds himself retracing Kant's deduction from the first *Critique* (particularly the pivotal chapter on the "transcendental schematism") and Kant's later, more explicit conception of "feeling" as a subjective universal in the realm of aesthetic production and judgment.[30] Thus Fichte admits that in order to "raise feeling to consciousness" the imagination must produce an "image" (*Bild* [1964–95, 2, 3: 297]) of that feeling, one whereby consciousness would be enabled to recognize its immediate "feeling of determinability" in objective form and thus take hold of a knowledge that had previously slumbered in the encrypted form of an "intellectual intuition." In apparent proximity to Schelling's and Goethe's conception of archetypes (*Urbild*), Fichte stipulates that such an image must be produced by the subject's imagination, a claim that ensures the ascendancy of aesthetics over logic in the business of transcendental philosophy.

And yet, once again, the problem of reflective recognition intrudes. For what, other than mere desire (which may afford consciousness transient pleasures, though surely no coherent self), could possibly underwrite the objective authenticity of the image that the imagination had produced? How could the self recognize the image as a genuine representation of *its own* "feeling" of determinability? And how can an image paradoxically charged with mediating this supposedly "immediate feeling of determinability" for the "I" (and thus promoting that "I" to outright self-awareness) be recognized as having *delivered* proof rather than having contrived it?[31] Fichte's own reflections—carefully edited out from the 1794 *Wissenschaftslehre*—falter on just that point as he worries that "the (productive) imagination itself is a faculty of the Self. Couldn't it be the only grounding faculty [*Grundvermögen*] of the Self?" (1964–95, 2, 3: 298).[32] Is the imagination a "faculty" of a rational, logically deducible subjectivity, or does it merely figuratively conjure or *pro*ject a self whose most abiding characteristic it is to think of itself as firmly, rationally grounded? Mocking the specious reasonings whereby "*Ich* and *Geist* are but the Christian and Sirname of his weak Iness, J. G. Fichte," Coleridge was to remark sometime after 1815 that Fichte had not shown his notion of immediacy (or feeling) "to be more comprehensible than the Anschauung, & the precious mechanis[m] of Selbstbewusstsein substituted for it." As he sums up his case, "how could Fichte have *made* these abstractions of Reason, Feeling, intuitive space, but from some absolute Entity? And what entitled him to abstract? (Coleridge, 1980–2000, 2: 610–11). Admittedly, though, Coleridge's qualms about Fichte's theory pertain not so much to "the *doctrine,* as to the Chasms in the Proof of it" (ibid., 607), and the latter effectively vitiate all talk of self-consciousness. In a short essay from 1816, Coleridge states the aporetic nature of self-awareness in particularly succinct form:

> *With* the Data of Reflection & with nothing more, there might, I say, be Consciousness; but there could not be Self-consciousness—on the other [hand,] Something more being granted, if this Something were a negatively simple entity, a *Same* throughout, there might be a Self, but not *Consciousness* or conscious Self-knowledge— and Knowledge without Consciousness is not *a Knowing* but a *Being,* and Consciousness is impossible without Distinction—either, namely, a distinction *of* the Scitum from the Sciens, i.e. an alterity of the former, or a Distinction *in* the former—as, for instance, in objects in which Form & Difference is superinduced on Color, Sound, &c.—But in the present case, i.e. the Soul's *Self*-consciousness, the first Distinction is precluded by the terms. The Subject here is one and the same with its object: the Sciens and Scitum are one. It follows therefore that the second Distinction must have place—We must attribute to the Soul, as a self-conscious personal Being, not only a unity that cannot be divided; but this unity must contain distinctnesses that cannot be confounded. The Soul must not only be distinct & therefore distinguishable, *from* other Souls & other Objects, but she must be capable of actually [so] distinguishing herself. But this is impossible, unless there be *in* herself what is ~~are~~ capable of being inter-distinguished. (Coleridge 1995, 1: 427–28)

For Novalis, the constitution of the "I" as a holistic self is forever elusive to philosophy, in that the latter can only grasp its objects by means of reflection. To that end, "we leave the *identical* in order to represent it" (wir verlassen das *Identische* um es darzustellen), which is to say, "we represent [being] by means of its nonbeing, something not identical—a sign" (wir stellen es durch sein Nichtseyn, durch ein Nichtidentisches vor—Zeichen [Novalis 1997, 90 / *WTB*, 2: 8]). Hence, all reflective representation (*Vorstellung*) can only ever attain its cause in etiolated, reified form—namely, *as* object—even as the "essence" of that object rests with its "ineffability: hence any word must put it to flight. [Originally,] any object is non-word, non-concept" (Alle Worte, alle Begriffe sind vom Gegenstande entlehnt—Gegenstände—und darum können sie ihn nicht fixiren. Namenlosigkeit macht gerade sein Wesen aus—darum muß ihn jedes Wort verjagen. Er ist Nichtwort, Nichtbegriff [*WTB*, 2: 110]). The original identity of the "I"—as such simply presupposed in earlier explanations of self-consciousness as a reflexive self-relation and self-recognition—thus falls outside the threshold of what can be authentically known or represented. Indeed, for the conscious subject, the only cue pointing back to his or her antecedent, original self-identity involves, "upon reflection, a curious, persistent longing for philosophical thought or for a systematic connection between thinking and feeling" (Die Reflexion findet das Bedürfnis einer Filosofie, oder eines gedachten, systematischen Zusammenhangs zwischen Denken und Gefühl [Novalis,1997, 97 / *WTB*, 2: 20]). Yet even that affective longing for self-signification and self-determination in systematic, philosophical form can only manifest itself in the alien (Novalis speaks of *Alienation* [Novalis 1997, 92 / *WTB*, 2: 11]) modality of reflective thought, since "it is impossible to represent the pure form of feeling" (Die reine Form des Gefühls ist darzustellen nicht möglich [Novalis 1997, 97 / *WTB*, 2: 21]).

Novalis's much-quoted observation that "*What reflection* finds *already* seems to have been there" (*Was die Reflexion* findet, scheint *schon* dazuseyn [*WTB*, 2: 17; emphases in original]) exposes philosophy's propensity to sleight-of-hand insight, to "anatomizing" (*WTB*, 2: 11) the grounding, affective quality of the "I" and thereby reifying it as an object, a proposition, or a concept. "The spirit of feeling is, then, gone" (Der Geist des Gefühls ist da raus [Novalis 1997, 96 / *WTB*, 2: 18]). Fichte's original act of autogenesis (*Tathandlung*), in which the self posits itself as self-positing and simultaneously demarcates itself from the otherness of the objective world or nonself, appeared to unify the cognate binaries of practice and knowledge, subject and object, intuition and concept, content and form, or substance and accident, all within a single flash of intelligent self-assertion. Fichte's problematic name for this coincidence is "intellectual intuition." Even as Fichte acknowledges the impossibility of grounding the "I" in a self-relation (i.e., in reflection), he is anxious to reclaim this contingent act of original self-creation for systematic, philosophical thought. Fichte clearly understands that "reflection . . . may only trace back to the understanding, wherein it will find *something given* to reflection as the material for its representation, yet it may not become conscious of the modality whereby such material had entered into our understanding"; (although the self "is conditioned in its being, its ability to afford that very being its proper determinations is unconditional" (Fichte 1794, 153, 197; my translation). The "contingency [*Abhängigkeit*] of the I, as intelligence, is to be overcome," and the *science of* knowledge aspires to "exhaust man in his entirety" by restoring "the *unity* and *coherence* to man that are lacking in so many systems" (ibid., 168; 202n; 212; emphases in original).

Not so for Novalis, whose *Fichte-Studien* permanently suspends the systematic pretensions of *Bestimmung.* For the coincidence of "feeling" and "reflection" (or intuition and concept) in an originary act of self-creation and self-assertion—Fichte's *Tathandlung,* which Novalis rechristens *Urhandlung*—can itself only be proclaimed from the vantage point of reflection: "The originary act is the *unity* of feeling and reflection, [seen from] within reflection" (Die Urhandlung ist die *Einheit* des Gefühls und der Reflexion, in der Reflexion [Novalis 1997, 99 / *WTB,* 2: 24)]. Echoing Rousseau's and Godwin's Enlightenment faith in *perfectibilité,* Fichte's proclamations of the self's intrinsic rationality and determinability seem motivated by an underlying, quasi-metaphysical dread—one that Novalis alternately portrays as the specter of linguistic indeterminacy and of interpretive contingency. "If the subject doesn't postulate the absolute I, it will perforce be swallowed up by an abyss of error—this, however, can only happen for reflection—which is to say, only for one part of the subject, the merely reflexive one" (Postulirt das Subject nicht das absolute Ich, so mußes sich in einem Abgrund von Irrtum verlieren—dis kann aber nur für die Reflexion geschehn—also für einen Theil des Subjects nur, dem blos reflectirenden [*WTB,* 2: 36]).[33] Novalis thus reads Fichte's philosophy as largely unaware of its partial, reactive, and self-legitimating structure, and therefore as a doomed attempt at "presenting a state of non-reflective [being] by means of reflection, and one simply never gets to non-reflection in this manner" (denn man will die Nichtreflexion durch Reflexion darstellen und kommt eben dadurch nie zur Nichtreflexion hin [*WTB,* 2: 27]).

"Instinct transfigured into art": Feeling, Drives, and Constructivist Aesthetics

As a thorough critique of the scope of reflective thought and the systematic philosophical ambitions connected with it, Novalis's *Fichte-Studien* alerts us to two shortcomings in the theory of knowledge as a reflexive (self-)relation.

First, reflective knowledge invariably covers only a part ("half") of the phenomena that solicit its scrutiny. Second, while the "drive" behind reflection—namely, to assign a determinate content to an inherently unconditional state—is itself unlimited in its aspirations, the knowledge produced by reflection invariably betrays its rhetorical, mediated character; all reflective knowledge necessarily effects a distortion or inversion of its objects: "Our entire faculty of perception is like the eye," Novalis remarks in his later collection of fragments, *Blüthenstaub.* "Objects must pass through opposite mediums in order to make their proper appearance on the pupil" (Die Objekte müßen durch entgegengesetzte Media durch, um richtig auf der Pupille zu erscheinen (Novalis 1999, 24 / *WTB*, 2: 229). Because all reflection involves mediation by signs, it inverts the absolute identity of the self's original condition (*Zustand*), one that it can only capture in the alien modality of predication isolating a determinate content (*Gehalt*).[34]

Hence, as Manfred Frank and Gerhard Kurz have so cogently argued, Novalis urges a second, supplemental reflection that qualifies the knowledge produced by ordinary, reflective thinking.[35] Such a reflection acknowledges the necessarily inverse relation between Being and Form, Feeling and Proposition in all representation (*Vorstellung*). Yet unlike Hegel, who institutes this secondary reflection as the very means whereby individual "opinion" (*Meinung*) yields up (*entäussert*) its contingent qualities and so is sublated into collective knowledge, Novalis does not invest this second-order reflection with systematic and absolute potential. To be sure, his *Fichte-Studien offers* the first philosophical argument "where the critique of reflection is itself effected by reflection. Yet, unlike Hegel's type of argumentation, . . . [Novalis's theory] actually issues a challenge to the autonomy of reflection. By negating itself, reflection may correct the false position of thought into its own truth, to be sure, yet it cannot claim to have been the originator of that truth" (Frank 1977, 79). Reflection, and hence systematic philosophy, merely holds a corrective, though never a properly creative authority; Novalis puts it bluntly: "[Philosophy] generates nothing" (Hervorbringen kann sie nichts [*WTB*, 2: 17]. For the truth of "feeling" as an identity primordially given preexists all conscious reflection and representation, no matter how cognizant (and shrewd in remedying) the latter may be of its own distortions.

Yet far from terminating in a philosophical pessimism (itself an absolute and hence illegitimate position), this inability of thought to reclaim the absolute identity of the self to which thought itself owes its driving, searching, and reflexive specificity gives rise to a new, aesthetically focused type of thinking. In an entry to a later manuscript group of the *Fichte-Studien,* Novalis articulates this break with systematic philosophy with stirring clarity:

> Philosophizing has to be a unique way of thinking. What do I do when I philosophize? I reflect upon a ground [*Grund*]. A striving toward the thinking of a ground is thus the ground of philosophizing. Ground does not, however, mean cause in the literal sense, but rather inner nature—connection to the whole. Thus all philosophizing must end at an absolute ground. If such a ground were not given, if this concept contained an impossibility, then the drive to philosophize would be an infinite activity. Thus it would be without end, because there would be an eternal need for an absolute ground, which could only be satisfied to a relative degree, and therefore would never cease. . . . Philosophy, the result of philosophizing, comes about through the *interruption* [*Unterbrechung*] of the drive for a knowledge of ground—through suspension at the point where one finds oneself. Abstraction from the absolute ground and the advancing of the actual absolute ground of freedom, validating it by means of interconnecting and reifying a whole [*Verknüpfung* <*Verganzung*>] of that which stands to be resolved into a whole." (Novalis 1997, 107–8; translation modified / *WTB,* 2: 180–81)

Bidding farewell to philosophy's delusive quest for "grounding" the "I" through a reflexive conversion of its original identity into an intellectual proposition ("feeling" into "form"), Novalis proceeds to articulate an alternate poetics of *erdenken* (Erdenken ist Dichten [Novalis 1997, 109 / *WTB,* 2: 182]). In it, the categorical assertions of logic give way to a temporal developmental praxis (*Wircksamkeit*) aimed not at "expressive" communication but at the formal-aesthetic or (in Müller-Sievers's reading) "epigenetic" construction of a self. Novalis is well aware that the impossibility of rendering the self transparent unto itself will necessarily also wreak havoc with mechanical theories of language as communication and their naïve premise of a timeless correspondence between word and object. The opening pages of his *Fichte-Studien note* how, if "sign and signified are completely separate . . . and if their relationship exists in the first signifying person alone, it is only by chance or miracle that the signified comes across to the second signifying person by means of such a sign" (Sind aber . . . Zeichen und Bezeichnetes völlig getrennt, ist ihre Beziehung blos im ersten Bezeichnenden, so kann es nur ein Zufall oder

Wunder seyn, wenn durch ein solches Zeichen das Bezeichnete dem 2ten Bezeichnenden übereinkommt [Novalis 1997, 93 / *WTB*, 2: 13]). The long passage quoted above emphasizes the hermeneutic chasm forever separating the intention entering into the production of signifiers from that underlying their reception. Thus a calculated wordplay on *Grund* (motive, cause, foundation) alerts us to the polysemy of all signs and to the open-ended temporality of all language-based *Darstellung*—and Novalis is quick to draw attention to the myriad cognitive possibilities and interpretive horizons opened up by that very fact. The rhetorical play and conceptual indeterminacy that attend all speculation about the limits of systematic, philosophical reflection account for the fundamental *temporality* of thought—a process whose analeptic and retroactive qualities Novalis finds nicely captured in the prefix of the German word for thinking, *Nachdenken,* literally an "afterthought." Indeed, Novalis's later fragments (e.g., *Blüthenstaub* and *Vorarbeiten 1798*) exhibit a verbal creativity within the domain of theory not seen again until Nietzsche and Wittgenstein. An example of Novalis's precursor role can be found in the following, brief fragment on the indelible temporality and linguistic materiality constraining thought from its very beginning:

> Aller wircklicher Anfang ist ein 2ter Moment. Alles was da ist, erscheint, ist und erscheint nur unter *einer Voraussetzung*—Sein individueller Grund, sein *absolutes Selbst* geht ihm voraus—muß wenigstens *vor* ihm gedacht werden. Ich muß *allem* etwas absolutes *Voraus*denken—voraussetzen—Nicht auch *Nachdenken, Nachsetzen? / Vorurtheil.* Vorsatz. Vorempfindung. Vorbild. Vor Fantasie. *Project.* (*WTB*, 2: 380; emphases in original)

> All actual beginnings are secondary moments. Whatever is there, makes its appearance, is and appears only under *one precondition*—its individual ground, its *absolute self* already precedes it—or must at least be thought as *prior* to it. I must at all times think of an absolute *in advance* of what I think—*pre*suppose—hence, [mustn't I] also *re*flect, *re*trace? / *Pre*judice. *Pre*conception. *Pre*sentiment. *Pre*figure. *Pre*fantasy. *Pro*jection.

Relative to the "chaos" of being itself, all cognition exhibits the traces of this secondariness in its precarious linguistic constitution. Because "words are a deceptive medium for some anterior cognition—unreliable vehicles for a determinate, specific stimulus" (Die Worte sind ein trügliches Medium des Vordenckens—unzuverlässige Vehikel eines bestimmten, specifischen Reitzes

[*WTB*, 2: 312]), all expressive practice, however skilful, will have to be favored by a magical sympathy or recognition on the part of its recipient. "Every word is an instance of conjury" (Jedes Wort ist ein Wort der Beschwörung [ibid., 313]), Novalis remarks, and for the individual to attain completeness as a self requires less the ministrations of formal logic than the magical charisma of art (Vollständiges Ich zu seyn, ist eine *Kunst* [ibid., 206; emphasis in original]).

The first order of business, then, becomes to expunge any residues of eighteenth-century "correspondence-theories" of language: "Logical concepts relate to each other as words do, without thoughts" while "metaphysical concepts relate to each other like *thoughts, without words*" (die logischen Begriffe verhalten sich aber zu einander, wie die Worte, ohne Gedanken. . . . Die metaphysischen Begriffe verhalten sich zu einander, wie Gedanken, ohne Worte [Novalis 1999, 51; *WTB*, 2: 317]). In their stead, Novalis conceives of aesthetic form as ceaselessly evolving, progressing, and imbued with a magical aura. In its syntagmatic organization as "text," the aesthetic emulates life itself. In literature, "words are not universal signs but, rather, tones—words of conjury" (Worte sind nicht allgemeine Zeichen—Töne sind es—Zauberworte [*WTB*, 2: 324]). Herein lies the epistemological relevance and authority of literature: it no longer submits to the government of systematic philosophy but offers itself as the fictional remedy for the imperiled authority, the indemonstrable "ground" of rational, reflective thought. Andrew Bowie calls this "the move from revelation to literature" (74). What had been so anxiously kept at bay by Fichte's efforts to ground the "I" strictly by means of purely logical, simultaneous reflexive determinations (*Reflexionsbestimmungen*), now points theory toward the aesthetic and helps philosophy recover from its "epistemological state-of-emergency" (Frank 1989, 269) through the medium of poesy.[36] Art, and specifically the art of narrative (romance, the novel), thus gives form to a subjectivity that has fully recognized and, in the productive medium of art, come to embrace its irreducibly temporal constitution. In Novalis's rigorously dialectical conception of developmental time, there is no expectation of a *parousia* in the guise of an immediate "feeling" or "intellectual intuition" and, consequently, no "ground" for Fichte's reflexive determinations and their pursuit of systematic and universal Enlightenment. Rather, the present is simply a virtual axis for the differential and open-ended determination of the self via its putative identity—an absolute state of self-identical being anterior to all reflective knowledge, seemingly recollected from the past and tenuously projected as an object of future recovery: "A universal system of philosophy must be constituted like time itself, a thread that guides us through infinite determinations" (Das Universalsystem der Filosofie muß wie die Zeit seyn, Ein Faden, an dem man durch unendliche Bestimmungen laufen kann [*WTB,* 2: 201]). The systematic ambitions of philosophy have thus for the first time been supplanted by the dynamics of presentation (*Darstellung*), "an expression of the inner state, of inner transformation, a manifestation of the inner object" (Darstellung ist eine Aeußerung des innern Zustands, der innern Veränderungen—Erscheinung des innern Objects [ibid., 195]). The self's estrangement from its own ineffable identity—manifest as a "feeling," yet irrecuperable for any finite, conscious individual—thus proves constitutive of its very being. To be a self is to occupy "a position [that] is not what it represents, and that does not represent what it is" ([Sein] Stand ist nicht, was er vorstellt, und stellt nicht vor, was er ist [ibid., 135]). Anticipating Heidegger and Sartre, this *ek-static* subjectivity is in its very essence nonbeing, forever on the verge of consciously grasping and giving expression to the very horizon of temporality that circumscribes all consciousness.[37]

For Novalis, the most apt generic expression of this philosophical predicament—which also opens up romanticism's sense of literature as an "absolute" opportunity—can be encountered in the novel, specifically when read as the generic transformation of romance. The latter genre's teleological quest for an idealized or eroticized other, a mythical, absolute presence that is to heal the wound of a provisionally alienated self, has been abandoned in the novel. Not surprisingly, Novalis is the first author mentioned and quoted in Georg Lukács's *Theory of the Novel,* a book whose opening pages reproduce with truly Joycean mimicry the Jena school's sententious prophecies and, more specifically, Novalis's depiction of philosophy's dream of "being at home everywhere." Philosophy, in its quest to pinpoint a "transcendental *locus*" on an "archetypal map" of its own devising, finds itself inexorably drawn toward a hypothetical state of "self-being . . . where there is not yet any interiority, for there is not yet any exterior, any 'otherness' for the soul." And yet, when looked upon as an epistemological quest-romance, "philosophy, as a form of life or as that which determines the form and supplies the content of literary creation, is always a symptom of the rift between 'inside' and 'outside,' a sign of the essential difference between the self and the world, the incogruence of soul and deed" (Lukács, 29).[38]

For Walter Benjamin, the romantic and post-romantic novel above all gives, "[i]n the midst of life's fullness, and through the representation of this fullness

. . . evidence of the profound perplexity of the living" (1968, 87). What Lukács, a decade earlier, had famously characterized as the novel's inherent condition of "transcendental homelessness" is now worked out, in Benjamin's essay, as the atrophying of experience by modernity's irresolvable web of contradictions. If, in the wake of World War I, the 1923 deflation, and the foibles of Weimar, "strategic experience [has been thoroughly contradicted] by tactical warfare, economic experience by inflation, bodily experience by mechanical warfare, moral experience by those in power" (ibid., 84), the storyteller's aura of absolute presence and oral immediacy now seems impossibly remote.

For Novalis, literature can only dream of absolute beginnings such as Fichte's "intellectual intuition," itself the basis for the self's epigenetic construction as it is to be advanced by what Fichte calls the logical drive (*Trieb*) and its "reflexive determinations" (*Reflexionsbestimmungen*). Novalis voices Fichte's (and philosophy's) predicament with epigrammatic concision: "To describe man has been impossible up to now because what a person is has not been known. As soon as what a person is becomes known it will also be possible to offer a genetic account of the individual" (Menschen zu beschreiben ist deswegen bis jetzt unmöglich gewesen, weil man nicht gewußt hat, was ein Mensch ist. Wenn man erst wissen wird, was ein Mensch ist, so wird man auch Individuen genetisch beschreiben können [*WTB*, 2: 281]). Foreshadowing Benjamin, who himself scrupulously studied and wrote on the fragments of the Jena romantics, Novalis conceives of fiction and the poetic word as a magical, virtual remedy for philosophy's inability to furnish a genetic account of the modern individual. Given that a rigorously causal and genetic construction of the individual proves impossible, the status of history and the value to be assigned to its experience turns out to be imperiled to the point of having vanished. Whereas Benjamin surmises that the storyteller in his "living immediacy" belongs to a mythical past (itself, perhaps, only a retroactive fiction), and as a result, experience "has fallen in value" (Benjamin 1968, 83–84), Novalis tells us outright that "the novel has its origins in a lack of history" (Der Roman ist aus Mangel der Geschichte entstanden [*WTB*, 2: 829]). Consequently, it can recover the inscrutable totality of its protagonist's inner world only through moments of serendipity, "conjury" (*Zauber*), or "magic" (*Magie*), qualities that Novalis regards as the unique property of the aesthetic.

Given its supplemental relation to the impasse of systematic philosophy, the novel unfolds as an infinite variation (*Variations Operation* [*WTB*, 2: 343]) whereby—through the detour or supplement of the aesthetic—the modern individual reflexively fashions him- or herself as *fiction:* "All chance events of our lives are materials from which we can make what we like. Whoever is rich in spirit makes much of his life. For the thoroughly spiritual person, every acquaintance, every incident, would be the first element in an endless series, the beginning of an infinite novel" ([Novalis 1999, 33; translation modified] Alle Zufälle unsers Lebens sind Materialien, aus denen wir machen können, was wir wollen. Wer viel Geist hat, macht viel aus seinem Leben. Jede Bekanntschaft, jeder Vorfall, wäre für den durchaus Geistigen erstes Glied einer unendlichen Reihe, Anfang eines unendlichen Romans [*WTB*, 2: 252]). Thus the novel can only offer itself as an extended prose signature of modernity's ironic constitution, namely, by enacting at the symbolic and thematic level the deeper recognition that any quest for an absolute and permanent ground is impossible, because categorically beyond the reach of presentation (*Darstellung*). Such a poetics is emphatically postclassical in that here "form is no longer the expression of beauty but an expression of art as the idea itself" (Benjamin 1996, 176). Faced with the impossibility of grounding self-consciousness in an immediate act of production, literature elects this very dilemma as the focal point of its own, extended prosaic constitution. Novalis embraces an essential and irremediable asymmetry between emotion and expression (or indexical reference): "Unrepresentable by any individual sign, emotion is represented by traces in a differential network. Textuality offers an alternative to expression and indication."[39] Stripped of its absolute, systematic pretensions, the principle of reflexivity has, in fact, been salvaged, inasmuch as it is now mediated by the artwork's dynamic polarities of *Darstellung* and *Kritik.* Benjamin calls such art *Reflexionsmedium.* As Novalis puts it, "if a given problem is of an insoluble character, then we solve it by presenting its insolubility" (Wenn der Caracter des gegebenen Problems Unauflöslichkeit ist, so lösen wir dasselbe, wenn wir seine Unauflöslichkeit darstellen [*WTB*, 2: 613]).[40] With its dialectical and infinite organization, the novel—a concept that names both a literary form and its critical effects—thus reveals the necessarily supplemental character of the aesthetic.

Once rechristened *Instinkt,* Fichte's inexorable logical drive (*Trieb*) is no longer legitimated by its putative telos (viz., self-consciousness) but, instead, unfolds as a variational, open-ended progression. If human "instinct is *unintentional* art," it can yet be "transfigured into *art*" (Instinkt ist Kunst *ohne Absicht.* . . . Der Instinkt läßt sich in *Kunst* verwandeln [*WTB*, 2: 520]). For the primordial character of the intellect lies in its persistent tendency to formal adaptation and developmental variation, thus conjuring up a dynamic progression that is above all committed to prolonging itself and so giving rise to ever more complex meanings. Seen within such a pre-Darwinian model, self-awareness and the symbolic forms by which it is progressively effected are simply so many formal devices created and ceaselessly refashioned for the purpose of self-preservation.[41] Amid the numerous fragments dedicated to physics, medicine, and the role of the central nervous system in Novalis's *Allgemeines Brouillon* (1798–99), the following entry argues for the epigenetic (self-creating and self-perpetuating) nature of human instinct as a dynamic principle ceaselessly in search of formal and material means for its own survival:

> Der Instinkt, als Gefühl des Bedürfnisses, des Incompletten—ist zugleich das Gefühl des Zusammenhangs, d[er] Stätigkeit—der *fortleitende*—sich tastend orientirende Sinn . . . der rohe, synthetisch complettirende Trieb—ein *transitorisches—Punctähnliches* Ich. (*WTB*, 2: 683)

> Instinct, as the feeling of need and incompleteness—is at the same time the feeling of a connection, of *continuity*—the sense of continuity and a quasitactile orientation. . . . It is the raw drive toward synthetic completion—a *transitional—quasi monadic* "I."

Aesthetic form thus serves the purpose of mediating the individual for him- or herself by providing "archetypes" (*Urbilder*) and "exemplars" (*Vorbilder*). This romantic conception of literature, not merely as an art, but as a formal-epistemological device for self-prolongation and survival would seem in some sense to adumbrate certain Darwinist ideas or even Heidegger's concept of the subject as an *Entwurf* ("project").[42] In Novalis, then, subjectivity attains reality only through its capacity of imaginatively "*pro*jecting" itself into concrete symbolic constructs and so "*re*membering" an inherently *dis*membered self. Literature's new function is to simulate the "ground" of subjectivity that had proven ineluctable for philosophy, a ground now reconceived as the object of aesthetic surmise, a lingering mood or "sense sublime of something far more deeply interfused"—a "feeling" (*Gefühl*). Subjectivity in Novalis appears above all taken up with generating signs, sounds, words, poetry, books—all simulations of a ground felt to be permanently inaccessible. Anticipating Hegel's well-known reference to the "cunning of reason" (*List der Vernunft*), "instinct" in Novalis is defined above all by its unrelenting creation of complex forms whose magical charisma (*Darstellung*) and interpretive effects (*Kritik*) seem no less compelling than the preternatural certitude of "feeling." Driven and guided by a prereflective "instinct," feeling reconstitutes itself in objective form as stylized, "artful" representation, literature.

The novel in particular lends formal-aesthetic specificity to an epigenetic model of subjectivity that had ultimately been theoretically indemonstrable in both Kant and Fichte. It is just this attention to the novel's sensuous amalgamation of the prosaic and the magical—the coincidence of banality and conjury in the operation of reference—that prompts Novalis to characterize his own speculations as the apotheosis of Fichtean philosophy. "To Fichtecize better than Fichte himself" (besser Fichtisiren als Fichte [*WTB*, 2: 314]), however, no longer means to beat systematic thought at its own game but, rather, to forgo such "intellectual contrivances" (*Gedankenkunststücke* [ibid.]) in favor of an open-ended presentation of feeling. Nowhere are the Jena school's misgivings concerning the ability of thought to ground and authorize itself by means of a decisive act of self-reflection or self-positing more evident than in the repeated instances of déja vu that permeate its fictions. A case in point would be Novalis's *Heinrich von Ofterdingen,* where the ineffable, partial recognition of déja vu effectively becomes part of what its author elsewhere calls "romantic rhythm"—a moment of serendipitous, albeit inconclusive, insight stimulating its subject to emotional or cognitive advance, albeit without any further possibility of being authenticated and consolidated as genuine knowledge.[43]

Both Kant and Novalis conceive of "feeling" as an irreducibly social phenomenon, simply because its very discernment and potential significance demand that it be exiled from its putative site of origin (the solitary individual) and transposed into the intersubjective and constructivist domain of the aesthetic work. Such a radically allegorical model of emotion—arguably *the* transformative event in romantic theory—sets the stage for the readings that will follow. For whether it is the concept of paranoia, trauma, or melancholy, we shall find romanticism looking upon emotional life as accessible solely if and when transposed into aesthetic forms that continually reaffirm the "textual difference between ideality and substance" (Terada, 45). If Novalis still claims a truth-content and an ethical mission for voice, he does so not in spite of but because of its apparent medial, textual dimension. For in reconstituting feeling in the virtual form of art, voice also prepares the ground for the social circulation and effectivity of emotion. Only as a text soliciting interpretive discernment and collaboration does the Kantian "feeling" actually attain its epistemological objective of facilitating "cognition in general" (*Erkenntnis überhaupt*)—namely, by ensuring its "communicability" not *through* but *as* textual form. Kant's ambivalent bequest to aesthetic theory thus involves his naming—in the precise way that the act of "naming" hovers between the creative and the recursive, the tropological and the referential—"pleasure" and "voice" as the nontranscendable conditions for the operation of criticism itself. The question of Kant's third *Critique* concerning the grounds and social legitimacy of "critical" knowledge is also its ambivalent bequest to nineteenth-century theory. Arguably, this question of how to conceive of a "voice" (*Stimme*) capable of investing the irreducible experience of "pleasure" with greater social significance amounts to a constitutive obligation of critical practice. The abiding significance of Kant's text lies in its conceptual struggle with the fundamental tension between the formal and material dimensions of all appearance. The aim of Kant's critical project is to draw a balance, however provisional, between our intuitive and our rational faculties, between our idiosyncratic inclination toward uniquely material textures of a world subjectively experienced and the crucial, if comparatively mediated, obligation to render that world more permanently inhabitable, or rational.

To recognize that there ought to be "balance" between these two stances—which adumbrates the ethical commitment of Kant's *Critique*—is also to acknowledge that aesthetic production and critical knowledge are rooted in the same impulse. For that reason, Kant sensibly chose to leave undetermined whether the voice of critique ought to be understood as an integral component of aesthetic experience or merely as one of its epiphenomenal effects. He did so not because he did not know how to answer the question but because he felt, intuitively perhaps, that it would be the wrong question to ask or, at the very least, a fateful one to answer. For any attempt to resolve the issue by pronouncing the work of critique to be wholly isomorphous with the contingent material experiences that gave rise to it or, alternatively, as sublating (*aufheben*) aesthetic experience into pure abstractions invariably forecloses on the ethical implications of critical practice. For such an embrace of a theoretical solipsism or, alternatively, a mystical or hedonistic materialism severs the dialectical ties between experience and cognition by either eclipsing the unique formal-material nature of aesthetic experience or becoming wholly absorbed in the latter, our capacity for articulating its significance. Yet precisely this attempt at reflecting on aesthetic experience as a complex embodiment of social and spiritual meanings positions the voice of critique at the margin of epistemology and ethics.

Coda: Linguistic Form and Mood as Dialectic in Wordsworth, Hegel, and Hölderlin

With an equanimity that may seem startling today, Wordsworth's *Preface* to *Lyrical Ballads* (1800–1802) remarks, almost in passing, it would seem, how cognition and emotion are intimately entwined: "our continued influxes of feeling are modified and directed by our thoughts, which are indeed the representatives of all our past feelings." Throughout the *Preface,* we witness a strategic alignment of "repeated experience and regular feelings" (Wordsworth 1992a, 744–45), it being Wordsworth's contention (not at all unlike Nussbaum's neo-Stoic view) that emotion or feeling relates to thought the way the climate relates to local weather conditions.

Shrewdly echoing Edmund Burke's paean to the "cold sluggishness of our national temper" (Burke, 187), Wordsworth fashions a deliberately understated lyric idiom so as to funnel potentially volatile emotions into "habits"—a term designating an unapparent social disposition, at once temporally enduring and holistic in scope: "So by the repetition and continuance of this act feelings connected with important subjects will be nourished, till at length, if we be originally possessed of much organic sensibility, such habits of mind will be produced that by obeying blindly and mechanically the impulses of those habits we shall describe objects and utter sentiments of such a nature and in such a connection with each other, that the understanding of the being to whom we address ourselves, if he be in a healthful state of association, must necessarily be in some degree enlightened, his taste exalted, and his affections ameliorated" (Wordsworth 1992a, 745). In so many words, this passage accords feeling a transcendental quality. Yet to be able to pronounce the foundational status of feeling as a fundamental mode of "being-in-the-world" (and we shall have occasion to return to Heidegger's conception of "mood" in the context of Keats and melancholy), Wordsworth briefly sketches the linguistic circuitry through which feeling constitutes itself. Unfolding as a metonymic series, the passage leads us from "feeling" to "sensibility" to "impulses" and "habits," all of which are treated simply as epiphenomena of a discursive practice in which feeling operates as a social, not private, phenomenon. What language achieves is a social connectivity that pivots not on logical propositions but on far more indirect and recondite processes. When "we address" ourselves to others, it is the mood of speech or, rather, the transference or projection of mood *through* and *as* speech aimed at realizing a post-Enlightenment social vision. Far from being "expressive" of a mood, aesthetic work proves generative—on a fundamental level that precedes discrete impulses, volitions, or conscious intentions—of what, in his revision of Kantian transcendentalism, Heidegger came to identify as the "mood" (*Stimmung*) of *Dasein:* a "mood" that circumscribes social life in a transcendental (or, for Heidegger, ontological) sense by conditioning a priori all possibilities of being. Significantly, a "mood" such as an aesthetic feeling of pleasure assumes in Kant a positive, constructive power, whereas in Heidegger, it appears as the invisible "horizon" of finitude that can be exposed only by a thoroughgoing "destruction" of metaphysics.

Hovering between the two positions, Wordsworth posits that the Enlightenement's key objectives of cognitive, moral, and social improvement ("enlightened," "exalted," "ameliorated") cannot be realized by the syllogistic and abstract machinations of reason. Rather, they demand a constructivist aesthetic and, corresponding to it, a heuristic model of literature as mandating engaged, rather than distracted, reading. Beginning with the "Advertisement" to *Lyrical Ballads* in 1798, which repeatedly characterizes the new literary paradigm as an "experiment," social progress is viewed as "insensibly" premised on, or mediated by, aesthetic construction. Crucially, such a reorientation of Enlightenment thought, which, for Wordsworth, was primarily defined by the French materialists and Encyclopedists, radically alters the status and role of emotions. For in the passage quoted above, emotions no longer constitute a given individual's exclusive domain and expressive resource but, instead, reveal themselves as a Jamesian "figure in the carpet" of discursive life. Feeling is an inferred, not autonomous, value, one whose ideality can only ever be asserted ex post facto. Already in Wordsworth, feeling is being understood as the ontological "mood" that shapes social life (the Lacanian "Real") itself, as something that arises, unbeknownst to itself, from the continuously evolving interplay of a myriad, simultaneously existing, semi-independent genres of speech and writing (discursive or literary, religious, political, journalistic, professional, etc.). "Feeling" in Wordsworth thus orients a priori the discursive and expressive behavior of individuals and communities. For that very reason, *Stimmung* (mood) proves inaccessible to cognition except by a peculiar "awakening" of the kind attempted by Kant's transcendental method and Heidegger's ontological rethinking of metaphysics.[44] Wordsworth's *Preface,* meanwhile, is particularly concerned with recalibrating the relation between a fundamental conception of feeling such as mood and its vicarious encryption in language, especially in the obliquely constructionist "poetics" of the ballad. As we shall see in Chapter 4, Wordsworth values deceptively simple genres because they mediate individual and communal identity as a belated interpretive struggle with volatile determinants abruptly surfacing from the past. The ballad and its permutations (inflected as pastoral in "Michael" and as gothic in the Lucy poems) thus provide a sphere for complex, interpretive collaboration between author and reader. Poetry here positions mood as the focal point for sustained hermeneutic engagement, a virtual infrastructure mediating social existence as interpretive process. Through the lyric's and the ballad's formal experimentation with multiple, often incompatible fictive personae and voices, "mood" is being crystallized, neither as the diametrical opposite nor as a mere prolegomenon of rationality, but as the historically specific quality of what Heidegger was to elaborate as being-in-the world.

While he has thus far not been invoked in person, Hegel's philosophy has already figured in my argument by implication, namely, as the epitome of early-nineteenth-century theoretical optimism committed to dialectically redeem emotions, like all other particulars, from their contingent, oblique, and idiosyncratic nature. Such, at least, is the stated goal of Hegel's *Encyclopedia* where, in § 447, we learn that "the form possessed by spirit in feeling is the lowest and the worst, that of self-absorbed [*selbstisch*] singularity, within which spirit lacks the freedom of infinite universality, its capacity and content being contingent, subjective, and particular" (Hegel 1978, 121; translation modified). Emotion here is construed as palpable evidence of an "as yet" incomplete movement of self-conscious universality; it is, in Hegel's characteristic parlance, "still devoid of spirit" (*noch geistlos* [ibid., 124]). Even so, it is a systematic imperative of Hegelian thought that any given disposition of mind, however deficient vis-à-vis the overarching objectives of speculative thought, must yet contain within it fuel that will keep the dialectical machine running. Feeling, in other words, cannot simply be itself but must, however obliquely, already contain within itself an impetus toward self-reflection and conceptual externalization (*Entäußerung*). A latent measure of perceptual acuity or "attentiveness" (in the Addendum to § 448 of the *Encyclopedia,* Hegel introduces the term *Aufmerksamkeit*) must already be contained within even the most ephemeral and self-absorbed emotive state. For it is only out of such speculative seeds that reflective thought can acquire its energy and direction. Yet to make that observation is to concede a peculiar, as it were, retroactive, dependency of speculative thinking on supposedly contingent and inferior particularities, a dependency that speculative thinking itself can never fully assimilate.

Wordsworth's contention that "our thoughts . . . are indeed the representatives of all our past feelings" thus also holds true for Hegel.

It is instructive in this regard to observe Hegel's discussion of lyric poetry in the *Aesthetics* struggle with a tension that opens up between the systematic *cum* historical objectives of its overall narrative, on the one hand, and evidence that the lyric might effectively amount to an alternate, perhaps complementary mode of cognition, on the other. Rather than restricting the lyric to a merely "immediate" and as yet unreflective expression of feeling, Hegel posits the genre as the medium most suited to extracting the intentionality and lucidity encrypted by a given feeling. The lyric's peculiar cogency is thus understood to reside precisely in conveying a knowledge altogether unattainable if one were to disregard its phenomenal presentation *as a sustained feeling or mood.* Unlike philosophical thought, which can treat emotions only in a prosaic form that denies them their essential qualities, lyric poetry is capable of grasping (*begreifen*) feeling *as* feeling; the lyric "gives words and language to this enriched inner life so that *as inner life* it may find expression." Inwardness in lyric form is not mired in its affective or emotive particulars but, through the conduit of lyric (figural) language, has advanced far in articulating the perception of values and conflicts encrypted in emotional life, albeit without denying their mode of appearance as emotions. Hence, in Hegel's precise diction, the lyric's task is "to liberate the spirit not *from* but *in* feeling. The blind dominion of passion lies in an unconscious and dull unity between itself and the entirety of a heart that cannot rise out of itself into ideas and self-expression. Poetry does deliver the heart from this slavery to passion by making it see itself, but it does not stop at merely extricating this felt passion from its immediate unity with the heart but makes it an object purified from all accidental moods [*ein von jeder Zufälligkeit der Stimmungen gereinigtes Objekt*]" (Hegel 1975, 1111–12 / German: 1986, 3: 417). Poetry constitutes a unique phase in the evolution of philosophical self-consciousness, one potentially inimical to Hegel's overarching systematic interests, according to which art is merely a dress-rehearsal for a philosophical prose of the world deemed best for expressing the idea of freedom as it animates and guides the entire dialectical movement of Hegelian thought. For lyric poetry here presents itself as a form of expression that reproduces the comprehensive social knowledge dormant in emotional life without simply jettisoning the emotional, "felt" quality of that knowledge. This it achieves by embodying emotions in a language that always reflects on its own medial character *as language.* Long before Roman Jakobson's conception of the "poetic function" as a focus on language as phonetic matter, Hegel's theory of the lyric asserts poetry's reflexive relationship to its linguistic and rhetorical underpinnings. Precisely because of its sustained reflexivity, poetry is capable of articulating the representative, exemplary knowledge encrypted in what would otherwise remain contingent emotional states of an individual.

It is important to note that here, as in part 3 of the *Encyclopedia* or in the early sections of the *Phenomenology,* feeling or emotion must strike the Hegelian subject with traumatizing force, or, more precisely, that emotion specifies the moment where history does so. For the obliquity of emotion is not a shortcoming to be identified and overcome by the ministrations of reflective consciousness and philosophical prose; it is not a vacuum, a "not yet" merely presaging the plenitude of philosophical cognition. Rather, to be fully consistent with the Hegelian regime of phenomena, the material and psychophysical concreteness of a given "feeling" attests to a highly condensed knowledge striking the subject with its full complexity—one not pared down *by,* and perhaps permanently uncontainable *by,* any concept. In short, feeling comprises an over- not underdetermined knowledge of how the subject is embedded in the world.[45]

For Raymond Williams, mapping the nearly imperceptible but ceaseless transformation of historical existence calls for tracing an essential affective dimension through its aesthetic embodiment. Setting aside the rigors and orthodoxies of vulgar Marxist or Hegelian theory that polemicize from the vantage point of "fixed social generality" against everything "'subjective' and 'personal,'" Williams takes note of "an unmistakable presence of certain elements in art which are not covered by . . . other formal systems." In his view, the "'aesthetic', 'the arts' and 'imaginative literature'" grant access to "structures of feeling. . . . We are talking about characteristic elements of impulse, restraint, and tone; specifically affective elements of consciousness and relationships: not feeling against thought, but thought as felt and feeling as thought: practical consciousness of a present kind, in a living and interrelating continuity." Foreshadowing Williams's subsequent definition of "structures of feeling . . . as social experiences in solution" (Williams, 132, 133), Hegel cites the ballad as an example of feeling as an obliquely intersubjective and intentional form of social and historical experience. In the genres of folk poetry, and ballads in particular, "what is made recognizable . . . is not a single individual poet with his own peculiar manner of portraying himself artistically, but a national feeling [*Volksempfindung*] which the individual wholly and entirely bears in himself because his own inner ideas and feelings are not divorced from his people or its existence and interests" (Hegel 1975, 1124 / German: 1986, 3: 433).

Lyric poetry thus achieves the twofold goal of drawing out the oblique intentionality of feeling, its representative and exemplary force, without betraying the fact that the social knowledge in question can only properly disclose itself as emotion. Thus, far from absorbing the aesthetic into the autonomy and formal transparency of the idea, the 1,200 pages of Hegel's *Aesthetics* present what Tilottama Rajan has called "an interrupted and deferred teleology," a narrative in which discrete art forms stage a "subversion of aesthetics, [just] as phenomenology is a sub-version of idealism" (Rajan 1995, 173–74). In taking into account that important qualification in its formal-aesthetic design, poetry effectively achieves a cognition that may be viewed as superior to philosophical thought, even by Hegel's own standards, inasmuch as it doesn't relate indifferently to the medium of cognition. The capacious social knowledge is objectively rendered as the lyric's rhetorical form, with its intricate figural operations, rhythmic patterns, verbal echoes, and sonorities—a form sufficiently complex to reconstitute the "mood" in the form of which the holistic knowledge of historical existence had made itself felt. Here "the cognitive grasping is not produced by the emotional experience, it is embedded in it" (Nussbaum, 243).

In addition to being so cognitively complex, lyric poetry (like all genuine art) also discredits all sentimental or philistine claims of the petit-bourgeois subject to "feeling" as personal, inalienable property. For the "inner life" of the lyric subject now appears divided, being "partly the individual's pure unity with himself," while at the same time finding itself "fragmented and dispersed into the most diversified particularizations, insights, etc.; and their linkage consists solely in the fact that one and the same self carries them, so to say, as their mere vessel. Therefore, in order to be the centre which holds the whole lyric work of art together the poet must have achieved a *specific* mood [*Bestimmtheit der Stimmung*] or specific situation, while at the same time he must identify *himself* with this particularization of himself as with himself, so that in it he feels and envisages himself" (Hegel 1975, 1133 / German: 1986, 3: 443–44). The aesthetic, especially lyric poetry, thus not only guarantees speculative progress in Hegel's philosophical narrative; it simultaneously preserves the actual quality in which the knowledge drawn out into lucid expression first announced itself. Not only does the lyric extricate the cognitive elements from the life of emotions that would expire in narcissism if left to the contingent drift of mere inwardness; it also draws out the intersubjective cognitive element that slumbers in the emotive fabric of individual life, without forgoing the force with which such knowledge first announced itself *as emotion.*[46] It preserves the integrity of such knowledge as something that can never be analytically captured as it was affectively experienced, inasmuch as it comprises innumerable political, economic, religious, and cultural vectors and forces. Not at all unlike the Kantian aesthetic, with its premise of an underlying intentionality geared toward (future) "communicability" (*Mitteilbarkeit*), Hegel's aesthetic theory claims for the lyric a fundamentally intersubjective cognitive mission, albeit one that remains faithful to the way in which a knowledge that one may be tempted to cast in purely prosaic and universal form of "criticism" actually manifested itself. Lyric knowledge reconstitutes an emotive dimension, not out of some misguided nostalgia, but because the knowledge in question proves so comprehensive and overwhelming as to inhere in consciousness only in the "felt" quality of "mood" (*Stimmung*). If poetry encrypts history as "an experiential complexion" (*Erlebniszusammenhang*), to recall Dilthey's compound, it does not do so because it lacks the hermeneutic cleverness of (new) historicist critique or because it has not yet attained to the Hegelian "labor of the concept"—itself the original, if frequently unacknowledged matrix of (new) historicist analysis. Rather, the holistic grasp of the Real that endures in emotional life is captured as a heuristic proposition, now to be transformed by and into formal-aesthetic *work*—taking that term in its conjoined meanings of "labor" and "oeuvre."

In its origins, this constructivist model of the lyric, whose full development ultimately continues to be stifled by Hegel's systemic and narrative imperatives, can be traced back to Friedrich Hölderlin's superbly differentiated conception of "feeling" in his theoretical writings from Homburg around 1799. What Hölderlin calls "organized feeling" (*organisirtes Gefühl* [1943–85, 4, i: 235 / 1987, 47]) constitutes a holistic cognition that has dialectically incorporated into itself, and now holds in a poetic, formal-aesthetic equilibrium, myriad discrete kinds of awareness. As such speculative progression, the lyric poem "is a continuous metaphor of a feeling" (ist eine fortgehende Metapher eines Gefühls [Hölderlin 1943–85, 4: 266 / 1987, 83]). The intentionality slumbering in a given emotive state will reveal itself only when transposed into the materially alien, yet highly manipulable, order of tropes, metaphors, and signs, as well as larger syntactic units. "Feeling is both bridle and spur of thought" (ist Zügel und Sporn dem Geist). It is "divine, because it is neither mere consciousness, mere reflection (subjective or objective) with the loss of inner or outer life, nor mere striving (subjectively and objectively) with the loss of inner and outer harmony, nor mere harmony like the intellectual intuition and its mythical, figurative subject-object, devoid of consciousness and hence of unity; but because it is all this at once and can exist for itself in a feeling which is transcendental" (Hölderlin 1987, 77–78 / German: 1943–85, 4: 259). To securely and holistically grasp the dynamic relation between self and world requires the transposition of feeling into an organized textual construct. In his dialectical theory of the alternation of tones (analogous to Novalis's theory of the novel), Hölderlin conceives of the lyric as an objective simulation of emotional life, an "echo of the original living feeling . . . purified into a pure, formal mood" (Wiederklang der ursprünglichen lebendigen Empfindung . . . zur reinen formalen Stimmung geläutert (1943–85, 4: 261–62 / 1987, 80). Echoing Kant's third *Critique,* Hölderlin identifies such feeling as "transcendental." The following passage, whose apparently unwieldy syntax is not accidental or pathological but, on the contrary, is accounted for by its very claims, analyzes the mysterious transposition of a focused but as yet unselfconscious subjectivity into the lyric form, which Hölderlin views as a quasi-holographic reconstitution of mood. Lyric voice (*Stimme*) dialectically raises a holistic mood (*Stimmung*) beyond all subjective contingency by reconstituting it as the lawful calculus of poetic language, though in the full awareness that it can do so only in the etiolated, because strictly textual, modality of aesthetic form:

> For if, prior to the reflection on the infinite subject matter and the infinite form, there existed for [the poet] some language of nature and art in specific form, then he would to that extent not be in his sphere of influence; he would step outside of his creation. . . . [Yet] the artist's creative reflection consisted in that, out of his world, out of the sum of his outer and inner life, which is also more or less mine, he took the subject matter in order to designate the tones of his spirit, to evoke out of this mood the fundamental life through this related sign; that, by naming this sign for me, just as he borrows the subject matter from my world, he causes me to transfer this subject matter into the sign. (Hölderlin 1987, 81–82; translation modified / German: 1943–85, 4: 264)

Inasmuch as reflective cognition "presages" (*ahndet*) language, language "recalls" (*erinnert*) cognition. The transposition of feeling into aesthetic form does not amount to an analytic isolation of the myriad shades of awareness comprised in a feeling. Rather, it reconstitutes a complex knowledge whose experience has always pivoted on (not just been accompanied by) a distinctive charge of affect. The sign—writ large as the "formal calculus" (*gesezliche Kalkül*) of a complex triadic hymn—preserves and sublates the subject's emotionally suffused relation to a world that, as "infinite subject matter" and as the "total sum of one's outer and inner life," demands an aesthetic construct of equally infinite formal and interpretive complexity (*unendliche Form*). Far from being the antithesis of cognition, poetry captures the very "mood of thought" (to borrow Heidegger's phrase). For Hölderlin, and, at his most lucid and receptive, for Hegel also, the poetic text encrypts an anterior reflective disposition (*Stimmung*) in the alien modality of a voice (*Stimme*). Once transposed into and henceforth consubstantial with the "lawful calculus" of poetic form, feeling for Hölderlin is both epistemologically and materially indistinguishable from an early version of modernism's constructivist aesthetic.[47] Hence Hölderlin also paraphrases this calculus as a "system of feeling" (*ein Empfindungssystem* [1943–85, 5: 196]). For what Hölderlin designates as "creative reflection" (*schöpferische Reflexion* [1943–85, 4: 264]) in the longer passage quoted above no longer purports to "express" a feeling but constructively realizes feeling as an objective aesthetic artifact. A voice so understood can produce knowledge only insofar as it also continues to reflect its liminal position between the spontaneous and the providential, between the affirmation of subjective intelligence and the heteronomy of material signs and "hints." As Hölderlin puts it in his ode "Rousseau":

> [A]uch dir, auch dir
> Erfreuet die ferne Sonne dein Haupt,
> Und Stralen aus der schönern Zeit. Es
> Haben die Boten dein Herz gefunden.
>
> Vernommen has du sie, verstanden die Sprache der Fremdlinge
> Gedeutet ihre Seele! Dem Sehnenden war
> Der Wink genug, und Winke sind
> Von Alters her die Sprache der Götter. (HÖLDERLIN 1943–85, 2, 1: 13)
>
> Your crest too, though but once, yours too
> Is gladdened by the light of a distant sun,
> The radiance of a better age. The
> Heralds who looked for your heart have found it.

You've heard and comprehended the strangers' tongue,
Interpreted their soul! For the yearning man
The hint sufficed, because in hints from
Time immemorial the gods have spoken. (HÖLDERLIN 1994, 125)

If "Rousseau embodies the tension between an isolated subjectivity and the imperatives of social life" (Nägele, 171), Hölderlin's strophic reflection on the citizen of Geneva shows how the development of one's own voice necessitates the cautious detour through an other, even one as seemingly close as Rousseau. In the end, that otherness is only realized through the objective medium of a language shot through with historical, generic, and contextual determinants outside anyone's control. If the ode credits Rousseau with having been visited by the "rays" of the "distant sun," such semantic plenitude can be claimed figurally, in what Derrida characterizes as the quintessential philosophical "heliotrope" of light and illumination. Moreover, the knowledge to which Rousseau is said to have been privy can be imagined only a posteriori, not by Rousseau himself but only transferentially, with Hölderlin speaking *for* Rousseau. Thus mediated through its own other (Rousseau), Hölderlin's voice does not establish itself in propositional form but, instead, motions toward a revelation that is itself perched between an unverifiable past and an anticipated future. Poetry here is presented as a type of scripture that expressly forgoes the desire for closure, as evidenced by the carefully open-ended reception of "the strangers' tongue" (*die Sprache der Fremdlinge*) that was "heard . . . comprehended . . . interpreted" (*vernommen / verstanden / gedeutet*). The revelation at issue may indeed come to the "longing" man (*Dem Sehnenden*), but it does so only if we believe the Rousseau of the *Reveries* to have attained the perfect ratio of curiosity and restraint. For to discern meaning in a "hint" (*Wink*), that enigmatic sign of the gods, involves more than outright indolence and passivity. It demands a complex echo—what Hölderlin is to Rousseau—whereby the intimations of the other's voice are transfigured into the comparative specificity of a text. Hölderlin's aesthetic can thus be characterized as an attempt to fuse poetry and critique—to "grasp" (*fassen*) and articulate the otherness of his own voice in a textual "version" (*Fassung*) and thus to achieve an instance of subjective "composure" (*Fassung*) for which Rousseau's repose is the archetype. By means of its transferential, figural detour through the other (Rousseau), Hölderlin's poetry offers the very apotheosis of Kant's and Novalis's critical project with its shrewd rhetorical balancing of the emotive and rational dimensions of knowledge. As his poetry ponders the interdependency between a material existence, past and future, conjured up by the operation of tropes and images and the simultaneous reflection on the rational, or "critical," truth-value of those images, Hölderlin's voice appears genuinely informed by Kant's critical enterprise. Like the philosophical idiom of late-Enlightenment critique, his poetry shows the dialectic of intuition and concept, as well as the corollary tension between an imagistic and a propositional style, to be necessarily open-ended. Poetry so understood transcends (in a strictly nonteleological sense) the arid and self-privileging claims of pure theory, yet it also avoids any hedonistic attachment to its own voice and, for that matter, the epigone's blind worship of aesthetic tradition.

Part I / Sublime Politics

Paranoia

CHAPTER TWO

Anxious Inspiration

Radical Knowledge in Godwin and Some Contemporaries

> The voluntary actions of men are under the direction of their feelings.
>
> — WILLIAM GODWIN, *Enquiry Concerning Political Justice*

> Symptoms are meaningless traces, their meaning is not discovered, excavated from the hidden depth of the past, but constructed retroactively—the analysis produces the truth; that is, the signifying frame which gives the symptoms their symbolic place and meaning . . . Thus things which mean nothing all of a sudden signify something but in a quite "different domain. What is a "journey into the future" if not this "overtaking" by means of which we suppose in advance the presence in the other of a certain knowledge—knowledge about the meaning of our symptoms—what is it, if not the *transference* itself? This knowledge is an illusion, it does not really exist in the other, the other does not really possess it, it is constituted afterwards, through our the subject's—signifier's working; but it is at the same time a necessary illusion, because we can paradoxically elaborate this knowledge only by means of the illusion that the other already possesses it and that we are only discovering it.
>
> — SLAVOJ ŽIŽEK, *The Sublime Object of Ideology*

One way of gauging the temper of a particular period, and thus establishing a fixed chronological span such as the 1790s *as* a period or as a more compressed "hot chronology" (to use James Chandler's term), is to identify a dominant rhetorical or formal-aesthetic pattern. The symptomatic and, potentially, evidentiary value of such a pattern increases to the extent that it can be traced across a wide spectrum of writings, especially where such a pattern surfaces independent of the writings' political claims and perspectives.[1] I propose that paranoia constitutes both the paradigmatic mood of the 1790s in England and the most effective rhetorical strategy for containing—in the modality of an embattled, lucidly defensive inwardness—the anxious perception of history as a welter of uncontainable and malevolent forces. In order to verify the hypothesis of paranoia as a vicarious mode of historical cognition, this chapter explores number of discrete examples. Some we shall look into only briefly, while others (particularly William Godwin's *Political Justice* and *Caleb Williams*) will be read more closely.

Already, however, the attempt to secure our hypothesis with a compelling array of "examples" and through single-minded interpretive scrutiny—without first securing the criteria that establish and underwrite their "exemplarity"—verges on the fallacy of imitative form. Must an account of paranoia necessarily replicate the very affective and rhetorical conditions that it seeks to elucidate? Paul Smith is surely right to caution against a structural complicity "between the interpretative strategies of the humanist and those of the paranoiac . . . a kind of 'metaparanoia' in humanist practices. The 'subject' in these practices, as in paranoia, is an interpreter, unable and / or unwilling to recognize the condition of its own interpretations as constructs, fictions, and imaginary narratives. Such a 'subject' not only constructs the order of reality in which it wants to live, but also has to defend itself against the otherness of that very world."[2] In assigning paranoia a paradigmatic role in the intellectual and discursive formations of early romanticism, we must bear in mind Smith's caveat that, whether it is applied to unlocking so-called "clinical" cases or merely to quotidian forms of culture, what is known as a hermeneutics of suspicion remains formally unchanged. Recently, Peter Logan has restated the problem both with reference to the intrinsic form of narratives generated by the "nervous bodies" of the later eighteenth century and as regards the interpretive dilemma that such narratives visit on their readers. Arguing that the so-called "nervous body" and its symptomatic manifestation in narrative form "enjoyed its clearest moment of cultural ascendancy in the late Georgian period, when middle-class disorders became part of the official discourse of medicine" (5), Logan states this dilemma in ways particularly apposite to the writings of the 1790s:

> These narratives strain to avoid the negative implications of the narrator's hysterical speech, as the hysteria threatens the authority to speak. However, the texts also pose an opposite and more intractable problem caused by the relationship between the speaker's illness and the speaker's voice. In each case, the narrator's illness serves a positive purpose, for it gives rise to the narrative voice. Without the disease there would be no narrative, not even one with the social utility of warning against the social conditions that created it in the first place. And so,

> paradoxically, the nervous narrative promotes, in its formal structure, the same disorder it cautions against by transforming the narrator's debility into a narrative premise. This problem only intensifies as the narrative gets increasingly convincing. The more compelling it is aesthetically or intellectually, the more valuable the nervous condition ultimately appears as a precondition to the act of speech. Thus, these narratives have to negotiate two contradictory problems, one in which hysteria implicitly undermines the authority to speak, the other in which it becomes the basic condition of speech. (Logan, 3)

That Logan should be speaking of hysteria, not paranoia, does not so much pose a conceptual difficulty as identify a persistent interpretive tension at work within, and formally defining of, (allegedly) paranoid narratives. Those who read Edmund Burke's *Reflections on the Revolution in France* and his later *Thoughts on a Regicide Peace* as symptoms of the author's disintegrating psyche—and there have been many, not all of them confined to the 1790s—have tended to depict him in terms usually associated with female irrationalism. Famous, much-discussed instances would include Mary Wollstonecraft's association of Burke with the ornate language of romance, James Gillray's depiction of him as a feminized, ineffectual Don Quixote, and Tom Paine's persistent association of the *Reflections* with "painted" theatrical shows. Now, as Peter Logan points out, "for the purposes of cultural history, the value of hysteria as an object of study lies precisely in its protean, wide-ranging, and frequently unrestricted semiology. This conceptual flexibility allowed the disease construct to be adapted to the different circumstances of time and place. Hysteria is always thought to be enigmatic, and so it is necessary to account for the local context in which it is deployed, the individual decision that *this* is hysterical, and *that* is not."[3] Likewise, paranoia is at once enigmatic and prolific, inscrutable in its origins yet copious in its manifestations. It appears as an oblique psychological condition but quickly rebounds on any observer who ventures it as a hypothesis about the formal-aesthetic peculiarities of someone else's discourse. Indeed, as an urgent, counterfactual narrative bent on stripping the real of its deceptive symbolic veneer, paranoia constitutes an early form of phenomenological reasoning, one where appearances are by definition, in Heidegger's words, "occurrences in the body which show themselves and which, in showing themselves *as* thus showing themselves, 'indicate' something which does *not* show itself" (Krankheitserscheinungen . . . Vorkommnisse am Leib, die sich zeigen und im Sichzeigen als diese

Sichzeigenden etwas indizieren, was sich selbst *nicht* zeigt [Heidegger 1962, 52 / 1979, 29]).

However, as a formal principle organizing and compelling a particular narrative, paranoia appears strictly confined to *that* narrative, and it imputes to its audience an analogous type of emotively fueled cognition. Without such a transferential model, the authorial affect of conspiratorial anxiety could hardly be rationalized as plausible, indeed probable, knowledge, and it would be impossible to justify the extravagant causal claims about the world entertained by the narrative in question. To impute paranoid delusion to a particular narrative demands an extensive commitment of the reader's interpretive (that is, formal-narrative) resources, which in turn will expose such a critique to the same diagnosis. Yet insofar as a counterfactual mode of reading shifts the emphasis from casual observation to systematic interpretation, and eventually to a counterconspiratorial narrative that verges on the fallacy of imitative form, the feeling of paranoia constitutes a fundamentally social, not private, state. What at first seems a contingent (affective) "state" must, if it is to signify properly, be revealed as a collective "disposition": a mood. Its discernment, however "objective" and avowedly "critical," already implicates the observer within the same nexus of social and cultural forces that produced his (or her) paranoid other. What the colloquial phrase "It takes one to know one" unwittingly throws into relief, then, is not simply the observer's (still contingent) affinity with the observed but, rather, the paranoid symptom's deep-structural logic and social connectivity; we might also say, its intrinsic, if vicarious rationality. Hence it is difficult, if not impossible to distinguish between paranoid narratives and narratives committed to identifying the paranoid character of some other narrative; it is always "some one else's" narrative in which one is asked to locate the condition that, by the 1790s, had become all but coterminous with the project of "critique." Like any special or "private" language, the formal poignancy of paranoia inheres, not in its alerting us to some unique content of knowledge well concealed *out there,* but in a specific formal way of knowing that has already been operative *in us* for some time and hence proves constitutive *of* all of us.

Given the ambivalence yet to be explored in the 1794 treason trials of members of the London Corresponding Society and also in Freud's remarks on the curious efficacy of the paranoid symptom, the following readings most certainly *do not* posit paranoia as a self-evidently or even covertly "pathological" condition. Rather, "paranoia" in my account names a situation of extreme interpretive agitation and urgency whose specific historical tensions are legible in the (narrative) way in which it dreams their solution in specific literary-aesthetic forms. Inasmuch as the romantic individual appears both engulfed within a volatile historical situation *and* struggling to defend against the impinging recognition of his or her own volatile modernity, the formalization of a particular kind of inwardness (paranoia being no exception here) oscillates between a pathogenic state and a strategy for recovering from it. Far from being ahistorical, like the general post-Aristotelian theory of humors that prevailed from the time of Theophrastus in the third century B.C.E. to the late seventeenth century, the condition popularly known as paranoia involves a productive tension between the subjective experience of history as a welter of inscrutable and inchoate forces and the subject's reactive, formal-symbolic struggle with modernity—now experienced as reaching into and defining of the subject's innermost recesses. Early in his *The Political Unconscious,* Fredric Jameson categorically states that "the literary or aesthetic act . . . cannot simply allow 'reality' to persevere inertly in its own being, outside the text and at a distance[, but] must rather draw the Real into its own texture" (1981, 81). On the face of it, such a view reiterates the originally Kantian premise that the "real" can only ever be brought into focus by symbolic means. Yet it is just this lingering debt, however oblique at the moment, to Kant's critical project that complicates Jameson's well-known contention that literature "constitutes a symbolic act, whereby real social contradictions, insurmountable at the level of material practice or official discourse, find a purely formal resolution in the aesthetic realm" (ibid., 79). For the "Real"—here juxtaposed to the Lacanian symbolic as its enigmatic antecedent "ground"—continues to operate like a more refined cousin of a more primitive, vulgar-Marxist notion of "authentic" and inert "materiality."

To distinguish between (the hypothesis of) an extrinsic material reality and its (appearance as) symbolic representation, between fact and value, is to ignore the fact that both terms already operate within a preconscious, subjective economy—a "mood"—where, in Kant's words, they have manifested themselves as a "feeling of determinability" and potential "communicability." The difference between Kant and Jameson here is simply that what the former seeks to analyze and communally cultivate as "reflective judgment," the latter characterizes as an ideological act.[4] At issue, then, is less a difference in the description of a cultural practice than the question of its evaluation. Thus romantic writing ought to be read not so much as an expression of "still properly formal *contradictions*" (Jameson, 1981, 77) but, rather, as a discourse whose formal—and ideological—reflexivity effectively presages the very contradictions that a Neo-Marxist critique purports to reconstruct after the fact. Elsewhere in *The Political Unconscious,* Jameson effectively concedes as much, arguing "that if interpretation in terms of expressive causality or of allegorical master narratives remains a constant temptation, this is because such master narratives have inscribed themselves in the texts as well as in our thinking about them" (ibid., 34). The literary text, and its underlying aesthetic mode of production, thus anticipates, enables, even baits the cognitive structure (and scope) of the interpretations that are subsequently visited upon it. Its relation to the interpretive practices committed to discerning and exposing its ideological entanglements appears cannily prescient. Indeed, as I have argued elsewhere, texts of the early romantic era appear particularly eager to anticipate and control their own posthumous reception.[5]

It is worthwhile bearing in mind that popular culture of the past two decades has been filled with conspiratorial narratives—many of them revolving around late capitalism's transnational corporations scheming to conceal the presence of alien organisms within the community of the "human." In an update on earlier, strictly political conspiracies (*Seven Days in May, The Manchurian Candidate, Three Days of the Condor, The Parallax View*), popular cinematic culture of the 1980s and 1990s dramatizes paranoia as a condition experienced by individuals or groups who feel their very status as "human" to be under siege. From Ridley Scott's *Alien* films to James Cameron's *Terminator* bonanza, from *Blade Runner* to *X-Men* and *The X-Files,* from Stanley Kubrick's *2001: A Space Odyssey* to Steven Spielberg's *AI* (Artificial Intelligence) and the unsettling image of Arnold Schwarzenegger beholding his own clone in "his" suburban living room celebrating "his" birthday (*The Sixth Day*), conspiracies shrewdly conceived and robotically executed by the abstract forces of global capital ultimately target for elimination the very idea of our "essential" humanity.[6] That the "human" should have come under such pressure and, moreover, that the anxiety over such prospects should specifically play itself out in the medium of film and cyberpunk fiction warrants closer attention. For the pressure brought to bear on the human, the suspicion that human-like effects can be usurped by alien intelligences or mimicked by unheard-of advances in mechanical ingenuity, ultimately converges in the dreadful hypothesis of a terminal confusion of image and referent, the soulless mechanics of representation and the once spiritual core of the human. Thus, in the end,

Schwarzenegger's character learns that he "himself" had been a clone. His terror at such recognition is a late-twentieth-century's version of the horror of artifice familiar from gothic texts of the early romantic era, which under the influence of DNA technology has become positively autonomous, self-aware, and hence prone to confounding earlier notions of the "essentially" and "inalienably human" as mere wishful dreaming of a fabled, mythic past.

The ultimate specter of the paranoiac thus involves finding his totalizing interpretation confirmed—utterly, and in every detail—and thus being forced not only to accept the radical transformation of a cherished order but also to recognize his own anxious and defensive interpretations as precisely the means for the unraveling of that fantasy. For paranoia is above all a process of transition, away from the ideological fiction of a timeless past (so succinctly embodied in Burke's nomenclature of "custom," "the method of nature," "tradition," and the "antient constitution") and toward a wholly deregulated concept of historical time. Part of that transition involves the paranoiac's recognition that the very transformation he had sought to defend against by indicting it as someone else's as yet unconsummated design has already succeeded and, consequently, has also shaped his anxious outlook on it, perhaps even made him an unwitting co-conspirator in it. A number of features, then, are likely to prove elementary to any paranoid vision:

- *Rethinking representation:* In anxiously reconceptualizing the *medium* of representation, paranoia also wrestles with the *process* of representation, both in its technical-material sense and as regards the infrastructure for its dissemination as essential features and evidence for their conspiratorial intent (e.g., commercial mass printing, the dissemination of pamphlets by the Corresponding Societies, Blake's reading of Reynold's Royal Academy as a "counter-arts conspiracy").
- *Discrediting intuition:* Paranoia reevaluates the habitual, quasi-instinctual modes of knowing and doing. Thus Burke's anti-theoretical "method of nature," which defines social processes as "tradition" or "inheritance," prompts his contemporaries to read the *Reflections* not simply as the expression of a superannuated social vision but as perpetrating a full-fledged conspiracy against any politics that centers on the free and rational deliberation of constitutional arrangements.
- *Rethinking linear time:* Paranoia reconstructs dominant forms of civic, cultural, and religious life as long-standing and almost successful con-

spiracies perpetrated against what had been an original, uncorrupted state of "authentic" humanity (Paine, Wollstonecraft, Godwin). Civilization and tradition here *are* the conspiracy retroactively understood as having surreptitiously estranged humanity from its (putative) Rousseauian origins.

- *Scrambling causality:* The paranoid subject gradually comes to recognize its own suspicious intelligence as the unwitting instrument for bringing about an outcome that it had sought to preempt by its contestation of established values (e.g., custom, habit, honor, virtue, etc.). The conspiratorial imagination shuttles back and forth between an undisclosed, nefarious past intention and a dreadful future (*prolepsis*), which it views as determined by the former. Yet such remedial agitation—for example, by criticizing an overdetermined history, such as Burke's concept of "tradition"—effectively produces its own cause (*analepsis*) by soliciting the state's reactionary and repressive intervention to which such a critique had previously imagined itself to be the response.

All of these features reveal an emphatically *analytic* quality at the very core of paranoia, confirming Martha Nussbaum's overall view of emotion as a covertly evaluative phenomenon that is expressive of an acutely human intelligence, but one that is now forced to respond to a world in which cause and effect, intention and outcome, agency and perceptible reality are no longer aligned. "In emotion," says Nussbaum, "we recognize our own passivity before the ungoverned events of life" (78). The strained intensity of the paranoiac's "meanings" appears imbued with what Hegel calls "the cunning of reason," inasmuch as its sublime and menacing knowledge is brought about precisely by the paranoiac's own active struggle to defend against it.

For a first example, let us turn to Edmund Burke's *Reflections on the Revolution in France* (1790), a work that might be said to fit our bill too obviously. The following long passage seeks to offer an ambitious cluster of causal explanations for the revolutionary events that suddenly erupted in Paris during the summer and fall of 1789:

> Along with the monied interest, a new description of men had grown up with whom that interest soon formed a close and marked union—I mean the political men of letters. Men of letters, fond of distinguishing themselves, are rarely averse to innovation. Since the decline of the life and greatness of Louis the

> Fourteenth, they were not so much cultivated, either by him or by the regent or the successors to the crown, nor were they engaged to the court by favors and emoluments so systematically as during the splendid period of that ostentatious and not impolitic reign. What they lost in the old court protection, they endeavored to make up by joining in a sort of incorporation of their own; to which the two academies of France, and afterwards the vast undertaking of the Encyclopedia, carried on by a society of these gentlemen, did not a little contribute. The literary cabal had some years ago formed something like a regular plan for the destruction of the Christian religion. This object they pursued with a degree of zeal which hitherto had been discovered only in the propagators of some system of piety. They were possessed with a spirit of proselytism in the most fanatical degree; and from thence, by an easy progress, with the spirit of persecution according to their means. What was not to be done toward their great end by any direct or immediate act might be wrought by a longer process through the medium of opinion. To command that opinion, the first step is to establish a dominion over those who direct it. They contrived to possess themselves, with great method and perseverance, of all the avenues to literary fame. Many of them indeed stood high in the ranks of literature and science. The world had done them justice and in favor of general talents forgave the evil tendency of their peculiar principles. This was true liberality, which they returned by endeavoring to confine the reputation of sense, learning, and taste to themselves or their followers. I will venture to say that this narrow, exclusive spirit has not been less prejudicial to literature and to taste than to morals and true philosophy. These atheistical fathers have a bigotry of their own, and they have learned to talk against monks with the spirit of a monk. But in some things they are men of the world. The resources of intrigue are called in to supply the defects of argument and wit. To this system of literary monopoly was joined an unremitting industry to blacken and discredit in every way, and by every means, all those who did not hold to their faction. To those who have observed the spirit of their conduct it has long been clear that nothing was wanted but the power of carrying the intolerance of the tongue and of the pen into a persecution which would strike at property, liberty, and life. (Burke, 211–12)

Burke's well-known arguments against atheists, infidels, "stock-jobbers," and literati exhibit a characteristic tension that appears one of the more distinctive features of any conspiratorial vision. On the one hand, Europe's and especially France's sharply divided ideological landscape is attributed to the machinations of a small handful of individuals, "a cabal" bent on the "destruction of the Christian religion." Here Burke's argument almost desperately clings to a traditional model of causation, though, like many of his contemporaries, we find ourselves without an adequate explanation as to *why* a small cabal should have conceived this intent. That cause Burke is only able to provide in the mythic form of a proper name (*causa efficiens*)—a few individuals, a cabal, with Baron d'Holbach, Helvetius, Diderot, and La Mettrie at the very center, and perhaps featuring the Reverend Richard Price, that "spiritual doctor of politics" (Burke, 97) as head of the conspiracy's English branch (as parodied by Gillray's cartoon of Burke's bespectacled visage intruding into Price's nocturnal studies [fig. 1]).[7] What cannot be proffered for this individually conceived plot is a plausible *motive* (*causa finalis*). The brute, unselfconscious zeal or passion attributed to a hypostatized cabal here operates as a

Fig. 1. James Gillray, *Smelling out a Rat;—or—The Atheistical Revolutionist disturbed in his Midnight Calculations.* The specter of Edmund Burke intrudes on the lucubrations of the nonconformist Reverend Richard Price. Copperplate engraving published by Hannah Humphrey, 3 December 1790. Reproduced by permission of *The Huntington Library, San Marino, California.*

strictly self-authorizing force, thus relieving Burke from the obligation of critically analyzing the cabal's alleged aims, objectives, and motives in relation to his own cherished vision of English politics as a "sort of family settlement, grasped as in a kind of mortmain for ever" (Burke, 120).[8]

On the other hand, the simplicity of Burke's conspiratorial model of agency and its inscrutable passions is contradicted by the technological sophistication and shrewd planning allegedly employed by Dissenters and Jacobins in pursuit of political and religious subversion. Incongruously, that is, Burke charges the cabal with the utmost fanaticism and irrationality while simultaneously crediting them with craftily masking that very passion by their abstract, "geometric" politics. Nowhere does this contradiction emerge more glaringly than in Burke's discussion of the contemporary literary scene. For his argument clearly implies that writing—which, needless to say, is also *his* chosen medium—constitutes a wholly unregulated domain, a technology for disseminating all kinds of opinion, itself susceptible to appropriation and manipulation. Simultaneously, the persona and authority of the disinterested civic man (in the tradition of Shaftesbury and Harrington) appears likewise subject to impersonation and manufacture by the novel commodity known as "literary fame." Rather than assailing England's supposedly timeless order of local government, collective sentiments, manners, opinions, and prejudice, the new regime of literati appears to have exposed the inauthentic and hence vulnerable fabric of tradition. Abandoning the customary antithesis of a benign civilization whose legitimate edifice is suddenly besieged by pseudo-rational forces from without, Burke's passage progressively unravels the antithesis between a hereditary polity and upstart "men of theory." For it now turns out that the threat to the former issues not from the outside; rather, it appears that the political appeal and putative "authenticity" of traditional Englishness had always hinged on the favorable manipulation of collective opinion—an inherently artificial process inseparable from what Burke and his contemporaries understood as the aesthetic. Yet by 1790, "this oblation of the state . . . in buildings, in musick, in decoration, in speech, in the dignity of persons" (Burke, 196–97) has become increasingly hard to control in its effects, inasmuch as its principal medium, writing, has slipped from the closed circuits of the Augustan patronage system into the public domain.[9]

The terror lurking everywhere in Burke's *Reflections* thus no longer involves some oblique cabal pursuing social and religious dissolution—with malice (cause) supposedly aiming at pervasive disorder (effect). Rather, the previously natural, self-evident, hereditary "mixed system of manners and opinions" (170), which Burke shrewdly conflates as both body and dress—"our natural entrails" (197) and the "coat of prejudice" (183)—has suddenly attained self-awareness and come to see itself as artificial, not human, and hence infinitely manipulable. As Claudia Johnson has argued, Burke's *Reflections,* in attaching "massive political urgency . . . to affectivity of an exorbitantly erotic sort," had effectively mobilized "chivalric sentimentality—'that generous loyalty to rank and sex'—[as] the affective front of ideology" (6). However conspicuous in Burke's late writings, the function of the erotic in the *Reflections* extends well beyond a defensive reaffirmation of gender distinctions and their metaphoric role in a starkly polarized ideological sphere. Anticipating Adorno's arguments in *Minima Moralia,* erotic motifs in Burke involuntarily lay bare the instability and atrophied status of the human. From Burke all the way through Hazlitt and Keats, eros serves as the last line of defense for a concept of autonomous and inalienable subjective agency that is on the verge of being absorbed into ever-more-complex technologies of representation, including literary (gothic, sentimental) simulations of the human. Ultimately, it is the medium of print and the profoundly contingent, stylistically wayward nature of Burke's writing that further energizes the very ideological specter from which it recoils, namely, the structural rather than personal nature of agency in the drama of historical change.[10] Taking up the Burkean cause after its author's death, Arthur Young's 1798 *Enquiry into the State of the Public Mind Amongst the Lower Classes* restates the conspiratorial force of print and time and again lambastes "a licentious press, vomiting out daily the atheistical tenets of jacobins" and the "multitudes employed in the distribution" of such writings (31–32). Young repeatedly expresses fear of literacy as a wholly unregulated economy in which writing is freely disseminated and just as recklessly imbibed, especially by the poor who, "if they resort to an ale-house kitchen to hear a newspaper read . . . have the *probable chance* of swallowing the poison of seditious prints in the pay of the French Government" (ibid., 7).

Not surprisingly, Burke's first readers sensed that his "pen . . . let loose in a frenzy of passion," in the words of Tom Paine (*RM,* 39), and very much partook of the conspiracy of writing for which it sought to indict various, ill-assorted enemies. John Thelwall echoes this conspiratorial assessment of Burke's style as fraught with "much deep design and insidious policy. . . . It is his intention at once to instruct and to confuse" (Thelwall, 396). What Novalis was to call Burke's "revolutionary book against the revolution" (*WTB*, 2: 279) came to be read as symptomatic of a new understanding of style as a political message. More insidious than its propositional content, it was Burkean form that caused the *Reflections* to be perceived as a synecdoche for an entire aesthetic and system of manners whose design (and, above all, its author's excessive preoccupation with that design) appeared to conceal darker, more sinister political motives. "Is this the language of a rational man?" Paine exclaims (*RM*, 49), and he proceeds to lampoon and indict Burke's stylistic obliquities with various witty comparisons to New England's elusive coastline ("point-no-point") and the excesses of "tragic" and "horrid" "paintings" and "theatrical representation" (*RM*, 49–50). Paine vacillates as to whether we ought to read Burke's theatrical prose as merely pathological ("Mr. Burke should recollect that he is writing History, and not Plays" [*RM*, 50]) or as outright conspiratorial. In favor of the latter speaks the consistency of the *effect* wrought by Burke's oblique figural oratory, particularly his persistent reference to an otherwise unexplained "antient constitution" (Burke, 117), set up as a "sort of political Adam in whom posterity are bound for ever" (*RM*, 44). Burke's self-indulgent harangue on behalf of the "manuscript assumed authority of the dead" and against "the rights of the living" (*RM*, 42) ought to be read, Paine tells us, as merely so many "subtleties, or absurdities [whereby] the divine right to govern has been imposed on the credulity of mankind. Mr. Burke has discovered a new one, and he has shortened his journey to Rome, by appealing to the power of this infallible parliament of former days" (*RM*, 43).[11] For Thomas Jefferson, writing in 1791, Burke's *Reflections* was itself a revolution: "The Revolution in France does not astonish me so much as the revolution of Mr. Burke. I wish I could believe the latter proceeded from as pure motives as the former. . . . How mortifying that this evidence of the rottenness of his mind must oblige us now to ascribe to wicked motives those actions of his life which wore the mark of virtue and patriotism."[12] Just as for Jefferson the suspicion of a concealed motive in the present instance compels a sweeping reevaluation of Burke's entire public persona since he had come onto the political stage, Paine suggests that Burke's nonlinear prose conceals its true allegiance. Cannily fusing legitimate objections to Burke's notion of an "antient constitution" with popular suspicions of Burke's alleged crypto-Catholicism, Irish loyalties, and material greed, Paine thus sets up an instantaneous connection between political beliefs openly professed by Burke (e.g., support of hereditary monarchy) and his religious and political fanaticism, for which the former are merely the stalking horse. In the end, there is little difference between Paine's suspicious allusions to Burke's "journey to Rome" and Burke's paranoid fixation on Adam Weishaupt's Illuminati or his late embrace of the *Urtext* of French Royalist conspiracy theories, the abbé Auguste Barruel's anti-Masonic and counterrevolutionary *Mémoires pour servir à l'histoire du jacobinisme.*[13]

Similarly, in what amounts to a classic reversal of the Burkean charge that the revolutionary events in France are the product of a conspiratorial "cabal," Paine insists that "no plot was formed against . . . the exiles who have fled from France." Rather, they were plotting against others; and those who fell, met, not unjustly, the punishment they were preparing to execute" (*RM* 56). As regards the cause that prevented earlier generations from "trac[ing] the rights of man to the creation of man," Paine's conspiratorial imagination is quick to settle the point: "I will answer the question. Because there have been upstart governments, thrusting themselves between and presumptuously working to *un-make* man" (*RM,* 66). For Paine, whose "political theory was vintage liberalism," there was "but one villain: government" (J. Kramnick, 154; 157), and the state's habitual abuse of its institutional monopoly is his principal target. It was natural for Paine to locate the principal cause of and medium for the state's successful usurpation of the rights of the living by the dead in language itself. Throughout the *Rights of Man,* no other argument is pursued more insistently than the conspiratorial hypothesis that the ancien régime's metaphoric contrivances—with Burke's *Reflections* as their most glaring and symptomatic *summa*—had created purely fictitious meanings and realities. As Paine argues with regard to particular titles, as well as such fetishized *singularia* as "crown" and "constitution," the "imagination has given figure and character" to social distinctions where none should exist. For "when we use a word *merely as a title,* no ideas associate with it. What respect then can be paid to that which describes nothing" (*RM,* 81). Such a "nothing" is, in Paine's view, to be read as a conspiracy to distract and deceive the public. By contrast, the delegates to the French National Assembly "have not to hold out a language which they do not themselves believe, for the fraudulent purpose of making others believe it. Their station requires no artifice to support it" (RM 92).

It will not do to read the conspiratorial designs that Burke and Paine impute to one another as the mere symptoms of an underlying subjective and pathological disposition. Rather, we ought to approach their views as literary devices—*advanced in the guise of a deeply held belief*—that seek to conjure up and sustain conspiratorial fears among a gullible audience. Far from being the cause for the overwrought representations of the text, conspiratorial anxiety emerges as the effect of the text's transferential designs on the affective economy of its audience. In exposing the hidden designs of Burke's "flowery" oratory, Paine routinely charges Burke and the Pitt government with bad faith, as for example when alleging (like contemporary satiric prints) that wars were being provoked merely as a rationale for increased taxation and, by extension, for keeping up economic pressure on liberal, reform-oriented middle-class professionals, merchants, manufacturers, many of them dissenters.[14] In Paine's ever-timely observation, "War is the art of conquering at home: the object of it is an increase of revenue; and as revenue cannot be increased without taxes, a pretence must be made for expenditures" (*RM*, 77). Like James Mackintosh and Mary Wollstonecraft, Paine perceives Burke's style and aesthetic theory as a symbolic plot aimed at securing a perpetual reign for the unequal and often inscrutable workings of constitutional monarchy.[15] For Paine, the oblique British aesthetic of "mixed," "irregular" design—hailed by Burke as expressing "a conformity to nature in our artificial institutions" (*Burke*, 121)—amounts to a conspiracy of the past against the present, of a cyclical against a developmental concept of time, of the undifferentiated *durée* of aristocratic pleasure against the Enlightenment's model of cognition-by-rational-disputation.[16] Because rationalism as a thoroughgoing critique is so axiomatically wedded to the ontological coherence of what, in rough-and-tumble life, typically appears inchoate and haphazard, it recoils from the terrifying, sublime possibility that this axiom of coherence—advanced under such disparate names as "reason," "benevolence," "perfectibility," or even "utility"—might itself be a fantasy, an elaborate dream. We recall the basic dialectic of Enlightenment thought, first mapped by Adorno and Horkheimer, according to which, in "extricat[ing] itself from the process of fate and retribution," the Enlightenment voids the specificity of all particulars, only to reenact, in the paradigm of causation ("the equivalence of action and reaction") the mythic force of repetition. "Abstraction, the tool of the Enlightenment, treats its objects as did fate, the notion of which it rejects: it liquidates them."[17] The putative rationality of the sign thus demands that it be sharply demarcated from the mythic sensuousness of the image, which the Enlightenment holds to an ever more restrictive standard of mimetic accountability.

Few writers of the 1790s exhibit reason's proclivity to conceptual and rhetorical hypertension more readily than Mary Wollstonecraft. In her *Vindication of the Rights of Woman* (1792), a conspiratorial logic uneasily struggles to coexist with another, emergent model of discourse—that of a social psychology that was to be more fully developed by Nietzsche, Durkheim, Weber, and Veblen. To be sure, the style of the 1792 *Vindication* often appears to partake of the excessive sentimentality and "those pretty feminine phrases" (82) behind which, as her familiar argument insists, the "slavish dependence" of the female sex is being concealed. It is not Wollstonecraft's emphasis on the political significance of gender-specific public morality, however, that sets her apart from Burke's *Reflections*, where, most notoriously in his overwrought tribute to Marie Antoinette, an overtly gendered and sentimental diction had also been deployed. Rather, it is Wollstonecraft's proposition that the language of sensibility, of male-authored and -dominated sentimentality, ought to be read as a conspiracy against female enlightenment that sets her apart. "Because in Britain the definition of gender was seen to be fundamental both to the Jacobin prospects for reform and to the Anti-Jacobin attempt to maintain a natural order, the debate over sensibility became a key issue in British politics" (Barker-Benfield, 360). Wollstonecraft's central claims amount to nothing less than a definition of ideology as the effect of subtly, if unconsciously, coordinated causes ("a variety of concurring causes" [79]) operating in the lower regions of the mind, and thus eluding reflexive scrutiny, even as they coordinate the practices of a vast number of otherwise anonymous individuals. Thinking perhaps more of Jane Austen's novels than of Wollstonecraft's puritanical strictures, Lionel Trilling nonetheless finds himself making the same argument a century and a half later:

> Somewhere below all the explicit statements that a people makes through its art, religion, architecture, legislation, there is a dim mental region of intention of which it is very difficult to become aware. We now and then get a strong sense of its existence when we deal with the past, not by reason of its presence in the past, but by reason of its absence. As we read the great formulated monuments of the past, we notice that we are reading them without the accompaniment of something that always goes along with the formulated monuments of the present. The voice of multifarious intention and activity is stilled, all the buzz of implication which always surrounds us in the present, coming to us from what never gets fully stated, coming in the tone of greetings and the tone of quarrels, in slang and humor and popular songs, in the way children play, in the gesture the waiter makes when he puts down the plate, in the nature of the very food we prefer. . . . We feel that the truth of the great preserved monuments of the past does not

> fully appear without it. . . . What I understand by manners, then, is a culture's hum and buzz of implication. I mean the whole evanescent context in which its explicit statements are made. It is that part of a culture which is made up of half-uttered or unuttered or unutterable expressions of value. . . . In this part of culture assumption rules, which is often so much stronger than reason. (Trilling, 105–6)

One strongly suspects that Mary Wollstonecraft would have wholeheartedly agreed with this characterization, though she might have faulted Trilling for the apparent tone of acceptance, even resignation, in his last sentence. Her 1792 *Vindication,* after all, tells just this kind of story of a conspiracy of the unsaid against the explicit, of Burkean "prejudice" against reason, and of an entire "dim mental region of intention" continually forestalling the objective of a *civitas* comprised of rational, virtuous, self-aware middle-class individuals.

What proves most unsettling to Wollstonecraft, however, is not the apparent irrationality of the Burkean "method of nature" (Burke, 120) with its paralyzing brew of manners, opinions, and prejudices to be mindlessly imbibed. Rather, her 1792 *Vindication* appears troubled by the lateral impact of Burke's ideology, by the fact that it may already have been successfully grafted onto the unconscious of an entire people. For the collective efficacy of the Burkean regime of "custom" as both system and anti-system has to do with its self-authorizing *habitus,* something loudly proclaimed (rather than concealed) by the *Reflections* themselves. Burke's protective "coat of prejudice" amounts to a "form of thought whose ontological status is not that of thought, that is . . . some Other Scene external to the thought whereby the form of thought is already articulated in advance." In other words, the conspiracy of the unconscious against reason involves two mutually reinforcing vectors: first, it disables reflection and critique under the guise of the self-evident and commonplace ("custom," "tradition"), that is, a "reality whose very ontological consistency implies a certain non-knowledge of its participants."[18] At the same time, however, this imperceptible cluster of fears, assumptions, and fantasies that structures the apparent normalcy of everyday life also replicates itself laterally, that is, across a vast spectrum of otherwise different individuals. The specious consistency of ideas begets an apparently more real coherence at the level of material life. Regional "variety" and "irregularity" thus establish themselves as the comforting, mythic signature of a nation whose economic and imperial machinations and ambitions have long transcended popular comprehension and hence have undermined the comfort level (the "cold sluggishness of our national character" [Burke, 181]) that is the ideological prerequisite for their implementation *by* the populace.

For a rough analogy, we may call to mind how CEO's and politicians funded by their transnational corporations have seized the stage with folksy vignettes conjuring up a "global village," a sentimental trope that for the past quarter century has anchored the capitalist romance of a homely and sympathetic middle-class culture achieving contentment through the consumption of goods produced by faceless, third-world producers. In embracing an ever more differentiated economy of customized services and commodities, the mythic inhabitants of the "global village"—who in this regard recall Burke's vision of a happily obtuse John Bull—accept what already by 1790 had taken shape as an anxiety-inducing, because inscrutable, system of far-flung economic speculation. Rather than militating against the complexity of trade and financial speculation—as J. G. A. Pocock reads the *Reflections*—Burke's paean to an emotive contentment that middle-class individuals are to achieve in the mythic cocoon of timeless Englishness mostly seeks to stabilize (and thus implicitly supports) the continued expansion of advanced manufacture, trade, and commercial speculation. The same can be said of the contemporary discourse of globalization with its shrewd embrace of regional and ethnic "variety," for such ideological countermeasures effectively obscure the cost to inadequately compensated third-world labor and an increasingly ravaged environment.[19]

Wollstonecraft's challenge, then, is to trace back the irrational assumptions that have so successfully ordered eighteenth-century life, not merely at the level of ideas but, above all, at the level of material practice. As a result, all regional, local, or idiosyncratic habits (of education, division of labor, religious worship, reading, writing, or idle conversation) must ultimately be read metaphorically. Oddly enough, however, it is just this charmingly oblique, if oppressively coherent, aesthetic of Georgian England, so volubly defended by writers like Burke, Johnson, and Reynolds, that conspires against the intervention of rational critique. Through "the diffusion . . . and mediation of [courtly] manners, compliancy with social rules is secured invisibly within the subject him- or herself" (C. Johnson 1995, 35). The conspiracy, in other words, is not so much revealed *in* as perpetrated *by* the oblique *habitus* of late-Augustan manners, sentiments, and prejudices as these find symptomatic expression in patterns of speech, gestures, and indeed the entire psychosexual constitution of the human body. "Sexuality and pleasure are narcotic inducements to a life of lubricious slavery."[20] Conservatives, like the physician Thomas Trotter in his *A View of the Nervous Temperament* (1807), and radicals such as William Godwin and Mary Wollstonecraft herself substantially converge in reading the physiology of the human body itself as a social symptom and as the most compelling speculative (Godwin) or statistically quantifiable (Trotter) evidence of Britain's unhealthy social composition. Bodies, writes Peter Logan, "are reservoirs for the social narrative, which is gradually written upon them and hoarded into the structure of their nerves. Each is the product of a slowly accumulated sequence of sensations rather than of a single catastrophic event." Thus Caleb's adversary Falkland, in Godwin's *Things as They Are, or, The Adventures of Caleb Williams,* is "not traduced 'in a moment' into the act of murder but is led into it, ineluctably, through a lifetime of socially acquired conventions, particular incidents, and recent aggravations that finally accumulate to produce the disordered fit that constitutes murder itself" (Logan, 49).[21] Social description of the kind undertaken by Wollstonecraft's 1792 *Vindication,* in other words, less involves the exposure of an irrational or antagonistic core underneath the deceptively placid surfaces of ordinary life than confronts the fact that the symptom actually "works" in highly effective ways—much like the warm and fuzzy digital gauze by which transnational news-information-entertainment-retail conglomerates of our own time paralyze the cerebrums of their consumers while continually stimulating their economic desires. Heidegger's expression for the symptom's seamless efficacy is that of a "being thrust into its 'there' (Geworfenheit dieses Seienden in sein Da [1979, 135]), its basic affective disposition of "being in the world" (*In-der-Welt-sein*). From an ontological perspective, the total a priori determination of the limits and possibilities of both, social and private life can never be known but nevertheless abides within each subject and community as a "mood" (*Stimmung*).

From the very start of her 1792 *Vindication,* Wollstonecraft seeks to identify synecdochic relations between discrete phenomena and larger, fundamentally irrational causes. The "cause of [women's] barren blooming I attribute to the false system of education" and to men "anxious to make [women] alluring mistresses" (79). Given that these pernicious causes operate in every nook and cranny and at all levels (apparent and unapparent) of culture—in manners, decorum, habits of speech, practices and theories of education, religion, reading, writing, and so on—Wollstonecraft's conspiratorial hypothesis also implies an unprecedented thematic expansion of writing into an all-encompassing sociological analysis. This project, in turn, all but coincides with discourse analysis, inasmuch as the idioms of custom, gallantry, politeness, sensuality, vanity, false modesty, and so forth have by now metastasized into all areas of writing (the novel, romance, the ballad, and theatrical spectacles), thereby continually foisting "false sentiments and overstretched feelings" on a preponderantly female audience consuming such writing. Notwithstanding Wollstonecraft's exasperated disclaimer to the contrary ("I shall be employed about things, not words"), her 1792 *Vindication* leaves no doubt that the conspiracy against the intellectual and social autonomy of women is seated in the complex and invidious tendencies of print language itself. "Artificial feelings" and "flowery diction," we are told, "has slided from essays into novels, and from novels into familiar letters and conversation" (82).

As was the case with Burke's *Reflections,* Wollstonecraft's *Vindication of the Rights of Woman* mobilizes the explanatory model of a conspiracy in order to bridge the widening gap between cause and effect, between a traditional model of rational and self-conscious agency and a vast spectrum of ideologically cognate effects. At the farthest remove, the very history and transmission of Englishness as a cultural memory *is* the conspiracy in question. As Emerson was to remark (albeit in more conventionally gendered language), "society everywhere is in conspiracy against the manhood of every one of its members" (29). Proceeding from that very premise two generations earlier, Wollstonecraft insists that one must "go back to first principles in search of the most simple truths, and to dispute with some prevailing prejudice every inch of ground" (91). Yet what is the nature of such prejudice? Is it a deep-seated pathology that afflicts men, and indeed most women, as Wollstonecraft certainly suggests at various junctures in her argument (e.g., "deeply rooted prejudices have clouded reason" [91])? Or are we to read the polite and ephemeral show of manners, decorum, and seemingly "natural" practices as a ruse? Is prejudice itself a sly contrivance, a political strategy masquerading as habit, an ideological design dissembling as a collective memory? Does prejudice, however unenlightened, belong to the order of genuine "affect," or does it rather manipulate the stock of authenticity that has long been invested in words like "feeling," "sentiment," and "sensibility," so as to obfuscate a darker ideological purpose? In Wollstonecraft's conflicted account, the scale repeatedly tips in favor of this latter view, such as when she contends, in her 1790 *Vindication of the Rights of Men,* that "sensibility is the *manie* of the day, and compassion the virtue which is to cover a multitude of vices" (6) or, in her 1792 *Vindication of the Rights of Woman,* how "Men, in general, seem to employ their reason to justify prejudices, which they have imbibed, they can scarcely trace how, rather than to root them out" (92).[22] Affect—that is, a (putative) "feeling" subjected to and transformed by insistent formalization into something like "manners," "gallantry," "sentimentality," or outright "affectation"—alternately presents itself as the source or progeny of a collective cultural history. As the latter, however, it is a changeling, a mere simulacrum of emotion introduced for deeper-seated ideological ends. While proof of this conspiratorial hypothesis cannot always be delivered, the 1792 *Vindication* indicts and proscribes "feeling" with barely veiled Puritan zeal as synecdoche of all things illicit. The book targets pleasure as something of a meta-feeling, since "pleasure" functions as an affective substratum underlying any particular conscious experience to begin with (as is also the case in Kant). Precisely because of its unwholesome proximity toward narcissistic self-awareness, Wollstonecraft proscribes pleasure as void because unproductive, merely self-replicating and thus prone to reinforcing a wasteful aristocratic *habitus* that, even in 1792, remains the gold standard of social ambition.[23]

Behind the deceptively static, topical antitheses of masculine / feminine, mind / body, rationality / prejudice, Wollstonecraft thus claims to have unearthed a conspiratorial plot. Such customary oppositions prove false, inasmuch as they seduce men and women to conceive of them as timeless essences. To accept them as such is to remain unaware of how one term in the dyad invariably conspires against the other. Rationality is enlisted so as to justify prejudice; mind construes the (female) body as an agency ever forestalling the intellectual improvement of woman under the guise of "innocence, as ignorance is courteously termed" (132). The nomenclature of late-eighteenth-century society thus constitutes a structural conspiracy of ephemeral sensations indulged in, and affective values affirmed, by the "public" against Wollstonecraft's gold standard of a civic, inalienable, and timeless truth variously identified as "virtue" or as "the grand ideal outline of human nature" (104). At its most incisive, the 1792 *Vindication* locates this conspiracy against female Enlightenment in the medium of social exchange: spoken language. In women given to desultory consumption of reading matter but barred from the serious intellectual pursuit of writing, the "muddy current of conversation" can yield only "the crude fruit of casual observation" and "superficial knowledge" (105).[24] With language as its ultimate repository, Burkean custom is read as the virtual agency of a far-flung conspiracy against reason. Both in their obliquely ideational and materially concrete qualities, sensibility, gallantry, and manners, or decorum, are to be read as weapons wielded in civilization's extended campaign against the female half of humankind. Ultimately, Wollstonecraft argues, in ways echoed by Blake, Thelwall, Paine, and Godwin, that the source and agency of such a conspiracy must be located in history itself.

Notwithstanding their urgent political occasion, even Burke's, Paine's and Wollstonecraft's paranoid modes of argumentation appear less to be indulged (and thus pathological in kind) than consciously mobilized so as to account for, and impress on their audience, a historical shift whose complexity threatens to defeat traditional models of causality and individual agency. Instead, their writings build on and extend on paranoia as a "style" or "mode of causal attribution" (Wood, 409), which during the second half of the eighteenth century became truly ubiquitous in political, social, philosophical, and religious writing. For Gordon Wood, who has charted this tendency across a widespread array of prerevolutionary and revolutionary writings in America and England, "the commonplace image of figures operating 'behind the curtain' was the consequence of a political world that was expanding and changing faster than its available modes of explanation could handle" (429). What emerges is the image of a society straining to restore intelligibility to its own world, one whose inscrutability appeared to be a correlate of what was otherwise hailed as "progress," particularly in the areas of financial speculation, social mobility and demographics, mathematics, legal theory, and above all the diversified production and expanded dissemination of all kinds of literature. As Wood notes, "far from being symptomatic of irrationality, this conspiratorial mode of explanation represented an enlightened stage in Western man's long struggle to comprehend his social reality." Indeed, "in retrospect, [it was] a last desperate effort, to hold men personally and morally responsible for their actions," specifically, as happened with growing frequency, when the declared intentions and actual effects of such actions were at odds. While Wood's account offers ample and compelling evidence for this thesis from a range of historical and popular writings, we also ought to trace this "paranoid style" in writings concerned less with intractable political or economic controversies than with shifting paradigms of knowledge in established disciplines or instituting new modes of social cognition altogether.

Arguably, no other writer's oeuvre is more richly informed by paranoid and conspiratorial figures than William Blake's, a fact frequently remarked upon by critics as early as Northrop Frye and, more recently, in rich and rewarding historical and critical detail by Jerome McGann, Morris Eaves (in his study of Blake's *Counter-Arts Conspiracy*) and Saree Makdisi, whose capacious exploration of Blake and the "impossible" history of the 1790s is a landmark achievement. As Makdisi points out, Blake's early prophecies, particularly *America,* "confirm Blake's attack on the old regime *and* his disruption of the philosophical conceptual, and political narratives underlying the discourse of 'liberty,' and in particular his critique of the narrow conception of freedom animating much of 1790s radicalism" (2003, 19–20). Given the unique interpretive challenges presented by Blake's "mixed-media" productions—among them an unprecedented metastasizing of paranoia into a reading process confronted with so many discrete material "performances" of a given illuminated book—I can only highlight a few aspects of conspiratorial imagination in Blake. To attempt more would unbalance the proportions of the present study, not only on account of the wealth of relevant material but because of the unique challenges that Blake presents to any study seeking to claim him as a "representative" figure in some larger argument. Though a cursory reading of Blake will quickly reveal his acute and increasingly conspiratorial view of politics, religion, and (an increasingly commercialized) model of the arts, his conspiratorial relationship to creative work strongly resists the latter's appropriation by any critical narrative. For by intellectual and artistic temperament, Blake remained vehemently opposed to any kind of generalizing and abstract argumentation throughout his life, an opposition that positively structures his major works. Contrary to liberal and more or less secular late-Enlightenment intellectuals like Price, Paine, Thelwall, Wollstonecraft, or Godwin, Blake does not exhibit any commitment to theoretical principles and abstract rights as a promising strategy for delivering Britons from the tyranny of custom, tradition, and established opinion. Indeed, his oeuvre positively repudiates theoretical modes of argumentation and abstract models of value within political, economic, and cultural life as something of a conspiracy in its own right. To be sure, Blake leaves no doubt about his distaste for the "mixed system of manners and opinion" (Burke, 170) that during the mid-century dominance of the Whigs amalgamated itself with a "Commercial Nation" filled with "Impostors." Who but Blake could wax as indignant against "the fatal Slumber into which Booksellers & Trading Dealers have thrown [Englishmen] under the artfully propagated pretence that a Translation or a Copy of any kind can be as honourable to a Nation as An Original" (*CPP,* 582; 576). And yet, it would be erroneous to read Blake's attacks on "Sr Joshua [Reynolds] & his Gang of Cunning Hired Knaves"

(*CPP*, 636) and the "mystery" of Anglicanism as implying a commitment to a liberal-progressive vision of social history. Far from it, Blake regards the secular strains of artisan and bourgeois radicalism as equally conspiring against "truth," "justice," and "eternity," terms dear to him yet noticeably absent from the secular discourse of his contemporaries on such topics as the rights of man, expanding the franchise, or repealing the Test Act.

Long before Walter Benjamin remarked that "generalization . . . contradicts the nature of justice" (1996, 247), the antinomian Blake posited that what confers spiritual urgency on a contingent empirical perception and thus turns it into a genuine "issue" is necessarily some deep-seated metaphysical concept. "Truth can never be told so as to be understood, and not be believ'd" (*CPP*, 38). Yet truth, as Blake insists time and again, is by definition "minute and particular." Both in its combative tone and its local, intuitionist, and anti-rationalist thrust, statements such as "Every Eye Sees differently," "To Generalize is to be an Idiot," and "To Particularize is the Alone Distinction of Merit" (*CPP*, 645; 641) show Blake, on this specific count anyway, to be closer to Burke's misgivings about "men of theory" (128) than to the arguments proffered by the artisan and bourgeois radicals and intellectuals with whom a long tradition of secular academic criticism has sought to connect him.[25] Contrary to what one can observe in Burke, Paine, or Wollstonecraft, however, paranoia in Blake does not merely organize some theoretical or anti-theoretical perspective on social and cultural change. For even as Blake's *Songs* and his early prophecies keep those arguments in view, his writings also expose the limits of theoretical argumentation (including arguments *about* Blake) itself. Blake's oeuvre not only launches into conspiratorial narratives about the usurpations of spiritual and artistic life by state, church, and commerce but tenders these narratives in hybrid forms whose verbal and visual complexity and internal discontinuity (multiple versions) effectively conspire against their interpretive reduction to stable, fully socialized meanings (cf. Paul Smith's observation of a "meta-paranoia" organizing critical argumentation in the humanities today).

The most widely recognized conspiratorial narrative in Blake arguably involves his critique of Anglicanism as a long-standing, systematic conspiracy aimed at defrauding true believers of their unique and inalienable spiritual intuitions. For the small communities in which radical dissent survived in late-eighteenth-century London, antinomianism was "a way of breaking out from received wisdom and moralism, and entering upon new possibilities," E. P. Thompson notes, and he goes on to describe "a spiritual conflict which wears temporal disguises, but which is the more real for being spiritual" (1993, 20; 62).This conflict found strong and "determinate" artistic expression in Blake's *Songs of Innocence* (1789). One may think of the self-serving, numbingly choreographed procession of London's orphaned poor in "Holy Thursday" (*Songs of Innocence* [*CPP*, 13]), or of little chimneysweep Tom Dacre's dispiriting embrace of his economic exploitation as a test of his faith: "And the Angel told Tom if he'd be a good boy, / He'd have God for his father & never want joy" (*CPP*, 10). Other poems, particularly in *Songs of Experience,* push the critique of Anglicanism's institutional monopoly in spiritual matters toward a proto-Nietzschean critique of religious psychology as ressentiment, such as when Blake traces the evolution of "humility" into a figural monstrosity (the British Oak?) casting its "dismal shade" over all true believers, a "Mystery" that can only ever "bear the fruit of Deceit" (*CPP*, 27). Perhaps the most linear presentation of Blake's antinomian and anti-institutional conception of institutional religion can be found in plate 11 of *The Marriage of Heaven and Hell,* which warrants quoting in full:

> The ancient Poets animated all sensible objects
> with Gods or Geniuses, calling them by the names and
> adorning them with the properties of woods, rivers,
> mountains, lakes, cities, nations, and whatever their
> enlarged & numerous senses could percieve.
> And particularly they studied the genius of each
> City & country. placing it under its mental deity.
> Till a system was formed, which some took ad-
> vantage of & enslav'd the vulgar by attempting to
> realize or abstract the mental deities from their
> objects; thus began Priesthood.
> Choosing forms of worship from poetic tales.
> And at length they pronounced that the Gods
> had ordered such things.
> Thus men forgot that All deities reside
> in the human breast. (*CPP*, 38)

On the face of it, this narrative follows a familiar "rise-and-fall" pattern by offering a self-assured account of a bounteous and intuitive existence enjoyed in paradisiacal innocence, a Rousseauian "state of nature," only to be incrementally usurped and perverted by a caste of self-styled spiritual guardians. As in Wollstonecraft's 1792 *Vindication,* historical development and its confining of spontaneity and intuition within ever-more-sophisticated institutional frames *is* the conspiracy that Blake's narrative aims to expose. Yet Blake's conspiracy markedly differs from the more familiar imposition of Augustan customs, manners, and prejudices, which secular and literate Enlightenment intellectuals viewed as preemptive of their own rational and linear narratives of political and social improvement. Hence, Blake's cryptic narrative—echoing Robert Lowth's archeology of the Hebrew prophets' "parabolic style"—targets what Adorno and Horkheimer would eventually scrutinize as the Enlightenment's obsessive, "mythic" drive toward totalizing (and potentially totalitarian) "thorough-rationalization" (*rationale Durchorganisierung*) of all human experience, including its spiritual dimension.[26] In its institutional and hence political weight, theory itself—Blake speaks of a "system" bent on "abstract[ing] the mental deities"—effectively intensifies the conspiracy against a pluralist and intuitionist model of spiritual life.[27] The paranoid logic culminates in Blake's indictment of theory and "system" as achieving outright autonomy and legitimacy when it is "pronounced that the Gods had ordered such things." Implicit in Blake's narrative is an acute distrust of narrative insofar as that concept is understood as a metonymic series in which one set of terms is calmly supplanted by another and so forth, and as conceiving time as linear, progressive, and strictly chronological matter. Makdisi rightly notes how in Blake's oeuvre, "freedom from the cyclical time of the working day is transfigured into freedom from the linear time of the working life. The moment of deliverance is located in the gap, the no-time in which repetition slides into interruption, and diachrony into synchrony—a no-time in which freedom is celebrated neither at the beginning nor at the end of narrative (whether linear or cyclical), but in the disruption of narrative and the implosion of historical time" (161).

Blake's early prophecies display a commitment to "illumination" that appears to be cued by the alleged spiritual and political oppression said to have issued from Albion's mythic "past." "Illumination" and artistic "execution," in turn, reflect the artist-writer's hope for a retroactive "correction" or "redemption" of that past from the stranglehold of priestcraft, tyranny, and reason. In *The (First) Book of Urizen,* the faultline separating the chiliastic beliefs of London's underground millenarian dissenters from the secular rationalism associated with radicals like Paine, Priestley, Thelwall, Holcroft, Godwin, Wollstonecraft, and Spence is artistically framed as a Pauline tension between faith and law. In this sumptuously visual project, the radical antinomian "energy" of Blake's counter-commercial illuminated books emerges as the "contrary" to the imperial and commercial hubris of the state and the abuses of institutional Anglicanism, yet also to the one-sided and invariant rationalism that by the 1790s had come to dominate opposition to the established powers. If Blake's own artistic project is organized by a conspiratorial or paranoid logic, it is so in an unusually complex, quasi meta-discursive sense—what McGann terms its "*critical* edge" and "fundamentally satiric and critical posture" (1988b, 162). For Blake's vision (and visualization) of "words articulate, bursting in thunders" refuses to be framed in a single opposition of secular and religious meanings. Examples of this conceptual innovation—which can also be found to organize writings by Goethe, Hölderlin, and Hegel—abound. On Bishop Watson's refutation of Paine's brazenly secular *Age of Reason* (1795), Blake laconically observes that "Paine has not Attacked Christianity. Watson has defended Antichrist" (*CPP,* 612). Paine's logical dissection of Christianity holds neither positive nor negative value in Blake's thinking since it fundamentally misidentifies its object. Likewise, "Christ comes as he came at first to deliver those who were bound under the Knave not to deliver the Knave," just as "we do not find any where that Satan is Accused of Sin he is only accused of Unbelief & thereby drawing Man into Sin that he may accuse him." Blake's "Vision of the Last Judgment" thus confounds the Christian habit of indicting, of predicating righteousness on accusation, identity on difference. "At the judgment Seat of Jesus the Savior . . . the Accuser is cast out. Not because he Sins but because he torments the Just & makes them do what he condemns as Sin & what he knows is opposite to their own identity" (*CPP,* 564–65). Similarly, at the level of writing as both material and conceptual practice, Blake's "visible language" not only seeks to reconcile the dichotomy of speech and writing but "is also designed to undo certain oppositions within the world of textuality, most notably the gap between the pictorial and the linguistic use of graphic figures."[28]

In Blake, then, the "mood" of paranoia is formally objectified above all in the theoretical notion of the "contrary." In Hazard Adams's (sensibly hypothetical) wording, "a 'contrary' would be an opposition in which the distinction itself (or the reasoning that creates it) is on one side, and on the other is the denial of the distinction in favor of the identity of the two things in the term 'energy,' with neither side negated."[29] By contrast, the formal expression of a paranoid "mood" as it prevails in most other writings of the 1790s (e.g., by

Burke, Wollstonecraft, Paine, Thelwall, Godwin) revolves around competing interpretations of historical "causality." That Blake's conspiratorial imagination refuses to get bogged down in questions of causation has to do with his radically different relationship to time. For in Blake, as Makdisi points out, "clarity is achieved . . . by bringing the flow of empty, homogeneous historical time to a momentary pause" (2003, 156). Blake's writings prove just as wary of the self-authorizing opposition between the linear and progressive model of time employed by the secular discourse of 1790s liberalism and radicalism and Burke's mystification of society as embedded in cyclical, organic, and recurrent time ("a great mysterious incorporation of the human race . . . never old, or middle-aged, or young, but in a condition of unchangeable constancy" [Burke, 120]). Blakean prophecy functions as the contrary to these oppositions by continually shifting back and forth between implementing belief as an unconditional intuition and critically reflecting on a past now understood to have significantly constrained all belief in the rigid institutions of the Anglican Church and its "Book / Of eternal brass, written in . . . solitude" (*CPP,* 72).

Overall, the Lambeth books predict no plausible or fantasized future, nor do they aim to ensnare their audience in myths of a forever reenacted and codified in fixed institutional forms. Instead, the Lambeth prophecies offer a startling reconfiguration of visual and rhetorical signs that helps "illuminate" and so retro-activate a past that never was. Much like contemporary critiques of ideology, that is, Blakean prophecy seeks not to predict a determinate future but to dislodge the false determinacy of the past. Similar to Godwin's "Of History and Romance" (1797), to which we shall soon return, Blake demurs the "dull way that some Historians, . . . weakly organized themselves" misconstrue spiritual events as historical facts: "all is to them a dull round of probabilities and possibilities; but the history of all times and places, is nothing else but improbabilities and impossibilities" (*CPP,* 543). Blake's prophetic oeuvre thus aims to recover the "vision" of an as yet unrealized imaginative past from the one that has usurped its place and that has gradually reproduced itself through the oppressive psychopolitical institutions of "priestcraft" and a regime of representation premised on memory, allegory, and state-sponsored arts.

As an esoteric critique (or, as McGann holds, parody) of the Book of Genesis, Blake's *(First) Book of Urizen* opens with an indictment of state religion as an institutionalized conspiracy dating back to the roots of Christianity: What Blake conjectures as "the primeval Priests assum'd power" (with a characteristic pun on "prime evil") was reluctantly yielded by the "Eternals" who had "spurn'd back his [Urizen's] religion / And gave him a place in the north, / Obscure. shadowy. void. solitary." Yet the prophecy quickly moves beyond this more familiar conspiratorial narrative—already familiar from *The Marriage of Heaven and Hell*—to a mystical critique of embodied creation itself, now seen as a desperate proliferation of finite and vagrant particulars by a deity that Blake imagines fearful of its "Self-closd, all-repelling . . . abominable void" (*CPP*, 70). Embodied, finite creation—of which the institutional authority of the modern church is but a late reflex—becomes necessary once eternity has been misconstrued as an empty void—that is, when mind attains self-awareness as a "soul-shuddring vacuum" now struggling to fill itself. Blake's *Book of Urizen* gives vivid expression to this conflict in the recurrent visual and textual motif of division or "sund'ring" (*CPP*, 73 [fig. 2]). Yet beyond its radical politics, there is also a metaphysical dimension to Urizen's fragmentation of eternity into history ("dividing / The horrible night into watches" [*CPP*, 75) and Los's agonized recollection of eternity ("White as the snow on the mountains cold") now rapidly consumed by general "Forgetfulness, dumbness, necessity!" (*CPP*, 75). Exaggerating Urizen's instinctual fear of the "myriads of Eternity" contained in everything particular, Blake rewrites received myths of creation and rationalist theories of progress by challenging the defensive, even vindictive conception of the human body that these accounts had once inaugurated. Sensual, embodied humanity can now be remembered only as the physiological torment of birth and aging so vividly captured by Blake's skeletal figure in figure 2:

> A vast Spine writh'd in torment
> Upon the winds; shooting pain'd
> Ribs, like a bending cavern
> And bones of solidness, froze
> Over all his nerves of joy.
> And a first Age passed over,
> And a state of dismal woe. (*CPP*, 75)

To the prophetic voice of Blake's *Book of Urizen,* the past ultimately begs to be redeemed from its "primeval" distortion as a distinctly embodied, transient particularity. History itself arises only as a problem of understanding, or as a "tradition" to be administered by state and church, to the extent that eternity has been misunderstood or forgotten. Consequently, redemption in Blake demands an art form that does not "represent" particulars, does not arrange historical constellations in some readily familiar narrative perspective, and does not seek truth by merely rearranging the material specifics of Urizen's "petrific abominable chaos" (*CPP*, 71). For Blake to remain within a model of art-as-representation and as linear narrative would inevitably reenact Urizen's primeval usurpation of eternity. Blake clearly recognizes the complicity of the eighteenth-century modes of visual and narrative representation as part of Urizen's conspiracy against "eternity," a conspiracy that dates back to the very beginning of time ("time on times he divided" [*CPP*, 70]) and that finds authoritative textual expression in the Book of Genesis. For that reason, Blake's especially vivid designs in *The Book of Urizen* opt for a purposely nonperspectival technique where the Eternals and eventually the figure of Los ("howling" as "Urizen was rent from his side" (*CPP*, 73–74), gazing into the void of historical time, recognize it as an ineffable monstrosity—a history that should never have been. Blake's retroactive imagination thus shares an important feature of paranoid reasoning with Wollstonecraft and Paine, namely, a preoccupation with history and tradition as finite processes that have conspired against a vision of plenitude that should have been. Yet when it comes to naming the latter, Blake's visions quickly shift away from the concrete and secular concepts of an inclusive, enlightened, and participatory polity found in his liberal counterparts. For such intellectual projects merely reinstate reason (Urizen) in a slightly different guise but do not recognize how any kind of "system" by definition conspires against the infinity and integrity of the "human form divine." For Blake, any attempt to capture infinity in a linear or cyclical model of time—which is to say, any narrative—proves inherently complicit in the Urizen's frenetic quest to capture eternity as embodied creation. The scrambling of linear, narrative order—observable throughout Blake's Lambeth books—thus amounts to a deliberate avoidance of Urizen's "primeval" mania for possessing eternity as causality. To Blake, the bipolar disorder of 1790s political discourse ultimately converges in the originally Urizenic quest for containing all human "energy" within a rigid institutional and narrative ordering framework. Lukács's remark that the "creation of forms is the most profound confirmation of the existence of a dissonance" (1971, 172) finds an early expression in Urizen's hyperactive attempts ("surging sulphureous / Perturbed Immortal mad raging" [*CPP*, 74]) at controlling the volatility of the past in determinate forms of the present. For Blake, the Enlightenment's secular project—which just then was beginning to take formal and institutional ex-

Fig. 2. William Blake, *The Book of Urizen,* copy G, pl. 13. Lessing J. Rosenwald Collection, Library of Congress. Copyright © 2004 the William Blake Archive. Used with permission.

pression as "historicist method"—of overcoming and completing history as "critical knowledge" appears no longer viable.

And yet, all is not lost, for Blake's idea of the book is itself an attempt to mobilize what Walter Benjamin was to call our "*weak* Messianic power," that is, the materially and spiritually vivid illumination of a catastrophic history which, *from its very beginning and by virtue of that beginning,* has compromised all means for our recovery from it. To grasp that inescapable "guilt context of the living" (*der Schuldzusammenhang des Lebendigen* [Benjamin 1996, 204])—a phrase defining what Benjamin understood as fate and what we may call ideology—is to contemplate, actively and imaginatively, a past of which we, our curiosity, and our expressive capabilities are all joint and irremediably corrupted effects; Blake's *Book of Urizen* dramatizes just that moment:

Thus the eternal prophet was divided
Before the death image of Urizen
For in changeable clouds and darkness
In a winterly night beneath
The Abyss of Los stretch'd immense
And now seen now obscured to the eyes
Of Eternals the visions remote
Of the dark separation appear'd.
As glasses discover Worlds
In the endless Abyss of space
So the expanding eyes of Immortals
Beheld the dark visions of Los,
And the globe of life trembling. (*CPP*, 78)

Illustrating the primordial crisis of a mind "rifted with direful changes," Blake depicts Los, "Groaning! gnashing! groaning!" over his "wrenching apart" in a plate whose iconic force, reminiscent of medieval nonperspectival art, grows out of the violent contrast between the "depthless" gestalt of "dreamless night" and Los's terrified gaze (fig. 3). His eyes show Los craving nothing so much as perspective and distance from "formless unmeasurable death." Blake's figure anticipates Walter Benjamin's account of Paul Klee's *Angelus Novus,* in which Benjamin identifies the "angel of history": "His eyes are staring, his mouth is open[.] . . . His face is turned toward the past. Where we perceive a chain of events, he sees one single catastrophe which keeps piling wreckage upon wreckage and hurls it in front of his feet. The angel would like to stay, awaken the dead, and make whole what has been smashed. But a storm . . . irresistibly propels him into the future to which his back is turned, while the pile of debris before him grows skyward. This storm is what we call progress" (Benjamin 1968, 258). In Blake, as in Benjamin, the image itself offers the most vivid and forceful perspective on a conflict between the fantasy of an authoritative and conclusive mode of historical cognition and the abject intuition that any intellectual promise of epistemological self-sufficiency inevitably

Fig. 3. William Blake, *The Book of Urizen,* copy G, pl. 9. Lessing J. Rosenwald Collection, Library of Congress. Copyright © 2004 the William Blake Archive. Used with permission.

resurrects the rationalist (Urizenic) conception of history from which it was purported to redeem us.

In their vivid generation of an interpretive gestalt out of the fluid interplay of word (itself split into a textual and iconic dimension), image, and color (discontinuous from one "version" to the next), Blake's designs also undertake a radical reevaluation of romantic pathos. No longer is pathos conceived as the affective property of a self, a psychological "event" to be transfigured into aesthetic semblance (*Schein*). Instead, Blake's designs "illuminate" pathos as the moment of catastrophic recognition that no image, concept, or narrative—aesthetic *or* critical—will ever reconstitute the spiritual and cognitive equilibrium whose loss these forms themselves dramatize with such intensity. In the Lambeth prophecies, subjective, contingent pathos dissolves into impersonal, deep-structural awareness—a mood. Art no longer *represents* a fleeting "state" but instead reenergizes word and image as the conduits to the modern individual's tormented spiritual "disposition." The vision materially realized in Blake's prophetic books presages Benjamin's ninth thesis on the concept of history, a notion Geoffrey Hartman calls "the written space of a contradiction" (1980, 77). There, too, history generates a wholly new kind of pathos, whose sufferers are "denied the image as a place of repose or as an icon blasted out of the past" (ibid., 78). Blake's conspiratorial rereading of Scripture as a Word whose potentialities have been hijacked and betrayed by the institutions devoted to its "historical" and "causal" explication anticipates Benjamin's characterization of historicism as caught up in a phantasmagorical interplay of danger and redemption. Like Blake, Benjamin insists that "to articulate the past . . . means to seize hold of a memory as it flashes up at a moment of danger. . . . Th[at] danger affects both the content of the tradition and its receivers. The same threat hangs over both: that of becoming a tool of the ruling classes. In every era the attempt must be made anew to wrest tradition away from a conformism that is about to overpower it" (1968, 255). And yet, insofar as the narratives of Burke and his liberal or radical opponents revolve around an "image of happiness [that] is indissolubly bound up with the image of redemption," their promise to sort out historical and social processes and antagonisms remains necessarily incomplete and unstable. For the very past that these either cyclical or progressive narratives posit as "timeless" and organic or as inexorably leading up to the present extirpation of all ancient "prejudice," already carries within itself the "temporal index by which it is referred to redemption," Benjamin says. "There is a secret agreement between past generations and the present one. Our coming was expected on earth. Like every generation that preceded us, we have a *weak* Messianic power, a power to which the past has a claim" (Benjamin 1968, 254). Echoing Blake's conspiratorial reading of scriptural authority as simply a means of redeeming subjects from their (alleged) lapse into sinful, historical time, Paine's *Age of Reason* raises the "probability" that "the whole theory or doctrine of what is called the redemption . . . was originally fabricated for the purpose to bring forward and build all those secondary and pecuniary redemptions upon; and that the passages in the books, upon which the idea or theory of redemption is built, have been manufactured and fabricated for that purpose" (Paine 1976 [1795], 27). Inextricably woven into the texture of Blake's early prophecies, "critique" thus emerges as a moment of interference between an intuitive commitment to "action" and an encroaching consciousness of metaphysical abjection. The latter arises as soon as we grasp that "the field of action . . . includes the past: its relation to the crisis at hand" and so causes "criticism [to] approach the form of fragment, pensée, or parable: it both soars and stutters as it creates the new text that rises up, prankishly, against a prior text that will surely repossess it" (Hartman 1980, 75, 82).

For a last short example of paranoia, taken from late-eighteenth-century theory, let us turn to Immanuel Kant's Copernican revolution in epistemology. As is well known, both the stated goal of and the intellectual hypothesis driving his *Critique of Pure Reason* (1781) tell us that Kant's very narrative will constrain the audience to reevaluate its cognitive relationship to phenomena ostensibly external to their subject-position. Kant's *Critique* thus opens not so much with an outright rejection of the concept of experience but with the curious hypothetical statement that "experiential knowledge might quite possibly be already something composite [*ein Zusammengesetztes*] of what we receive by way of intuition and what is spontaneously furnished by our cognitive faculties [*Erkenntnisvermögen*]." The involvement of the latter, meanwhile, is said to constitute "an additive [*Zusatz*] that we cannot distinguish from the basic matter of experiential data until extended practice has drawn our attention to this circumstance and has schooled us to make discriminations in this manner" (Kant 1965, 41–42). Kant's opening remarks already advance *two* claims that reciprocally confirm each other. First, he argues that the possibility of knowledge rests on something logically prior to the deceptive primacy of experiential data and to our intuitive mechanisms for the reception of such data. Second, Kant posits that in order to grasp so counterintuitive a theory of knowledge, we must effectively abandon all hope of speedy proof and submit to the "extended discipline" (*lange Übung*) of transcendental reflection. Ultimately, Kant's *Critique* proposes itself as the only available manual for this new type of cognitive proficiency. For Kant's *Critique,* Stanley Rosen observes, "*constructs* theoretical entities that serve his purpose. There is no empirical confirmation of Kant's hypothesis, however, since what counts as experience, and also as confirmation, is created by our acceptance of that hypothesis."[30] In this manner, the Kantian project of a "critique" of reason, of setting limits to the kinds of claims that can responsibly and autonomously be made by and for the modern individual, comes at the expense of a pervasive disorientation that, in the domain of empirical, socioeconomic phenomena the sociologist Anthony Giddens has called "disembedding," a "'lifting out' of social relations from local contexts of interaction and their restructuring across indefinite spans of time-space" (Giddens, 21).

Kant's concept of experience as something grounded in an imperceptible synthesis of our intuitive and conceptual powers would yet have to confront its ultimate, repeatedly deferred presupposition: whether to view mind itself strictly as one more *effect* of this synthetic, transcendental operation or, alternatively, to argue that mind (as "pure self-consciousness") actually governs this synthesis itself a priori. At issue is whether the rationality of Kant's (or, for that matter, any other) hypothesis is sufficiently guaranteed by the coherence of its discrete elements, or whether rationality demands that its own, intrinsically hypothetical structures attain self-awareness. Recognizing that his term "transcendental" has for some time functioned in ways that make it virtually indistinguishable from "hypothetical," Kant asks: does mind exercise rational governance over "its" representations (including those of "itself"), or is it merely a contingent and logically belated effect of its own subterranean synthetic activity? Given the apparent impossibility of justifying a project whose internal organization rests on our acceptance of a hypothesis about matters *prior* to experience—thereby precluding all verification or falsification *by* experience—Kant introduces a new type of preconscious symbolization that is to ensure both the self-presence of the philosophical subject known as apperception and the rationality and legitimacy of its representations as knowledge.

This symbolic activity is introduced under the name "schematism" and is characterized, in the words of Ernst Cassirer, as a "product and, as it were, a monogram, of pure a priori imagination, through which . . . images themselves first become possible."[31] Posited as the hidden capstone for Kant's analytic edifice, however, this schematism, so poignantly captured in the trope of a "monogram," derives its authority from an activity—theory instantiated by *writing*—that has already been unfolding in a self-consciously hypothetical manner for some time. At the same time, the idiosyncratic connotations of "monogram" suggest that it will necessarily remain inscrutable and indemonstrable. As Kant notes, "in its application to appearances and their mere form . . . [the schema is] an art concealed in the depth of the human soul, whose real modes of activity nature is hardly likely ever to allow us to uncover, and to have open to our gaze" (183). The Kantian schema curiously anticipates Blake's Urizen—that cocooned embodiment of reason—philosophy's ultimate presupposition of "silent activity / Unseen in tormenting passions; / An activity unknown and horrible / A self-contemplating shadow / In enormous labors occupied" (*CPP*, 71).

In Kant's transcendental account, then, all justification is necessarily internal, and his overall account takes shape as a metonymic chain of interlocking hypotheses that, by virtue of their repeated usage as (pseudo-)explanations, progressively validate what Kant calls "transcendental reflection." Having charged all possible experience with conspiring to claim independence, when, in fact, it is utterly incapable of representing itself, Kant's *Critique of Pure Reason* seeks to remedy the situation by offering its own hypothetical account as a logically viable answer to this conundrum. Kant's answer comes in the form of his "schematism," a subterranean, synthetic activity designed to restore the epistemological coherence of the subject and its world, from which Kant's argument, until just now, had taken such pains to estrange us. As Philippe Lacoue-Labarthe and Jean-Luc Nancy point out, "if the Kantian *schema* was the never *truly* explained union of concept and intuition, the romantic *character* is its explication and the figure provided for its truth" (119). Hence, as my earlier reading of Novalis aimed to show, Jena romanticism grasps such a character as a fiction, in both the psychological and formal-aesthetic senses. Its truth-value resides in its self-reflexive status *as construction.* Again, Lacoue-Labarthe and Nancy: "Construction attains the heart of what it constructs or reconstructs; it seizes, articulates, and presents its concept and its intuition as one" (111).

In his more discursive writings, Kant not only accepts the fact that the agency of apperception is never transparent to itself, but he actually builds up this seeming predicament into a dialectical theory of history. "Idea for a Universal History with a Cosmopolitan Intent" (1784) opens with a veritable blueprint for the epistemological possibilities and disciplinary innovations that follow from an axiomatically conspiratorial understanding of social process:

> Whatever concept one may form of *freedom of the will* in a metaphysical context, its *appearances*, human actions, like all other natural events, are certainly determined in conformity with universal natural laws. History—which concerns itself with providing a narrative of these appearances, regardless of how deeply hidden their causes may be—allows us to hope that if we examine *the play of the human will's freedom in the large,* we can discover its course to conform to rules as well as to hope that what strikes us as complicated and unpredictable in the single individual may in the history of the entire species be discovered to be the steady progress and slow development of its original capacities. . . . Individual men and even entire peoples give little thought to the fact that while each according to his own ways pursues his own end—often at cross purposes with each other—they unconsciously proceed toward an unknown natural end, as if following a guiding thread; and they work to promote an end they would set little store by, even if they were aware of it. (Kant 1983, 29)

Not only does this extraordinary opening intimate the sudden rise of demographic and statistical theory, barely in its beginnings at the time; it also presages the transgenerational and entirely unconscious transmission of cultural memory units that the evolutionary theorist Richard Dawkins would almost two centuries later identify as the principal mission of the body in Darwinian theory: to serve as a "survival machine" for genetic information and, potentially, for more capacious "cultural" information (what Dawkins calls *memes*). Most immediately germane to our purposes, however, is Kant's apparent embrace of the fact that individual subjects acquire historical efficacy precisely insofar as their conscious intentions or "meanings" miscarry, producing effects whose deep-structural logic and purposiveness can be uncovered only by a retrospective and axiomatically distrustful interpreter. Yet where Kant's essay adopts a cautiously dialectical view of history, and where a decade later, Novalis and Schlegel would flamboyantly embrace the wholly imaginary status of human agency, Burke's, Wollstonecraft's, and Godwin's philosophical fictions lack the ironic qualification according to which truth produced by narrative is understood to inhere precisely in the latter's status as a *construction.* The kind of conspiratorial hermeneutics taking shape in Kant's first *Critique,* and bequeathed to most social and political theoreticians and novelists of the 1790s, has persuasively been described as a "method for begging the question on a grand scale," which is to say, a "method for proving things, independent of empirical appeals, by demonstrating that they are self-evidently presupposed by what is (supposedly) self-evident" (Herrnstein-Smith 1988, 128). Similarly, Slavoj Žižek sees "the transcendental subject . . . confronted with the disquieting fact that it depends, in its very formal genesis, on some inner-worldly, 'pathological' process—a scandal corresponding perfectly to the 'scandalous' character of the Freudian unconscious, which is also unbearable from the transcendental-philosophical perspective" (Žižek 1989, 17).

Retroactivity as Romance: William Godwin and the Pleasures of Paranoia

Within the tumultuous politics of 1790s Europe, paranoid or conspiratorial logic spans the entire gamut of writing—from didactic literature to sociological treatises on female manners and education, innovations in philosophy, mathematics, economics, and law, and from the radically secular and materialist political arguments of the French Encyclopedists and some of their British sympathizers (Priestley, Godwin) to radical critiques of established and natural religion and their allegedly false biblical scholarship and translation (Alexander Geddes, Richard Brothers, and Blake). The two antithetical strands of secular and spiritual radicalism appear particularly receptive to conspiratorial modes of narration and to "a last desperate effort" (Wood, 411) at integrating the Enlightenment paradigm of intentional, self-conscious human agency and linear causation with an inchoate or inscrutable social reality. No accident, then, that for William Godwin the years 1793–97 marked an important transition away from rational and systematic mode of philosophical writings and its totalizing aspirations and toward a new, radical paradigm of literature whose modernist implications one could easily trace not only in the later poetry of Shelley but also in the skeptical epistemologies of Fyodor Dostoyevsky and Robert Musil. Like the contemporaneous crisis of rationality as it unfolds in the Jena romantics' skeptical reading of Fichte's *Science of Knowledge,* Godwin's last attempt at formulating a coherent social and political theory in his revised and much enlarged edition of *Political Justice* (1795) neatly illustrates the collapse of self-consciousness and intentionality as the Archimedian point for a coherent and comprehensive social theory. Indeed, few treatises of the time seem to call for a deconstructive reading more loudly than Godwin's magnum opus. To respond to that call, however, means more than charting that text's growing awareness of its own programmatic impossibility. For the retroactive (so-called paranoid) mode of cognition so reluctantly identified as an inescapable condition of human consciousness and "rational" agency in *Political Justice* effectively compels Godwin and his contemporaries to turn to literature—itself taken in a radically speculative *and* concrete sense—as the only plausible formal strategy for remedying that epistemological crisis. Among the "Principles" with whose summation *Political Justice* begins, section 6 offers these curious epistemological premises:

- The voluntary actions of men are under the direction of their feelings.
- Reason is not an independent principle, and has no tendency to excite us to action; in a practical view, it is merely a comparison and balancing of different feelings.
- Reason, though it cannot excite us to action, is calculated to regulate our conduct, according to the comparative worth it ascribes to different excitements.
- It is to the improvement of reason, therefore that we are to look for the improvement of our social condition. (*GPJ*, 77)

Given the overtly contingent status of reason ("not an independent principle"), the remedial aspirations of *Political Justice* as a whole imply a new, palpably diminished concept of "progress." With reason no longer operating as a necessary premise (as it still does for Kant), the progress of individuals or entire communities, like that of rationality itself, hinges on the contingent formation of character and on "the cultivation of knowledge" (*GPJ*, 77).[32] Rather than underwriting the a priori coherence and "communicability" (to borrow Kant's pivotal concept) of knowledge and other contingent acts of individual understanding, reason itself fades away into the twilight of utopian thought—itself merely a wish or, at most, a postulate whose realization hinges on the serendipitous convergence or arduous coordination of innumerable empirical practices and actions.

Godwin proceeds to analyze the internal structure of the individual whose discrete efforts ("cultivation of knowledge") he hopes to enlist in this Herculean task of salvaging the linchpin of Enlightenment thought, and things go from bad to worse. At first glance, the chapter "Of the Mechanism of the Human Mind" looks like any other of the chapters in book 4, "Of the Operation of Opinion in Societies and Individuals." Indeed, it follows on the heels of a chapter drawing "Inferences from the Doctrine of Necessity" whose deterministic aspirations put further, if rather nervous, pressure on the ensuing discussion.[33] For while Godwin never tires of reminding us that "it would be of infinite importance to the cause of science and virtue to express ourselves upon all occasions in the language of necessity," he concedes that "the contrary language is perpetually intruding, and it is difficult to speak any two sentences, upon any topic connected with human action, without it" (*GPJ*, 359). As remains to be seen, either term in Godwin's antithetical pairing of necessity and contingency will prove equally pernicious to the notion of a rational, intentional self-conscious agency. Such is the disturbing outcome of a chapter clearly aimed at recovering at the level of individual thought what Godwin was no longer willing to presuppose at the level of transcendental reflection or communal practice.

From the outset, Godwin hopes to assimilate the structure of cognition to that of causation, such that the "mechanism" of the human mind is "nothing more than a regular succession of phenomena, without any uncertainty of event, so that every consequent requires a specific antecedent, and could be no otherwise in any respect than as the antecedent determined it to be" (*GPJ*, 360–61). And yet, while Godwin's unsettling illustration of a hot iron "applied" to the body of an infant may seem to affirm the principle of causation in the form of pained screams, the effect here is less one of thought than of outright sensation. To ascend to the plateau of voluntary reflection or thought properly speaking is to inquire into the "traces made upon the medullary substance of the brain, by means of which past and present impressions are connected according to certain laws, as the traces happen to approach or run into each other" (*GPJ*, 361). It is nothing less than the question concerning the possibility of reason that stands to be answered here, for cohesive and purposive thought demands that the operation of "necessity" or determinism within the human mind be itself observable *by* that mind. There must be "a constancy of conjunction" within mind that will allow it to proceed from "antecedent to consequent" (*GPJ*, 362) with a sense of prolepsis, of anticipation, rather than continual surprise.

The potential success or failure of Godwin's larger political project—which the 1795 revisions of *Political Justice* had scaled back from the utopia of wholly rational, autonomous, and benevolent individual agency to the mere imagining of an "eventual" rationality within social life—appears to pivot on whether consciousness-as-agency ("thought") is itself monitored by consciousness-as-reflection. Thus Godwin momentarily draws a distinction between "thought" and a sort of supplementary reflection, by which the mind not only has the thought, but adverts to its own situation, and observes that it has it" (*GPJ*, 364). Like Edmund Husserl in his *Logical Investigations,* Godwin regards self-consciousness strictly as a "tracing" back (361) of actions that the mind could not reflexively grasp at the time of their occurrence because it itself was utterly consumed by them at that time.[34] In other words, since "mind" *in actu* "is always full" (367), self-consciousness can only ever occur as "a second thought" (364). Mind *qua* reflection is forever catching up with its own origin, an epistemological dilemma well known to Godwin's contemporaries Kant, Fichte, Novalis, and Schelling. Indeed, the distinction between "thought" and "reflection"—between consciousness *of* an object and consciousness *as* its own object—once again begs the question of mind on a grand scale rather than settling it. For as Godwin himself readily concedes, we do not as yet know "whether the mind can ever have more than one thought at any one time" (*GPJ*, 364–65).

Even the older and seemingly accepted paradigm of mind as a train of associations ultimately begs the question, for at every one of its nodal points of transition or intersection between one content and another, the same problem arises: "Have they any communication? Do they flow separately, or occasionally cross and interrupt each other? Can any reason be given . . . why the same man should not, at the same time, be both Newton and Shakespeare" (*GPJ*, 365). Godwin's earlier, physiological characterization of mental life as "medullary"—"pertaining to, of the nature of, or resembling marrow" (*OED*)—casts much doubt on this possibility of a stratum of apperception or self-consciousness supervening and at all times monitoring the countless "traces" of "how past and present impressions are connected." For if the organic meaning appears to signal a tight nexus of cause and effect, thought and action, the same word also denotes "encephaloid or soft cancer" (*OED*). Consistent with this skeptical meaning, Godwin's argument displays a growing awareness of how the mind's acute receptivity to all kinds of influxes undermines its capacity for autonomous self-reflection. Such metastasizing of peripheral sensation virtually guarantees that what Godwin calls "thought" will never achieve definitive self-awareness. The entire chapter ultimately deteriorates into a desperate quest on Godwin's part to formulate a solution to the dilemma that mind, however much it may wish to imagine itself as governing its representations in the same way that a cause necessitates a determinate effect, may in the end be merely the effect of a welter of stimuli and subconscious influences—even, perhaps especially, when it purports to transcend such chaos in the "supplementary" guise of reflection.

It is worthwhile to observe how Godwin's remedial introduction of two time-honored philosophical concepts miscarries. On the heels of his concession that, relative to the fatal spontaneity of action and volition, all consciousness amounts simply to "second thought," he proposes association as a means of ensuring that all representation ("thought") is accompanied by a supervening stratum of self-awareness ("consciousness"). While the fact of the mind's propensity to associate one thought with another, either because of some "external impression" or because of some property intrinsic to the first thought itself, is hardly in doubt, no proof exists that the mind observes itself as it proceeds along this path of vicarious contiguity. Associationism simply begs the question of "some link between" its sequential representations. Godwin himself notes that some "very curious questions will here arise (e.g., "Have the [representations] any communication? Do they flow separately, or occasionally cross and interrupt each other?"). Moreover, inasmuch as associationist thought rests on an implicitly temporalized concept of mind, the point in contention is less whether one representation may be observed to connect with another than whether there is any limit to such cross-referencing. For if, as Godwin maintains, no temporal gap ever intervenes between one thought and its associated neighbor ("the mind is always full" [*GPJ*, 367]), then how is consciousness ever to reflect in timely fashion on the associative relationship between its discrete representations?

Godwin's second attempt at recovery involves his appeal to Locke's distinction between simple and complex ideas. Though "the mind can only apprehend only a single idea at once . . . that idea needs not be a simple idea. The mind can apprehend two or more objects at a single effort, but it cannot apprehend them as two" (366–67). Contrary to Locke, for whom the move from simple to complex ideas constitutes a significant epistemological advance, Godwin finds that the complexity lurking behind the deceptive singularity of any one thought actually forestalls any conscious, reflective awareness of its true nature. The distinction between simple and complex ideas is no longer one of kind but a question of lacking awareness of their actual complexity at the instance of volition and action, and of a belated awareness upon reflection ("second thought"). In short, consciousness is by definition an awareness of complex causes belatedly inferred from the deceptive simplicity of their effect (viz., volition, action). Reflection, and by extension the writing of rational political philosophy, constitutes "an operation of science . . . altogether foreign to our first and original conceptions" (*GPJ*, 367). Indeed, the susceptibility of any individual to innumerable peripheral influences and more or less insistent associations soon thereafter compels Godwin to suspend his quest for a "mechanism" of mind—and by extension his vaunted project of political justice predicated on the doctrine of "necessity." For to have conceded that "the mind is always full," is to confront thought as the epicenter of ten thousand conflicting fault lines, some ephemeral and of scarcely measurable effect ("the pinch of a shoe . . . a pain in my head"), and others reaching very deep. It simply will no longer suffice to claim that the mind passes "from one [representation] to another without feeling the minutest obstacle, or being in any degree distracted by their multiplicity" (*GPJ*, 369). For the question is no longer whether mind is distracted by the heterogeneity and cross-fertilization of its discrete representations, but whether there is anything deserving to be called mind *except for that welter of thoughts.* In accepting the irreducibly temporal character of consciousness (in ways strikingly prescient of the early Husserl), Godwin ultimately qualifies consciousness as merely a subsidiary, "one of the departments," of memory:

> An infinite number of thoughts passed through my mind in the last five minutes of my existence. How many of them am I now able to recollect? How many of them shall I recollect tomorrow? One impression after another is perpetually effacing from this intellectual register. Some of them may with great attention and effort be revived; others obtrude themselves uncalled for; and a third sort are perhaps out of the reach of any power of thought to reproduce, as having never left their traces behind for a moment. If the memory be capable of so many variations and degrees of intensity, may there not be some cases with which it never connects itself? If the succession of thought be so inexpressibly rapid, may they not pass over some topics with so delicate a touch as to elude the supplement of consciousness?[35]

The anarchy that the 1790s knew to have been raging for some time beneath the polished veneer of late-absolutist display and genteel manners and customs can thus be traced back to a fundamentally epistemological chaos that, as *Caleb Williams* makes clear, also contaminates the republican model of subjective agency premised on notions of progress, benevolence, and sympathy.[36] If the above passage raises serious doubts about the ability of any individual consciousness to excavate the mostly oblique or altogether unconscious impressions that converge in the deceptive singularity and presence of so-called "thought," what prospects remain for ordering the political and social universe at large? Godwin's treatise, and more insistently yet, his political novel *Caleb Williams,* anticipates post-Freudian theory by showing how "the supplement of consciousness" is not only belated in the familiar, Hegelian sense of the word; he also reveals that the truth-value of such consciousness—even as it legitimates itself by loudly proclaiming itself to have awakened *from* an error or dream state—remains itself circumscribed by the very blindness that it purports to have overcome. "When we awaken into reality after a dream," Žižek reminds us, "we usually say to ourselves 'it was just a dream,' thereby blinding ourselves to the fact that in our everyday, wakening reality we are *nothing but a consciousness of that dream*" (1989, 47). Godwin himself remarks how in sleep, the individual may "actually find the ineffectual calls that are addressed to us, as well as various other sounds, occasionally mixing with our dreams, without our being aware from whence these new perceptions arose." In the absence of as yet undiscovered theories of hypnosis, sleep nonetheless illustrates the boundless receptivity of mind to subconscious influences and impressions. More important, the "rational" doings of consciousness themselves are premised on a notion of awakening—or, writ large, Enlightenment—as utter emancipation from everything that had entered into the mind prior to that break. Inasmuch as thought is a composite of "the most minute impressions" (*GPJ,* 373), its distinctness and simplicity as "one" thought is deceptive, to be sure, yet also essential, in that without such economy any transition from feeling to thought to volition to action would remain impossible.[37] In its formal integrity, thought, like the subject itself, constitutes a "fantasy-construction which serves as a support for our 'reality' itself: an 'illusion' which structures our effective, real social relations" (Žižek, 1989, 45).

As the notion of self-transcendence via reflection fades as no more than a utopian wish, Godwin's argument settles on a new, monstrously overdetermined model of subjectivity. In it, "every perception is complicated" not only "by a variety of simultaneous impressions, but every idea that now offers itself to the mind is modified by all the ideas that ever existed in it." What Godwin calls the "insensible empire of prejudice" (*GPJ,* 372) will reappear as the "pit" of memory in Hegel's *Encyclopedia* and as an epoch-making experience for the young Sigmund Freud attending Jean-Martin Charcot's experiments with hypnosis in 1885–86. For the subjectivity of mind, in Godwin's view, stems, not from some idiosyncratic perspective that it may be thought to maintain on its experiential world and thoughts, but rather from the fact that it is wholly incapable of rational self-transcendence, being at all times "overpowered and swallowed up by other sensations or circumstances" (*GPJ*, 373). While the relation of thought to volition or action may yet obey the laws of cause and effect, those laws can only be traced long after a myriad of intersecting sensations, desires, fantasies, and associations have congealed into an instance of volition that, in turn, has taken objective form as action. A characteristic example can be found in Mary Hays's *Memoirs of Emma Courtney* (1796), in which the protagonist recalls having "spent the night in self-examination." Only in "solitude"—for which the written "memoirs," a derivative of the early- and mid-eighteenth-century genre of the conduct book, provide the formal blueprint—is Emma able to grasp the extent to which her conscious persona has been shaped by inscrutable compulsions: "my reason was but an auxiliary to my passion, it persuaded me, that I was only doing justice to high and uncommon worth; imagination lent her aid, and an importunate sensibility, panting after good unalloyed, completed the seduction."[38]

The belated efforts of reflective consciousness to analyze the "mechanism" of thought can only infer a given state of mind a posteriori, and only by laboriously reconstructing the infinitely variegated causal sequence leading up to it: "If thought, in order to be the source of animal motion, need not have either the nature of volition, or the concomitant of consciousness, and if a single thought may become a complex source, and produce a variety of motions, it will then become exceedingly difficult to trace its operations, or to discover any circumstances in a particular instance of animal motion which can sufficiently indicate that thought was not the principle of its production" (*GPJ*, 374). With this final admission—that thought can never be ruled out as the cause of an action—Godwin retains, albeit in seriously atrophied form, the principle of causality for the inquiry into human agency and social practice. Yet given the ultimate inscrutability of mind, any future inquiry into the causes of action will prove formally open-ended and politically invasive as it engulfs the analyst in a vertigo of paranoid and reflexive suspicion. For inasmuch as the inferential tracing of presumed elusive "causes" (thought) is premised on likewise presumed visible "effects" (actions), there will have to be something curiously amiss or "symptomatic" about these actions. Any speculation about the "mechanism of the human mind" and its adaptability to rational, social purposes must therefore begin by scrutinizing the symptomatic surfeit, the conspicuous detail or action, that stands out within the muddy current of quotidian practice. At the same time, the obverse proposition also holds true: no practice, no act of volition, however trivial or fleeting, can be viewed as simply innocuous.

It is this reciprocity of ubiquitous symptoms (actions) and unrelenting inquiry (consciousness as "second thought") that accounts for Godwin's professional shift from the writing of political philosophy to that of fiction. The key document for this transition is his "Of History and Romance," an essay written in 1797, just as "the progressive sector of England's public sphere was about to collapse, and the machinery of the publications industry that had been central to it was being taken over by a new generation of sophisticated conservative intellectuals" (Klancher, 1995, 146). With this text, Godwin restates his earlier intimation, in the preface to the 1797 *Enquirer,* that a systematic and exhaustive political treatise in programmatic form is "incommensurate to our powers" (vi). If the 1795 account of the "Mechanism of the Human Mind" had seemingly held on to that vision, even as the argument confronted the inexorable self-deconstruction of individual agency, Godwin's speculations concerning "republican" romance as an alternative to the "cumbrous and unwieldy" (*GCW,* 361) abstractions of Scottish historiography now make him seem eager to stylize the impasse of systematic thought into an intellectual virtue. The weakness of "general history" lies in the fact that it has nothing to offer but repetition, thus allowing custom to atrophy cognition. Its principal characters "are disciplined to dull monotony. They are cast together in one characteristic mould. There is something of the nature of modern governments and institutions that seems to blight in the bud every grander and more ample development of the soul. . . . It is the history of negotiations and tricks, it is the history of revenues and debts, it is the history of corruption and political profligacy, but it is not the history of genuine independent man" (*GCW,* 365, 367).[39]

To this abstract and invariant procession of history as the sum of *res gestae,* Godwin opposes his conception of history as the archeology of individual motives, wherein all the political, social, and cultural forces of a given moment crystallize or, at least, can be traced from their present, necessarily encrypted form. Methodologically, this new dispensation involves a shift away from description and progressive narration toward inferential, indeed retroactive, analysis. "The study of individual men can never fail to be an object of the highest importance," because "when we return home to engage in the solemn act of self-investigation, our most useful employment is to produce the materials we have collected abroad, and, by a sort of magnetism, cause those particulars to start out to view in ourselves, which might otherwise have for ever lain undetected." All historical knowledge centers around "activity and motive" (*GCW*, 361). Godwin here may be echoing a position that Mary Hays, herself an avid student of his earlier *Enquiry Concerning Political Justice*, had articulated in the preface to her *Memoirs of Emma Courtney* (1796): "Whether the incidents or the characters are copied from life, is of little importance—The only quest is, if the *circumstances*, and situations, are altogether improbable? If not—whether the consequences *might* not have followed from the circumstances?" (Hays, 4).

For Godwin as for Hays, making pronouncements about society requires "us to scrutinise the nature of man, . . . [to] observe the empire of motives, whether grovelling or elevated; and [to] note the influence that one human being exercises over another" (*GCW*, 361, 363).[40] Romance, which Godwin here uses in ways not obviously distinguishable from the novel, presents itself as the most fitting medium for this new type of historiography. Godwin's essentially Aristotelian plea in favor of fiction over history is grounded in the greater value placed on "instruction" rather than empirical truth. Whereas general historiography offers a "mere skeleton of history," romance involves the mobilization of narrative and psychological technique in the service of simulating the human in exhaustive psycho-physiological concreteness ("the muscles, the articulations, everything in which life emphatically resides" [*GCW*, 368]). Overall, historical knowledge for Godwin involves the writer's incrementally obtaining exhaustive information about his individual subject, dissecting motive and action, and by means of such figural vivisection laying bare the historical determinacy of the modern individual.

If, as has been argued, Godwin's program for fiction demands a totalizing and invasive gaze, it does so to confer the greatest probability on historical romance; the more scrupulous the study of the individual, the greater the legitimacy of the fiction that brought it into focus. In Godwin's theory, romance not only gravitates from mere plausibility to the probability and the eventual proof for its thematic inventions but in so progressing authorizes and legitimates the initial act of curiosity—a key term in *Caleb Williams*—that had first brought its fictional subject into focus. What Godwin calls "the genuine scholar" thus constitutes a principle of unrelenting surveillance: "His curiosity is never satiated. He is ever upon the watch for further and still further particulars. Trembling for his own fallibility and frailty, he employs every precaution to guard himself against them." Godwin's acknowledgment of the radical interdependence of writing and surveillance, of fiction and suspicion, invention and self-legitimation, soon thereafter leads him to commit his own persona to this program:

> There are characters in history that may almost be said to be worth an eternal study. They are epitomes . . . of its best and most exalted features, purified from their grossness. I am not contented to observe such a man upon the public stage, I would follow him into his closet. I would see the friend and the father of a family, as well as the patriot. I would read his works and his letters, if any remain to us. I would observe the turn of his thoughts and the character of his phraseology. I would study his public orations. I would collate his behavior in prosperity with his behavior in adversity. I should be glad to know the course of his studies, and the arrangements of his time. I should rejoice to have, or to be enabled to make, if that were possible, a journal of his ordinary and minutest actions. (*GCW*, 364)

If writing here is equated with surveillance, it is so less for the purpose of ascertaining some truth about its individual subject than in order to prove that narrative is capable of producing ex post facto the very past that it had initially posited as its hypothetical point of departure. Having shed its traditional association with leisure, entertainment, and distraction, romance reconstitutes itself as an epistemological principle, a heuristic fiction whose medium, print, also seeks to overcome the contingent status of its discrete parts, such as author, character, and setting. By means of surveillance, fiction aspires to emancipate itself from the taint of leisure and caprice, the merely conjectural or plausible. In its retroactive drive and formal organization, romance seeks to confirm the very past that, initially, it could only conceive and approach as fiction. If *Political Justice* had foundered on the conceptual aporia of individual agency, Godwin's project of republican romance advocates the exhaustive, retroactive analysis of a given individual as "that which alone can give energy and utility to the records of our social existence" (*GCW*, 363).

Like Kant and Bentham, Godwin grasps the empirical world as a welter of contradictory and often inchoate motives, competing narratives, and tenuous causal connections that can be given organization and direction only by means of critical, heuristic fictions: "It follows that the noblest and most excellent species of history, may be decided to be a composition in which, with a scanty substratum of facts and dates, the writer interweaves a number of happy, ingenious and instructive inventions, blending them into one continuous and indiscernible mass" (*GCW*, 368). We note the self-conscious attitude with which Godwin articulates the status of such historical romance and its probabilistic truth-value *as* fiction. Beyond that, Godwin makes clear that the production of fiction ultimately aims at realizing a past that will sanction the coherence of the present narrative. To read Godwinian romance is to accept the past's intrinsic fluidity, its receptivity to and malleability by the power of writing. It is only in approaching the concept of fiction and the practice of writing as one of unrelenting surveillance and scrupulous reordering of a hypostatized past "that we shall be enabled to add, to the knowledge of the past, a sagacity that can penetrate into the depths of futurity" (*GCW*, 363).

We are now in a position to articulate the structural resemblance between Godwin's romancing of the historical past and our overarching concern with paranoia as a model of historical cognition involving a formally distinctive literary practice. Godwin's plea on behalf of historical cognition through the medium of prose fiction intrigues because it seems to suspend one of our most habitual axioms, that concerning the categorical determinacy and irreversibility of the past. In visiting obsessive scrutiny on "individual incident and individual man and . . . hang[ing] upon that his invention or conjecture as he can," Godwin's romance historian appears motivated by creating the past as something whose determinants are neither objectively fixed nor ever independent of the observer (novelist). Yet what does it mean for Godwinian romance to suspend the basic assumption according to which, "when one thinks of an event as having taken place, that all possible determinations of it have already been used up, and that therefore it is no use doing anything now designed to make it have happened," in apparent contrast to future events where "we do not have the picture of all determinations of it being *already* used up" (Dummett, 328).

Before further considering Michael Dummett's critique of this commonsense model of the past as exhaustively determined, we ought to pause and inquire into the origins of our customary, quasi-mythical attachment to that notion. Arguably, our contentment with the idea of a "fixed" and "autonomous" past is bound up with our concomitant habit of viewing the future as indeterminate. For if we are to sustain a liberal and optimistic vision of the future as full of uncharted possibilities, it is imperative that we posit the past as the unchanging *ground* for all future pursuits. Were it otherwise, we would be denied any sense of capable agency vis-à-vis the future, since a contingent and mutable past would forever threaten to destabilize all future projects.

Beginning in 1794, however, Godwin's writings seem to take things in reverse. The present—"Things as they are"—is endurable only if we are granted the chance of recreating the past so as to explain *why* they are thus and, more important, to expose their being "as they are" as grounded in a primal instance of repression and in a steadily operating web of illusions, deceit, and lies. For, according to Godwin, if the past is posited as wholly fixed, then so are the present and the future. To open up the present for individual development and freedom, the past will have to be realized, for the first time, in its authentic form. That is, the past must be discovered to have been other than what it has been taken to be until now. Such an interpretive recreating of the past in turn opens up the possibility of disabusing one's contemporaries of their comfortable rapport with the prevailing ideological fantasy of "Things as they are." Presaging the critical thrust of Althusser's, Lacan's, and Fredric Jameson's notions of history, Godwin's novels and theoretical writings after *Political Justice* conceive of the past as an absent cause preceded by and traceable only on the basis of its own apparent effect, the present, itself a network of antagonistic forces and vectors from which subjects cannot extricate themselves without once again "altering" the past by means of representing it differently. To appreciate the full implications of that position, on which Godwin himself continued to dwell even decades after publishing *Caleb Williams,* it will help to briefly recapture the most salient points of Michael Dummett's intriguing study of retroactive causation. According to his account, there are two types of retroactivity, one in which an action is taken *so as to verify* that a different event had taken place previously, and another in which an action is taken *so as to bring about* the occurrence of an earlier event. Under the first category would fall actions such as flipping a light switch in order to ascertain whether a defective lightbulb has been replaced. Doing so does not bring about the past (i.e., does not cause the lightbulb to have been replaced or not) but merely ascertains the operation of a cause by exploring its expected effect.

Yet already here, the entire explanatory system of causality seems strangely volatile, less the guarantor of clarity and transparency within a heretofore enigmatic, quasi-mythical state of mind than a more elaborate occasion for such sublime enigmas to reappear at the level of theory itself. For if "on the ordinary Humean view of cause, a cause is simply a sufficient condition," we here have a case where "an event of a certain kind [i.e., the light going on] is a sufficient condition for an event of another kind [i.e., the lightbulb having been replaced] to have taken place previously, and why should we not then call the later event the 'cause' of the earlier?" (Dummett, 319). The apparent dilemma is rooted in the logical aporia of Humean causation itself: "If causes precede effects, it seems that there can never by any certainty that a cause will bring about its effect; since, during the interval, something might always intervene to hinder the operation of the cause." If, on the other hand, we postulate that causes must be "contemporaneous with their effects . . . then the cause of the cause will be simultaneous with the effect, and we shall be unable to trace the causal ancestry of an event back a single instant in time" (320). Dummett's initial solution to this dilemma merits close attention, for it bears on Godwin's novelistic and theoretical concern with the relation between the psychological factors involved in our ordinary acceptance of historical causation as linear and progressive. Arguing that much depends on how "the picture of causation . . . is to be interpreted," Dummett adverts to Newtonian mechanics, where what "requires to be explained by the action of a force is not, as in Aristotelian mechanics, any deviation from a state of rest, but a deviation from uniform motion in a straight line. What we here regard as 'going on as before' need not itself be an unchanging state, but may also be a process. Thus, although causes operate to bring about their immediate effects without any lapse of time, we are able to trace the causal ancestry of an event back in time without any arbitrary lacuna in our chain of explanations; for a cause may initiate a process, which will be terminated when it reaches an assignable point, and will then in its turn have some further effect. The temporal direction of causation, from earlier to later, comes in because we regard a cause as *starting off* a process: that is to say, the fact that at any one moment the process is going on is sufficiently explained if we can explain what began it" (320–21). Dummett's obvious reference point is Hume's 1739 *Treatise of Human Nature,* which identifies contiguity, temporal priority, and necessity as the three criteria presupposed by all forms of causal explanation (Hume, 53–55). Hume, of course, famously calls into question the subject's ability ever to arrive at a "necessary" connection between cause and effect, since "the mind is determin'd by custom to pass from any cause to its effect" (ibid., 88). All causal explanation is thus intrinsically probabilistic, that is, unfolding within a general framework of "chance"—itself described by Hume as "the negation of a cause" (ibid., 87). Meanwhile, probability can be assessed in its fluctuations only inasmuch as the epistemological subject abides comfortably within the matrix of "past experience." "As past experience regulates our judgment concerning the possibility of . . . effects, so it does that concerning their probability; and that effect, which has been the most common, we always esteem to be the most likely." Yet Hume once again insists, "the supposition, *that the future resembles the past,* is not founded on arguments of any kind, but is deriv'd entirely from habit" (ibid., 92).[41]

To be sure, we see how causation is intimately entwined with the psychological constant of temporality, and with the logical fiction of time as a continuum. Yet it is by no means a foregone conclusion which of the two extreme points of that continuum ought to be considered the beginning and which the end. To settle that question, one is constrained to make reference to entirely different criteria, such as what constitutes a "normal" process and, especially, which explanatory model—which genre of representation—requires less effort. By way of illustrating the operation of such psychological factors in any causal ordering of the world, Dummett takes the example of a shot in billiards where simple physical laws (force, direction, along with the coefficients of friction, elasticity, masses of balls) "determine the motion of the balls." By contrast, were we "to imagine the whole sequence of events as taking place in reverse, the theory needed to explain the behavior of the balls would have to be far more complex, and prediction would depend on far more recondite observations."[42] Even so, the process unfolding in between is essentially the same, regardless of whether it is represented in the conventional "forward" or in the counterintuitive "reverse" mode. With this important qualification, we happen upon the second, more obviously puzzling model of retroactivity, exemplified by Dummett as follows:

> Someone who believes in magic has some extremely plausible grounds for doing so; he has noticed, after careful observation, that his spells and incantations are invariably followed by the results in order to produce which he carries them out. He has among his spells a formula for producing good weather in a particular place on a particular day; this formula works without fail. . . . An occasion arises when he has reason for wanting the weather at, say, Liverpool to have been good on the previous day, but he does not know whether it was or not; he therefore recites his spell, putting in yesterday's date. Subsequently, he finds out that there was fine weather at Liverpool on that day. If, to this idea of treating the occurrence of some event as an explanation of the occurrence of an earlier event we feel a strong objection, as most people probably do, this is because the accept-

ance of such a model of causation would also render it sometimes reasonable to *bring about* the occurrence with the intention of guaranteeing the occurrence of a previous event (Dummett, 324–25; emphasis added).

Again, the peculiarity of all this lies in the fact that our objections to such reasoning are premised on commonsense assumptions regarding the strictly progressive nature of causation for which proof is no easier to produce than for the apparently spurious idea of retroactive causation. For to argue, as we most likely would, that "either the event has taken place, or it has not" is premised on the assumption that "when one thinks of an event as having taken place. . . all possible determinations of it have already been used up." This argument, Dummett reminds us, "gets its strength from this picture that we naturally use—of the past as fixed, and the future as fluid; and this makes the argument valueless, for what it was intended to do was not to appeal to but to *justify* this picture" (Dummett, 328). What matters, for our purposes, is the fact that with the second type of retroactivity "the absurdity lay not in the action but in [our] method of describing it" (ibid., 327).

Precisely this will to transform the past through the sheer intensity of our present locutions brings into play the talismanic, mythic power of literary language, its capacity to conjure up the past as something decided only by the vividness, acuity, and persuasiveness of present articulation, as Coleridge's "Rime of the Ancient Mariner"—arguably one of the most powerful conjunctions of paranoia, magic, and retroactivity in English romanticism—impresses on us so strongly.[43] Similarly, the magician's seeming capacity for bringing about the past appears substantially vested in his highly formalized and idiosyncratic form of speech (a spell, a recitation). As demonstrated so powerfully by the "glittering eye" and "strange power of speech" of Coleridge's Mariner or by Godwin's repeated scientific references to the "magnetical sympathy" (*GCW*, 117) that Caleb's probing locutions create between him and Falkland, literary language by its very nature conjures up the past in strictly hypothetical and a posteriori form. In its programmatic and structural insistence on the uniqueness of the sign (Coleridge's "symbol," Godwin's "romance"), literature seeks to conjure up *for the first time,* and thus to create, the past as a matter of present urgency. If Dummett maintains qualified allegiance to the commonsense model of causation—one wherein causes have temporal priority and autonomy, while their effects prove secondary and contingent—he does so not because of decisive logical objections to the more perplexing alternative.

Rather, the commonsense model of causation prevails only conditionally, that is, as long as a speaker or writer is invested in producing the simplest and most generalizable proposition. A linear and progressive model of temporality and causation appeals because it renders it "much easier" to describe processes whose "continuance is not regarded as requiring explanation" (Dummett, 321, 322).

Yet a readily interpretable "customary" narrative model susceptible of general application is precisely *not* the aim of Godwin's *Caleb Williams.* Rather, the prose here seeks to undo "things as they are" and, where necessary, to expose the repressed criminality of the past, on which the deceptive normalcy of the present is allegedly premised.[44] The aim is to end the present's complicity with a past whose systematic obfuscation has conferred such specious consistency and commonsense coherence on the present. In its syntagmatic organization, *Caleb Williams* must expressly part ways with the commonsense model of progressive causation, on account of that model's formally undemonstrable and ideologically complacent acceptance of the past as exhaustively and irreversibly fixed. If one is to contest the assumption of the past (and, by implication, the present) as fixed within a framework of "tradition," then the Scottish historiographers' highly generalized "official" paradigm of Britain's glorious political past as inexorably moving forward, and so sanctioning its imperial and commercial present, constitutes exactly the wrong representational strategy. At the same time, Godwin's attempt at devising a counterintuitive account in which "we may observe that the occurrence of an event of a certain kind is a sufficient condition for the previous occurrence of an event of another kind" (Dummett, 322) invariably requires a far greater cognitive effort. Moreover, a retroactive narration committed to altering the past also forecloses on the possibility of developing "any kind of general hypothesis that could serve as a starting-point for further experiments and for developing a *theory* to account for the phenomena" (Dummett, 324). In short, retroactive causation—effects producing their own causes, action taken so as not only to verify but actively to realize the past that in turn will render an otherwise inchoate present intelligible—is not so much logically impossible as its representation seems unwieldy, laborious, and ungeneralizable. Such a narrative experiment may generate a fascinating story and plot, and it may even resist attempts at logical refutation. Yet it can do so only at the expense of the kind of generalization—itself premised on epistemologically suspect notions of "habit" and "custom"—

that would assimilate the story's local and contingent events to larger and more conventional patterns of social knowledge. Recalling Godwin's dissatisfaction with the abstractness and "prolixity of dullness" of the Scottish historiographers, we find his alternative of scrutinizing history in "abridgment" and allowing "ourselves to be deliver[ed] over to the reality of romance" (371) to suffer from the obverse difficulty. Romance, with its intense surveillance of the sole authentic, because causally most inscrutable, factor, "man's character" or the "Mechanism of the Human Mind," may indeed furnish the reader with a scrupulous kind of ideological critique. Yet in focusing on a given "case," wholly unique and hence never susceptible of representation in any "generic" and socially accepted ("customary") form, the knowledge so attained seems forever barred from social acceptance and legitimacy.

Quite possibly, Godwin's insistence on the absolute particularity and intrinsically novel(istic) quality of all genuine knowledge may also have precipitated the dramatic eclipse of his own authorial fame. As Hazlitt was to muse, in ways descriptive not only of Godwin's dramatic vanishing act from the arena of literary fame but also of the repressive inwardness of Godwin's principal characters in *Caleb Williams:* "Is truth then so variable? Is it one thing at twenty and another at forty? Is it a burning heat in 1793 and below *zero* in 1814?" Still, following on the heels of *Political Justice* (1793), which had propelled Godwin to "the very zenith of a sultry and unwholesome popularity" (Hazlitt, 7: 87–88), *Caleb Williams* constitutes a genuine landmark in the development of British fiction. In ways and with an intensity not previously encountered, the novel traces the innumerable ways in which social realities (e.g., differences of class) and the evaluative nomenclature that traditionally supported these realities remain fragile and susceptible of speculative scrutiny that may unearth a sublime netherworld of unconfessed crimes, motives, and desires. As Falkland so involuntarily puts it: "Honour, justice, virtue are all the juggle of knaves!" (*GCW,* 122). In rehearsing the strenuous self-justification of two nearly interchangeable characters (Falkland and Caleb), the novel identifies narrative and—in a radically new, speculative sense—the textual domain of "literature" itself as an existential condition of being. In the wake of Hume's expurgation of causality from the domain of knowledge, literature announces the flourishing of the human in the domain of the "probable." Fictionality and performativity emerge as novel means for producing self-awareness and socially relevant knowledge. "Beginning with the Augustans and the Scottish theorists of their literature," Douglas Patey has argued, "the literary work [becomes] a structure of signs organized in such a way as to lead the mind to their causes—a structure . . . of probable signs. Where the work is a fabric of signs, interpretation, the movement from formal features to meaning, will be a process of sign-inference.[45] Well beyond the political meaning of the term, which Godwin is often credited with having originated, "anarchy" now defines the epistemological situation of every individual, and thus of every community. Formally, *Caleb Williams* impresses this point on the reader through the distinctly paranoid narrative of its eponymous protagonist, whose epistemological zeal in leaving no feature or event causally unaccounted for is punctured by curious blind spots, moments of utterly unconscious action that alert the reader to a deep-seated ambivalence and a persistent irrationality lurking within the program of political protest and reform. Attentive readers will likely be disconcerted by the acts of hyperrational self-justification repeatedly merging with strands unconscious fantasy. In so fusing ennobling programmatic and erratic performative elements, the novel casts doubt on Godwin's reputation as a fervent rationalist seeking to ground political philosophy in a tightly wrought web of internally consistent, abstract propositions. Rather, it depicts all political and social relations as a welter of conflicting fears, fantasies, and memories, and as foreshadowing not merely the demise of the ancien régime but, equally so, the profound irrationality and menace of Jacobinism under whose slogan "Liberté, Egalité, Fraternité" the old order is currently being vanquished.

"Full of a thousand conjectures": Causation and Emotion in *Caleb Williams*

Few committed anti-Jacobins allow their ostensibly noble-minded writing to explore the abyss of irrational compulsions and wayward desires as thoroughly as the reputed radical Godwin was to do in *Caleb Williams.* In so exploring the potential interference between a political and an epistemological (or psychological) radicalism, Godwin unfolds a new paradigm of literature. His 1794 novel reconstitutes romance—until now the generic vehicle for the Burkean alchemy of politics and aesthetics—as a hypothetical and progressively self-legitimating creation of the past based on the present, of causes traced from their effects. Godwin implements this entirely new theoretical *cum* fictional program in meticulous and utterly deliberate ways. As he was to recall, nearly four decades later, in his preface to the Standard Novels edition of his novel *Fleetwood, or, The New Man of Feeling,* the beginning of 1793 found him "obliged to consider my pen the sole instrument for supplying my current expenses" (*GCW,* 347). Like the novel's eponymous protagonist, Godwin embarked on the writing of *Caleb Williams* with an evident desire to control the plot and outcome as carefully as his theoretical arguments in the recently published first edition of *Political Justice:*

> Pursuing this idea, I invented first the third volume of my tale, then the second, and last of all the first. I bent myself to the conception of a series of adventures of flight and pursuit; the fugitive in perpetual apprehension of being overwhelmed with the worst calamities, and the pursuer, by his ingenuity and resources, keeping his victim in a state of the most fearful alarm. This was the subject of my third volume. I was next called upon to conceive a dramatic and impressive situation adequate to account for the impulse the pursuer should feel, incessantly to alarm and harass his victim. . . . This I apprehended could best be effected by a secret murder, to the investigation of which the innocent victim should be impelled by an unconquerable spirit of curiosity. . . . I felt that I had a great advantage in thus carrying back my invention from the ultimate conclusion to the first commencement of the train of adventures upon which I purposed to employ my pen. An entire unity of plot would be the infallible result; and the unity of spirit and interest in a tale truly considered, gives it a powerful hold on the reader. (*GCW,* 349–50)

As Godwin's retrospective account suggests, all detail in *Caleb Williams* must be subordinated to the narrative's overarching purpose and design. As a minute, indeed obsessive tracing of its eponymous protagonist's history (in his own words) through that of his double (Falkland), the novel already implements what Godwin's "Of History and Romance" was to formulate later in more categorical terms. Political and ideological knowledge always amounts to a *special kind* of knowledge and hence, as a reviewer of the novel in 1794 already noted, "between fiction and philosophy there seems to be no natural alliance." Indeed, what the same reviewer termed the "skilful management . . . of the story" exemplifies Godwin's overall paradigm of fiction, for the first time realized in *Caleb Williams* in particular, involves the audience's coming to understand knowledge as the art of detecting and representing wholly particular events in their rhetorical and ultimately textual guise.[46] Just as Blake was to assert, in his "Public Address" of 1809, that "Ideas cannot be Given but in their minutely Appropriate Words" (*CPP*, 576), Godwin and his protagonist's intense advocacy of gothic romance over traditional historiography aims at elucidating a historically specific ideological constellation. Rather than inhering in generalizations, objectivity, and distance, such knowledge is a coefficient of political and psychological interestedness—something to be attained not by impartiality but by a narrative that crystallizes a monstrous suspicion concerning the placid surface of "things as they are." Another early reviewer's observation that "few readers will have sufficient coolness to lay down the book before they have it" (later echoed by Hazlitt's remark to the same effect in his 1825 essay on Godwin) confirms Godwin's success in shaping the book's affective hold on the reader.[47]

In remarking that the novel's "powerful interest" for its prospective audience "could best be effected by a secret murder" (*GCW*, 349), Godwin effectively concedes that Falkland's alleged crime does not so much constitute a moral or empirical fact as serve a formal-epistemological function. Murder amounts to a heuristic premise designed to throw into relief the formal-interpretive complexities—at the levels both of *récit* and of the novel genre itself—bound to vitiate any project that aims to expose, discredit, and ultimately vanquish the ancien régime through the exposure of its alleged criminality. If, "through Caleb as reader, Godwin inscribes a model of reading as the unearthing of truth and *the correction of past misrepresentations*" (Rajan 1990, 185), *Caleb Williams* also shows that project of a thoroughgoing and uncompromising critique of ideology to be premised on the epistemological fantasy of an utterly transparent mode of representation.[48] Inasmuch as Caleb fancies himself to have succeeded on that count, his epistemological triumph coincides with an equally absolute loss of his own inwardness and "character." Intimations of the novel's formally self-consuming nature emerge early on, as Caleb legitimates his surveillance of Falkland with the same hypothesis (Falkland's murderous past) also advanced by the novel's author. In both cases, the motive force driving the formulation and attempted verification of that hypothesis is not its intrinsic truth but rather its capacity for securing and sustaining audience "interest." Inasmuch as both novelist and protagonist fashion the hypothesis of Falkland's crime so as to secure "a powerful hold on the reader," the moral questions posed by the novel's thematic developments are only means to an end. Neither author nor protagonist (especially not the latter) is able to grasp the motive force that fuels and shapes a narrative whose preoccupation with its probability and "entire unity of plot" (*GCW,* 350) often threatens to displace the social values and moral conflicts thrown into relief by its actual empirical events.

Both as regards their narrative technique and affective constitution, the author and his protagonist and antagonist work in startlingly symbiotic fashion, with each alternately occupying the position of pursuer and pursued, plaintiff and defendant. If, as Tilottama Rajan observes, "Falkland and Caleb are not simply antagonists but also doubles," readers are put in a position to "apply to [Caleb's] text whatever methods of reading he applies to Falkland's representation of himself." Reading thus evolves into a "correction of past misrepresentations" (Rajan 1990, 184) or, more accurately, into the production of causes that have been preceded by their (symptomatic) effects. Each agency appears consumed with seizing control over a narrative first set into motion by the protagonist's acknowledged "curiosity"—itself simply a colloquial name for the paranoid affect that presupposes a narrative controlled (and shrewdly obfuscated) by some other agency to be already in progress. As was to prove the case in the 1794 treason trials, the narrative voice of *Caleb Williams* locates agency by definition in the other, indeed considers agency synonymous with otherness. Hence, in Caleb's account, Falkland's malevolent and dissembling ingenuity and energy initially makes only the most ephemeral appearance ("it was but a passing thought" [*GCW,* 112]) in the mind of his alert, though professedly *passive,* intellectual respondent, Caleb himself. Yet within the space of a few sentences, in an instance of aristocratic caprice here indulged by the servant, Caleb remarks that "the idea having once occurred to my mind, it was fixed there for ever" (*GCW,* 112). Confessedly enthralled with his optional "employment" as a "spy"—for which the hypothesis of Falkland's murderous past and his subsequent conspiracy to hide that past is simply a self-privileging justification—Caleb renders his own narrative voice, as well as all the alleged "discoveries" that it relays to its audience, permanently unreliable:

> The instant I had chose this employment for myself, I found a strange sort of pleasure in it. To do what is forbidden always has its charms, because we have an indistinct apprehension of something arbitrary and tyrannical in the prohibition. To be a spy upon Mr. Falkland! That there was danger in the employment served to give an alluring pungency to the choice. I remembered the stern reprimand I had received, and his terrible looks; and the recollection gave a kind of tingling sensation not altogether unallied to enjoyment. The further I advanced,

> the more the sensation was irresistible. I seemed perpetually upon the brink of being countermined, and perpetually roused to guard my designs. The more impenetrable Mr. Falkland was determined to be, the more uncontrollable was my curiosity. (*GCW,* 112–13)

Curiosity is formal epistemology's dignified nom de plume for what in a more quotidian setting would likely be termed "passive-aggressive" behavior, and "Caleb's sympathy is no neutral or innocent" state but "an irrational and exploitative byproduct of political power" (Bender, 268). Once again, Caleb's own locution paves the way for such critical insight, such as when he acknowledges how curiosity was "the spring of action which, perhaps more than any other, characterised the whole train of my life. It was this that gave me my mechanical turn; I was desirous of tracing the variety of effects which might be produced from given causes" (*GCW,* 6). From the start of the novel's action all the way through the closing scenes of trial and fatal imprisonment (original ending) or courtroom vindication (revised ending) that initiates the action of telling itself, the projected critique of "things as they are" is expressly entwined with a formal-epistemological inquiry into the "mechanical turn" of mind itself.

Exactly this structural bifurcation of the novel between the official value and hidden motive that inform the act of telling—between the narrative's programmatic commitment to political and social critique and its inadvertent betrayal of deeper-seated motives of its own narrative production—circumscribes the modernity of Godwin's fiction and sets it apart from other, more transparently didactic political novels of the same period, such as those of Robert Bage and Thomas Holcroft. The same split may also be recast as that between the novel's "objective"-criminal and its "subjective"-erotic dimension. For Caleb's "insatiable curiosity" regarding Falkland is not legitimated by the outcome of his (purported) discoveries concerning the past but, on the contrary, aims to bring about that past as a post hoc ergo propter hoc rationale for the affective enigma of that very "curiosity." The professed object of inquiry, Falkland's potential guilt, is merely the hypothesis crafted in order to legitimate a curiosity whose unconfessed, unspeakable, "sublime" motives are located in the unconscious of the protagonist—itself the ultimate object of inquiry in this Jacobin gothic romance. For at no point is it being suggested that Caleb wishes to bring Falkland "to justice" or moral accountability for his putative crime. Instead, he is consumed with obtaining Falkland's approval of his, Caleb's, peremptorily suspicious narrative, and hence of the very curiosity that constitutes the narrative's ineluctable affective origin. In partial acknowledgment of his own ineffable motivation, Caleb observes how, just as he imagines having obtained proof of Falkland's guilt, "my animal system had undergone a total revolution. My blood boiled within me. I was conscious to a kind of rapture for which I could not account. I was solemn, yet full of rapid emotion, burning with indignation and energy. In the very tempest and hurricane of the passions, I seemed to enjoy the most soul-ravishing calm" (*GCW,* 135). Yet this uncompromising elucidation of the narrator-protagonist's inner life—itself forever beyond his timely reflexive reach—also reveals the deeper entanglements of Godwin's paradigm of fiction as the representation of a wholly unique and hence ungeneralizable situation. For it now appears that the chimerical nature of political and social reality ("things as they are") mirrors an equally deceptive and opaque "calm" within the mind of a given individual's mind (Caleb's no less than Falkland's). Far from being a positive state or achievement, however, such calm recalls Godwin's troubled concession, in *Political Justice,* that "the mind is always full" and hence constitutively barred from knowing the causes (motives) that shape and fuel its conscious representations, especially those of itself. In so indexing an epistemological void, Caleb's "calm" also delineates, as it were *ex negativo,* a genealogy of irrationalism that extends from the late Enlightenment all the way to Freud's 1915 metapsychological writings on the unconscious.

The same epistemological predicament also vitiates the rational authority of the protagonist's Jacobin sympathies, as evidenced by numerous slips, irrational glitches, and oversights whose opaque causality steadily undermines Caleb's avowedly rational pursuit of truth. Not incidentally, the novel's central quest is being characterized as "a kind of fatal impulse that seemed destined to hurry me to my destruction" (*GCW,* 127). Caleb's pivotal transgression, his prying open the content of Falkland's "chest" arises out of "some mysterious fatality" (*GCW,* 135) that directs his steps toward his employer's private apartment during a house fire. Likewise, his attempt at conscious reflection ("to take a survey of the various circumstances of my condition" [*GCW,* 152]) while on an errand for Falkland leads him to the residence of Falkland's brother, a mishap that, as Caleb readily grasps, is bound to intensify his master's suspicions. In a particularly fateful instance, Caleb feels "unaccountably impelled" to deposit some of his personal belongings in a seventeenth-century "priest-hole" prior to fleeing the Falkland estate. With its overt reference to the mid-seventeenth-century persecution of Catholics in England, the closeted space "of the most secret nature not uncommon in houses so old as that of Mr. Falkland" (*GCW,* 161) aptly mirrors the irremediable opacity of Caleb's own consciousness, the agency that appears "unaccountably impelled" to hasten the undoing of his own social persona. Finally, in an effort at reconstituting that persona in the guise of the anonymous London writer, Caleb recalls how, "by a fatality, for which I did not exactly know how to account, my thoughts frequently led me to the histories of celebrated robbers" (*GCW,* 268). As these repeated irruptions of contingent and opaque motives into a narrative otherwise consumed with its own causal and rational functioning make clear, to explain Caleb's curiosity merely through the vicarious (and ultimately unverifiable) circumstantial evidence that it yields is to miss an important part of the story. For his belated acknowledgment of having repeatedly acted under the sway of ineffable passions and uncontrollable impulses attests to the persistent operation of a deeper, fundamentally ineluctable power within his own mind. Indeed, one is tempted to read Caleb's histrionic references to Falkland's predatory yet ever-elusive power of surveillance as figural acknowledgment of the conspiracy of his, Caleb's, unconscious against his professed quest for "truth."

Moreover, Godwin's authorial decision to compose his narrative strictly in reverse and "in a high state of excitement" not only mirrors the formal and affective (he is "thrilled to my very vitals" [*GCW,* 9]) process of Caleb's first-person narrative in the novel itself; it also frames the entire project of Jacobin ideological critique as intrinsically equivocal and ambivalent with regard both to its epistemological veracity and its moral-political valuation. Caleb's overwrought attachment to his narrative project of self-vindication casts him in the same light of female and irrational behavior that Jacobins of the 1790s typically employed to characterize the ancien régime's system of manners and conventions. From the "curiosity" so programmatically introduced in the novel's opening pages to the "rapidity, perturbation, and vehemence" (*GCW,* 342) of Caleb's failed attempt at narrative self-exculpation during the novel's original ending, "the speaker's effeminization appears a formal precondition for the production of narrative. Without that nervous body, there would be no narrative launched into the world, not even to warn readers against the social conditions that brought it into being" (Logan, 54–55). The question of the first-person narrator's state of mind obviously impinges on the debate concerning the novel's two endings. As is well known, the original ending (set aside by

Godwin only days before the book was to go into print) has Caleb remanded to prison, where he proceeds to write the remaining portions of what is, in sum, the novel itself. In an apotheosis of the novel's structural principle of paranoid suspicion, Caleb's closing paragraphs feature manic conjectures as to his being poisoned and his manuscript about to be purloined by the implacable Falkland. By contrast, the published ending features Falkland's memorable courtroom confession ("'Williams,' said he, 'you have conquered'" [*GCW*, 335]), thereby for the first time introducing an instance of public corroboration for the novel's central hypothesis concerning Falkland's crime.

In the original version, then, nothing ever offers extrinsic and objective confirmation for Caleb's key hypothesis regarding Falkland's guilty past; hence, too, it is not entirely accurate to dismiss that ending's closing "figure of imprisonment [as] simply the rhetorical reverse of a simplistic and utopian desire for liberation" (Rajan 1990, 185). In fact, Caleb's closing reflections on the potential reception of his story admit both its epistemological volatility and its consequent undecidability as a text: "Perhaps I am beguiling myself during all this time, merely for want of strength to put myself in the place of an unprepossessed auditor, and to conceive how the story will impress every one that hears it. My innocence will then die with me! The narrative I have taken pains to digest will then only perpetuate my shame and spread more widely the persuasion of my nefarious guilt" (*GCW*, 345). Consumed by the formal mystery of causation, Caleb's highest good lies in the internal consistency of his narrative. Yet such an attempt at achieving absolute causal control over his thematic materials and their narrative representation now points back at the obsessive, deeply irrational constitution of a subject so motivated. Hence a number of irrational decisions and acts (already discussed above) are being interpolated throughout Caleb's story, thus allowing him at once to maintain a firm retrospective hold on the story's successive developments *as narrator* while clearing him *as protagonist* of all involvement in the narrative's inexorable development and catastrophic outcome. The story's representation of events successively unfolding in the course of forward-moving empirical time is governed by the agency of the unconscious and probability—themselves the Enlightenment's cautious update on the mythic notion of fate. Indeed, a central feature of late-Enlightenment radicalism involves its schizoid perception of the ancien régime as simultaneously mystified and hyperlucid, a state of mind at once meandering, indolent, and capricious, *as well as* methodical, resourceful, and malevolent. In first sketching how his own career appears utterly entwined with the history of the aristocratic Falkland, Caleb sees all development shaped by an agency whose perspicacity, relentlessness, and inscrutability was not to be met with again until Freud introduced his 1915 audience to the unconscious.[49] In his own words, Caleb meets with "the uninterrupted persecution of a malignant destiny, a series of adventures that seemed to take their rise in various accidents, but pointing to one termination" (*GCW*, 18).[50] As in Michael Dummett's image of balls on a billiard table moving in reverse, Caleb's narrative concerns itself with elucidating only those causes that have been (allegedly) preceded by their effects. That is, while ostensibly concerned with tracing the (allegedly) antecedent cause of Falkland's crime from its (once again alleged) present effects—Falkland's symptoms—Caleb's provocative domestic conduct and overbearing interpretive habits at the beginning of volume 2 are effectively meant to *bring about* that cause.

As Caleb himself admits, "I was . . . watchful, inquisitive, suspicious, full of a thousand *conjectures* as to the meaning of the most indifferent actions. Mr. Falkland, who was most painfully alive to everything that related to his honour, saw these variations and betrayed his consciousness of them now in one manner and now in another, *frequently before I was myself aware, sometimes almost before they existed*" (*GCW*, 128; emphasis added). Already early in the novel, Caleb preemptively guards against any doubts readers might entertain concerning his reliability as a narrator, as well as any potential demands for independent corroboration of his claims. Adverting to Falkland's alleged fits of rage and manic depression, Caleb cautions his readers that "it must not be supposed that the whole of what I am describing was visible to the persons about him; nor, indeed, was I acquainted with it in the extent here stated but after a considerable time and in gradual succession" (*GCW*, 9). The interjection suggestively links its refusal to furnish external proof for its allegations with a renewed pledge to the principle of retroactive narration. Causes attain their explanatory authority only because and inasmuch as they are susceptible of integration into a narrative that will offer a coherent accounting for their supposed effects, which in the temporal order of cognition always come first.

In what bears a striking resemblance to the state prosecution's of the London Corresponding Society later that same year, Godwin's protagonist does not desire the revolutionary correction of aristocratic depravity but, on the contrary, seeks confirmation of a "secret wound" (*GCW*, 114) in order to usurp the power needed to shape an alternative political future. If "there is something tyrannical in the prohibition" (e.g., against prying open Falkland's "chest"), the elixir (or aphrodisiac) of such tyranny aptly mirrors Caleb's own conduct, whose rational objective (to verify Falkland's hypothetical past crime) remains forever subordinate to the tyranny of paranoid desire, namely, to bring about Falkland's criminal past. Thus, like his master, Caleb too "pays obedience to the principle which at present governed me with absolute dominion" (*GCW*, 121). His "new state of [my] mind" anticipates exactly the central conundrum ("the mind is always full") that the second edition of Godwin's *Political Justice* was to unearth within the mechanism of the human mind a year later. For "when one idea has got possession of the soul, it is scarcely possible to keep it from finding its way to the lips." Consequently, Caleb remarks, "I had only a confused apprehension of what I was doing" (*GCW*, 118). The result is a charismatic narrative, at once irrefutable but, as it appears, no longer representative of anything beyond its own immediate thematic and ideological confines. In the final court scene of the novel's original version, Caleb himself notes that "I depended for my success upon the consistency and probability of my narrative." In that ending, confirmation of the Falkland's murderous past once more eludes the public eye, whereas Caleb is vexed to observe how Falkland's guilty "shuddering . . . was partly counteracted by the firmness of his mind, and partly by the general relaxation of his frame incapable either to receive or convey strong impressions" (*GCW*, 340–41). Evidently oblivious to such physiological symptoms (if they exist at all), the judge listening to Caleb's narrative—which effectively comprises the totality of the novel itself—acknowledges the story to have been "told with great artifice and consistency" (*GCW*, 341), thereby hinting at the extent to which the story's formal coherence has been secured through a system of strictly internal justifications and pieces of evidence.

Yet this formal-epistemological shift to tracing causes from effects said to have preceded them comes at the expense of his narrative's demonstrability, probability, and representative character. The dilemma recalls Kant's transcendental method, which, in a capricious reclassification of empirical matter as *factum probandum* and no longer *factum probans,* had suddenly redefined the very data of "experience" (*Erfahrung*), not as the cause of knowledge, but as symptomatic "effects" of an as yet unspecified, perhaps forever inscrutable, transcendental "schematism" governing a priori the work of all synthesis (i.e., representation). Kant had scrutinized the operational coherence of representation per se—taken as effect or symptom—so as to isolate the so-called transcendental and inherently prerational "conditions of possibility" of all social knowledge. Thus the presumptive "effect" of experience, *which reaches the philosopher only in the guise of interpretable representations,* constitutes the only inroad toward discovering its underlying, putatively "transcendental" causes. Transcendentalism's first item of business must therefore be to instruct its readers in learning to fathom the inherent *unreality* of what until now they had accepted as experience, to grasp its inherently unreliable, symptomatic quality. All empirical matter awaits to be redeemed from its deceptive quotidian, not to say banal, appearance and from its speciously self-evident manifestation *in* and *as* the present ("things as they are").

In the original version of *Caleb Williams,* the narrative that for some 300 pages had sought to unveil a monstrous past smoothed over by an infuriatingly tranquil present terminates in a trial scene in which Caleb's "inflamed mind" (*GCW,* 342) struggles to convince judge and audience of his story. Indeed, Caleb's *j'accuse* can be imagined to comprise the totality of everything the reader has read thus far. The narrative doubles back on itself as it creates the final conflict that necessitates and shapes its well-known opening with a desperate first-person plea ("My life has for several years been a theatre of calamity" [*GCW,* 5]) delivered with "incredible eagerness" (*GCW,* 342). Given the nature of Caleb's story—in which, as in Kant's *Critique,* "there is no empirical confirmation of [the central] hypothesis . . . since what counts as experience, and also as confirmation, is created by our acceptance of that hypothesis" (Rosen, 25)—the misgivings expressed by the judge presiding at the novel's concluding trial scene may well echo those already experienced by readers at the novel's beginning. For Caleb imposes on his audience with preemptive urgency from the start, arguing that "my story will, at least, appear to have that consistency which is seldom attendant but upon truth" (*GCW,* 5). In fact, the equivocal "seldom" concedes that the appeal of Caleb's ensuing psychohistorical narrative, contrary to the generalizations and abstractions of Scottish historiographers, remains necessarily and terminally confined to the realm of probability.[51] Moreover, given that everything mentioned in the narrative serves the dual purposes of information and self-legitimation, Caleb may well have taken to heart the distinction between truth and probability that Falkland's brother, Forester, had explicitly drawn for him during an earlier instance of narrative distress: "Reserve what you have to say to the proper time. Make the best story you can for yourself—true if truth, as I hope, will serve your purpose; but, if not, the most plausible and ingenious you can invent" (*GCW,* 169). Provided one retains the novel's original ending, Caleb's narrative remains categorically indemonstrable on any other grounds than those furnished and approved by his own narrative industry. In ways that prove startlingly prescient of the treason trials of Thomas Hardy, John Horne Tooke, John Thelwall, and others later that year, all evidence is being fitted to corroborate the intent, as well as to account for and hence discredit the innocent *appearance*, of Jacobin defendants whose "normal" conduct the law peremptorily views as a mere effort to dissemble their criminal intentions. Part of the formal and ideological lucidity of Godwin's novel lies in the fact that the Jacobin agitator and the aristocratic murderer stand in perfectly symmetrical and hence equivocal relation to one another. The result is a dynamic of Blakean contraries, in which Jacobins and aristocrats labor under structurally cognate paranoid fantasies of which they seek to disburden themselves through isomorphous conspiratorial and self-privileging accounts of retroactive causation.

The preceding attempt at isolating the formal and psychological characteristics of narratives concerned with unearthing social, political, and epistemological knowledge leads to a number of conclusions. First, it appears that paranoia is not simply a new type of interpretive conundrum produced *by* the narrative in question, as it were in contingent and eccentric fashion. Rather, it is a historically specific mood of social cognition that discloses itself to us in the specific formal organization and coherence of writing. In order to relate to any of the competing narratives during the 1790s, readers must jointly subscribe to the formal hypothesis of "reality as a 'text' or system of misrepresentation, but also of ideology as a form of textual desire" (Rajan 1990, 167). To make that reticent textual system work, to hold it accountable and mine it for all the knowledge it is capable of disclosing, the reading process shifts from one of distraction to one of detection. Constrained to approach all textual matter in an axiomatically suspicious and probabilistic manner, readers must commit themselves a priori to a conspiratorial paradigm of the real. In the age of suspended, even reversed, causal explanation, all cognition demands an interpretive and counterintuitive positioning of "things as they are" within a new narrative script. The textual autonomy of Jacobean narrative is thus fundamentally opposed to the specious ordinariness and stability of empirical perception whose significance has been preemptively dulled by its complicity with Augustan notions of "tradition," "custom," "manners," and "common sense." By objectifying itself in idiosyncratic, causally indeterminate, and hence ungeneralizable narratives (e.g., the ballad, the novel, and the sociological, political, or epistemological treatise), paranoia offers a first instance of how a distinctive historical period can be secured by observing a distinctive mode of formal-aesthetic production. Paradoxically, that very mode aims to forestall the very consciousness to which it vicariously gives rise. For in the age of revolutionary terror and government repression (1789–98), knowledge is achieved dialectically, namely, by suspecting, investigating, and potentially indicting surface appearances and representations as mere clothing draped over the irrational. Such agitation on behalf of particulars, as proposed above all by Kant, Godwin, and Blake, cannot, however, consider itself exempt from the eccentricity, irrationality, and conspiratorial thrust that it aims to expose within the official symbolic representations of the real. Rather, the investigative principle itself appears fueled by irrational motives that will remain inscrutable and ungeneralizable. Thus, beginning with the 1790s, literature and the aesthetic emerge as the sole media for realizing an epistemological advance for which there can never be any systematic and rational justification outside of the eccentric, situationally specific terms and characters that it provides. It is in the 1790s pervasive affiliation of paranoia and narrative, too, that we find Novalis's key insight confirmed, according to which all "emotion" acquires distinctness only if formalized and given *durée* in an aesthetic form whose own interpretive volatility, complexity, and open-endedness "magically" conform to those of the feeling in question.

CHAPTER THREE

Paranoia Historicized

The Dialectics of Treason and Political Representation in 1790s London

> The connexion of intention and the circumstances is plainly of such a nature, as more to depend on the sagacity of the observer, than on the excellence of any rule. The pains taken by the civilians on that subject have not been very fruitful; and the English law writers have, perhaps, as wisely, in a manner abandoned the pursuit. In truth, it seems a wild *attempt to* lay down any rule for the proof of intention by circumstantial evidence; all the acts of the party; all things that explain or throw light on these acts; all the acts of others relative to the affair, that come to his knowledge, and may influence him; his friendships and enmities, his promises, his threats, the truth of his discourses, the falsehood of his apologies, pretences, and explanations; his looks, his speech; his silence where he was called to speak; every thing which tends to establish the connexion between all these particulars;—every circumstance, precedent, concomitant and subsequent, become parts of circumstantial evidence.
>
> — EDMUND BURKE, *Report from the Committee of the House of Commons,* 30 APRIL 1794

This chapter seeks to establish communications among three structurally related issues. The first, strictly historical in kind, involves the trial of the shoemaker and political activist Thomas Hardy for high treason in 1794 and focuses specifically on how the efforts throughout that trial to legally determine the allegiance between individual and government came to expose a significant theoretical crisis within the larger paradigm of the law. Considerations of the ideological pragmatics served by the formal composition of judicial argument take us to the next, closely related issue, namely, the role of transferential and self-privileging narratives as a model of historical comprehension during the early romantic period. Both the formal and theoretical significance of the notably paranoid model of narrative here at issue—as well as the epistemological tensions inherent in it—would eventually pose a theoretical and disciplinary problem in Freud, specifically in his reading of Schreber's *Memoirs of My Nervous Illness.* In his efforts to conceptualize the general mechanism of paranoia, Freud encountered epistemic convolutions remarkably similar to those that produced the reversal of fortune in favor of the defendants during the 1794 treason trials. There the defense was able to expose the prosecution's self-confirming, "constructive," and distinctly narrative modes of inferential legal argumentation. Notwithstanding its local-historical context, Thomas Erskine's defense of Hardy explores whether the law can ever verify the hypothesis of pervasive conspiracy without arbitrarily converting the myriad particulars that make up daily reality into symptoms and, ultimately, into evidence. What for Erskine was especially a legal conundrum has a strong bearing on the problem of "disciplinarity" in the humanities and social sciences today, specifically the problem of a lingering, structural and inextricable complicity between *any* method of interpretation and its proposed "objects" of analysis. To what extent do the currently dominant models of historicist scholarship, materialist analysis, and rhetorical reading open up more authentic and historically durable vistas on the antagonistic sociopolitical and aesthetic scene of romanticism? Or, alternatively, are the disciplinary, methodological, and theoretical rigor and reflexivity that characterize such approaches but further, if distant echoes of romanticism's ideological dispensation? Do our scholarly and critical engagements of romanticism constitute an authentic "overcoming" or simply another repetition of romanticism? Is our knowledge of romanticism objective and abiding or does it amount to a pragmatic and transferential representation of that "past"?

From another perspective, these questions appear to converge with the particular causal accounts and ambitiously plotted narratives by means of which historical subjects—ourselves no less than individuals in England during the 1790s—represent their experiences of a contingent and agonistic present. As we shall find, it is in their ambitious efforts at coping with comprehensive ideological transformations of which they are only ever partially *conscious* that specific interpretive communities generate the rhetorical symptoms that now, belatedly, solicit our aesthetic and ideological "interest." Thus it is the formal and rhetorical organization of narratives, rather than their professed content, that emerges as the symptomatic material on which any analytic relationship to romanticism will ultimately pivot. The formal-rhetorical structure of these accounts *is* their historical content, which is to say, it is the *mode of appearance* of the consciousnesses produced by historical change. The logical and formal tensions that characterize the legal narratives and counternarratives of the prosecutors and the defense during the context of the 1794 treason trials thus throw into relief the affective and cognitive imbalance of subjects produced *by* and participating *in* their precarious historical moment. What renders their rhetoric at once cogent *and* symptomatic is the significantly unconscious "knowledge" of their historically contingent and tenuous disposition. The subjects of this legal and political drama are all caught up in a moment of impending recognition, to which they respond by revising existing or generating new rhetorical strategies capable of diffusing the ultimately *un*bearable knowledge of their historicity.

An analysis of the astonishingly imaginative accounts produced by the "disciplines" of the law and psychoanalysis is complicated by the fact that we ourselves are just as inextricably caught in a web of transformations as the historical communities that an earnest and urgent historicism aims to reconstruct. Indeed, as Clifford Siskin has suggested, we seem just as bewildered by what our own technologies of information are doing to us as were the communities of the eighteenth century as they adjusted to the proliferation and rapidly changing authority of writing.[1] For we, too, react to these transformations by mobilizing, revising, and fine- tuning concepts such as experience, perception, explanation, generalization, and justification. In so doing, our hyperreflexive methods of historical investigation—still dedicated to the project of defining and administrating a distinctive and "functional" body of social and cultural knowledge—ultimately continue to operate as further displaced effects of the ultimate impossibility of such knowledge. The early phase of romantic culture in England focuses this epistemological dilemma in the peculiar rhetorical form of anxiously prophetic and conspiratorial accounts. This tendency is especially apparent in late-eighteenth-century legal reasoning on treasonous conspiracy and in early-twentieth-century psychoanalytic reflections on paranoia. Though separated by a full century and by topic, these two discourses converge in their representation of historical change, namely, by objectifying such change in the bilateral temporality of narratives at once suspicious and prophetic. In many ways, then, rhetoric aims to "disburden" (Arnold Gehlen's term) people from having to recognize their ideals of historical stability and a homogeneous relation between self and culture as imperiled or outright illusory. To that end, the politicized subjects of the 1790s conceive their specific social knowledge in prosecutorial form (Freud was to call it "projection"), namely, by ascribing the failure of their ideal to some other subject's or community's complex and malignant intentions and doings. As we shall see, such narrative detours not only produce and effectively control that other but, in a genuinely Hegelian mode, also enable the agents of representation to produce their historical "truth" without consciously having to "mean" it.

Following his close reading of the strange case presented by the onetime superior court justice Daniel Paul Schreber with a characterization of the mechanism of paranoia, Freud made two general observations potentially very disruptive to his overall conception of psychoanalysis as a discipline. First, he conceded that "the psychoanalytic investigation of paranoia would be altogether impossible if the patients themselves did not possess the peculiarity of betraying (in distorted form, it is true) precisely those things which other neurotics keep hidden as a secret" (*FCH,* 104). Oddly enough, the functional mechanism characterizing paranoia appears preemptive of the work of analysis; indeed, it seems all but structurally cognate with the investigative rigors of psychoanalysis. Sensing that their mode of production of psychological knowledge all too closely resembled the procedures of psychoanalysis, Freud declared cases of paranoia all but impossible to treat. Surely no one knew better than Freud how frequently and with what intensity psychoanalysis had been branded a pseudo-science, premised on always unverifiable hypotheses about hidden connections and inscrutable machinations, that conspired against the established science of psychiatry. It was supposedly a science devoid of any moral core, precariously cosmopolitan, dissociated in its sensibility, and in the final analysis—a charge that was to dog Freud throughout much of his life and career—a Jewish science. Seen in this light, Freud's decision to delve into the subject of paranoia in anticipation of his metapsychological writings seems especially risky. For to attempt a theoretical account of paranoia almost inevitably risks a precarious reversal whereby the condition of paranoia, rather than functioning as the "object" of psychoanalysis, might well emerge as the unacknowledged source of that science itself.[2] After all, his readers might well consider the "object" or "issues" of psychoanalysis to be merely the effects of an elaborate explanatory practice that, in classically paranoid fashion, continually projects these "objects" (i.e., neuroses) onto its social environment as the presumptive cause of its analytic industry. The question thus arises of whether psychoanalysis constitutes the legitimate science of the *symptom,* or whether it too belongs to the domain of the symptom, a possibility it deflects by framing the symptom in objective, disciplinary form—that is, as so many "case histories."

Opening his general discussion of the subject, Freud noted that "the distinctive character of paranoia (or of *dementia paranoides)* must be sought . . . in the particular form assumed by the symptoms [*die besondere Erscheinungsform der Symptome*]." Indeed, inasmuch as "the mechanism of *symptom-formation* in paranoia requires that internal perceptions, or feelings, shall be replaced [*ersetzt*] by external perceptions" (*FSA,* 7: 183, 186 / *FCH,* 161, 166), the symptom's mode of appearance is virtually identical with the paranoid condition itself. Freud calls it "projection." A close relative of the more general psychic function of displacement, "projection" constitutes "the most striking characteristic of symptom-formation in paranoia." In it "an internal perception is suppressed [*unterdrückt*], and, instead [*zum Ersatz*], its content, after undergoing a certain degree of distortion, enters consciousness in the form of an external perception" (*FSA,* 7: 189 / *FCH,* 169). As Freud argued time and again about all cognates of displacement, their representational structure is organized by the overriding functional aim of "staving off *consciousness,*" which also suggests that the "symptom" signifies only retroactively, compelling the inferential reorganization of a past in response to an insistent, menacing perception of the impending future.[3] As Naomi Schor has argued, the Freudian concept of "displacement" (*Verdrängung*) assumes a point of contact between the consciousness forestalled by the operation of displacement and the details furnishing the material conditions for that operation in the first place. Freud's term for this contiguous element linking the psychic operation and its representational focus is *Anlehnung.* In a more general theoretical sense, that word may be translated as "contiguity," an essentially rhetorical device ensuring the mediation-by-resemblance of the (traumatic) consciousness forestalled *by* "displacement" with the consciousness resulting *from* that very operation of "displacement." *Anlehnung,* in other words, enables us to forget the difference between the consciousness that should have been and the consciousness that is. It suspends the subject between the virtual and not-yet-recognized import of a past preemptively deferred/displaced into the future (whence it will return as a "symptom") and the *specious* integrity of the consciously experienced present that is predicated on that exclusion.

Still, to construe the relationship between the "feeling" displaced and the external, distorted perception projected in its stead as one of *Anlehnung* is to ignore the substitutive meaning of *Ersatz* and *ersetzen,* the very words chosen by Freud to describe the dynamics of "projection" in cases of paranoia. To be sure, Freud conceives of the paranoiac's projections, his or her ideas and representations, as *metonymic* traces or marks that are contiguous with the repressed *archē* of the unconscious. Yet his choice of the word *Ersatz* actually suggests that "projection" actually involves a fundamentally independent signifier and signifying frame (discourse).[4] Though he clearly struggles to control the dynamics between feeling and displacement in metonymic terms, Freud can offer no theoretical proof of why the representational surface of displacement ought to be authentically related to the psychic "content" allegedly displaced. Moreover, it is only on the grounds of that unproven assumption that Freud can invest such psychic "content" with a priori authenticity. Indeed, the matter has rather unsettling implications for Freud's larger endeavor. For the disciplinary and interpretive coherence of the "science" of psychoanalysis is predicated on the assumption of an essential contiguity between the welter of affective charges (his "System Unconscious") and the surface representations that comprise conscious existence. In other words, Freud asserts his disciplinary jurisdiction over the representational excess of the symptom (i.e., the Freudian detail) on the assumption that the relation between "feeling" and "displacement" is metonymic rather than metaphoric. The relation is not to be taken as one between two heterogeneous orders—the silence of affect and the clamor of representation. Rather, Freud has in mind an indissoluble bond between a legitimate (though displaced) authoritative signifier and a subsidiary counterfeit signifier that has temporarily usurped the timeless office of the unconscious. Freud posits, as it were a priori, a relation of "contiguity" (*Anlehnung*) between the truth of the unconscious and metonymic representations such as allegedly have prevented that truth from operating by emulating its appearance. In so doing, psychoanalysis seeks to shelter its integrity as a discipline and its institutionalized mode of cognition from the contingencies of reading. An alternative vision would conceive of the symptom as an independent, "free-floating" detail—a sign of contingent and open interpretive import rather than an integral component within a closed economy of knowledge. Yet to do so would be to put at risk the disciplinary and scientific authority of psychoanalysis altogether and to challenge its presumptive theoretical and descriptive authority over psychic phenomena.

Freud's palpable investment in theoretical closure and in a systematic paradigm of disciplinary practice warrants further reflection. For to strip-mine contingent empirical phenomena with the stated objective of excavating determinate affective meanings from them suggests that the subjects of psychoanalysis and that discipline itself pursue fundamentally the same objective.

In its programmatic self-presentation as a scientific "discipline"—with that term's attendant connotation of *askesis*—psychoanalysis ultimately amounts simply to a different style of response to (and, hence, symptom of) an overwhelmingly complex social reality. Like the distracting and allegedly inauthentic representations of its "case" subjects, that is, the voice of psychoanalysis also aims to dominate the convolutions and antagonisms of its historical situation through its elaborate interpretive procedures. In a significant and sensible qualification of Freud's model, Lacan would thus rethink psychoanalysis as an open-ended dynamic between patient and analyst who construct each other's subjectivities in a dialectical speech-process. Rather than granting one discipline authority over what is called "symptom," Lacan understands the symptom as a historical process, infinitely complex and susceptible of ever-new interpretations, that has yielded the identity and epistemic authority of the addressee whom it has framed beforehand.[5]

For Lacan, these qualifications of the Freudian enterprise are, in fact, intrinsic to its original text, if only in the form of sudden reversals or disclaimers. Thus it may not come as a surprise to see Freud, in his opening account of paranoia, suddenly abandon all further inquiry into the figural status of the displaced and the projected consciousness. Perhaps he noted that to probe any further into the unstable dynamic between psychological and rhetorical values might compromise his larger project of a metapsychological theory. In any event, he notes, projection "makes its appearance not only in paranoia but under other psychological conditions as well, and in fact has a regular share assigned to it in our attitude towards the external world. For when we refer the causes of certain sensations to the external world, instead of looking for them (as we do in the case of others) inside ourselves, this normal proceeding [*dieser normale Vorgang*] also deserves to be called projection" (*FSA*, 7: 189 / *FCH*, 169). Indeed, Freud is quick to draw attention to the ostensibly "normal" character of paranoid representations. For contrary to cases of neurosis, the subject of paranoia tends to betray rather than conceal, to elaborate highly coherent plots exhaustively rather than to be cryptic, erratic, and inchoate in its representations. Hence there may, in fact, be nothing distinctly pathogenic or structurally unique about the operation called "projection." Indeed, even the otherwise sacrosanct premise of psychoanalysis that all neuroses are ultimately sexual in their origins does not appear secure either. With the "sexual etiology by no means obvious . . . strikingly prominent features in the causation of paranoia, especially among males, are social humiliations and slights" (*FSA*, 7:

183 / *FCH*, 162). And so, resolving "to postpone the investigation" of projection and turning instead to "the mechanism of repression," Freud first unfolded the tripartite sequence of repression, subsequently amplified in his 1915 metapsychological essay on that concept. That sequence leads from "fixation" to "repression proper" and terminates in what he called "the most important phase . . . of miscarriage of repression, of irruption [*Durchbruch*], of the return of the repressed (*FSA*, 3: 190–91 / *FCH*, 170–71). As Freud eventually argues, the mechanism of paranoia is, in fact, nothing but this third phase, the "return" of the repressed, writ large and formally organized as a symptomatic representation. In other words, the paranoid subject's representations are not simply stories relegated to a subsidiary role by the affective truths they displace. Rather, their eloquence amounts to a self-authorizing substitute (*Ersatz*), a fully independent system of empirical perceptions, causal explanations, and ethical justifications.

Having, perhaps, offered thus far little more than standard psychoanalytic fare, this review of Freud's session with the troubled Dr. Schreber will now go into recess until I have shown sufficient cause for rehearing a case history that has already undergone plentiful critical review. I have yet to strengthen the connections between some structural problems endemic to psychoanalysis and my larger concern with tracing historical change through its aesthetic formalization as romantic interiority. More needs to be known about that seemingly timeless figure of legal interpretation known as high treason and set down in English law as the statute 25 Edward III of 1354, originally brought about by shrewd negotiations between the king and his *magnes.* Meanwhile, the eighteenth-century Blackstonian conception of the treason statute under which Hardy, Thelwall, Tooke, and others stood indicted in 1794 is distinguished by its circular and 'constructive' mode of (self-)authorization. Thus Blackstone would not define outright a "declarative" statute ostensibly concerned with defining "the highest civil crime" (Blackstone 1979 [1765–69], 4, chap. 6: 75). Instead, he treats the statute in accordance with his overall legal philosophy, namely, to explicate what "the common law is and ever hath been" (quoted in Barrell 1992, 122). As the belated transcription of a supposedly preexisting social consensus, the treason statute authorizes itself as a summary articulation of past legal practice, only to treat such a de facto interpretation as confirmed and accepted fact and extending into the indefinite future. Such an "epigenetic" mode of theoretical argumentation typically amounts to a "last instance, the sheer possibility of mundane origination, void of all substance" and hence to an "ideological operation" par excellence (Müller-Sievers 1998, 6).[6] Yet this inherently self-authorizing substitution of a fixed text for "what *we* [emphasis here added] call *natural* allegiance" (Foster, 183) also alerts us to the ex post facto logic and consequent material danger of "constructive" treason as the defendants in the 1794 trials experienced it. For how can the treason statute safeguard citizens against the "constructive" misconstrual of innocuous material acts and practices when, allegedly in response to a perception of imminent political revolt, the state chooses to convert *all* material acts into legal facts and *all* citizens into defendants?

Blackstone's benign objective is "to prevent the inconveniences which began to arise in England from this multitude of constructive treasons" (Blackstone 1979 [1765–69], 4, chap. 6: 76) and, to judge by his concluding elaboration of the four-step ritual of execution for those convicted of high treason, these "inconveniences" were rather considerable. Both from the perspective of the perpetrator and the law, then, treason constitutes a strictly imaginary act, namely, "to compass and imagine the death of our Lord the King, or of our Lady his Queen," provided that "there be upon sufficient proof (*provablement*) attainted of open deed by people of his condition."[7] A multitude of problems arises at once: if the crime is an imaginary act—Blackstone defines the crucial word "compass" as "signifying the purpose or design of the mind or will, and not, as in common speech, the carrying such design into effect" (ibid., 78)—much seems to depend, in Michael Foster's succinct formulation, on that elusive question of "what doth or doth not amount to an open deed" (Foster, 207).[8] Given what Thomas Erskine was to call the "complete anomaly" of a crime "wholly seated in unconsummated intention" being construed as high treason (*STT,* 896), thus leaving us merely with the presumptive evidence of its having been contemplated, how is one to tell apart material and legal facts, evidence and crime? In Foster's famous characterization of this epistemological dilemma, "the law therefore tendereth the safety of the King with an anxious concern, and, if I may use the expression, with a concern bordering *upon jealousy.* It considereth the wicked imaginations of the heart in the same degree of guilt as if carried into actual execution, from the moment *measures appear to have been taken to render them effectual* (Foster, 195). For the first time, in a moment of self-conscious rhetorical license ("if I may use the expression," Foster says), the law, taken as a discipline comprised of self-supporting formal propositions, discloses the seemingly paranoid nature of its commerce with the real.

For an empirical act is transfigured into "a legal fact" (*factum probans*) by the "jealous" concern of the law as expressed in the statute of high treason. Having transformed an axiomatic and peremptory suspicion into a disciplinary mode of knowledge, the law seems at liberty to impute criminal intent a priori to potentially any material act and, in so doing, to "construct" the very criminal intention relative to which the now "legal" fact will subsequently be adduced as evidence and confirmation.[9]

Unlike Sir John Scott—crown prosecutor during the 1794 trials and, as Lord Eldon, better known to romanticists as an exhibit in Shelley's gallery of state villains in "The Mask of Anarchy"—and Sir James Eyre, whose notoriously biased "Charge" to the grand jury we have yet to consider, Foster appears keenly aware of the self-consuming and "constructive" excess of this statute and thus struggles to draw a sharp line between the treasonous intent with which the defendant is charged and any "constructive" reading of the statute whereby a material act *is said to constitute* the very crime for which, later on, that same act will be adduced as evidence. To that end, Foster specifies a number of restrictions regarding what may or may not, in and of itself, be taken as sufficient evidence of "compassing and imagining" the death of the king. With scrupulous legal reasoning, he insists that insofar as "overt acts [are] the means made use of to effectuate the purposes of the heart" (Foster, 194, 203), they must bear not merely a symptomatic but indeed an instrumental relation to the crime itself. Otherwise, the law effectively creates the crime, an act of disciplinary transference commonly referred to as "constructive treason" and repeatedly criticized by Foster as an abuse of the rules of evidence. "Under no circumstances," he insists, "can a man be *argued* into the penalties of the acts by inferences and conclusions drawn from what he affirms" (201–2).[10] That is, to merely have an individual affirm that he or she did X, Y, and Z (e.g., wrote a pamphlet on behalf of a national convention, deriding the king, and also purchased a pike) does not entitle the courts to infer the existence a priori of some treasonous intent. The post hoc ergo propter hoc illogic (and the curious projection of criminal intent from the prosecutor onto the defendant) that characterize such argumentation as inherently paranoid are still kept in check in Foster's 1762 *Discourse,* though not for much longer.

Indeed, if "loose words, *not relative to any act or design, are* not overt acts of treason" (Foster, 200), Foster already reduces the state's burden of proof when suggesting that they may be so "with publication" (198). His rationale for imputing greater criminality to print than to speech is grounded in the assumption that the evidentiary potential of discrete acts hinges on their proximity to one another. Such proximity is perhaps most in evidence where acts of mind—intentions—present themselves in metonymic form: that is, as a narrative presented in print form. The viability of the treason statute pivots on the ability of the judicial process to establish a "direct" or significantly "proximate" relationship between discrete and possibly innocuous or even incompetent acts. The principal struggle of any future trial for high treason thus will likely revolve around what kind of text is more compelling: the prosecutor's narrative of a defendant's highly coordinated and hence in their tendency criminal acts or the defense's critical interpretation of that narrative as an expression of the state's delusional fears.[11] It is the peremptory and imaginary (or, as we might now put it, the politically unconscious) conception of the crime that effectively shapes the disciplinary instruments concerned with its adjudication. The stage is set for a game of mutual suspicion and paranoia in which the secretive industriousness of alleged conspirators is countered by the narrative and interpretive agility of all participants in the legal process.

A concise illustration of this hermeneutic conundrum is furnished by Blackstone's *Commentaries,* that first magisterial attempt to implement a holistic sense of disciplinary and professional coherence in a heretofore alarmingly random and capricious legal and legislative universe.[12] Discussing the special branch of "counterfeiting" within 25 Edward III, Blackstone affirms that "counterfeiting the king's money . . . is treason, whether the false money be uttered in payment or not" (Blackstone 1979 [1765–69], 4, chap. 6: 84). In a remarkable footnote appended to later editions, Blackstone decides to enlarge the particular conditions under which the material act of counterfeiting the king's money would fall within the purview of the treason statute: "The monies charged to be counterfeited must resemble the true and lawful coin, but this resemblance is a mere matter of fact, of which the jury are to judge upon the evidence before them; the rule being, that the resemblance need not be perfect, but such as may in circulation ordinarily impose upon the world. Thus the counterfeiting with some little variation in the inscription, effigies, or arms, *done probably with the intent to evade the law,* is yet within it; and so is the counterfeiting a different metal, if in appearance it be made to resemble the true coin" (ibid., 56n; emphasis added). As Worcester in Shakespeare's *King Henry IV, Part One,* 5.2.13, says of the king's unrelenting suspicion, "stuck full of eyes": "Interpretation will misquote our looks." Blackstone's account presupposes the reality of the crime from the outset rather than inferring the crime from the evidence at hand. His probabilistic reading of the evidence (note the crucial word "done *probably* with the intent to evade the law") aims above all at securing the legal, disciplinary hypothesis of imaginary treason. By implication, such a priori reasoning also affirms the treason statute's claim to interpretive autonomy and, perhaps, the increasingly totalizing claims of the law as an autonomous interpretive discipline. It is on the verge of becoming *the* new paradigm of political agency, charged above all with defining the terms of allegiance between citizens and the state, and thus far more than just another administrative mechanism occasionally employed by the social and civic sphere. Acts of inadequate counterfeit, we learn, no longer negate the charge for lack of requisite evidence. Rather, any potential deficiency of evidence (including, as we shall soon see, the very absence of evidence altogether) is now interpreted as merely an attempt to circumvent the reach of the statute—a concealment of traitorous purposes, which can potentially be ascribed to any action whatsoever. The same mode of argumentation was to be used by the prosecution of the defendants in 1794 when the discussion turned to the procurement of weapons by some members of the London Corresponding Society. That the evidence presented in this regard was scant indeed—some rusty halberds and daggers that, in Erskine's words, had "retired to their ancient office of carving"—came to be interpreted by the prosecution as yet another instance of the defendants' concealing their treasonous conspiracy.[13] This self-authorizing and self-privileging move of the law—its constitution as wholly autonomous and practical—points to a wider trend within social theory subordinating and absorbing all empirical and heterogeneous matter within the emergent paradigm of modern professionalism and disciplinarity at the end of the eighteenth century. Indeed, through its own formal inauguration as an a priori interpretive authority that is to transform random appearances into symptoms and free individuals into defendants, the law more than any other discipline signals the radical revaluation of theory as the regulative model for all types of social cognition and practice.[14]

Foster's cautionary insistence that evidence in cases of high treason bear not merely a conjectural or symptomatic but, in a far more proximate sense, an instrumental relation to the crime charged did not, in the end, prevent the law from once again establishing its hegemony over the real. Blackstone insists that the crime is consubstantial with an "intention," a term he invests with such integrity as to preclude its disconfirmation by the potential inadequacy of the material steps allegedly undertaken to implement that intention. The materiality of so-called evidence, in other words, is rapidly being demoted to mere empirical surfeit for a criminal design implacably transferred by the law onto the defendant's mind. However insufficient the "means" employed by the defendant in pursuit of his alleged traitorous "designs," the law will only ever be prepared to acknowledge his incompetence, never his innocence. More likely yet, the appearance of incompetence will in turn be construed as evidence of a second-order intentionality: that of concealment.[15] For similar reasons, Blackstone also rejects Foster's requirement that writing only be regarded as traitorous "under some circumstances *with publication*" (Foster, 198). While appearing to concede the contingent status of all words, spoken or written, Blackstone nonetheless maintains that *scribere est agere,* though "in this case the bare words are not the treason but the *deliberate* act of writing them" (Blackstone 1979 [1765–69], 4, chap. 6: 53; emphasis added).[16]

The same self-confirming suspicion operative in Blackstone's intriguing footnote and, throughout the *Commentaries,* evidence of the expanding professional and disciplinary scope of the law, was to reappear in Sir John Scott's opening statement for the prosecution during the 1794 trials. There Scott remarks that "it is not necessary to prove, that the means were as competent to the end, as they were *thought to be* [emphasis added] by those who used them" and that the London Corresponding Society was diabolically well organized, "prepared for emergencies and exigencies [and] . . . acting with a secrecy calculated to elude observation." Scott's lax conception of evidence would be challenged by Thomas Erskine, who correctly saw that whether or not evidence adduced was deemed "competent" to sustain the charge of high treason would depend on whether judge or jury were to find law in this matter: "Whatever, therefore, is relevant or competent evidence to be received in support of the traitorous intention is a legal overt act, and what acts are competent to that purpose, is (as in all other cases) a matter of law for the judges; but whether, after the overt acts are received upon the record as competent, and are established by proof upon the trial, they be sufficient or insufficient in the particular instance, to convince the jury of the traitorous compassing or intention, ought not to be so transferred to the judges, and converted into matter of law" (*STT,* 894–95).[17]

A year after the treason trials were concluded, Coleridge was to summarize the politics of English law by remarking, with millennial hyperbole, how "the old Treason Laws are superseded by the exploded commentaries of obsequious Crown lawyers[;] the commentary has conspired against the text: a vile and useless slave has conspired to dethrone its venerable master." In Coleridge's nearly paranoid account, the present state of British law *was* the conspiracy, and judges ("what will not Judges do?") would routinely "endeavour to transfer to these laws their own flexibility." Against their "strange interpretations" there existed only one defense: juries ("But English juries could not, would not understand them" [Coleridge 1971, 288]).

"The Contingency of a Scratch": Indicting the Political Unconscious in 1794

We now turn to the circumstances surrounding the arrest of Hardy, Thelwall, and other members of the London Corresponding Society on 12 May 1794. As E. P. Thompson (1966), Albert Goodwin (1979), and John Barrell (2000) have shown, the arrest in Edinburgh in December 1793 of Joseph Gerrald and Maurice Margarot, the emissaries of the London Corresponding Society to the Scottish National Convention, followed by their trial and sentencing to transportation to Australia, stimulated the corresponding societies in London and in Sheffield, Norwich, Liverpool, and other provincial towns into unprecedented activity. It was a climate highly charged with visions of political upheaval, as reflected in the particularly strident tone of resolutions adopted by the London Corresponding Society at its general meeting at Chalk Farm on 14 April 1794 under the leadership of John Thelwall. Resolution 5 of that meeting rejected the "arbitrary and flagitious proceedings of the court of justiciary in Scotland," the "Tyranny of Courts and Ministers," as well as the "Corruption of dependent Judges." Such abuses "ought to be considered as dissolving entirely the social compact between the English nation and their Governors; and driving them to an immediate appeal to that incontrovertible maxim of eternal justice, *that the safety of the people is the* SUPREME, and in cases of necessity, the *ONLY* law."[18] Pitt's government responded on 12 May with a wave of arrests throughout the country that included the apprehension of Thomas Hardy, John Thelwall, John Horne Tooke, and other leaders of the reform movement. A vast number of papers were seized, particularly at Hardy's house. Habeas corpus was suspended on 22 May. Broadsheets headed "Treason, Treason, Treason" were sold, and ballad singers were commissioned by Pitt's administration to further strengthen public acceptance of the government's charge that a pervasive and well-engineered conspiracy had been uncovered. Responsible for it were, allegedly, various kinds of radicals, millenarian visionaries and misguided reformers, all operating in collusion with the French Jacobins, whose atheistic beliefs and regicidal acts abroad the government regarded as incontrovertible proof of the threat now posed to crown and constitution in England. In response, "Church and King" mobs attacked houses of the London Corresponding Society's members, including the dwelling of Thomas Hardy, whose wife died, according to the malignant surmise of one London newspaper, "in consequence of being haunted by visions of her dear Tommy's being hanged, drawn, and quartered."[19] While mocking the "honest men" evading arrest with guilt-stricken apprehension, Gillray's 1798 etching *Search Night; or State Watchmen Mistaking Honest Men for Conspirators* (fig. 4), also draws attention to the crude investigative methods of Pitt's government (whose payroll included Gillray).[20] Gillray's choreography of bullying investigators and embarrassed suspects hiding under tables or scrambling up ladders has something decidedly burlesque and staged about it. The etching depicts politics as a farce, a game of mutual suspicion and apprehension in which, it appears, all parties must play their assigned roles over

Fig. 4. James Gillray, *Search Night; or State Watchmen Mistaking Honest Men for Conspirators.* Etching published by Hannah Humphrey, 20 March 1798. Reproduced by permission of The Huntington Library, San Marino, California.

and over ad nauseam.[21] In the case at hand, it took investigators nearly half a year to review and connect all the written records and documents seized from the London Corresponding Society, and even then the prosecution's case continued to look weak. Indeed, in the eyes of many, there was something staged and fabricated about indicting a shoemaker for "compassing the death of the king," even as government officials struggled to produce the material and "overt" acts that would allow the attorney general to sustain the indictment.

Opening the legal proceedings on 2 October, the presiding judge, Sir James Eyre, launched into an extensive discussion of 25 Edward III and the legal principles that, in his view, ought to attend the adjudication of any charge of high treason. Adopting a tone of peremptory legal suspicion that would soon be familiar, Eyre affirmed that the seeming inscrutability of intent, the "wicked imagination of the heart," was no impediment; on the contrary, it gave judge and jury alike extraordinary latitude in assessing charges of high treason. In Eyre's words, "with respect to the question, whether the fact has relation to the design, so as to constitute an overt act of this species of treason . . . it is impossible that any certain rule should be laid down for your government; overt acts being in their nature all the possible means which may be used in the prosecution of the end proposed; they can be no otherwise defined, and must remain for ever infinitely various" (*STT,* 202). Eyre's refusal of "any certain rule" for the "government" of the grand jury, and his prejudicial characterization of evidence in matters of high treason as "infinitely various"—provided a narrative can be produced that will create a persuasive connection between "overt acts" and the legal fact in question—are significant. For such an approach also implies that the adjudication of the charge of treason is no longer governed by inferences that a jury might be compelled to draw based on the material evidence presented to them. Rather, the case is to be decided de jure by the allegedly treasonous "end proposed." In other words, the material evidence produced by the state need not prove the treasonous intent but, on the contrary, its evidentiary status already presupposes a holistic criminal "design." Indeed, the complexity of the defendants' (alleged) treasonous design and the government's elaborate case history are viewed as mutually authorizing. *Acts* represented by a particular prosecutorial narrative as favoring a certain outcome shall, in Eyre's view, be taken as evidence that such an (imaginary) outcome was already inherent, a priori, in the very intentions and purposes concluded to have inspired these acts to begin with.[22] Hence, for the jury to regard empirical facts as a mere "veil, under which is concealed a traitorous conspiracy" (*STT,* 205) is to convert, by default, "matters of fact" into "matter of law" and to conclude that a traitorous intention sponsored a given act, even though such an intention could only be retroactively inferred *from* that act.

To call James Eyre's and Sir John Scott's mode of reasoning paranoid is neither to dismiss it as false nor to pathologize it as deluded relative to some otherwise unexamined criteria of objective truth and health. On the contrary, the conspiratorial surfeit in the state's case reveals the high degree of narrative productivity and epistemic coherence achieved *within* the prosecutorial mode, the ultimate product of that effort being a significantly delayed consciousness of the inevitability of historical change on the part of its speakers. As Gordon Wood has argued, in social usage, the term "conspiracy" and its cognates became rapidly more common and amorphous during the last two decades of the eighteenth century. In his view, the period's unusual investment in conspiratorial theories may be understood as a "last desperate effort to hold men personally and morally accountable for their actions" in a world that was palpably "outrunning man's capacity to explain it in personal terms."[23] In this rapidly evolving, postrevolutionary world where "true motives had to be discovered indirectly, had to be deduced from actions," and where "causes had to be inferred from effects," historical knowledge was, invariably, dialectical in nature (Wood, 411, 423). That is, historical explanation could no longer be achieved in the form of conscious propositions but only as a highly mediated, elaborate, and counterintuitive practice of narrative transference.[24] Which returns us to the 1794 trials and Sir James Eyre's analysis of the British constitution—one "so framed, that the imperial crown of the realm is the common centre of the whole; that all traitorous attempts upon any part of it are instantly communicated to that centre, and felt there" (*STT,* 204). Consistent with this holistic constitutional model, Eyre exhorted the jurors to avail themselves of an organic mode of reasoning by examining the evidence "very carefully, to sift it to the bottom; to consider every part of it in itself, and as it stands connected with other parts of it; and to draw the conclusion of fact, as to the existence, the nature, and the object of this project of a convention, from the whole" (*STT,* 207). The charge that they had planned to convene a national convention of delegates from chapters affiliated with the London Corresponding Society throughout England was the very core of the government's case against Thomas Hardy and his co-defendants. Could a convention be called without those doing so thereby usurping the role of government?

Could reform be demanded without such demands sounding like an ultimatum to the king and thus posing a direct threat to his office and person?

> If a conspiracy to depose or to imprison the king, to get his person into the power of the conspirators, or to procure an invasion of the kingdom, involves it in the compassing and imagining of his death and if steps taken in prosecution of such a conspiracy are rightly deemed overt acts of the treason of imagining and compassing the king's death: need I add, that if it should appear that it has entered into the heart of any man who is a subject of this country, to design, to overthrow the whole government of the country, to pull down and to subvert from its very foundations the British monarchy, that glorious fabric which it has been the work of ages to erect, maintain, and support, which has been cemented with the best blood of our ancestors; to design such a horrible ruin and devastation, which no king could survive, a crime of such a magnitude that no lawgiver in this country hath ever ventured to contemplate it in its whole extent; need I add, I say, that the complication and the enormous extent of such a design will not prevent its being distinctly seen, that the compassing and imagining the death of the king is involved in it, is, in truth, of its very essence. (*STT*, 203–4)

Such extended legal parataxis reveals the emergent conception of the law as a self-authorizing discipline that recognizes no limits to its hermeneutics of suspicion. Its baroque syntax relies on Burke's conception of an organic, irregular, and highly intricate concept of the polity ("that glorious fabric"), even as it shows this myth of the "antient constitution" to be acutely nervous and unstable. For Eyre, to contemplate *any* reform under the prevailing constitutional arrangements would necessarily (however unintended) "subvert from its very foundations the British monarchy," which in turn would inexorably bring about the "death of the king."[25] As Thelwall, who was himself indicted and put on trial shortly after the opening trial of Hardy, observed, the entire case showed the panicked imaginary of the state running amok. "Legal sophisters" were putting forward a "pretended treason" in which the criminality of the defendants was recklessly inferred from consequences that might "possibly" ensue: "because people may *possibly* become unreasonable in their demands, and the government may *possibly* oppose their wishes, and a contest may *possibly* ensue, in which the King may *possibly* be deposed or slain" (Thelwall, 11). Even to his own legal advisors, Eyre's legal reasoning appeared forced, and several of them had already expressed misgivings that Attorney General Sir John

Scott had possibly "over-charged" the defendants. Anxiety about the outcome of the trial ran high in government circles, and many felt that a conviction was more likely to be obtained on the lesser charge of sedition.

Maintaining, nonetheless, the more ambitious charge of high treason, Attorney General Scott proceeded to build his case against the defendants in an opening argument that, for nine full hours, elaborated a plot of deceptively simple design. Focusing on the London Corresponding Society's plans to hold a national convention as his central piece of evidence—the "overt act" that was to prove the "principal" fact or criminal intention of high treason itself—Scott reiterated Eyre's organic view of the British constitution. It was because of the extraordinary connectedness and coherence of Parliament, the law, the electoral system, and the monarchy, he argued, that *any* challenge issued to *any* one of these institutions would necessarily imperil the office and, in due course, also the natural person of the king. Speaking of the 1795 Treason Bill, which expanded yet again the list of treasonable acts, Coleridge observed that "to make such a law . . . is arming a man cap-a-pee [i.e., cap-à-pie: from head to foot] with cumbrous steel, to prevent the contingency of a scratch! Is not this a confession, that so bad is the state of his body, that a scratch might eventually terminate in a mortification" (Coleridge 1971, 293). Many years later, Coleridge was to offer a strikingly similar parable when contradicting Anna Laetitia Barbauld's assessment of the "Rime of the Ancient Mariner" as wholly "improbable" and having "no moral." Quite to the contrary, Coleridge remarked, "the chief fault of the poem was that it had too much moral, and that too openly obtruded on the reader. It ought to have had no more moral than the story of the merchant sitting down to eat dates by the side of a well and throwing the shells aside, and the Genii starting up and saying he must kill the merchant, because a date shell had put out the eye of the Genii's son" (Coleridge 1971, 272–73). The off-handed parable echoes what the "Rime" had so effectively dramatized some thirty-two years before, namely, the Enlightenment's propensity to entrust itself wholly to the power of abstract understanding and, hence, to over-apply the principle of causation and elaborate inferential reasoning. More than any other of Coleridge's major poems, the "Rime" ought to be read as a literary (i.e., purposely concrete, intuitive) meditation on the paranoid excess of Enlightenment rationality. Challenging Bishop Jeremy Taylor's (d. 1667) account of original sin, Coleridge observes in his *Aids to Reflection* how "altogether incompatible the principle of judging by General Consequences is with the Idea of an Eternal, Omnipresent, and Omniscient

Being! that he should be made aware of the absurdity of attributing *any* form of Generalization to the all-perfect Mind. . . . Generalization is a Substitute for Intuition, . . . a gift of inestimable value to a finite Intelligence, such as *Man* in his present stated is endowed with and capable of exercising; but yet a *Substitute* only, and an imperfect one to boot" (Coleridge 1993, 275n). Or, as Blake had put it, "General Knowledge is Remote Knowledge[;] it is in Particulars that Wisdom consists & Happiness too" (*CPP*, 560). For Coleridge, Blake, and the counsel for the defense in the trial of Thomas Hardy, the reckless application and overextension of inferential reasoning, as well as the perilously "remote" or "abstract" nature of knowledge so obtained, could ultimately be traced back to an a priori embrace of the concept of intentionality. The excess of inferential and probabilistic argumentation is the price ultimately paid for wishing to inhabit a universe of exhaustive causal determinacy in which there can be no accidents, no coincidences, and hence no such things as "innocent" acts like a contingent "scratch" or a carelessly disposed of "date shell."

Similarly, as chief counsel for the defense in the trial of Hardy, Thomas Erskine—to whom Coleridge addressed a sonnet—seethes at the state's peremptory and abstract construal of any discrete act by the defendants as merely a subterfuge for some hidden treasonous scheme.[26] As he put it in a show of exasperation, "how are men to express themselves who desire a constitutional reform?" (*STT*, 936). Yet Attorney General Scott brushed aside any such objections:

> It seems to me to follow not only that those who conspire to remove the king out of the government altogether, but that those who conspire to remove him, unless he will govern the people according to laws, which are not statutes in Parliament agreed upon, and the laws and customs of the same, or as the head of a government framed and modified by any authority not derived from that Parliament, do conspire to depose him from *that royal state, title, power, and government, which the indictment mentions,* and to subvert and alter the rule and government *now established* in these kingdoms. He *ought not* so to govern—I say he cannot so govern—he is bound to resist such a project at the hazard of all its consequences; he must resist the attempt; resistance necessarily produces deposition, it endangers his life. (*STT*, 245)

Such argumentation appears curiously unconcerned with the heavily inferential, not to say transferential, logic of his case—one substantially rooted in the narrative imaginary of the attorney general. For it is he, rather than the defendants, who "constructs" the traitorous conspiracy and the legal "fact" of high treason by first outlining a nightmare vision of comprehensive political and social change. Insofar as such change appears too sweeping and pervasive to be acceptable to the state, even as a mere hypothesis or act of imagination, it is being objectified as the *legal* matter of high treason. What produces this "highest civil crime" (as Blackstone had called it) is the prosecution's extended narrative transference. That is, the state projects its unendurable knowledge of the British constitution as historically contingent and temporal—which is to say, its own political unconscious—onto defendants by charging the latter with the "crime" of having intended to turn that knowledge into reality all along (cf. Žižek in the epigraph to Chapter 2). Yet precisely because the state cannot bear to acknowledge the tenuous and changeable nature of its present disposition, it must mediate this knowledge through a shoemaker, a pamphleteer, and a linguist as the conspirators who allegedly "intended" that knowledge in the form of a highly sophisticated and far-flung plot. As Erskine's defense pointed out time and again, "a supposed attack upon the king's civil authority has been transmuted, by construction, into a murderous conspiracy against his natural person; in the same manner, and by the same arguments, a conspiracy to overturn that civil authority, by direct force, has again been assimilated, *by farther construction,* to a design to undermine the monarchy by changes wrought through public opinion, enlarging gradually into universal will" (*STT,* 882).

In what proved an inevitably circumstantial case, the prosecution's construction of such a plot hinged almost exclusively on the interpretation of written evidence. In particular, the state had to establish a kinship of design between the resolutions and letters drafted by the London Corresponding Society and the notorious, in some cases proscribed, publications of John Thelwall and Thomas Paine, from which, ironically, the attorney general proceeded to quote, and thus enter into public record, hundreds of paragraphs. Thus Sir John Scott made extensive reference to writings both published and unpublished, including deliberately inflammatory letters written by government infiltrators of the London Corresponding Society to some of its members and now adduced against these members—now defendants—as proof of *their* treasonous intentions. Sensibly, the attorney general opened his case by stressing "the principles upon which construction is to be given to the written evidence that will be adduced," namely, that "the language they use, ought to be considered according to its obvious sense. If the language admits, and naturally admits, of a double interpretation, it must then be considered according to the nature of the *principle* which that language is calculated to carry into execution.'"[27] The jury is thus held to an otherwise unspecified standard of "obvious sense," to "the ordinary course of things," or to the "common experience of mankind" (*STT,* 254, 256).[28] Above all, then, the prosecution had to establish in the jury's collective mind its master narrative of a constitution beleaguered by regicidal conspirators, lest the jury should elect to read the evidence submitted as simply the expression of innocuous "commonsense" politics.

For Scott, however, the conspirators' "publications are either brought into the world with such a secrecy as baffles all prosecution,—published without names of authors or of printers,—published by contrivance . . . in the dead of night" or, alternatively, in quantities that confound all government regulation. Such a paranoid mode of argumentation closely corresponds to Freud's (likewise text-based) analysis of paranoia as a conspicuously productive mode of interpretation. Unsurprisingly, then, Sir John Scott proceeded to engulf the jury in a blizzard of written matter which, as Erskine wearily noted in his opening statement for the defense, "consumed four days in the reading . . . the unconnected writings of men unknown to one another, upon a hundred different subjects" (*STT,* 891). Upon hearing of the prosecution's nine-hour opening presentation, Former Lord Chancellor Thurlow was said to have exclaimed: "Nine hours? Then there is no treason by God!"[29] Once committed to the charge of high treason (rather than of sedition), however, the prosecution knew that it had to proceed by building a highly circumstantial, inference-driven, and elaborate *narrative* case; for only in this manner would it be possible to overcome the resistance *within* the very writings entered into record—"all this handsome language" (*STT,* 296), as Scott characterized it—to yielding up its evidentiary import. In an effort to demonstrate the objective existence of a conspiracy (the very imagining of which occasions and formally shapes the prosecutorial art of telling), Scott repeatedly stressed the need for a correspondingly metonymic imagination on the part of the jurors: "each paper must be considered with reference to the context of the same paper, and with reference to the contents of all other papers that form the evidence of the same system, which the paper produced is meant to prove" (*STT,* 276). What connects papers in "spirit and letter" is inferentially to be taken as evidence of a conspiratorial connection among all individuals somehow associated with *any one* of these papers, be it as author, recipient, or merely as a member of the organization in whose name such papers were drafted. As Scott put it, "in a conspiracy as widely extended as this is, I shall undoubtedly insist, before you and the Court, that the acts of individuals . . . [and] what they do in reference to these acts is evidence against all of them; and likewise that letters which the persons write relative to the same addresses, are evidence against each of them whether written by the particular individual or no, as being in prosecution of the same purpose" (*STT*, 320).[30]

In their strenuous resistance to any rules governing the admissibility of evidence or its subsequent narrative connection, Eyre's "charge to the jury" and Scott's case for the prosecution reproduce a familiar dilemma. Edmund Burke had confronted the same obstacles while pursuing the impeachment of Warren Hastings, governor-general of British India, between 1788 and 1795. Frustrated by six years of compulsive yet inconclusive gathering of evidence and legal maneuvering, Burke made a passionate plea for narrative latitude and challenged the then operative rules of evidence laid down by Blackstone in his *Commentaries,* which prohibited hearsay (albeit with some exceptions) and insisted on the independent integrity of each item of evidence. In particular, Burke objected to what he considered a deliberate fragmentation of his narrative account by the defense counsel, who, at every step of the way, constrained Burke to justify each piece of evidence *separately* as truly pertinent to the crimes alleged. To do so, Burke contended, is "to break to pieces and garble those facts, upon the multitude of which, their combination, and the relation of all component parts to each other, and to the culprit the whole force and virtue of . . . evidence depends."[31] By seeking to define the nature of a crime and form of judicial process via the "collective effect" of narrative representation, Burke shows that he is "already committed to a closed narrative of human affairs" (Welsh, 34–35).

As might be expected, Jeremy Bentham viewed such "constructive" and overly narrativized forms of legal reasoning with great skepticism. Several decades later, in his *Rationale of Judicial Evidence* (1827), Bentham once again rejects narrative approaches to legal reasoning as overly self-privileging. As he notes, the (Burkean) model does not provide for evidence to be introduced *into* a legal narrative; rather, evidence tends to be produced *by* the prosecution's narrative. Attempts to discriminate categorically between indirect and direct evidence are bound to fail, since what counts as evidence is determined not by its (supposed) nature but by its "position in the argument." As Bentham puts it, "in this way a chain of facts, of any length, may be easily conceived, and chains of different lengths will be frequently exemplified: each such link being, at the same time, with reference to the preceding link, a principal fact, and with reference to a succeeding one, an evidentiary fact."[32] To be sure, Bentham is more concerned with defining a rational and transparent judicial process, and much less so with accomplishing a spectacular political feat. Still his contention that evidence is always by definition *indirect* and therefore to be kept separate from the actual crime bears directly on the core problem of the 1794 treason trials. Inasmuch as all crime inheres solely in an intention, it proves inaccessible save by means of a cautious inferential process (excluding, for the sake of argument, the possibility of outright confession).

Of the many observers witnessing the 1794 trials, no one seemed more aware of the hermeneutic prejudice with which the prosecutor's narrative transmuted empirical facts into evidentiary matter than William Godwin. When his close friend Thomas Holcroft was indicted among the members of the London Corresponding Society, Godwin hastened to London, where he published a trenchant analysis of the crown's case entitled "Cursory Strictures," directly challenging Eyre's circular, post hoc ergo propter hoc style of legal reasoning, which Godwin treats as acknowledging in *symptomatic* form the inescapability of social and political change.[33] In questioning whether Eyre's charge is "reasoning respecting law, or respecting a state of society" (*STT,* 214), Godwin reversed the charge to the point where the "treason, real or imaginative" is the justice's and, by extension, the state's "own mere creation" (*STT,* 220).[34] He left conspicuously open the question of whether the principle of "constructive treason" set out in the charge in "the most unblushing and undisguised manner" (*STT,* 222) amounted to a deliberate narrative distortion of the facts and the law—based on "forced constructions . . . . ambiguous and deceitful words"—or to the more deeply seeded "delusions of a practiced sophister" (*STT,* 220). Eyre's and Scott's mode of legal reasoning,, Godwin argues, proceeds "not forward from general rules of action to the guilt or innocence of particular men, but backward from actions already performed to the question, whether or no they shall fall under such or such provisions of the law" (*STT,* 219–20). Eyre's charge invents "a kind of accumulative or constructive evidence, by which many actions, either totally innocent in themselves, or criminal in a much inferior degree, shall, when united amount to treason" (*STT,* 222). In order to expose how a presumptive ideological consensus is being enforced in the seemingly objective and dispassionate explication of the statute on high treason, Godwin dwells on the prosecution's "profusion of fiction, hypothesis, and prejudication . . . [designed] to bewilder the imaginations" of the jury and the nation (*STT,* 225). Such metonymic compulsion reveals the law to be itself a symptom of an ideological trauma, one of which it seeks to disburden itself by projecting it, "in the nature of an *ex post facto* law" (*STT,* 230), onto defendants as a malignant and criminal intention. The rhetoric of legal knowledge, the "accumulative" presentation of evidence—the equivalent of *Anlehnung* in Freud's discussion of paranoia, and otherwise known as metonymy—is thus reconstructed by *Godwin's* critique as a social symptom: "There is a figure of speech, of the highest use to a designing and treacherous orator, which has not yet perhaps received a name in the labours of Aristotle, Quintillian, or Farnaby. I would call this figure encroachment. It is a proceeding, by which an affirmation is modestly insinuated at first, accompanied with considerable doubt and qualification; repeated afterwards, unaccompanied with these qualifications; and at last asserted in the most peremptory and arrogant terms" (*STT,* 224). Undeniably, Godwin's fervent rationalism helps him expose the state's self-confirming narrative transformation of matters of fact into matters of law, as well as its tendency to project treasonous intent into otherwise quite possibly innocuous actions on the part of the defendants.

Still, the analytic optimism that permeates Godwin's strictures does not agree well with the construction of English politics as it emerges from the pages of his *Caleb Williams.* For as a novelist, Godwin situates his characters in a web comprised of deceptive experiences, inscrutable, unconscious desires, and overtly hostile political forces, with the result that any character's intentions and actions produce results so fraught with contingency as to verge on the bizarre. Rather than placing much faith in the integrity, let alone transparency, of anyone's intentions, Godwin's fiction also portrays its subjects' actions as circumscribed—well in advance of their inward origination or material execution—by powerful moral, social, and disciplinary narratives, the law being only the most prominent of these. Appeals to good faith or authentic convictions such as supposedly impel a given individual to act one way or other stand no chance against the overwhelming forces of disciplinary and political suspicion that now define social relations. We recall the advice of Falkland's brother, Forester, to the embattled Caleb Williams: "Make the best story you can for yourself—true, if truth, as I hope, will serve your purpose; but, if not, the most plausible and ingenious you can invent. That is what self-defence requires from every man, where, as it always happens to a man upon his trial, he has the whole world against him, and has his own battle to fight against the world" (*GCW*, 169). Remarking on the pervasive usurpation of spiritual values by rhetorical performance (and thus of universals by particulars) in late-eighteenth-century England, James Epstein writes that "it was not the 'happiness of nations' but the sacred act of narrating the story of a particular nation's happiness that was persuasive" (Epstein, 31). Godwin's "Cursory Strictures," meanwhile, remains in the older, if updated, constitutionalist idiom, a dialogic wrestling for the interpretation of a supposedly venerable and (in his view) perfectable body of legal and political rules. Godwin quotes, via Hume, the words of the seventeenth-century earl of Strafford against constructive treason: "Let us be content with what our fathers left us; not our ambition carry us to be more learned than they were" (*STT*, 219). Godwin shrewdly appeals to the more traditional sensibility of potential jurors, politicians, and to that of the defense counsel (Erskine, Gibbs). His reasoning thus differed markedly from the Painite republican rhetoric that dismissed the constitution outright as nonexistent, a fiction, and hence in need of being written for the first time.

The Dialectics of the Quotidian: Retroactivity in Law, Satire, and Psychoanalysis

Substantially cued by Godwin's essay, Erskine's brilliant defense began with a nine-hour opening argument that exhausted not only all pertinent aspects of the law but, by all accounts, also the jury and spectators. Expanding on the core implication of "Cursory Strictures," Erskine again protests against "all appeals to speculations, concerning *consequences*, when the law commands us to look only to intentions" (*STT*, 878), "the crime created by the statute not being the perpetration of any act, but being, in the rigorous severity of the law, the very contemplation, intention, and contrivance of a purpose directed to an act" (*STT*, 897). Erskine draws on what Godwin had captured as the most salient rhetorical symptom of the state's paranoid case history against the defendants—the master trope of "encroachment." Thus Erskine points out that the jury's judgment will be "swept away" by the state's inflated narrative "into the fathomless abyss of a thousand volumes" (*STT*, 892). It is crucial, he argues, for the jury to be in control over matters of fact and matters of law. Only the jury, that is, may legitimately dispute whether an alleged "overt fact" bears a provable, direct, and competent relation to the criminal intention alleged. As Erskine insists time and again, it must be understood "that the province of the jury over the effect of evidence ought not to be . . . transferred to the judges, and converted into matter of law" (*STT,* 895). For "it is the act with the *specific intention,* and not the act alone which constitutes the charge. The act of conspiring to depose the King, may indeed be *evidence,* according to circumstances, of an intention to destroy his natural existence, but never, as a proposition of *law,* can constitute the intention itself. Where an act is done in pursuance of an intention, surely the intention must first exist; a man cannot do a thing in fulfillment of an intention, unless his mind first conceives that intention" (*STT,* 880). What should matter to the jury, then, is "whether, even if you believed the overt act, you believe also that it proceeded from a traitorous machination against the life of the king.—I am only contending that these two beliefs must coincide to establish a verdict of guilty . . . and that the establishment of the overt act, even if it were established, does not establish the treason against the king's life, BY A CONSEQUENCE OF LAW" (*STT,* 895–96).[35]

It is, in other words, impossible "to pronounce *as a matter of law,* what another man intends" (*STT,* 899); or, to quote from Shakespeare's *The Rape of Lucrece,* "thoughts are but dreams till their effects be tried" (line 353). With the defendants themselves having affirmed that they intended to hold a national convention, the jury now had to evaluate whether such plans had specifically been contrived as direct expedients *"for the purpose alleged, of assuming all the authority of the state, and in fulfilment of the main intention against the life of the king."* Unless "this double intention" could be verified, Erskine time and again contended, the indictment could not be maintained. Referring to his successful defense of Lord George Gordon against the charge of high treason in 1782, Erskine recalled how even in cases of pervasive civic unrest such as the Gordon riots, "it is the end therefore for which the war is to be levied, and not the conspiracy to do any act which the law considers as a levying of war, that constitutes an overt act of treason" (*STT,* 906). Once again, that is, intent must not be inferred retroactively as the presumptive cause for the "overt" material acts, acts that in the Gordon case were far more conspicuous than in the present instance, where "the conspiracy imputed was not to effect reform by violence, but . . . by pamphlets and speeches, which might produce universal suffrage, which universal suffrage might eat out and destroy aristocracy, which destruction might lead to the fall of monarchy, and, in the end, to the death of the king.—Gentlemen, if the cause were not too serious, I should liken it to the play with which we amuse our children. 'This is the cow with the crumpled horn, which gored the dog, that worried the cat, that ate the rat,' &c. ending in the 'house which Jack built'" (*STT,* 906).

As in the children's rhymed sing-song story, the prosecution appears to rely on the monotony of repetition to cover up the utterly mechanical nature of its reasoning. Erskine's witty example works all the better given that it shows the same progression from the trivial and innocuous to the monstrous and grotesque. Finally, though, the children's rhyme seems more lucid than John Scott's overblown deductions. For by repeating its individual steps *in reverse,* the children's ditty exposes its intrinsic artificiality and absurdity. Erskine, in other words, is anxious to put distance between the defendants and Scott's elaborately conceived case history of their supposedly treasonous intentions and "overt acts." Erskine, it would seem, was altogether aware that to rebut the prosecution's case point by point would mislead the jurors into believing that they were witnessing a genuine and rational contest of ideas. Instead, they are to view the defendants as subjects to machinations at once farcical and monstrous, a delusive scheme that one might prefer to dismiss as an overly elaborate practical joke, were it not for the violent tactics of the police and the specter of capital punishment facing the defendants.

In so splitting its strategy between reasoned argumentation and calculated satire, the defense aims to expose the state's case history as wildly imaginative and paranoid, a kind of retroactive prophecy obsessed with reconstructing heterogeneous events large and small as the effects of one hidden cause.[36] To confirm their fears of a comprehensive transformation of the present ideological dispensation, then, the "alarmists" in Pitt's government might, for example, infiltrate the London Corresponding Society with agents provocateurs (which they did). In their persistent efforts at steering the organization toward issuing more radical resolutions and instigating what might subsequently be interpreted in court as the taking of material steps ("overt acts") toward the implementation of a treasonous intent, these agents did not so much function as a means of verifying that a past event *had* occurred (i.e., that the treasonous intent had already and independently been conceived by Hardy, Thelwall, and Tooke) as "bring about an event in order that a *past* should have occurred" (Dummett, 324). The motive behind the state's case, in other words, is not one of empirical verification of the past but the unselfconscious and retroactive creation of a past as the origin of the kind of pervasive conspiracy that will legitimate the state's reactionary dealings with the ideological dissensions in the present.

Erskine's defense, then, exposed the prosecution's attempts to indict the state's ideological other as a paranoid projection into the empirical world of a wish for change latent in the collective mind of the government and the ruling class. As Erskine noted, the conspiratorial paradigm was fundamentally absurd, for it presumed intent and conscious manipulation where such behavior would serve no purpose. Challenging the evidentiary merit of private correspondence among various members of the London Corresponding Society—intercepted or seized by the state upon the arrests of Hardy and Thelwall and alleged to have been written with such ambiguity as to evade the charge of treason, Erskine commented:

> When the language of the letter, which is branded as ambiguous, thus stares them in the face as an undeniable answer to the charge, they then have recourse to the old refuge of *mala fides;* all this they say is but a cover for hidden treason;—but I ask you . . . what reason upon earth there is to suppose, that the writers of this letter did not mean what they expressed? . . . [I]f this correspondence was calculated for deception, the deception must have been understood and agreed upon by all parties concerned, for otherwise you have a conspiracy amongst people who are at cross purposes with one another: consequently the conspiracy, if this be a branch of it, is a conspiracy of thousands and thousands, from one end of the kingdom to the other. (*STT,* 935)

In his own defense against the same charge of high treason, Thelwall was to capture the paradox by dwelling on the contiguity between the reform movement's pursuit of more inclusive political "representation" and its written "representations," published and disseminated in pursuit of that goal: "What does the charge amount to? Simply to this: that we attempted so to organize the public opinion that it might be made known to the representative. . . . If this is a crime, Representation is itself High Treason" (Thelwall, 27). To construe written correspondence among members of the London Corresponding Society in question as legal evidence—in the double sense of an "overt act" and the concealment of the very intention that the act would otherwise confirm—is to presuppose, Erskine's argument implies, that the state and the treasonous conspirators share one and the same imaginary. In other words, ideological struggles and historical transformations do not unfold within separate and distinct empirical formations, classes, or communities—venerable aristocrats, guileless constitutionalists, and conspiring artisans. On the contrary, the analytic work performed by Erskine's defense on the case history of Sir John Scott suggests a pervasive transference. Erskine does not so much defend his clients as interpret the prosecution's case as a symptomatic longing for its unacknowledged, indeed unconscious, fears to be established as historical truth. In the words of Lacan, Erskine compels the state to "recognize [its] unconscious as [its] history." This objective the defense accomplishes by helping the prosecution "perfect the contemporary historicization of the facts which have already determined a certain number of the historical 'turning points' in [its] existence" up to the present (Lacan 1968, 23).[37] In reading the state's case history as the transferential projection of a wish for change entertained on the part of the political establishment, Erskine's most effective evidence was provided, not suprisingly, by a representative of the state. Calling the duke of Richmond to the witness stand, Erskine had him read extensively from documents attesting that the Tory administration itself had been contemplating for some twelve years precisely those kinds of political and electoral reforms now charged as a treasonous conspiracy against the corresponding societies.[38] In further questioning this extraordinary and (to make matters worse) perfectly obliging witness, Erskine followed up on his earlier, shrewdly elliptic admonition to the prosecution that they "ought . . . to proceed with more abundant caution, lest they should be surprised by their resentments and their fears" (*STT,* 892).

Erskine conceives historical change as a series of almost imperceptible shifts in the national imaginary. Such shifts gain symptomatic distinctness as they begin to be projected in various rhetorical and institutional settings (the court, the popular press, pamphlets, satiric prints, etc.) onto individuals and communities. In defending those accused of high treason in 1794, Erskine is mindful to predicate his legal arguments on a much wider theory of social processes that are governed by structural, unreflected processes of displacement and transference. However rigid and repressive the state may be in its partial and dispassionate enforcement of the law and in its exclusionary notion of social and political representation, Erskine insists that the state apparatus has only very limited influence on the current of social affect. Ultimately, though, it cannot control the nation's complex imaginary altogether:

> In times, when the whole habitable earth is in a state of change and fluctuation,—when deserts are starting up into civilized empires around you,—and when men, no longer slaves to the prejudices of particular countries, much less to the abuses of particular governments, enlist themselves, like the citizens of an enlightened world, into whatever communities in which their civil liberties may

> be best protected; it can never be for the advantage of this country to prove, that the strict, unextended letter of her laws, is no security to its inhabitants.—On the contrary, when so dangerous a lure is every where holding out to emigration, it will be found to be the wisest policy of Great Britain to set up her happy constitution,—the strict letter of her guardian laws, and the proud condition of equal freedom, which her highest and her lowest subjects ought alike to enjoy; it will be her wisest policy to set up these first of human blessings against those charms of change and novelty which the varying condition of the world is hourly displaying and which may deeply affect the population and prosperity of our country. (*STT*, 967)

Erskine's ardent and humane caveat urged the judiciary and the jury to become aware of the dialectical nature of legal and partisan politics throughout the 1790s. Weary of the rapid disciplinary ascendancy of the law as *the* dominant symbolic instrument for the construction of authoritative social knowledge, Erskine repeatedly argues that the treason statute's authority rests on an unproven, indeed unprovable, hypothesis of criminality. For every subject inhabits his or her own world of "change and fluctuation," and the collective psyche of millions of Britons is inevitably divided in its allegiance to the unequal "blessings" of the present and the elusive "charms of change and novelty" of countless imagined futures.

This heterogeneity of social interpretation also organizes the highly performative medium of satiric prints and political caricature during the 1790s and the romantic period more generally. Such prints reached the peak of their popularity just around the time of the 1794 treason trials, often providing a running a commentary on the ideological fault lines of British politics. Etymologically linked to subterranean, conspiratorial, and (at least in a colloquial sense) unconscious forces, the "grotesque" style of the satiric prints so popular during the 1790s very much reflects Erskine's conception of political and social reality as a spectrum of competing interpretations. Yet in prints by James Sayers, James Gillray, and, somewhat later, George Cruikshank, we also find a persistent ambiguity that makes it nearly impossible to determine the artist's views of the ongoing social, religious, or political debates. Many of the prints in question show subjects ensnared by their own fixations and prejudices when it comes to interpreting and positioning themselves within their culture. This relatively novel medium effectively produces metarepresentations of British society by throwing into relief the idiosyncrasies and compulsions at work beneath the (supposedly rational) interpretations that various individuals and communities have fashioned of a reality perceived as intrinsically threatening. Behind the work of caricature there invariably lurks a whole panoply of conspiratorial, anxious, or outright paranoid (sublime) imaginings. Hence it would be a misreading to suppose that prints by Gillray and Sayers merely impose an element of caricature on hapless, otherwise sober subjects. Quite the contrary, their works articulate the reductive caricature that supported the various competing viewpoints of British society during the 1790s.[39] Like the mutually suspicious legal narratives examined thus far, satiric prints also strain the conventions of mimesis by their sheer visual excess or eccentric fixation on a particular feature, with the implication that fuller consideration of it is indispensable to a better grasp of politics. Satiric representation thus disrupts the more traditional or familiar forms of mimesis and, in their stead, confronts its viewers with a lesser reality, a "nature . . . worse than the actuality" (Paulson, 182). Time and again, the satiric prints published during the 1790s confound the hermeneutic expectations of a public characterized by considerable political and aesthetic literacy, to be sure, though often viewed (by a whole spectrum of dissenting intellectuals) as dull, conformist, and driven only by the prospect of material gain. What needed to be instilled in the usually obtuse-looking John Bull was a consciousness of the *excess that is the political.* In this regard, the aesthetic practice of Gillray and Sayers accords with the self-conscious poetic theories of Blake and the early Wordsworth. These satiric prints do not so much aim at frivolously hyperbolizing a rational order of things as seek to expose the obsessive and histrionic mood of 1790s Britain. Rather than claiming what it uncovers as "truth," satire sheds light on an all-encompassing emotive framework (what Lacan calls "the Real") to account for the curiously identical patterns of representation ("the symbolic") shared by unselfconscious agents on all sides of the political spectrum.

James Sayers's 12 May 1791 etching *Mr. Burke's Pair of Spectacles for Shortsighted Politicians*—which could be alternatively titled *The World According to Burke*—features most of the prominent political figures of the 1790s, the majority of them depicted in association with their writings (fig. 5).[40] Mirrored in Burke's spectacles (a regular standby in prints of the period) are Charles Fox (left) and Richard Sheridan (right), with conspirational expressions on their faces. Joseph Priestley, astride a demon sailing through the sky,

Fig. 5. James Sayers, *Mr. Burke's Pair of Spectacles for Shortsighted Politicians.* Etching published by Thomas Cornell, 12 May 1791. Reproduced by permission of *The* Huntington Library, San Marino, California.

holds *Priestley on Civil Government.* Richard Price, just passed away and already rising from the dead, is predictably linked with a quotation from his notorious *Discourse on the Love of our Country.* A demon is tempting the duke of Portland with the French constitution, inscribed in blunt Burkean shorthand as "Atheists, Demagogues, the Mob." Real and imaginary titles by Thomas Paine (*Rights of Man* and *Treasonable, Seditious Sermons)* provide the devil with a seat, Sheridan extinguishes the religious symbol of Anglicanism, and Fox prepares to chop down the British Oak. As a condensed visual metacritique of the already lurid imagery of Burke's *Reflections,* the print is complicated by its interpretation of "vision" as both empirical beholding and paranoid projection, indicated by the looming, disproportionate presence of Burke's spectacles discerning his enemies. Averting to the kind of rhetorical and ideological excess that Mary Wollstonecraft, Catharine Macaulay, Thomas Paine, James Mackintosh, and others had exposed as the pathology of the *Reflections,* Sayers depicts Burke's unbalanced mind as a gothic stage spectacle in which countless personal and political enemies crowd around of the usual icons of sedition and treasonable writing.

Another Sayers print, *Thoughts on a Regicide Peace* (14 October 1796 [fig. 6]), shows the now retired and aged Burke asleep in his seat, his head spewing smoke and flames, as well as assorted lines from Shakespeare's *King Richard II* (1.1.40ff.).[41] It includes a resigned Dutchman (or, rather, frog) on the left, kept in line by the classic sansculotte—who in turn is being treated to the competing tunes of the British lion's roar and the latest opera (which begins with a "Peace Overture"). All these are condensed into the nightmare world that produced Burke's recent publication and is now being refracted in the print. That is, the rigid ideological divide that characterizes the waking life and mental reality of Edmund Burke appears, as it were, an imaginary realm guaranteed by the nightmare of its potential and quite possibly imminent disintegration. The central historical reference here (the dove bearing a passport and olive branch) concerns Lord Malmesbury's mission to negotiate peace with the French Directoire, a mission to which Burke's widely anticipated pamphlet of 19 October 1796 was about to respond. Implicitly construing Burke's harangue as the textual projection of an ideological nightmare, the print dramatizes Burke's unconscious so as to locate the Tories' profound ambivalence regarding any prospects for peace with their revolutionary other. Burke's dream—which the print holds to be his pamphlet's content—projects such peace as the disastrous prospect of an actual end to the ideological oppositions that

Fig. 6. James Sayers, *Thoughts on a Regicide Peace.* Published by Hannah Humphrey, 14 October 1796. Reproduced by permission of The Huntington Library, San Marino, California.

support Burke's and England's political reality, indeed, *are* that reality. If the print appears to visually reenact the deeply paranoid argumentation of Burke's *Thoughts on a Regicide Peace,* it also exposes the pamphlet's unconscious production of political meanings by revealing the political position of Burke and his Tory allies as wholly mediated and thus guaranteed by the fixity of their

Jacobin and Whig opponents—a realization that Burke cannot admit, however, and that his polemic effectively works to keep at bay.

Gillray's etching *Promis'd Horrors of the French Invasion—or Forcible Reasons for Negotiating a Regicide Peace* (20 October 1796 [fig. 7]) hovers somewhere between the complex social texture found in Hogarth's sketches of London life and the apocalyptic imagery of Blake's Lambeth prophecies.[42] Confounding any static ideological opposition with its extremely unbalanced text/image ratio, the print strongly suggests that political reality and the choices to which that reality is preemptively reduced are founded on paranoid speculations about the apocalyptic prospects of a possible, even imminent, future. Gillray's print gives rise to a series of questions. Is Burke, by dreaming the nightmare of a "regicide peace," suffering from his personal delusions, or do such paranoid fears allow him to come to terms with a changing political

Fig. 7. James Gillray, *Promis'd Horrors of the French Invasion,—Or Forcible Reasons for Negotiating a Regicide Peace.* Etching published by Hannah Humphrey, 20 October 1796. Reproduced by permission of *The Huntington Library, San Marino, California.*

world? Does a "regicide peace" serve to stave off the terrifying prospect of a French invasion and of England succumbing to French atheism and anarchy? Or might considerations of such a peace amount to a (perhaps necessary) form of therapy that will spare Burke and other orthodox Tories from having to retell (like Coleridge's Mariner) the same paranoid vision of social apocalypse over and over again?[43] Can Burke bear to wake up from his lifelong dream of irreconcilable conflict with England's perennial other? Alternatively, can he afford *not* to wake up from it? Is peace being simultaneously explored by some and opposed by other Tories because there is no longer a genuine Tory consensus on England's politics vis-à-vis France? Is the political establishment at long last prepared to accept that a continuing imaginary projection and material confrontation of England's revolutionary other might turn out to be more exhausting and unbearable than having to wake up from it? Do Burke and Pitt sleep better dreaming that dream or not dreaming it? Will a regicide peace give them a purchase on calmer sleep, and, if so, won't it by the same token also bring them closer to those whom they must loathe and continue to represent as the most pernicious threat to everything British? Eventually, these questions all collapse into the issue of the status of this print as representation. Does it send a distinct political message or does it invoke and then confound countless interpretive scenarios so as ultimately to render *any* political message suspect? Is politics an integral element of the real, or does the print show us that politics, if only inadvertently, already contains the textual and visual symptoms of its own intrinsic irreality?

Gillray's etching *Opening of the Budget or: John Bull giving his Breeches to save his Bacon* (17 November 1796 [fig. 8]) exhibits a similarly equivocal line of questioning.[44] While focusing on the particular issue of heavy and obviously unpopular wartime taxation, the print seeks to estrange the beholder from any settled perspective on the current war or taxation by advancing two competing models of causation in the domain of politics. To argue that Fox, ostensibly signaling to the French invasion fleet at Brest, is "the object of the artist's indignation" (Paulson, 185), though tenable as a partial reading, abridges the print's far more intricate performance. An inversion of Paulson's empirical reading is just as plausible, namely, that the depiction of Fox's treason might constitute a projection, a pseudo-cause floated before the public so as to sanction "Master Bill's" (Pitt's) heavy taxation. Is Fox *really* signaling the fleet, and, if so, is his doing so the cause for Pitt's levying heavy taxes in order to defend a noticeably dull-looking John Bull from Britain's treasonous Whigs and their

Fig. 8. James Gillray, *Opening of the Budget;—or—John Bull giving his Breeches to save his Bacon.* Etching published by Hannah Humphrey, 17 November 1796. Reproduced by permission of The Huntington Library, San Marino, California.

(alleged) Jacobin cohorts in France? What, after all, are we to make of John Bull's quizzical expression and his obtuse pledge ("—a coming?—are they? nay then take all I've got at once") so monotonously echoed by Pitt and his associates ("Ay! They're a coming . . ."), a reference to taxes levied and collected in unprecedented quantity? If we take Fox's signaling the French fleet as a probable, or at least plausible event, might it not be argued that he does so precisely in order to liberate John Bull from unprecedented wartime taxation and conscription of soldiers by Pitt's Tory administration? To entertain such a reading would furthermore prompt one to read Pitt's warmongering as a calculated strategy for continually disenfranchising and splitting the domestic political opposition—Whigs, dissenters, artisans, millenarians, Catholics, and so on. Paine, of course, had done that when lambasting "the intrigue of Courts, by which the system of war is kept up" and Burke's preference for governing the people by "fraud . . . force . . . and contrivance" (*RM,* 146, 167). In juxtaposing these incompatible readings, the print also discriminates between paranoia as a subjective-pathological condition, on the one hand, and paranoia as an objective-disciplinary category, on the other. Bent on exposing the fictitious nature of the political process, Gillray's satire scrambles cause and effect and so exposes a contingent ideological perspective that supports any given line of political argumentation. It also lets us glimpse the mechanisms of resistance by means of which any political philosophy fends off a conscious recognition of its irreducibly contingent nature. Gillray's sketch of incompatible models of causation in British politics thus opens with a first, "innocent" reading of the present political actions (Pitt's taxation and Fox's treason) as *real* effects of an equally *real* cause (the French revolutionary threat). From here the print advances us toward a more reflexive or "experienced" reading in which the adversarial nature of English political discourse masks the subterranean dialectic of imaginary Tory fears and Whig desires (invasion), as well as Tory desires and Whig fears (taxation). In highlighting the physiological, raw, and self-absorbed motivations of *any* political subject—French or British, Foxite or Pittite, Whig or Tory, artisan or noble, rural, provincial, or metropolitan—Gillray's satire invariably undercuts the transcendent and universalizing pretensions of political rhetoric. Consequently, it calls into question the possibility of *any* significant and organized development of national and cultural life. The undecidability so frequently observed by commentators on Gillray is generated by the continued interference between image and text, situation and rhetoric, and the contingencies of the body and the face, all of which are certain to betray the ideological mask of aesthetic and rhetorical form.

All this brings us back to Freud's reading of the Schreber case. By now we can more fully appreciate how what seemed merely another dull and procedure-ridden deposition of that compulsive confessor might nonetheless result in a surprise vindication. Having reviewed the transcripts of Schreber's case, Freud renders the verdict in the name of psychoanalysis: "not pathogenic." He refers to the subject's highly imaginative and analytical quest for an all-encompassing cause that would account for his overwhelming sensation of inhabiting a fractured and antagonistic reality. Such a quest takes the form of a metonymic process, alternatively defined by Freud as "projection," as the "return of the repressed," and sometimes just as paranoia. Through narrative industry, the subject struggles to objectify an "inner" affective catastrophe as a disastrous, albeit empirically distinct, perception. And yet, in his articulate description of schemes supposedly devised to hasten the utter collapse of a cherished social and cultural order to which the paranoiac retains a strong allegiance—"the end of the world is the projection of [an] inner catastrophe"—the subject of paranoia also recovers from this fear. For precisely the narrative labor of his projections allows the paranoiac to reclaim that world and, consequently, his own damaged subjectivity—not in any more authentic or definitive sense, to be sure, but undoubtedly in a more functional one. He rebuilds his world,

> not more splendid, it is true, but at least so that he can once more live in it. He builds it up by the work of his delusions. The *delusion-formation, which we take to be a pathological product, is in reality an attempt at recovery, a process of reconstruction.* . . . We may conclude, then, that the process of repression proper consists in a detachment of the libido from people—and things—that were previously loved. It happens silently; we received no intelligence of it, *but can only infer it from subsequent events* [emphasis added]. What forces itself so noisily upon our attention is the process of recovery, which undoes the work of repression and brings back the libido again to the people it had abandoned. In paranoia, this process is carried out by the method of projection. It was incorrect of us to say that the perception which was suppressed internally was projected outwards; the truth is rather, as we now see, that what was abolished internally returns from without. (*FSA*, 193 / *FCH*, 173–75)

As Freud realized, the symptom cannot be discounted as the mere (albeit distorted) effect of an authentic (albeit absent) past—what we might call the "genealogical" and conspiratorial construction of the political unconscious—primarily because the symptom is itself fundamentally dynamic and productive. More crucial yet, with regard to its epistemological status, the symptom precedes both the interpretive efforts of psychoanalysis and the *archē* of an unconscious primary repression (*Urverdrängung*) that analysis subsequently hypostatizes as the original cause of that symptom. Hence, to argue that the subject's narrative practice is a metonymic displacement of a primordial, unconscious cause amounts to a hypothesis fundamentally triggered by the dynamic structure of the symptom itself. What Freud explores as the paranoiac's displaced representations and what the state's indicts as its treasonous other in 1794 are hypothetical entities whose existence—as a conspiratorial threat issuing from the past—effectively authorizes the interpretive curiosity and disciplinary authority of psychoanalysis and the law respectively. For it is only on the premise of a seamless temporal and causal trajectory leading from past repression to present distortion to future recovery that legal and psychoanalytic analysis can claim to adjudicate and so remedy that (allegedly misrecognized) past as the cause of an impending sociopolitical catastrophe.

What is systematically obscured by Enlightenment progression from an unconscious cause (feeling) to its effect—a symptomatic mode of representation—is the crucial fact that any consciousness of that cause, which is to say, the disciplinary knowledge of psychoanalysis, owes its epistemological authority to that original miscarriage. Yet while the latter is necessarily an inference drawn, something Freud's metapsychological writings of 1911–15 often admit, psychoanalysis *as a discipline* must treat the miscarriage of representation (i.e., repression) as a theoretical axiom. Put differently, what Freud sometimes calls "primary repression" (*Urverdrängung*) is not only the subject matter of psychoanalytic knowledge but also the limiting condition for psychoanalysis as a discipline. Freud's explication of the paranoiac's representations as an exaggerated structure of causal attributions can succeed only by reproducing, albeit in reverse order, the very explanatory mechanisms alleged to characterize the paranoiac himself. Where contradictory affect was projected into symptomatic external perceptions, the work of analysis purports to redress the effects of the operation of displacement itself. That is, it redirects the subject's articulate representations to the rightful authority of the unconscious whom they sought to evade. In a revealing turn of phrase, Freud concedes, however, that the process of repression proper consists in a detachment of the libido from people—and things—"we can only infer from subsequent events." The oblique institutional authority and totalizing interpretive procedures of Freudian psychoanalysis and Blackstone's vision of English law as imbued with timeless coherence thus operate on the same ideological axis. For both, the analyst who examines an autobiographical account of paranoia by a judge and the attorney general committed to the inferential reconstruction of a pervasive treasonous conspiracy, are themselves the *conscious* (though not self-conscious) effects of what post-Freudian theory understands by a "symptom." For however sincere and technically refined their interpretive pursuit of the symptom may be, their conscious practice always takes "after" the symptom (in the temporal and causal sense that the French captures as *depuis* and *selon*). The institutional and disciplinary consciousness of the symptom remains itself, at all times, an effect of the very symptom for which that consciousness seeks the interpretive cure. The disciplinary and cognitive authority of legal and psychoanalytic interpretation concerned with conspiracies of the unconscious or otherwise disenfranchised political agencies thus remains predicated on a precariously self-authorizing, inferential mode of reasoning. In a fundamental sense, both the patient's and the analyst's narrative practices are structurally and functionally cognate. Each agent's analytic efforts are stimulated by a quasi-axiomatic sense of distress at the phenomenal organization of a present replete with eccentric and antagonistic empirical determinants, a present that both wish to be unified and noncontradictory. Inasmuch as the antagonistic structure of the present forecasts the future as irreducibly contingent and uncontrollable by *any one* ideological consensus, it is traumatic, unthinkable, except insofar as its heterogeneous determinants can be represented as the symptoms or distorted effects of an as yet undisclosed causality. Schreber, Eyre, Scott, and to a significant extent even Freud thus shaped the institutional and disciplinary structure of legal and psychoanalytic interpretation precisely so as to secure their intrinsically unprovable hypothesis of a conspiratorial agency located in a terminally inscrutable past.

The promise of these disciplines to salvage an embattled present from the past's subterranean conspiratorial stranglehold points to their grounding Enlightenment utopia of realizing a wholly determinate, noncontingent future.[45] To qualify or disqualify *any* representation as pathogenic thus constitutes an irremediably contingent event, a grasping for ideological hegemony whose contingent and self-privileging nature no amount of scientific method and no legal rationale can ever overcome. Indeed, such contingency is certain to infect these sciences themselves, for it was an attempt to stave off the consciousness of an inescapably open and contingent future that produced these sciences in the first place. What appeared to be a symptom of a psychopathological affliction clinically referred to as *dementia paranoides* thus turns out to be a quasi-Blakean "contrary" to the self-confirming conceptual logic of health and disease. The symptom is its own cure and, as such, equally resists interpretive delimitation as a wholly irrational suffering or as a readily curable ailment. This situation is roughly consistent with the postmodern notion of an irremediably scrambled causality elaborated by Slavoj Žižek. Under such circumstances it becomes imperative that we abandon the cause-effect model as a valid explanatory mechanism for the adjudication of either psychoanalytic symptoms or legal evidence. For the romance of recovery—taking "recovery" here in the double sense of archeological technique and spiritual restoration—that motivates and structures the practices of analyst and prosecutor alike was itself produced by their peremptory or (dare we retain the word) paranoid reading of their respective worlds as a fundamentally antagonistic environment, fraught with hypercharged details that defy mastery unless they can all be referred back to the plenitude of an originary (if shrewdly concealed) plot. To move beyond this closed vision requires that one abandon the metonymic paradigm of *Anlehnung*, the presupposition of a seamless causal link between the unconscious and its projections. The result is a fundamentally open economy of interpretation where all we can (and should) hope for is to relate one order of effects to another, and where symptom and signifier remain forever interchangeable and equivalent terms.

Overall, then, the 1794 trials chart the rapid ascendancy of speculative, theoretical forms of explanation as a social and political practice in its own right. This development hastened the demise of empiricist theories of perception and in their place left the rising disciplines of legal, political, and esthetic representation to contend for the interpretive monopoly on the real. Hence Burke, Eyre, and Scott show a marked preference for cultivating the rhetorical coherence of their narrative presentation rather than relying on the force of material evidence. Holistic, autonomous, and richly performative, narrative allows for the construction of essentially irrefutable worlds bounded by a chain of circumstances where each new piece of discrete evidence is instantly confirmed by the cumulative authority of the narrative already in place and immediately proceeds to further corroborate the holistic vision spun by that very narrative. The precarious evidentiary logic that supports the legal reasoning on the statute of high treason and is at the very heart of Burke's passionate plea for evidentiary license (see the epigraph to this chapter) thus reflects a capacious epistemological transformation. As the conceptual equivalent of the Napoleonic bon mot "Je suis mon ancêtre,"[46] so to speak, theory has inaugurated itself as an authority that lives on the boldness of its imaginings, a mode of discursive production that is at once self-launching, self-confirming, and intrinsically narrative in kind. It is also preemptively suspicious of any future threat to its claims for a priori autonomy—so much so that it has, in effect, made it its business to head off or prepossess such potential encroachments by pathologizing the real in the forms of legal, epistemological, and psychoanalytic suspicions. As the romantic texts and contexts examined here suggest, the only discourse to *defend* us against the traumatic recognition of an irreducibly contingent future is that of a "pure" theory unrelentingly enacting the dream of our having been all along awake, lucid, and reflexive. As Novalis was to put it so succinctly: "We are close to awakening when we dream that we are dreaming" (1978, 2: 232).

Part II / Lyric Awakenings

Trauma

CHAPTER FOUR

"Long before the time of which I speak"

Traumatic History and Lyric Awakenings, 1800–1815

> I look into past times as prophets look
> Into futurity, a [?Scroll] of life runs back
> Into dead years, the poetry of thoughts,
> The lyric Spirit of philosophy,
> Leads me through moods of sadness and delight.
>
> — WORDSWORTH, DC MS. 30

> ". . . every history [must] begin with awakening; in fact, it should treat of nothing else."
>
> — WALTER BENJAMIN, *The Arcades Project, trans.* HOWARD EILAND AND KEVIN MCLAUGHLIN

> Would this situation be conceivable: someone remembers for the first time in his life and says "Yes, now I know what 'remembering' is, what it *feels like* to remember."—How does he know that this feeling is 'remembering'? Compare: "Yes, now I know what 'tingling' is." (He has perhaps had an electric shock for the first time.)—Does he know that it is memory because it is caused by something past? And how does he know what the past is? Man learns the concept of the past by remembering.
>
> And how will he know again in the future what remembering feels like?
>
> (On the other hand one might, perhaps, speak of a feeling "Long, long ago," for there is a tone, a gesture, all of which go with certain narratives of past times.)
>
> — LUDWIG WITTGENSTEIN, *Philosophical Investigations,* TRANS. G. E. M. ANSCOMBE

The following chapter turns a new page in this book's attempt at redrawing the extended, insecure borderline between literary, historical, and psychoanalytic modes of explanation. With the emphasis being on theoretical comprehension—which ought to include articulating the limits of theory vis-à-vis the practice of interpretation—the following readings of English and German romantic lyric poetry do not seek to import psychoanalytic theory into literary texts. Neither do I wish to rehearse the typological story of how Western literature supposedly scattered the seeds for the eventual rise of psychoanalysis, only to have the latter impose its interpretive method on the literary tradition itself. As has often been noted, the circular epistemology of psychoanalytic reading only tends to undermine the authority of the very discipline that sponsors the reader's interpretive activity. At the same time, Freud's basic psychoanalytic conceptions are far too rich in their speculative potential to be dismissed along with the mostly discredited models for their "application." In what follows, then, I examine a process of constructing knowledge that is primarily located in the poetic genre of the ballad, a genre particularly remarkable for the way in which its interpretive effects of a momentous awakening foreshadow the same, crucial figure in psychoanalysis. Again, the aim is to show why certain kinds of knowledge refuse to be embodied in discursive, propositional statements and, instead, demand the circuitous form of the ballad and its open-ended economy of reading.

The ballad form typically revolves around a moment of interpretive crisis, which, however local, incidental, or even apocryphal, may be considered as a symptom of deep-seated historical antagonisms.[1] In Wordsworth's *Lyrical Ballads*, for example, tensions at the level of economic and regional history are repeatedly reproduced as the formal enigma of a lyric voice bordering on the unintelligible. As the last poem in the 1800 edition of *Lyrical Ballads*, however, "Michael" struggles and ultimately breaks with the constraints that the genre imposed on Wordsworth. If earlier ballads seem exemplary in their allegiance to anonymous, incidental folk knowledge, their contingent and ephemeral world ultimately interferes with Wordsworth's professional ambitions. Exasperated and positively stimulated into action by Coleridge's failure to complete "Christabel"—which had been slated to be the closing piece in the 1800 *Lyrical Ballads*—Wordsworth conceives of and identifies "Michael" as "A Pastoral Poem."[2] More than most poems in that collection, "Michael" appears as a formal hybrid, combining elements of the credal poetry deriving from a particular strain of the ballad with those of pastoral and elegiac writing. Formally, "Michael" completes and reflexively sublates (in the Hegelian sense) the project of *Lyrical Ballads.* For it takes as its proper object the limitations of the ballad form by dramatizing, at the level of action, its protagonist's precarious transition from the self-enclosed world of local (balladic) knowledge into the unbounded world of agrarian capitalism and its myriad connections with urban commerce and speculation. As we shall see, the historical valence and the limitations of the ballad genre are themselves at the very heart of the story told by Wordsworth's "Michael." Rather than constituting an evasion of history—which new historicism has rather schematically construed as an evasion of referentiality—the symbolic overdetermination at work *in* "Michael" and the explicit generic marking *of* "Michael" as "A Pastoral Poem" strongly suggest that some kind of awakening is imminent.[3] In their own ways, both the author of *Lyrical Ballads* and his protagonist are about to awaken from the rhetorical and epistemological limitations of the ballad genre. At an authorial and professional level, Wordsworth is about to reflect (and thereby transcend) the apparent incommensurability of the ballad genre with his literary and cultural ambitions as these take shape around 1800. Simultaneously, his characters appear increasingly restless (e.g., Leonard in "The Brothers") within the manifestly closed system of social cognition associated with the ballad (e.g., "low and rustic life," "slow feelings," and "simple and unelaborated expressions"). Subjectivity in these late ballads is no longer embedded *in* and identified with its rustic setting; rather it is *haunted* by the incipient recognition of this world as palpably anachronistic ("Simon Lee" and "Hart-Leap Well") and suffused with disquieting markers of sexual guilt and death (Lucy and Matthew poems).

It is in this context that I invoke Freud's conception of "trauma," whose distinctive symptomatic feature of "repetition compulsion" is said to respond to a past so catastrophic at the time of its original occurrence as to have precluded its conscious assimilation by the subject. As a result, an enigmatic past continues to trace the conscious history of its subject with an oblique insistence for which "haunting" seems just the right word. Subjected thus to an inscrutable (because never consciously experienced) causality, the subject is obliged, in Freud's words, "to *repeat* the . . . material as a contemporary experience instead of . . . *remembering* it as something belonging to the past," and he or she typically does so with "unwished-for exactitude" (1920, 18). As Cathy Caruth has recently argued, Freud's theory of trauma allows us "to recognize the possibility of a history that is no longer straightforwardly referential (that is, no longer based on simple models of experience and reference)"; the formal eloquence of literature may itself be taken as a "parable of trauma" and, indeed, as "a parable of psychoanalytic theory itself as it listens to a voice that it cannot fully know but to which it nonetheless bears witness" (Caruth 1996, 11, 9). Caruth's argument amounts to a new prescription for close, scrupulous reading of the literary text, and for an insistent listening to literature's characteristic tonal mix of vocal urgency and textual reticence, a dynamic of which the hybrid genre of the ballad is a particularly striking manifestation. I concur that to approach the text as "an address that remains enigmatic yet demands a listening and a response" may indeed allow "*history* . . . [to] arise where *immediate understanding* may not" (ibid., 11; emphasis in original). Like Freud's controversial account of the origin of Judaism and a distinct community of the Jewish people—for which his conception of trauma is marshaled as an analogy—Wordsworth's "Michael" remembers the disintegration of a seemingly timeless familial, economic, and spiritual order. Its story tells of the protagonist's "traumatic departure" (ibid., 15) from his phantasmagorical order of time and place. Exodus here is realized as a narrative of progressive disillusionment that continues to point back at an instance of catastrophic *méconnaissance* in the protagonist's past. As will be seen, the world of "Michael" is the kind of place where "history can be grasped only in the very inaccessibility of its occurrence" (ibid., 18).

Like his yet humbler literary and social counterpart in the 1798 *Lyrical Ballads,* Simon Lee, Wordsworth's Michael is a survivor; and like the stubborn huntsman, Michael is presented in such a way as to make us doubt that he ever fully comprehends the "accident" that he has survived. Indeed, it is only with considerable unease that we embark on our analytic quest for a knowledge that we suspect has continued to elude Wordsworth's archetypal protagonist. For right from its beginning, the poem stages our belated initiation into Michael's world with such scriptural concision as to make us shrink from obtruding with the discursive, secular agenda of "critical" reading. To persist, we feel, is to perpetrate an almost sacrilegious disturbance of the past. For the symbolic order of this "history / Homely and rude" (line 35) seems to conspire against all analytic interest and against the potential disruption of a tacit covenant between text and reader. The story of Michael, who survives the traumatic disintegration of a world of which he believed himself to be a permanent inhabitant, is designed to compel and chasten us. It does so by hinting, subtly yet persistently, at a profound connection between the psychological enigma of survival and the ethical burden of remembering. Clearly, readers are invited to premise their critical response to "Michael" on the terms so insistently furnished by the poem itself: its biblical imagery, the rhetoric of intergenerational covenant, and the opposition between country and city—itself embedded in what Geoffrey Hartman has called "an immemorial covenant between man and the land" (Hartman 1971, 265). Hartman was also among the first to view the poem's rustic idyll as besieged by the growing forces of industrialization, though he preferred to consign that threat to the periphery of the poem's ostensibly autonomous affective order. For him "Michael" is "Pastoral in the most genuine sense," a text whose "care of nature" and "of the human" has only been "heightened by the spirit of the time" (262).

More recent historicist criticism has questioned what Hartman, with critical empathy, identifies as the poem's opening mandate to the reader: namely, to separate the wheat from the chaff by discriminating sharply between spiritual and economic, familial and social, past and present matter: in short, to divide the essential (human) from the contingent (historical).[4] Where Hartman appraises Wordsworthian symbolism as the embodiment of an inalienable spiritual "knowledge" (in ways that deconstructive readings a decade later were no longer prepared to), the first exponents of a revived romantic historicism have tended to view aesthetic form as the possibly unconscious evasion of a latent social knowledge. To some extent my reading of "Michael" is aimed at a (dialectical) reconciliation of these views. As I mean to argue, what we typically subsume under the category of aesthetic form cannot but *produce* knowledge, though that knowledge (as Freud was to observe) may indeed be achieved only by the subject's persistent attempts to evade it or, at least, to evade being dominated by it. The particular narrative and symbolic organization that gives a poem like "Michael" its unmistakable character—its "form"—may thus be understood to break down a traumatic knowledge that not merely slumbers beneath the symbolic surface of Wordsworthian narrative but also conditioned the text's formal production and eventual reception. Such knowledge, at once overwhelming and inescapable, is processed at several levels in the poem, ranging from the characterization of Michael himself to the text's symbolic predetermination of the reader's performance. In what, we ask, does this knowledge consist, and why must the poem stage its experience as a dialectical process in which the formal defenses against the knowledge in question effectively turn out to be the instruments for its critical realization?

Just when the Wordsworthian still life of agrarian self-sufficiency seems complete—a pastel of "endless industry" and familial bliss realized in a cottage that "as it chanc'd . . . on rising ground / Stood single"—the balance suddenly tilts:

> Long before the time
> Of which I speak, the Shepherd had been bound
> In surety for his Brother's Son, a man

Of an industrious life and ample means,
But unforeseen misfortunes suddenly
Had press'd upon him, and old Michael now
Was summon'd to discharge the forfeiture,
A grievous penalty, but little less
Than half his substance. (WORDSWORTH 1992a, 260, LINES 219–27)

The shock of these disclosures is about more than economic contingencies; for Michael's seemingly incidental financial reversals also impress on us how the "hidden valley" (line 8) with its archetypal streams, its rocks and "common air" (line 66) is affiliated with the intricate and hazardous urban world of manufacture, trade, and credit-based speculation. Rather than rounding off the scene of pastoral containment with a tribute to the values of consanguinity and kinship loyalties, the family connections so belatedly and abruptly introduced into the narrative effectively reposition Michael as an unwitting participant in a historically distinctive phase of England's evolving political economy.

This recognition, at once inescapable and unbearable for Michael, warrants more precise elaboration. To begin with, Michael's embrace of agrarian self-sufficiency runs counter to the declining share of agriculture within Britain's overall national economy. As Eric Hobsbawm remarks, by 1800, agriculture "occupied no more than a third of the population and provided about the same fraction of the national income." At the same time, Michael's vision of permanent independence as a freeholder highlights the amphiboly of the terms "soil" and "landed interest" in late-eighteenth-century Britain. For another reason for the "prominence of agriculture was that the 'landed interest' dominated British politics and social life. To belong to the upper classes meant to own an estate and a 'seat.'"[5] In Wordsworth's pastoral, Michael's dominant fantasy of landownership seems to rest on the reverse conclusion, namely, that to own land will elevate one's social position. At the same time, Michael's tenacious commitment to this fantasy of landownership and permanent social accreditation as a freeholder also echoes a siege mentality that was beginning to spread among the agrarian producers toward the end of the century. For by then agricultural improvements were rapidly expanding productivity and thus squeezing the profits of an excessively large agrarian sector. Seen against the background of a "growing surplus of the rural poor," Wordsworth's Michael, though sensible of changes wrought in the local economy, remains unable to conceptualize their macroeconomic causes. Many of the rural poor, Michael being quite typical in this respect, thus proved "slow to abandon the life of their ancestors, the life ordained by God and fate, the only life traditional communities know or can conceive."[6]

Michael suddenly experiences the complex effects of what Adam Smith had already analyzed as a deep-structural process, "a revolution of the greatest importance to the public happiness" that was gradually brought about by "the silent and insensible operation of . . . commerce and manufactures" (1976 [1776] [vol. 1, bk. 3, chap. 4], 440). This revolution not only accounts for the gradual decline in feudal landownership and the simultaneous transmutation of landed wealth into mobile capital. It also ensured that an attachment to the older, feudal notions of inalienable property relations—underwritten not by distant markets but by consanguinity, "connections," and local knowledge—would sooner or later become a costly illusion. Smith's analyses deserve close attention, for they suggest that effective management of small estates, a skill so abundantly displayed by the industrious Michael, is also an economically self-defeating proposition: "A small proprietor . . . who knows every part of his little territory, who views it with the affection which property, especially small property, naturally inspires, and who upon that account takes pleasure not only in cultivating but in adorning it, is generally of all improvers the most industrious, the most intelligent, and the most successful." At the same time, however, "the law of primogeniture, and perpetuities of different kinds" remain a powerful reality. Consequently, Smith concludes, there is at any given point in time only a very limited quantity of land available for acquisition, "so that what is sold always sells at a monopoly price. The rent never pays the interest of the purchase-money, and is besides burdened with repairs and other occasional charges." In characteristically dispassionate language, Smith thus concludes that "to purchase land is everywhere in Europe a most unprofitable employment of small capital" (ibid., 441) and, even where it does not lead to ruin, will forever consign its proprietor to economic and social marginality. A writer for the *Commercial and Agricultural Magazine* put the case rather more bluntly: "A wicked, cross-grained, petty farmer is like the sow in his yard, almost an insulated individual, who has no communication with, and therefore, no reverence for the opinion of the world."[7] Put in more genteel terms, this dismal portrait has been echoed by many contemporary historians. Remarking on the declining price of basic food costs that had resulted from increased agricultural productivity, Roy Porter sees such developments as a major factor in the growing rates of bankruptcy experienced by families that had farmed their lands for generations. His characterization of the pressures felt by late-eighteenth-century small farmers could well serve as a plot summary for Wordsworth's "Michael." "Minor gentry and freeholders unable to diversify felt the pinch most. Many farmers went out of business, otherwise got into debt . . . rents fell into arrears, or had to be lowered, some farms became tenantless, and incomes in the landed sector stagnated or dropped" (Porter, 203–4).

By 1800, the cult of "improvement" had largely faded, but Smith's 1776 analyses of small freeholders' habitual overestimating of the value of landed property (and so subscribing to an illusion bound to undermine their economic base) remained valid. The "distressful tidings" that suddenly reach Michael's ear cannot, then, be written off as mere contingencies. Rather, they confront Michael with the traumatic recognition that his lifelong pursuit of agrarian self-sufficiency has, literally, been a bad investment of his only capital—many decades of arduous physical labor.[8] At the same time, the deceptive simplicity of a life spent plowing patrimonial fields and shearing flocks of sheep under the "Clipping Tree" has effectively prevented Michael from recognizing that, although he has sought to fortify his life against the impingements of urban commerce and speculation by his labor, he has involved himself in much larger and infinitely more complex economic realities. Michael's life illustrates what Pierre Bourdieu calls the "homogeneity of habitus," an "immanent law, *lex insita,* laid down in each agent by his earliest upbringing, which is the precondition . . . for the co-ordination of practices" (Bourdieu 80–81). Like the Lacanian unconscious, the "objective intention" of such a habitus resembles the structure of a complex language that conditions the "actions," "works," and "conscious intentions" (ibid., 79) of individuals and, for that very reason, falls outside the range of subjective understanding. Consequently, Bourdieu insists, one must safeguard against "all forms of the occasionalist illusion which consists in directly relating practices to properties inscribed in [a given] situation." In truth, "interpersonal relations are never, except in appearance, *individual-to-individual* relationships and . . . the truth of the interaction is never entirely contained in the interaction" (ibid., 81). The latter point is especially germane to Wordsworth's poem. For in choosing to underwrite his nephew's economic ventures in the city, Michael characteristically and dangerously confuses familial and economic motives by assisting the extended family with a show of financial support. What may have been a gesture of loyalty, however, also amounts, however unwittingly, to a risky investment of the very returns yielded by decades of unalienated labor. As Michael now finds, the risk extends all the way to his very "substance."

With the day of Luke's departure drawing near, Michael offers his son a revealing account of his long and inconclusive march to economic independence:

> 'tis a long time to look back, my Son,
> And see so little gain from sixty years.
> These fields were burthen'd when they came to me,
> 'Till I was forty years of age, not more
> Than half of my inheritance was mine.
> I toil'd and toil'd; God bless'd me in my work
> And 'till these three weeks past the land was free.
>
> (WORDSWORTH 1992a, 265, LINES 382–88)

Even now, that is, Michael cannot acknowledge that the land was only ever "free" in a highly conditional sense. Nor does he seem fully conscious of the fact that the imperiled status of "half his substance" is the result of his own vicarious involvement in a market economy whose financial logic continues to elude him. This structural illusion or "blind love" (line 78) at the heart of Michael's conception of property, and his consequent incapacity to recognize that his entire adult life has been predicated on that very illusion, leads to a series of peculiar decisions that effectively repeat the original *méconnaissance.*[9] Begotten late and, it seems, groomed strictly for the role of the heir to whom Michael could bequeath his landed property, Luke constitutes in his father's imaginary a repetition of his own life: "from the Boy there came / Feelings and emanations / . . . / that the Old Man's Heart seem'd born again" (lines 210–14).

Now, following the discovery of his land's impending seizure by distant creditors—and, along with it, the traumatic shock of having to recognize his entire economic and familial history as a prolonged illusion—Michael chooses to put up Luke as collateral for what was to be his landed inheritance. In so entrusting his son to yet "another kinsman" in the city—who once again is presumed to be "a prosperous man / Thriving in trade" (lines 259–60)—Michael uncannily repeats the very act that had led to his present insolvency. Lest we miss the point, Wordsworth interpolates Isabel's daydream of one Richard Bateman, who "with a Basket on his arm" was sent to London and, having been successfully apprenticed, grew "wondrous rich" and returned to adorn the chapel of his birthplace with "marble" floors (lines 266–80). Isabel's generic reverie ("These thoughts and many others of like sort / Pass'd quickly through the mind of Isabel" [lines 281–82]), so evocative of connections between capitalism and romance, only stages at a more transparent level what, at bottom, are also Michael's defensive illusions. The circular pattern continues as Michael, prior to Luke's departure, rededicates himself to initiating his son into a life that will essentially repeat Michael's own, as well as the lives of his ancestors: "I wish'd that thou should'st live the life they liv'd," he tells Luke, and he affirms the intergenerational covenant by noting that "herein / I but repay a gift which I myself / Receiv'd at others' hands" (lines 381, 372–74).

Finally, there is the "Sheep-fold" itself, so programmatically hailed as "An emblem of the life thy Fathers liv'd," as "anchor" and "shield," a wall devised both to contain the property within and to keep at bay the entropic world without. Indeed, the sheepfold is at once the very heart of Michael's illusion *and* the object that will precipitate his awakening to the illusory character of his economic and familial "habitus." For as an attempt at enclosure, the wall intimates the land's implicit status as a form of capital rather than as inalienable "soil." At the same time, Michael's preoccupation with enclosing his patrimonial field constitutes the objective expression of a deeply personal and genealogical covenant between himself, his son, and what he considers to be an immutable nature. The ambivalent status of the sheepfold—at once material evidence of the encroaching capitalist forms of agrarian production and symbolic evidence of an anti-modern, defensive mode of being—exemplifies what Anthony Giddens has described as the modern disjunction of space and place:

> In pre-modern societies, space and place largely coincide, since the spatial dimensions of social life are, for most of the population, and in most respects, dominated by "presence"—by localised activities. . . . The advent of modernity increasingly tears space away from place by fostering relations between "absent" others, locationally distant from any given situation of face-to-face interaction. In conditions of modernity, place becomes increasingly *phantasmagorical:* that is to say, locales are thoroughly penetrated by and shaped in terms of social influences quite distant from them. What structures the locale is not simply that which is present on the scene; the "visible form" of the locale conceals the distanciated relations which determine its nature. (Giddens, 18–19)

Like all *phantasmata,* however, the sheepfold—as well as the elaborate archetypal world of Michael's household and the "hidden valley" to which it stands in synecdochic relation—constitutes no mere illusion. For even as it throws into relief Michael's devotion to labor and an intergenerational covenant, the sheepfold also facilitates the reader's gradual awakening to the protagonist's inescapable modernity. For as the narrative progresses, readers become more acutely conscious of the disjunction of space from place described by Giddens. Rather than functioning as an intact symbol, that is, the sheepfold progressively unveils and so demystifies its architect's overinvestment in a homespun, defensive symbolism. Furthermore, when considered as the summa of the entire collection of *Lyrical Ballads,* the crisis of the sheepfold—namely, that soil and land no longer coincide with the space in which property relations constitute themselves—also throws into relief the preceding ballads' apparent overinvestment in oral and folk culture. In short, the crisis of Michael the protagonist is also expressive of limitations intrinsic to the ballad genre and, hence, of the relative modernity of the romantic lyric.[10]

On the face of it, however, enclosing the sheepfold appears both to sustain and fortify Michael against the calamitous recognition of his present situation. Yet what seems a constructive type of labor gradually discloses a compensatory, defensive reaction on Michael's part. We recall Freud's claim that "attempts to bring the trauma into operation once again—that is, to remember the forgotten experience or, better still, to make it real, to experience a repetition of it anew, or . . . to revive it in an analogous relationship" are one of the positive effects of traumas. Such efforts, Freud suggests, can be summarized "under the name of 'fixations' to the trauma" (1964, 75). Like the root of a dead tree in "Simon Lee" (itself the double of Simon's body, "dwindled and awry" and perched "upon ankles swoln and thick"), the forever incomplete sheepfold negotiates for its architect what Freud was to call "the complete devastation or fragmentation of [his] ego" (ibid., 78). In its permanent incompleteness, the sheepfold also recalls Proust's observation that the past "is somewhere beyond the reach of the intellect, and unmistakably present in some material object (or in the sensation which such an object arouses in us)."[11] Taken as an object of abortive labor and contingent perception, that is, the sheepfold embodies Michael's failure to recognize the ideals of permanent ownership and agrarian independence as illusory and to acknowledge that their collapse was the result of his own actions rather than of contingent circumstance.

Foremost among these actions ranks the curious *Fort! Da!* game that Michael is playing with his son. Thus we find him affirming the inescapable affective bond that "will be between us" even as he prepares to invest the son in an alien and, to judge by the evidence, dangerous environment. Given the distress that his economic reversals have already brought him, Michael's decision to repeat this ill-fated speculative act seems at the very least perplexing. Freud was similarly puzzled to observe in a number of cases a "repetition compulsion" (*Wiederholungszwang*) operating in apparent contradiction of his earlier postulate of the "pleasure principle" as the supreme regulative of all psychic activity. Freud specifically connected the subject's compulsive reenactment of a profoundly disturbing scenario to case histories where it was known that the patients had previously undergone a terrifying experience, a "trauma." As Cathy Caruth notes, the modern usage of that term shifts emphasis away from its ancient physiological meaning and toward a notion of trauma as a "wound of the mind," a "breach in the mind's experience of time, self, and the world." As such, traumatic experience constitutes not "a simple and healable event, but rather an event that . . . is experienced too soon, too unexpectedly, to be fully known and is therefore not available to consciousness until it imposes itself again, repeatedly, in the nightmares and repetitive actions of the survivor. . . . [T]rauma is not locatable in the simple violent or original event in an individual's past, but rather in the way that its very unassimilated nature—the way it was precisely *not known* in the first instance—returns to haunt the survivor later on" (Caruth 1996, 4).

This initial characterization of the concept also hints at a deeper connection between trauma as an inassimilable experience of disintegration (both of the ordered world without and, ultimately, of mind itself) and neo-Marxism's influential conception of history "as an absent cause [that] is inaccessible to us except in textual form," as Fredric Jameson puts it.[12] History thus manifests itself, not only affectively but also cognitively, as a complex aggregation of effects that both circumscribe and constrict the subject. In just that sense, Freud's theory of trauma also develops an axiomatically suspicious view of the conscious subject, whose symbolic actions Freud tends to read as the belated, symptomatic reverberations—manifest at the level of conscious *practice*—of a past disturbance that went unwitnessed at the time.[13] What alerts us to the possibility of a traumatic past, in other words, is not the subject's avowed (or even concealed) state of mind but his actions. Beginning with *Beyond the Pleasure Principle* (1920), Freud thus comes to view the conscious ego as the belated structural echo of an antecedent rupture within the subject's psyche. In a reflection subsequently extended by Lacan, the Freudian ego is thus defined as the producer of symbols, indeed, an entire symbolic order designed to shield its future from terrors (*Schrecken*) that continue to issue from a past that has never been consciously experienced or worked through. Extending his earlier topological conception of mind as a multilayered construct, Freud thus insists that consciousness ought to be understood as an epiphenomenon of "memory-traces" deposited elsewhere in the mind. As he remarks, "such memory-traces . . . have nothing to do with the fact of becoming conscious; indeed they are often most powerful and most enduring when the process which left them behind was one which never entered consciousness. . . . We lay down the proposition that *consciousness arises instead of a memory-trace*" (1955, 25). Angelika Rauch sees Freud's psychoanalytic model closely entwined with the concept of tradition, a view that indirectly foreshadows the present thesis about an incipient conservative strain within European romanticism—fixated on the mythic powers of tradition and advanced as a "renewal" of poetry as secular scripture—and the traumatic origin of that cultural and aesthetic development. Rauch's critical summation of Freud's account bears quoting in full:

> In the psychoanalytic model, the mark of a primary event or experience imprints itself in the individual's psyche, a process that, as stated, will never become conscious in itself. This impression leaves a memory trace (*Gedächtnisspur*) behind. As it interacts with other such traces of impressions, it forms the matrix for (belated) significant experiences which shape the individual's history. Resembling an unconscious text, these marks effect future perceptions of events or experiences in the sense that by being recalled they prefigure their interpretation and significance. Since the event that caused the impression will never become conscious, it can only be inferred or posited in the analysis of a later element of significance. Even though the spatio-temporal constituents of the second event are different from the first, the event in the subject's perception is a repetition of the first. Repetition does not suggest a duplication of the experience, for the temporal forward displacement of a primary event has changed the latter's character and significance over time, adapting it to the life-history and circumstances of the subject. The difference here results from the event's displacement which shifts the assumed originary event into different contexts and onto different levels of signification. This difference in repetition marks the difference between an unconscious structure of significance, based on the unconscious capacity of memory, and conscious understanding in the form of perceivable and interpretable signs. (Rauch 2000, 43)

In speaking of a "difference" between unconsciously assimilated memories and the conscious, interpretive relation to signs whose significance is tacitly shaped and enriched by the former, it is important to bear in mind that that difference itself can never become an object of knowledge proper; rather, it circumscribes the agency of conscious knowledge like the "mood" discussed earlier. Beginning with Kant and Novalis, aesthetic form furnishes the virtual means whereby theory can differentiate between the unconscious hieroglyphic order of the "event" and its belated, reflexive articulation by and for consciousness.

To begin with, consciousness is determined by its supplemental relation to a traumatic past for which it has unwittingly substituted the ultimately specious integrity of the ego—here variously incarnated as husband, father, freeholder, and representative of a distinctly Wordsworthian aesthetic. Yet such a substitution proves taxing, precarious, and forever incomplete, as evidenced by the poem's curious vacillation between a narrative and a sententious style, and between an event-driven and a didactic logic of production. At once pointedly humble and ambitiously symbolic, the style of "Michael" attains its peculiar cohesion and distinctiveness less by aesthetic design than by epistemological default. For Wordsworth's idiom can be understood as the protagonist's (and perhaps also the speaker's) expressive defense against the insistent claims of a history that, once admitted, would inexorably lead to the unraveling of their conscious, ordered existence in the present. Perhaps it is the fear of such discomposure that accounts for the curiously elaborate, at times mannered, quality of Michael's and the narrator's language. Yet because of its intrinsic overdetermination, the poem's style also exhibits a tendency toward disintegration, thereby allowing memory traces of a traumatic past to surface that the conscious subject's "endless [symbolic] industry" had struggled to keep at bay. Two instances of such a rupture in the fabric of Michael's affective and cognitive illusions will help illustrate my point. Both involve quasi-aphasic tremors disrupting his speech, and both occur as Michael struggles to articulate—first to Isabel and then to Luke—a precise rationale for his decision to substitute his son for the land, a sacrifice by proxy, as it were:

> As soon as he had gather'd so much strength
> That he could look his trouble in the face,
> It seem'd that his sole refuge was to sell
> A portion of his patrimonial fields.

Such was his first resolve; *he thought again,*
And his heart failed him. "Isabel," said he,
Two evenings after he had heard the news,
"I have been toiling more than seventy years,
And in the open sunshine of God's love
Have we all lived; yet if these fields of ours
Should pass into a Stranger's hand, I think
That I could not lie quiet in my grave.
Our lot is a hard lot; the sun itself
Has scarcely been more diligent than I,
And I have lived to be a fool at last
To my own family. An evil man
That was, and made an evil choice, if he
Were false to us; and if he were not false,
There are ten thousand to whom loss like this
Had been no sorrow. I forgive him—*but*
'Twere better to be dumb than to talk thus.
When I began, my purpose was to speak
Of remedies . . .

(WORDSWORTH 1992a, LINES 231–53; EMPHASIS ADDED)

The second passage occurs later, as Michael seeks to reinforce the triangular covenant between Luke, the land, and himself. The archetypal nature of the action (laying a stone on the sheepfold) here tends to distract from Michael's curiously faltering speech on this crucial occasion:

But lay one stone,
Here lay it for me, Luke, with thine own hands.
I for the purpose brought thee to this place.
Nay, Boy, be of good hope:—we both may live
To see a better day: at eighty four
I still am strong and stout,—do thy part,
I will do mine.—*I will begin again*
With many tasks that were resigned to thee,
Up to the heights and in among the storms
Will I without thee go again, and do
All works which I was wont to do alone,
Before I knew thy face—Heaven bless thee, Boy,

Thy heart these two weeks has been beating fast
With many hopes—it should be so—yes—yes—
I knew that thou could'st never have a wish
To leave me, Luke,—thou hast been bound to me
Only by links of love, when thou art gone
What will be left to us!—*But I forget*
My purposes. Lay now the corner stone . . .
(WORDSWORTH 1992a, 265–66, LINES 396–414; EMPHASIS ADDED)

The repeated breakdown of Michael's speech—precisely when he struggles to trace the genesis of his problems, articulate a solution, and prognosticate a future recovery—marks a surreptitious awakening of sorts. As we learn how Michael "thought again," a lacuna opens between his premeditated "purposes" and the contingent drift of his actual locutions. Pondering the elusive causes of his dilemma, Michael slowly realizes that such misfortune can no longer be attributed to a single human agency ("an evil man"). At the same time, Wordsworth understandably presents his protagonist as someone unacquainted with the theories and vocabulary required for a full analysis of the economic circumstances in which he is presently caught. The seemingly timeless moral and physical strength of this quintessentially Wordsworthian freeholder—labor, frugality, sensitivity to local conditions, and so on—no longer guarantees economic and familial stability. Suspended over the void that separates intention from outcome, virtue from reward, and cause from effect, life must be sustained by "remedies" (line 249) where timely analysis and logical anticipation have manifestly collapsed.

Still, Michael's pledge to Luke that he "will begin again" only deepens our suspicion that his proposed "remedies" will prove futile. For by trading the son for the land and pledging to rededicate himself to tasks that had already been "resigned" to Luke, Michael—whose economics oddly resemble the visionary pursuits of the French physiocrats—acts on an inherently utopian desire: to reverse the direction of historical time.[14] Besides exposing the anti-modern illusions at the heart of his quest for absolute economic self-sufficiency, Michael's affirmations also raise serious questions about what to make of the interpretation of "Michael" proffered by Wordsworth himself in a letter to Charles James Fox in 1801, in which he appears to reproduce Michael's ethos of preservation and recovery, hailing the economic and domestic arrangements of the "statesmen" in the north of England as the ideal antidote for an increasingly compromised national "spirit."[15] We do not know, of course, whether Wordsworth was merely conjuring up a scenario that he expected to appeal to Fox or whether he was himself unequivocally committed to such a view. Still, when considered as an independent text, his epistolary vision of a pastoral, even nostalgic self-containment on which Fox ought to predicate his reading of "Michael" effectively mirrors the illusions of the poem's eponymous hero.

To return to Michael's speech, we note how in the very act of declaring his intentions to Luke, his locution falters as it advances toward its core implication: namely, that Luke's familial and economic status, indeed, his very life, be interchangeable with that of his father. Michael's own diction, however, already betrays the ambivalence that tends to emerge in wishes once they have been cast in determinate rhetorical form. All that Michael ever knows of Luke is his "face." The trope disconcerts, for it alerts us to the possibility that the encounter of father and son—in analogy to the earlier "face to face" (line 5) of poet and landscape, reader and text—may prove an irremediably opaque event, no more than two ships passing in the night. Moreover, Luke, we learn, when he "had reach'd / The public way . . . put on a bold face" (lines 436–37), a harbinger of disasters to come that further stresses the inscrutability of the "face." No wonder, then, that between voicing his "many hopes—it should be so—yes—yes—" and his fears ("thou could'st never have a wish / To leave me, Luke"), Michael should "forget [his] purposes." The uneasy, halting, and self-revising character of Michael's locutions bespeaks an incremental shift in his consciousness; we might say that he is in the process of becoming aware *of* the consciousness that *should have* been his. What Michael encounters, in other words, are memory traces whose previously unwitnessed and hence unreflected status enabled him to consciously persist in his utopian quest for an utterly independent and self-sufficient existence. It is a utopia as remote as the "hidden valley" in which the freeholder's dreams are said to have unfolded. Once these memory traces begin to assert themselves, as they invariably will, they gradually confront consciousness itself with the terrifying knowledge of its own precarious and partially inauthentic nature.

It is this very awakening that constitutes the larger subject matter of "Michael" and so defines the poem's place in a history that conceives romanticism as a distinct phase in the evolution of modernity. This awakening also identifies the dual status of trauma itself. For apart from the specific material recognition that precipitates Michael's awakening at this very moment, the freeholder's industrious, morally upright persona also helps Wordsworth to stage the modern middle-class subject's confrontation with emotion as the index of a previously unrecognized past that forms an ultimately inescapable component of his or her very being. In Martha Nussbaum's distinction, Michael's dual awakening involves both a recognition of Michael's "background emotion [that] is the wound" and the "situational emotion [of] the world's knife entering the wound" (75). Both as narrative and as an aesthetic artifact, Wordsworth's poem does not merely conform to but in significant measure anticipates Cathy Caruth's model of traumatic narrative as "a kind of double-telling, the oscillation between a *crisis of death* and the correlative *crisis of life:* between the story of the unbearable nature of an event and the story of the unbearable nature of its survival" (Caruth 1996, 7). Michael is constrained to awaken *from* his conscious, "official" history as an independent statesman or freeholder, a history suddenly invalidated by his belated recognition of the extent to which his local economy had been implicated in a national economy all along. To come to this realization, however, also means awakening *to* the new, negative awareness that his conscious identity has itself been elaborately designed to stave off precisely that catastrophic recognition. The carefully wrought environment of cottage, shepherd's staff, semi-enclosed fields, and, above all, the seemingly endless tradition of "Forefathers," are now on the verge of being devalued as a no longer sustainable symbolic order. Indeed, it is the formally overwrought, symptomatic character of Michael's patrimonial landscape—the dream of timeless property and absolute economic stability as a freeholder—that precipitates the awakening. Or, as Caruth notes of Freud's famous dream of the burning child, "it is *the dream itself . . . that wakes the sleeper*—an awakening not to, but against, the very wishes of consciousness. . . . To awaken is thus precisely to awaken only to one's repetition of a previous failure to see in time" (Caruth, 1996, 99–100).

For Slavoj Žižek, this awakening announces a more profound grasp of why the shock of modernity must be symbolically reenacted. For contrary to "epistemologically naïve" models of repetition, it is essential to understand how "so-called historical necessity itself *is constituted through misrecognition,* through the initial failure of 'opinion' to recognize its true character—that is, the way truth itself arises from misrecognition. The crucial point here is the changed symbolic status of an event: when it erupts for the first time, it is experienced as a contingent trauma, as an intrusion of a certain non-symbolized Real; only through repetition is this event recognized in its symbolic necessity—it finds its place in the symbolic network; it is realized in the symbolic order" (Žižek, 1989, 61). The symbolic dream world of the "hidden valley," with its trappings of a permanent familial and economic order, is neither simple self-delusion nor a Wordsworthian gesture of ideological obfuscation (as new historicists have supposed). Rather, the carefully wrought symbolic order becomes the condition for an awakening that could never take place were it not for the overdetermined symbolism *from* which and *by means of which* the subject is finally awakened. Concomitantly, Michael faces the shock of awakening to the sum of his illusions, of being conscious only of a dream that he had mistaken all these years for his real life.[16] Inasmuch as trauma leaves the subject stranded on the threshold between inside and outside, it does not so much constitute a neurotic state as name a precarious, transitional process.[17] Thus, during the weeks between the initial shock discovery of his devastating economic obligations and Luke's impending departure, Isabel notes "how [Michael] was troubled in his sleep" (line 301).

"Passions that were not my own": Wordsworth's Pastoral Art of Equivocation

Dreams, however, are only one way in which to repeat a traumatic scene. Luke's imminent sacrifice on the distant altars of metropolitan commerce or, simply, to the temptations of the city offers another, perhaps more promising perspective on traumatic history and symbolic repetition in Wordsworth's ballad. The apparent connection between Michael's act and Abraham's and God's patriarchal struggles with filial sacrifice suggests that repetition eventually compels its subjects to interpret their lives by articulating significant differences within a deceptively invariant sequence of events. In "Michael," repetition operates on at least two distinct levels. The first of these involves Michael's repetition of precisely those acts that had rendered his conscious history so traumatic, most obviously his sacrifice of Luke. More than anything, that act shows Michael's life to be implicated in a typological history of filial sacrifice in the Old and New Testaments and in the timeless exegetical struggle over the relation between the value sacrificed and the value affirmed by that act. As that goes, Michael's surrender of his son appears misguided, not to say hubristic. For it neither affirms his unconditional faith (Abraham's value) nor can claim to serve the greater good of humanity itself (God's value). Instead, the sacrifice appears to support little more than a father's nostalgic attachment to his land, while also betraying a merely conditional attachment to his son. As Marjorie Levinson notes, "the parallel between *The Akedah* and Wordsworth's explicit narrative breaks down in that Michael, by sending Luke to town, substitutes his son for the land, whereas Abraham had substituted the ram (property) for Isaac. Michael substitutes up in the scale of being, while Abraham substitutes down" (71).

One is reminded, in this context, of Max Weber's observation that the high esteem for agriculture, also especially consistent with piety, which the Puritans shared, applied . . . not to the landlord, but to the yeoman and farmer, in the eighteenth century not to the squire but the rational cultivator" (Weber, 173). Does Michael fail the Puritan conception, which in Weber's reading emphasizes labor as a rational enactment of religious asceticism, because he becomes obsessively fixated on the reward or "object" of his industry? The question is not easily answered because of the ambiguous status of property in the Protestant work ethic. On the one hand, it rejects "the pursuit of riches for their own sake." Yet at the same time, it cannot do without the objective manifestation of labor in the form of property and wealth, for "the attainment of it as a fruit of labor in a calling was a sign of God's blessing" (ibid., 172). As John Wesley saw it, the only justification of material property consisted in being simultaneously "diligent and frugal," in short, "to exhort all Christians to gain all they can, and to save all they can; that is, in effect, to grow rich" (quoted in Weber, 175). There is thus a sacrificial logic built into the process of methodical accumulation that has defined Michael's life of "endless industry." What spiritual time Michael has expended on husbandry and management is to be legitimated by the material fruits of labor. Yet these fruits are not to be enjoyed (consumed) but instead must themselves be preserved as the objective correlative of their producer's spiritual state. In other words, the ethos of frugality complements the ethos of accumulation, and to that end the material possession is not so much an object of possession as it is one of perpetual transmission to future generations. Only so is it conceivable that Michael should put up his son as collateral for the property, however erroneous and fateful that decision will ultimately prove to be.

The poem's uneasy fit within the long spiritual and exegetical tradition of filial sacrifice indicates a second level of repetition (i.e., of typology) that also operates throughout "Michael." It concerns reiteration of formal-symbolic values, such as the text's recurrent archetypal images (soil, winds, shepherd's staff, laying stones, etc.). As early structuralists (Jan Mukarovsky and Roman

Jakobson, among others) suggested long ago, reiterating a restrictive lexical and syntactic inventory incrementally establishes a sense of proximity, connection and, eventually, equivalence among various parts of a poetic text.[18] Even in an idiom as reticent as Wordsworthian blank verse, the principle of repetition accounts to a significant degree for the progressive consolidation of a palpably open-ended *story* into the tacit authority of a poetic *genre.* As we saw earlier on, at the level of reading, the poem's spiritual character and its formal organization tend to converge, indeed, collapse into each other. For as the poem's opening makes clear, the history of "Michael" is driven by a spiritual urgency that solicits the reader's quasi-testimonial collaboration with the symbolic and narrative order of the protagonist's story. History and story—the fluctuating aggregation of memories and the evaluative symbolism that undergirds their transmission as *text*— here converge in the obliquely artifactual genre of the pastoral ballad. It is a genre that is both fragmented and, precisely for that reason, urgently calling out for the supplemental ethos of scrupulous scholarship and sympathetic exegesis. As a distinctly middle-class mode of cultural production, the ballad encrypts history as a matter of strictly vicarious, perhaps serendipitous *revelation.* Thus it presents us with an individual's contingent account that, upon closer and cautious inspection, proves to be simply the repetition of a significant past that had never been experienced as a lived "presence." The transposition of story into history, of contingent matter into representative (if still local) knowledge, thus runs parallel to the coalescence of story and form, testimonial and genre.

Yet in the finite world of Wordsworth's "Michael," that transition pivots on material ephemera, such as a dilapidated sheepfold or "the useless fragment of a broken bowl" ("The Ruined Cottage"). Put differently, the possibility of relocating Michael's personal story in a nexus of economic and psychological determinants—the move from objective fate to subjective choice—will forever depend on serendipity in the shape of an object fortuitously encountered in an otherwise recalcitrant landscape.[19] Itself the enfeebled successor to the once rugged metaphysical idea of providence, serendipity per se is, of course, not a fact but a specific perception generated by an equally specific mode of reading. It arises inasmuch as the audience of a poem like "Michael" is steadily cued by its repetition of symbols, images, forms of speech, actions, and such. As the poem's opening makes clear, stories are told only to be retold, written to be read and reread. For only by means of that simultaneously aesthetic and social process of repetition can we hope to articulate why a seemingly incidental narrative should continue to haunt us with intimations of an antecedent, more capacious, knowledge—the mere "*sense* / Of something far more deeply interfused."

Having thus far articulated the logic of repetition that informs, indeed, shapes the poem as narrative (*syntagma*), we must now account for the ballad's generic manner (*paradigma*) of (re)constructing history as an involuntary memory. Authorless, incomplete, and "distressed" by its merely conjectural relation to a past that oscillates between an opaque memory and folkloric confabulation, the ballad is uniquely suited to dramatize the relationship between memory, knowledge, and survival. As Susan Stewart notes, its "text goes on to become symptomatic. It is a fragment of a larger whole that is a matter not only of other versions, but of the entire aura of the oral world—such a world's imagined presence, immediacy, organicism, and authenticity."[20] Inasmuch as the ballad is constitutively anonymous—a haunting appeal from the void that separates voice and text, cognition and construction, history and fantasy—it emulates the structure of trauma. For the dynamics of trauma involve precisely the belated "calling" of a past never before consciously experienced, and precisely for that reason capable of exposing the symbolic order of our conscious present as intrinsically unreal. Inasmuch as it shows the subject being overtaken by the *méconnaissance* of its own "proper" history, Wordsworth's "pastoral poem" inflects the habitus of ballad reading as one of witnessing the operation of a Proustian *mémoire involontaire.* As Walter Benjamin first noted, Proust's concept is itself an expression of the historical forces of modernity with its characteristic dispersion of economic causality and its erosion of conscious agency. For in this new psychological dynamic, the contingent and the personal converge without advance warning: "Man's inner concerns do not have their issueless private character by nature. They do so only when he is increasingly unable to assimilate the data of the world around him by experience." Such "atrophy of experience" accounts for the replacement of "older narration by information, of information by sensation," Benjamin argues (1980, 158–59). Knowledge has now ceased to operate via direct lines of oral narrative transmission. Instead, it is realized through affective simulacra of memory such as sympathy, nostalgia, and similarly oblique forms of "sensation." As a result of this development, Benjamin contends, knowledge has become a matter of contingency, of flashes of awareness triggered seemingly at random. What Proust calls *mémoire involontaire* is thus "part of the inventory of the individual who is isolated in many ways." When taken "in the strict sense of the word," Proust notes, "experience" names the moment when "certain contents of the individual past combine with material of the collective past."[21] Benjamin reinforces the point by remarking how "experience is indeed a matter of tradition, in collective existence as well as private life." However, as such, it depends less on "facts firmly anchored in memory than [on] a convergence in memory of accumulated and frequently unconscious data" (Benjamin 1980, 157).

Wordsworth's decision to preface the actual history of Michael with an extended meditation on the paradoxical structure of memory—at once inherently accidental, yet imbued with profound ethical responsibility—bears out my present contention: namely, that the practice of reading stands in supplemental relation to the ballad's theme of "survival." Considered from a strictly formal perspective, that is, "literary" reading transforms a putatively local oral "tradition" into symbolically condensed "information" (in Benjamin's sense of the term), a virtual (or aesthetic) knowledge that will haunt the audience with flashes of recognition no less insistent than those experienced by the story's protagonist. To read is to produce a vicarious type of knowledge, at once deceptively contingent and inescapably personal: Freudian trauma. The text of "Michael" thus mediates the Wordsworthian program of sociological analysis *qua* aesthetic tourism by giving rise to a highly deliberative mode of reading. Urged into a role of extensive collaboration, the audience must also face the hazards of unsuspected recognition, of sudden "transport" across the psychological and temporal divide that separates its own economic security, affective stability, and interpretive confidence from the tenuous livelihood, contingent struggles, and precarious existence of its rural ancestry. Michael's world, we learn, can only be reached by means of a decidedly lyric (and inherently textual) "turn . . . from the public way." Like the mental topography of the subject of trauma, this *ou topos*—an "utter solitude" (line 13) where the mountains have "made a hidden valley of their own"—proves to be essentially uncharted territory. It is located somewhere between exile and sanctuary, between the history *from* which one awakens and an as yet unknown and terrifying state *to* which one has awakened:

It is in truth an utter solitude,
Nor should I have made mention of this Dell
But for one object which you might pass by
Might see and notice not. Beside the brook
There is a straggling heap of unhewn stones;

And to that place a Story appertains,
Which, though it be ungarnished with events,
Is not unfit, I deem, for the fire-side
Or for the summer shade. It was the first
The earliest of those Tales that spake to me
Of Shepherds, dwellers in the Vallies, men
Whom I *already* lov'd, not verily
For their own sakes, but for the fields and hills
Where was their occupation and abode.

(WORDSWORTH 1992a, 253, LINES 13–26; EMPHASIS ADDED)

As Proust was to observe of his *mémoire involontaire,* such unsuspected recognition is triggered by "some material object" the encounter with which "depends entirely on chance." Indeed, he notes, it is by no means clear "whether we come upon it before we die or whether we never encounter it."[22] Thus fronted "face to face" by the mountains and suddenly halted by that "straggling Heap," Wordsworth characteristically locates the significance of the encounter in the passage from "see[ing]" to "notic[ing]" the remainder of the sheepfold. What matters about that material object is not so much its narrative potential as, rather, its capacity for triggering in the poet and his audience a reflexive awakening of sorts—an unexpected receptivity to "those Tales that spake to me." Though "ungarnished with events," the story of Michael's unsustainable attachment to his land points to the subterranean demographic and cultural transformations that in the course of time came to shape the poet's identity and, ultimately, that of his audience too. It is the old story of the complex, fluid connection between economics and affect, the story of how the lives of writers and readers—professionalized, sophisticated, and always forward-looking—had always been premised on their *not remembering* the affective, spiritual price exacted by the dramatic transformation of England's demographic and cultural landscape during the past two generations. "Not remembering" here should be taken in the preemptive, "strong" sense of what Nietzsche calls "forgetting." For it was precisely by so "forgetting" the deep-structural connection between a subsistence and a speculative economy, between the timeless rhythms of rural existence and the inscrutable fluctuations of urban commodity culture, that the poet and his audience came to imagine their lives as stable and meaningful.

Wordsworth's decision to sublate the ballad's formal and cognitive limitations into a "pastoral poem" meanwhile ensures that the awakening *from* this imaginary order will be gradual—a matter of symbolic *bathos* rather than existential *pathos.* For in repeating a past previously misunderstood, namely, by exposing the poet and his audience to a seemingly "other" narrative, the ballad encourages the listener's partial identification with its ostensibly anonymous, haunting subject matter. At the same time, however, its stylized textual form and the reverential, artifactual, and archeological qualities of the ballad genre also ensure that the awakening will be a controlled, rather than retraumatizing, experience. "Form" thus delineates a virtual zone of safety in which such recognition is to unfold vicariously. Not surprisingly, we are told that the "objects" of this ostensibly alien landscape were "already" (line 24) familiar to the poet, a claim that renders his entry into this "hidden valley" a déja vu experience. In this manner, the belated cognition of misdirected labor that had brought such existential distress to Michael is being attenuated, its traumatic force absorbed into the virtual experience of "reading" and its inherently compensatory pleasures. To that end, the "voice" of the pastoral ballad strives for balance, distance, and elegiac composure. On the one hand, the poem hints that the subject's contingent migration into a seemingly alien place and time ("Vallies, men / Whom I already lov'd" [line 25]) is imbued with reflexive, indeed retroactive significance. At the same time, the pastoral interpolates its own partially inherited symbolic order as a halfway house for the subject struggling to adjust not only to the belated recognition of his past conscious existence as delusive but also to the epistemological abjection entailed by such an awakening. Small phrases betray this dilemma, such as the speaker's assertion that "natural objects led me on to feel / *For* passions that were not my own," (lines 30–31). Like the "wound" of the mind in Freud's account of trauma, the speaker notes how the barren landscape haunts its subjects with an aura of incipient recognition. At the same time, however, the text itself mediates the potential shock of that event by allowing historical self-knowledge to unfold only in oblique, aesthetic form. If poetry exposes its subjects to "passion," it does so no longer in the strong, Aschylean sense of *pathein* but via the late Enlightenment's key strategy for the mediation of anonymous middle-class subjects as a (virtual) community: "sympathy." Affect has become essentially textual in nature, a *deictic* process whereby—in Wordsworth's cunningly attenuated phrase—the poet is "led . . . *on* to feel / *For* passions."

It is important now to locate Michael's traumatic awakening, precisely *because* it is so visibly mediated and attenuated in form and force in a larger system of (psycho)historical coordinates. Consistent with this book's hypothesis of "mood" as possessing historical specificity and therefore granting us, in its formal encryption as writing, access to the qualitative shifts that give the term "history" its substance and meaning, the halting locutions of Wordsworth's "Michael" and its eponymous protagonist should be at once specific and representative testimony about the experience of historical change around 1800. Yet to invest the voice and text, character and pastoral, with the talismanic force of a concrete universal—even if undertaken in pursuit of historical knowledge that often seemed anathema to the new critical embrace of poetry as both specific and representative—requires independent confirmation. A shift in scenery from England to the Continent will soon buttress my claims about a structural relationship between individuals gradually awakening to the traumatic recognition of historical change as something only ever to be grasped in untimely (belated) utterances. Yet in the English literary context, Coleridge offers some independent confirmation for this hypothesis in a curious little essay entitled "Insensibility of Public Temper," published in the *Morning Post* on 24 February 1798, which immediately calls attention to the public's *lack* of response to historical change ("insensibility," "read[ing] without emotion") as a "very remarkable *symptom* of the public temper" (1978, pt. 1, 20–21; emphasis added). The incomprehensibility of historical transformations abroad is matched, precisely and symptomatically, by the "languor and lethargy" (ibid., 22) of English politicians and their subjects. Numbed by the sublime terrors unfolding daily on the stage of European politics, Britons look upon the manifest folly of their own government with "passive acquiescence" (ibid., 23). In a particularly acute and prescient comment, Coleridge speculates that "this familiarity with revolutions may perhaps one day be found to be fraught with the most important consequences" (ibid., 22). Above all, the symptomatic "insensibility" and its as yet unimagined consequences appear to be the result of the formally invariant representation of historical events in literature and the periodical press—what Coleridge would later call "the two public *ordinaries*" feeding the public (Coleridge 1972, 38). Precisely this failure of most writing, literary or journalistic, to develop a reflexive relationship to its form accounts for the failure of reading audiences to develop a timely affective response to the historical transformations all around them.

"It is with nations as with individuals," says Coleridge (1972, 15). Wordsworth may have been among the first to consider what it would mean for an individual to inhabit a world in which the "important consequences" of historical change—and one's own role in such change—would only become apparent after the fact. Yet unlike his journalistic counterparts, Wordsworth understands that to dramatize the tension between an abiding *méconnaissance* and a belated awakening requires an intrinsically divided textual and literary form. For this reason alone, it bears reiterating that, in its eventual finished form, "Michael" effectively transmutes the comparatively less artful idiom of balladic speech into the more settled cadences of the pastoral. In one of several fragments relating to the composition of "Michael," Wordsworth actually comes close to articulating the volatile relation between the ostensibly uncensored rural idiom in which the story of Michael and Luke supposedly first reached him and the need for his authorial intervention. Rather than entrusting himself to "Two shepherds . . . two wits of the dale / Renown'd for song, satire, epistle and tale," the task of textually reconstituting the "cause of Michael's decay" demands the professional ministrations of the poet. The resulting text is thus positioned as a stylized defense against the alleged "taunts" and "sly malice" that depict Michael as suffering more from his capricious and self-involved metaphysics than from any economic reversals:

> Perhaps the old man is a provident elf,
> So fond of bestowing advice on himself
> And of puzzling at what may befall,
> So intent on making his bread without leaven
> And of giving to earth the perfection of heaven
> That he thinks and does nothing at all.
>
> (DC MS. 15, WORDSWORTH 1992a, 319)

The eventual text of "Michael" thus appears to rewrite earlier, more unequivocally local versions of the same story. Well beyond staving off the story's imminent lapse into obscurity, the polished cadences of the final version seem designed to counterbalance the allegedly common and trivializing rendition of "that pastoral ballad" ("So thoughtless a falsehood it grieves me to hear"). At the level of form, Wordsworth's thoroughgoing revisions of "Michael" thus reenact the same defensive logic that also supported the affective and economic illusions of Michael's deceptively contingent personal history. That is, in content *and* form, the revision of ballad into pastoral yields the aesthetic equivalent of a Freudian "screen-memory" (*Deckerinnerung*). Rather than obfuscating the raw forces of economic history outright, the pastoral allows its readers to reconstruct oblique social and psychological causation in the virtual domain of a highly sophisticated, if also rather hermetic aesthetic form.

Knowledge is vested, not in propositional forms, but in the author's and, ideally, the audience's remedial intervention in the raw data of a crude orality and the unedited textures of a native ballad culture. In so redeeming an allegedly deeper, more capacious knowledge encrypted in casual, not to say mindless, forms of local balladic speech, narrator and audience also give reality to the new, distinctly Wordsworthian paradigm of poetry as a uniquely purposeful type of productivity. For not only does their collaboration extend the individual's range of spiritual experience, but it also consolidates a middle-class model of the British nation by affirming—in the subtly authoritative modality of the Wordsworthian text—the representative demographic value of that experience. A short fragment from the manuscripts for "Michael" dramatizes the mediating powers of this new aesthetic model through the indeterminate gestalt of the sheepfold itself:

There is a shapeless crowd of unhewn stones
That lie together, some in heaps and some
In lines that seem to keep themselves alive
In the last dotage of a dying form
At least so seems to a man that stands
In such a lonely place. (DC MS. 31, WORDSWORTH 1992a, 329)

Stranded amid the miscellaneous debris of Michael's failed enclosure, the speaker readily acknowledges his tenuous epistemological vantage point. The choice, we are told, is between reproducing the inchoate rustic locutions of a "shapeless crowd" and attempting to reproduce a coherent outline that is understood to have existed only as a feeble, impossibly nostalgic wish ("the last dotage of a dying form"). Wordsworth's carefully wrought image works only with mezzotints, shades, and the merest intimations of representational art. With a technique that seems to anticipate late impressionism, the above passage shows how narrative form and social purpose emerge, or vanish, in strict accordance with the distance maintained between the medium of description and the object described. Inasmuch as such distance can only achieved by a superior technique, it is clearly unavailable to the local populace and its culture of ballad speech. Not surprisingly, the revisions of "Michael" show Wordsworth take pains to distinguish his blank-verse, textual approach to narrative from the local culture of "Rhymes pleasant to sing or to say" (DC MS. 15, Wordsworth 1992a, 319].

Moreover, with its images carefully perched on the threshold between mimesis and allegory, the pastoral ballad haunts its audience in the same way that the sheepfold haunts Michael.[23] It confronts the reader with an object whose ability to induce sudden recognition hovers between the contingent and the providential. Sensibly, Wordsworth's "Michael" opens by drawing our attention to what is at stake in the way we choose to respond to the haunting appeals of the past. For the price of the "text"—a cultural commodity that exacts our sustained interpretive labor—we are put in a position to adjust our precarious "distance" to the past, and thus to come to know it even as the text's aesthetic form serves to qualify the knowledge thus produced. At the same time, by engaging in "serious" commerce with the ballad as a "deep" aesthetic form, the audience also acknowledges its errant, superficial, or "public way[s]," an obliquely confessional step that leaves readers poised to repossess a past whose forgetting had lent such specious consistency to their conscious present. The ballad form, that is, at once reconstitutes and redeems its audience by enabling it vicariously—in the overtly disinterested modality of lyric transport—to repeat a history that had been preemptively forgotten. To awaken to the belated consciousness of that loss is also to atone by confronting (up to a point) the larger significance of a historical causality previously occluded from view. Rather than merely perpetrating the "loss of history," as the new historicism has argued, the cultural logic of the Wordsworthian ballad and its pastoral self-transcendence mobilizes the form of dedicated, "serious" reading itself as a partial atonement for that loss.

Admittedly, Wordsworth's aesthetic entails a deeply equivocal ethos of reading—one promising us recovery both *of* and *from* history. Even so, it would be reductive to pathologize the Wordsworthian model as something to be redeemed either by the rhetorical finesse or the archival scrupulousness of deconstructive or historicist criticism respectively. For by meticulously encoding an ineffable, though unrelenting, historical causality in its overarching narrative and embedded speech situations, "Michael" effectively presages the very hermeneutics of suspicion that, over the past half century, has established itself as both the axiomatic method and the institutional justification for literary studies broadly speaking. In fact, it is the careful deployment of trace narratives—first remembered, it bears pointing out, in Michael's faltering monologues—which would eventually be writ large as a supposedly groundbreaking (to use the appropriate agrarian trope) advance on the part of a new historicist method that aspires to restore memories and material facts allegedly obfuscated by romantic lyricism. The inadvertent irony of such methodological righteousness can hardly be overlooked once we recall that "Michael" itself dramatizes the process of remembering, albeit with the conclusion that all recollection is partial and even then endurable only in heavily mediated form. To read "Michael" is to witness the drama of a subject embattled by an elusive yet insistent (traumatic) causality struggling to historicize his own life and existence, something Michael's recapitulation of his past for Luke aptly illustrates. Yet here no less than in the institutionally cloistered and methodologically cautious proceedings of new historicist reading, remembering always means to grasp life only retroactively by tentatively opening oneself to the possibility that reconstructing a previously blocked past may bring it into focus, for the first time, as involving us, as *our* past. "Michael" does just that and, no less than its latter-day interpreters, sets about its task from a position of prearranged safety for which, at its specific historical moment of 1800, the pastoral offered a particularly congenial mediating form. Attenuated in the measured narrative cadences of the pastoral, the cogency of balladic speech—still interspersed at various points in "Michael"—proves no more evasive than do the highly specialized models of critique (including the present argument) developed by various interpretive communities and circulated to small subsets of equally specialized readers today.

Around 1800, Wordsworth's pastoral or elegiac inflection of the ballad in poems such as "Michael," "The Brothers," and "Heart-Leap Well" proves far more complex and ambivalent than one is led to expect by his theoretical statements about the genre in the 1800–1802 "Preface" or in his 1801 letter to Charles James Fox. Whereas his prose disquisitions insist on a stable and determinate message—to "make the incidents of common life interesting by tracing in them, truly though not ostentatiously, the primary laws of our nature" (Wordsworth 1992a, 741)—the ballads in question often conspire against the apparent idealization of a quasi-Burkean economy of "permanent feelings."[24] For to claim a direct causal relationship between the "spreading of manufactures . . . heavy taxes . . . workhouses, Houses of Industry, and the invention of soup-shops" and "the rapid decay of domestic affections" (Wordsworth 1984, 41) is to ignore the obvious and startling implications of most of the ballads in the 1800 volume: namely, that "the bonds of domestic feeling," prior to their formalization in balladic speech and pastoral narration, are fundamentally self-deceiving and illusory. It is just this obsessive orderliness so characteristic both of pastoral life in "Michael" and of Wordsworth's subsequent epistolary specification of the poem's rationale (namely, to dramatize the freeholder's "almost sublime conviction of the blessings of independent domestic life" [Wordsworth 1984, 42]) that functions as a symptom of romantic trauma. For the symbolic order that, according to Wordsworth, defines the aesthetic of lyrical ballad and pastoral narrative and the affective economy of northern freeholders' whose "little tract of land [that] serves as a kind of permanent rallying point for their domestic feelings" effectively guarantees that the "great transformation" (Polanyi) of socioeconomic existence will go unnoticed for a perilously long time. Michael's illusion of affective immunity from such change, which the Wordsworthian poem extols as both aesthetically and spiritually ennobling, is the prima facie reason for his delayed and hence traumatic recognition of the changes wrought by Adam Smith's "invisible hand," not only in the world without but, by "grievous" implication, within Michael's own material and affective world as well. In this manner, the pastoral at once perpetrates the very illusion from which Michael must awaken and, in the course of the narration proper, evolves into the medium that precipitates that awakening.

In 1800, Wordsworth's conception of "feeling" as the ideal focus for the writing and reading of poetry is still highly volatile. Though rather worn by much careless citation, the references to "spontaneous overflow of powerful feelings" and the "manner in which our feelings and ideas are associated in a state of excitement" (Wordsworth 1992a, 744–45) found in the 1800 "Preface" hardly accord any predictable or settled qualities to the current of emotions. In fact, rather than reiterating Burke's inherently skeptical, not to say desperate, endorsement of "inbred sentiments," "untaught feelings," and the "cold sluggishness of our national character" (Burke, 181–83), Wordsworth's embrace of a subjectivity strictly guided by its affective and intuitive resources seems rather equivocal. Not only does the "Preface" advance that view only conditionally ("if he be in a healthful state of association"), but the potential gains of a purely emotive relation to the world ("in some degree enlightened . . . his taste exalted . . . his affections ameliorated") are attained at the expense of any preparedness for historical change and contingency. For to live life strictly according to affective cues is to "obey blindly and mechanically the impulses of those habits" (Wordsworth 1992a, 745). It is only right that Wordsworth's *Preface*, after an extended interspersed discussion of meter and formal conventions, should end up qualifying its earlier claims regarding the cognitive and representative value of emotions. Thus, far from tranquilizing "upheavals of thought" (to borrow the phrase from Nussbaum's Proust-derived title), it is an integral and crucial function of poetry to resurrect the volatility and complexity of emotions: "I have said that Poetry is the spontaneous overflow of powerful feelings: it takes its origin from emotion recollected in tranquility: the emotion is contemplated till by a species of reaction the tranquility gradually disappears, and an emotion, similar to that which was before the subject of contemplation, is gradually produced, and does itself actually exist in the mind" (Wordsworth 1992a, 756).

Contrary to the deceptive tranquility that characterizes Michael and ostensibly makes him the representative "estatesman" of an anti-modern and anticapitalist lyric economy of feeling, both the writing and reading of ballad and pastoral demand a slow and laborious decoding of a likely antagonistic complexion of meanings that have lain dormant and encrypted as "durable feeling." By insisting on the constitutive volatility of emotions whose intermittent "tranquillity" actually belies their volatile and antagonistic composition, Wordsworth anticipates a crucial insight in Freud's metapsychological writings of 1914–15.[25] There, particularly in his essay on repression, Freud concedes (very much to the detriment of his overall theoretical project), that the relationship between a repressed meaning and an acceptable "substitute-formation" can never be seamless or fully symmetrical. On the contrary, the eventual breakdown in the work of repression already announces itself in cracks and fissures that open up within the "official" representation, a predicament that does not go entirely unnoticed by the subject but, on the contrary, explains why the language of Freud's subjects, aside from its surface meaning, continually reveals the presence of a nonsemantic "affective charge" (*Affektbesetzung*). Clearly, the pastoral text of "Michael," notwithstanding its programmatic attempt at closing off the 1800 edition of *Lyrical Ballads* by absorbing the formally and historically plain and direct idiom of the ballad, reveals at critical junctures the unfathomable and uncontainable potential of emotions associated with a traumatic awakening (Michael's dream, his faltering speech, his tears, Luke's "proud face"). Indeed, it is just this involuntary disclosure of an emotive substratum running counter to the intentional and propositional thrust of everyday locution that poetry reveals in operation, even if doing so means complicating or atrophying its own surface order. In his 1800 note to "The Thorn," Wordsworth states the matter in rather peremptory language: "The Reader cannot be too often reminded that Poetry is passion: it is the history or science of feelings: now every man must know that an attempt is rarely made to communicate impassioned feelings without something of an accompanying consciousness of the inadequateness of our own powers, or the deficiencies of language" (1992a, 351). Behind the vaunted claim that poetry is "the history . . . of feelings" lurk two equally startling concessions: (1) that feeling itself is historical, not universal, and (2) that its emergence within poetry, in the genuine (i.e., Wordsworthian) sense of the word, pivots not on the expressive or evocative manipulation of words but, rather, on the persistent reification of "words, not only as symbols of the passion, but as things, active and efficient, which are of themselves part of the passion" (1992a, 351). As Wordsworth's subsequent scriptural examples (Judges 5: 12–28) are meant to show, emotion is structurally embedded in language, not as its expressive source, but as homologous with its syntactic patterns (parallelism, anaphora, etc.). Hence, like language, emotion must be understood as inherently social, something that acquires reality and significance only inasmuch as it is bound up or homologous with the aesthetic construct of a poem, and hence as the virtual, heuristic embodiment of a value *for* another, *for* a community.

Not until 1815 did Wordsworth articulate in programmatic terms how his poetry was meant to generate interest by first perplexing and eventually focusing the attention of readers on precisely this affective surcharge that runs through the speech of his balladic and lyric personae and characters. The 1815 "Preface" thus identifies "a commutation and transfer of internal feelings, co-operating with external accidents" as the principal objective of all those lyrics now classified as "Poems of the Imagination" (Wordsworth 1989, 639). Speaking of "imagination [as] the faculty which *images* within the mind the phenomena of sensation," the "Preface" reaffirms the eighteenth-century view (developed and popularized by Robert Lowth, John Newbery, Hugh Blair, and J. G. Herder, among others) that a strong bond exists between all affect and figural speech (Wordsworth 1989, 635). Yet the question that remains open is whether to read "affective charge" as the cause of figural speech and writing, or whether the latter alone is the condition through which volatile yet insistent passions and feelings attain any epistemological validity to begin with.

Its canonical and often divisive conservatism notwithstanding, Wordsworth's 1815 "Essay, supplementary to the *Preface*" opts for the more radical position here. Setting aside lesser kinds of poetry (encompassing much of the poetry *not* written by Wordsworth) as merely "occasional recreation," "a specious of luxurious amusement," or "consolation for the afflictions of life," Wordsworth turns to another, far more ambitious kind of poetry. It emphasizes the ethos of labor and study, of dedicated and sustained interpretive commitment to a language that "treat[s] of things not as they *are,* but as they *appear;* not as they exist in themselves, but as they *seem* to exist to the *senses* and to the *passions.*" Such an ennobling commitment to poetry as part of "general literature" and hence "*as a study*" naturally encounters the same problem that had already beset the 1800 "Preface," namely, how to distinguish between an affective charge that may lead to hidden and complex strata of historical causation and mere sensationalism ("transient shocks"). Far less defensive than the earlier "Preface," the "Essay, supplementary" to the 1815 *Poems* not only concedes that such confusion between "temptations to go astray" and truly complex feelings is not only "unavoidable [but] no doubt eminently useful to the mind as a process" (Wordsworth 1989, 643). Hence the labor ("study") of "the higher poetry" that Wordsworth himself claims to provide justifies not only the canonical arrangement of the 1815 *Poems* into a set of loose psychological categories (Poems of the Imagination, Fancy, Sentiment and Reflection, etc.) but also necessitates and sanctions a new, quasi-professional form of sustained interpretive reading.

It is not until he has safeguarded his poetics against the lingering threat of its appropriation by or subordination to some narrow theological position that Wordsworth articulates the critical paradigm of emotion supposedly in play throughout the "higher poetry" of his 1815 volumes: "There are emotions of the pathetic that are simple and direct, and others—that are complex and revolutionary; some—to which the heart yields with gentleness, others,—against which it struggles with pride: these varieties are infinite as the combinations of circumstance and the constitutions of character. Remember, also, that the medium through which, in poetry, the heart is to be affected—is language; a thing subject to endless fluctuations and arbitrary associations" (Wordsworth 1989, 656). More than anywhere in his prose or letters, the "Essay, supplementary" reveals Wordsworth's proto-Hegelian conception of lyric poetry as possessing historical depth, not unwittingly, but out of the deeper recognition that historical meaning can be realized only as a kind of (Protestant) interpretive labor, as a *re*membering of the *disjecta membrae* of history encrypted in the "endless" and enigmatic rhetorical nuances of literature. For Wordsworth, the significance of feeling deepens in direct proportion to the labor that is exacted by its interpretive discernment and articulation. "It is not to be supposed that the Reader can make progress . . . like an Indian Prince or General—stretched on his Palanquin, and borne by his Slaves" (Wordsworth 1989, 656).

The disciplinary structure of philological, historicist, and rhetorical analysis thus stands in complementary relation to the transferential design or, we might say, responds to the covert intentionality of "feeling" itself. For what Wordsworth calls the "commutation or transfer of internal feelings" into a poetic diction whose exemplarity grows as its rhetorical nuances proliferate and yield up "endless fluctuations and arbitrary associations" is ultimately what Kant had called taste. Taste thus constitutes the condition of possibility for any future improvement in social relations and knowledge. As Wordsworth puts it, "to create taste is to call forth and bestow power, of which knowledge is the effect" (ibid., 656). Knowledge thus constitutes the tranquil recollection of the "missed," because all-encompassing, traumatic shock of modernity. It is a shock whose historical causality readers—understood as a "people," not a "public"—should strive to reassemble from its philological and rhetorical bits and pieces. As objects of a wholly serendipitous encounter, such textual or material fragments open up vistas on a previously occluded past because of their seismic reverberation as *forms*—such as slips of the tongue or pen, persistent ambiguities, or curious symbolic fixations. Such is the transferential process set in motion by romantic lyricism: genuine poetry, in Wordsworth's definition, encrypts a volatile and far-flung affective complexion that begs to be redeemed from its own obliquity. To the extent that the labor of interpretive reading succeeds, it also ensures that readers, like Michael, must recognize their own present as no less contingent and potentially inauthentic than the official knowledge of an increasingly spurious past from which the consciousness of that present derives its legitimacy.

The Aura of the Romantic Image: Poetic Cliché as Memory and Revelation

The preceding discussion of Wordsworth's pastoral conclusion to his "experiment" in *Lyrical Ballads* will have to suffice as interpretive synecdoche for a host of other possible readings of British lyric writing from around 1800. A rather similar logic of trauma could also be shown to underlie and formally organize Coleridge's "Dejection" (1802), beginning with its portentous storm imagery in the epigraph and the opening stanza and its near-programmatic definition of trauma as "A grief without a pang, void, dark, and drear, / A stifled, drowsy, unimpassioned grief, / Which finds no natural outlet, no relief."[26] Such a trauma-based curricular trajectory might well proceed from here to Wordsworth's "Resolution and Independence," like Coleridge's "Dejection" written between May and July 1802 (Wordsworth 1983, 123–29). Again, the opening figure is that of a cataclysmic storm, though here the ravages have been wrought and the voice reflexively doubles back upon itself to find a "nothing" or mere "dejection" (line 25) where there ought to be joy at the apparent renewal of nature. The dominant trope here and (a likely next stop on such a potential syllabus) also in the "Intimations" ode is that of a missed or unowned experience: "My old remembrances went from me wholly" (line 20), a scene of physical and psychological maiming that is brought into objective focus only through the figure of the Leech Gatherer who, inexplicably, "Wandering about alone and silently" (line 138) reflects back to the Wordsworthian traveler the sheer and persistent fact of survival, even and especially where the survivor is unable to articulate the trauma that he or she has survived. For the Leech Gatherer, the catastrophe is fundamentally economic, just as in "Michael." Aside from the many such characters found in *Lyrical Ballads* (1800), further instances of traumatized subjects—manifestly displaced, apparitional, nearly aphasic in demeanor—include the discharged soldier in book 4 and the blind beggar in book 7 of *The Prelude* and Margaret in "The Ruined Cottage," to name only the most obvious.

At first glance, rather different historical and cultural factors would appear to be at work in literary production after 1803 on the Continent, specifically in Napoleonic Germany. There, after a long period of delay due to the singularly recalcitrant political and economic organization of the old *Reich* and its superannuated patterns of *Herrschaft* (to which we shall return below), modernization happened suddenly and, uncharacteristically, was mostly imposed from above. The drastic changes wrought by Napoleon's sweeping territorial reorganization of Germany in 1803 were most significant, of course. They were soon followed by the ambitious Prussian reform movement, launched immediately upon Prussia's stunning defeat at Jena and Auerstädt in 1806 and aimed at modernizing the state with a view to emerging from Napoleonic rule. Heeding the call of German romanticism's programmatic declarations rather than that of its momentous history, readers have long construed that epoch as the very apotheosis of aesthetic autonomy or, if critical of that value, as succumbing to strictly theoretical contradictions.[27] Except for obligatory token references to the threat of the French Revolution and the pervasive disorder of the Napoleonic era, criticism has generally been reluctant to relate the period's artistic or theoretical output to its momentous history. Just how to configure aesthetic production and the experience of historical change has long been a hotly debated question.[28] My aim in the following pages is to sketch and exemplify how to read literature as a critical medium for historical cognition, which is to say, to approach literature as maintaining a dialectical (rather than an evasive or otherwise reactive) relation to history. To help set the stage, we may recall Theodor Adorno's prescient warning against a historicism that deems literature generically incapable of historical cognition and, with its rich methodological armature, purports to redeem literature from its unconscious obfuscation of ideological positions. Early in his *Aesthetic Theory,* Adorno remarks on something both profound and enigmatic that lies at the heart of all claims for aesthetic autonomy. By way of qualifying his earlier optical metaphor "there is no aesthetic refraction without something being refracted," Adorno observes that

> the communication of artworks with what is external to them, with the world from which they blissfully or unhappily seal themselves off, occurs through non-communication; precisely thereby they prove themselves refracted. . . . Even the most sublime artwork takes up a determinate attitude to empirical reality by stepping outside of the constraining spell it casts, not once and for all, but rather ever and again, concretely, unconsciously polemical toward this spell at each historical moment. That artworks as windowless monads "represent" what they themselves are not can scarcely be understood except in that their own dynamic, their immanent historicity as a dialectic of nature and its domination, not only is of the same essence as the dialectic external to them but resembles it without imitating it. . . . Art's double character as both autonomous and *fait social* is incessantly reproduced at the level of autonomy. It is by virtue of this relation to the empirical that artworks recuperate, neutralized, what once was literally and directly experienced in life and what was expulsed by spirit. Artworks participate in enlightenment because they do not lie: they do not feign the literalness of what speaks out of them. They are as real as answers to the puzzle externally posed to them. Their own tension is binding in relation to the tension external to them. (Adorno 1997, 5)

Most salient here, perhaps, is Adorno's claim that the artwork's recalcitrant, seemingly autistic relationship to the "tension" permeating what is "external" to it ought to be understood not as a defensive and escapist maneuver but, rather, as born of the deeper awareness of history itself as a welter of chaotic, traumatizing forces. In forgoing the complacency of the "literal" (of language as "communication"), art draws closer to understanding history as profoundly enigmatic. Whatever history may turn out to be, it is never just "context" or some empirically recoverable set of references at which one might hope to arrive *ex negativo*—that is, via the critique of some putative aesthetic ideology.[29] So as to sharpen these as yet rather abstract remarks, one must scrutinize the rhetorical organization of the lyric to the point where it becomes legible as an *affective response* to a historical situation whose urgency and complexity belatedly strike the expressive subject with traumatic force. Yet doing so is only a first step. For beyond approaching literary form as the symptomatic encryption of a historical tension seeking poetic release, we must also remain alert to the enabling, generative power of cultural forms. To take that crucial second step—one frequently ignored, even disparaged, by romantic historicism—is to recognize historical cognition (rather than the vaunted "evasion of history") as a salient, indeed motivating, force within romantic aesthetic production itself.

In short, the transition from the rhetorical analysis of a specific poetic idiom to historical cognition—or, in Kenneth Burke's nomenclature, from a grammar of symbols to a grammar of motives—is only the first step in a more complex itinerary. For the dialectic of literature and history, form and function, remains in turn susceptible to, indeed demands, integration into a larger and forever evolving history of human relations. In what follows, I approach the romantic lyric as a dialectical form struggling to articulate its speaker's and audience's belated and hence precarious cognitive relationship to their own historical moment. Rather than striving for historical "truth" intentionally, the lyric word, untrammeled by the banal certitudes of communication and "events," divulges its historical import with a clarity at once belated and serendipitous, yet also inescapable. What Lacan says of Freud holds equally true of the performance of the word in the romantic lyric. Recognition here "is not a question of biological memory, nor of its intuitionist mystification . . . but a question of rememoration, that is, of history. . . . It is not a question of reality, but of Truth, because the effect of the full Word is to reorder the past contingent events by conferring on them the sense of necessities to come" (Lacan 1968, 18). In what follows, then, I argue that the romantic lyric mediates, rather than occludes, historical consciousness. It does so out of the recognition that history can only ever be known as a moment of "depth" unexpectedly and inescapably opening up amid the surface order of waking quotidian life. In grasping history as "mood," the romantic lyric posits the subject as an inwardness (*Innerlichkeit*) that bears nearly eponymous affinity to the spontaneity of remembrance (*Erinnerung*). Put differently, romanticism can postulate the affective depth of its subjects *only by historicizing them,* a process that begins, in Germany no less than in England, with a comprehensive recovery and advocacy of "ancient" folk culture.[30] The latter forms part of the late-eighteenth-century European "invention of tradition," to borrow Eric Hobsbawm and Terence Ranger's phrase, and it is dialectically related to the repudiation of sentimental literature.

Chronologically, the mobilization of folk culture as a strategic resource for an aesthetic and political "rebirth" of Germany coincides precisely with the collapse of the old *Reich* in 1806, and its "ground zero" is the intellectual circle of romantics at Heidelberg. Among those preeminently associated with the Heidelberg school, Ludwig Achim von Arnim offers a prefatory account of his and Clemens Brentano's epoch-making collection of folk poetry, *Des Knaben Wunderhorn* (1806–1808), whose intent often resembles Wordsworth's slightly earlier defense of his poetics in the "Preface" to *Lyrical Ballads* (1800–1802). In von Arnim's view, sentimentalism and the allegedly mannered forms of writing associated with a late-eighteenth-century system of literary patronage are nothing but "illness and annihilation" (*Krankheit und Vernichtung*)—a mere "imitation . . . of feeling" (*das Nachahmen . . . des Gefühls*).[31] By contrast, the "authentic tone" (*wahrer Ton*) of folk poetry is posited as a vital resource for an eventual German national community, a project that pivots on attuning a collective reading-audience to memories at once imperiled yet magically preserved in the archetypal form of the *Volkslied:* "Dear God! Where are the old trees under which even yesterday we found rest, the ancient signs of firm borders; what has happened, is happening to them? Almost forgotten by the people, we make painful contact with their roots" (Arnim 1975, 409; my translation). Not surprisingly, perhaps, this programmatic cultivation of romantic interiority via the resurrection of once spontaneous literary forms, of once again hearing "people sing who were no poets" (was ich von Leuten singen hörte, die nicht Sänger waren [409]), entails a formalization of folk song itself. Thus the *Volkslied* is postulated as the spontaneous expression of a timeless naïveté—that is, of an affect impervious to the dialectical model of time-as-difference (Hegel's *absolute Unruhe*).[32] Upon closer inspection, however, this postulated "naïveté" constitutes no original value but, rather, bespeaks the romantics' will to think the lyric's (supposedly) intuitive foundations in explicit disjunction from historical time. Hence von Arnim also laments the disappearance of "ancient forests" irretrievably leveled by the economic forces of modernity. The "ancient signs" of folk culture have been "almost forgotten," and their recovery is said to pivot on precisely the kind of archival industry, philological technique, and aesthetic reflections belatedly furnished by the editors of the *Wunderhorn* collection. In short, immediacy and spontaneity alone no longer guarantee cultural value. Conceived only ex post facto from the alienated perspective of modernity, folk culture's naïveté is here formalized and institutionalized as an "ancient" wisdom encrypted in linguistic artifacts whose integrity can no longer be produced and can only be recovered through serendipitous encounters on the order of what Proust was to name *mémoire involontaire.*

As we have already seen in the case of Wordsworth's "Michael," the peculiar efficacy and lucidity of the romantic lyric involve its representing its own agonistic modernity *for* its initial readers in thematic, topical form and reflecting that audience as a protonational community defined by its shared cultural avocation. This the lyric effects transferentially, that is, by unconsciously projecting visions of social and cultural health into a hypostatized past and recovering such values through sophisticated literary forms and institutions concerned with allowing an embattled community to awaken to its cultural "memories." As remains to be seen, the high romantic lyric conceives of its subjects as uneasily perched on the threshold between a state of pure presence, consciously experienced and widely cherished as middle-class inwardness (*Innerlichkeit*), and unsolicited yet insistent fragments of recollection (*Erinnerung*) that point back to an antecedent trauma to which lyric writing and reading respond with a formal concision that we must not misconstrue as a defensive aestheticism. Approached as a richly speculative, textual strategy, romanticism's reflexive transposition of folk culture into high lyric art—its conditional recovery of a lost organic presence through contingent moments of recollection: song into text—is anything but naïvely teleological or didactic in intent. Far from proclaiming the outright recovery and reinstatement of medieval folk culture, Wordsworth in England and von Arnim, Brentano, Joseph Görres, Friedrich Creuzer, and Joseph von Eichendorff in Germany premise their literary productivity on a moment of inspiration ("spontaneous overflow of powerful feelings . . . recollected in tranquility"). Inasmuch as the formulation promises the containment of subconscious turmoil within the studied, textual affect of repose, the latter remains merely the printed image, and hence the trace, of a negative whose insistent claims the writer's expressive locutions sought to contain (though never to disavow outright) and, in so doing, continually reproduced. Precisely this dialectic also shapes the language of high romantic lyricism. Here, too, we note a quasi-schizophrenic split between the quotidian and the magical, the blandly descriptive and flashes of conjury. The lyric serves both politics and revelation; it is at once a record of local-material ephemera (Wordsworth's "real language of man") and a holograph capable of unveiling the supersensible depths encrypted in history's fleeting detail; indeed, it appears to be *the only* repository for a notion of the supersensible that is not opposed to but distilled from historical experience.

Rather than abridging historical awareness, this basic schema—first proposed by the ballad revival of the late eighteenth century and, by 1815, fully amalgamated either with the more speculative form of the lyric or the more discursive genre of the historical novel—constitutes a powerful strategy of historical cognition in its own right. Foregoing historicism's gluttonously accumulative and naïvely leveling faith in history's material concreteness and transparency, the romantic lyric cultivates a richly dialectical relation to historical process that strikingly foreshadows Walter Benjamin's unique rewriting of historical materialism as a type of critique bent on "the salvation of phenomena" by the "idea." For Arnim and Brentano no less than for Benjamin, the critical reconstruction of phenomena is not aimed at a "totality." Rather, critique aims to cultivate a historical fact to the point where "its innermost structure appears to be so essential as to reveal it as an origin." If one is to establish a rapport between concrete phenomena and truth, one must find in the former the unique quality of *Intentionslosigkeit* (lack of intentionality). The goal of literary-historical study, in Benjamin's words—and they might just as well have been Brentano's—is "not therefore one of intention and knowledge, but rather a total immersion and absorption in [truth]." Above all, "the state of being, beyond all phenomenality, to which this power belongs, is that of the name." In close proximity to Plato's ideas—which, Benjamin argues, "might be considered . . . nothing but deified words and verbal concepts"—poetic language presents its subject with the uncanny and unsuspected ("intentionless") authority of "almost forgotten" memories whose claims prove both arresting and unsettling.[33] In Brentano's and von Arnim's programmatic statements about *Des Knaben Wunderhorn,* the ancient memories miraculously preserved *in,* and suddenly again conjured up *by,* the poetic word also rekindle the conflict between the collective truth of the past, represented by the "people" (*Volk*), and the dispersed knowledge of modern individuals, commonly known as the "public."[34]

Reiterating what David Wellbery has analyzed as Goethe's and Herder's myth of "primordial orality," von Arnim conjures up the image of artless songs woven into the fabric of quotidian existence, say, of miners and chimney sweeps.[35] Only later, Arnim notes, did he understand "that their songs had already achieved what [artificial] songs strive for in vain, namely, that one tone should resonate in many people and unite them all" (Später sah ich den Grund ein, daß in diesen schon erfüllt, wonach jene vergebens streben, auf daß ein Ton in vielen nachhalle und alle verbinde [Brentano, 6: 409]). In the lucid encryption of lyric form, itself "bound" up with the objective materiality of text and book, romanticism mediates a complex and conflict-laden historical situation, and it typically does so by staging that situation as a hermeneutic crisis provoked by the unsuspected resurgence of ancient meanings within the damaged psyche of the modern subject.[36] If Benjamin tells us that "historical knowledge should treat of awakening . . . and nothing else" (1999, 464), the "greater Romantic lyric" anticipates and fulfils that exigency with uncanny precision.

It is this very enjambment of heuristic and archival matter, of a traumatic awakening triggered by the deceptively innocent memories embodied in folk culture, that prompts romantic authors like Brentano and von Arnim (and Wordsworth in England) to characterize their literary productions as "experiments." In appealing to a deep interiority that springs from the modern subject's abrupt encounter with archaic memories uneasily slumbering within a folk song (balladic) tradition, romantic writing claims a strong hermeneutic role for itself. Not surprisingly, Freud was quick to acknowledge and capitalize on the apparent correlation between the inscrutable efficacy of romanticism's articulate forms and his own theory of the unconscious's "deferred" (*nachträglich*) efficacy. Indeed, Freud's decision to credit romanticism with having first mapped, at the level of literary *practice,* those psychological substrata that he himself sought to reclaim through and for his new theoretical *discipline,* is little less than shrewd. Still, subsequent generations of readers have pointed out with growing precision how romanticism—rather than being a folksy embryonic precursor of modern psychoanalysis—developed a highly reflexive and programmatic grasp of the modern subject as the unwitting vessel of his or her own past.[37] Precisely this *already reflexive* tendency in romantic writing—evident in the work of Novalis, Friedrich Schlegel, Brentano, and von Arnim—suggests a deep-rooted epistemological mission intrinsic to romantic cultural production. For these writers, the poetic word was imbued with the unsettling power of projecting the past into the present regardless of the modern subject's conscious intentions or avowed beliefs. As an insistent, though "intentionless," agency silently shadowing the modern subject's conscious existence, the past functions somewhat like the Freudian unconscious. As Robert Schumann puts it so laconically in an 1828 diary entry, "the past is the present's angel of death" ("die Vergangenheit ist der Würgengel der Gegenwart" [1971, 1: 89]). Alluding to his first encounter with the outline of folk poetry, von Arnim conjures up the revealing image of "a firm foundation still shimmering through from beneath the waves, the old streets and piazzas of the submerged city" (als ich dieses feste Fundament noch unter den Wellen, die alten Straßen und Plätze der versunkenen Stadt noch durchschimmern sah).[38] Von Arnim's figuration of the past as a virtual agency forcing the subject to receive previously unwitnessed memory fragments joins up with Freud's conception of a "trauma" whose distinctive symptomatic feature of "repetition compulsion" is said to respond to a past so catastrophic at the time of its original occurrence as to have precluded its conscious assimilation by the subject.

At first glance, my conjunction of romantic lyricism with concepts of traumatic awakening would seem to credit the cultural matter professedly remembered with a degree of authenticity that a number of recent and highly accomplished critics have justly called into question. Susan Stewart treats the late-eighteenth-century ballad as an example of what she calls "distressed genres," distinguished by its tendency to "rescue forms that seem to be disappearing—that is, to effect a kind of archeology of speech forms . . . [and] to place such 'specimens' as curiosities, characterized by fragmentation and exoticism, against the contemporary."[39] Katie Trumpener has remarked on "a long history of pseudo- documentary fictions framed, in their prefaces, by pseudoeditorial authenticating devices" and reads the literary archetype for this practice, James Macpherson's *Ossian* poems, as "a new way of conceiving the unevenness of character, and of textuality, as historical testimony, as an inadvertent record of historical upheavals and endurance, survivals and extinction. This model understands witnesses to history, whether human or textual, as inherently passive and mute on the subject of their sufferings." By contrast, "the broader Ossianic tradition—and the Ossian controversy itself—makes available a rather different model, in which the representatives of the old order loudly challenge the representatives of the new; their way of life may be doomed, but they will go down fighting" (Trumpener, 111, 117). And yet, as Trumpener's last statement affirms, the urgent need and consequent capacity of such cultural memories for awakening modern subjects to their own alienated condition lies in the widespread endorsement of their authentic *appearance*, not in their de facto authenticity (assuming that could ever be authoritatively established).

In accord with Freud's shrewd distinction between memories dating *from* and those relating *to* childhood, "authenticity" must thus be read as self-conscious fiction—a "fantasy" in Slavoj Žižek's definition—and hence an *effect* performatively wrought by specific literary, figural means. In other words, the archival ethos that proclaims them to be fragments of folk culture serendipitously recovered *in* and *for* the present is itself the effect wrought by imaginative literary writing, whose fictitious nature that ethos subsequently neutralizes by the sheer *gravitas* of philological work on cultural "traditions" miraculously preserved or recovered (yet never actually produced). In this manner, the late-eighteenth-century archival cult of authenticity—seizing upon ballad, romance, and eventually the historical novel and what M. H. Abrams long ago christened the greater romantic lyric as its generic linchpins—effectively realizes the collective fantasy of a timeless social order and, as remains to be seen, the new ideological formation of romantic conservatism. The abovementioned genres add a crucial new dimension to such ideological dream work, namely, that of an adventitious belated awakening. In these forms, aesthetic inventiveness is naturalized inasmuch as it conceives and proclaims itself to be an awakening to a deeper historical truth slumbering within its thematic surfeit. In this manner, a literary topos is quietly transfigured into cultural value; *inventio* becomes *traditio.* Consequently, the acutely "literary" quality of reconstituted fragments of (a putatively vanishing) folk culture does not threaten to expose such materials as "inauthentic." On the contrary, their "literary" presentation crucially instances *and* affirms their broader social value as fragments of a *collective* memory, something that nonliterary discourse, with its different standards of authenticity and verifiability, would find difficult to do.

In the high romantic lyric, past experience continues to determine a priori the conscious history of its subject with oblique but unrelenting tenacity. Subjected to an inscrutable, because never consciously experienced, causality, the conscious subject is obliged, in Freud's words, "to *repeat* the . . . material as a contemporary experience instead of . . . *remembering* it as something belonging to the past," and it typically does so with "unwished-for exactitude" (Freud 1955, 18). Like Freud's controversial account of the traumatic origins of Judaism (Freud 1964), the literary production of the Heidelberg romantics

(Creuzer, von Arnim, Brentano, and, for a brief but significant period, Eichendorff) centers around the involuntary remembrance of a catastrophe that had suddenly erased an entire seemingly timeless economic, cultural, and spiritual order. Time and again, these writings tell of their protagonists' "traumatic departure" from some phantasmagoric order of time and place. Exodus here is realized as a narrative of progressive disillusionment that continues to point back at an instance of catastrophic *méconnaissance* in the protagonist's past—and the formal concision of lyric writing furnishes a self-consciously fantasized vantage point from which "history can be grasped only in the very inaccessibility of its occurrence" (Caruth 1996, 15, 18). To conceive the disruptive impact of a contingent memory within the structure of conscious experience in terms no less explicit than Freud's archeological metaphors is to locate poetry within a broad disciplinary and programmatic context. In the case of the Heidelberg romantics—Arnim, Brentano, Görres, Creuzer—the reflexive power of the poetic word establishes an implicit rapport between the contingent moment of its own production and the vast historical aura of its linguistic materials. Or, as Kevin Newmark argues, poetry oscillates "between the punctual defensiveness of the consciousness that produces it and the retentive duration of the memory it serves to replace." Referring to Walter Benjamin's account of "Some Motifs in Baudelaire," Newmark contends that the symbolist lyric raises the

> fundamental question of the *historical* relationship between tradition and modernity. When the formal patterns of continuity that are presumed to have been grounded in traditional experience by the assimilation of consciousness to memory are disturbed by the truly alien experience of modernity, the coherence of subjective experience is itself displaced in unexpected ways. Consciousness and memory, whatever their relationship in some more or less mythic past, are no longer able to function as associative elements within the same system of individual and collective identity. According to this model, then, modernity would itself be structured like a historical "accident" that has at some prior moment befallen and disrupted the homogeneous structure of experience. And the traces of this accident manifest themselves whenever consciousness . . . can no longer be made compatible with memory. (Newmark, 238–39)

Insofar as the romantic lyric articulates the modernity of its subject as a recurrent tension between consciousness and memory, it is bound to stage the intrusion of the latter as an unexpected, haunting intervention. In Newmark's definition, the lyric would be one such "place where the wholly unexpected and accidental can happen to the subject" (Newmark, 239). Still, the past does not only obtrude on consciousness as something that has not yet been consciously known. Rather, what Newmark refers to as "the homogeneous structure of experience"—with all its deceptive coherence and authority as socially valid knowledge—can only constitute itself *because and insofar as it has not acknowledged* its dialectical other: the past.

More than any other German romantic writer, Joseph von Eichendorff (1788–1857) centers his lyrics around this irruption of past memories into the patterns of quotidian conscious existence—a strategy not only calculated to intensify our perception of psychological depth *qua* "recollection" (*Erinnerung*) but also our sense of an untranscendable covenant between subject and history. The past sings and "murmurs" (*rauschen*) everywhere in Eichendorff's writings. Yet the poetry also suspends that unconscious dynamic between the subject's belated awakening to a strictly negative knowledge—that is, of one's having failed to develop a timely grasp of the past when it was still "event" (*Ereignis*)—and a mystification of that very awakening as a purely natural revelation. As we read in Eichendorff's "Liebe in der Fremde" ("Love in a foreign world"), "Everywhere in the trees / The furtive whisper of remembrance bestirs itself" (Erinnernd rührt sich in den Bäumen / Ein heimlich Flüstern überall ([*EW*, 1: 72]). In what follows, I shall explore first how the romantic subject's traumatic awakening to its own disorienting modernity is being contained in lyric form and, subsequently, how Eichendorff's distinctive affiliation of lyricism and memory relates to the emergence of romantic conservatism (*Altkonservatismus*). Indeed, it was primarily with this often misunderstood movement that Eichendorff came to be associated late in his career. Similarly, and at a rather early point (1806), von Arnim already remarks how the "whirlwind of innovation, the lightening-quick presumption of being able to fashion paradise on earth" (in diesem Wirbelwind des Neuen, in diesem vermeinten urschnellen Paradiesgebären auf Erden) of the French Revolution had virtually extinguished all folk song (Brentano 1975, 408). At least from the moment of Prussia's utter defeat, the culture of romantic lyricism begins to edge progressively closer to the discourse of conservatism. Both languages are preoccupied with a traumatic disjunction of past and present, memory and experience.

If the *ideologeme* of early conservatism marks the outer limits of my inquiry into the operation of traumatic affect in romantic writing—that is, beyond its historical motif (*Erinnerung*) and its psychological effect (*Innerlichkeit*)—the evidence for these larger claims must ultimately always be found in the literary text. A reading of a first Eichendorff poem may help us develop a sharper outlook on what Mannheim calls the *tensio* of thought toward "contents surviving from the past." The first lyric is entitled "Vesper" ("Evening Meal") and was first published in Eichendorff's 1837 collection *Gedichte*, though first included in his play *Ezzelin von Romano* (1828):

Die Abendglocken klangen
Schon durch das stille Tal,
Da saßen wir zusammen
Da droben wohl hundertmal.

Und unten war's so stille
Im Lande weit und breit,
Nur über uns die Linde
Rauscht' durch die Einsamkeit.

Was gehen die Glocken heute
Als ob ich weinen müßt?
Die Glocken, die bedeuten,
Daß meine Lieb gestorben ist!

Ich wollt, ich läg begraben,
Und über mir rauschte weit
Die Linde jeden Abend
Von der alten, schönen Zeit! (*EW*, 1: 250)

The evening bells sounded
Already through the quiet vale,
While up there we sat together
well-nigh a hundred times.

Down below it was so quiet
Throughout the whole land far and wide,
And only the lime tree above us
Rustled through this solitude.

Why will the bells ring today
As if I should have to cry?

The bells that tell
Of my love that has died!

I wish I lay already entombed,
And each evening far above
The lime tree rustling would
Speak of the dear old time! (MY TRANSLATION)

The four stanzas break down into two halves, each marked by the concluding, archetypal image of the "rustling lime tree." The overall coherence of the lyric is ensured by its temporal dimension, initially brought into focus through the notion of a recursive, potentially empty event: "While up there we sat together / Well-nigh a hundred times" (Da saßen wir zusammen / Da droben wohl hundertmal). In contrast to such routine sociability, the concluding image of the tree's "rustling" points to a rupture between the rhythm of the quotidian present and "the dear old time" (die alte, schöne Zeit). This phrase, or rather cliché, is Eichendorff's veritable poetic signature. Through it, the poetic "I" sets a limit to all historical time and voices the wish for its own interment ("Ich wollt, ich läg begraben") in an immaculate, mythic past. The peal of the church bell that resonates through the ominously "silent vale" (das stille Tal) positions the voice at the threshold between empirical perception and metaphysical intuition. Gauging the spatial depth of the valley, the faint, distant sonority of church bells prefigures the concluding, funereal vision. More important, though, it exhorts the voice to specify the nature of its "loss." The local and particular dimension of affect, bereavement at the loss of a beloved ("Die Glocken, die bedeuten, / Daß meine Lieb gestorben ist"), only enters in hypothetical form. The loss of *die Lieb* may refer either to a beloved or to the capacity to love. Thus the scene of evening oscillates bewilderingly between an intensification of affect ("loss of the beloved") and its complete erosion (the incapacity to feel love). Twice in this short lyric, we thus have affective states bracketed by subjunctive constructions: "Als ob ich weinen müßt" and "Ich wollt, ich läg begraben." Precisely this hypothetical notation of affect as the last bastion of authentic subjectivity- -the last rampart to defend the subject against its imminent awakening to the knowledge of its own atrophied interiority—is truly defining of early-nineteenth-century lyric writing.

Meanwhile, the bells also serve as the emblem of a specifically lyric form of attentiveness. Just as the spatial depth of the "land far and wide" (Lande weit und breit) is gauged only through the migration of sound, the peal of the bells also gives rise to a fundamental subjective self-awareness. In Husserl's *Logical Investigations,* the colloquialism of "attentiveness" (*Aufmerksamkeit*) is suddenly introduced as the pivotal condition allowing so-called "intentional acts" to be promoted to objective status, and hence to become accessible to an "inner perception." In short, without the constitutive leap to such attentiveness, consciousness itself would remain merely a contingent signified of its (supposedly) "intentional" objects, unable to arrive at a coherent representation of their quality and, consequently, barred from ever becoming conscious of itself as a cognitive agency.[40] It is precisely in this sense of "attentiveness"—a belated calling-away of the subject from its mundane "contents" and so awakening it to its inscrutable historical situatedness—that is enacted in Eichendorff's lyrics. Time and again, the subject is subtly extricated from its precarious absorption in the mythical bond that fuses regional and local existence, religious beliefs, and cultural values. Rather than merely symbolizing a vague "mood" or outright mystical state of affect, Eichendorff's spatial and aural figurations always point toward a rupture in the fabric of human time. Far from indulging in the myth of a purely affective, timeless interiority, a poem like "Vesper" effectively encodes—in the image of the bell tolling—the imminent passing of that self-enclosed dream world. If a desire for total immersion in this imagistic world takes us into the poem, the lyric's excessive accommodation of that desire—a kind of hypersimulation to be explored in further detail—effectively compels us to awaken to its status as a text-based fantasy.[41] Thus Eichendorff's characteristic choice of the subjunctive has already qualified affect as dangerously mesmerizing and wholly self-privileging.

To be sure, it is tempting to frame the entire lyric within an opposition between the empty, repetitive time of social existence ("Da saßen wir zusammen / Da droben wohl hundertmal") and an absolution from all temporality marked by the bells' distant sonority. Yet to proceed in this manner is to ignore that a phrase as overtly clichéd as "the dear old time" has been carefully framed in a subjunctive syntax, thereby alerting us to interpretive pitfalls that lurk beneath clichés encountered in lyric writing. To escape from empirical social time is to express a desire for transcendence that can only take the textual form of a paradox: to escape to a state of being that could only be realized as nonbeing (i.e., death). Thus the epistemological collision of two worlds characteristic of all traumatic awakening finds objective lyric expression in the interference between image and grammar, between the banal certitude of the poetic cliché and the prevarication of the subjunctive. Even the lyric image per se resonates with such tension by alternately ensnaring its readers in inauthentic clichés or consigning them to the epistemological vagaries of an anxious and disorienting modernity where experience and memory are no longer aligned. Indeed, the suspicion that Eichendorff's poetry might be little more than an array of clichés skillfully deployed dates back a long way, something echoed by Adorno's remark that "when one first hears many of Eichendorff's lines . . . they sound like quotations, quotations learned by heart from God's primer."[42] Richard Alewyn expands on this point by offering a short catalogue of what Adorno had called the "stage-prop quality of the linguistic elements" in Eichendorff's poetry (Adorno 1991, 1: 70). For Alewyn, these lyrics

> operate altogether in the external world of visible and audible things, which is one of the reasons why they appear so "slight." At the same time, Eichendorff is certainly no "realist." His poetry contributes little to our knowledge of some straightforward reality. It has often been remarked how narrow a segment of life and world he seems to content himself with. Readers have responded with even greater annoyance—though scarcely attuned to the true scope of the matter—to the fact that the same motifs recur in endless repetition. Forever we have forests rustling [*rauschen*], nightingales singing, fountains murmuring, rivers shimmering. Time and again, light reflexes and harmonies from summits, from down below, or from among the treetops waft over to us or enter through the window. All this is pushed to the point of formulaic rigor.[43]

Alewyn's characterization is at once accurate and, as he himself concedes, in need of further reflection. For the presence of images as overtly schematic as Eichendorff's confounds the plausible attitude of an "empathetic reception" (reading as *Einfühlung*) by alerting the audience to the lyric's quotation-like quality. To do so is to press, within the form of the lyric itself, the question of literariness—of what shall count as "literary value" and the purposes to which it appears so obliquely committed. As it turns out, this very question: "Does a specific poem belong to the order of invention or quotation?" correlates with the subject's epistemological condition: can it grasp (*begreifen*) experience by means of autonomous categories of rationality, or is it at the mercy of an "almost forgotten" past, at once unfathomable and inescapable? Clichés disconcert because of their conspicuous enjambment of form and cognition. They no longer communicate referentially but, instead, appear bent on dismantling the audience's faith in stable referential connections between affect and form, interiority and expression, pathos and its communicability. The cliché stages the subject's troubled awakening to precisely those depths of its language that are not "expressive." Beneath its placid, seemingly unruffled rapport with inherited rhetorical models, the cliché unmasks (allegorizes) an earlier period's excessive faith in linguistic mastery over the contingent world of intuition and perception. It is romantic allegory sensu stricto—stripped of all wit and social effectivity: that is, of all irony. Its baroque mournfulness, so powerfully at work throughout Eichendorff's lyric oeuvre, resides in its imperceptible ability to estrange us from any residual faith in a (supposedly inalienable) affective rapport (*Einfühlung*) between self and world. By disarticulating the myth of a language wholly self-sufficient and untrammeled by any contingencies of perception, the poetic cliché effectively subverts the mimetic principle on which its overconfident surface representations continue to be predicated.

We shall have further occasion to consider whether this unsettling proximity of poetry to outright quotation or cliché may indeed constitute the underlying aesthetic and ideological signature of European writing during the era of the Regency in Britain and the *Restauration* in Germany. For the time being, it remains imperative to listen to the peculiar idiom of Eichendorff's lyrics and so close in on their construction of a specific affective economy. At first glance, the voice that constitutes itself so unmistakably in these poems seems to conjure up an impossibly remote past with an attitude of deep nostalgic longing. Yet as one slows down the reading of this poetry, a peculiar reversal of cause and effect, image and referent, affect and expression can be found to occur. Rather than presenting itself as the timeless and unimpeachable *source* of writing, affect here seems to emerge as an epiphenomenon of eerily familiar stylistic patterns. Indeed, Eichendorff's lyrics seem bent on rehearsing for us what Paul de Man describes as moments of interference between the referential or expressive function of language and its performative reconstitution of being in the form of textual simulacra.[44] Almost imperceptibly, the lyric's official faith in a symbolic coincidence of word and referent begins to shift and decompose, because techniques mobilized for the representation of affect work, in effect, too well. That is, the poetic cliché hastens the demise of the mimetic principle, for it lays bare how that principle works to begin with. Here we see *in actu* what Adorno meant by saying that the artwork is "not only of the same essence as the dialectic external to [it] but . . . resembles it without imitating it" (1997, 5). Thus the excessive "fit" of word and referent in Eichendorff's lyrics disrupts the reader's initial assumption that to read is to enter a domain of quasi-sensory perception. Asked to witness the operation of *Vorstellung*, we effectively become aware of mimesis as an effect of hypersimulation. If "mimesis [is] the presentation of an ideal reality" [Darstellung eines ideell Wirklichen], David Wellbery argues, then the "simulacrum [asserts] the reality of the presentation" itself [*Wirklichkeit der Darstellung*]. Thus Eichendorff's lyrics ought not to be approached as "mood-based [*Stimmungslyrik*] in any conventional sense, but as thematizations of the lyric medium." Wellbery convincingly locates Eichendorff's poems "perched on the threshold between two worlds," that of an unconscious, dreamlike immersion in the principle of mimesis and that of an awakening to the medial character of the lyric image as simulacrum—its reflexive detachment from all faith in mimetic and expressive technique (Wellbery 1998, 452, 460, 458; my translations).

Yet without contesting de Man's basic claims concerning the aporetic nature of poetic language, which he came to regard as the manifestation of a pervasive and insoluble epistemological dilemma, my aim here is somewhat more complex in nature. To begin with, moments of rhetorical instability ought to be grasped—albeit with a caution that befits all speculative proceedings—as symptomatic condensations of a larger historical dilemma. Indeed, it is only on the basis of a deeper affinity between formal-aesthetic and historical processes that we can begin to grasp romanticism as a specific phase in the evolution of modernity. Above all, we find the period conceding interiority to its post-Enlightenment subjects only in supplemental form. Rather than collapsing inwardness into a purely imaginary order—a quasi-maternal and allegedly unimpeachable, affective origin—romanticism during the Napoleonic era and beyond stages the inwardness of its subjects as a progressive awakening to their traumatic history. A strictly literary-historical narrative ought thus to approach Eichendorff's lyrics as the second stage in an epistemological crisis, first apparent in the way that Goethe's lyrics struggle to name and thus affirm an absolute source and origin for all expressive and creative acts. For quite some time, readers have been remarking on the fact that the romantic lyric's formal-rhetorical antagonisms, such as its subject's deeply personal investment in affective experiences (melancholy, indolence, longing, dejection, etc.), seem oddly generic and are rendered in curiously mannered images. This paradox of escapist desires not concealed but curiously accented in lyric speech ultimately is not so much symptomatic of the romantic lyric as constitutive of it. That is, far from being a mere rhetorical accident randomly vitiating the expressive agenda of a given poem, the paradox in question is being rehearsed *by* the text and *for* an audience whose longing for a state of pure inwardness the text itself qualifies rather than indulges. As we have already seen, one of the principal rhetorical strategies for such a reflexive agenda is the poetic cliché, and few poems stage this process of the subject's self-demystification more effectively than Eichendorff's poem entitled "Sehnsucht" ("Longing") in the 1837 collection:

Es schienen so golden die Sterne,
Am Fenster ich einsam stand
Und hörte aus weiter Ferne
Ein Posthorn im stillen Land.
Das Herz mir im Leib entbrennte,
Da hab ich mir heimlich gedacht:
Ach, wer da mitreisen könnte
In der prächtigen Sommernacht!

Zwei junge Gesellen gingen
Vorüber am Bergeshang,
Ich hörte im Wandern sie singen
Die stille Gegend entlang:
Wo die Wälder rauschen so sacht,
Von Quellen, die von den Klüften
Von schwindelnden Felsenschlüften,
Sich stürzen in die Waldesnacht.

Sie sangen von Marmorbildern,
Von Gärten, die überm Gestein
In dämmernden Lauben verwildern,
Palästen im Mondenschein,
Wo die Mädchen am Fenster lauschen,
Wann der Lauten Klang erwacht
Und die Brunnen verschlafen rauschen
In der prächtigen Sommernacht.— (*EW*, 1: 66)

Amid the stars' golden effulgence
I stood alone at the window
And from far realms I heard

A post-horn calling through the still land.
As my heart inflamed with passion,
I secretly bethought myself:
Ah! who wouldn't join these travels
Amid the splendors of this summer night!

Two young apprentices passed
Over a mountain ridge,
I heard them singing while journeying
Throughout quiet regions:
Of dizzying ravines,
And forests rustling ever so gently,
Of springs leaping from chasms
Deep down into the forest night.

They sang of marble statues,
Of gardens grown wild over rocks and stones
And expiring in dusky foliage,
Of moonlit palaces,
Where young maidens at the window,
Harken to the sound of lutes awakening
And to the dreamy rustle of fountains
Amid the splendors of a summer night. (MY TRANSLATION)

Poised beneath the stock-in-trade "golden stars" and framed by the inevitable window that limns the oblique passions of so many of Eichendorff's lyric subjects, the voice issuing from the page of this text assumes a peculiar status indeed. It seems less expressive of some authentic, if secretive ("da habe ich mir heimlich gedacht . . .") nostalgia for spontaneous travel and comradeship than it impersonates that longing by citing it, by distilling its lyric composition out of a series of topoi. Indeed, the precarious status of the fantasy is rendered obvious not only by the thoroughly domestic setting of the speaker but also by the perilous journey of the two apprentices said to pass along a ridge and dizzying ravines ("am Bergeshang . . . / Von schwindelnden Felsenschlüften"). Beyond the reach of the eye, these emblematic wanderers haunt the speaker with their calling, an appeal to break out of a terminally uneventful, bureaucratized, and domesticated middle-class existence. The tension between the speaker and wanderer correlates with that between the eerily familiar (*heimlich*) precision of the lyric text and the wayward and ultimately inscrutable motions of folk song. Lyric writing thus constitutes itself by tracing its other, the folk song whose origins are forever occluded by the informal sonority of nature, be it the gentle rustle of far-flung forests or the murmur of ineluctable springs / sources (*Quellen*) flowing into the dark of night.

It is just the schematic imprecision of Eichendorff's landscape that prompts its being read as an allegory of lyric production during the postrevolutionary era. It highlights the distance between lyric and folk song, alienated speech and its flashbacks to an ostensibly authentic cultural practice (*singen*) that was never consciously witnessed but can only be *re*constructed in a conjectural, indeed, overtly transferential process of listening. Because the lyric overtly dramatizes the distance between its own notably formalized contemplation and some nonspecific past, that past can no longer be thought of as the authentic point of reference for expressive, representational writing. With the lyric drawing attention to the instability of historical time, the apprentices' journey, at first so longingly traced by the speaker, oscillates in an ideally indeterminate present—perched between a blank future and an inscrutable past. As Peter von Matt notes, "the temporal structure of the [subject's] ground . . . consists in the potential presence of everything past. . . . The seemingly innocuous longing for times past becomes aware of itself as the perilous longing for a place of utter simultaneity—along with everything that such a place would entail: erotic ecstasy, dissolution of the self's boundaries, and personal catastrophe."[45] Rather than proceeding from a belief in imaginative transport—motion as *e*motion—Eichendorff's dominant rhetorical and psychological strategy is that of explicit transference. No longer does the furtive thought (*heimlich gedacht*) of an escape into other regions constitute a desire accidentally disclosed. Rather, it is transference articulated with a reflexivity that, in Eichendorff, time and again takes the form of the interrogative and the subjunctive ("Ach, wer da mitreisen könnte . . ."). The poem acknowledges its own unreality by overstating a utopian desire for its folkloric other (the singing students, the call of distant horns, etc.). Longing (*Sehnsucht*) constitutes less a straightforward psychological attitude unwittingly implemented *in* the text than a transferential process reflexively exposed *by* the text. Crucial in this regard is the third stanza, with its random array of nostalgic images ranging from marble statues to fading French gardens, gazebos at twilight, moonlit palaces, and so forth. Like a set of Chinese boxes, the stanza mirrors the attentive listening posture that had solicited the speaker's attention (*Aufmerksamkeit*) to begin with. Thus we read of young women listening to the forlorn harmonies of the lute and spellbound by the sleepy murmur of distant fountains.[46] The motif of awakening belatedly to an impossible desire thus surfaces as a motif *within* and as the organizing principle *of* lyric form itself.

CHAPTER FIVE

Phantasie

The Postmodernity of Romantic Lyricism and Political Conservatism

> Intérieurs . . . are residues of a dream world. The realization of dream elements, in the course of waking up, is the paradigm of dialectical thinking. Thus, dialectical thinking is the organ of historical awakening. Every epoch, in fact, not only dreams the one to follow but, in dreaming, precipitates its awakening. It bears its end within itself and unfolds it—as Hegel already noticed—with cunning.
>
> — WALTER BENJAMIN, *The Arcades Project, trans.* HOWARD EILAND AND KEVIN MCLAUGHLIN

> The ambiguity of the . . . revelation of the past does not depend so much on the vacillation of its content between the Imaginary and the Real, for it locates itself in both. Nor is it exactly error or falsehood. The point is that it presents us with the birth of Truth in the Word, and thereby brings us up against the reality of what is neither true nor false. . . . For the Truth of this revelation lies in the present Word which testifies to it in contemporary reality and which grounds it in the name of that reality. Yet in that reality, it is only the Word which bears witness to that portion of the powers of the past which has been thrust aside at each crossroads where the event has made its choice. . . . [Historical anamnesis] is not a question of reality, but of Truth, because the effect of a full Word is to re-order the past contingent events by conferring on them the necessities to come, just as they are constituted by the little liberty through which the subject makes them present.
>
> — JACQUES LACAN, *Speech and Language in Psychoanalysis, trans.* BY ANTHONY WILDEN

Notwithstanding their seemingly self-contained idiom and form, the figural organization of Eichendorff's lyrics closely resembles some disciplinary developments in philology and general psychology during the first two decades of the nineteenth century. The intellectual response to the collapse in 1806 of the sprawling, superannuated, and altogether peculiar behemoth known as the Heiliges Römisches Reich deutscher Nation, or Holy Roman Empire of the German Nation, shows lyric writing mediating the traumatic historicity of its romantic subjects, rather than evading it. Within days of reaching Heidelberg in May 1807, Joseph von Eichendorff and his brother began to attend lectures by Joseph Görres (1776–1848).[1] A highly charismatic rhetorician, lecturer, and wide-ranging essayist, as well as a student of Kant's and Herder's cosmopolitan writings and a radical advocate of Enlightenment ideals, Görres established himself as a central figure during the short-lived but influential period of romantic lecturing and collaborative writing at Heidelberg (1806–8). Like Brentano and von Arnim, Görres was a beneficiary of the dramatic reorientation of the German lyric in Goethe's *Sesenheimer Lieder* of 1771 and, among other writings, in Herder's *Auszug aus einem Briefwechsel über Ossian und die Lieder alter Völker* (1773). At issue was more than just the quest for a poetry untainted by the alleged artifice and esotericism of mid-eighteenth-century literary writing (Wieland, Gleim, Haller, et al.). Goethe and Herder saw their literary innovation as integrally related to the broad cultural objective of nation-building, and their resolve was strengthened by publications in England, in particular, Thomas Percy's *Reliques of Ancient English Poetry* (1765). Herder's invective against "doctrines rendered dry, lifeless dogma" (Lehren in trockner, schläfriger dogmatischer Form) expressed the view of a cosmopolitan, enlightened, and educated community, whose utopian hopes, frustrated in 1807, would be appropriated by a new and politically more circumspect generation of romantics.[2] For the generation of intellectuals that followed Goethe and Herder, Napoleon's resounding defeat of Prussia and his military and administrative domination of most German territories mandated the redefinition of nationalism from a political into a cultural strategy. Of strategic concern to the new patriotic culture that rapidly took shape after 1804 was healing the split between two linguistic systems: the refined, latinate language of courtly society and scholastic learning, on the one hand, and a comparatively unsophisticated, long-disparaged vernacular German culture, on the other. Von Arnim's postscript to *Des Knaben Wunderhorn* speaks of a linguistic divide (*Sprachtrennung*) that is both philological and political in character. Thus, the books in which folk culture had allegedly survived were hampered both by "capricious, foolhardy government restrictions" (von Regierungen willkührlich leichtsinnig beschränkt) and by the "learned classes having adopted a peculiar, mannered language of their own" (die Gelehrten indessen versassen sich über einer eigenen vornehmen Sprache [Brentano, 6: 430–31]).

Romantic medievalism and the resurgence of Catholicism among intellectuals (including Eichendorff, Schlegel, Novalis, Görres) during the romantic period must be understood as a strategy aimed at identifying and popularizing cultural values ostensibly antecedent to the split between these two linguistic systems. At the same time, radicals like Görres made it quite clear that nationalism, medievalism, and the vision of an essentially classless society would all go hand in hand. Here, too, lie the roots for the almost seamless transition of anti-Napoleonic radicalism into an educated conservative dissent from both Metternich's Machiavellian restoration politics and the equally secular, albeit more idealistic and attenuated, agenda of German liberalism after 1819. As early as 1805, with Herder's and Goethe's stress on the cosmopolitan European character of "folk song" (the term *Volkslied* actually being Herder's coinage) and folk culture rapidly fading, the emphasis shifted to an allegedly distinctive German vernacular culture. As late as 1804, von Arnim 's search for old manuscripts suitable for inclusion in *Des Knaben Wunderhorn* had still taken him to London, Paris, and Zurich, but his 1805 postscript to the first volume of the collection left little doubt about its allegiance to German national values. Shortly after the publication of the collection, and caught up in the chaotic retreat of Prussian troops from the battlefields at Jena and Auerstädt in 1806, von Arnim provided soldiers with wartime poems that he had rewritten from old manuscripts.[3] It is hard to imagine a scene more poignant than the editor of a just published collection of medieval folk poetry distributing battlefield songs to the retreating troops. Notwithstanding the quixotic idealism of von Arnim's gesture, the commitment of the Heidelberg romantics to the recovery and rehabilitation of folk song and medieval popular culture represented a deliberate effort to wrest control over the redefinition of German culture away from politicians and place it in the hands of intellectuals. Between 1806 and 1819, the formative years for an entire generation of romantic intellectuals and writers, that attempt was doggedly pursued, though ultimately defeated at the hands of Metternich's restoration politics. Speaking of his and Brentano's collection, von Arnim notes how "[m]any of the poetic idioms [*Singweisen*] point back toward a vanished dance, just as the ruins of a castle point toward a magic formula that will emerge some day when we hit upon it and solve it. . . . Who is to say when Germany is to be reborn; yet whoever carries it within himself feels it stirring powerfully. Just as a strong fever resolves itself in a feeling of thirst . . . so the health of a future period appears to greet us in these songs. Often we encounter images that are more than that, images that grope toward us and address us, [saying], "If only this were true" (Brentano, 6: 436–37; my translation).

Even at this relatively early point, however, German romanticism's cultural and political ideals seem compromised by the figurative language in which they are set forth. Thus, while the appeal for a national rebirth pivots on the familiar trope of a feeling "stirring powerfully," the content of that feeling is grammatically elusive: "whoever carries *it* within himself." Rather than being validated by a determinate content, patriotic affect is quite literally (pro)nominal. What is more, the passage reveals the epistemological significance of nationalist emotion to be wholly contingent on some serendipitous encounter with cultural objects transmitted from the past—cryptic, ruined, faded, and continually awaiting redemption by the future. Much later, in one of his most widely quoted and programmatic lyrics, Eichendorff again evokes the suspension of the romantic subject in a temporal structure spanning from a past imbued with archeological possibilities to a desire for future redemption. Recalling von Arnim's notion of a world filled with historical debris "point[ing] toward a magic formula that will emerge some day when we hit upon it and solve it," Eichendorff's "Wünschelrute" ("Divining Rod") conceives of the present as illusory, repetitive dreaming (*fort und fort*) that can only be overcome by magical access to the historical "aura" (as Benjamin calls it) slumbering in all "things":

Schläft ein Lied in allen Dingen,
Die da träumen fort und fort,
Und die Welt hebt an zu singen,
Triffst du nur das Zauberwort. (*EW*, 1: 132)

Slumbers there a song in all things
That dream forever on and on,
And all the world shall launch into song,
If only you divine the magic word. (MY TRANSLATION)

While Eichendorff's gnomic verse qualifies eschatological hope with a shrewdly conditional syntax, it originates in the same basic conception of historical cognition set forth by von Arnim.[4] As the latter insists, any appeal issuing from the past takes the form of images that haunt the modern subject by virtue both of their urgency and their (at least partial) unintelligibility. Romantic subjectivity is here intimately entwined with the project of historical hermeneutics. Far from evading history and seeking refuge in some putatively autonomous aesthetic domain, the authorial subject conceives of the past as a cryptic memory best negotiated via the complex hermeneutic medium of the lyric image. It is in the writings of Görres, Eichendorff's first and most influential teacher at Heidelberg, that we find the historicity of the image, specifically the lyric image, forcefully asserted. Only a year after the appearance of Brentano's and von Arnim 's collection of folk poetry, Görres published *Die teutschen Volksbücher* (1807), a collection of folktales that is particularly significant because of the author's explicit statements about the relationship between historical recollection (*Erinnerung*) and the modernity of romantic affect (*Innerlichkeit*). That these folktales "enjoy an immortal, unassailable life," as Görres argues, is at least in part due to their being exempt from all social division. "Pulsating through all social strata" (alle Stände durchpulsierend), folk literature is said to have effectively survived all fluctuations of literary taste, even if for extended periods it had been ignored or disparaged by high culture's arbiters of taste and, "thus banned, had to seek shelter among the common people. . . . If you wish to seek these exiles, you will have to look for them among the people where they still survive, as well as amid the dust of libraries where they have hibernated for many centuries" (Görres, 173, 291–92; my translation).

Time and again, Görres insists on the basic ideological mission underlying the project of philological recovery. Apart from salvaging the calcified practices of philology—later lampooned by Eichendorff as "an old man grown childish and given over to arcane literaria [*Silbenstechen*] and interminable variations on a long forgotten theme" (Eichendorff 1984, 5, 4: 147)—the rehabilitation of folk literature furnishes disenfranchised and often displaced intellectuals with the needed objective correlative for their protodemocratic populist agenda. Already disillusioned by Napoleon's betrayal of the revolutionary idea, which he had witnessed firsthand while serving as the representative of his native city, Koblenz, in Paris between 1799 and 1800, Görres conceives of folk literature as the "magic word" (*Zauberwort*) that allows the romantic subject to awaken to the meaning of modernity. Thus *Die teutschen Volksbücher* imagines medieval culture as a carnivalesque society unencumbered by economic and professional specialization, territorial and religious schisms, and the rising specter of philistine ressentiment that was to flourish during the restoration age:

> William of Poitou led off the procession, . . . and a bustling procession comprising all ranks followed suit: priests, laymen, kings, dukes, knights, women, all harmonized in this dithyramb. As though a magic wand had touched all of humanity, the people rose up with beautiful enthusiasm, and for two centuries the choruses traveled through forests, castles, and cities, all the while rejoicing and swinging the Dionysian baton. Everything resounded to their call, all earthbound and previously muted creatures had found their language, and everywhere there was an abundance of song, surging, sounding, pulsating as if a harmonious tempest of sound had taken hold of these times. . . . Indeed, in this lyric culture all social difference had been reconciled. (Görres, 283; my translation)

Görres's romanticism conceives of knowledge as an archeological endeavor, irreducibly historical—not by choice, but because it is necessarily hindsight.

In the same year that saw Hegel finish his *Phenomenology of Spirit* to the rumble of artillery outside Jena, Görres and his romantic collaborators at Heidelberg also conceived of knowledge as the subject's continual, if never conclusive, awakening to the fact of its intrinsic belatedness.[5] While the romantic medievalism of *Die teutschen Volksbücher* strikes us as fantastic, and with good reason, we should take care not to dismiss the project outright. For precisely this phantasmagoric status of the past, its inherently opaque and figural character, also enables the modern subject to envision a form of cognition beyond the disciplinary and institutional constraints of the present. Against the Enlightenment's fervent attempts at correcting the mythical and inscrutable palimpsest of history with the covert mythology of rational universals—Görres conceives of history as a process of philological reconstruction and imaginative rewriting. Inasmuch as history circumscribes the individual's material existence and interpretive possibilities alike, this individual can awaken to his or her intrinsic belatedness vis-à-vis history only if that fact is given objective and concrete expression in distinctive aesthetic forms. For Görres and his fellow romantics, historical knowledge cannot be located in a deceptively factual, though ultimately lifeless, aggregation of dates, tables, and genealogies.[6] Rather, it arises through the concerted philological mapping of idioms and styles serendipitously preserved and transmitted only in folk literature. Far from constituting an objective other awaiting appropriation at the hands of some dispassionate scholastic method, history is to be located in the evolution, transformation, and tacit endurance of diverse idioms, languages, and folkloric styles. Understood as a process of unconscious semiosis, history amounts to a dynamic principle in its own right, a haunting appeal urging the subject to awaken from the quasi somnambulist logic of its modernity: "Schläft ein Lied in allen Dingen / Die da träumen fort und fort."

Görres's philological recovery of folktales revolves around an attentive listening to the submerged call of the past. At their farthest remove, the rhetorical forms and idioms of folk culture "speak in dark hieroglyphs . . . with an elemental meaning and significance, though not as the human tongue, in articulate sounds" (sie sprechen in dunkeln Hieroglyphen . . . wie die Elemente sprechen, sinnvoll und bedeutend, aber nicht mit Menschenzungen, nicht mit artikulirten Tönen [Görres, 275]). Inasmuch as old heroic narratives (*Sagenpoesie*) are said "to have persisted like a quiet murmur throughout all generations until the last of these raised it to a complete language" (wie ein leises Murmeln fortlief durch alle Geschlechter, bis der Letzten Eines sie zur vollen Sprache bildete [ibid., 181]), the modern subject's capacity to merge consciously into a linguistic and political community depends on scanning the forms of quotidian, popular language for unsuspected historical depth. Time and again, it is the trope of the nearly inaudible, "almost forgotten" voice—the persistence of folk culture as a historical unconscious—that lends potential depth to the modern subject.[7] Like a holograph of successive rhetorical epochs and submerged aesthetic traditions, the modern subject's interiority (*Innerlichkeit*) pivots on a sustained, speculative listening to the calling of the past and on the subsequent preservation (*Aufhebung*) of its serendipitous disclosures:

> Their call resembles a stirring breeze, the ear listens to the wondrous sounds, even as understanding is granted only to the inner senses or mind. . . . And once the present rises anew from the soil, the hieroglyphs have ripened; like leaves, a dark and cool breath of wind loosens them from their branches and quietly blows them across the soil. Indeed, all of humanity gathers the magic writings and recognizes in them beloved traits of the past. Phantasmatic voices [*Geisterstimmen*] arise and, in a quiet whisper, hold communion with the past. (Görres, 275–76; my translation)

Most significant about Görres's arguments, and consequential for our own reading, is the ambivalent character of the awakening sketched out in this passage. The awakening call of "spirit voices" said to be intelligible only "to the inner sense" effectively anchors the fate of an entire collective (*das ganze Geschlecht*) within the affective spontaneity of each individual. An awakening of this kind proves both involuntary and dynamic in that its subjects are caught up—like the leaves in Dante's *Inferno* and in Shelley's Dantean "Ode to the West Wind"—in an irresistible progressive motion ("treibt sie still vor sich an der Erde hin"). With their movement governed by the wind, these subjects resemble Benjamin's *Angelus Novus,* facing the past while caught by an irresistible storm that propels them into the future. Görres here explicates, as it were avant la lettre, the inherently ambivalent logic of modern ideology. Ostensibly unpremeditated, a collective movement is said to arise in consequence of an inscrutable calling "felt" within each individual. Spellbound by the poignancy of his or her own affective response and transfixed by the ancient sources of the calling itself, the individual quietly communes both with the past and with all those anonymous subjects who exhibit the same kind of response. Overall, the passage quoted above combines features of the patriotic radicalism for which the young Görres was best known with the mystical overtones of a Catholic conservatism (*Altkonservatismus*) that, shortly after 1800, was to rise in opposition against Napoleon's and eventually Metternich's political and economic reorganization of central Europe.[8] Unlike the bureaucratic and officially sanctioned conservatism that was to prevail in Austria and Prussia after 1819, the movement sketched out in this passage is much closer to the conservative ideology articulated by Karl Mannheim.

Profoundly opposed to the false choice between aristocratic dissipation and bourgeois greed, which would sooner or later be shown to be the true motivations of so-called conservative "beliefs," Eichendorff (following his teacher Görres) understands conservatism as an affective calling—a poetic "vocation" issuing from the magical of past writings (*Zauberschriften*). Indeed, it is only by heeding this faint but insistent voice and allowing it to awaken one to the traumatic scene of modernity that what we call "interiority" (*Innerlichkeit*) begins to constitute itself. Eichendorff's short lyric "Der Abend" ("Evening"), the figuration of which is strongly reminiscent of Görres's *Die teutschen Volksbücher,* also enjambs spatiotemporal and affective qualities in highly distinctive locution:

Schweigt der Menschen laute Lust:
Rauscht die Erde wie in Träumen
Wunderbar mit allen Bäumen,
Was dem Herzen kaum bewußt,
Alte Zeiten, linde Trauer,
Und es schweifen leise Schauer
Wetterleuchtend durch die Brust. (*EW,* 1: 69)

Mankind's noisy pleasures silenced,
Earth, as in dreams, rustles
Marvelously with all the trees;
The heart scarcely conscious,
Old time, faint mourning,
And quiet shudders like distant lightning
Rove through one's bosom. (MY TRANSLATION)

Concise, impersonal, and almost modernist in its radical figuration, this lyric is dominated by aural images ("Schweigt . . . laute Lust / Rauscht die Erde / . . . leise Schauer"). And yet, it is the *materiality* of sound—not sound itself—that is represented. In its quintessential sonority, Eichendorff's primal "rustling" (*rauschen*) refuses to be partitioned according to Saussurean concepts of "acoustic image" and "concept."[9] For here the acoustic image functions strictly on its own behalf, and not as the vehicle for some abstract sense. With the medium taking center stage, the relation between lyric speech and its subject matter shifts from a model of mimesis to one of simulation. Thus it is quite impossible to tell whether the chthonic murmur of the earth serves as a simile for the unconscious ("wie in Träumen . . . / Was dem Herzen kaum bewußt") or vice versa. Even more directly, the "faint showers" said to rove through "the breast" do so not *like* lightning but (as the gerund implies) *as* lightning (*wetterleuchtend*). A deep-structural link between the obliquity of material sound and that of ancient times (*alte Zeiten*) thus emerges—again, not as outright metaphor—but in a poetic idiom so studiously impersonal and nonpropositional as to embody that affinity at the level of the medium. To call a phrase such as "wetterleuchtend durch die Brust" metaphoric, or to read "wie in Träumen" as a straightforward simile, is to resolve the materiality of the image into a determinate meaning and construe an empirical phenomenon as simply an expedient for communicating some putatively abstract content.[10] And yet, in ways that would not surface again until Georg Trakl's lyric poetry almost a century later, Eichendorff effectively denies his readers a controlled experience of his tropes and figures. Rather than mediating and tempering sense, the poetry confronts us with the complexity of the (linguistic) medium itself. Recollecting and "interiorizing" (*erinnern*) a faint yet insistent past, lyric speech appears poised between a materially vivid experience and the tentative distillation of its significance. Perched between the referential and a purely positional function (to recall de Man's distinction), the poetic sign here assumes the character of a simulacrum, a copy (or pseudo-memory) for which no original can ever be produced. What the lyric recovers, then, is not the past but its symptomatic reverberation as a "mood" that circumscribes the entire spread of formal decisions that inform lyric figuration (*Darstellung*). Precisely because it is irrecuperable (and, indeed, unverifiable) in any referential or mimetic sense, the past haunts its belated subjects in the medium of lyric signs perched between materially vivid phonation (*rauschen*) and a tentative promise for intellectual closure.[11]

In 1817, precisely when his teachings were formally published in the philosophical compendium entitled *Enzyklopädie der philosophischen Wissenschaften im Grundrisse,* Hegel gave up the position at Heidelberg that he had assumed only two years earlier and moved to the capital of a Prussia eager to reconstruct its political and cultural authority.[12] In delivering his inaugural lecture at Berlin on 22 October 1818, he was quick to acknowledge how—following many delays and reversals in his professional career during the Napoleonic era—"this [Prussian] state has now accepted me into its community" (dieser Staat, der mich nun in sich aufgenommen hat).[13] He insists on the hegemony of philosophical thought vis-à-vis "quotidian and material interests, as well as the vanity of mere opinion" (die Interessen der Not und des Tages, andererseits aber die Eitelkeit der Meinungen [401]). In its dialectical form, philosophy is not merely the other of such needs, interests, opinions, or feelings; as "rational thought"(denkende Vernunft), it comprehends these psychological states in their relative and foreign-determined character.

Within the heavily compartmentalized *Enzyklopädie,* which served as Hegel's philosophical breviary, the proclaimed hegemony of conceptual thought is demonstrated most concisely and forcefully in part III ("Philosophy of Spirit), section C ("Psychology") and its subsections α ("Intuition") and β ("Representation"). Section β, in turn, is further broken down into (1) Recollection, (2) Imagination, and (3) Memory. Palpably bureaucratic in its design, Hegel's *Encyclopedia* embodies the intellectual and institutional confidence that undergirds his overall conception of philosophy. Aspiring to become the blueprint for an entire discipline, it thus stakes out ambitious claims for a subjective "intelligence" elsewhere defined by Hegel as the "power over the fund of images and presentations belonging to it" (die Macht über den Vorrath der ihr angehörigen Bilder und Vorstellungen).[14]

Whereas the Heidelberg romantics only a decade before had stressed the mystical and haunting appeal of the past, without which the psychology of the modern subject would remain depthless, Hegel's account at every turn asserts the speculative superiority of the present. This is not to say that dialectical thinking is in any simplistic sense fixated on the present, or that, according to popular yet reductive accounts, Hegel's philosophy exhibits a rigid teleological orientation toward the future. On the contrary, the dialectical method recalls Plato's notion of *anamnesis* as an awakening to the full conceptual determinacy of the present—which invariably means a painstaking "recollection" (*erinnern*) of the past. Where dialectical argumentation departs in categorical, even peremptory, ways from romantics like Creuzer and Eichendorff is in its axiom that recollection purges the past of all contingent, serendipitous qualities. Like all matters of state, the interiority of the Hegelian subject must submit to an intricate disciplinary scheme, here set forth in a bureaucratic prose that assigns each psychological state its own category, epistemological rank, and relative authority. It helps to juxtapose the intertwining of psychology and semiology in Hegel with the far more tentative, even skeptical, relationship between inwardness and image as it emerges in Eichendorff—who, in December 1819, embarked on a long and uneasy career in the Prussian bureaucracy. Doing so allows us to grasp Eichendorff's image-centered poetry and Hegel's speculative narratives as expressions of two distinct and increasingly incompatible models of conservative thought. One offers a skeptical vision of the psychology of the romantic individual entirely circumscribed and dominated by the traumatic force of history, whereas the other embraces modernity in an administrative mode by reconceptualizing philosophy as an essentially bureaucratic process concerned with the progressive socialization of the subject within the emergent nineteenth-century nation-state.

§§ 446–462 of the *Encyclopedia* sketch a sequence of cognitive forms and, implicit in it, a gradual increase of autonomy enjoyed by a subjectivity at first dominated by the heterogeneity of material sensation. In Hegel's account, all cognition involves the assimilation of otherness to the order of intelligence, a process mediated by the concurrent development of increasingly abstract semiotic forms. Thus any given stage in Hegel's progression of representational forms is matched by a distinct semiotic operation (diagram 1). As the *Encyclopedia* makes clear time and again, the autonomy of what is called "intelligence" depends on its ability to purge representation of all foreign material determinants. Indeed, the strategic objective of transfiguring substantiality into subjectivity could not be realized without the differential progression of *semiosis*. For only by means of a detour through the medial advance from gaze to image, symbol, allegory and, finally, the sign can the assimilation of matter into intelligence unfold as a seemingly logical and inevitable development. For our purposes, Hegel's treatment of the image is of particular interest. "Although they still have a *sensuously concrete content* . . . *images* are already more universal than intuitions," he notes (1978, 167). For the image "no longer has the complete determinateness of intuition, and is arbitrary or contingent, being generally isolated from the external place, time and immediate context in which intuition was involved" (ibid., 149). This assertion of a categorical divide between intuition and image is crucial. Both in its material and cognitive import, the image is by definition incompatible with the being *of* which it is the image. While it may recall the contingent material sensation to which it owes its existence, the image as such has irrevocably transcended that origin. Indeed, it exemplifies the transitional function of representation overall of which Hegel tells us that it "is the middle between the immediacy of intelligence finding itself determined, and the free intelligence of thought" (ibid., 145).

Like any other semiotic operation, then, the image constitutes itself as a specific moment of "sublation" (*Aufhebung*) insofar as it distils a psychological content from the raw data of intuition. Still preserved (*aufgehoben*) within the image, this content remains at first unreflected or "unconscious"—even though the "*clarity* and *freshness* . . . and firmly determined singularity" of its original

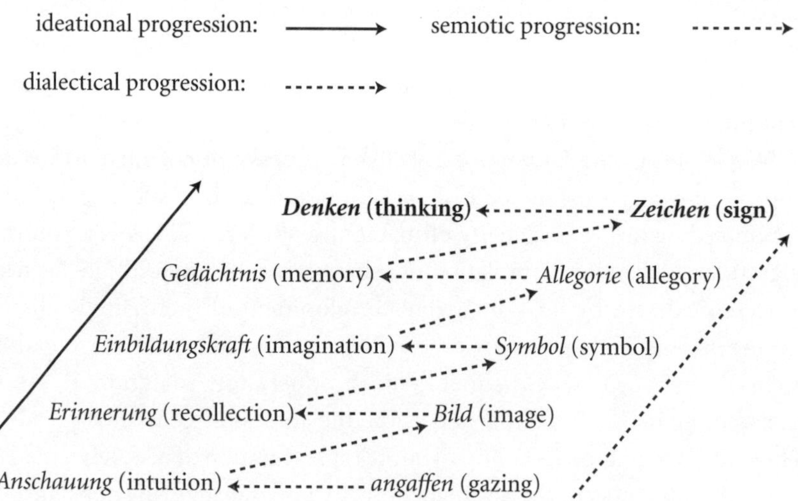

Diagram 1. Hegel's dialectical model of cognition and semiosis (representation).

material have already been "canceled" (*aufgehoben*). For "everything that happens acquires *permanence* for us only in that it is taken up into the representing intelligence [*vorstellende Intelligenz*], and that happening which intelligence does not deem worthy of being thus taken up becomes wholly of the past" (Hegel 1978, 151). As Jacques Derrida puts it, "intelligence . . . is the name of the power which produces a sign by negating the sensory spatiality of intuition."[15] As the *Aufhebung* (sublation) of intuition, the sign also replaces the spatial character of intuition with a temporal logic intrinsic to all signifying systems. The "essence" (*Wesen*) of intuition yields to an awareness of its deeper historicity (*Gewesenheit*). At the same time, this transfiguration of material intuition into the subject's interiority remains as yet unreflected. Consequently, the past merely slumbers within the subject as a sumptuous repository of images, almost as random in their assembly as the contents of Warhol's "time capsules."

Given the larger stakes of a conclusive and totalizing theoretical progression, Hegel must demonstrate step by step how the image is recognized, assimilated, and dominated by philosophical thought. These recurrent transitional moments in the *Encyclopedia* also allow us to pinpoint the divide separating Hegel's bureaucratic and operational state conservatism from the *ideologeme* of romantic conservatism (*Altkonservatismus*). In characteristic manner, Hegel capitalizes on the speculative possibilities of the root *-inner* in the words *Innerlichkeit* ("interiority") and *Erinnerung* ("recollection") when he remarks how "recollected within intelligence [*in ihr erinnert*], the image is no longer existent, but is preserved unconsciously."[16] At first glance, Hegel seems to assign the image essentially the same function that it held in the work of Brentano and Görres—of a semiotic corollary for the unconscious:

> The image is mine, it belongs to me: initially however, this is the full extent of its homogeneity with me, for it is still not *thought,* not raised to the *form* of *rationality,* the relationship between it and myself still stemming from the standpoint of intuition, and being not free but a relationship according to which I am merely the *internality,* while the image is something *external* to me. Initially, therefore, I still have an imperfect control of the images slumbering within the abyss of my inwardness [die im Schacht meiner Innerlichkeit schlafenden Bilder], for I am unable to recall them *at will.* No one knows what an infinite host of images of the past slumbers within him. Although they certainly awaken by chance on various occasions, one cannot,—as it is said,—call them to mind. They are therefore only *ours* in a formal manner" (Hegel 1978, 153–55).

The assimilation and further purification of the image *by* and *into* thought effectively raises the image from a merely formal "property" (*Eigentum*) to an "actual possession" (*wirkliches Besitztum* [ibid., 155, 156]). In what follows (§ 454), Hegel's argument thus centers on the appropriation of the image and its sublation (*Aufhebung*) into thought, a crucial step designed to strip the image of its vestigial materiality and its contingent, potentially disruptive impact on the subject as a still unreflected (*unbewußt*) form. For Hegel, the subject is not to be "stirred" (*bewegt*) by emotions associated with images and "awaken[ed] only by chance." Located at the center of a rational and teleological "movement" (*Bewegung*) from intuition to recollection, the subject's psychological progression toward universality is instead taken as the blueprint for a complex cultural policy.

The objective of Hegel's entire argument is to break the image, to strip it of its iconic force, and to denude it of its contingent, magical presence—its "aura." Casting the totality of the subject as the interiorized (*erinnert*) and reflected history of its progression, Hegel's Protestant universe of *Bildung* thus requires a mode of representation untrammeled by referentiality and, even at the provisional stage of the image, already gesturing toward self-referentiality. "The more cultured [*gebildeter*] the person the less he lives in immediate intuition [but] . . . in recollections [*Erinnerungen]*" (ibid., 157). To absolve the image from its vestigial relationship to the contingent matter of the past—to promote it from a medium that merely preserves (*aufheben*) the past to one capable of overcoming it—the image has to be utterly reconstituted. By way of further approximating the denuded, prosaic quality that, for Hegel, defines philosophical (that is, fully autonomous) thought, the image is to be reworked into a simulacrum. To be sure, the image still allows the subject to maintain a cognitive relationship with the empirical world, yet this relation is no longer materially determined. Instead, having been rendered wholly interior (*erinnert*), the image reconstituted by the "productive imagination" merely implies that such a relation had occurred in the past. Referentiality is strictly a function of recollection, and as such it does not emerge *from* the past but can merely relate *to* it in a retroactive (*nachträglich*) manner. Going beyond its initial, "merely reproductive" operation of "recall[ing] the images present within it," the imagination proceeds to transfigure "them into *general* presentations by *relating* them to *one another.*" Finally, "[t]he *third* stage . . . is that at which intelligence endows its *general* representations with an *imaged determinate being* by positing them as identical with what is *particular* in the image. This sensuous determinate being has the dual form of *symbol* and *sign,* so that this third stage contains the *fantasy* that symbolizes and also *engenders signs,* the latter constituting the *transition* to *memory* [so daß diese dritte Stufe die symbolisirende und die *zeichenmachende Phantasie* umfaßt, welche letztere den *Übergang* zum *Gedächtnis* bildet]" (ibid., 163; translation modified).

Considered from the vantage point of memory (*Gedächtnis*), that is, images are no longer determined by their referential ties to the subject's empirical history. Rather, as *simulacra,* they are now equivalent and interchangeable with one another and, to the extent that they are understood as such, they are no longer images at all but signs (*Zeichen*). Hegel specifically emphasizes that the transfiguration of image into sign should not be misconstrued as some hazy amalgamation of each form's ingredients. As he puts it, this "*universalization* of the *image* . . . comes about not through the general representation's unifying itself with the image to form a *neutral* or so to speak *chemical* product, but by its activating and proving itself as the image's *substantial power* [substanzielle Macht], by its subjugating it [sich unterwirft] as an accidental, constituting its soul" (ibid., 169–71; translation modified).

It is here that the concept of "fantasy" (*Phantasie*), which will be of ongoing concern to us, is introduced as a key psychological function. It is the agency responsible for converting images into simulacra that no longer answer to empirical intuitions from the past but, instead, mediate subjective intelligence with itself as strictly autonomous agency. As such, fantasy at once identifies a sequence of crucial substitutions or, as the case may be, displacements: sensation → intuition → image → symbol → allegory → sign. At the same time, however, this sequence of conceptual shifts is reified under the categorical authority of *Phantasie,* thereby concealing the intricate and indeed problematic relationship between psychological and linguistic forms. Hegel's account, that is, cannot make the discrete steps of this progression known to the individual for at least two reasons. First, there is the logical objection that a subject cannot be conscious of the very progression to which it owes its status as intelligence except, of course, after the fact. Second, subjective insight into the (psychological and rhetorical) origins of intelligence must also be suspended until its completion, lest Hegel's encyclopedic account of this process should appear wholly redundant. According to the *Encyclopedia,* true cognition is never immediate and contemplative but, on the contrary, always reflexive and mnemonic. Or, as Hegel notes, "the image produced by fantasy is only subjectively intuitable. In the *sign* fantasy adds proper intuitability, and in *mechanical* memory it completes this form of *being* within it." Through "the dialectical motion" of first embracing the symbol, then mediating it "by means of the image," and finally grasping it in its abstract import as an "objective being in and for itself," the "general representation [has become] liberated from the content of the image" (ibid., 173; translation modified). The result is a form of subjectivity strictly predicated on discursive signs (*Zeichen*) and mnemonics (*Gedächtnis*).

Hegel's development of intelligence is dialectically bound up with the Protestant repudiation of the image, of sensuous being, and of materiality as possessing only a deceptive or, at most, provisional objectivity. Dialectically mediated and reflected, intuition yields to image to memory to symbol / allegory, terminating in the prosaic domain of an *allgemeine Vorstellung* ("universal representation" [ibid., 174]), thereby bringing closure to a progression continually fueled by what Hegel calls a "logical instinct" (ibid., 181). The abstract rigor of Hegel's argument, its bureaucratic inflection of Enlightenment optimism, lends itself to a more general comparison between Hegel's paradigm of a pure "intelligence" and a more intuition-and affect-based romantic interiority. In Hegel, the purgation of all particularity from the image—whose kinship with materiality is limited to its retroactive conjury of an intuition—constitutes a fundamental prerequisite for language in its ultimate, philosophical dimension. In detailing this entire progression with such authority and bureaucratic exactitude, the *Encyclopedia* aims at the autonomy of intelligence and its complete "sublation" (*Aufhebung*) of all things past. With "spirit" (*Geist*) emerging as the new assignment for a new, intrinsically bureaucratic model of disciplinary work, "psychology" resolves itself into a matter of due process. For Hegel, what matters is the essential abstractness of alphabetic writing—the fact that it "designates tones, which are already signs" and "therefore consists of signs for signs" (Zeichen der Zeichen [ibid., 183]). In consigning its subject to the virtual (that is, strictly textual) domain of philosophical prose, Hegel's *Encyclopedia* reaffirms the nullity of all material being for philosophy to the extent that the latter had thought of matter as something independent and external.[17] Taking an ostensibly different view, Slavoj Žižek suggests that "the 'last secret' of dialectical speculation" effectively requires the persistent imposition of precisely that kind of contingent, aconceptual external matter to which Hegelian philosophy tends to respond in such peremptory and irritable manner. Like the bureaucracy of the modern nation-state or the gatekeeper of Kafka's famous parable, dialectics teems with the manifestations of a paradox that it cannot acknowledge. It exists solely for the purpose of addressing the needs of those petitioners (matter) who come before it. Yet it will acknowledge their concerns only in a (bureaucratic, conceptual) language fundamentally indifferent to the concerns that brought the petitioner into its orbit to begin with, and it consequently resents and ultimately rejects that other to the extent that it persists as an independent entity. In the final analysis, speculative thought attains its systemic authority and legitimacy "not in the dialectical mediation-sublimation of all contingent, empirical reality, not in the deduction of all reality from the mediating movement of absolute negativity, but in the fact that this very negativity, to attain its 'being-for-itself,' must embody itself again in some miserable, radically contingent, corporeal left-over" (Žižek 1993, 207). Speculative dialectics demands contingency and alterity, but only so as to be able to reject their importunate demands. With unwitting self-irony, however, Hegel's prosaic outline of a fully bureaucratized subjectivity also attests to the impoverished existence that could be expected in the social sphere of restoration-era Germany where bureaucratic and political processes must continually disavow the alterity and contingency of whatever matter comes before them. In aesthetic terms, the self-certainty of Hegelian reason (as Adorno never tired of showing) is not so much premised on as dedicated to the eventual realization of a uniform concept of civic agency. It is a paradigm of subjectivity that, like its formal-semiotic medium of exchange—writing, or the "prose of the world"—appears denuded of all sonority, voice, tone, and music.

Encryption and Disclosure: The Serendipitous Historicity of the Romantic Image

We are now in a position to return to Eichendorff, for whom, in contrast, the image remains irrevocably (*unaufhebbar*) linked to the past, even though special care is taken *not* to suggest that the image could ever return us to the past outright. For Eichendorff, the word oscillates between image and sign. While it cannot be contained within a dialectical theory of the sign, its ability to relate the subject *to* the past must be carefully distinguished from a naïve supernatural model that would regard the word as directly issuing *from* the past. The relation between subject and history—the presence of the poetic sign and the past ostensibly referred to—is not a seamlessly genealogical one. Rather, it is a relation of substitution. In it, the past is brought into focus, not as an empirical reference point for nostalgic or speculative reacquisition, but as a simulacrum enabling the subject to mediate (albeit strictly ex post facto) its own traumatic exodus into the present. Characterized by the persistent oscillation of its conceptual and material features, the lyric image dramatizes a subject haunted by modernity. Like the sonority of the lyric voice, the effects of modernity arise without premeditation and prompt the lyric subject to awaken to the inherently unreal character of its existence; as a catalyst for that precarious transition, the lyric exhibits the same preternatural lucidity as the symptom in post-Freudian psychoanalysis. With good reason, Georg Lukács credits Eichendorff with having wrought "radically new forms to evoke world-historical changes in human feelings." For Lukács, Eichendorff's lyrics constitute a formal-aesthetic objectification of a pervasive, historically determined "unease . . . a feeling without a concrete object." Notwithstanding his deterministic approach, Lukács is right to grasp Eichendorff's lyrics as the objective constructs through which otherwise oblique and antagonistic historical forces ("the dark, sinister nature of the 'unfathomable' that intervenes in men's lives, shaping their destiny") suddenly achieve a crystalline outline (Lukács 1993, 56–59).

Eichendorff's preferred strategy for identifying this potentiality of the word is to stress its contiguity (not identity) with material sensation. Time and again, the figures in his poetry appear mesmerized by a past that oscillates between the uncanny quality of déjà vu and that of an outright projection or fantasy. At a rhetorical level, this undecidability reproduces itself as a lyric voice suspended between the seductive presence of its sonority (*Klang*) and fleeting intimations of a deeper and more expansive significance (*Bedeutsamkeit*). The short lyric "Im Walde" ("In the Woods"), first published in 1836, and memorably set to music by Robert Schumann in 1840, throws into relief this spectral and ephemeral quality of the lyric image:

Es zog eine Hochzeit den Berg entlang,
Ich hörte die Vögel schlagen,
Da blitzten viel Reiter, das Waldhorn klang,
Das war ein lustiges Jagen!

Und eh ich's gedacht, war alles verhallt,
Die Nacht bedecket die Runde,
Nur von den Bergen noch rauschet der Wald
Und mich schauert im Herzensgrunde. (*EW* 1, 49)

Along the mountain a wedding moved,
I heard the birds in song,
Horsemen flashed by, a bugle called,
What a merry hunting there was!

And ere I knew, it all ebbed away,
Night has descended all around,
Still from the mountains the forest rustles,
And I shudder to the depth of my heart (MY TRANSLATION)

Rather than conferring mimetic stability on appearances previously witnessed, the first stanza's rendition of a distant wedding procession and its ambient, vivacious sociability is immediately qualified as a spatiotemporal echo—at once vivid and fleeting. "Es zog eine Hochzeit den Berg entlang" conjures up being as a fugitive apparition (*Darstellung*) rather than a stable representation (*Vorstellung*)—an aspect brilliantly captured by Schumann's entries of *ritardando* and *diminuendo* into the piano accompaniment to the opening lines of each stanza.[18] Pointedly ephemeral, the opening image throws into relief the lyric's underlying temporal dimension, according to which the image was never consciously taken in but can only be grasped retroactively—as the inward echo ("verhallt") or reverberation ("mich schauert"). Indeed, with the subject never consciously attuned to the image as presence ("eh ich's gedacht"), it may even be too much to speak of an echo. The archetypal image of marital promise and mirthful sociability has only been secured a posteriori. Strictly speaking, it is subject to recall only through the quasi-hypnotic murmur of forests on distant hilltops. The temporal marker "noch" (still) thus surmises that the image that went unwitnessed is yet preserved—or encrypted—in the oblique sonority of forests "murmuring" ("Nur von den Bergen noch rauschet der Wald").

Characteristically, Hegel's *Encyclopedia* invokes *rauschen* as a choice example to corroborate its basic hypothesis that the advancement of the Enlightenment and its preordained termination in the pure textures of philosophical prose depend on the silencing of any residual "murmur" of language:

> For the *elementary material* of language, while on the one hand the presentation of mere contingency has extinguished itself, the principle of imitation has confined itself to its narrow range of sound-making objects. Yet one can still hear the German language praised of its wealth of particular expressions for particular

> sounds,—rustle, whiz, creak, etc. Possibly a hundred or more of these have been collected, and new ones can be coined at will on the spur of the moment, but such a superabundance in respect of what is sensuous and insignificant ought not to be regarded as contributing to what constitutes the resources of a cultured language. (Hegel 1978, 181)

The rustle of language, to borrow Roland Barthes's memorable title *Le Bruissement de la langue,* is invoked only as an example of its own "insignificance" and, allegedly, as the very antithesis of a "cultured language." Precisely where the Hegelian sign refers only back to other signs—such as the alphabetic script that merely evokes the "idea" of sonority (*Töne*) untrammeled by the material specifics of articulation— Eichendorff's lyrics draw our attention to a persistent murmur within language. Indeed, it is only because a murmur still persists ("noch rauschet der Wald") that the lyric can take its turn toward reflection. Haunted by what it construes to be the echoes of a onetime social plenitude, the lyric voice reveals itself as an involuntary recollection that can be preserved only in textual form. As in Hegel, the interiority of affect can indeed only abide in the domain of the lyric as text, but for Eichendorff that text encrypts and preserves the very contingency of the past that the bureaucratic process of Hegelian thought and Prussian nation-building aim to overcome.[19] In the materiality of sound and voice, recollection (*Erinnerung*) revives dormant, mythic or magical forces that the Enlightenment and its Hegelian apotheosis sought to contain within a secular, fully socialized, and processual conception of rationality. The underlying tension is that between romanticism's mystical and materially suffused notion of the poetic image as an involuntary reflex of its historical unconscious and the assimilation of the individual's contingent interiority and its affective memories to an administrative and institutionally organized model of civic existence.

Another lyric further crystallizes the radical contingency within the relation between text and history, between conscious existence and those "memory-traces" (Freud) on whose displacement the stability of quotidian conscious life is typically premised. Bearing the very idea of allegiance in its title, Eichendorff's "Treue" once again deposits its subject at the very threshold between recollection and projection:

> Wie dem Wanderer in Träumen,
> Daß er still im Schlafe weint,

Zwischen goldnen Wolkensäumen
Seine Heimat wohl erscheint:

So durch dieses Frühlings Blühen
Über Berg' und Täler tief
Sah ich oft dein Bild noch ziehen,
Als ob's mich von hinnen rief;

Und mit wunderbaren Wellen
Wie im Traume, halbbewußt,
Gehen ew'ge Liederquellen
Mir verwirrend durch die Brust. (*EW*, 1: 240)

How to the wanderer in dreams,
Amid the silent tears of sleep,
Framed by golden clouds
His homeland must appear:

So through this blossoming of spring
Over mountains and deep valleys
I often saw your image moving
As if calling me hence;

And with marvelous surges
As in a dream, half-conscious,
The eternal sources of song
Bewilderingly rove through my breast. (MY TRANSLATION)

The poem's title already intimates a basic antagonism. "Fealty" and "fidelity" (*Treue*) as the conscious allegiance to an individual or a collective may well constitute ideal values. Yet such allegiance subsists only in the opening figure (simile) of the traveler conjuring up phantasmagorical visions of his distant homeland ("Wie dem Wanderer in Träumen . . ."). Likened to a longing at once clichéd in its literary derivation (evoking Novalis) and improbable as regards its fulfillment, "loyalty" here lacks the certainty and confidence of the virtue that goes by that name. Instead, it points up the inescapable hold of the unconscious as it manifests itself, a posteriori, at the level of affect. Echoing his Heidelberg teachers (Görres, von Arnim, Creuzer), Eichendorff conceives of affect as a "half-conscious" repository of cultural sources ("ew'ge

Liederquellen") whose belated resurgence accounts for the inherently confused nature of the subject's interiority ("verwirrend durch die Brust"). The lyric itself appears a belated effort on the part of the conscious subject to understand its own historical unconscious. To that end, the lyric voice endows the historical unconscious with the barest contours of a beloved ("dein Bild")—truly but a hypothetical figure imagined to haunt the modern self with its insistent calling ("als ob's mich von hinnen rief"). Transcribed into the medium of lyric writing, the lyric voice attempts to grasp the uncertain source of its inspiration in discursive form only to recognize such *Liederquellen* as terminally inaccessible. Quite centrally, that is, the entire lyric revolves around an "image" (*Bild*)—the word itself is found precisely at the middle of the poem—belonging to a past that is at once inscrutable and inescapable. Contrary to Hegel, Eichendorff imagines the lines of interpretive authority between past and present reversed, with the past and its insistent harbingers (the images of folk culture) permanently eluding the bureaucratic and uniform "immanent rhythm of the concept" (Hegel 1989, 36). Both "Im Walde" und "Treue" show how romantic knowledge is not merely defined by its coming *after the fact* but, in its contents and epistemological scope, constrained to awaken to the very reality of its belatedness. It follows that such a conflicted transition can in turn be realized only in lyric, philological, or philosophical writings that will figuratively reproduce that very predicament. For Eichendorff, as for Novalis, Schleiermacher, and Hegel, the structure of romantic knowledge—staged as a mood of a recurrent, traumatic awakening—is irreducibly textual. Yet in the case of the lyric, especially those of Eichendorff, the voice that bestows such figural charisma on writing actually acknowledges its own phantasmagoric status. Thus the constant recurrence of words like *verwirrend* (confusing) or *irrend* (deluded or wayward) attests to a fundamental lack of synchrony between the lyric voice and an ineluctable past to which it returns in the same way that traumatized subjects must revisit the scene of a catastrophic disruption: unable to remember it, they will reenact it. At the same time, the lyric voice also provides the one remaining formal resolution whereby the subject—in the vicarious, dreamlike modality of scrupulous poetic writing and reading—calls out to itself in order to awaken from that cycle of repetition.

Having relied both in this and the preceding chapter on the theory of trauma as a framework for the historical role of literary production, particularly during the Napoleonic era, we may now move from scrutinizing the symptomatic character of romantic lyricism between 1800 and 1815 toward articulating the traumatic event that had been "missed." What was the disruption whose insufficient assimilation by those caught up in it is being attested to by the insistent, if oblique, callings of the romantic lyric? Having studied the recurrent formal manifestations of a traumatic disruption—which for Eichendorff involved the sudden and all-consuming arrival of economic, sociocultural, and political modernity between 1789 and 1815—we now need to retrace a macrohistorical narrative of that traumatic disruption itself. To be sure, any such account will prove inadequate in some respects, a mere synecdoche for what it cannot show, and what those caught up in Germany's utter transformation over just two decades could witness only belatedly and unexpectedly. At the same time, the ubiquity and prominence of lyric writing in popular culture attest to the fact that individuals continually *felt* that transformation, that it *affectively* seized them and profoundly shaped their historical (self-)awareness. As Heine's friend and mentor Karl Immermann was to comment so perceptively: "For the social body, unconscious impressions are frequently the most powerful ones; indeed the collective affect of the social body is more delicate than that of the corporeal organism."[20] The principal points where Eichendorff found himself overtaken by the reorganization of Germany's social, cultural, and economic landscape involved his family's estates and his own career in the regional administration of East Prussia, which was oddly erratic and, for that very reason, also representative of a larger struggle within Germany. That struggle revolved around what kind of allegiance ought to be maintained by the rapidly expanding caste of civil servants (*Beamtenstand*) vis-à-vis the competing projects of a moderately inclusive, modernized, liberal nation-state and an embattled though surprisingly resilient estate and guild culture.

Joseph von Eichendorff's life, like those of all the romantics, was intertwined in the turbulent decades following the French Revolution, the prolonged and ultimately disastrous war of the "Holy Alliance" against the revolutionary and eventually Napoleonic regime and, above all, by the utter disintegration of the old Reich. Born and raised on his family's estate at Lubowitz in Silesia, on the eastern outskirts of the Empire, Eichendorff witnessed the abrupt intrusion of sweeping political, economic, and cultural change. At the heart of the radical transformation of the entire German-speaking world between 1803 and 1815 was the concept of the *Land*, "a collection of institutions, laws, and customs peculiar to itself . . . enmeshed with, rather than self-consciously superior to, a variety of institutions beyond and within itself" (Sheehan, 25). From time immemorial, the governance of the land in this preponderantly agrarian society had embodied the peculiar political organization of the Reich itself—ordinarily referred to (with characteristic simplicity and self-assurance) as *Herrschaft* (dominion). Leaving further local variations aside, one must bear in mind the basic distinction between *Grundherrschaft* and *Gutsherrschaft*—the former denoting the gentry's dominion over landed property, while the latter also encompassed the landed nobility's juridical authority over their realm and their proprietorship of present and future generations of serfs living on their land.[21] Particularly in East Prussia and Silesia, where the Eichendorff family had settled around 1626, *Gutsherrschaft* was the dominant model of civic, economic, and social relations "in ways substantially different from most of the other aristocracies in Europe; binding them more closely to their estate, it caused noble landowners to see possession and control as essential to their preservation as a class" (Berdahl, 21).

Characteristic of Eichendorff, and defining of his *altkonservativ* ideology is, above all, the conception of the past as the site of a disruption so violent and traumatic as to have been unimaginable and inassimilable by those caught up in it. A long passage from his late autobiographical essay "The Nobility and the Revolution" will help us distinguish romantic conservatism both from a nostalgic Rousseauian longing for a primordial, natural state and from the later state-sponsored conservatism whose tenets were mostly defined by capitalist greed and fear of labor unrest:

> This was more or less the state of affairs during the last decades of the previous century. As mentioned before, a portent of thunderstorms hung over the entire land. Everyone sensed that something grand was approaching, and a tacit, unsettling apprehension, nobody knew of what, had more or less taken hold of everyone's mind. In this stifling atmosphere, as always before impending catastrophes, there appeared some peculiar figures and outlandish adventurers, such as the Count St. Germain, Cagliostro, and so on, self-styled emissaries of the future, so to speak. This indeterminate unease, lacking anything external that it might form or shape, could only continue to eat deeper and deeper inwards. The Rosicrucians appeared on the scene, as did the Illuminati, and people contrived various secret societies in an attempt to advance the happiness and education of mankind, such as we see them, for example, at Lothario's castle in Goethe's *Wilhelm Meister.* However silly and childish, these [societies] nonetheless constituted symptoms and prophetic intimations of an approaching epoch. For the

> ground had long been rendered unstable by clandestine mines, which were to explode both past and present. Everywhere one could hear an uncanny, subterranean hammering and knocking [*ein spukhaftes unterirdisches Hämmern und Klopfen*], even as grass continued to grow merrily on the surface, with fat herds peacefully grazing on it. (*EW*, 1: 910; my translation)

Eichendorff's look back at the French Revolution characteristically forgoes the outright *narratio* of its arrival in favor of a vivid description of how the aristocracy and gentry failed to notice the portents of that impending cataclysm. Like the new academic disciplines of historical poetics, philology, and idealist philosophy that he had studied in his youth, Eichendorff's retrospective rests on a deeply ambivalent model of the subject as a ratio of act and quality, recollection (*Erinnerung*) and inwardness (*Innerlichkeit*). It is an agency unconsciously and inescapably determined by a past whose occurrence it was unable to assimilate in its time. Nowhere would this prove more apparent than in the case of the approaching revolution. For, as Eichendorff repeatedly stresses, the social and cultural coherence of the aristocracy and gentry—who by 1800 were finding their socioeconomic mission and political legitimacy seriously atrophied—was predicated on *not heeding the urgent call of the past.* Given the historical failure of the gentry and, especially, the aristocracy, the sudden defeat of regionally differentiated cultural, political, and economic practices, first by Napoleon and then (at least partially) by the ambitious reforms of Baron Karl von Stein and Prince Karl August von Hardenberg, almost appears just retribution. And yet, characterized above all by a pervasive loss of history, modernity seems the very antithesis of an *altkonservativ* order, even if the latter breaks with the often crudely Machiavellian politics of post-Napoleonic conservatives, such as the Viennese aristocracy or the East Prussian landed nobility, or Junkers. "Ideal loyalty" has been displaced by "monetary forces" ("Die Stelle der idealen Treue wurde sofort von der materiellen Geldkraft eingenommen" [*EW*, 1: 899]). Eichendorff thus feels caught between a phantasmagorical past whose resources and once-legitimate order had been squandered long before by the upper echelons of society, on the one hand, and a modernity similarly largely shaped by the basest craving for economic and political ascendancy among anonymous and competitive subjects, on the other. The resulting sense of historical abjection is acutely felt in "Auf einer Burg" ("The Watchtower") a poem also memorably set to music by Schumann in 1840:

Eingeschlafen auf der Lauer
Oben ist der alte Ritter;
Drüber gehen Regenschauer,
Und der Wald rauscht durch das Gitter.

Eingewachsen Bart und Haare,
Und versteinert Brust und Krause,
Sitzt er viele hundert Jahre
Oben in der stillen Klause.

Draußen ist es still und friedlich,
Alle sind ins Tal gezogen,
Waldesvögel einsam singen
In den leeren Fensterbogen.

Eine Hochzeit fährt da unten
Auf dem Rhein im Sonnenscheine,
Musikanten spielen munter,
Und die schöne Braut die weinet. (*EW*, 1: 64)

Gone to sleep while on the watch
Above there sits the ancient knight;
Over yonder rain is showering,
And woods rustle through the trellis.

Inward grown his beard and hair,
Turned to stone his breast and ruffle,
He sits for many hundred years
Aloft in the noiseless cell.

Outside it is still and peaceful,
All have moved into the vale,
Little wood birds sing all forlorn
In the empty window arches.

Far below a wedding glides along
Bathed by sunlight on the Rhine;
Musicians play, oh, so gaily,
And the lovely bride is weeping. (MY TRANSLATION)

With its ironic opening ("Eingeschlafen auf der Lauer . . ."), the lyric swiftly establishes its overarching focus on the inexorable *and* inscrutable nature of historical change.[22] The fossilized feudal body of the ancient knight who has fallen asleep on his watch is a veritable schoolbook example of romantic allegory. Rendered wholly impersonal, even generic, by the passage of time and by the advent of change, for which his faltering vigilance was no match, the once individual knight has been utterly transformed by the fluctuations of historical time. To the speaker's archeological gaze, "der alte Ritter" is no longer the representative of a coherent social formation. Indeed, it is only now that he has turned to stone and involuntarily become a statue that the knight fully embodies a feudal order whose historical mission, it seems, can only be articulated from the vanishing point of the postrevolutionary lyric. "Ingrown and calcified" (Eingewachsen und versteinert), the feudal body marks Eichendorff's "rediscovery of an allegorical tradition beyond the sensualistic analogism of the eighteenth century," Paul de Man observes. "[T]he prevalence of allegory always corresponds to the unveiling of an authentically temporal destiny," de Man continues. "This unveiling takes place in a subject that has sought refuge against the impact of time in a natural world to which, in truth, it bears no resemblance." The meaning of allegory can "consist only in the *repetition* . . . of a previous sign with which it can never coincide" (de Man 1983, 205–7). The lyric allows us to grasp the knight's representative character only as something accidental, perhaps serendipitous. The ability of the feudal body to represent its authentic "destiny" thus requires its estrangement, its vivid, almost tactile, transfiguration from a flesh-and-blood individual into an accidental monument. Hence the knight's two bodies—the "real" and evidently overwhelmed individual and his fossil form—reflect the ultimate ineluctability of historical time, a fact that can be illustrated only by means of a visible discontinuity between two embodied states. In the third stanza, this fundamental evacuation of determinate (human) meaning from the passage of historical time is captured in the empty windows occupied only by the natural, asemantic song of the birds.

Yet how does the voice of Eichendorff's lyric modernity position itself vis-à-vis this disconcerting conception of historical change as inherently unknowable and hence uncontestable by any individual or community, however intently vigilant (*auf der Lauer*) these may have been? What does it mean to grasp history only a posteriori, as a failure to have "seen in time" (Caruth) and, more specifically here, as the traumatic demise of a social order that cannot be reconstituted but only mourned wherever we happen upon its stony debris? Both Wordsworth's "heap of unhewn stone" and Eichendorff's *versteinert* knight (to say nothing of Keats's Saturn) are cultural artifacts that confront these questions.[23] And, like Wordsworth in the elegiac closure of "Michael," Eichendorff envisions lyric form as a means of forging the passage from the modern subject's traumatic recognition of his or her irremediably estranged historical condition to a more attenuated and faintly promising scene of "mourning" (see the discussion below of Freud's concept of *Nachträglichkeit*, or "retroaction").[24] Thus the location where the feudal order met its unanticipated demise has been abandoned—"alle sind ins Tal gezogen"—and now figures as the objective site of the modern subject's belated and insistently mournful recollections (*Erinnerung*).

The final stanza's wedding party observed from afar, a quintessentially romantic image, projects the continuity of a modernity that is buoyantly committed to its quotidian rituals and pursuits but sometimes dismayed by inexplicable moments of grief, which may surface without warning. Thus the speaker's vision of the bride in the distant sunlight "down below" is subverted by the unsettling fact that she is weeping: "Und die schöne Braut die weinet." Far from being a recuperation of modernity, the wedding yields tears that at the level of affect portend a knowledge already conveyed by the marmoreal figure in the castle above: the inexorable and nonteleological progression of betrayal, miscognition, and unpredictable change that is historical time. Robert Schumann appears to have had a keen understanding of this dynamic when setting this lyric to music. For Adorno, Schumann's setting of the poem "is distinguished by its bold dissonances . . . which result from the collision of the melodic line and the chorale-like ties in the accompaniment, which moves step-wise; it is as though the modernity of this harmonization were an attempt to protect the poem from aging" (Adorno 1991, 1: 77). Crucial for our purposes here is to understand Eichendorff's often proclaimed (and usually discredited) "conservatism" more accurately; it should be seen, not as a naïve (or possibly self-righteous and self-serving) nostalgic longing for the past, but as a self-conscious attitude of *Nachträglichkeit* vis-à-vis a past understood to have lost sight of its historical mission long ago.[25] This failure to adhere to its legitimating values, Eichendorff suggests, accounts for the evident imperceptiveness of *Herrschaft* as regards the rising threat of radicalism, factionalism, and burgeoning class-specific mobility that culminated in the French Revolution and its impact on the rest of Europe. Static and seemingly impenetrable to outsiders, the system of *Herrschaft* had been premised on a truly labyrinthine array of centuries-old covenants, special clauses, exemptions, and highly varying modes of representation. Thus some wealthy members of the landed gentry had no more access to the parliament (the Reichstag) than a simple freeholder, while an impoverished knight could mire the Reichstag in procedural trivia simply because his ancestors had negotiated the coveted privilege of *Reichsunmittelbarkeit.* With its political institutions nearly paralyzed and its regional monarchs (the rulers of Prussia, Saxony, the Palatinate, Württemberg, Bavaria, etc.) unable to expand their revenues in the face of an intransigent and legally resourceful gentry, the consequent lack of coordination between local, regional, and federal interests left the Reich all but defenseless against the military and political genius of Napoleon. Even before the final defeat of Prussia and Austria in 1806 and 1809, Napoleon had launched an unparalleled territorial and administrative reorganization of what was, then as now, the largest language-community in all of central Europe. His organization of the Rhenish Confederacy (Rheinbund) and the radical alignment (*Mediatisierung*) of several dozen minor principalities and small and medium-sized secular and ecclesiastic territories in 1803 suggested that the long-smoldering conflict between the old system of *Herrschaft* and a new paradigm of nation-building, or *Staatswesen,* was finally being resolved.[26] Not foreseeing that the modernization of the German-speaking territories would also result in a substantially stronger and more decisive Germany, and thus hasten his own demise, Napoleon tapped a vast potential of long-frustrated economic and intellectual potential that today might be lumped together under the catchall category "middle class" (*Bürgertum*).

As is usually the case with class formation, this new educated class evolved so as to meet an array of civil functions without initially having any marked consciousness of its own demographic specificity.[27] If, as James Sheehan puts it, information was the "essential lubricant" of the variegated system of local and regional *Herrschaft,* then it "had to be gathered, remembered, communicated; files, forms, statistics became more extensive," and by the end of the eighteenth century, "bureaucrats had become the chief instruments of the state's authority and the personification of its distinctive character" (Sheehan, 35). The demise of the old Reich in 1806, however, not only confirmed the timeliness of Napoleon's sweeping territorial reorganization three years earlier. It also provided the opportunity for one of the most ambitious and cogent instances of state-sponsored reform in the entire nineteenth century. Between 1807 and 1810, first under the leadership of Stein and later under Hardenberg, Prussia abolished all forms of serfdom, instituted the unrestricted right of acquisition and sale of landed property by any subject, as well as the free choice of professions (*Gewerbefreiheit*) without further interference from the guilds. Concurrently, a thorough reform of the armed forces and plans for a coherent and unified tax law were being pursued, though the latter in particular met with fierce opposition from the East Prussian Junkers. As Thomas Nipperdey has argued, the reforms sought to extricate the individual from the tangled, paralyzing web of old privileges, local customs, and regional idiosyncrasies and to release the subject into a modernity where self-determination (*Bildung*), rather than inherited privileges and obligations, would define one's social position:

> The impetus for the new education [*Bildung*] emerged from the small social class consisting of the educated, the civil servants and the liberal professions. Since a strong commercial bourgeoisie was absent, this was the only class besides the nobility which could justifiably stake a claim to leadership. In the more sophisticated social and cultural environment, it gradually took upon itself the function of an intelligentsia outside of the church. The objective of the new education was a new society. Turning its face against the old world of the estates and aristocracy, it sought to promote talent and achievement . . . [and] to release people from their existing social constraints, liberate them from the tyranny of family background and land. (Nipperdey 1996, 46)

However, this ambitious, albeit partial, deregulation of social barriers and, even more so, the abolition of age-old economic and professional constraints eventually succumbed to European politics. Until 1815, the reforms continued to make significant advances in most areas, with the issue of taxation arguably proving the most intractable of all. Still, both by his noxious territorial presence and by his example of administrative efficiency, Napoleon continued to energize the reform movement, which ultimately aimed to rebuild Prussia to the point where it could shake off his yoke.[28] Following Waterloo, however, the emphasis quickly shifted in favor of reconsolidating the powers of a limited monarchy and its traditionally landed base of political support. One by one, the reformers and their various project met with the same fate: first ignored, they were soon forced into retirement or, in some cases, even exile. By 1819, that notorious year of conservative retrenchment across Europe, the reform movement was essentially defeated. What remained, however, was a substantial constituency of mid- and upper-level bureaucrats who had formerly entered the civil service with a strong commitment to reforms. However traditional the shape of its internal and foreign policy, government was no longer conceivable without this new professional "estate" of civil servants (*Beamtenstand*).

The preceding historical *narratio* is made necessary by this book's overarching concern with the relation between a deep-structural "mood" and the experience of history. For as part of such an inquiry, we must also consider to what extent the historical energies codified in structures of feeling and subsequently represented in encrypted, "literary" form actually define a specific demographic spectrum. Rarely do we find a mood as peculiar and agonistic as the one prevailing in the Prussian bureaucracy, particularly after 1815. To the members of the nobility and gentry, economically disenfranchised by the revolutionary wars and, in part, by the reform project, going into the civil service seemed one way to reclaim at least some of their recently lost material and social privileges. Throughout the first half of the nineteenth century, one can observe how the upper echelons of the bureaucracy, "as a result of their own system of legal privileges . . . had themselves evolved into an estate, and this accorded not only with their self-assessment but also that of the rest of society."[29] Yet, as the list of privileges secured by the civil bureaucracy continued to expand (including special courts of law, separate codes of punishment, marital alliances with the nobility, partial exemption from taxation, etc.), the bureaucracy's claim to broad-based political reform and leadership succumbed to the lure of social and economic ascendancy. At the same time, its consolidation as a new quasi-estate came at the expense of compromising the social ideals of individual self-determination and socioeconomic advancement based on professional and educational attainments. In response to its perceived loss of moral authority, particularly after 1819, the bureaucracy began to fragment, with the first-generation, idealistic *Bildungsbeamtentum* gradually losing influence to a more opportunistic and socially ambitious *Staatsbeamtentum*. For the reform-minded civil servants who had incubated their social ideals during the age of reforms and anti-Napoleonic resistance under the commander of the Lützower Freikorps resistance, Ludwig Adolf von Lützow—among whose men we also find Eichendorff—were forced to witness the gradual strangulation of their youth's expansive vision of social and cultural regeneration. By contrast, the calculating and efficient approach cultivated by the *Staatsbeamtentum*—so aptly embodied in the bureaucratic style of Hegel's

Fig. 9. G. W. F. Hegel (1770–1831). This 47-mm medallion, widely distributed in Germany during Hegel's lifetime, was commissioned in 1830 by Hegel's students at the University of Berlin to commemorate his rectorship there and executed by August L. Held (1805–1839) on the basis an earlier bas-relief. The reverse side celebrates the eternal friendship of Christian faith and *Wissenschaft* (true philosophy) in a Grecian motif.

Encyclopedia and its author's quasi-institutional stature (fig. 9)—secured the social ascendancy of its members by implementing decrees, policies, and laws mostly designed to ensure the lasting political disenfranchisement of the professional middle class, including the reform-oriented government bureaucrats. The result was an abject professionalism afflicted by a sense of structural (rather than incidental) collaboration and self-betrayal.[30]

As the memories and promises of his student days and subsequent involvement, in "a patriotic fit" ("Anfall von Patriotismus"),[31] with Lützow's struggle against Napoleon (1813–14) receded, Eichendorff's lyrics condense (*verdichten*) history into a rich, albeit bewildering, texture of affective states. A poem dating back to his participation in Lützow's force (1814) already attests to the phantasmagorical character of historical experience. Keeping watch, the lyric voice peers into the void, baffled by a landscape that is tantalizingly opaque and uneventful:

Mein Gewehr im Arme steh ich
Hier verloren auf der Wacht,
Still nach jener Gegend seh ich,
Hab so oft dahin gedacht!

Fernher Abendglocken klingen
Durch die schöne Einsamkeit;
So, wenn wir zusammen gingen,
Hört ich's oft in alter Zeit.

Wolken da wie Türme prangen,
Als säh ich im Dunst mein Wien,
Und die Donau hell ergangen
Zwischen Burgen durch das Grün.

Doch wie fern sind Strom und Türme!
Wer da wohnt, denkt mein noch kaum,
Herbstlich rauschen schon die Stürme,
Und ich stehe wie im Traum. (*EW*, 1: 163–64)

Weapon in arm, I stand
Lost here on guard,
Quietly I gaze toward that region,
Where my thoughts have often tended!

Distant evening bells are sounding
Through the beauteous solitude;
Thus, when we jointly walked,
I often heard it in old times.

Clouds gleam like towers there,
As if through mists I beheld my Vienna,
And the Danube serenely wanders
Among castles through the green.

Yet how distant are the river and towers!
Whoever lives there scarcely thinks of me,
Autumnal storms already rustle,
And I am suspended as in a dream. (MY TRANSLATION)

Eagerly sought after by the subject's gaze, history always appears to occur elsewhere. As the soldier's vigilance is becalmed by distant church bells and inscrutable cloud formations, history bypasses the modern subject whose earnest watchfulness stands in ironic contrast to its quintessentially "lost" (*verloren*) position. Above all, "Auf der Feldwacht" intimates this rising intuition that, rather than being constituted as a progressive sequence of momentous events, history unfolds underground, leaving the modern subject marooned in a phantasmagorical zone where watchtowers and cloud formations seem fully interchangeable ("Wolken da wie Türme prangen").[32] The similarity between the stony watchtower occupied by a fossilized relic of the old *Herrschaft* in "Auf einer Burg" and the glittering towerlike clouds envisioned by the brooding student patriot in "Auf der Feldwacht" serves to heighten the irony. Conceived as a missed and therefore "unclaimed experience" (to recall Cathy Caruth's titular phrase), the enigma of history reaffirms the demise of feudal *Herrschaft* but treats its vanished representatives as the counterparts of the alienated, hallucinating postrevolutionary subject: "Und ich stehe wie im Traum." Eichendorff's poem thus attests to a basic asymmetry between history seen as an underground structural process of coordinated labor and the older, obviously defunct, model of history as a series of conspicuous and heroic individual actions.

For individuals to become cognizant of this asymmetry means not only to "feel" or "intuit" their own alienation but, through the persistence of that very mood, to become sentient of a deep-structural historical shift. As various social and intellectual historians have argued, the kind of alienation at issue here had been building, at least among the educated and professional classes, since the late eighteenth century. Preeminent among its early manifestations ranks sentimentalism (a.k.a. the "Werther syndrome"), a cultural movement so apposite to alienation because it appears to indulge in a set of ostensibly "personal" feelings while simultaneously revealing their origins in collective habits of writing and reading. With the old Lutheran ideal of morally stalwart inwardness revealing its complex alliance with fluctuations of rhetoric, taste, and fashion, the truth-value of affect rapidly erodes. Not surprisingly, the mid-eighteenth-century genesis of bourgeois and middle-class professional communities goes hand in hand with an unprecedented commitment to literary and aesthetic pursuits. As has often been observed, this rapidly growing investment in literary and related cultural projects, and the earnestness and urgency of its collaborative pursuit by writers and readers, sought to realize existence in the supplemental, virtual domain of "spirit and letter." As often as not, this new, symbolic dwelling was already recognized as inherently supplemental and compensatory. Yet this ironic or melancholic insight also ensured that the quest of disenfranchised and alienated middle-class communities for cultural (in lieu of political) self-representation in the realm of "taste" and "imagination" could never succeed. While middle-class reading habits after 1800 became more homogeneous and self-conscious—both in Germany and, even more so, in England—the projected, strategic "payoff" of this project of *Bildung*—that is, the merging of cultural into political action—never materialized.[33] Rather than providing the middle class with a remedy for its growing sense of political alienation and apparent irrelevance, literary practice turned out to be co-originary with these very frustrations. As a result, during the 1820s and 1830s, the once ambitious project of romantic *Bildung* threatened to deteriorate into a mere simulacrum of political action.

The decline of the ambitious aesthetic programs of early German romanticism ought to be considered in relation to the concurrent defeat of the Prussian reform movement. Both succumbed to what Thomas Nipperdey has called the "tragical dialectic of the reform": "The constitution presupposed a bourgeois society within a greater state, no longer particularist or based on estates. But this society first had to be created. It was a society of the future. The way to such a society and to the participation of the nation in its politics seemed to lie in a bureaucratic dictatorship by educational means. Policies of modernisation could not be advanced by the representatives of the old society ... [yet] for reasons of financial and national policy, it was not possible to manage without them" (Nipperdey 1996, 54),

By 1819, the Prussian reformers' ideals sounded distant and abstract, evidence that Stein's and Hardenberg's political and economic reforms had met with defeat at the hands precisely of those whom they had been designed to liberate. *Bildung* had become something specialized, separate, and essentially private: "The more one identified with 'culture', the sooner it could appear to be detached from general existence. Cultural life became the separate 'domain' of a certain type of nineteenth-century bourgeois, alongside work and political activity" (Nipperdey 1996, 235; translation modified).[34] As an increasingly peripheral phenomenon—a *vita contemplativa* standing in "complementary and compensatory" (ibid.) relation to the *vita activa* of professional and public life—culture effectively embraces the defeat of political and social ideals that, at Weimar and Jena, had been perceived as inextricably intertwined with aesthetics. Heine's shrewd amalgamation of "high-cultural" topics with the irreverent journalistic idiom—such as in *Die Romantische Schule, Zur Geschichte der Philosophie und Religion in Deutschland,* and *Schwabenspiegel*—effectively recast the vaunted progression of German *Geist* and *Bildung* as an integral component of that larger historical defeat. Overall, the transition from Eichendorff's formative years (1806–19) to Heine's (1819–27) appears to be defined by the shift from a traumatic confrontation of historical change to the melancholic awareness that an entire people had betrayed precisely those social and cultural opportunities that Napoleon's drastic reorganization of the Reich had opened up.

Both for its philistine proponents and for the policymakers of the Austro-Prussian *Reaktion* calculating the costs and benefits of their repressive policies, this restrictive definition of *Kultur* as a historical agency by symbolic proxy had its appeal. At once fiercely partisan and pragmatic in its preemptive stifling of political and cultural opposition throughout Germany, Metternich's administration was a peculiar hybrid of ancien régime and modern bureaucratic state, aristocratic *hauteur* and nervous partisanship.[35] Yet in its prolonged confrontation with the major cultural movements and eminent writers of the 1820s and 1830s, it seems to have settled on expedient levels of surveillance and intervention. Either the character of a particular cultural formation or initiative (e.g., "das Junge Deutschland") would be so transparently political and provocative as to have forfeited its claims to genuine cultural (i.e., "aesthetic") quality—in which case government action in the form of censorship and imprisonment could easily be defended—or the work of individual writers merely sketched a faint, imaginary equality among individuals in their respective private spheres, while leaving uncontested the inequalities in public, political life—in which case there was no obvious need for government intervention.[36]

Retroactivity: Lyricism, Conservatism, Fantasy, and Romantic Postmodernity

Bound by an inexorable logic that is revealed only in larger, demographic shifts, Eichendorff's professional career and his development as a writer unfold within this quintessentially "modern" struggle between the visionary politics of the Jena and Heidelberg romantics and the post-Napoleonic reorganization of power as bureaucratic, secular, and reactionary. Following the financial collapse of his family estate at Lubowitz in 1818, Eichendorff came to experience the gradual extinction of the culturally centered patriotism of his student days at the hands of a new, harshly pragmatic political order that was to dominate German and Austrian life for decades to come.[37] Once again confronting dire financial straits, he had little choice but to embark on what would prove an often-agonizing bureaucratic career in the Prussian and Viennese administrations. Both during his ten years (1821–31) of service under the important reformer Theodor von Schön, chief regional administrator (*Oberpräsident*) of East Prussia, and subsequently from 1831 to 1844, Eichendorff held various advanced administrative positions, including one in the chief censorship bureau (*Oberzensurkollegium*). Making his transition from provincial Königsberg to the Prussian capital, Eichendorff became acutely aware that his own career was enmeshed with an ideological confrontation between the regional power base of a culturally sophisticated and reform-oriented bureaucracy (*Reformbeamtentum*) and the often opportunist and ambitious politics of the centralist bureaucracy (*Staatsbeamtentum*) that was to prevail and dominate German politics through 1918.

More than anything else, this struggle between regional and centralist forces within the Prussian state threw into relief the writer's precarious situation as a public advocate of "cultural values" and, more generally, the delicate kinship of literature and politics.[38] In distinguishing between his own conservative tendencies and those of the restoration (*konservativer Legitimismus*),[39] Eichendorff also recoiled from the increasingly widespread and often crude involvement of literature with politics during the 1820s and 1830s, which struck him as both naïve and self-destructive, a view shared by the altogether differently situated Heine. Responding to a wearied assessment of the times by his superior, Schön, Eichendorff observes that "in this blissfully conformist [*gemeinheitsseligen*] age, a truthful voice like yours . . . offers a security that the longing for something greater is still alive and will yet prevail. Poetry, too, gradually succumbs to this universal paralysis. It has accepted the philistines' invitation and, in their company, is growing altogether political, the most pathetic fate with which this child of the gods could meet, now that politics is no longer poetic, as in the years 1807–1813" (Eichendorff 1984, 12: 132; my translation).[40]

This indictment of his own times as trivializing and vulgarizing poetry by forcibly conjoining it with politics would seem to be the very hallmark of a staunch Catholic conservative. Indeed, a casual reading of the section entitled "Geistliche Gedichte" in Eichendorff's 1837 collection of his lyrics would seem to exemplify "the familiar romantic finale," as Nietzsche puts it, the "break, breakdown, return and collapse before an old faith, before *the* old god" (Nietzsche 1993, 11). The remainder of this chapter is less concerned with proving or disproving this popular (if also facile) position, however, than with probing its epistemological assumptions and aesthetic consequences.

What exactly was romantic conservatism (a term first coined by Chateaubriand's journal *Le Conservateur* in 1818 and soon popular throughout central Europe)? Was it merely an anti-modern reaction, a transparently regressive form of symbolic behavior? The eagerness of contemporary criticism in the humanities to uncover certain thought formations or strategies of writing as "conservative"—and, in so doing, to presume that it has effectively discredited them—frequently leaves the actual nature of conservatism unexamined. The ambivalent suspension of conservatism between a purely affective, unselfconscious disposition and a distinctive rhetorical practice already points to a critical problem. Is the recursive temporal structure of *Erinnerung* as it resonates in many of Eichendorff's titles ("Erinnerung," "Rückblick," "Letzte Heimkehr," "Vergebner Ärger," "Verlorne Liebe," "Trennung," "Abschied," etc.) merely an expression of a nostalgic longing, a desire for something as implausible as an outright reversal of historical time? Both Görres's amalgamation of mythography and historicism and Eichendorff's self-consciously hypothetical acts of lyric introspection speak against this hypothesis. Particularly in the latter, the highly reflexive formalization of interiority as a holograph of spontaneous recollection, historically conditioned anxiety, and utopian, spiritual longing strongly militates against interpreting conservatism as a case of naïve and unqualified nostalgia. Nor, it turns out, is the phenomenon of romantic conservatism fully captured by Hegel's speculative thesis of the bureaucratic nation-state as a world-historical force that has preserved and contained the past in institutional form. For the Protestant "can-do" spirit of Hegel's historical inventory-taking appears ultimately geared toward enhancing the authority of the Prussian nation-state and as such seems notably impatient with both Friedrich Schlegel's cultural conservatism and Joseph Görres's mythical or Catholic figurations. What, then, are we to understand as the ideological place of romantic conservatism, and how are its affective, rhetorical, and cognitive spheres to be demarcated from one another?

In what may at first seem counterintuitive and startling, I propose to understand romantic conservatism in close proximity to postmodernism. Doing so means, first of all, discriminating sharply between the ideational character of romantic conservatism and its Machiavellian counterpart—the politics of reaction. What sets the two apart is, among other things, their radically different conception of temporality. To the pragmatic sensibility of the post-Napoleonic reaction, temporality meant little more than a menacing future, an impending modernity manifest in the importunate clamor of liberal, socialist, and radically nationalist (and nascently anti-Semitic) constituencies. The most popular expression of this "threat" of the modern involved the movement of German liberalism, which beginning in the 1820s kept pressing for a national constitution and parliamentary system. By and large, Germany's agonistic politics before 1848 involved struggles over political and economic reform and the meaning of the "constitution" similar to those that had unfolded in England prior to 1832. And, as the participants in these debates all understood, romantic political discourse found its primal scene in the French Revolution. Even for Eichendorff, who had seen the gentrified world of his childhood and youth swept away by Napoleon's revolutionary transformation of Germany's political and economic landscape, the dismantling of the old Reich was inevitable and indeed long overdue: "Small wonder, then, that German life and the German Reich, both of which rested primarily on these invisible foundations, began to sag precariously at all ends and finally sustained such fatal cracks that, at the behest of the authorities, the edifice had to be condemned and torn down. Thus the entire old structure had already collapsed at the beginning of our century. The storm of the French Revolution and subsequent foreign rule only served to sweep away its useless debris" (*EW,* 1: 920; my translation). Sentiments like these were common to the representatives of romantic conservatism and, as the case of Friedrich von Gentz reveals, they were even entertained by the official policymakers of the *Reaktion.*[41]

Yet for pragmatic, truly Machiavellian reasons, the established, albeit nervously vigilant, powers in Vienna and Berlin felt impelled to combat all political and cultural manifestations of modernity with everything that the rich conceptual reservoir of a received tradition (*Tradition* and *Überlieferung*) provided. Writers across the entire political spectrum, from the conservative Eichendorff to the cosmopolitan Goethe, to a radical like Ludwig Börne or an ideologically noncommittal voice like Heine's, nothing seemed more distasteful than the reaction's continual fusion of sentimentalism and expediency. They all recoiled from that peculiarly German tendency to philistine (and Christian) ressentiment or "cultivation of hatred" (to borrow Peter Gay's phrase) that Nietzsche was to subject to ruthless scrutiny in his *Genealogy of Morals* at the end of the century. For Eichendorff, Germany's political landscape in the 1820s was being divided between a superannuated aristocratic and feudal class and new communities of mostly unimaginative and self-righteous middle-class opportunists. As he remarks, "it is in any event erroneous to describe the aristocracy of that time as an exclusively conservative party. Already at that time, as we have seen, the aristocracy had only a feeble idea and awareness of its original meaning and purpose—little more, indeed, than a vague tradition of arbitrary formalities—and consequently lacked all belief in itself" (*EW,* 1: 911; my translation). At the same time, with the rise of its philistine petit bourgeoisie, Germany appears on the verge of succumbing to an "imperishable sentimentality that continually brawls with the terrorism of a vulgar patriotic fervor" (die in Deutschland unsterbliche Sentimentalität, in beständigem Handgemenge mit dem Terrorismus einer groben Vaterländerei [*EW,* 1: 906]).

Standing in sharp and self-conscious antithesis to the politics of the *Reaktion,* romantic conservatism sought less to indulge the anti-modern prejudices that undoubtedly formed part of it than to articulate an organic vision that combined diverse elements of a precapitalist and even a preschismatic social formation. Hence, romantic *Altkonservatismus* must be distinguished from the period's established politics of restoration and reaction. For conservatism encompassed prima facie an aesthetic, and often stridently anti-capitalist, program.[42] At the same time, it appears not so much to have aimed at some future utopia as to have stressed the persistence of history in a holistic sense. Though ultimately irretrievable in any objective sense, the past was nonetheless inescapable. That is, romantic conservatism did not actually seek to implement its peculiar cultural vision of an implicitly Catholic, ideally stratified precapitalist society. It did not purport to reverse the flow of historical time. Rather, the past was conjured up—in the medial form of a Platonic allegory—as a system of values conceivable only from the shadowy (discursive) perspective of the abject modern individual. Rather than capturing incidental empirical matter, *Erinnerung* amounted to a self-conscious "fantasy." Fully aware of its terminal confinement in the cave of modernity, romantic conservatism embraced history and tradition as something mesmerizing—not despite but because of the fact that they had been irretrievably lost and, indeed, had never been consciously experienced to begin with.[43] "[T]he psychoanalytic notion of fantasy cannot be reduced to that of a fantasy scenario which obfuscates the true horror of a situation"; if fantasy "conceals" the "horror of the Real," it also and "at the same time . . . creates what it purports to conceal, its 'repressed' point of reference" (Žižek 1997, 7). Furthermore, if we are to accept Žižek's definition of "fantasy [as] the primordial form of *narrative,* which serves to occult some original deadlock," romantic conservatism can certainly be interpreted as a narrative of just this kind. For it was above all a bourgeois, not a feudal, phenomenon.[44] As the successor of a feudal age that had alternately missed or squandered its historical opportunities, the protobourgeois subjects of the modern, bureaucratic capitalist nation-state continued to be haunted by the revolutionary trauma to which, in effect, they owed their very existence. Forever distraught over the loss of a simpler and happier past, the "sadder and wiser" ideology of romantic conservatism could only consolidate itself in dialectical relation to a modernity whose cultural and social ramifications it continued to deplore.

Yet as regards the precise affective and rhetorical forms of such historical mourning, *Reaktion* and *Altkonservatismus* were strikingly dissimilar. The former, Friedrich Heer argues, was distinguished by the prevalence of "monastic traits"; every reactionary was "a failed monk, a secularized monk," who bore "within him the original sin of the monastic order—acedia, or melancholy, which the fathers of the church had already struggled with" (Heer, 51; my translation). In contrast, romantic conservatism typically conceded the overtly fantasized nature of what it called tradition, as well as the interpretive contingencies that determine the transmission of historical "values." For according to a critical genealogy extending from Justus Möser through Friedrich Schleiermacher all the way to Gadamer's *Truth and Method,* historical understanding has always been conceived as a methodologically open-ended and partially fantasized ("divinatory") process. In Schleiermacher's words, "all understanding contains a powerful motive for the conjunction of speculative with empirical and historical elements."[45] For the methodological and theoretical underpinnings of *any* historicism prove themselves inescapably historical. The past that is being reconstructed in the textual productions of literary and political *Altkonservatismus* can never be grasped as an authentic entity. Rather, it constitutes a textual, and indeed fantastic, simulacrum of the mournful affect that confirms its status as something irretrievable by us.

Peripheral to Eichendorff's career unfolds that of Adam Müller (1779–1829) who, building on the work of Justus Möser in the previous generation, emerged as the most prominent representative of German romantic conservatism. For Müller, *Staatswissenschaft* had to be kept out of the hands of technocrats and managers, lest it become a mere "aggregate of the institutional apparatus" (Herzählung des gesamten . . . Apparats); the state had to be captured in its "soaring dynamic" (*Fluge seiner Bewegung*), rather than being conceived of as simply an "accumulation of concepts" (*Anhäufungen von Begriffen*) (Müller 1931, 7, 16). Müller strongly echoes his political idol, Edmund Burke, repeatedly pleading for a fluid and holistic conception of politics in which the "lifeless concepts" are to yield to the "living idea" said to unify the discrete spheres of politics, law, culture, and finance.

The aesthetic—that "oblation" of the crumbling British state in an era of mounting revolutionary challenges—is already treated in Burke's *Reflections on the Revolution in France* (1790) as a strategy of "consolation" rather than salvation.[46] Rather than throwing in his lot with the shrewd pragmatism of his friend Gentz (Burke's first translator) who, as political secretary to Metternich, had established himself as the preeminent strategist of the Austrian *Reaktion*, Müller pursued an erratic, at times near-fraudulent, trajectory as a political writer and lecturer. Beginning around 1807, his writings set forth a vision of political conservatism whose utopian and figural presentation seems curiously to foreshadow postmodernism's notion of late-capitalist subjects trapped in a "posthistorical" existence.[47] Conservatism here emerges as a virtual reality determined not by objective memories but by ever-shifting states of hermeneutic desire vis-à-vis the past. Or, more precisely, conservatism's ideological "fantasy provides a *rationale* for the inherent deadlock of desire" (Žižek, 32). To conservative thought, the cradling pleasures of tradition can only be enjoyed in allegorical form, as borne out by Eichendorff's lyrics and autobiographical prose, such as his remarkable "Chapter about My Birth" ("Kapitel von meiner Geburt"), to which we shall soon return. Müller's peripatetic career often suggests the close affinity between his notorious political and personal opportunism (Carl Schmitt calls him an "untrustworthy and superficial littérateur" [45]) and his self-consciously figural modes of political argumentation.[48]

Müller's facile anthropomorphic conception ("The organization of the state must altogether mirror that of the human subject" [1931, 101]) opposes the Enlightenment model of the state as a social contract instituted by fully formed, independent, rational subjects. For Müller, the "artificial constitutionalism" (*Konstitutionskünstelei*) that dominated postrevolutionary (and eventually post-Napoleonic) political debates had merely contrived a "surrogate" for the "invisible unity of will" (*unsichtbare Willenseinheit* [Müller 1931, 102–3]) said to have defined the state as an organic, affective community. Yet in what would prove an enduring trait of conservative thought, such a community—grasped as a utopian or, in any event, no longer available concept—is said to depend on an intricate web of rationality and fantasy (*ein inniges Verwobensein von Gefühl, Verstand, Phantasie und Wille* [101]).[49] Müller's argument rests on an implicit collapse of time into absolute duration, with "time immemorial as such [serving] as the ultimate basis of right" (Schmitt, 62). Inasmuch as time itself is conceived as an "irrational abyss that brings forth the cosmic event out of itself" (ibid.), conservative thought may justly view its embrace of the past as an instance of wholly contingent and involuntary recollection (*Erinnerung*). Indeed, understood as a *punctum* within a limitless temporal duration, the past can only be constituted rhetorically, sustained by tropes and figures that remain necessarily devoid of all objective reference.

In his 1806 lectures on science and literature, Müller's notion of an "invisible unity of [political] will"—itself a kind of shorthand definition of ideology—is extended into a vividly figural account of cultural and, specifically, literary production. Deploying the well-worn antithesis of (dead) letter and (living) spirit, Müller remarks how the "letter of modernity, intrinsically devoid of meaning as such" (*der für sich bedeutungslose Buchstabe*), is raised to the "living word" only by the "traditions and histories of a past world" (*die Traditionen, die Geschichten der Vorwelt*). Everything thus depends on "letter and tradition" (Buchstabe und Tradition) and on a people's serendipitous discovery of "an authentic, well-preserved sign" (*ein echtes wohlerhaltenes Zeichen*) from the past. Yet to be receptive to the processes of tradition also requires a given community to accept and embrace the "infinite number of variations" and competing senses for the palimpsest of history. A strictly literal methodological approach to isolated particulars of history would fail to grasp the holistic and irregular nature of historical process. Overtly systematic conceptions of history amount to a "false Protestantism" (*falscher Protestantismus*), whose literal and legalistic emphasis on the letter's technical rather than historical dimensions invariably reifies tradition as a mere form of understanding, Müller argues (1967, 1: 87–89). In contrast, conservatism's exegesis of tradition shuns such ramrod literalisms in favor of a holistic model of the state as an organic "idea."

Aside from repudiating modernity's alienated logic of possessive and competitive individualism, Müller's self-conscious fantasy of a conservative *Ideenstaat* (ibid., 97) also envisions the restoration of a precapitalist feudal order on the model of the patriarchal family, albeit without "even mentioning, much less advocating, serfdom" (Berdahl, 169). Likewise, the projected return to a monarchical system politely sidesteps the excesses of absolutism, preferring instead to locate the monarch's "humble authority figure . . . at the center of the unfettered pursuits of proud servants" (*der bescheidene Herrscher . . . im Zentrum des freien Getümmels stolzer Diener* [Müller 1967, 1: 101]). Based on a tradition said to resemble a palimpsest of infinite exegetical possibilities, conservative thought thus fantasizes the state as an organic family of individuals and communities. Yet because of its overtly fantasized presentation, Müller's model of conservatism is able to credibly dissent from the reaction's crude calculus of expediency, coercion, and self-interest: "Duration, which only the spirit . . . can bequeath, cannot be grasped by any exterior emblem, nor will it submit to any official, enforced restoration of the church, senate consultation, law of succession, improvised family, or some federal system spawned by idle invention and sheer coincidence" (Müller 1967, 1: 96; my translation. Not surprisingly, Müller's most rhapsodically figural paragraph concerns itself with conjuring up the capacity of language to evoke a state of ideological kinship and permanence, even as he concedes that "the majority of our contemporaries might choose to obey other imperatives" (ibid., 103). Here the distinctly figural (or "allegorical") character of romantic *Altkonservatismus* begins to emerge.

Speaking of conservatism as a "historical-dynamic structural complex," Karl Mannheim has elaborated the curious genealogy of this ideology. Rather than falling back on realist or nominalist models, according to which conservatism was either received as an already finished quasi-metaphysical construct or conceived as a theory by supposedly autonomous individuals, Mannheim interprets conservatism as a dynamic mode of "retroaction." For Mannheim, conservatism presents itself as a Heideggerian "mood of thought" intimately entwined "with the actual existence and destinies of human groups and appearing as their product." Having achieved its conceptual integrity only "in relation to [a] particular course of experience," the "stylistic design" of conservative thought is necessarily something "historically embedded."

Presaging Freud's concept of *Nachträglichkeit*, romantic "conservatism" thus partially compensates for and partially repeats a pervasive traumatic disruption for which the French Revolution, Napoleon's radical reorganization of Central Europe, and the depressing economic and ideological realities of the post-Waterloo era constitute successive phases.

As evidenced by its densely figural and metaphoric articulation, early-nineteenth-century *Altkonservatismus* responded to its historically distinctive experience of modernity in the mode of an incipiently self-conscious ideological fantasy. Given that this intellectual fantasy unfolds in tandem with such historical disruptions, conservative thought "may well be nothing more than [its] conceptual effect." The distinctive characteristic of conservatism, meanwhile, lies in the fact that here "past and trauma are treated as if they were one and the same" (Rauch, 113). Seen as the development of a "traditionalism [that has] become self-reflective" (Mannheim, 88), romantic conservatism bespeaks its proponents' awareness of their "authentically temporal destiny" (de Man's phrase).

Consistent with Eichendorff's self-conscious amalgamation of "tradition," "recollection," and "fantasy," J. G. A. Pocock remarks that "a tradition," which "in its simplest form, may be thought of as an indefinite series of repetitions of an action," does not so much require an original point of reference as the fiction of one: "it may well be that it is the assumption, rather than the factual information, of previous performance that is operative; each action provides the grounds for assuming that it had a predecessor." Later in the same essay, Pocock persuasively distinguishes between "tradition" as stressing "either the continuity of the process of transmission, or the creative and charismatic origin of what is transmitted. The two are conceptually distinct, . . . but they are dialectically related, and are often—perhaps normally—found together within the same tradition. A distinction may be drawn between traditions which conserve highly specific and significant images of the creative actions with which they began and of which they are in some way the continuation, and traditions which depict themselves as sheer continuity of usage or transmission and conserve little or no account of their beginnings" (Pocock 237; 244).

Like a more mature embodiment of Friedrich Schlegel's concept of irony, romantic conservatism knows of its own intrinsic and irremediable allegorical constitution. Like the Stoics long before, the representatives of *Altkonservatismus* are resigned to the fact that the certainty of open-ended, unpredictable historical time cannot be countered by *any* politics, liberal or reactionary.[50] Instead, with its logic of "retroaction" (*Nachträglichkeit*), romantic conservatism anticipates a criterion repeatedly invoked to define postmodernism: that of a fundamentally "posthistorical" era. Moreover, though arguably at a more intuitive level, romantic conservatism also seems to know of a profound (if ultimately ineluctable) relation between the languages of theory, fantasy, politics, and aesthetics. Hence it looks "for breaks, for events rather than new holds, for the telltale instant after which it is no longer the same . . . for shifts and irrevocable changes in the *representation* of things and why they change." It only "clocks the variations themselves, and knows only too well that the contents are just more images" (Jameson 1993, ix):

> Cultural production is . . . driven back inside a mental space which is no longer that of the old monadic subject but rather that of some degraded collective "objective spirit": it can no longer gaze directly on some putative real world, at some reconstruction of a past history which was once itself a present; rather, as in Plato's cave, it must trace our mental images of that past upon its confining walls. . . . It is a realism that is meant to derive from the shock of grasping that confinement and slowly becoming aware of a new and original historical situation in which we are condemned to seek History by way of our own pop images and simulacra of that history, which itself remains forever out of reach. (Jameson 1993, 25)

As we saw early on, Eichendorff's oeuvre is shot through with "pop images," or clichés evocative of a history known to be irrecuperable, and, in response to that impasse, positing conservatism as a strictly virtual reality: a fantasy. To be sure, it is tempting to read Eichendorff's political prose—specifically his late treatise on the *Folgen von der Aufhebung der Landeshoheit Bischöfe und der Klöster in Deutschland*—as conservative propaganda. What else could be meant by his patriotic *laudatio* of the "German tendency, one of more profoundly inward character, that venerates its own while respecting everything sacred and showing consideration for all tradition" (*die deutsche Richtung, tiefsinniger nach innen gekehrt, und sich selber ehrend achtet . . . alles Heilige, berücksichtigt alles Herkömmliche* [Eichendorff 1958, 4: 1155])? Indeed, few writers exemplify better the tendency of "mythical transcendence" that Karl Mannheim identifies as a salient characteristic of romantic conservatism (56). While other post-Napoleonic European nations appear like "well-adjusted palaces that impress on us a certain ennobling feeling of order and security," German politics, mostly aimless where it is not outright repressive, furnishes the observer with

> a lovely view from the mountain[s] into the boundless space, precipitous cliffs, rivers, a chiaroscuro of forests and states, out into the immeasurable cerulean distance, where heaven and earth mysteriously touch [in die unermessene blaue Ferne hinaus, wo Himmel und Erde einander rätselfhaft berühren], every single appearance . . . as a whole for itself, every stream and river searching for its own path to the eternal ocean, and yet all together building in a colorful tone the blossoming depth, which, though it may confound the naked eye with its opulence, wonderfully exalts and refreshes the heart with an imperishable feeling of nature. (Eichendorff 1958, 4: 1155–56; my translation)

Precisely this apparently clichéd nature of Eichendorff's writing, however, ought to serve as a check to the familiar critical impulse in the humanities today, whereby an overtly aestheticized idiom is quickly repudiated as an instance of ideological obfuscation and conservative delusion. For a passage like the one quoted above does not so much appear to indulge in aesthetic mythmaking as to rehearse for us how it is done. For what better way to exemplify the mythical structure of conservatism and draw attention to the metaphysical desire underlying the entire passage than with a citation of German romanticism's archē text or (if a bad pun may be permitted) architect: Novalis. Surely, the reference to "the immeasurable cerulean distance where heaven and earth miraculously join" (*die unermessene blaue Ferne hinaus, wo Himmel und Erde einander rätselfhaft berühren*) constitutes a pointed reference to *Heinrich von Ofterdingen,* the text that defined romantic longing for Eichendorff's generation. Yet citation is a distinctly self-conscious form of repetition, and Eichendorff's specular image not only reenacts the impossible nostalgia of early romanticism: it also recalls a widely quoted image in one of his own best-known poems, "Mondnacht": "It was as though heaven had / Held earth in quiet kiss" (*Es war, als hätt der Himmel / Die Erde still geküßt*). Suspended between its own, inscrutable affective origins and an expressive language that proves overtly allusive of an earlier text, Eichendorff's Old Germanic (*altgermanisch*) political community constitutes an exemplary instance of Freudian "retroaction" (*Nachträglichkeit*). It renders an ideological fantasy in an overtly allegorical (that is, self-consciously textual) form. Not surprisingly, Eichendorff's essay demurs the hegemony of the "understanding" (*Verstand*) in Protestant culture, advocating instead the liberation of "fantasy" (*Phantasie*) from the constraints of "stale sentimentalism or outright political madness" (Eichendorff 1958, 4: 1160). In the modality of lyric form—the smaller-scale image of an agonistic modernity inhabited by the writer and his projected audience—fantasy simulates original creation as involuntary recollection. As Adorno puts it, "through fantasy, as recollection, genius continuously restores original creation—not as the creator of its reality but by the reintegration of its given elements in an image. . . . Through recollection, fantasy transforms the traces of the collapse of a sinful creation into a sign of hope for one that is whole and without sin and whose image it forms out of ruins." In his early Kierkegaard essay, a first attempt at formulating an aesthetic theory, Adorno stresses the miniature-character of the aesthetic vis-à-vis creation itself ("Fantasy imitates creation through miniaturization"), a bit of speculation borne out by lyric writing in particular. Moreover, the discrepancy in scale between the magnitude of a ruined creation and its "reintegration" in a dialectical, rather than Platonic, "domain of the image" (*Bilderreich*) stands in strict correlation with temporal discontinuity. Adorno quotes Kierkegaard: "Art consists in producing an enjoyment which never actually becomes present, but always has an element of the past in it, so that it is present in the past. This has already been expressed in the word: posthumous (*nachgelassen*)" (*Adorno 1989*, 139).[51]

Given its twofold sense as *nachgelassen*—that is, as self-consciously "posthumous" at the level of both form (creation as simulation) and historical time—Eichendorff's conservatism is *nachträglich* in a more complex sense even than Freud's own usage of that term.[52] For a conservative aesthetic—taking the term in its strong, reflexive sense—does not merely understand the representations of its disaffection as "belated," since doing so would assume a basic continuity between history and the present, between the plenitude of times past and the conscious impoverishment of the here-and-now. A reflection of this kind would still be, in essence, a type of (epistemological and political) *Reaktion* and thus would bear all the customary traits of a delusional formation. True to the rich semantics of *Nachträglichkeit,* however, Eichendorff's stress on conservatism's "retroactive" or allegorical status (which, no doubt, also inspired his late project of translating Calderon) takes history to be by definition a missed experience.[53] As such, it can be recovered only via the (truly necessary) fantasy of a specular, mythical "depth" ("jene blühende Tiefe"). Like Proust's *mémoire involontaire,* the insights of conservative thought appear legitimate and authoritative only if their serendipitous occurrence is construed as a sign of (metaphysical) providence. Yet Eichendorff's writings typically do not take that leap. Instead, as the following lyric makes all too clear, the longing for a heroic past invariably succumbs to the insistent, polyphonous ("tausend Stimmen") and "disorienting" ("verwirrend") calling that haunts the wayward and wandering romantic poet—always found *extra urbe:*

Ich wollt im Walde dichten
Ein Heldenlied voll Pracht,
Verwickelte Geschichten,
Recht sinnreich ausgedacht.
Da rauschten Bäume, sprangen
Vom Fels die Bäche drein,
Und tausend Stimmen klangen
Verwirrend aus und ein.
Und manches Jauchzen schallen
Ließ ich aus frischer Brust,
Doch aus den Helden allen
Ward nichts vor tiefer Lust.

Kehr ich zur Stadt erst wieder
Aus Feld und Wäldern kühl,
Da kommen all die Lieder
Von fern durchs Weltgewühl,
Es hallen Lust und Schmerzen
Noch einmal leise nach,
Und bildend wird im Herzen
Die alte Wehmut wach,
Der Winter auch derweile
Im Feld die Blumen bricht—
Dann gibt's vor Langerweile
Ein überlang Gedicht! (*EW*, 1: 119)

I sought to compose in the forest
A heroic song full of splendor,
Intricate stories,
Quite cleverly thought out.
There the trees were rustling, streams
Leaping from precipices,
And a thousand voices resounding

Bewilderingly all around.
And many gleeful cheers issued
From my vigorous breast,
Yet all those heroes were eclipsed
By my profound enjoyment.

Once I return to the city
From fields and forests cool,
Then all the songs return
From afar through the bustling world,
Pleasure and pain quietly
Reverberate once more,
And creatively within my heart
The old yearning awakens,
Meanwhile winter also snaps
flower stalks out in the field—
Then, out of boredom, we are presented
With a poem far too long! (MY TRANSLATION)

If the professional goal of paying expressive tribute to a heroic past has lured the writer out of the city, the resulting poem already concedes the impossibility of such programmatic art by the end of the first stanza ("Doch aus den Helden allen / Ward nichts vor tiefer Lust"). Yet this opening—quite possibly a caricature of the nationalist agitation (*Deutschtümelei*) that had become associated with the notorious 1817 Wartburg festival—yields to a far more complex second stanza. For in returning to the city both richer and disillusioned, the speaker finds his affective center by reflecting on the conventionality of songs written in lieu of those that cannot be written because of their enigmatic, ineffable point of reference. Consistent with this productive failure, the lyric's dominant affect of *Wehmut* (melancholy) emerges only vicariously. *Wehmut* in the sense of mourning or longing no longer constitutes some timeless emotive source for lyric expression. Rather, such states can only be isolated and understood retroactively, namely, from the conditional, perhaps utopian, perspective of an eventual return ("Kehr ich zur Stadt erst wieder . . ."). Both in its title, "Rückblick" ("Retrospection"), and in its astutely phrased second stanza ("Es hallen . . . / Noch einmal . . . nach"), the lyric premises its wistful interiority on the condition that the subject has always known of its constitutive belatedness. Its interiority is merely the echo chamber of voices and songs whose ideological desire—be it patriotic *Deutschtümelei* or a pathological immersion in nature (*Naturverfallenheit*) of the kind that Walter Benjamin ascribes to Goethe's Ottilie—has been unmasked as an outright fantasy.

Ultimately, Eichendorff's conservative voice knows itself to be trapped between its profoundly spiritual attachments to a past that it knows to be beyond recovery and emergent mass ideologies—the various socialisms of Feuerbach, Saint-Simon, Ricardo, Mill, Cabet, Fourier, Comte, et al.—that typically transmute their underlying nostalgia for a Rousseauian state of nature into some utopian vision of the end of history. As Adorno notes, in Eichendorff's poetry "the status of conservatism has changed in the extreme" and is "broad enough to embrace its own opposite."[54] Inasmuch as the conservative's epistemological situation of *Nachträglichkeit* is one of continual dissent, he experiences historical time as an unending present—be it as the void of a temporal *punctum* or that of empty *extensio*— that reveals nothing but "false, mendacious life" ("falsches, lügenhaftes Leben"). Both in a historical and formal sense, the subjects of Eichendorff's primal scene of a traumatic postrevolutionary romanticism attain knowledge only in the modality of deferral and retroaction. Hence their interiority reconstitutes itself—not in the imaginary order of desire but in the self-consciously figural (i.e., allegorical) domain of fantasy. Such individuals are condemned to self-awareness as wholly belated (*Epigonen* or *Nachgeborene*) and thus experience history as a temporal void whose depth can only be gauged in lyric miniatures, musing on the allegorical and ineffectual bulk of conventional poetry: "Dann gibt's vor Langerweile / Ein überlang Gedicht."

In some fragments from the 1830s, initially conceived as drafts of a new autobiographical novella with the curious title "Unstern" ("Ill-fated Star"), Eichendorff takes the epistemological dilemma of conservatism, its apparent historical improbability, to new imaginative extremes. Drafts of the novella's opening section—gathered under the curiously explicit heading of "Kapitel von meiner Geburt" ("Chapter about My Birth")—show Eichendorff crafting the veritable archetype of conservative fantasy. In sharp contrast to the cold, wintry world outside, the prose conjures up its cradled infant protagonist enveloped by the song of the redbreast, by his mother's large eyes, and (corresponding to these) by the lure of distant stars outside the window:

> For my part, I can only recall dimly lying there so perfectly cozy and warm, wrapped in my comforter in the well-heated chamber, staring mesmerized at the play of rings and figures projected by the nocturnal light onto the ceiling. The

> tame redbreast had been roused by the peculiar light and nocturnal murmuring, shook its feathers . . . and sang drowsily as if to wish me a Happy Birthday. My Mother, with her beautiful, pale face and wide eyes, bent tenderly over me, however, entirely enveloping me in her curls, through which I could see stars and silent snow shimmering through the window. Since that time, whenever I see a clear and starry, winter night, I feel as though I was being born again. (Eichendorff 1984, 5, pt. 4: 19; my translation)

It is difficult not to interpret this rendition of the maternal imaginary as the (conservative) fantasy of an immutable origin and inexhaustible, creative source. Similar to Wordsworth's "Bless'd the infant babe" episode in book 1 of *The Prelude,* to say nothing of the opening to Goethe's autobiographical *Dichtung und Wahrheit,* this fantasy would seem to furnish the authorial persona with a virtual shelter from the real vicissitudes of historical time. Indeed, the next set of drafts conjures up a scene of ghost-story-telling on a wintry night, with "everyone rejoicing in their safety" (*alles sich freut, hier so im Sichern zu seyn*). Yet the fairy tale of goblins wreaking terror in the castle is interrupted (and thus confirmed) by a "French officer" delivering the latest newspaper accounts "of the distant war" (ibid., 53). Eichendorff's idyllic rendition of his own birth as the eventual protagonist of his own text is obviously stylized and indebted to an entire tradition of literary autogenesis (Cardano, Grimmelshausen, Rousseau, Sterne, Goethe, Wordsworth, and Jean Paul, to name but a few). In short, the fantasy of a life sheltered from the terrors and imponderables of history takes on a strong reflexive (because intertextual) quality. With claims to imaginative authenticity clearly subordinated to inherited cultural models, Eichendorff's maternal fantasy amounts to a *citation* of desire—hence, "fantasy"—rather than actually indulging in it. It grasps the idyll of the aesthetic as dialectically wedded to the genial yet unsustainable "constellation" of a feudal mode of economic production and social organization. As if to sharpen that point, Eichendorff's chapter recounts how "an event of great importance for me, namely, my birth" was elaborately orchestrated to take place precisely at midnight. A band is assembled in the freezing courtyard, fireworks have been prepared, and the midwife is to wave a white cloth at the appointed moment. Yet by a series of minute deviations and errors, the ritual comes off "a minute and a half too late" and the ideal "alignment [of stars] had been missed" (ibid., 40). The baroque fascination with the alignment of the stars at the moment of one's birth here serves to highlight the protagonist's fall into a thoroughly historical world. No amount of feudal privilege and planning can restore the subject of modernity to the imaginary (maternal) shelter of a purely metaphysical order. Consigned to the vagaries of a traumatic history, the writer can recall the ideal planetary "constellation" (hence the novella's title, "Unstern") of his own birth only as a barely "missed experience": "I was born precisely one and a half minutes too late" (*ich wurde gerade um anderthalb Minuten zu spät geboren*).

As the drafts of the novella progress, however, the tone shifts from the picaresque and satirical to the elegiac. At the same time, the text undergoes a progressive formalization from loose prose paragraphs to iambic and even hexametric composition. The result is a rendition of self-consciously belated *Erinnerung*, that is, the retroactive fixation of a maternal order in the modality of the poetic image. Such transfiguration effectively reveals the agency of imagination, and indeed the aesthetic per se, as something dialectically bound to (and betrayed by) the flux of historical time. References to the writer's personal, affective moorings at Lubowitz become all but interchangeable with those to the French Revolution: "The castle of which I have sung so often, where elves dance on the forest's moss and deer graze on moonlit nights, etc. It's burned down now and only exists in lyrics and dreams" (*Das Schloß, von dem ich oft gesungen, wo die Elfen tanzen auf dem Waldesrasen, die Rehe im Mondschein grasen, usw. Nun ist's verbrannt, es existiert nur in Liedern und Träumen*).[55] A poem entitled "Letzte Heimkehr" ("Final Return") articulates the *nachträglich* (deferred) and *nachgelassen* (posthumous) status of romantic conservatism—that is, the self-conscious fantasy world inhabited by the subject of *Altkonservatismus*. The voice here returns from the seductive but deceptive lure of distant lands ("Ihm log die *schöne* Ferne") into a space of manifest irreality, in other words, a return from the illusions of nostalgic longing to what is now reflexively grasped as the *ou topos* (nowhere) of home:

Der Wintermorgen glänzt so klar,
Ein Wandrer kommt von ferne,
Ihn schüttelt Frost, es starrt sein Haar,
Ihm log die *schöne* Ferne,
Nun endlich will er rasten hier,
Er klopft an seines Vaters Tür.

Doch tot sind, die sonst aufgetan,
Verwandelt Hof und Habe,

Und fremde Leute sehn ihn an,
Als käm er aus dem Grabe;
Ihn schauert tief im Herzensgrund,
Ins Feld eilt er zur selben Stund.

Da sang kein Vöglein weit und breit,
Er lehnt' an einem Baume,
Der schöne Garten lag verschneit,
Es war ihm wie im Traume,
Und wie die Morgenglocke klingt,
Im stillen Feld er niedersinkt. (*EW*, 1: 81–82)

One radiant winter morning,
A wanderer approaches from afar,
Shivering from frost, his hair hoary white
The *beautiful* distance deceived him as,
longing finally for respite here,
He knocks on his father's door.

For dead are who once were inviting,
Transfigured the estate and all goods,
And strangers stare at him
As if he had risen from his grave;
He shudders deep within his heart,
Fieldward he rushes within the hour.

There no bird was singing anywhere,
He leant against a tree, while the
Beautiful garden lay covered with snow,
To him it all felt like a dream,
And as the bell of morning tolls,
He sinks to his knees in the field. (MY TRANSLATION)

Snow-covered, devoid of all life ("Da sang kein Vöglein"), the speaker's empirical home, and by extension his own affective interiority, appear wholly denatured.[56] With his quasi-posthumous existence ("Als käm er aus dem Grabe") confirmed by the alienated gaze of strangers, the lyric subject achieves not a return to the past but an awakening to its future as permanently unreal. Eichendorff's lyric meditation leaves its subject halted in a landscape that has been purposely evacuated of all historical markers. The vanishing of home and all its affective moorings marks the arrival of a radically different experience of history, namely, as empty time, a visible darkness whose negative force consists in having obliterated all empirical coordinates for subjective existence. Eichendorff's closing image depicts the traveler as having awakened both *from* the nostalgic dream of his "return home" and *to* the conservative, postmodern experience of romantic longing with full consciousness of its fantasy character. This progression becomes apparent if we consider the endings of each stanza. Having knocked "on the father's door" in a gesture of apparent futility (st. 1), the speaker hurriedly withdraws into the open field (st. 2) where, admonished by the funereal peal of the church bell he sinks to his knees (st. 3) in an attitude of worship that affirms no deity but, on the contrary, attests to an almost existentialist sense of abjection. So familiar is this scene that it can almost be taken for a generic transcription of motivic work encountered time and again in C. D. Friedrich's paintings (see, e.g., fig. 10).[57]

Fig. 10. C. D. Friedrich (1774–1840), *Cloister Cemetery in the Snow* (ca. 1819). Formerly in the National Gallery, Berlin; destroyed during World War II. Photo credit: Bildarchiv Preussischer Kulturbesitz / Art Resource, New York.

The final text by Eichendorff to be considered, and unquestionably one of his most distinctive and memorable lyrics, is entitled "Mondnacht." In what Adorno so aptly termed its "humble irrationality," this poem exemplifies the challenge of Eichendorff and, more generally, of the deeply engrained mystical strain in romantic writing for a contemporary audience:

Es war, als hätt der Himmel
Die Erde still geküßt,
Daß sie im Blütenschimmer
Von ihm nun träumen müßt.

Die Luft ging durch die Felder,
Die Ähren wogten sacht,
Es rauschten leis die Wälder,
So sternklar war die Nacht.

Und meine Seele spannte
Weit ihre Flügel aus,
Flog durch die stillen Lande,
Als flöge sie nach Haus. (*EW*, 1: 286)

It was as though heaven had
Held earth in quiet kiss,
That entranced in shimmering blossoms,
She now could only dream of him.

The breeze passed over the fields,
Grain stalks gently yielded,
Forests rustled quietly,
So clear was the starlit night.

Then my soul far
Extended its wings and
Passed over the silent lands,
As if bound for home. (MY TRANSLATION)

One must, above all, overcome one's "lazy unwillingness to muster up the energetic receptivity the poem requires" (Adorno 1991, 1: 57). How are we to read a lyric whose imagery is carefully poised at the threshold between naïvely empirical mimesis and a self-conscious textuality reminiscent of baroque topoi. At a strictly formal level, such oscillation between mystical longing and allegorical distance can be located in the poem's conditional syntax—sustained from the very opening ("Es war, als hätt . . .") through the last line ("Als flöge sie . . ."). Taken as a whole, the vision of "Mondnacht" appears decidedly qualified, a fantasy attenuated by *allegoresis* rather than a desire intensified by symbolism. Thus the opening image of the *Brautkuss* whereby heaven and earth are reconciled—far from overcoming the split between fecund perceptions and transcendent truths—only widens it.[58] For the image of reconciliation is itself a purely literary device, a baroque *topos* (archetype, commonplace, or perhaps cliché?). Likewise, the subsequent construction of an analogy between cornfields and treetops animated by a breeze and the soul spreading its figural wings for flight never allows us to forget that we are dealing with a rhetorical operation. Wary of any mimetic commerce with such overworked terms as history or nature, and governed by "the ruling Baroque metaphor of life as a dream" (Gillespie, 209), the poem "strip[s] the allegorical world book down to a few root words, its radical lexemes" (ibid., 204).

And yet, in this poem, Eichendorff (late in his career a dedicated translator of Calderon) anticipates Walter Benjamin remarks about the "contemplative calm" of earlier baroque allegory. Indeed, it is tempting to read "Mondnacht" strictly as an expression of baroque stoicism, a concise rendition of the basic topos of *nulla in mundo pax sincera* so memorably set to music by Vivaldi in his solo motet RV 630. Still, such a reading must take care not to reduce stoic and allegorical language to a mere commonplace or cliché. For the allegorical topos of the *Brautkuss* also gauges what Benjamin refers to as "the chasm between pictorial being and significance [*bildlichem Sein und Bedeuten*] where we find nothing of the flouting indifference that characterizes the deceptively similar intention of the sign" (Benjamin 1982, 144; my translation). Hence, the poem's capacity to hint at the elusive metaphysical kinship between perception and knowledge pivots on qualifying its own voice as intrinsically unreal and chimerical. Yet such qualities do not betoken indifference, and even less an evasion of the sublime discontinuities of history. Far from it, a surreal imagery hints at the poem's reflexive self-awareness as irremediably textual (allegorical). Recognizing the impossibility of either transcending or "knowing" history, the lyric holds in an equilibrium the two dominant conceptual strains of German romanticism: mysticism and historicism. It does so by placing the lyric voices—taken both as a spiritual and intellectual agency—in an overtly phantasmagorical relation to the temporal forces of history. The latter can be encountered only by chance, not by design. Given that any "knowledge" of history can only come in the form of an involuntary (and belated) memory act (*mémoire involontaire* or *Erinnerung*), one can easily be deceived by the poem's seemingly incidental naturalistic images. Yet the insistently conditional syntax and the persistent of allegorical topoi prevent any mimetic conflation of imagery with perception and, consequently, any reading of the overall poem as a symbolic revelation.

In Eichendorff, no less than in Blake or Wordsworth, revelation does not mark the end of temporal knowledge but, instead, signals the emergence of a deeper, quasi-stoic form of historical awareness: that of a traumatic belatedness.[59] Like the interiority of a subject traumatized by the apparent collapse of history as a stable field of reference, "the meaning constituted by the allegorical sign can . . . consist only in the *repetition* of a previous sign with which it can never coincide" (de Man 1983, 207). Hence, Eichendorff's deceptively simple opening ("Es war, als hätt der Himmel / Die Erde still geküßt") dwells precisely on the inaccessibility of "mood," or *Stimmung*, to propositional, discursive language. From the outset, "mood" is presented as incommensurable with any empirical perception and, hence, with any form of speech premised on the convergence of phenomenal and lexical matter. Heaven and earth embrace only in the virtual domain of an expressly conditional syntax and are further qualified inasmuch as their union, the fantasy *of* (not desire *for*) affective fulfillment, can only be figured as a received literary topos. Because its utopian character can no longer be denied, the idea of a paradisiacal interiority can be properly expressed only as self-alienated literary language. The romantic voice rediscovers itself as a baroque topos; lyric utterance finds itself transmuted into the involuntary memory of a purely literary citation.[60]

Yet if the self-demystification of allegorical topoi risks the outright demotion of nature and history (via the image) to mere clichés, the vestige of this operation—that is, the figural world of lyric writing—still exhibits traces of the totality whose disappearance it confirms. In his remarkable account of shifting conceptions of figural language, Erich Auerbach notes that "beside the opposition between *figura* and fulfillment or truth, there appears another, between *figura* and *historia. Historia* or *littera* is the literal sense or the event related; *figura* is the same literal meaning or event in reference to the fulfillment cloaked in it, and this fulfillment itself is *veritas,* so that *figura* becomes a middle term between *littera-historia* and *veritas*" (Auerbach, 47). Anticipating the French symbolists, Eichendorff's radical figural enjambment of such terms as heaven and earth, soul and wings ("Und meine Seele spannte / Weit ihre Flügel aus") unfolds with just enough self-conscious literariness and artificiality to keep the eschatological hopes of (Christian) symbolism at bay. Whereas "the symbol must possess magic power, . . . the *figura,* on the other hand, must always be historical," Auerbach notes, for "it is a product of late cultures, far more indirect, complex, and charged with [literary] history. Indeed, seen from this point of view, it has something vastly old about it: a great culture had to reach its culmination and indeed show signs of old age, before an interpretive tradition could produced something on the order of figural prophecy" (ibid., 57).

Such is the complex affinity between the formal-literary character of Eichendorff's poetry and the fantasy structure of romantic conservatism, when approached as a matter of ideation rather than quotidian politics. Both view the *punctum* of perception and the self-identity of a "feeling" as shot through with a temporal dimension, a past whose significance for the present and the future proves irresistible, if also incalculable. Notwithstanding its naturalist veneer, Eichendorff's image of a breeze sweeping over cornstalks and treetops, as well as its analogue of the soul (Gr. *pneuma:* breath, wind, soul) spreading its wings in flight reveals, upon closer inspection, an acutely temporal dimension. Suspended (in Auerbach's phrase) between *littera- historia* and *veritas,* Eichendorff's mystical *figurae* of natural and spiritual animation harbor intimations of unrest, of potentially cataclysmic historical change. A passage in Eichendorff's historical prose restates the mystical tranquillity of "Mondnacht" almost verbatim, though now the explosive historical forces seething just below the surface (or beyond the horizon) of romantic nature writing are impossible to ignore:

> Intermittently, from across the farmstead there wafted the noise of starlings frolicking in the trees, the gobbling of turkeys, the monotonous rhythm of the harvesters, and all the magical sonority of rural, peaceful life that, like the alpenhorns for the Swiss, leaves the traveler unexpectedly submerged in a state of profound longing. Down below in the valleys, the cornfields swayed quietly, an ominously humid atmosphere presaged thunderstorms, and nobody noticed or took heed that heavy weather was on the rise in the west and some initial lightning was already prophetically flashing above the bluff of trees in the distance. (*EW,* 1: 903; my translation)

Analogous to the fantasy character of romantic *Altkonservatismus,* Eichendorff's oeuvre derives its stylistic charisma and quintessentially romantic authority from one recurrent figural operation, that of presenting the symbolic-mystical and the allegoric-historical, revelation and history, in a state of conditional suspension. Are we, in the above passage, to read the breeze that momentarily enlivens a cornfield expectantly (viz., as a symbol of revelation) or anxiously (viz., as a scene of unpremeditated and unfathomable, traumatic memory)? Truth (*veritas*) is not captured by a single and definitive awakening *to* it but, instead, unfolds as a repeated formal-aesthetic enactment of such awakening itself. *Figura,* in Eichendorff, thus amounts to an ontological condition (rather than a contingent literary technique), a condition, however, that can only be traced in its distinctive formal-rhetorical presentation. We note how the prose text introduces both the "prophetic" (*prophetisch*) and the "nostalgic" (*Heimweh*) as affective qualities at once unpremeditated and inescapable (*unversehens*). With revolutionary terrors having given a permanently surreal quality to all of European culture and politics, the music of repose ("Musik des ländlichen Stillebens") is not mimetically *there.* Rather, like von Arnim 's "ancient signs of firm boundaries" (uralten Zeichen fester Grenzen), such an idyll marks the modern individual's estrangement from any putative affective foundation in fundamentally allegorical ways. Inasmuch as this estrangement takes the form of a traumatic awakening *to* history as the nontranscendable horizon of European culture, it demands a correspondingly volatile symbolic form: the lyric image. Variously positioned on the continuum that extends from cliché to topos to revelation, Eichendorff's images furnish both the cause and the medium for this awakening. Far more articulately and honestly than his prosaic conservative fellow writers, his poetry enacts Coleridge's programmatic characterization of poetry as "a rationalized dream dealing to manifold Forms our own Feelings, that never perhaps were attached by us to our own personal selves" (Coleridge 1980, # 2086).

Part III / Lyric Provocations

Melancholy

CHAPTER SIX

"The Purest English"

Serialization, Eros, and Melancholy in the Early Keats

Were I in such a place, I sure should pray
That naught less sweet might call my thoughts away,
Than the soft rustle of a maiden's gown
Fanning away the dandelion's down;
Than the light music of her nimble toes
Patting against the sorrel as she goes.
How she would start, and blush, thus to be caught
Playing in all her innocence of thought.
Oh, let me lead her gently o'er the brook,
Watch her half-smiling lips, and downward look;
Oh let me for one moment touch her wrist;
Let me one moment to her breathing list;
And as she leaves me may she often turn
Her fair eyes looking through her locks aubúrne.
What next? A tuft of evening primroses,
O'er which the mind may hover till it dozes

— JOHN KEATS, "I STOOD TIP-TOE UPON A LITTLE HILL" (EMPHASIS ADDED)

Nature and reconciliation communicate in melancholy; from it the "wish" arises dialectically, and its illusion is the reflection of hope. It is illusion because not happiness itself but only its images are given to the wish and in them the wish, which is nourished by them, is at the same time filled with longing because, according to Kierkegaard, the eye, the organ of the wish, "Is most difficult to satisfy."

— THEODOR ADORNO, *Kierkegaard: Construction of the Aesthetic*, TRANS. ROBERT HULLOT-KENTOR

Born of an excess of knowledge that ultimately renders it incommensurable with *any* form of representation, melancholy has long puzzled those inquiring into its constitution. Whereas the Enlightenment posits a lack of reflexivity as the distinguishing characteristic of all affect, melancholy appears to be so insistent and overdetermined a feeling that it must be viewed not as the opposite of self-consciousness but as its veritable apotheosis. With its attendant quality of exhaustion rather than possibility, of a lucid ending rather than sentient beginnings, melancholy confounds the eighteenth-century paradigm of conspicuous, theatrical, and unselfconscious passion inasmuch as it appears to have worked through and despaired over all methods of knowing and representing itself. Exceeding the scope of any one epistemological model that might be mobilized for the purpose of its explication, melancholy also seems to defy a Hegelianism that, in "grasping" (*begreifen*) an emotion, claims to raise it to the self-authorizing clarity of philosophical reflection. Turning the tables on the self-authorizing claims of late Enlightenment thought, melancholy instead appears to arise from a more categorical "insight" into the inadequacy of epistemological and representational techniques. To be sure, "insight" into the context of melancholia becomes a dubious, even aporetic, notion—a trope signifying its own impossibility—in that since the sixteenth century, melancholia has been characterized by profound despair over all representation fashioned by discursive understanding. Originating as a reflection on the inadequacy, even futility, of knowledge in a disenchanted world, melancholy fuses the experience of negation ("consciousness") with the quality of a persistent, albeit negative feeling (the "unhappy" in Hegel's unhappy consciousness) in quasi-Hegelian ways.

Upon close and patient reading, Hegel's 1807 *Phenomenology* continues to startle with its modernist psychology of subjects capable of realizing their initially unconscious telos of a transparent and enlightened community only through continual involvement with, and episodic estrangement from, "culture" (*Bildung*). If Hegel's modern individuals appear unhappily conscious of their permanent self-alienation, they ultimately embrace this new, constitutively artificial mode of being promised by the labor of *Bildung*. In Hegel's uncompromising formulation, "the existence of the world, as also the actuality of consciousness, rests on the process in which the latter divests itself of its personality, *thereby creating its world.* This world it looks on as something alien, a world, therefore, of which it must now take possession." As the *Phenomenology* points out at various turns in its narrative, self-awareness can be thought only as the effect (never, though, as the "ground") of self-alienation: "self-consciousness . . . has actuality only in so far as it alienates itself from itself." For Hegel, it is only through an "expressive divestment" (*Entäußerung*) of naïvely fictive or imaginary notions of the self as immediacy that the modern subject will realize itself in social relations—a step that inevitably will strip that subject of any unreflected sense of individuality. Through its social and essentially linguistic commerce with others, or indeed with language itself (irony, metalanguage, poetry), the self "gives itself the character of a universal, and this universality is its authentication and actuality. This equality with everyone is, therefore, not the equality of the sphere of legal right, not that immediate recognition and validity of self-consciousness simply because it *is;* on the contrary, to be valid it must have conformed itself to the universal by the mediating process of alienation" (Hegel 1977, 296).

Hegel's argument implicitly dismantles as utopian the liberal model of a community of educated, deliberative autonomous individuals. For to engage the public sphere as an educated, deliberative individual is to abandon the petit-bourgeois ideals of autonomy and immediacy as vestiges of a naïve, precritical concept of personhood. Even more radical than Marx, whose writings ultimately seek to contain alienation as a historically and materially determined aberration that may (and ought to) be corrected, Hegel conceives of alienation as the very foundation, the negative origin, of the modern, cultured individual. Setting the tone for the remainder of my study, the following quotation from the *Phenomenology* speculatively characterizes nineteenth-century culture as pivoting on the self's embrace of difference, including above all its capacity (and speculative obligation) to differ from itself. For Hegel, alienation is not a contingent fate suffered at certain times by only some individuals but, on the contrary, involves the self's delving deep into its own otherness, its denatured, deracinated constitution. Only so can subjectivity realize, in praxis and thought, its inherently productive engagement with and determinacy by the social: "It is therefore through culture (*Bildung*) that the individual acquires standing and actuality. His true *original nature* and substance is the alienation of himself as Spirit from his *natural* being. This externalization (*Entäußerung*) is, therefore, both the purpose and the existence of the individual. . . . This individuality *moulds* itself by culture into what it intrinsically is, and only by so doing is it an intrinsic being that has an actual existence; the measure of its culture is the measure of its actuality and power. Although here the self knows itself as *this* self, yet its actuality consists solely in the setting-aside of its natural self."[1]

For Hegel, culture does not simply negate the theoretical fantasy of immediacy and autonomy; it also reorients the experience of that negation toward productive ends by identifying expressive genres and techniques that allow the individual to articulate such self-alienation in objective and social form, namely, as aesthetic work. As we have already seen, it is lyric poetry in particular that in Hegel's account facilitates the transition from an aesthetic toward a philosophical "world already more prosaically stamped."[2] To recognize "culture" (*Bildung*) as structurally cognate with Hegelian negation, and hence as the linchpin of modern consciousness, primarily means to *feel* something (negation) that cannot, after all, be positively represented or known. In the particular context of literary (imaginative) writing, such feeling centers around a fundamental tension between the sensuous and intellectual dimensions of writing. Here, too, inasmuch as the feeling or (to use a musical trope) "dissonance" in question originates in an insoluble conflict, it cannot be "known" per se.

At the same time, however, one cannot oppose it to the work of knowing. Rather, in affectively grasping critical knowledge as a deeply ephemeral pursuit, melancholy rediscovers the kinship between time as a formal category indispensable to all knowledge and its metaphysical dimension of transience. What the baroque counterreformers and their secular, no less mournful humanist contemporaries articulate in usually hypertrophic, overwritten forms is the irremediably lapsed nature of representation. Foreshadowing Hegel's dynamic model of twofold negation, the baroque's understanding of melancholy as the inescapable affective substratum of all reflection—and, indeed, of all action premised on it—dismantles the false certitudes of empirical knowledge. Yet, unlike Hegelian thought, melancholy cannot integrate its peculiar lucidity with some metanarrative whose very impossibility the melancholic subject endlessly ruminates instead. What remains is Keats' "slow" and "aching" time (*KCP*, 533), which can be filled only with sifting through the debris of goals, methods, and images of a post-Waterloo culture that has defeated the very incarnation of heroic agency and historical change and thus is condemned to gorge on displaced cultural artifacts (e.g., the Elgin Marbles). Only by "tast[ing] the sadness" (*KCP*, 541) of knowledge in all its futile particularity can thought ascend to a new, conspicuously mediated or virtual plateau—that of an intellectual engagement "studiously" mindful of its own radical transience and hence bound to survey and expose the delusive permanence of a cultural literacy once again tethered to Augustan notions of taste, canonicity, and polite speech.

A synecdoche of that faltering model can be located in the so called "greater Romantic Lyric," identified by Meyer H. Abrams as "the earliest Romantic formal invention, which at once demonstrated the stability of organization and the capacity to engender successors which define a distinct lyric species."[3] If one accepts Abrams's characterization of this quintessentially romantic literary paradigm, one will also see why—for writers of Keats's generation—any contestation of literariness had to tackle the Wordsworthian model of lyricism, specifically its implicit creed that an inclusive and "permanent" (that most distinctively Wordsworthian criterion) conception of English cultural value be realized in a language that formally valorizes complex emotional experiences. Romanticism's success with establishing lyric poetry as the form that was not only to dominate the taxonomy of literary forms but, *qua* literature, would also exemplify a new middle-brow ethos of depoliticized self-cultivation is premised on a restricted economy of admissible, valid, and indeed representative emotions. Whatever these may be—Wordsworth's *Poems* (1815) provides an ample taxonomy both in its table of contents and in its "Preface" and ("supplemental") postscript—the emotions must yield some implicit intellectual progression.[4] An emotion that refuses sublation (*Aufhebung*) into a representative, socially "binding" (to recall Geoffrey Hartman's perceptive term) narrative would not only be void but potentially dangerous. Yet it was this "high Anglican" model of the lyric that came under pressure during the Regency. Beginning with Keats and Hazlitt, and eventually in the writings of Heinrich Heine and Charles Baudelaire on the Continent, the lyric acquired a new affective quality that was not only disruptive of the explicit moral purposes that Augustan writers were thought to have foisted on imaginative (i.e., "literary") writing but subverted the more obliquely fantasized social consensus that united figures like Adam Smith, Sir Joshua Reynolds, and Edmund Burke, that "mixed system of opinion and sentiment" (Burke, 170) whose final collapse took place during the years of the Regency. At this historical juncture, the social dimension of literary writing took on a special, crystalline sharpness in deceptively hermetic and ostensibly ahistorical forms, such as lyric poetry and verse romance. As Hegel (following Hölderlin's hints) observed, the lyric's intrinsically metalingual and metapoetic character makes it an intrinsically reflexive form of writing, a type of signification that unfolds by focusing on its medium. It thus comes close to grasping and articulating the historically specific antagonism to which it owes its existence, a speculative acuity that also explains the aura of melancholy that envelops much lyric writing throughout the Regency period. As Adorno puts it, melancholy does not merely arise from the writer's feeling sense of isolation and expressive failure vis-à-vis his or her culture; it also betrays "an alien quality" *within* the lyric, "a demise of its basic content in expression, the eloquence of something that has no language. What has been composed could not exist without the content falling silent, any more than it could without what it falls silent about" (Adorno 1991, 2: 112).

In what follows, I shall approach lyric writing as a deeply experimental form of writing enabling the subjects of a rapidly diversifying and highly literate post-Waterloo capitalist society to articulate a general continuity between its socioeconomic and its discursive abjection. Keatsian melancholy constitutes a simultaneously affective and reflexive response to the disparity between adverse historical conditions, exhaustively "known," and an inventory of expressive forms so stratified and rigid as to stifle any effective articulation of that knowledge. Walter Benjamin, it may be recalled, characterized tradition as an oppressive symbiosis of invariant historical time and sterile cultural values: "What are phenomena to be rescued from? Not only, and not in the main, from the discredit and neglect into which they have fallen, but from the catastrophe represented very often by a certain strain in their dissemination, their 'enshrinement as heritage.' . . . There is a tradition that is catastrophe."[5] And yet the genesis of romanticism as a distinctively "literary" event pivots on the progressive narrowing down of the very definition of literature, and of a seemingly autonomous "tradition" of imaginative writing that culminates, perhaps beginning with Wordsworth's 1807 *Poems in Two Volumes,* in a canonical model of writing marshaled against the formally and demographically subaltern fictions that had sprung up during the later eighteenth century (sentimental novels, Gothic fiction, theatrical "spectacles," sensational ballads). As part of its strategic consolidation and institutionalization of aesthetic and specifically "literary" value, romanticism began to shift emphasis from "textual effects" to "authorial behavior—what writers did instead of what writing could do." Such a shift from "the potentially disruptive power of the technology of writing to the supposedly disrupted personalities of people who wrote" (Siskin 1998, 15–16) also asks us to rethink the intense emphasis placed during the period in question on the literary formalization of affect (sentimentalism, paranoia, melancholy, etc.). Inasmuch as it reflects a deep-structural antagonism between individual subjects and the technologies governing their social and economic relations, affect ought to be understood—not as the expressive *content* of literature—but as a "mood" whose formal symptom is a crisis within the technology of expressive writing itself. The sheer monumentality of

Wordsworth's *Excursion* and his *Poems* suggests that by 1815 a threshold had already been reached beyond which lyric writing could develop only by adopting a metalinguistic and reflexive distance vis-à-vis an essentially invented "tradition" of middle-brow imaginative writing. It was a step Wordsworth was not prepared to take.

If literature for Wordsworth constitutes a teleological (and covertly providential) process—one that gravitates toward an exemplary and, by 1814, often prescriptive idea of moral and psychological order—jettisoning that view became for Keats a matter not only of principle but of writerly survival. What he says of Milton—"life to him would be death to me" (*LJK*, 2: 212)—also holds true of his more immediate precursor. Keats's poetry unfolds as an often irreverent reflection on the very paradigm of literariness that had been set forth by the earlier generation of romantics and for the first time marks the emergence of a crucial anti-literary strain within romantic literature. As a whole, Keats's oeuvre often comes close to casting doubt on the Coleridgean and Wordsworthian credo in poetry offering a metalanguage capable of binding otherwise heterogeneous, even antagonistic socioeconomic and experiential groups to one another merely on the grounds of its allegedly superior authenticity. To approach Keats's oeuvre in that manner also helps explain the vituperativeness of his early reviewers, who, it appears, clearly perceived that a system of cultural value and, by extension, the very conception of social order were being challenged by the rise of the "Cockney school." The following readings of Keats's so-called "early" poetry aim to illustrate his oeuvre's exposure of an antagonism intrinsic to lyric writing and, on a larger scale, to late romantic valorization of literature overall.

A distinctive threshold is crossed in the history of modern thought once this "feeling" of the phantasmagoric nature of thought inscribes itself into the very structure of sensory experience and into its representation. Beginning with Albrecht Dürer's and Lorenzo Lotto's depictions (figs. 11 and 12) of melancholia as the distinctive affective undercurrent of modern knowing, itself temporarily refigured as the Protestant indictment of the humanist's sinful aspirations in the popular chapbook versions of *Doctor Faustus* (1587) and Marlowe's eponymous tragedy, and finally writ large in Robert Burton's formally and methodologically sprawling *Anatomy of Melancholy* (1621), a new feature is added to modernity—namely, the experience of thinking as a process accompanied by a feeling of disorientation at once integral to and hence uncontainable by thought.[6] The metonymy between writing, reading, and a deep awareness of mortality is poignantly conveyed in Lotto's 1523 *Portrait of a Young Scholar,* with rose petals standing in for the transience of all study. The otherworldly, almost inaccessible, quality of the young man's countenance further reinforces our sense of learning as "abstraction"—that is, giving rise to an abstracted, distant brooding—or, to recall Keats's famous use of the word in "Ode to Nightingale" (lines 70–71), "forlorn" disposition.

It is to this melancholic recognition that intellectual and cultural practice responds, albeit in the full knowledge that it can never hope to expunge or overcome it, for the simple reason that the remedial operation of thought, having been called forth by that feeling, is forever bound to reproduce and prolong it. No effect can ever fully absorb and contain its own cause; or, as Adorno (whose entire oeuvre can be read as an extended meditation and enactment of modernity as the melancholia of thinking) argues in *Negative Dialectics,* an indivisible remainder of the mute, preconceptual object will forever persist vis-à-vis all epistemological models of cognition and, in so doing, will continually threaten to unravel them.[7] Similarly, Nietzsche's oeuvre, with its epic time frames and its fine ear for ambivalent feelings raging beneath the tranquil surface of modern consciousness—"no beautiful surface without a terrifying depth" (keine schöne Oberfläche ohne schreckliche Tiefe [Nietzsche 1980, 7: 159])—suggests, the trajectory of modernity from the Reformation onward ought to be read as simply a progressively refined variation on the Ur-motif of Socratic optimism that had sought to escape the undertow of cognitive and affective chaos, violence, and the Circe call of nothingness. If Nietzsche reads modernity as an unwitting, indeed self-deceived, movement of *décadence* ("Eine Epoche des Niederganges"), his philosophy unfolds as an extended meditation on melancholy's Janus-headed profile as suffering and aggression, loss and ressentiment—an emotive intentionality that constitutes both the motive force behind and, for that very reason, the eventual nemesis of rational thought.

Heidegger's term for the ontological "mood" *in* and *as* which *Dasein* finds itself to be wholly overdetermined is *Verstimmung,* a close cognate of his fundamental theory of "mood" (*Stimmung*) from *Being and Time* and his 1929 lectures on *The Fundamental Concepts of Metaphysics.* For Heidegger, the deep-existential melancholy or boredom of a subject "thrust" into a world exhaustively determined both as regards its practical possibilities and the expressive inventory in which one might wish to reflect on that very predicament lies at the very heart of "distemper" (*Verstimmung*):

> In *distemper* (*Verstimmung*) . . . *Dasein* becomes blind to itself, the environment with which it is concerned veils itself, and the circumspection of concern gets led astray. States-of-mind are so far from being reflected upon, that precisely what they do is to assail *Dasein* in its unreflecting devotion to the "world" with which it is concerned and on which it expends itself. A mood assails us. It comes neither from "outside" nor from "inside" but arises out of Being-in-the-world, as a way of such being. But with the negative distinction between state-of-mind and the reflective apprehending of something "within," we have thus reached a positive insight into their character as disclosure. *The mood has already disclosed, in every case, Being-in-the-world as a whole, and makes it possible first of all to direct oneself toward something.*[8]

"More categorically hermetic than any *non*-perception," something demonstrated by its opposite, Heidegger's *Verstimmung* already inheres in the deep-structural boredom as we find it organizing the Keatsian text *as language.* In Keats's lyric forms, too, melancholy thus constitutes an ontological predicament even (perhaps especially) where it may not be an obvious thematic concern. Throughout much of Keats's oeuvre, including his very first poetic attempts, we encounter a deep-structural mood of "distemper," an indication that the conceptual and aesthetic projects for a fundamental reconfiguration of the social framework, 1789–1815, have now—with the defeat of Napoleon—become depleted of all developmental energy. At the heart of Keats's poetry thus lies the insight that afflicts Saturn at the opening of Keats's *Hyperion*—albeit an insight that pays no future dividends and is not generative of any future action. As pure "negation," Keats's and Saturn's melancholy knowledge locates its object solely in the end of the Enlightenment's developmental paradigm of history as progressive and benevolent. When speaking of the "suddenness with which the "melancholy fit shall fall" (*KCP,* 539), Keats seems to gesture toward a Heideggerian "mood," an eruption of a melancholia that originates neither expressively from within a discrete subject nor intrudes upon it from without. Rather, melancholy encrypts a more fundamental "situatedness" (*Befindlichkeit*). Heidegger speaks of a peculiar nontransparency that characterizes "distemper" (*Verstimmung*), and Keats appears to have something quite similar in mind in his often-quoted phrase of "the feel of not to feel it" (*KCP,* 288).

Fig. 11. Lorenzo Lotto (1480–1556), *Portrait of a Young Man* (1530). Courtesy of the Galleria dell'Accademia, Venice. Photo credit: Scala / Art Resource, New York.

For the time being, however, it is important to be mindful of the multiple levels at which melancholy simultaneously operates. First, when approached as a distinctive type of feeling, melancholy is to be situated within a historically specific economy of pleasure. In Keats, both the representation of pleasure and the pleasures of representation appear to be coordinated by the same underlying melancholic intentionality. In his essay "The Fate of Pleasure" (1963), Lionel Trilling comments perceptively on the complicated relationship of pleasure to literature and literariness, and hence to the symbolic ordering of social and moral values as it prevailed and was continually reinforced in Regency England. Trilling situates pleasure within a broader historical narrative, marked by a progressive "downward spread of the idea of dignity." By the time of Regency culture, and so particularly legible in Keats's oeuvre, pleasure

Fig. 12. Albrecht Dürer (1471–1528), *Melancholia I* (1514). Photo credit: Bildarchiv Preussischer Kulturbesitz / Art Resource, New York.

had become "an idea that might be applied to man in general, [and] was advanced by *the increasing possibility of possessing the means or signs of pleasure*" (Trilling, 432; emphasis added). For Trilling, "that dialectic of pleasure . . . is the characteristic intellectual activity of Keats's poetry."[9]

Occasionally heeding the shrewd analytical hints of William Hazlitt, Sigmund Freud, Walter Benjamin, Lionel Trilling, and Julia Kristeva, one of the more specialized strands of Keats criticism (John Bayley, Christopher Ricks, and Marjorie Levinson) has earnestly sought to account for Keats's tendency to achieve pleasure vicariously through insistent, quasi-"motorial" (Benjamin) representations of melancholic displeasure. Indeed, the curiously mediated status of pleasure remains arguably the ideal point of departure for any inquiry into Keats's work. Yet to approach romantic melancholy as a resurgence of the baroque's pseudostoic despair over the projects of scholastic learning and authentic representation also means having to locate the former within a historically specific conception of writing, specifically "literary" writing. An entry in Coleridge's *Table Talk* dated 1832 may help establish these coordinates: "there have been three silent revolutions in England: 1. When the Professions fell off from the Church. 2. When Literature fell off from the Professions. 3. When the Press fell off from Literature."[10]

It would appear to be above all the third of these "revolutions" that defines the Regency scene of cultural production, and for once Hazlitt would agree with Coleridge: "The spirit of universal criticism has superseded the anticipation of posthumous fame, and instead of waiting for the award of distant ages, the poet or prose-writer receives his final doom from the next number of the *Edinburgh* or *Quarterly Review*" (*HSW,* 2: 97). However different their outlooks, both Hazlitt and Coleridge view the periodical press as both cause and symptom of the substantially damaged aura of literature per se. Stripped of its redemptive and charismatic force, literature and other high-cultural artifacts have now become objective correlatives for a post-romantic, or even anti-romantic, tendency in romanticism. It is a move beyond the traumatic awakening that had at once been forestalled and belatedly precipitated by the debris of a bygone folk culture reconstituted as the artifact of lyric and pastoral-elegiac writing, forms enabling the subjects to gauge the extend to which a covert economic and an overt political revolution had alienated them from their past and, hence, from themselves. Despairing over the ambivalent role of literature in the context of romantic trauma—namely, as the pastoral dreamworld that had prevented Wordsworth Michael from grasping economic change at the time of its occurrence, yet also as a means of awakening him to belatedly recognize that very failure—post-Napoleonic culture gradually abandons romanticism's earlier stress on the redemptive power of literature. If melancholy involves an intensely focused and self-deconstructing meditation on the irremediably damaged idea of "culture," Keats's "pseudo-Hellenic" poems written after his abandonment of *Hyperion* ought to be read as a deliberate revaluation of the very idea of "literariness." In jettisoning earlier standards of socially relevant knowledge—such as authentic, local, and genuinely "felt" experience—Keats's (and also Hazlitt's) explicitly and deliberately pseudo-antique writings presage Heine's and Baudelaire's deconstruction of an authentic subjectivity grounded in and drawing its strength from some putatively unique and unimpeachable affective source.

Walter Benjamin's reflections on melancholy in his 1923 book on *German Tragic Drama,* perhaps still unparalleled in their cogency, draw attention to the conspicuously "motorial" quality of the melancholy affect. Cued by a calamity, "an *a priori* object" (Benjamin 1998, 139) that remains itself strictly anterior and inaccessible to melancholy, that very feeling now "respond[s] like a motorial reaction to a concretely structured world." Indeed, Benjamin goes on, "this attitude . . . is only called a feeling because it does not occupy the highest place" in the "hierarchy of intentions." Nonetheless, "it is determined by an astounding tenacity of intention" and exhibits a "special intensification, a progressive deepening of its intention" (ibid., 123). Long before Martha Nussbaum was to comment on the focused, albeit oblique, intentionality of emotions that are, at bottom, encrypted value judgments, Benjamin identifies melancholy as perhaps the most defining affective characteristic of the modern era. It is a feeling that all but knows about its own bottomless nature, that knows itself to be, not the *ultima ratio* of the human, but rather a "pseudo-antique" (ibid., 124) or neostoic (e.g., Nussbaum) response to the loss of all feeling—a knowledge that, instead of a determinate object, revolves around the subject's confronting its epistemological abjection, which also includes its inability to localize and name the cause of that dilemma. "For sorrow is," as Robert Burton observed in his 1621 *Anatomy of Melancholy,* "both the cause and symptom of this disease" (Burton, 298). As Benjamin's epochal book shows, the study of melancholy coincides with the analysis of its symptomatic manifestation, which in turn was to lead Benjamin (and, following him, Paul de Man) to a radically new conception of allegory.

For Benjamin, allegory involves above all a profound loss of mystic-symbolic power in verbal and pictorial representation. Indeed, it is this very expiration of the symbol's claim to conjuring up and transfiguring its object in a single creative and affirmative instant that allegory itself enacts, and must do so over and over again. If, like Keats's Hellenic artifacts, melancholy injects "slow time" into the very medium of representation—and thus calls into question the symbol's claim to an instantaneous capture and redemption of being—the resulting allegorical mode shapes the experience of time as endlessly recursive and invariant. "Whereas in the symbol destruction is idealized and the transfigured face of nature is fleetingly revealed in the light of redemption, in allegory the observer is confronted with the *facies hippocratica* of history as a petrified, primordial landscape. Everything about history that from the very beginning has been untimely, sorrowful, unsuccessful is expressed in a face—or rather in a death's head. . . . This is the heart of the allegorical way of seeing, of the baroque, secular explanation of history as the Passion of the world" (Benjamin 1998, 166). It is tempting, though ultimately too obvious, to extend Benjamin's analysis to the early deconstructionist account of allegory and temporality in Paul de Man (whose "Rhetoric of Temporality" seems curiously reticent when it comes to acknowledging its debt to Benjamin's study). Instead, the proposed readings of Keats will benefit from Benjamin's strong concern with the compulsive, reiterative, indeed, purposely wasteful, treatment of linguistic material by the baroque allegorists. As early as Burton's *Anatomy of Melancholy,* melancholy is understood as thoroughly rhetorical in its constitution and as a conscious articulation of that very fact. Thus it unfolds as a recurrent, monotonous, indeed, serial, reenactment of the *vanitas* or futility not only of symbolic signification but of the very creation that the symbolic seeks to capture and, by that very means, redeem. Hence Benjamin's emblem of the "death-head," so oppressively passed on from Dürer's *Melancholia I* to Hamlet's Yorrick to Goethe's *Faust I,* not only signifies a denuded, indeed, denatured, creation but, more important, also points back to its own emptiness as an overdetermined sign forever bequeathed by one generation of authors to the next as a palpable reminder of the strictly negative estate of writing, specifically literary writing per se.[11]

Julia Kristeva (1991) has drawn attention to the striking correlation between a presupposed, albeit unspecified, "object loss" and the apparent "failure" of the signifier to articulate that loss in the melancholic subject's speech. What melancholic speech laments is less the loss of a specific object than "the real that does not lend itself to signification." Consequently, melancholic speech exhibits highly formalized, quasi-ceremonial rhetorical patterns and thus comes across not as charismatic speech or presence but as the simulation of a voice steeped in anterior writing. Melancholic speech thus exhibits "a recurrent breakdown in the metonymy of pleasure" that would, ordinarily, take the subject from an as yet unspecified "erotic thing" to a concrete "Object of desire." It is important here to note that melancholy is not merely informed by the failure of such metonymic, narrative progression but reconstitutes and positively displays that failure as an alternative expressive form. The "excess of affect," Kristeva notes, has "no other means of coming to the fore than to produce new languages—strange concatenations, idiolects, poetics." It must load signs with "affects . . . [by] making them ambiguous, repetitive, or simply alliterative, musical" (Kristeva, 42). A product of negative knowledge rather than irremediable blindness, the language of melancholy thus bespeaks the subject's grasp of a permanent insufficiency in the order of the signifier, of the established discursive order (political, economic, and aesthetic). As Kristeva puts it so succinctly: "melancholy persons are foreigners in their maternal tongue" (53). Her emphasis on the elaborately patterned nature of melancholic speech implies significant connections between melancholy and the formal repetitions that shape lyric speech and threaten to slant it toward a quasi-serial, mechanical type of signification. The contemporary critic John Gibson Lockhart's half-serious suggestion that Keats might have contracted the new disease of "metro-manie" captures the central point: namely, that the oddly constructed, reflexive formalisms of baroque and Regency-Restoration poetic language may be either expressive of a deep-seated melancholic affect or, alternatively, may owe their overwrought quality to the fact that there is nothing, no inward feeling, to be expressed whatsoever. With her suggestive enjambment of lyric and melancholy, Kristeva thus extends Freud's earlier view of melancholy as a cultural strategy arising from "a loss of a more ideal kind" (Freud 1963b, 166) rather than from that of a determinate object. Compare Keats's observation that "imaginary grievances have always been more my torment than real ones" (*LJK*, 2: 181).

At the same time, Freud's and Kristeva's accounts both also highlight some less auspicious tendencies in the psychoanalytic project, a certain tendency toward analytic quietism. For as it probes the subject's innermost guises and recesses, psychoanalysis vacillates between approaching its phenomena (e.g., symptomatic representations) as either contingent and pathogenic or purposive and strategic. Are they symptoms, or might the symptom's enigmatic purposiveness be read as a subject's sly technique for recovering from a condition whose (social rather than clinical) cause he or she cannot or will not name? At the very least, the insistent manipulation of expressive conventions by the melancholic subject cannot be viewed as wholly contingent and simply pathogenic. Rather than begging remedial explanation of the classical psychoanalytic variety, the eloquence of the melancholic subject reveals how the "symptom" fuses both suffering and a remediation into one and the same *form.*[12] Beyond its official indexing of an original loss and the open-ended suffering that results from the subject's inability to specify what has been lost, "symptom" also denotes the subject's reenactment of that crisis in studiously patterned, even mannered, rhetorical forms. As Lacan puts it, "the signifier, by its very nature, always anticipates meaning by unfolding its dimension before it" (1977, 153); or, as Žižek summarizes the point, "there is no symptom without its addressee" (1989, 73). It is this overtly symptomatic and transferential character of melancholic speech and writing that solicits—*is designed* to solicit—the hypothesis of a hidden cause for such suffering and, thus, a process of remedial intervention (psychoanalyst—symptom—patient; reader—text—author) that accommodates the subject's / patient's covert narcissistic desire. Yet in locating the symptom almost exclusively in the domain of individual speech, traditional psychoanalytic reading largely ignores how speech—and, even more so, formal writing—implicates its subject in a process of "selection" and "combination" (to invoke Roman Jakobson's terms) from a highly complex system of socially sanctioned or proscribed rhetorical conventions and techniques. Hence, to trace an allegedly symptomatic text back to a supposedly inward origin, such as the "condition" of melancholy, is to ignore the collective history of rhetorical forms, practices, and values as they circumscribe any given instance of speech or writing. In fact, to understand the persistent affiliation between melancholy and lyric writing, one must give due consideration to the lyric's internally divided profile. Marked, if not defined, by its recurrent patterns of imagery, figuration, and syntax, the nascently post-romantic and anti-literary Keatsian inflection of the lyric shifts the genre away from its until then dominant paradigm as authentic and expressive speech and toward an overt simulation of such personal, expressive effects.[13] These it achieves by drawing on an already existing inventory of iconic and stylistic conventions relative to which a given lyric text functions more as citation than invention, as mention rather than use.

Inasmuch as both its cause and symptoms pivot on a deep awareness of its strictly textual constitution, melancholy cannot be classified as a "feeling" in any ordinary sense. In a brooding, quasi-intentional way, it appears fixated on the "feeling of difference" without which, Kant argues, a subject can never "orient itself in thinking" at all. Because it "feels" its own categorical otherness, so to speak, whenever it is put to referential or expressive use, melancholy invariably tends toward endless reflexivity, and it adopts a fundamentally metalingual stance as poetry. As such it "knows" (albeit in a strictly negative sense) that it cannot possess being and, burdened with that knowledge, must continually disavow being in articulate form.[14] Here lie the metaphysical sources of the "marked unnaturalness" (Levinson) or "perverse" and "second-hand" (Byron) quality of Keats's poetry. In its articulate denaturing of being, Keatsian melancholy also stalls the dialectical machine of Hegel's contemporary theory with its conceptual mediation of being and the idea of freedom. For Keatsian melancholy proves categorically resistant to narrative movement and the Protestant Hegelian work ethic of speculative philosophical thought. Instead, melancholy in Keats's oeuvre stages what Robert Kaufman has called a "celebration of the actual" by drawing out into the open the unreal, phantasmagoric, and allegorical character of the real. Keats's formalist deracination of being, his objectification of the real *as text,* thus "appears as a first step toward what twentieth-century artists and critics will lament or praise as antiaesthetic *loss of aura, reification,* and *mechanical reproduction.*" Kaufman summarizes this as the "Keatsian dissolution of selfhood and [his] concomitant building up of form, which in turn serves an intellectual sensorium ultimately capable of dissolving the object-world" (Kaufman 2001, 380, 382).

Keats's poetry sets limits to the subjective fetish of "feeling" and "affect" by dramatizing, in the abject lucidity of the allegorical text, feeling's intrinsic and persistent tendency to point to some alien, different quality within itself. As evidenced by the hypertrophic array of citations and examples throughout Burton's *Anatomy,* melancholy—in its constructed, formal-aesthetic presentation—reflects the oppressive authority of a traditional system of writing that has effectively usurped the very domain of the human. As the principle of " 'structure' in the pre-structural age," allegory is the very substance of melancholic affect, since the subject confronts his or her own posthumous condition through reading, which "becomes melancholy in that it mortifies its objects and consequently perceives them as dead texture. Reading is melancholy in its 'perception' of the materiality of texts, in the contemplation of the dead letter" (Haverkamp 1996, 104). As so many of Keats's protagonists reveal (the knight-at-arms of "La Belle Dame sans Merci" or, most obviously, Saturn in *Hyperion*), melancholy leaves the sufferer "hollow-ey'd, pale, and lean, furrow-faced, [and with] dead looks, wrinkled brows, riveled cheeks, dry bodies" (Burton, 299). It does so *not* by dint of some adverse fate but because readers will experience these figures as typological echoes or citations of a wealth of earlier books and, thus, as emblematic of the self-conscious and self-alienated status of late romantic literature. Conscious that they lack all epistemological and political agency or efficacy, Burton's melancholic subjects, like the "undead" of Bram Stoker's unhappy imagination, "cannot die [and] will not live" (Burton, 449). Instead, they blankly stare at a world whose overdetermined textual constitution they acknowledge to be exhaustive and rigid (and covertly resent for being so).[15] The excessively emblematic quality of allegoric expression corresponds to a thoroughly overdetermined world in which all objects, identities, and possible forms of action appear owned and exhausted a priori.

From Burton through Freud, Benjamin, Adorno, de Man, Kristeva and beyond, melancholy is characterized by this "motorial" deployment of signs as the very emblem of their referential futility and spiritual emptiness. At the same time, however, the gesture that posits the sign as the legible symptom of its own nothingness must be enacted over and over, lest the negative knowledge contained within it should fade and yield to utopian hopes or longings. As Kristeva puts it, the language of melancholy is "repetitive and monotonous. Faced with the impossibility of concatenating . . . sentences are interrupted, exhausted, come to a standstill." The result is a symptomatic idiom of "recurring, obsessive litanies" (Kristeva, 33) so cultivated and stylized as to hint at a covert transferential design on its audience.[16] "Elaborated with the help of much knowledge and will to mastery," melancholic speech "seems secondary, frozen and arbitrary" (ibid., 43). In short, it expressly identifies as a self-conscious, fatigued, indeed symptomatic form that disables the (romantic) paradigm of spontaneity and expressivity before our very eyes. The melancholic idiom unravels the project of an authentically expressive poetics as an illusion of subjective mastery premised on an inaccessible pre-text. As with cubism's exaggeration of a pointillist technique wherein late impressionism had for a last time fulfilled art's representational covenant, the romantic image here disintegrates as its symbolic aesthetic is rendered in shards or fragments without any credible claim to a preexisting totality. These fragments seem to know of their own otherness, that is, of their having come into being solely as instances (*emblemata*) of repetition. As Benjamin puts it, in the allegorical language of the baroque,

> any person, any object, any relationship can mean absolutely anything else. With this possibility a destructive but just verdict is passed on the profane world: it is

> characterized as a world in which the detail is of no great importance. But it will be unmistakably apparent, especially to anyone who is familiar with allegorical textual exegesis, that all of the things which are used to signify derive, from the very fact of their pointing to something else, a power which makes them appear no longer commensurable with profane things, which raises them onto a higher plane, and which can, indeed, sanctify them. Considered in allegorical terms, then, the profane world is both elevated and devalued. This religious dialectic of content has its formal correlative in the dialectic of convention and expression. For allegory is both: convention *and* expression.... [Yet it] is not the convention of expression, but expression of convention. (Benjamin 1998, 175)

As the most concentrated manifestation of melancholia as a rhetorical, indeed literary, symptom, baroque allegory is deliberately unoriginal and monotonous. In its downward transposition of a revelatory symbol into a recursive emblem, melancholy paradoxically valorizes the latter's derivative and conventional status—appearance *as* appearance—because only so does the word properly acknowledge the metaphysical lapse of creation into historical time. Curiously, it is this metaphysical-*cum*-historical quality of allegorical time that largely drops out of de Man's and, similarly, Kristeva's accounts of allegorical writing and melancholic speech, respectively. To say that "in the world of allegory, time is the originary constitutive category" and that, consequently, "we have . . . a relationship between signs in which the reference to their respective meanings has become of secondary importance" (de Man 1983, 207), while not incorrect, obscures the deeper significance of that shift. For the lapse into allegory constitutes the descent from metaphysical expectancy into the lapsed finitude of history, a descent that has turned writing and the book into damaged repositories of invariant and profane signs and conventions. For Benjamin's reading of the German baroque, no less than our reading of Keats, must keep in sight the historical dimension of time. To be sure, to the strictly negative and stoic lucidity of the allegorical text, there is no such thing as historical specificity but only empty time, whose affective experience unfolds on a continuum between boredom and despair. Nonetheless, this affective perception of an invariant temporality—which constitutes the "feeling" of melancholy prima facie—can only express itself through a historical particular inventory of signs. Its textual organization must deploy an inventory of literary signs and expressive conventions that are, in their proper historical moment, recognizably that: convention.

Some initial examples taken from writers other than Keats attest that melancholia pervades a broad spectrum of British and continental, post-Napoleonic literature. In the figure of Anne Elliott, Jane Austen's *Persuasion* (1818) gives us a character whose entire outlook on the present is shaped by "a disappointment" (39) that occurred some eight years before the narrative gets under way. Her rejection at that point of Wentworth's proposal of marriage is less a personal choice than submission to Lady Russell's advice—and, as such, socially conventional and economically opportunistic. Anne's persona throughout the opening chapters of *Persuasion* has a posthumous and abstracted quality about it. Devoid of any sense of mission and agency—and yet, like most of Austen's heroines, acutely conscious of that very fact—Anne soon finds herself at Uppercross Cottage, the humble residence of her simple-minded, vain, and hypochondriac sister. Inimitably balancing the melancholic and the satiric, allegory and irony, Austen's prose in chapter 5 sketches a domestic scene filled with petty resentments, trivial displays of female "accomplishments," and a host of aimless, "confused" psychological impulses and signals. All these are aptly embodied in the very décor of the Great House of the in-laws, whose affluence and superior reputation Anne's sister so indelicately covets:

> To the Great House accordingly they went, to sit the full half hour in the old-fashioned square parlor, with a small carpet and shining floor, to which the present daughters of the house were gradually giving a proper air of confusion by a grand piano forte and a harp, flower-stands and little tables placed in every direction. Oh! Could the originals of the portraits against the wainscot, could the gentlemen in brown velvet and the ladies in blue satin have seen what was going on, have been conscious of such an overthrow of all order and neatness! The portraits themselves seemed to be staring in astonishment. . . . There was a numerous family; but the only two grown up, excepting Charles, were Henrietta and Louisa, young ladies of nineteen and twenty, who had brought from a school at Exeter all the usual stock of accomplishments, and were now, like thousands of other young ladies, living to be fashionable, happy, and merry. Their dress had every advantage, their faces were rather pretty, their spirits extremely good, their manners unembarrassed and pleasant; they were of consequence at home and favorites abroad. (Austen, 67)

All of the key features of melancholy as the very essence of post-Waterloo literature and culture are in place here; social life has become calcified, a mindless enactment of an unconscious, ritualistic template of "proper" behavior.

Conformity reigns supreme in the Musgrove's daughters who, with their "usual" accomplishments and routine polish, appear eerily phantasmagorical, inhuman, or perhaps posthuman—veritable replicants of a cultural ideal that has been bred into them since birth. A strong temporal and allegorical dimension enters the description as the narrative lingers over the "originals" preserved in painted form on the walls and staring down "in astonishment" on the petty, shadowy bustle of the present below. As with the "sculptured dead . . . Imprisoned in black, purgatorial rails" found in Keats's "Eve of St. Agnes" (*KCP*, 454), it is through the historical distance of the aesthetic artifact (Austen's portraits or Keatsian sculpture) that the unreality of present-day empirical "life" is unveiled. Reminiscent of the inventory of cultural artifacts and scientific tools so miscellaneously scattered in the foreground of Lorenzo Lotto's and Albrecht Dürer's depictions of melancholy, the objects or possessions so erratically distributed throughout the "Great House" in *Persuasion* only heighten the reader's consciousness of their inutility. In their random contiguity, piano, carpet, shining floor, and harp function less as the details guaranteeing a "realist" feel for the narrative than as symptoms of a despondent mood. At the core of this mood lies an insistent and dispiriting sense of temporality, a deep-structural sedimentation of time as invariant and endlessly recursive. Without congealing into a straightforward proposition or utterance by either a character or the implied author, this melancholy temporality covertly transfers onto readers of Austen's prose the holistic perception of the whole business of the human as consisting of mindless material acquisitions and the unconscious emulation and display of cultural forms and practices ("the usual stock of accomplishments"). Far from cradling copious human life in their midst, Austen's details conjure the human as a failed utopia, here visibly strangled by the derivative, petty, and unreflective nature of social process. Experiencing her hyperlucidity and acute perceptiveness as a profoundly melancholy gift, like all of Austen's female heroines, Anne Elliott is condemned to bear quiet witness to the dystopia of middle-class life as it is here instanced by the Musgrove family. In stark contrast with the mournful humanity preserved in the portraits "staring" down on them, the young ladies of the Musgrove household are blissfully unaware of their composite status. Their "essence" consists in an unconscious mastery of the grammar and lexicon that define the socially well-adjusted female: good spirits, unembarrassed manners, advantageous dress, and pretty faces. Contiguous with the ambient furniture, female identity is shown in Austen's subtly melancholic narrative to be a composite of social and material details—details, however, with which the lesser characters of Austen's fiction gleefully identify, rather than grasping them as symptoms of a wholly deracinated human experience.

In a far more acerbic and self-conscious, though no less melancholic mode, the language of conspicuous detail also shapes Stendhal's *The Red and the Black* (1830), arguably the most apposite work of French literature when it comes to post-Waterloo melancholia. Immured in a seminary for aspiring priests at Besançon, the novel's restless protagonist, Julien Sorel, finds himself initially baffled by the utter lack of spiritual commitments at this institution, in particular any dedication to active thought and considered judgment: "To their eyes, he was guilty of the monstrous vice that *he thought, he judged for himself*" (Stendhal, 192). Catching on, Julien realizes that thus far, "the major actions of his life were astutely managed; but he did not pay attention to details, and details were the only things the clever people in the seminary valued. Thus he was already known by his comrades as a *skeptical mind.* He had been betrayed by a host of little things." Realizing that "learning counts for nothing here," and that "progress in dogma, in sacred history, etc., matters only in appearance," Julien makes a developmental quantum leap when he embraces and internalizes the entire social and rhetorical grammar and lexicon of details that regulate quotidian life in this "sacred" institution. Stendhal takes care to inform his readers, that Julien does so, not in spite, but because of the utter emptiness of this formal inventory:

> From the moment Julien was disillusioned, the drawn-out exercises in ascetic piety, such as the rosary five times a week, performing canticles to the Sacred Heart, etc., which had seemed to him so deadly boring, became the most interesting fields of action. Thinking about himself rigorously, and above all trying not to overestimate his capacities, Julien did not even attempt at first, like the seminarists who served as models for the others, to constantly perform actions that would be *significations*—that is to say, demonstrative of some type of Christian perfection. . . . Julien tried at first to arrive at the *non culpa,* which is the state of the young seminarist whose mode of walking, whose ways of moving his arms, eyes, etc., have nothing worldly about them, but do not yet advertise the person as being absorbed by the idea of another world and the *pure nothingness* of this one. (Stendhal, 193–94)

Few texts offer more eloquent confirmation of Paul de Man's thesis concerning the deep-seated affinity between romantic allegory and irony. For

Stendhal's protagonist, embracing the material specifics of finite, institutionally circumscribed existence at the seminary becomes possible only once he has evacuated the intricate structure of social signifiers of all claims to spiritual meaning. Words, gestures, and looks begin to enthrall Julien only insofar as they are emblems of their own referential futility. Yet Stendhal's protagonist does not, therefore, deteriorate into a superficial or outrightly cynical persona. On the contrary, part of the complex irony of this passage (one of many similar ones throughout the novel) is that we are made to witness how Julien's insight into the "pure nothingness" of signification inadvertently opens up for him a far more profound, truly baroque dimension of spiritual life. It is no accident that his principal advisor, the abbé Pirard, belongs to the Jansenist movement, which by 1830 was on the verge of extinction. Indeed, the abbé's spiritual integrity and moral rectitude derive in large part from the fact that Jansenism, the source of his spiritual identity, has already been defeated. Like his improbable disciple Julien, for whom initially the defeated, banished, and deceased Napoleon fulfils an analogous function, Pirard cultivates a quasi-posthumous existence. This structural irony, of signifiers producing a deepening of human interiority precisely where hope of an authentic spiritual signified (i.e., genuine faith in election; the heroic code) has already been evacuated from them, is Stendhal's and Keats's artistic signature—supremely realized in the latter's portrayal of Saturn in *Hyperion*. It is also late romanticism's principal bequest to the great modernist novelists (Dostoyevsky, Mann, Proust, Musil). The formal term for this purposive disequilibrium is, of course, irony, which Georg Lukács so aptly characterized as "the self-correction of the world's fragility" (1971, 75). Julien's suddenly changed relationship to signs, his new perception of them as mere *emblemata* of their social and spiritual futility, actually moves him closer to the baroque culture of mourning so incisively explored in Walter Benjamin's meditation on the baroque "play of mourning" (*Trauerspiel*).

Yet the same conversion experience also precipitates a new and shocking consciousness of the human as denatured, stripped of genuine spiritual agency and self-determination. It is this secondary implication that makes Julien a fitting pupil for Pirard, the sole remaining representative of Jansenism, whose conflict-laden history primarily stemmed from its scandalous embrace of predestination. Yet for Julien, this very premise of theories of predestination—namely, the impossibility of the human individual being an authentic agent of his or her own spiritual destiny—also serves as the point of departure for an entirely new, almost postmodern, creation of the self as a self-conscious fiction. For "Julien continually conceives himself as the hero of his own text, and that text as something to be created, not simply endured. He creates fictions, including fictions of the self, that motivate action" (Brooks, 71). This secondary, generative, and enabling dimension of melancholy bears keeping in mind, not only because it is key to Keats's epigenetic conception of poetic work ("that which is creative must create itself" [*LJK,* 1: 374]), but because it also helps us distinguish the more radical and profound mood of melancholy found in Austen, Keats, and Stendhal from the more narrowly thematic invocation of melancholy in the work of Byron. Canto IV of *Childe Harold's Pilgrimage,* published in 1818, offers some of the most poignant images of melancholy, and it does so in a manner that, while unmistakably Byronic, also claims to be genuinely representative of the depressive mood of post-Waterloo Europe. Openly doubting (in the canto's prefatory note to John Hobhouse) whether, in the "late transfer of nations" at the Congress of Vienna, "England has gained something more than a permanent army and a suspended Habeas Corpus" (1980–93, 2: 124), Byron offers a wistful survey of restoration Europe, where "An Emperor tramples where an Emperor knelt; Kingdoms are shrunk to provinces, and chains / Clank over sceptred cities." With Venice serving as the apt emblem for the transience of political institutions and national power ("Statues of glass—all shiver'd—the long file / Of her dead Doges are declin'd to dust" (ibid., 128–29), the Byronic text offers itself as a generic invention of sorts—a dystopic update on the topographical writing of the previous century. With his own public persona thoroughly discredited in his native England, Byron's last two cantos of *Childe Harold* positively embrace the damaged aura of the heroic, public, and larger-than-life persona (Byron, Napoleon) as representative of a profound, seismic shift in the ongoing process of European modernity. He stands, Byron tells us, "A ruin amidst ruins; there to track / Fall'n states and buried greatness, o'er a land / Which *was* the mightiest in its old command" (ibid., 132).

If Byron brands his time as one of decline, this dystopic vision is proffered in overtly sentimental and nostalgic terms. As befits a writer who has reconstituted his aristocratic Augustan identity as a literary trope and commodity, Byron bemoans the loss of aura and of personal charisma. What is a still only an incipient notion in Byron, Nietzsche bluntly states as the melancholic consequence of a disenchanted Europe whose "democratization amounts to the creation of a type prepared for slavery in the most subtle sense" and, thus, "is at the same time an involuntary exercise in the breeding of tyrants."[17] Nietzsche's pessimistic vision of the "averaging" of Europe already surfaces in Byron's portrait of a society where "opinion," has become

> . . . an omnipotence,—whose veil
> Mantles the earth with darkness, until right
> And wrong are accidents, and men grow pale
> Lest their own judgments should become too bright,
> And their free thoughts be crimes, and earth have too much light
>
> And thus they plod in sluggish misery,
> Rotting from sire to son, and age to age,
> Proud of their trampled nature, and so die,
> Bequeathing their hereditary rage
> To the new race of inborn slaves, who wage
> War for their chains, and rather than be free
> Bleed, gladiator-like . . .   (BYRON 1980–93, 2: 155)

Byron's strength, his forthright indictment of the bankrupt political order of restoration Europe and of Regency Britain in particular, is also his weakness. For it is perplexing to see how, in a post-Waterloo Europe whose leaders have so obviously and recklessly squandered all kinds of political opportunities, and hence their moral capital, it is still possible to write poetry in the straightforward neoclassical cadences of (modified) Spenserian verse. In his superb edition of Byron, Jerome McGann remarks on how Byron's "choice of the Spenserian stanza was regulative, for he took its tradition as a sanction for tonal and structural flexibility." In recalling "examples of Ariosto, Thomson, and Beattie to guide him in the practice of mixing tones and moods 'in the style and stanza of Spenser,'" Byron appeared to look for and find "a model that would foster stylistic spontaneity and sincerity."[18] It is this premise of a possible and desirable alignment of traditional rhetorical forms with authentic emotions that consistently informs and shapes all of Byron's oeuvre except for *Don Juan*, a work that opens up far more radical, protoexistentialist psychological scenarios. By contrast, *Childe Harold* remains content to posit melancholy strictly as a rhetorical topos and thematic proposition, and little thought is given to the possibility that melancholy might effectively alter, perhaps irreparably damage, the very ideation of "literariness" itself. It is this fundamental presupposition of literary value as transhistorical that ultimately constrains much of Byron's writing, even as it secured the author temporary notoriety and unprecedented sales figures. For if one reads the last two cantos of *Childe Harold's Pilgrimage* as a lucid obituary to the morally and psychophysiologically damaged representatives of a fading Augustan order (e.g., Byron, Brougham, Castlereagh, Wellington), one must ultimately also acknowledge the composite nature of the Byronic stanza and imagery as a formal symptom of that cultural paradigm's manifest sterility. Reminiscent of the syncretistic prescriptions for neoclassical painting found in Sir Joshua Reynolds's *Discourses,* Byron's amalgamation of Spenser with Ariosto, Thomson, and Beattie betrays an uncertainty about the degree to which writing and authorship should ever exceed the display of tradition. Not until *Don Juan* did Byron decisively answer that question for himself. What T. S. Eliot lamented as Byron's "imperceptiveness . . . to the English word" (quoted in Manning, 115), and what European readers during the first half of the nineteenth century had appreciated as the unique susceptibility of Byron to translation, also troubled Keats. "Lord Byron cuts a figure—but he is not figurative," Keats notes in early 1819.[19] The epistolary aside not only highlights a weakness that inheres in literary production in which the meaning of literariness itself is not perceived to be at stake; it also sets up a contrast with the peculiar vulnerability of Keats's own almost diametrically opposed approach to writing, to which we can now return.

One strategy of responding to the peculiar vulnerability of Keats's early writing—that is, to its almost flamboyant courtship of critical censure on both moral and formal-aesthetic grounds—has been to adopt a preemptive focus on Keats's "later" work only. Numerous readers thus commend the odes of a twenty-four-year-old wise man for their "controlled experiments with sensation" (Vendler, 13) while quietly consigning the writings of the twenty-two-year-old man-child to oblivion. Alternatively Keats's "special kind of vulnerable endearing intelligence" (Bayley, 3) has also been read as an expression of his sociocultural alienation. Yet the purposes of Keats's sustained rumination of sensation and pleasure ultimately prove impossible to discern, unless one begins with a patient accounting of the symptomatic character and deep-structural function of verbal matter ("words are images of thoughts refin'd" [*KCP,* 6]) throughout his oeuvre. For that purpose, the famously "embarrassing" text of Keats's 1817 *Poems* offers a rich and instructive hunting ground, both on literary-historical and methodological-critical grounds. For here melancholy is not merely, not even primarily, a thematic preoccupation—that role is accorded to pleasure—but instead emerges as the intrinsic property of literature in an age of social stratification and competitive professionalism. Perhaps more than the writings of any other major nineteenth-century poet, Keats's work has been alternately cast as the supreme embodiment of a thoroughly objectified and purified inwardness or as the most consummate perversion of that ideal. Rather than leaving the opposition between an allegedly derivative, self-imitating, and embarrassingly sentimentalized style and an objective, quasi-Hellenic bathos unresolved, a resourceful strain of literary interpretation (the school Marjorie Levinson, following Morris Dickstein, identifies as the "Harvard Keatsians") has sublated that antithesis itself into the account of a profoundly humanizing development.[20] The resulting familiar master narrative—the organizing principle of virtually all biographies, memorials, anthologies, and most critical studies of Keats— tells of the poet's phenomenal evolution. The story begins inauspiciously enough with the writer's youthful effusions, famously savaged by John Gibson Lockhart as "calm, settled, imperturbable drivelling idiocy" (Reiman, pt. C, 1: 90) and, in Byron's canny phrase, as a representative of "the *second-hand* school of poetry" (Byron 1982, 254), doomed from the start by insurmountable social antagonisms. These notorious invectives are startlingly, even deliberately, imperceptive of Keats's sly allegorical performance as a writer who, fully cognizant of his lack of material resources and cultural accreditation, effectively turns the tables by emulating and thus exposing literariness as a specious good—a commodity as yet unconscious of its commodity status. From the outset, Keats identifies himself as an allegorical presence, a producer who approaches poetry deliberately (as the "expression of convention" [Benjamin]) and reflexively—namely, by reproducing poetic convention *as* convention.

Keats's poetry reinstates the baroque mode with disconcerting precision, notably in his early deployment of recognizable styles (Spenser, Chatterton, Shakespeare, Leigh Hunt, the Della Cruscans) as a cultural commodity. Jerome McGann perceptively notes that Keats may well have understood that verbal art can only simulate emotions: "Keats begins (as a poet) by sentimentalizing sentimentalism" (1996, 121). Following the hints of McGann and William Keach, and Lionel Trilling's much earlier ones, the following discussion will thus run counter to a variety of critical accounts that institute the rather implausible division between an "early" (1817) and a "late" (1819) Keats. Such developmental narratives typically seek to redeem the "early" Keats of the 1817 *Poems* and *Endymion* volumes by means of an archetypal humanist master trope. Keats is presented as an idiot savant who, being "morally intelligent" beyond his years, dialectically transports his readers toward the discovery and articulation of "good human purposes" simply on the strength of his poetic ineptitude and moral naïveté: "a particular strength of Keats is the implication that the youthful, the luxuriant, the immature, can be, not just excusable errors, but vantagepoints" (Ricks, 1; 12). Presaging later, more cautious, readings (Ricks, McGann), John Bayley's earlier provocative account ultimately retreats from a fully developed allegorical reading of Keats's *entire* oeuvre logically consistent with his premises. Instead, we are treated to the familiar nineteenth-century myth of Keats's as an idiot savant regrettably despoiled of his greatest endowments by an academically wrought classicist aesthetic that Regency reviewers had stipulated as the sole legitimate foundation for middle-class morality and taste. Drawing on the ancient myth of the unselfconscious bard, Bayley portrays the early Keats as a latter-day Ion reveling in "linguistic innocence" and gifted with an adolescent's "almost embarrassing tendency to mean what he says." Such a view reinforces a seemingly timeless divide between the happy obtuseness of the youthful writer and the melancholy knowledge of the critic. Indeed, inasmuch as Keats's earlier poetry is seen as the youth's "acceptance of the first eager brainwave, and a consequent unawareness that it might be modified or corrected" (Bayley, 9–10, 19, 20), the role of the critic becomes that of an adult guardian sheltering the author's literary effusions from the corrupting influence of adult critical reading.

Posited either as blissfully naiveté (1817) or "classically" unapproachable, with the teleological fantasy of the idiot savant mediating between the two—Keats seems to be forever sheltered from the cold vicissitudes of critical reading. Even a century after the heyday of Victorian fin-de-siècle appreciative writing, such professional concerns appear transgressive of Keats's fetishized Hellenic persona, whose death and transfiguration (as in Richard Strauss's eponymous tone poem) remain forever motivically entwined. Thus romantic studies (with Levinson's account as a still rare, though by no means unproblematic, exception) seem forever enthralled by Keats's death at age twenty-six in Rome.[21] The very apotheosis of romantic melancholy, the scene of Keats's premature passing is even now ritually commemorated by mournfully accented recitations of his "Lines Supposed to Have Been Addressed to Fanny Brawne" ("This living hand . . ." [1819]) read to momentarily enthralled academics at annual romanticism meetings.[22] Culminating in such mystification, the story of Keats's changing reception enacts the romantic master narrative of *Bildung* with eerie perfection; like the trajectory of Goethe's Wilhelm Meister,

Keats's life unfolds (even posthumously) as an aesthetic theodicy of sorts by progressively cleansing the author of the taint of the "common," a term that does not merely encompass Keats's humble social origins or his conspicuously sexualized and often prurient early writings (what he so self-consciously labels as writing "in a voluptuous vein" [*KCP*, 21]), but also the secular doings of an academic criticism given to ritual bouts of self-castigation for its self-confessed profanation of Keatsian scripture.[23]

James Chandler reads the sonnet "To Some Ladies," from which the phrase "in a voluptuous vein" derives, as "Keats's articulation of his own 'psyche' in response to a condition he saw emblematized by [Thomas] Moore and [Mary] Tighe." Building on the "fact" or "information" that Keats's sonnet was occasioned by his having received a transcription of Moore's *The Wreath and the Chain,* Chandler proceeds to argue that Keats's "notion of 'psychic' development became historicized . . . in relation to what we have been calling the 'spirit of the age'" (Chandler, 394). My contention throughout this chapter differs markedly from Chandler's view of Keats's "imitative" (ibid., 394n) early style, in that I perceive imitation not as a case of "use" but of "mention," in other words, not as a style emulated or copied, but rather as one consciously deployed as a damaged signifier. Keats's overtly derivative style does not posit "psyche" as its ultimate signified but instead exposes the derivative constitution of psyche itself—no longer an expressive origin but a recognizably "literary" product. Keats's poetic process turns out to be less "smokeable" (to recall Chandler's shrewd, Keats-derived metaphor) by historicist inquiry than baiting the latter. For the simulation of literary sentimentalism in Keats's early poetry does not simply target Moore and Tighe; in so doing, it also offers a canny critique of the then still recent and increasingly class-specific notion of "literariness." Rather than aiming at "relative transcendence" (ibid., 402) vis-à-vis these two immediate contemporaries, Keats's early style, like that of his German contemporary Heinrich Heine, conceives of literariness as an act of simulation, not expression. Keats's apt formulation for this process is "Soul-Making" (*LJK*, 2: 101). Both the consumptive attachment of Regency audiences to the verse romances of Tighe, Moore, and the early Byron and the belated skepticism of historicist readers rest on the same fundamental assumption of an expressivist paradigm that Keats's poetry has effectively begun to dismantle. Keats, Heine, and eventually Baudelaire acquire their eminent status in nineteenth-century culture, and in the history of melancholy as an aesthetic *and* ideological phenomenon, because in their poetry, literature begins to dissociate itself from itself, begins to historicize its ideological entanglements and acknowledge its ultimate impossibility.

Such a transvaluation of the very idea and institution of literature does not only reflect the "temper of 1819" (*LJK,* 2: 116) that Chandler reconstructs with such literal and synchronizing precision. Rather, Keats's aim is to "unwrite" (ibid., 323) literature as intrinsically (albeit obliquely) derivative of other literature and, in so doing, to expose the middle-class codification of morally and aesthetically "proper" sentiment and forms of sentimentality. If such a critique of Regency literature's moral and institutional claims, including its imperial mandate as the very essence of cultural value in a British-dominated world, takes shape in Keats, that argument need not be unfolded from the belated vantage point of post-Hegelian historicism. For in its formal *habitus,* Keats's poetry itself practices the methodological virtues of a reflexive, metalingual critical distance vis-à-vis its proposed object—poetry. This it does by unraveling literariness as it were from within, by exposing the self-cherishing, imperious, and ethically indifferent profile of the "high romantic" arguments for a blessed Wordsworthian or narcissistically sentimental (Tighe, Moore) psyche through its unrelenting imitation. It is this historicizing of aesthetic pleasure as a "specious good" (Trilling, 444) that confers on the poetry of Keats, Heine, and Baudelaire such a distinctive, modern beauty. Already in Keats's early poetry, the "bliss" of inwardness as spontaneous revelation becomes indistinguishable from the bliss of commanding the recognized and accepted "expressive" signs of such inwardness. The result is an invigoration of melancholy "around" 1819, a Heideggerian mood of lucid despair over the fact that not only literature but "culture" and *Bildung* more broadly had by then outlived their historical efficacy. Like the titans of *Hyperion,* these ideals find themselves alienated from their former promise and plenitude and now are condemned to get on in an ethically impoverished system unwilling to locate in aesthetic work anything more than a mercenary ideological use-value for the new Olympian order of British imperial culture. In exploring the "containment function" of a British literary and cultural curriculum in India, Gauri Viswanathan notes how "the claim that literature can be read meaningfully only when a high degree of morality and understanding is present in the reader implied that certain controlled measures were necessary to bring the reader up to the desired level. But paradoxically, those measures took the form of instruction in that same literature for which preparation was deemed necessary." A strikingly similar dynamic also characterizes the surveillance of the literary marketplace by the semi-official institutions of the Edinburgh reviewers during the Regency.[24]

Such formal-aesthetic dissent from within literature against its ideological appropriation as, I believe, can be found throughout Keats's *entire* oeuvre ("early" to "late") has, not surprisingly, been sharply curtailed by the dignified and edifying narratives of his authorial becoming. Another strategy of containing the anti-romantic and anti-literary strain that makes Keats's poetry so intriguing can be found to operate at the level of literary anthologizing. Anthologies, surely one of the most powerful instruments of institutional reproduction of literary and aesthetic values, have to this very day not only been responsive to but instrumental in enforcing the key premise that Keats's aesthetic rehabilitation requires us to sharply discriminate between his allegedly derivative, phony sentimentalism and the authentic, classical affect of his late odes. It was not enough simply to foist on Keats the distinction between what *Blackwood's Edinburgh Magazine* had referred to as a "species of emasculated pruriency that looks as if it were the product of some imaginative Eunuch's . . . melancholy inspiration" and a worthier mature Keats. Rather, the capacity of criticism to tell "Right from Wrong in matters of moral Taste" (*LJK*, 2: 182), as Keats's friend John Taylor had so strenuously insisted in the context of his "Eve of St. Agnes," had to be deduced from a considered reading of Keats's "mature" or canonical poetry. The resulting separation of the "early" Keats's serial offenses against the (presumptive) laws of stylistic and moral propriety from the (equally presumptive) genuine classical passion of his late odes has been with us ever since. A particularly dramatic result of such self-privileging interpretation has been a radically foreshortened (no pun intended) Keats, produced by tight canonical supervision and represented nowadays by no more than a dozen poems out of well over a hundred and fifty.

Bad Grammar and Unnatural Feelings: Keats's Phantasmagoric Style of 1817

To this day, Keats's allegedly discordant styles identify a still lingering crisis of "literary" value—not just particular, local values but, rather, a crisis of what ought to count as literary value. Gerard Manley Hopkins was among the first to express dismay at Keats's verse for apparently "at every turn abandoning itself to an unmanly and enervating luxury" and the poet's only late in his short life taking "an interest in higher things and . . . powerful and active thought."[25]

Happily drawing on Keats's apparent decision to reform his ways ("I hope I am a little more of a Philosopher than I was, consequently a little less of a versifying Pet-lamb" [*LJK,* 2: 116]), much literary criticism of the twentieth century not only followed Hopkins in peremptorily separating the "enervated" luxuries of Keats's early verse from his putative dedication to "active thought" in 1819 but in so doing also excluded the possibility that an aesthetic offense might constitute a purposeful political strategy.[26] Against this dominant strain, Jerome McGann, William Keach, David Bromwich, and Nicholas Roe all have asserted the political valence of Keats's early writing, its flamboyantly subaltern esprit. Yet in seeking to rehabilitate the poetry that had reached the public through Keats's 1817 *Poems,* criticism effectively reaffirms the divide between politics and aesthetics. The aesthetic, to be truly worthy of critical attention, must contain a determinate political message or, at least, yield a determinate political effect. Thus Keats's supposed indebtedness to Hunt, his at times dandyish aesthetic in the 1817 volume, can only be redeemed as an anti-aesthetic, which readers like Bromwich, Roe, and Keach in turn welcome as evidence of at bottom liberal political credentials and hopes. Drawing much support from John Wilson Croker's and John Gibson Lockhart's reactionary yet shrewd ("malice can be discerning malice" [Bromwich, 199]) identification of Keats's compulsive "metro-manie" with the upstart claims of the "Cockney school of politics," an axiomatically liberal-and progressive-minded critical establishment takes solace in "Keats's inseparable poetical and political vices."[27]

To a critique premised on "vulgar Marxist" axioms about the political responsibility of art, Keats's own vulgarity ensures his political and, by a curious reverse logic, also his aesthetic salvation. A flamboyantly anti-literary poetry surely must be the (sly) expression of a covert anti-establishment politics. However ennobling and edifying to preponderantly liberal academic practitioners and readers today, historicism remains largely mired in a merely topical and occasional model of politics and, as a further consequence, conceives of aesthetic and literary form in strictly instrumental terms. That is, Keats's poetry is read, not as the expression of a reflexive process of complex and purposively equivocal signification, but as either proffering a proper evaluation of (putatively germane) material and political constellations or, worse, as an unconscious and hence pathological prevarication or outright repression of political meanings. For the first and arguably decisive choice made by any interpretive reading of literature is whether to evaluate the textual object vis-à-vis a peremptory notion of what it *should have said* or, alternatively, whether to see it as a dynamic negotiation of ideological antagonisms in a symbolic form that solicits and demands a *nuanced and process-based* interpretive response from its implicit reader. Much ingenuity may and has indeed been expended to discern "iconographical details" (Keach, 194) in "To Autumn" from which to draw conclusions about its author's likely preoccupation with and disgust at the recent Peterloo massacre in Manchester on 16 August 1819.[28] Yet, however momentous and disconcerting in its day, it is the very particularity of that calamitous event that also renders it ill suited as a semantic framework for the carefully stylized, melancholic imagism of "To Autumn" with its insistent juxtaposition of sensual plenitude and barren emotions, a pungent material world encoding a denatured psyche.

Through formally elaborate simulations of tactile, olfactory, and aural sensations, the Keatsian subject "fade[s] away" into a formal constellation. Yet it will not do to explain this quintessentially Keatsian poetic signature as mere evidence of a late romantic aesthetic operating in unconscious complicity with the repressive political forces of post-Napoleonic restoration Europe. For the affect in question is too acutely reflexive and rhetorically stylized. Being so meticulously composed—not just a poem but a veritable case study of synaesthetic, protodecadent poetic effects—"To Autumn" does not ask us to construe the relationship between politics and art as one of authentic (material) causes and displaced (formal) effects. Rather, Keats's poetry suggests that any expressive or critically suspicious alignment of politics and aesthetics will necessarily prove to be a *misalliance* in the end, regardless of the particular historical conditions under which it is attempted. Nicholas Roe's recent study *John Keats and the Culture of Dissent* is arguably the most erudite and forceful historicist attempt at recovering the politically engaged Keats. To that end, Roe adopts a "form of close reading which might properly be called a literal archeology" that aims "to return (so far as possible) to the original inflections of Keats's language, imagery, and poetic style in order to understand how his poems were once understood to be loaded with controversial meaning" (ix). Yet reclaiming the Keats manqué from the grip of late-nineteenth and twentieth-century aestheticism and formalism commits Roe and those historicist readers who have embraced that agenda to reading all poetry from an axiomatically *referential* vantage point, which "has the effect of highlighting [*sic*] the explicit topicality" of Keats's language and allows the critic to demonstrate how "Keatsian themes and motifs . . . can be located within a broader revolutionary discourse" (Roe, x).

The present reading of Keats declines any such peremptory placement of Keats's diction within either a referential or an expressive model of signification. For the same reason, my readings do not frame melancholy as a thematic preoccupation in Keats's poetry but, instead, as a psychohistorical phenomenon that attains legibility in the poetry's formal design. Fundamentally, Keats's aesthetic originates in and keeps in play the referential and ideational futility of the poetic word. One need only read closely the mischievous choreography of mutual promises and betrayal between Lamia and Hermes to pick up on the deep-seated mood of melancholy as it arises from the transience of all verbal representations of (putatively) authentic inward states. With "rosy eloquence," Hermes seeks to tease out of Lamia, the "smooth-lipped serpent," the unknown whereabouts of his coveted nymph. Words beget more words as Hermes swears to compensate Lamia for divulging information by contriving her humanity: "Light flew his earnest words, among the blossoms blown." True to his distinctive portfolio as the messenger of the gods, as well as the god of thieves and merchants, Hermes renews his oath (sworn "by my serpent rod") in language that inevitably becomes a metacommentary on the simulated commerce of modern literature with the real: "Then, once again, the charmèd God began / An oath, and through the serpent's ears it ran / Warm, tremulous, devout, psalterian" (*KCP*, 620–21). As Garrett Stuart summarily notes how "words in Keats are the theater of a world interfused with affect and its vanishments, mutable layered, elusive. When transposed to poetry, these are the effects of which his late poem *Lamia* is a parable" (Stewart, 140).

Not surprisingly, then, Keats's late cadences are closer to the existentialist psychology of Camus or Ingmar Bergman's cinematic evocation of a post-theological world than to the utopian rhetoric of revolutionary romanticism. Given the persistent tendency of Keats's poetry to slip into such metacommentary on referentiality as simply a simulated, unenforceable contract, any critical alignment of his oeuvre with the cultural and political discourse of Regency England must proceed with great caution. For a poetry that so radically qualifies itself as sonorous, perhaps euphonious ("warm, tremulous, devout, psalterian"), phonetic matter is likely to resist instrumentalist co-optation for political ends—be it by a (lesser) poet or a naïve critic. For the same reason, Keats's idiom also marks a radical departure from the high romantic aesthetic that, after 1815, was principally associated with Wordsworth, Coleridge, Southey, and their political apologists in Edinburgh.[29]

Jerome McGann's influential essay on Keats soon qualifies not only his conclusions but, fundamentally, his entire methodological reasoning, although cautiously pursuing the historicist recuperation of Keats's "bad" early poetry for "good" political ends. While reaffirming that our grasp of the "significance of this Cockney style" hinges on "reading such poetry in a sharply specified historical frame of reference," McGann effectively aims at recovering not a political message ("abstract characteristics") but something rather more elusive that he calls "the felt *qualities* of its poetic structure" (McGann 1988a, 28). Consistent with much of what has already been observed about melancholy, McGann follows Croker's October 1817 review of "The Cockney School of Poetry," which had acknowledged Keats's early style as "self-consciously 'smart, witty . . . and learned' " (ibid., 30). Yet following his meticulous philological exposition and interpretation of "La Belle Dame sans Merci" and the Paolo and Francesca sonnet, McGann concludes that the poem in question offers "a grim assertion which emerges as a terrible function about the poem's ideas about love, the 'world', and poetry. For the sonnet's 'melancholy' tone also asserts that the conflicts between the World and romantic Love cannot be resolved in the terms defined by the poem. Poetry itself is affected by these conflicts. The sonnet tells us—finally, desperately—that poetry's power to see these contradictions carries with it the fate of ineffectuality. Here, at all levels, we see a situation in which everything is to be endured, but nothing is to be done" (ibid., 42). In a revealing, if only momentary, suspension of the political and methodological optimism that otherwise dominates his argument, McGann's conclusions here startlingly resemble those of a very different critical genealogy (Benjamin, Adorno, and de Man, Kristeva, and Haverkamp, among others). Rather than churning Keats's Cockney aesthetic as mere fuel by means of which critics belatedly rekindle the noble fires of political protest from August 1819, McGann hints at an arguably more profound, because no longer politico-instrumental, understanding of Keatsian melancholy.

A complementary passage from Adorno's late *Aesthetic Theory* serves to underline the critical connection for our purposes. Lyric writing, for both McGann and Adorno, knows—in ways that a "vulgar Marxist" critique, superficial even on genuinely Marxist grounds, does not—how profoundly art despairs over its unconditionally mediated character, a despair that includes, indeed is deepened by, the awareness that a superior form or method of engagement with life and the world simply does not exist. "Because meaning, whenever it is manifest in an artwork, remains bound up with semblance, all art is endowed with sadness; art grieves all the more, the more completely its successful unification suggests meaning," Adorno writes. "Melancholy is the shadow of what in all form is heterogeneous, which form strives to banish: mere existence. . . . In the utopia of its form, art bends under the burdensome weight of the empirical world from which, as art, it steps away" (Adorno 1997, 105). Far from being a pure and immediate human emotion susceptible of authentic literary representation, for Adorno, melancholy is the affective correlate of a certain type of "literary" writing— the lyric—whose noninstrumental genres (particularly lyric and romance forms) are proffered as virtual sanctuary to modernity's embattled subjects. Adorno extends his argument about the obliquely social character of lyric form by noting how it is precisely the "semblance" (*Schein*) of the work that compels its reader to "reflect over what speaks in art." "Semblance" is simply a more general term for what Adorno elaborates as the "linguistic quality" of a work, one that is foregrounded within the work in ways that critics like Jakobson and de Man, working from different critical genealogies, were beginning to articulate throughout the 1960s.

Following de Man, Forest Pyle speaks of "a pervasive noncoincidence between a human domain and the material, nonhuman operations of language, a noncoincidence disclosed in the poetry itself" (Pyle 1995, 136). Keats's poetry does indeed foreground its linguistic material and its formal (rhetorical) conventions with such emphasis as to obtrude on its projected audience poetry's strictly simulated commerce with the real. In so laying bare its technique of hypersimulation as the mode of access to a world with which it can never coincide, Keatsian lyricism baits its audience's critical and melancholic recognition of poetry as semblance, and semblance as socially determined. Such semblance in turn transforms the reader's relationship, not only to the text, but to its producer, who can no longer be credited with an unmediated, expressive pathos. Far from an origin or "source" of lyric expression, the writer's subjectivity is, as Adorno puts it,

> constituted in the work through the action of the work's language; in relation to the work, the individual who produces it is an element of reality like others. The private person is not even decisive in the factual production of artworks. Implicitly the artwork demands the division of labor, and the individual functions accordingly. By entrusting itself fully to its material, production results in something universal born out of the utmost individuation. The force with which the private I is externalized in the work is the I's collective essence; it constitutes the linguistic quality of works. The labor in the artwork becomes social by way

of the individual, though the individual need not be conscious of society; perhaps this is all the more true the less the individual is conscious of society.[30]

The critical problem, then, is how to conceptualize a melancholic quality intrinsic to literature, which Keats may be among the first to have drawn out. Doing so involves much more than the posthumous dispute over Keats's troubled "legacy" as it became absorbed into the broader Victorian and Edwardian consolidation of what properly ought to count as aesthetic and literary history (Gerard Manley Hopkins, Mathew Arnold, David Masson, Leslie Stephens, George Saintsbury). For this very instability of literary value also constitutes an intrinsic, indeed an enabling, feature of the Keatsian text itself. What distinguishes Keats's oeuvre from other post-Napoleonic literary and critical writing is his decision to dramatize the modern individual's atrophied interiority in his poetry. Keats appears to connect this diminished capacity for sensation, feeling, and desire—be it cultural, economic, or psychosexual—with the overdetermined literary and cultural conventions that govern its written expression. Thus Keats's earlier poetry does not so much accidentally run afoul of the censorious middle-brow model of feeling, what Wordsworth's *Prelude* (1805) so canonically calls "vernal promises, the hope / Of active days, of dignity and thought, / Of prowess in an honorable field, / Pure passions, virtue, knowledge, and delight, / The holy life of music and of verse" (1992b, 1: 50–54). Rather, Keats hints at how desire attains distinctness only through its perilous commerce with a notion of literariness that—as Wordsworth's passage (sounding, after all, so unmistakably "Wordsworthian") exemplifies—invariably creates the impression of a language imitating itself. In fact, spiritual and emotive depth is merely a hypostatized value retroactively inferred from the melancholy event of its stylistic miscarriage, the event of a putative interiority flattened out by recursive, quasi-serial tropes and conventions.

Late romantic feeling comes into its own only inasmuch as it confronts its determinacy by intrinsically social techniques of writing and reading. Only in the abject condition of the text, that is, can the subject realize the meaning of its desire as that with which it can never coincide. Constitutively alienated from its projected, inward truth, Keatsian desire begins its quest for adequate self-expression by traversing a labyrinth of aesthetic norms, generic prescriptions, conventions, and traditions that we associate with the lyric and, ultimately, with the system of "Literature" in general. In the course of that journey, desire recognizes its claims to authenticity and truth to be insupportable and, ultimately, utopian. As we shall see again in Heinrich Heine, it is precisely this sense of an utopia perceived to have failed, and thereby to have created a radically novel, dystopic sensibility, that defines late romantic melancholy as simultaneously an aesthetic and an ideological watershed. Keats's writing—whose "marked unnaturalness" Marjorie Levinson has rightly characterized as "aggressively literary" (Levinson 1988, 230, 5)—is predicated on the perception that desire, far from being an essential and inward quality, is cued by the material riches and social prospects manifestly unattainable for the writer. Beyond that, however, Keats's poetry reinforces the unattainability of the object of desire by giving us protagonists (Lorenzo, Porphyro, Lycius) whose conspicuous voyeurism not only reveals their social estrangement but, indirectly, also forecloses on the Wordsworthian poetics that proclaims its superior, indeed providential, vision to ennoble—and, in turn, be redeemed by—its literary representation.

Almost from the start of his lyric career, Keats responds to that predicament, not by attempting to overcome it, but rather by representing it. He compels us to witness the near instantaneous dissolution of desire into the indifferent, serial structure of a glaringly "public" text. Isn't this forcible subordination of affect to the implacable demands of a deep-structural, preordained social and aesthetic grammar at the heart of melancholy? If so, one must conceive melancholy in ways radically different from traditional Freudian psychoanalysis with its hypostatized paradigm of a pure ("prelinguistic") affective value redeemed from its allegedly mute and subterranean dwelling only by the work of analysis. Keats actually points to a very different conception. To illustrate my claim, let me turn to Keats's early (c. 14 February 1816) sonnet "To—" (with the addressee significantly unspecified):

> Had I a man's fair form, then might my sighs
> Be echoed swiftly through that ivory shell
> Thine ear, and find thy gentle heart, so well
> Would passion arm me for the enterprize.
> But ah! I am no knight whose foeman dies,
> No cuirass glistens on my bosom's swell;
> I am no happy shepherd of the Dell
> Whose lips have trembled with a maiden's eyes.
> Yet must I dote upon thee—call thee sweet,
> Sweeter by far than Hybla's honeyed roses

When steeped in dew rich to intoxication.
Ah! I will taste that dew, for me 'tis meet
And when the moon her pallid face discloses,
I'll gather some by spells and incantation. (*KCP*, 32)

The generic character of desire in Keats's early writings is striking—or, in John Bayley's words, "rich and *disconcerting*." We cringe or (to use Keats's preferred term) "blush" at the disclosure of a desire so transparently self-focused and seemingly self-absorbed. To begin with, there is no clear object of desire here; no persona, feminine or masculine, ever attains distinctness beyond a bland, pronominal "thee." Nor should we settle on the statuesque male body as the actual object of desire—notwithstanding the editors' obligatory reference to Keats's misgivings about his diminutive stature (5′¾″). The latter option is already disqualified by the lyric's self-negating opening syntax. Rather than identifying masculinity as the focus of desire, the poem's shrewdly conditional syntax ("Had I a man's fair form") shows that such desire has already been recognized as altogether unattainable. So as to reinforce the subjunctive grammar of terminally suspended desire, the lyric also points to the incommensurability between the chivalric and pastoral codes (fleetingly called up in the second quatrain) and an affective longing for which, in fact, there is no longer any authentic code or language. Lyric writing here commemorates feeling as an utopian delusion that is to be overcome in the very medium and social sign—"literariness" per se—that had caused such emotion to unravel into a cliché to begin with. More unsettling yet, the sestet's opening lines ("Yet must I dote upon thee—call thee sweet, / Sweeter by far than Hybla's honeyed roses . . .") show the lyric persona suspended between the interrogative and the compulsory, between an indeterminate and a mechanical kind of affect. In short, the sonnet disturbs by confronting us with the explicitly negative aura of a rigorously formalized, quasi-mechanical eroticism.[31] Having lost its aura of intuitive certitude, desire seems little more than a tangled mess of oblique compulsions and futile petitioning—"a gordian complication of feelings" (*LJK*, 1: 342) that renders Keats's voice alarmingly depersonalized. The lyric appears mired in the liminal space between an opaque intuition and its imminent own assimilation to traditionally high- and middle-brow literary forms (ode, hymn, elegy, loco-descriptive poetry) that will only reinforce a (Heideggerian) "mood" of social and aesthetic alienation into which the writer's and reader's subjectivity finds itself "always-already" thrust. If anything, the dubious reference to "spells and incantation" at the end of the sonnet reinforces the melancholy condition of a writer mobilizing his own curious lyric idiom as a virtual response to deeply alien norms of authentic sensibility and stylistic propriety.

A first feature of melancholy, namely, its overdetermined and hence abject consciousness of the citation-like, rigorously textual constitution of affect thus comes into view. Following Benjamin's hints, Theodor Adorno's early work on Kierkegaard makes the point forcefully and, at the same time, begins to draw attention to yet another feature of melancholy central to the discussion of Keats: the apparent evaporation of the material world or, rather, melancholy's implicit repudiation of the realist model that posits the empirical world as an authentic epistemological source. Foreshadowing Adorno's theoretical model, Keats's phantasmagoric images do not stand on the opposite side of the real; rather, they serve to draw out the intrinsic otherness, the fantasy character that lurks within all comforting talk about social, political, and moral "realities." For the young Adorno, writing on Kierkegaard, poetic language mourns its inability to share in the fantasy of the real, and it copes with such mourning by giving it objective character as an aesthetic construction—a poem: "No truer image of hope can be imagined than that of ciphers, readable as traces, dissolving in history, disappearing in front of overflowing eyes, indeed confirmed in lamentation. In these tears of despair the ciphers appear as incandescent figures, dialectically, as compassion, comfort, and hope. Dialectical melancholy does not mourn vanished happiness. It knows that it is unreachable. But it also knows of the promise that conjoins the unreachable, precisely in its origin, with the wish: 'Never have I been happy; and yet it has always seemed as if happiness were in my train'" (Adorno 1989, 124 / *AGS*, 2: 179).

Adorno's reading of Kierkegaard, himself an unwitting heir of Keats's startlingly similar conceptions, proves helpful in that it exposes optimism and spontaneity to be erroneous attributes of such feeling. In fact, with its desperate yet futile longing for an objective, material ground, all wishing, desiring, and longing effectively hastens the subject toward confronting the intrinsically unreal nature of such feeling itself. The "ah! could I tell the wonders of an isle" (*KCP*, 4) in his first, self-consciously entitled "Imitation of Spenser" already signals for a poetics that views inauthenticity as the sole remaining road of access to psychological and intellectual "depth." Keats here anticipates Freud's eventual association of the melancholiac's laments with narcissism ("The self-torments of melancholiacs . . . are without doubt pleasurable" [Freud

1963b, 172]). The outwardly confident opening of Keats's verse epistle to George Felton Mathew ("Sweet are the pleasures that to verse belong" [*KCP*, 24]) is followed by a vivisection of these pleasures, all of which are expressly identified as substitutes for the erotic lure of a sadly reticent and "coy muse." Consumed above all with its own prolongation, erotic desire can realize that goal only in the allegorical medium of the literary artifact. As Novalis had already noted in his late fragment collections, desire can possess itself and, consequently, can secure the reality of the "human" *qua* feeling only in the simulated rhapsodizing of literature. Hence Keats's early poems characteristically vacillate between the dystopia of a wish rendered self-conscious by its aesthetic formalization and an erotic compulsion forever imitative of more writing: "If this is vain—O Mathew, lend thy aid / To find a place where I may greet the maid, / Where we may soft humanity put on, / And sit and rhyme, and think on Chatterton" (*KCP*, 26).

Keats's next poem betrays this incongruity between stylistic and social dynamics in its very title, "Specimen of an Induction to a Poem." This self-consciously generic ("Specimen") emulation of Spenserian chivalric romance pays strange tribute indeed to the genre's Elizabethan master. If Spenser holds a firm and authoritative position within the evaluative taxonomy of contemporary literary history (Campbell, Southey), Keats's title leaves little doubt that Spenserian romance has ceased to function as a viable strategy for knowing and writing.[32] Indeed, the title warns us that the following lines will tell us nothing, least of all a story. As with the famously abortive *Hyperion,* this early narrative shows how Keats "cannot put his characters to work and cannot make his poem work. [The] poems are oppressively static, afflicted not by indolence but by its darker side, which Maurice Blanchot was to call worklessness or *désouvrement*" (Rajan 1998, 335). Such "loitering" (Keats's motional trope for the uncertain epistemological status of emotion) turns out to be purposive rather than pathological. Tilottama Rajan convincingly reads the "workless" and explicitly indolent character of such poetry as evidence that Keats was "more aware than Levinson supposes of both the preciousness (in a double sense) of 'poetry' and of the irrelevance of the life it signified" (ibid., 337). Extending Keats's epistolary remark that "I am quite disgusted with literary Men and will never know another except Wordsworth" (*LJK,* 1: 169), "Specimen" alerts us to the distance between the disenfranchised writing subject and a literary authority suspect not only on account of its historical remoteness but also because of the serial reproducibility of its idiom. The poem's forced opening—"Lo! I must tell a tale of chivalry / For large white plumes are dancing in mine eye"—is repeated with embarrassing monotony throughout the poem, even though, needless to say, no such tale ever emerges. Such repetition throws into relief the modern writer's abject relationship to a style whose expressive charisma he compulsively emulates as a utopian wish, fully conscious of both the commodity character of Spenserian romance and the impossibility of its revival. If literary styles have "become *signatures:* not audible voices but visible, material *signs* of canonical voices" (Levinson 1988, 15) in Keats's early oeuvre, they do not do so as a quasi-accidental entailment of the writer's alleged immaturity, social disenfranchisement, or lack of formal education. Rather, the poetry itself effects a critique of vestigially latinate and socially restrictive norms of expressive technique and propriety. As the supreme emblem of Britain's social and imperial strategy of policing alterity (social or ethnic) by cultural means, the lyric's

> affirmation of an ideal self and ideal political state . . . is essentially an affirmation of English identity. But that identity is equally split along the lines of actual and ideal selves, and the Englishman actively participating in the cruder realities of conquest, commercial aggrandizement, and disciplinary management of natives [and, we might add, Cockneys] blends into the rarefied, more exalted image of the Englishman as the producer of the knowledge that empowers him to conquer, appropriate, and manage in the first place. . . . In a parodic reworking of the Cartesian axiom, the Englishman's true essence is defined by the thought that he produces, overriding all other aspects of his identity—his personality, actions, and behavior. His material reality as subjugator and alien ruler is dissolved in his mental output; the blurring of the man and his works effectively removes him from history. (Viswanathan, 20)

With its flamboyant display of fraudulent (Chattertonian) emotions, the "Cockney school" in general, and Keats as its temporary aficionado, counters the absorption of subjectivity into a Protestant cultural work ethic of the kind described by Gauri Viswanathan.

For Keats, writing poetry both constitutes a compulsion and, as a rigorously formalist mode of production, furnishes the object that will enable him to grasp the psychosocial motives underlying it. In the most genuine Hegelian sense, writing is the "medium of reflection" (*Reflexionsmedium*). Nowhere does this fact seem more apparent than in Keats's epistolary references to the writing of *Endymion,* a project at once strategically grasped as "a test, trial of my Powers of Imagination" and tactically implemented through a wholly mechanical reproduction of invariant and equivalent poeticisms: "I must make 4000 lines of one bare circumstance and *fill them with Poetry.*"[33] It is one thing to admit to such mechanical ambitions in correspondence. Yet Keats repeatedly draws attention in *Endymion* itself to a strange fusion of mass production as his mode of authorial production with metonymy and romance as the corresponding master trope and master genre, respectively.

Many and many a verse I hope to write
Before the daisies, vermeil-rimmed and white,
Hide in deep herbage; and ere yet the bees
Hum about globes of clover and sweet peas,

I must be near the middle of my story.
Oh, may not wintry season, bare and hoary,
See it half finished, but let autumn bold,
With universal tinge of sober gold,
Be all about me when I make an end.
. . . .
Upon the sides of Latmos was outspread
A mighty forest, for the moist earth fed
So plenteously all weed-hidden roots
Into o'er hanging boughs and precious fruits.
And it had gloomy shades, sequestered deep,
Where no man went . . . (*KCP*, 122–23)

Generously partaking of the unsolicited piece of advice that he would eventually tender to Shelley ("load every rift of your subject with ore") Keats not only does that but also bares the device within the poem itself; his production quota of fifty lines per day is openly avowed in the verse paragraph's curious opening ("Many and many verses").[34] This inherently capitalist mode of production seems less to aim at tendering the resulting commodity to a literary marketplace already flooded with poetic articles of every conceivable kind, however, than to expose the seriously damaged aura of the modern vernacular poetic word. Hence "Keats's materialism" does not involve 'a materialist poetics' that yields 'materialist knowledge' but the eruption of a materialist disposition through the faultlines of an idealist (humanist and aestheticist) poetics" (Pyle 1995, 139).

Imaginative writing no longer secures its social effects through a laborious genealogy of primordial feelings, tranquil recollections, and their diligent transcription. Rather, it unfolds performatively through forms whose authority pivots on their vivid literariness rather than on their referential faithfulness vis-à-vis some putative antecedent experience. Such is the clear implication of "Adam's dream," that most congenial parable of Keatsian *poiesis* ("he awoke and found it truth"). For Keatsian beauty is the act of formalization grown wholly self-aware of its own arbitrary and "groundless" nature and, consequently, of its articulate dissent from the popular axiom (still reverberating in the projects of new historicism and cultural studies) that art has to be politically accountable: "What the imagination seizes as Beauty must be truth—whether it existed before or not" (*LJK*, 1: 185–86). Writing to John Taylor, Keats concedes that a famous passage from *Endymion* ("Wherein lies Happiness?") "must I think have appeared . . . as a thing almost of mere words" (ibid., 218). Yet the abject status of the word—its referential vacuity—also grants it increased, quasi-talismanic powers in the eyes of a radical formalist for whom truth can never be anchored in an operation of reference and its underlying premise of a fundamental correspondence between word and object. Rather, the truth of an utterance, and consequently its sole claim to social validity and political relevance, lies in its "intensity" ("The excellence of every Art is its intensity, capable of making all disagreeables evaporate" [ibid., 192]). It is telling to observe Keats restate and reflexively sharpen this position within the same sentence when, in a letter of January 1818, he writes: "with a great poet the sense of Beauty overcomes every other consideration, *or rather obliterates every other consideration*" (ibid., 194; emphasis added).

Arguably, the most elaborate image of the Keatsian axiom ("that which is creative must create itself" [ibid., 374]) can be found in a letter of February 1818. Rejecting the genealogical conception of originality and socially exemplary cognition associated with Wordsworth and Coleridge, Keats develops an expressly constructivist aesthetic that is to serve, not as a refuge from the real but as a dynamic principle for salvaging the real from the calcified Wordsworthian and Burkean regime of memory and custom: "Memory should not be called knowledge—Many have original minds who do not think it—they are led away by Custom—Now it appears to me that almost any Man may like the Spider spin from his own inwards his own airy Citadel—the points of leaves and twigs on which the Spider begins her work are few and she fills the Air with a beautiful circuiting: man should be content with as few points to tip the fine Webb of his Soul and weave a tapestry empyrean-full of Symbols for his spiritual eye, of softness for his spiritual touch, of space for his wandering[,] of distinctness for his Luxury" (ibid., 231–32).

Keats's implicit avant-gardism does not posit poetic language as a means of escape from the melancholic knowledge of terminally insoluble social and economic antagonisms. Rather, it posits literary form as a self-authorizing and endlessly dynamic principle of reflexive simulation, a principle of incessantly generative and consumptive productivity that operates outside the scope of all referential obligation ("as few points to tip the fine Webb"). Keats's tapestry seems to weave itself and pointedly disavows any referential and sociopolitical obligation. Instead, the overtly constructed form of poetic writing simulates tactile ("spiritual touch") and natural properties ("leaves and twigs") as means for conjuring up distinctive psychological qualities in an empirical world whose objects of possible experience have all dissolved into commodities. Long before Benjamin's profound insight into the language of the German baroque as the "*facies hippocratica* of history as a petrified, primordial landscape," Keats's poetic idiom enacts that critical insight in poetic form by visiting on the objective world and its inhabitants the reflexive knowledge of their damaged aura and irreversible self-alienation.

Foreshadowing Thorstein Veblen, Walter Benjamin, and Theodor Adorno, many of William Hazlitt's essays similarly view the exhausted interiority of the modern metropolitan subject as a direct consequence of the commodification of styles, expressive conventions, and a ubiquitous print culture. In such pieces as "On the Literary Character" (1813) and "Of Londoners and Country People" (1823), Hazlitt offers an intricately melancholic portrayal of Regency print culture that could just as plausibly have emerged from the pen of John Keats. The printed book, Hazlitt remarks, seems to "place the object at a distance, and embellish it at pleasure," while simultaneously suspending the reading subject in a "dim twilight existence" (*HSW*, 8: 134). For both, Keats and Hazlitt, this key feature of Regency print culture also serves as the premise for a subtle analysis of individual and group psychology in this aggressively capitalist and incipiently post-romantic era: "Wherever there is a very large assemblage of persons who have no other occupation but to amuse themselves . . . all profound thought, and all serious affection, will be discarded from their society" (*HSW*, 2: 131). For Hazlitt, the "constant intercourse with books" and "constant pursuit of little gratifications" inexorably atrophies the very notion of "individuality" in a highly stratified capitalist society and so exposes it the antagonisms intrinsic to that term. "Abstraction and refinement" in social and material practice begets indifferent, exchangeable subjectivities, such that "there is no difference between M. Grimm [i.e., Friedrich Melchior, to whose 1812–14 *Correspondence* Hazlitt responds] and the giddy girl" (ibid., 132). Yet, contrary to what one might expect, Hazlitt's objective is not to plead with or cajole the urban body politic into rehabilitating its imperiled psyche. Rather, he advocates an intensification of this new ephemeral and phantasmagoric relationship between self and world through "the *intellectual* dissipation of literature and of literary society. . . . It is the province of literature to anticipate the dissipation of real objects, and to increase it. It creates a fictitious restlessness and craving after variety, by creating a fictitious world around us, and by hurrying us, not only through all the mimic scenes of life, but by plunging us into the endless labyrinths of imagination" (ibid., 133). However, belated, lapsed, and atrophied in sensibility, Regency England, Hazlitt tells us, can only ever attain self-awareness through highly mediated symbolic practices and professional modes of representation (journalism, reading, conversation, fashion, flattery, etc.) that, upon closer inspection, turn out to have produced that subject's "character" in the first place. It is in the often disingenuous, though never uninteresting, theater of public conversation and private reading that emotions are "virtual" and figural sensu stricto. With the self-conscious artifice of "literariness" as its veritable apotheosis, print culture reconfigures subject and world as equally and purposely unreal. Here feelings, perceptions, desires, and especially expressive practices are all "seen through that general medium which reduces them to individual insignificance" (*HSW*, 2: 135).

Hazlitt's thesis is more fully developed in his 1823 "Of Londoners and Country People," an essay remarkable for its explicit and self-conscious mobilization of aesthetic and perceptual categories for the purpose of sketching the elusive psychological profile and, hence, political coherence of an entire social class. Mocking "Mr. Blackwood"'s divisive conception of the Cockney "as a person who has happened at any time to live in London, and who is not a Tory," Hazlitt opposes such reductive views of London's politically volatile lower-class citizenry with a startlingly postmodern conception that, quite serendipitously, also furnishes a rationale for Keats's early poetics. Having "never travelled beyond the purlieus of the Metropolis," the Cockney's world is comprised of substitutes: "Primrose-Hill is the Ultima Thule of his most romantic desires; Greenwich Park stands him in stead of the Vales of Arcady" (*HSW,* 8: 61). Far from afflicting consciousness with feelings of social disenfranchisement, Hazlitt's principle of deliberate substitution reconfigures the material domain of London and its suburban retreats into an aggregate of essentially equivalent visual signs. Cued by his visual commerce with a cornucopia of material and social detail, the Cockney's unrelenting, though perpetually shifting, gaze transfigures such matter into a sign. "He sees every thing near, superficial, little, in hasty succession." For Hazlitt, the Cockney's peculiar power of sight as much constitutes a transcendental framework for all possible social experience as names an ordinary empirical habit. For the Cockney's gaze, involuntarily transfigures all matter into image out of habit. "Figures glide by as in a *camera obscura,*" and the shopman, though "nailed all day behind the counter," from where he "sees hundreds and thousands of gay, well-dressed people pass," nonetheless "enjoys their liberty and gaudy fluttering pride." To Cockneys—regardless of whether they dwell in Lambeth, Cheapside, or Highgate—these are not simply anonymous and impenetrable others.

Hazlitt's verdict on such sights, absorbed as an endless stream of moving pictures (an "endless phantasmagoria," in which people and things only ever "swell into reality" as images [ibid., 61, 63]), anticipates Walter Benjamin's shock of a cinematic modernity, in which the unconscious dissolves all economic and class distinctions into equivalent moving quasi-celluloid images.[35] Indeed, Keats's epistolary reference to "the Spider spin[ning] from his own inwards his own airy citadel" (*LJK* 1: 231) resonates with Hazlitt's image of the real Cockney as simultaneously "the poorest creature in the world, the most literal, the most mechanical, and yet he too lives in a world of romance—a fairyland of his own. . . . and though a dwarf in stature, his person swells out and expands into *ideal* importance and borrowed magnitude" (ibid., 62).

What makes Hazlitt's argument so intriguing and relevant for present purposes is its conception of psychological depth as a fantasy achieved at the expense of what might be called the dematerialization of the world. The restless, quasi-mechanical agency of sight in Hazlitt's essay fully corresponds to Keats's compulsive assimilation of the material world to the virtual realm of his poetic "tapestry empyrean." In what appears an outright inversion or, perhaps, perversion of the creation myth, the melancholic gift of the Cockney consists in his manic decreation of his material sphere, its conversion into "phantasmagoria." The result is a self-consciously artificial world, one where empirical perception positively *enacts* (rather than counters) fantasy—the flesh become word. If there is a melancholic dimension to Hazlitt's Cockney psychology, it involves the latent knowledge of the perceptual phantasmagoria as just that—an artificial fabric of visual markers that are, for all intents and purposes, interchangeable and hence intrinsically "fallen." Such is the price exacted for the Cockney's furtive acquisition of an interiority that no longer *expresses* "fantasy" outward but, rather, recognizes itself *as* that fantasy. For Hazlitt and Keats, the substitutive logic of that fantasy deploys semiotic equivalences so as to erase all material and social distinctions. Hazlitt himself italicizes the point: "*Your true Cockney is your only true leveller*" (*HSW*, 8: 62). The result is a radically new, postmodern subjectivity. For "fantasy" here does not name something to which an otherwise intact subject has given expression. Rather, it is *only by means of and as that fantasy* that Hazlitt's and Keats's subjects experience their life world and acquire self-awareness. Marjorie Levinson's shrewd thesis, namely, that "what was, initially a substitute *for* a grim life became for Keats a substitute life: a real life of substitute things—simulacra" (Levinson 1988, 9), while coming close, does not fully capture the point. For neither Keats nor Hazlitt's Cockney shopkeepers and footmen could accept the distinction as valid, and to do so would mean retaining a traditional (Marxist) juxtaposition of "real" and "substitute." Yet it is precisely this critical distinction whose legitimacy "fantasy" by its very nature disavows. For, as Levinson herself concedes, fantasy names a process in which a subject is *reflexively* engaged, and it must therefore be sharply distinguished from the Marxist concept of illusion or ideological (self-)deception. Keats and Hazlitt's model of the Cockneys' substitute perceptions and identity cannot be opposed to some alternate, materially "real" acts of perception. Rather, in its reflexively poetic, textual manifestation, the logic of phantasmagoria has established itself as a new, quasi-postmodern framework conditioning perception and cognition alike. Structured like a language, its artificial and constructed nature has been effaced, indeed, rendered invisible, by habit. Once again revealing his acute sense for the Cockney's distinctive psychology, Hazlitt observes how by "com[ing] so often into contact with fine persons and things . . . he rubs off a little of the gilding, and is surcharged with a sort of second-hand, vapid, *tingling*, troublesome self-importance." The cumulative result is a purely fantastic interiority "by proxy" (*HSW*, 8: 61; emphasis added).

While conceding the Cockney's flamboyantly superficial aesthetic—"his imagination is jaded," and he is "pert, raw, ignorant, conceited, ridiculous, shallow, contemptible" (ibid.)—Hazlitt also draws out the psychological rewards of such a mode of being, as well as its latent political force. Like Keats, he too aims "to construct a counterpublic sphere" (Rajan 1998, 343), stripping material things of the symbolic charisma that they may ordinarily claim as unique artifacts, personal property, or "spiritual" values and rendering them interchangeable, not to say indifferent, markers within the deregulated sphere of his uninhibited social gazing. Yet this practice also enacts a type of ressentiment that Nietzsche was to analyze so powerfully. For there is an unconsciously vengeful thrust to Hazlitt's and Keats's anti-aesthetic that exposes the full extent to which the socioeconomic structure of Regency England has estranged matter from itself by turning it into commodity. Keats's complex meditation on the conversion of all things material into mere appearance in "Lamia" is a fine example of such poetic ressentiment (which we shall explore in more detail in the work of Heine). A closer exploration of that poem's endless play of substitutions and economic exchanges would also have to take into account the Bullion Debate over whether or not to reinstate the gold standard that had been suspended since 1797, though always with the promise that government bonds issued to finance the long campaign against Napoleonic France would eventually be redeemed in specie.[36] Such a conversion of romanticism's ultimate economic phantasmagoria, paper money, into genuine substance (gold), of course, never took place. Yet what the radical populist and publisher William Cobbett indicted as a government-perpetrated pyramid scheme—"a paper-bubble" which "the Borough Bank can *never pay in specie* without blowing up the whole system" (Cobbett 4: 135)—becomes for Keats and Hazlitt an irreversible condition of cultural and economic existence after Waterloo. However melancholy its implications, Hazlitt and Keats recognize the phantasmagorical constitution of Regency society to be so deeply and firmly entrenched by 1817 that any critique must formally mirror that very state of affairs. "Ressentiment" is the apt name for a mode of critique that no longer seeks redress, no longer hopes for a return to some "natural" state, but, instead, can only ruminate on the antagonistic and mendacious logic that sustains the political status quo. As Nietzsche was to remark, "to confabulate 'another' world makes no sense whatsoever unless an instinctual longing for libel, deprecation, insinuation of life itself powerfully works in us. In that case we take revenge against life itself by means of the 'phantasmagoria' of another, 'better' life."[37] In a very similar sense, Hazlitt's Cockney also thrives psychologically and politically: "His senses keep him alive," and as a result

> man in London becomes, as Mr. Burke has it, a sort of "public creature". He lives in the eye of the world, and the world in his. . . . In London there is a *public;* and each man is part of it. We are gregarious, and affect the kind. We have a sort of abstract existence; and a community of ideas and knowledge (rather than local proximity) is the bond of society and good-fellowship. This is one great cause of the tone of political feeling in large and populous cities. There is here a visible body-politic, a type and image of that huge Leviathan the State. We comprehend that vast denomination, the *People,* of which we see a tenth part daily moving before us; and by having our imaginations emancipated from our petty interests and personal dependence, we learn to venerate ourselves as men, and to respect the rights of human nature. (*HSW,* 8: 70)

Cognizant of the ongoing erosion of his or her own interiority, the modern urban subject lives a volatile, restless, and palpably unreal proxy existence (of which more later). Keats's and Hazlitt's avatars roam the metropolis—which resembles the melancholy "paper world" of the baroque so volubly deplored by Goethe's Faust—like Bram Stoker's undead: "the life of a mere man of letters and sentiment appears to be at best but a living death; a dim twilight existence: a sort of wandering about in an Elysian fields of our own making; a refined, spiritual, disembodied state, like that of the ghosts of Homer's heroes" (*HSW,* 2: 134). Well before Baudelaire, Hazlitt expressly fuses the phantasmagoric world of capitalist print and commodity culture with an affective model comprising melancholy and boredom as the dominant speculative and perceptual responses to the world.

For Benjamin, boredom constitutes "the external surface of unconscious events" and, as such, consists "in the readiness to savor, on one's own, an arbitrary succession of sensations." It is "a warm gray fabric lined on the inside with the most lustrous and colorful of silks" (Benjamin 1999, 106; 804, 105). This uncannily reproduces Keats's portrayal of himself sitting "by my fire after a day's effort, as the dusk approached, and *a gauzey veil seemed dimming all things*" and surrendering himself to the phantasmagoric as "faces of the mighty dead crowd into my room" (*LJK,* 1: 124; emphasis added). Overall, Keats's and Hazlitt's writings significantly prefigure Benjamin's and the Frankfurt School's conception of a formalist aesthetic that aims not to escape the real but, on the contrary, to gauge—both in thought and feeling—the depth of the subject's alienation from the real. Their texts linger over the phantasmagoric textures of late romantic modernity, a world composed of derivative print commodities and "frivolous" sentiments. Such substitute formations can no longer be dismissed as (pathogenic or merely accidental) distractions but, instead, actively promote distraction to a self-willed and self-created psychological condition. Unlike Wordsworth, Byron, or Marx, who—however disparate their political and cultural visions—read the subject's relegation to the "infernal din" of urban cultural and capitalist hyperactivity as a fall of near-biblical proportions, Keats and Hazlitt find an enabling dimension in melancholy.[38] For them, melancholy amounts to a quasi-intentional affective knowledge about the unreality and futility of all things, including any Tory, liberal, or socialist utopia that aspires to redeem the individual from finite, temporal, and chimerical perceptions and feelings by some programmatic and concerted action. Instead, Hazlitt's closing paean sketches a virtual Cockney republic held together by self-consciously imaginary modes of sensation, pleasure, and cognition. In ways not again seen until Baudelaire's *Fleurs du Mal,* Hazlitt's and Keats's phantasmagorias celebrate the demise of the traditional opposition of literal and figural properties. For both, life has become simulated and textual to its very core. Such a position, moreover, is not conceived of as contradicting or denying the reality of the material and empirical world; rather, it rigorously qualifies the terms of our access to that world.

If this ostensibly "new" cultural epistemology reinstates the baroque affect of melancholy, albeit without its onetime moral stigma of acedia, its most conspicuous casualty is arguably the erotic. Throughout Keats's short career, from the 1817 *Poems* to the title poem of his 1820 *Lamia* volume (to say nothing of "The Eve of St. Agnes"), one finds a startling enjambment of affective purity and deliberate imitativeness, of high pathos and generic writing, and its principal target is the erotic. From Petrarchan humanism to its petit-bourgeois afterlife in Keats's and Austen's time, the erotic appears as the last, sacrosanct bastion of authentic and permanent "human" meanings, the fantasy of a self immune to socioeconomic and psychological antagonisms. Yet for Keats—and, following him, Hazlitt, Byron, Heine, Baudelaire, and Flaubert—eros is the frontier beyond which a poetics of melancholy is to be extended. Far from designating a naïve and cherished affective domain, the erotic becomes a heuristic fiction by means of which the reading and writing subjects of a disillusioned Regency culture may gauge the full extent of their self-alienation. For Keats's new, reflexive embrace of self-alienation as a negative yet powerful source of formal-aesthetic productivity—what Marjorie Levinson calls his "double alienation from the textual interior and from his audience" (1988, 21)—reorients the erotic away from the material possession of an "object" and toward its simulation in poetic images about whose constructed proxy character neither author nor reader can entertain any illusions. With melancholic abandon, Keats's poetry treats romance as a locus where the alienated individual acquires reflexive distance from his or her abjection by means of an overtly performative and serialized model of literary production and consumption. An early and revealing example can be found in the poem that succeeds Keats's "Specimen of an Induction to a Poem," the short and abortive romance entitled "Calidore." Having embarked on his nervous quest for sensation, the protagonist's "healthful spirit eager and awake" paddles across the lake in what unfolds as a restless metonymic series of sensory distractions greedily absorbed so as to keep nothingness at bay. His alter ego momentarily surfaces in the form of a "black-winged swallow" that "dips so refreshingly its wings, and breast / 'Gainst the smooth surface, and to mark anon / The widening circles into nothing gone" (*KCP*, 36–37). To Calidore's frantically responsive gaze, all objects, regardless of their material particularity or social significance, "looked out invitingly" (*KCP*, 38). Yet precisely their equivalence and indifference to the protagonist's consumptive gaze also betrays their allegorical status. With its "lonely turret, shattered and outworn, / . . . too proud to morn / Its lost grandeur," the castle that marks the ostensible goal of Calidore's sensual quest also attests to the poem's blatantly utopian perspective. Keats's ersatz medievalism signifies the unreality not only of this particular narrative but the generic futility of romance and, by extension, of a paradigm of literature claiming to originate in authentic sensation and to sublate it into permanent and exemplary cultural meanings and values. The moment of this crisis, where melancholy reveals itself as a constitutive dimension of literariness in a terminally profaned world, comes as Calidore abruptly enters onto the scene whose depiction of chivalric love brings to mind the flamboyantly cheap props and overwrought affective stylizations of Tim Burton's 1994 *Ed Wood,* and indeed those of that B-movie director himself:

> Into the court he sprang
> Just as two noble steeds and palfreys twain
> Were slanting out their necks with loosened rein,
> While from beneath the threatening portcullis

They brought their happy burthens. What a kiss,
What gentle squeeze he gave each lady's hand!
How tremblingly their delicate ankles spanned!
Into how sweet a trance his soul was gone,
While whisperings of affection
Made him delay to let their tender feet
Come to the earth. With an incline so sweet
From their low palfreys o'er his neck they bent,
And whether there were tears of languishment,
Or that the evening dew had pearled their tresses,
He feels a moisture on his cheek and blesses,
With lips that tremble and with glistening eye,
All the soft luxury
That nestled in his arms. A dimpled hand,
Fair as some wonder out of fairly land,
Hung from his shoulder like the drooping flowers
Of whitest cassia, fresh from summer showers,
And this he fondled with his happy cheek
As if for joy he would no further seek— (*KCP*, 40)

The prosody's slackness and off-handedness, the willful abandon with which rhymes are either wholly predictable ("flowers . . . showers") haphazardly slanted ("eye . . . luxury,") or imposed in brazen indifference to sound, meter, or sense ("gone . . . affection") cumulatively maneuvers Keats's readers into a delicate and potentially volatile interpretive position. For the poetry in question is not "bad" in any accidental, pathological, or socially conditioned sense. Rather, its badness appears deliberate, "constructed," thereby intimating a new strain in nineteenth-century cultural production. Keats's "new romance," for which "Isabella" and "Lamia" offer more developed and equally grotesque examples, infuses a new rhetorical strain that proves covertly hostile and corrupting of middle-brow culture precisely because of its hypersimulation of those artistic fetishes (e.g., lyric poetry, romance, opera, etc.) by and with which such a culture identifies itself. Like the equivalent of a modern computer virus, "Calidore" shows Keats "creatively hacking" (Alan Liu's recent term) into the established and deeply conventional network of recognizably "literary" writing. The result is a model of romance whose internal bemoaning of its own antiquated, indeed anachronistic, status as a literary genre (and as the generic marker of "literariness" per se) recalls Freud's characterization of the melancholiac's laments as "plaints that are really complaints" (Freud 1963b, 169: "Klagen sind Anklagen"; translation modified / *FSA*, 3: 202). Keats's generic writing opposes the generic certitudes of Regency literary culture with an inherently anti-literary strain. The prereflexive domain of feelings, hitherto the linchpin of cultural value and "good human purposes" (Ricks), now appears as an epistemologically specious, because highly constructed, good. The estrangement of feeling from its presumptive and cherished immediacy unfolds in Keats's poetry through image simulacra that operate on the principle of citation rather than reference, and through narratives fueled by the associative (rhymed) and hence equivalent materiality of words and phrases rather than experience and wisdom.

While such an aesthetic spells death for the seemingly timeless and sacrosanct notion of eros, it also opens up vistas on a new eroticism—one textually mediated and possessed as a fantasy. In this new guise, eros subsists on image simulacra mechanically produced and frantically projected into a metonymic series. The resulting narrative no longer originates in experience but, instead, appears fueled by second-order images that confirm the sudden decline of experience in capitalist culture. The conspicuously abortive nature of Keats's narrative efforts, especially prominent in *Hyperion*, suggests that, like the storyteller in Walter Benjamin's eponymous essay, the romantic poet is also experiencing the death of "the epic side of truth, wisdom." In the profusion of essentially equivalent and interchangeable images, Keats's poetry attests, not only to the atrophying of experience and its displacement by ephemeral "information," but also, in its fragmentary and spasmodic narrative ambitions, to the "profound perplexity of the living" (Benjamin 1968, 87). Like Austen's novelistic project, Keats's poetry captures eros as a subtly dystopic, strictly "literary," and overdetermined sign. While more aggressive and flamboyant in its formal demeanor, Keats's poetry echoes Austen's and Stendhal's novelistic capturing of eros as a dystopic, because overdetermined and manifestly self-conscious, "literary" sign. Erotic experience no longer constitutes the origin of narrative but a quasi-intended, fantasized effect of literary production and consumption. If "to write" fiction means "to carry the incommensurable to extremes in the representation of human life" (ibid.), then, beginning with Keats, and continuing in the work of Heine and Baudelaire, literariness is recognized and embraced with melancholy satisfaction as a new type of sensation: *feeling by proxy.* The very slackness of Keats's early verse exposes its underlying motivation—namely, to disestablish or (in Keats's happy phrase) to "unwrite" the social value of literariness. Keats's text introduces each discrete image as overtly substitutive and hence interchangeable with all surrounding images. The swallow that dips its "wings and breast so refreshingly" into the water is not a swallow but a linguistic marker valued for its capacity to simulate material, tactile sensation and, in so doing, to keep at bay a metaphysical sense of nothingness that forever hovers in the margins of Keats's poetry threatening to reassert its metaphysical rights. Arbitrary details, such as the "dimpled hand," surface inasmuch as they may be indifferently rhymed with, and stand as metonyms for, the utopian plenitude of romance ("fair as some wonder out of fairy land"). Likewise, it no longer signifies whether "moisture" on the protagonist's cheek derives from some female's "tears of languishment, / Or that the evening dew had pearled their tresses." With the epistemological scaffolding of cause and effect, origin and telos, and the foundation of moral value wholly leveled, Keats's writing mediates all material experience as literary and prima facie verbal matter. Susceptible of endless manipulation and metonymic extension, such literature enables the Keatsian (or Hazlitt's Cockney) subject to realize the fantasy of "a life of sensations" in socially recognized form. Transposing Benjamin's theory of baroque melancholy and allegory to the mid-nineteenth-century bourgeois domain, Adorno's early work on Kierkegaard (whose hyperreflexive attitude toward affect and desire strongly resembles Keats's) helps articulate the proxy character of affect once we begin to think its representative images in historical-dialectical fashion:

> Nature and reconciliation communicate in melancholy; from it the "wish" arises dialectically, and its illusion is the reflection of hope. It is illusion because not happiness itself but only its images are given to the wish and in them the wish, which is nourished by them, is at the same time filled with longing because, according to Kierkegaard, the eye, the organ of the wish "is the most difficult to satisfy." This insatiability as aesthetic . . . this [aesthetic] sphere, painfully furrowed by a subjectivity that leaves its traces behind in it without every mastering it, receives its structure from images that are present for the wish, without having been produced by it, for the wish itself originates in them. This realm of images constitutes the absolute opposite of the traditional Platonic realm. It is not eternal, but historical-dialectical; it does not lie in perfect transcendence beyond nature, but dissolves darkly into nature; it is not imageless truth, but promises paradoxically unreachable truth in opposition to its semblance; it does not open

> itself to eros, but shines forth in the moment of disintegration [*Zerfall*]—in the historical disintegration of the mythical unity of unmediated existence. The figures that assemble themselves at this point carry marks of a suffocating, objectless inwardness.[39]

Adorno's lucid characterization of late romantic melancholy and its radically altered conception of the written word and literariness urges us to attend to the constructed, deliberate, and intrinsically lucid nature of Keatsian text, rather than settling for the circular model of a hypostatized "early" Keats whose writings betray a likewise hypostatized "badness." In this alternative reading, Keats's poetics of the "shabby genteel" (Byron's phrase) emerges neither as the psychological default value of access to social and educational venues foreclosed (Levinson) nor as a temporary want of aesthetic maturity and moral refinement soon to be compensated (Stillinger, Vendler) nor, finally, as a fortunate fall into an earnestly forthright Cockney culture whose guileless and flamboyant expressiveness some critics (Bayley, Ricks) read as serendipitously yielding Keats's distinctive grasp of the human and, hence, as contributing to the moral-aesthetic edification of his reading audiences, starting with the publication of his *Poems* in 1817.

Instead, Keats's early poetry unfolds as an internally consistent, shrewd, and deliberate body of work that is by and large continuous with his so-called "later" writing, produced just two years afterward. From his beginnings, Keats consciously and deliberately aims to unravel the affective moorings of high romantic argument and, by extension, to level the self-privileging middle-brow conception of literary value as esoteric, spiritually and formally complex, and sheltering its projected middle-class readers from the taint of the commodity culture on which their material affluence, social exclusivity, and moral righteousness are based. To that end, his poetry depicts dismayingly interchangeable protagonists—Calidore, Lorenzo, Porphyro, Lycius, the knight-at-arms in "La Belle Dame sans Merci"—plotting their improbable advances on a world at once idolized yet redoubtable, materially alluring yet morally repulsive. The pointlessness of such quest-romance is thrown into relief by the metadrama of the Cockney author who can possess this middle-brow literary culture only by exposing its unconscious commodity character through a technique of purposely "impure," serial, and compulsively eroticized reproduction. At the levels both of *sujet* and *récit*—that is, as the production of a story that mediates (allegorizes) the story of its own production—alienation and ressentiment come into view as the Janus faces of melancholy. Keats's deracinated Cockney protagonists covertly indict a depraved world, to which they relate by reproducing and deflating its value through acts of verbal "finery." The psychological type that is the linchpin of Keats's programmatically abortive "new" romances ("Calidore" being just an early instance) thus remains suspended between a deep, ineffable knowledge (a Wordsworthian and Coleridgean poetics) and a material experience of literary traditions and middle-brow notions of cultural work as permanently closed to him, as well as hostile to his manic simulation of such "work" within his own oeuvre. Having thus far followed the Spenserian precedent "with due reverence," the speaker ultimately "start[s] with awe at mine own strange pretence." Indeed, Keats's poetics of possession-by-simulation begins on the first page of his 1817 volume, which bears an engraved portrait of Spenser.[40]

"A figurative version of our native tongue": Keats's Literary Simulations"

Long before Adorno or even Kierkegaard, Keats perplexes and disturbs his readers with protagonists whose inwardness is awash in substitute feelings, all packaged in ready-made, pseudoliterary forms that leave the category of "experience" denuded of any intuitive or perceptual specificity. With this remarkably consistent formal-rhetorical habit of demoting Platonic *eidos* to *physis*, the Keatsian text disestablishes the claims of an earlier romantic paradigm of literature as originating in a timeless, inalienable, and socially beneficial type of affective experience. In premising all inwardness on material sensation, Keats's 1817 *Poems* place their subjects in a simultaneously addictive and distracted relation to material sensations that are paradoxically both specific *and* generic. Yet because material sensation in Keats does not merely seek to appease an ineffable subjective longing but, through its compulsive rhetorical enactment as the prototypical Cockney's "gossamer-work" (John Gibson Lockhart, quoted in Reiman, 3, 1: 92) actually reveals itself as the very ground of such inwardness, it can never reach a state of rest or contentment. Rather, through Keats's persistent and self-conscious transmutation of "old prose in modern rhyme more sweet" (*KCP*, 335), literature becomes the figural proxy for a notion of inward sensation that is not its ground or "source" but its vicarious and perilously devalued effect or product. In this manner, the startlingly generic work of Keatsian romance also exposes the illusory nature of subjectivity that appears to gain access to its own interiority only through an inherently contrived pathos. To recall Keats's late simulation of life in "This living hand," his lyrics *are* that hand—that is, an "earnest grasping" that performatively *instantiates* the subject's interiority. If eloquence begets pathos, it no longer refers to such pathos (by the rhetorical figure of analepsis) as the putative source of its expressive urgency. Keats's poetry establishes an almost postmodern model of feeling as intrinsically supplemental, with the generic textures of his romances providing evidence of a subjectivity that embraces the artifice of literature as the sole remaining yardstick by which to gauge the scope of its own alienation. As Shelley had put it, love is a compensatory quest undertaken once "we find within our thoughts the chasm of an insufficient void" (473).

It is this conscious and deliberate recognition of life and literature as equally and thoroughly mediated processes, as only ever affording their subjects a proxy existence, that resonates in Keats's programmatic declaration of how he means to conquer with "the armour of words and the Sword of Syllables" (*LJK,* 1: 157). Keats's early verse epistle to Charles Cowden Clarke (September 1816) offers an unvarnished transcript of his ambivalent quest to be "in the mouth of fame," a quest that made poetry "a Refuge as well as a Passion" (*LJK,* 1: 139; 141):

> Because my thoughts were never free and clear,
> And little fit to please the classic ear;
>
> . . . .
>
> to try my dull, unlearned quill.
> Nor should I now, but that I've known you long,
> That you first taught me all the sweets of song:
> The grand, the sweet, the terse, the free, the fine;
> What swelled with pathos, and what right divine;
> Spenserian vowels that elope with ease,
> And float along like birds o'er the summer seas;
> Miltonian storms, and more, Miltonian tenderness;
> Michael in arms, and more, meek Eve's fair slenderness. (*KCP,* 55–56)

With its characteristic entwining of literary and erotic possession in the closing line, the veritable signature of Keats 1817 *Poems,* the fetish character of literature per se is not accidentally but deliberately underscored. Literature emerges in the lines quoted above as a supplement to an interiority that cannot exist independently or even be conceived except for the mournful baroque catalogue of poetic passions ("The grand, the sweet, the terse, the free, the fine") attainable only as a generic inventory of epic, romantic, chivalric, satiric, or balladic locutions. Fundamentally, then, Keats relates to writing as a material craft, as the insistent and strategic manipulation of verbal matter. The approach here is self-consciously mediated, originating in and driven by the profound recognition of language as *res* and, as remains to be seen, to some extent also as *res publica.* Arguably, some basic grammatical categories make the case most efficiently: nouns are converted into adjectives; adjectives into nouns; adjectives into adverbs; singulars into plurals, with each instance amounting both to a distortion of grammatical and a violation of social norms:

- *Nouns into adjectives:* "lawny crest" (*KCP,* 3); "spherey strains" (*KCP,* 11); "lawny fields" and "pebbly water" (*KCP,* 17); "moonbeamy air" (*KCP,* 18)
- *Adjectives into nouns:* "The melting softness of that face, / The beaminess of those bright eyes" (*KCP,* 7); "morning shadows streaking into slimness" (*KCP,* 17); "sips its freshness" (*KCP,* 17)
- *Verbs into adverbs:* "The light dwelt o'er the scene so lingerlingly" (*KCP,* 36)
- *Adjectives into adverbs:* "shining beamily" (*KCP,* 4); "scantily hold out the hand" (*KCP,* 21)
- *Singulars into plurals:* "slopings of verdure" (*KCP,* 3); "archings of her eye-lids charm" (*KCP,* 31); "slopings of verdure" (*KCP,* 5); "shiftings of the mighty winds" (*KCP,* 32)
- *Cockney neologisms, vulgarisms, and eroticisms:* "leafiness" (*KCP,* 26); "boundly reverence" (*KCP,* 31); "full often" (*KCP,* 37); "untainted gushes" (*KCP,* 3); "a trembling diamond" (*KCP,* 15); "goodly states" (*KCP,* 18); ". . . when I sit *me* down to rhyme" (*KCP,* 9); "rich lys'd goblets, that incessant run" (*KCP,* 11); "the music of her nimble toes" and "fondling nips" and "tremulous eyes" (*KCP,* 22f.); "Catch the white-handed nymphs . . ." (*KCP,* 74); "The beaminess of those bright eyes" (*KCP,* 7); "passionate gushes" and "moonbeamy air" (*KCP,* 18); "the lance points slantingly / Athwart the morning air" and "the half-seen mossiness of the linnet's nest" (*KCP,* 34); "The light dwelt o'er the

scene so lingerlingly" (*KCP*, 36); "The sidelong view of swelling leafiness" (*KCP*, 38); "tears of languishment" (*KCP*, 40)

Keats's poignant remark that "words are images of thoughts refined" (*KCP*, 23) and that "I look upon fine phrases like a lover" (*LJK*, 2: 139) reveals his consciously manipulative relationship to verbal matter, a position that seems to belie readings of his 1817 *Poems* as outgrowth of an as yet immature or overheated or "manic" adolescent phase. What emerges from this catalogue is Keats's approach to literary language as wholly material and, consequently, as the unconscious other of those idealizing purposes attributed to literature by the preceding generation of writers (Wordsworth, Coleridge, Southey). To Keats, literature is above all verbal matter, a potential aggregate of formal equivalences, which Roman Jakobson would much later identify as poetry's constitutive feature. Jakobson's well-known thesis tells us that poetry "projects the principle of equivalence from the axis of selection into the axis of combination." In precise inversion of the metalinguistic function, whose focus is on a given linguistic "code," the poetic function involves the mobilization of equivalences (synonymity, similarity, or strictly quantitative equations of syllables as "units of measure") to create a message whose meaning is surreptitiously, almost hypnotically fixated on the phonetic charisma of words and phrases.[41] As Jakobson observes, for example, "without its two dactylic words the combination '*in*nocent *by*stander' would hardly have become a hackneyed phrase" (Jakobson, 71–72). Yet by constituting itself as a "reiterative figure of sound" (Jakobson here draws on Gerard Manley Hopkins's influential conception), the poetic function is hardly limited to poetry in any narrow or generic sense. In fact, the formal characteristic not only involves the mobilization of material equivalences but also intensifies them to the point where meanings of otherwise disparate signifying units begin to converge. Jakobson's use of "hackneyed" for the abovementioned colloquialism thus hints at a disconcerting, if also inescapable, propensity of formalized speech, namely, to allow "equivalence" to collapse into "indifference" (tellingly, the German *Gleichgültigkeit* can mean either). Indeed, to accept Jakobson's eventual conclusion that "equivalence in sound, projected into the sequence as its constitutive principle, inevitably involves semantic equivalence" also means to endorse his earlier observation that, in promoting "the palpability of signs," poetry effectively "deepens the fundamental dichotomy of signs and objects" (Jakobson, 83, 71). As M. R. Ridley said of "Isabella," "there are too many words which we feel uneasily are where they are not because Keats wanted their sense but because he needed their sound" (Ridley, 28).

With its serial emulation of literary effects, Keats's early poetry comes close to fulfilling both Jakobson's criteria for a metalingual *and* for a poetic operation. It throws into relief both the poetic code that dominated the reading culture of Regency England and the material base whose manipulation (into a sequence of equivalences) effectively produced the literary and affective values that define literariness around 1817. "A bowery nook / Will be elysium—an eternal book / Whence I may copy many a lovely saying / About the leaves and flowers" (*KCP*, 72). If "copying" down the verbal simulacra of material sensation from *books* renders the resulting textual signs at once equivalent and indifferent, the Keatsian text (even in its "early" phase) appears strangely aware of a poetics that is forever bound to widen the gap between sign and object. Take, for example, the long sequence of conjectured experiences ("were I in such a place, / I sure should pray / That naught less sweet might call my thoughts away, / Than the soft rustle of a maiden's gown"). Not only are these sensations overtly hypothetical, sustained only by literary signs that convey at once desire and frustration, affect and disaffection, but the litany of simulated experience is abruptly halted by an interjection that betrays the authorial detachment from the process of composition: ". . . as she leaves me may she often turn / Her fair eyes looking through her locks aubúrne. / *What next?* A tuft of evening primroses . . ." (*KCP*, 90; emphasis added). Though he probably never encountered Keats's work, Walter Benjamin captures the abject, hyperlucid textures of melancholia more honestly and perceptively than most of Keats's "critics." The baroque, he tells us, "expected that works of art could be absorbed in the midst of ordinary every day affairs, and devotion to them was less a private matter, for which account did not have to be given, than it was later to become. Reading was obligatory, and it was educational. The range of the products, their intentional bulkiness and lack of mystery should be understood as a correlative of such an attitude among the public" (Benjamin 1998, 181). In startling resemblance to baroque poetics, the Keatsian text, too, seeks "not so much to unveil material objects as to strip them naked. The emblematist does not present the essence implicitly, 'behind the image'. He drags the essence of what is depicted out before the image, in writing, as a caption, such as in the emblem-books, forms an intimate part of what is depicted" (ibid., 185).

The ultimate antagonist in the early Keats's radical reconceptualization of literary authority, however, was less a Coleridgean idea of complex inwardness than the cultural authority of the English language as expressed in its lyric tradition. Beginning with Milton and, as John Guillory has shown, steadily consolidated in the age of Gray and Johnson, the aesthetic and social valuation of English continued to increase, even as it appeared to drift further away from rhetorical and syntactic conventions associated with Latin and the Romance languages. Yet the emergence of English from its long period of aesthetic minority was premised on a strong bond, so powerfully reaffirmed in Milton and Gray, between the writer's capacious learning, authentic experience, and proper expression. If the revisions of Gray's "Elegy" had progressively anglicized the text between 1750 (the Eton MS version) and the revised and expanded text that had reached its twelfth edition by 1763, the authority of the text rested on its circumspect anglicizing of rhetorical models and countless citations and allusions that were yet recognizable. In short, the imagination of English as an aesthetically viable language was premised on the covert grounding of its locutions in classical sources of authority. Between 1750 and 1850, the institution of literary English and English literature (the durability of whose products remained as yet relatively unproven) remained premised on vestigial Latin authorities with which even writers like Gray, and to a lesser degree even Wordsworth, maintained delicately allusive commerce. The motive behind this amalgamation of modern and intrinsically professional models of vernacular writing with a canon of classical literary source texts is partly sociological. As Magali Larson notes, classical education around 1800 "served the professions . . . as the intellectual sanction which Oxford and Cambridge bestowed upon the gentry's hegemony . . . a gate keeping mechanism for the most prestigious professional roles."[42] The sedimentation of literary-historical continuities throughout a text by means of strategically placed allusions—particularly well executed in Wordsworth's *Prelude*—reassures an audience fundamentally uncertain of the criteria regulating literary value and the authority of its professional producer by offering "spot-translations" of modern verse into its putative classical sources. Christopher Anstey provided an unusually literal instance of such furtive relegitimation of a modern, vernacular poetics when, in 1762, he undertook to translate Gray's entire "Elegy" (back) into Latin. Some forty years later, Wordsworth commences the *Prelude* (1805) with careful allusions to Milton that once again betray the lingering obligation of English to identify the sources of its aesthetic and literary legitimacy.[43]

Keats's own relationship to classical materials has been subjected to close scrutiny. Nicholas Roe offers a particularly detailed and balanced account, including a judicious appraisal of the notorious depiction of Keats by the anonymous reviewer known as "Z" in *Blackwood's Edinburgh Magazine* (October 1819) as a writer possessed by "a sort of vague idea, that the Greeks were a most tasteful people, and that no mythology can be so finely adapted for the purposes of poetry as theirs."[44] The question is whether Keats aspired to classical learning or whether antiquity for him was rather a complex sign variously denoting a political utopia, linguistic immediacy, and a social order where beauty and art had (allegedly) not yet been usurped by commerce.

Keats's reading and writing habits point us in the right direction. As is well known, his principal sources of classical literary and mythological information were John Lemprière's *Classical Dictionary,* Joseph Spence's *Polymetis,* and Andrew Tooke's *The Pantheon . . . Fabulous Histories of the Heathen Gods, and the Other Most Illustrious Heroes of Antiquity*—in short, primers and reference works that captured antiquity in a digest-style, translated form that quite "evidently contrasted with tuition modeled on the practice at Eton" (Roe, 67). It would be precipitous to conclude, however, that his use of translation of classical Greek, Latin, and Renaissance authors (Homer, Virgil, Dante, Tasso, Ariosto, et al.) was merely a compromise. For though "his Homer was Chapman, his Dante was Cary, his Provençal ballads translations in an edition of Chaucer, his Boccacio Englished" (Levinson, 7), these were not simply the expedients of a young man who by the fall of 1818 had little reason to expect longevity. Rather, translation frees Keats's emergent authorial persona from the Procrustean bed of classical originals to which no modern lower-middle class writer could hope to fit himself without giving up his own distinctive modernity. A letter of 27 April 1818 to J. H. Reynolds shows Keats musing in highly equivocal terms on how "I long to feast upon old Homer as we have upon Shakespeare. And as I have lately upon Milton.—if you understood Greek, and would read me passages, now and then, explaining their meaning, 't would be, from its mistiness, perhaps a greater luxury than reading the thing one's self" (*LJK,* 1: 274). The foreign and classical text is specifically *not* approached as a model and exemplar but as a source of unfamiliar sensation and inspiration. The ancient and foreign languages are merely to furnish the stimulation that will help Keats devise a truly modern, vernacular, and autonomous poetic idiom.

A year later, Keats sharpens the point: "I shall never become attach'd to a foreign idiom so as to put it into my writings" (*LJK,* 2: 212). Challenging and if possible undoing the subservience of English literature to classical models was not only essential to Keats's future as a writer but also defined the means by which he might hope to advance toward that future. In other words, the Keatsian text does not accidentally or pathologically violate (or fall short of) classical models. Rather, it conceives a new, unapologetically vernacular literature precisely through a sustained, purposive, and readily legible deviation from these classical models. "There is no other crime, no mad assail / To make old prose in modern rhyme more sweet. / But it is done—succeed the verse or fail" (*KCP,* 335). The translation and transvaluation of classical models so defiantly expressed in "Isabella" is thus not a compensatory strategy. Far from reveling in a "life of substitute things" (Levinson 1988, 9), Keats's radically modern conception of literary Englishness is part of a stylistic insurrection that organizes his entire oeuvre. In some letters of 1819 that appear to revive his early project of an essay "On the limits of language," Keats imagines a "genuine English Idiom in English words" untainted by "French Idiom" (*LJK,* 2: 167) or Dantean symmetry. His projected literary language is also to prove its independence from "Chaucer's gallicisms." Even more, it seeks to extricate itself from Milton's *Paradise Lost,* that "grand Curiosity" of a "northern dialect accommodating itself to greek and latin inversions and intonations." Keats's dream of literary writing, that is, can only unfold in a utopian space impervious to cultural and poetic traditions and conventions, a space that Keats's poetry must therefore create and, in a virtual sense, also embody. Contrary models, such as poetry steeped in capacious historical learning (Milton) or in unique and inalienable experience (Wordsworth), would inevitably vanquish Keats's cultural and authorial persona from the outset. As Keats remarks of Milton, "Life to him would be death to me."

And yet, if Keats envisions a literary idiom beyond Milton's "corruption of our language"—freed from all the constraints of history, tradition, and *heteroglossia*—this model is not an absolutely private but, on the contrary, an utterly public language. It is public in the way that Thomas Chatterton's consummate act of literary forgery had placed its desperate producer in the eye of a public whose official policies of "taste" and "propriety" he knew would forever leave him disenfranchised. Keats's sonnet "To Chatterton" (written in early 1815) thus stakes his own literary and social authority on the posthumous defense, even rehabilitation, of Chatterton, who, after all, had dissembled his creative powers by projecting himself into the public sphere of letters only as the editor and commentator of his own texts. As Keats clearly recognized, the central and enabling characteristic of Chatterton's short-lived quest for literary renown involved his conquest of a tradition of literary and cultural learning that repudiated his authorial ambitions from the outset. To overcome the social barrier of such tradition required a sustained and ingeniously presented simulation of antiquity, a more intense version of James Macpherson's Ossian poems. Chatterton's "Excellente Balade of Charitie: as wroten bie the gode Prieste Thomas Rowley, 1464" nicely exemplifies how the manufacture of the author's social persona demands the forging of an entirely new literary idiom, one whose aura of antiquity is realized with truly postmodern self-awareness.

> In Virgyne the sweltrie sun gan sheene,
> And hotte upon the mees did caste his raie;
> The apple rodded from its palie greene,
> And the mole peare did bende the leafy spraie;
> The peede chelandri sunge the livelong daie;
> 'Twas nowe the pride, the manhode of the yeare,
> And eke the ground was dighte in its most defte aumere.
>
> (CHATTERTON, 173)

Chatterton's textual notes offer help with some of the more elusive words (e.g., "chelandri=Pied goldfinch" or "dighte=dressed"). Most significant about this opening—and arguably also the seed for the exposure of Chatterton's literary fraud as early as 1777—is a nature imagery that was just then beginning to make its way into British and German poetry (Goethe's *Sesenheimer Lieder* of 1771 come to mind). The connection between Chatterton's blossoming landscape and the author's apparent delight in his literary and sexual prowess ("the pride, the manhode of the yeare") is palpable enough. Yet such descriptive reveling in the virility of organic and human nature, aside from striking us as improbably forward for a fifteenth-century monk, also seems to betray an unadulterated pleasure in the generative power of the word, its capacity to conjure up or "make" (Grk. *poein*) reality by positing it in verbal forms whose social and referential accreditation appears guaranteed by their (forged) antiquity. Having already defended Chatterton's "fair name" from the "cold blasts" of critical exposure in his early 1815 sonnet (*KCP*, 10–11), Keats was to return to the failed genius in some of his most revealing epistolary comments. His letter of 21 September 1819 to John Hamilton Reynolds, exactly contemporaneous with his "Ode to Autumn," unfolds a revealing metonymic chain that takes us from a passing reflection on the autumnal season to a metareflection on the psychological "mood" of that season, to the evocative power of pictures to the purity and melancholic aura of Chatterton's English:

> How beautiful the season is now—How fine the air. A temperate sharpness about it. . . . I never lik'd stubble fields so much as now—Aye better than the chilly green of spring. Somehow, a stubble plain looks warm—in the same way that some pictures look warm—this struck me so much in sunday's walk that I composed upon it ["To Autumn"]. I hope you are better employed than in gaping after weather. I have been at different times so happy as not to know what weather it was—No I will not copy a parcel of verses. I always somehow associate Chatterton with autumn. He is the purest writer in the English Language. He has no French idiom, or particles like Chaucer[s]—'tis genuine English Idiom in English words. I have given up Hyperion—there were too many Miltonic inversions in it—Miltonic verse cannot be written but in an artful or rather artist's humour. I wish to give myself up to other sensations. English ought to be kept up. (*LJK*, 2: 167)

Key to a reading of this letter, and by extension to a reading of "To Autumn" and the slightly earlier great odes, is to excavate the underlying logic that allows for this singular fusion of season, representation, "purest" English, and the impossibility of epic writing. To formulate an answer is to return to the overarching mood of melancholy, one that Keats's letter is on the verge of making explicit. To hazard a paraphrase of Keats's beautiful and enigmatic meditation, all genuine poetry originates in a holistic awareness of how we are situated in the world. Contrary to what Heidegger was to call "being in the world," and what Keats recalls as having been "so happy as not to know what weather it was," the formal productivity of lyric writing in an intrinsically contested and partially alien medium also ushers poet and (at least potentially) audience into a fuller knowledge of their historical embeddedness or mood. At a more topical level, of course, autumn serves as the archetypal threshold connecting life and death. It impresses on us a baroque and mournful awareness of the transient quality of all material and organic life, "the clammy cells" and "ripeness to the core" of Keats's "To Autumn," which so conspicuously hint at impending decomposition ("Thou watchest the last oozings hours by hours" [*KCP*, 653]). Such emblematic meaning is soon transposed into a more complex, critical register as Keats, quoting from his own poem written just two days before, muses on the equivalent psychosomatic effect of perception and image: "somehow a stubble plain looks warm in the same way that some pictures look warm." Yet to secure and sustain the full potential of the "picture," it must be isolated from all referential obligations to historical matter or literary precedent, and it is here that Keats finds Chatterton enabling. For Keats (and in ways to which Keats could relate all too well), Chatterton had experienced his world as wholly overdetermined, a dystopic space in which all means and forms of social, economic, and cultural production had already been distributed and all venues for creative self-realization foreclosed. To recover from this seemingly all-encompassing melancholia, one had to create anew the very means of poetic (self-)production: language. As Keats was to reiterate in another letter, written three days later (24 September 1819), "the purest english I think—or what ought to be the purest—is Chatterton's" (*LJK*, 2: 212). The qualifying hortatory inflection also makes clear just how conscious Keats is of the necessity of moving beyond the overdetermined model of Englishness as a timeless sociocultural and linguistic tradition.

Like Chatterton's "Rowley Poems," Keats's deliberately overwrought lyrics communicate, not specific literary meanings, but the meaning and urgency of a new kind of literariness. In conceiving of literature as an inventory of stylistic effects, the aggressively artifactual demeanor of the Keatsian oeuvre aims to devise new possibilities—what Hölderlin calls "the open" (das Offene)—for poetry, though only by first unwriting the fixity of linguistic, literary, and cultural traditions and norms whose continued acceptance would consign him to terminal marginality. Not surprisingly, writers from reviewers for the most conservative Edinburgh periodicals to celebrity outcasts like Byron closed ranks, rightly sensing that such "redundancy of poetical decoration" (as an 1817 reviewer for the *European Magazine* put it) was simply a bid for social advancement. Keats himself appears fully conscious of the proximity between his self-consciously "literary" approach to lyric writing and Regency culture's dominant paradigm of a wholly public language: journalism. Keats's oeuvre, which bears a striking resemblance to the scandalous linguistic and stylistic hybridization of literary German by his German-Jewish contemporary Heine, continually posits the lyric as a strategic renegotiating of its producer's consciously abject relation to the seemingly impenetrable institutions of letters.

In a letter of July 1819, Keats makes a particularly strong connection between his exotic reading taste, the eroticized melancholia of his social existence, and his serial pursuit of poetry. The letter bears quoting at some length:

> I have been reading lately an oriental tale of a very beautiful color—It is of a city of melancholy men, all made so by this circumstance. Through a series of adventures each one of them by turns reach some gardens of Paradise where they meet with a most enchanting Lady; and just as they are going to embrace her, she bids them shut their eyes—they shut them—and on opening their eyes again find themselves descending to the earth.... The remembrance of this Lady and their delights lost beyond all recovery render them melancholy ever after. How I applied this to you, my dear; how I palpitated at it; how the certainty that you were in the same world with myself, and though as beautiful, not so talismanic as that Lady; how I could not bear [that] you should be so you must believe because I swear it by yourself. I cannot say when I shall get a volume ready. I have three or four stories half done, but as I cannot write for the mere sake of the press, I am obliged to let them progress or lie still as my fancy chooses. By Christmas perhaps they may appear, but I am not sure they ever will. 'Twill be no matter, for Poems are as common as newspapers and I do not see why it is a greater crime in me than in another to let the verses of a half-fledged brain tumble into the reading-rooms and drawing room windows. (*LJK*, 2: 130)

Most striking about this passage is Keats's refusal to articulate any causal relation between its discrete narratives: the progression of the text of romance from desire to deception to melancholic abjection; the more doubtful progression of his personal romance; and the distant prospect of invading drawing rooms with the metered products of a "half-fledged brain." Of the three performative selves—those of reader, lover, and writer—the middle one is surely the most oblique here. If anything, it mediates the quest of reading with that of writing and publishing, namely, by confirming for Keats that melancholy is a collective condition rather than a contingent fate. After apprising us of Keats's virtual kinship with a "city of melancholy men," the letter forges a transition from that mournful community to Keats's identity as a writer. Prolific, self-replicating, and published without aesthetic self-censorship, writing becomes the strategic response to an all-encompassing disillusionment. Robert Burton, whose *Anatomy of Melancholy* Keats was studying around this time—had long before described melancholy as a suffering without cause and had recommended writing as a remedy: "I writ of melancholy, by being busy to avoid melancholy" (Burton, 17).

Meanwhile, within the texts that result from such remedial authorship, it is usually women who figure as the ineffable origin of melancholy, a symptomatic rhetorical decision for a writer whose oeuvre time and again imagines women as objects of both stylized devotion and furtive ressentiment. At the heart of Keats's poetry and letters—and defining for the century's subsequent debate concerning the separation of lyric and prosaic writing—we find the axiomatic bond between the public persona of the writer and a culturally motivated hostility to women. Having found inherited notions of aesthetic purity and authentic poetry to be unattainable, Keats reorganizes his melancholic awareness of that circumstance into a prolific, serial poetic industry. Within the figural order of sonnets and romances, disillusionment is reconstituted as an erotic betrayal, and unattainable ideals resurface as self-imposed illusions. Eventually, the protagonists of Keats's romances must either abandon these illusions or be consumed by them. It helps here to recall Nietzsche's and Freud's insight into the passive-aggressive character of a highly formalized lament. Keats's oeuvre offers complex confirmation of that hypothesis inasmuch as his melancholic lyricism reveals a hostility toward women that seems less pathological and spontaneous than deliberative and textually constructed. If the Cockney poet is trapped between a social knowledge for which there is no form, and aesthetic norms whose inadequacy only heightens the urgency of that knowledge, his audience is to experience that antagonism no less. "When I am among Women I have evil thoughts, malice spleen—I cannot speak or be silent—I am full of Suspicions," he writes (*LJK*, 1: 341). Such resentful silence amounts to a precise inversion of the writer's public persona, one eager to haunt his readers with the same invariant story of his aesthetic and psychosexual exclusion from society. This particular issue reflects what Forest Pyle terms "the fundamental and inherent *textual* incompatibility between the ethics and linguistics of poetry." The consequence is a "materialism that questions the truth claims made for the imagination and takes this 'waking dream' to its breaking point" (Pyle 1995, 134; 129). As Keats so defiantly puts it in a letter, "I am determined to spin—home spun anything for sale. Yea, I will traffic. . . . I shall be able to cheat as well as any[one . . . in] the Market and shine up an article on anything without much knowledge of the subject, aye like an orange" (*LJK*, 2: 178–79). Keats's bequest, then, lies in his deliberate confusion of "genuine" aesthetic luster with the awkward "shine" of serialized poetic "articles."

In forging his prolific transition from an ineffable melancholy to the "richly disconcerting" (Ricks) language of social and gendered ressentiment, Keats recovered the lyric as a resource for the representation of social and cultural antagonisms. As he felt, the antagonisms that circumscribed his identity had to be converted into a social, public knowledge. To that end, his audience had to experience the full force of his social and cultural ambition—its embarrassing urgency, even vulgarity. More important yet, the strategic objective of his lyric writings is to exhibit his as yet incomplete quest for a technical mastery of literary writing. With his aggressive pursuit of formal-aesthetic competence as a social commodity, Keats forces into public consciousness the causal relation between his social ascendancy and his calculated infringement of a supposedly autonomous aesthetic domain. This unique fusion of melancholy and ressentiment not only informs all of Keats's work (including the *Hyperion* poems, the odes, and, perhaps most brilliantly, *Lamia*); it also presages and enables the cosmopolitan lyric writing of a materially and sexually volatile culture in the work of Heine, Baudelaire, Wilde, Trakl, and T. S. Eliot, among others. It would be another project to show the extent to which modernism retraces and capitalizes on the originally Keatsian insurrection of lyric writing against the deceptively "classless" Coleridgean paradigm of the organic text in which rhetorical technique and psychological effects ought to be fully integrated. What Keats calls the "purest English" is at once a brilliant assault on the false utopia of a "pure" aesthetic and a shrewd way of recovering from the melancholy to which acceptance of that model would otherwise consign him.

CHAPTER SEVEN

Melancholy into Ressentiment

Aesthetic and Social Provocation in Heine's *Buch der Lieder* (1827)

> Action is the offspring of the word, and yet all of Goethe's beautiful words prove childless. Such is the curse afflicting everything that has been merely the product of art. The statue assembled by Pygmalion was a beautiful woman, to be sure; indeed, the master himself fell in love with it and, with all his kissing, even brought her to life. Yet as far as we know, she never had any children. . . . yesterday when, roaming through the lower halls of the Louvre, I contemplated the sculptures of the old gods. There they stood, with their expressionless white eyes, and in their marble smile, there lurked a faint melancholy, intimating, perhaps, a pale recollection of Egypt, the realm of death from which they sprang; or a painful longing for the life from which they have been expelled by other divinities; or perhaps also the pain caused by their deadly immortality. They appeared to yearn for the word that would restore them to life and redeem them from their cold, rigid lifelessness. Strange as it may sound, these antiquities reminded me of Goethe's poems, themselves just as perfected, splendid, tranquil, and just as melancholically aware that their rigor and coldness separate them from the warm, animated life of our present day. [Goethe's poems], that is, cannot suffer and rejoice with us; indeed, they are no human beings but only miserable hybrids of divinity and stone.
>
> — HEINRICH HEINE, *Die Romantische Schule* (1833)

With its characteristic fusion of eloquent figuration and satiric irreverence, Heine's Oedipal sketch[1] of Goethe's monumental presence in—indeed, his stony embodiment of—German literature makes for a fine segue into the rich, convoluted terrain of restoration politics and Biedermeier culture. Goethe's capacious presence in German letters and society is figured both as monumental and, more furtively, as yearning to be liberated from its own archaic and lifeless aura. Ancient sculpture in the Louvre reminds Heine of what Keats called "the shadow of a magnitude." Awaiting "the word that would restore them to life," the stony divinities of ancient Egypt and Greece invite Heine to sharply distinguish between the remote self-sufficiency of Weimar classicism and his own mercurial role as a postclassical writer. Assuming a self-consciously belated persona during his self-imposed exile (from 1831 until his death in 1856), Heine knows that the "perfected" (*vollendet*) and "splendid" (*herrlich*) model of artistic creation associated with Weimar is no longer available to him. The "art period" (*Kunstperiode*) of Goethe and Schiller, as well as the concurrently advancing theoretical projects of the Jena school, had all drawn to a close, or, at least, appeared to be wholly exhausted.

Still, the opening, polemical assertion of Goethe's "childless" language—referring above all to Goethe's alleged lack of *political* consequence—reveals Heine's conception of writing as one of conscious and explicit aesthetic dissent. In its casual, yet altogether lucid, deployment of classical imagery, Heine's paragraph further signals the urgent need for a decisive break with Weimar classicism's myth of aesthetic autonomy. Rejoicing in his belatedness vis-à-vis the esoteric brilliance of Goethe's lyric oeuvre, Heine nonetheless ponders (almost wistfully) how Goethe's language itself already "seems to feel with nostalgia that its own rigor and coldness have separated it from the animated warmth of our current life" (und ebenfalls mit Wehmut zu fühlen scheinen, daß ihre Starrheit und Kälte sie von unserem jetzigen bewegt warmen Leben abscheidet). Unlike the ardent republican Ludwig Börne,[2] his fellow Jewish exile, Heine perceives Weimar classicism as warranting an ironic transformation rather than blunt repudiation.

Still, one wonders with Heine exactly why Goethe's perfectly balanced cadences should yet give rise to a "secret melancholy" and "murky recollection" (eine geheime Melancholie, eine trübe Erinnerung)—to some antecedent and higher quality now lost? In characteristically sharp-edged manner, Heine views Weimar classicism as stranded between a point of origin that it can barely recall (Ägypten, das Totenland, dem sie entsprossen) and the plenitude and agility of contemporary life (leidende Sehnsucht nach dem Leben) to which it no longer bears any functional relation. Goethe had passed away only a year before the publication of *Die Romantische Schule*, but Heine combatively asserts the demise of that allegedly timeless Weimar "art period" as a confirmed and accepted fact. As an aesthetic and social paradigm, Goethe has been displaced both by changing times and by the emergence of other divinities (andere Gottheiten). The latter (so labeled with subtle yet unmistakable irony by Heine) are no doubt the liberal writers associated with the *das junge*

Deutschland movement (Gutzkow, Mundt, Laube, Wienbarg), critics like Wolfgang Menzel and Ludwig Börne, and—surely most unclassifiable of all—Heine himself. Rather than naming a determinate affective content, a first aspect of melancholy involves the volatile relationship between the allegedly complacent monumentality of Goethe's classicism and Heine's alternative conception of the writer as a mercurial harbinger of troubled modernity. As Hegel had argued in his *Lectures on Fine Art*—begun around 1823 in Berlin, just as Heine became acquainted with his philosophy and with Hegel personally—the modern artist is afflicted by an excess of knowledge. He is the epigone, "born too late" as Heine puts it, referring to his own generation as "wir Spätergeborenen" (*HSS*, 3: 425). Far from being an exclusive insight of Hegel's theory of romantic art, the notion of the 1820s as a fundamentally belated period reverberates in the works of countless writers. At once oppressed by the abundance of aesthetic models generated since the age of Lessing and distressed by their evident inadequacy for the present, the subjects of the early restoration era (1815–19 to 1830) struggle with a new adversary: the idea of culture as a monolithic heritage. As Martin Greiner puts it, "the epigone is a wealthy subject starved by an excess of riches" and "struggling with the problem of culture as heritage—*Bildung* as an estate."[3]

In a world where "life has become so utterly clogged with projects, tendencies, and so self-conscious as to smolder like a covered kiln, without flames ever feeding on the open air" (Immermann, 5: 237), it is not surprising that Goethe's idiom, like Milton's English for Keats, has declined into "a grand curiosity." As Heine would put it years later,

> My old prophecy of the end of the art epoch that commenced at Goethe's cradle and will conclude with his burial seems about to fulfill itself. Contemporary art must perish, because its principles are still rooted in a superannuated, worn-out regime, in the Holy Roman imperial past. Like all faded remains of this past, it stands in the most unproductive contrast with the present times. It is this contradiction, rather than the dynamism of present times per se, that is so harmful to art. In fact, the dynamic present ought actually to benefit art, just as long ago, in Athens and Florence, the arts flourished to an unprecedented degree in the midst of brutal war and partisanship. (*HSS*, 3: 72; my translation)

Rather than indicting Goethe's aesthetic philosophy and practice as a merely delusive achievement, however, Heine invokes Goethean classicism as the very sundial that helps the "later-born" writer tell the time of history (to appropriate Adorno's famous image). Similarly, Karl Gutzkow imagines a critique of Wolfgang Menzel's selective and biased literary history as having "to name those cesurae where W. Menzel forgot to wind his pocket-watch" (die Einschnitte der Zeit zu nennen, wo W. Menzel seine Uhr aufzuziehen vergaß).[4] For Heine, Börne, and most of their contemporaries, the leap from the timeless symbolic order of Weimar classicism into the politically engaged, if ephemeral, productivity of the modern *Zeitschriftsteller* was one taken consciously and deliberately. Were it not for the "most unsettling contradiction" between what Heine terms the "faded remains" of the Weimar "art period," it would prove impossible to grasp the present as a distinctive caesura within the inexorable flux of historical time (*Zeitbewegung*). Precisely because of that historical caesura, then, the stylistic and philosophical ideals of Weimar, Jena, and Heidelberg suddenly appear to lack their formerly commanding presence. What was until recently *the* aesthetic paradigm now seems simply a faded cultural memory, one that no longer signifies life itself but instead is experienced solely as a cultural "heritage," and hence as symptomatic of the modern individual's forever perplexed relation to history. Indeed, given some skill and effort, Goethe's idiom can now be repeated almost at will. As Heine puts it in the brash opening of a letter to his new friend Rudolph Christiani: "If I make an effort, it should be possible for me to produce a few delicate sentences of bona fide authentic, grand-ducal Weimarian court prose, and so to put into suitable words my feelings toward you" (*HB*, 1: 138; my translation).[5]

Heine's gibe at Goethe's prose style—perhaps triggered by his evidently cool reception at the latter's house in Weimar the year before—appears restrained when compared with Menzel's anti-Goethean jeremiad in his 1828 survey of German literature *Die deutsche Literatur* or Börne's periodic outbursts in his *Briefe aus Paris.* In his review of Menzel's book, Heine discriminates sharply between "the Goethean form of thought, that flower that is destined to bloom with ever-increasing splendor on the dungheap of our present age," and the pathetic servility of the Goethe cult, saying, "by the word 'Goetheanism' [*Goethentum*], we specifically mean Goethe's manner as we find it regurgitated by his insipid ephebes, as well as the slack imitation of those tunes that the Great One used to whistle" (*HSS,* 1: 455; my translation). While the Austro-Prussian administration's repressive measures persistently linked Heine with the movement of liberal-republican writers known as *das junge Deutschland,* his actual position vis-à- vis Goethe and his liberal-republican detractors was complex—even cunningly ambivalent.[6]

Continuing political persecution and censorship between 1819 and 1835 usually forced liberal and republican intellectuals to choose either apostasy or exile. Writers like Menzel and Friedrich von Raumer recanted their one-time liberal convictions, and the former notoriously went on to carve out a role for himself as one of Germany's most aggressively nationalist, francophobic, and anti-Semitic literary and cultural critics. Metternich's regime, which was not without its own literary connoisseurs, eagerly sought out talented writers for employment in the ever-expanding *Zensurkollegium* or as hired mouthpieces. At one point, even the inveterate republican Börne was to be recruited; as Rahel Varnhagen writes in a letter (8 May 1819), Metternich's political secretary, Friedrich von Gentz, had strongly recommended Börne's new periodical, *Die Wage,* to her. Although he had been arrested in March 1820 by the Austrian authorities (following an informant's false report), Börne was still receiving invitations to "switch sides" as late as 1821.[7] The Viennese authorities were most taken with Heine's writings, thus showing considerable literary discrimination. As Metternich himself remarked, "As regards style and presentation, Heine's book [*On the History of Religion and Philosophy in Germany* (1835)] is a true masterpiece. Among the conspirators, he is clearly the greatest mind" (quoted in Sengle, 1: 167). In the end, of course, both Heine and Börne had to spend their later years in Paris, where they struggled—albeit in very different ways—to cope with their linguistic and geographical distance from German politics and letters. "[W]hatever doesn't involve masses of people or individuals representing entire communities and general interests lies entirely outside my sphere; for it doesn't in the least concern my duties," Börne wrote defiantly, perhaps sensing his gradual estrangement from the finer socioeconomic gradations and demographic shifts in his native Germany (Börne 1977, 3: 383; my translation). Yet such an approach, as Heine shrewdly observed, invariably resulted in an often shrill, one-dimensionally politicized idiom devoid of the stylistic nuances and responsiveness to complexity that mark the genuine writer. Far from regarding a commitment to literary form and the aesthetic more generally as incompatible with political advocacy, Heine viewed it as indispensable if one's politics were to have any decency whatsoever. "I'll only say this much, namely, that to write truly accomplished prose also requires great facility in metrical forms," he remarks in his 1840 commemorative essay on Ludwig

Börne. "Without it, the prose writer lacks a certain tact and is prone to slips in phrasing, diction, rhythm, and idiom that are only permissible in prosodic form. The result is a latent dissonance that only offends a few truly sensitive ears" (*HSS,* 4: 12; my translation).

Figurally claiming for himself the status of a conventional "guillotine" in all debates cultural and political—as opposed to what he lampoons as Börne's all-devouring "steam guillotine" (*Dampfguillotine*)—Heine also maintains a far more differentiated relation to Goethe.[8] Whereas Börne had so intemperately denounced Goethe for the political and aesthetic complacency of his classicism—"a cancer on the German body politic" and "cataracts in the German eye" (Börne 1977, 3: 70–71)—Heine refuses to decide the merits of any writer on merely political grounds. He does so, however, not in order to exclude politics from the domain of letters, but, on the contrary, to bring about their complete amalgamation. Inasmuch as for Börne and other members of *das junge Deutschland,* art ought to answer politics, their thinking perpetuates classicism's treatment of these two spheres as fundamentally distinct and incompatible. As Heine perceived it, regardless of a writer's specific politics, any partitioning of the actual craft of writing from the rough-and-tumble world of politics invariably benefits the political status quo. For such a divide not only perpetuates the hold on political power of those who have grown accustomed to wielding it but localizes and isolates the representatives of "culture" as what Julia Kristeva has termed "specialists of the negative." From Heine's point of view, the finer discriminations between Weimar, various romantic schools, and their recent detractors—poetic theory at Jena, medieval mythologizing at Heidelberg, Catholic revival in Vienna, and the anti-aesthetic partisanship of *das junge Deutschland*—are all equally harmless. It is in his risky polemic against Börne that Heine states his misgivings about a politics beyond art most clearly. Alluding to Börne's public mockery of Raumer's *Briefe aus Paris* (which appeared a year before Börne's own publication of the same title), Heine muses how

> upon encountering the first two volumes at that time, I was taken aback by the ultraradical tone, something I had least of all expected from Börne. This fellow, who perpetually inspected and monitored his proper and nicely groomed style, and who would punctiliously weigh and take the measure of every syllable prior to writing it down—whose style always retained characteristics of the provincial petit-bourgeois philistine, to say nothing of the timidity of his former office—

> this former police actuary from Frankfurt—now hurled himself head first into a Jacobinism of thought and expression the likes of which had never been witnessed before in Germany. Good heavens! What terrifying turns of phrase, what treasonous verbs! What regicidal accusatives and metaphors whose very shadow alone would warrant twenty years of incarceration. And yet, notwithstanding their horrific impact on me then, these very same letters also stirred up memories so cheerful as to nearly make me burst out laughing. (*HSS*, 4: 66–67; my translation)

However noble and courageous his declared liberalism, Börne is unmistakably a German philistine, who, even in the most frantic gestures of civic protest, is sure to calibrate each sentence, metaphor, exclamation point, or question mark according to an official standard of expressive propriety. In Heine's sly reading, the author of the notorious *Briefe aus Paris* emerges less as an instigator or prophet of political unrest than as an unwittingly Quixotic figure deluded by what, in fact, is little more than a heroic pose. Heine is lampooning the idea of the writer as someone who can be readily identified, categorized, and, if necessary, isolated by means of slander, exile, and / or censorship, a proposition that can be contested only at the level of literary form. To be sure, no text (least of all Heine's own writings) can claim to transcend its performative nature altogether and to satisfy some utopian standard of direct political efficacy.[9] Yet Börne's particular shortcoming is that he mistakes his "ultraradical tone" for the main event, and far from disparaging the performative character of his writings, Heine merely criticizes his lack of the ironic self-awareness that befits a postclassical writer. To underscore his point, Heine extends the above passage into a reminiscence about an old constable of his boyhood days who one day succumbed to the mad notion of being a mischievous young boy himself and proceeded to demonstrate to the amused children what "stirring up real trouble looks like," only to be locked up in an asylum.

The question astutely and provocatively raised by Heine remains valid to this day. Is a commitment to radical politics inextricably connected with a prosaic Jacobinism and a generally iconoclastic outlook on aesthetic form? Does a critical perspective on literature necessarily mandate an anti-literary form? And if so, what are the grounds on which that mandate's axiomatically anti-literary and anti-aesthetic model of critique is premised? Indeed, wouldn't a liberal activist or protosocialist political critique of the vaunted project of

Bildung risk being deceived about its own underlying pathos? Börne's insistence in his 1816 essay "Für die Juden" that "matters of sentiment must be turned into matters of reflection" valorizes rational and uncompromising inquiry without sufficiently grasping the Enlightenment's mythic pursuit of abstract and essentially equivalent rational propositions (later evoked by Adorno and Horkheimer) that reverberates in the "must." For Sander L. Gilman, Börne's transformation from ghetto Jew into "Lutheran journalist" ultimately betokens an acceptance that Judaic culture would have to be among the casualties of intellectual, social, and economic mobility. While I ultimately concur with Gilman's rather Procrustean thesis—which views Börne as yet another case of Jewish self-hatred—the wary perspicacity with which Börne looks upon the political contentment and mystical spirituality of many German Jews as late as 1816 stands him in good stead with regard to his larger project of producing a sharp-edged, journalistic critique of German gentile culture. For there, too, Börne mercilessly exposes the parochial, exclusionary, and often vindictive spirit in which the German petit-bourgeoisie embraced Goethe's and Schiller's concept of *Bildung.*

As Jürgen Habermas has noted, Heine's career confronted German audiences with a new paradigm of the writer as a public intellectual bent on exposing the false and arrogant notion of politics as just another bureaucratic task or professional skill and on dismantling the belletristic conception of literature as a strictly formal, ivory-tower avocation. From the early nineteenth century until 1945, certain politicians and aestheticians (Habermas names Curtius, Hesse, Jaspers, Weber, Theodor Heuss, Georg Lukács, and even Johannes Becher) resisted this "confusion of categories."[10] Indeed, in what may well be the most tortuous reception of any writer in German literature, Heine's writings were soon recognized as paradigmatically different and rejected, often with nationalist and anti-Semitic overtones, because his language was perceived to subvert notions of aesthetic autonomy and affective integrity. That traditional model, it turns out, proved curiously indispensable for conservatives and liberals alike. Political and cultural conservatives from the later F. Schlegel, Achim von Arnim, Clemens Brentano, and Adam Müller to Adalbert Stifter and Jeremias Gotthelf embraced the distinction as the basis for their respective visions of a culture that aspired to transcend politics altogether. On the other side, liberals associated with the *jungdeutsche* movement (Arnold Ruge, Theodor Mundt, Heinrich Laube, Ludolph Wienbarg, Karl Gutzkow) valued the distinction, since their repudiation of an autonomous aesthetic and of intrinsic literary values could logically never proceed without it.[11] Aside from furnishing a basic axiom for the left and the right, the premise of a properly separate aesthetic sphere also linked various social strata, extending all the way from the aristocratic regimes of Metternich and Wilhelm III to the bureaucratic and educated middle class (*Beamtenbürgertum, Bildungsbürgertum*).

Heine's entire career can be seen as a prolonged assault on the notion that the aesthetic is autonomous, a proposition he saw as shared by otherwise sharply opposed political constituencies. The axiom that art and politics were spheres that were both intrinsically separate and should remain so was held alike by the representatives of a sentimental Biedermeier romanticism (e.g., Rückert, Lenau, Chamisso), German nationalists (e.g., Jahn, Fries, the late Görres), those advocating the restoration of a mythical (preschismatic and emphatically Catholic), organic romantic *Volk* (e.g., Brentano, Arnim, Adam Müller, the late Schlegel), and the liberal and reform-oriented novelists and dramatists of *das junge Deutschland,* as indeed by the emergent "left-Hegelians." For all of these, whether from the perspective of nostalgia, reaction, reform, or rebellion, an aesthetic sansculottism seemed an indispensable correlate of their ideological and spiritual sincerity.

For the liberal intellectuals of the pre-1848 era (known as *Vormärz*), rejecting Goethe's political complacency and the Jena romantics' esoteric speculations also meant (at least implicitly) rejecting poetry. Of all the writers named in the Bundesrat's 1835 resolution outlawing the writings of *das junge Deutschland,* Heine was the only one to have a stake in the genre.[12] Even truly accomplished, sophisticated prose could not replace political action. In the words of Karl Gutzkow, "we must do something that will substitute for what we would really do. At the very least, it must equal the scope of our conceptions. Hence we reach for the quill."[13] The novels and plays of the liberal writers in question thus naturally tended to perpetuate a general ressentiment toward all aesthetic practice, to the point where Gutzkow himself conceded that the movement "contains far more enthusiasm than actual talent" (Gutzkow, 1: 1179). If political apostasy exacted the price of prolonged self-justification and self-loathing, expressing political dissent in the etiolated forms of literature typically entailed underlying hostility toward those forms' inadequacy. It is here that we begin to note the homology between the political and cultural vectors that circumscribe a historical phase and the psychological effects of its collective experience. Quoting Karl Immermann's remark that the "founders of the more recent German family are all more or less developed Hamlet characters," Friedrich Sengle speculates that traumatic disruptions of the collective unconscious may well have been the most significant cause of their pervasive melancholy.[14]

Wolf Lepenies has offered a broad sociological analysis of melancholy. Rather than conceiving of it as a contingent, strictly individual type of affect, Lepenies associates it with a "retreatism" that is "diametrically opposed to both conformity and rebellion" (Lepenies 1992, 4)—in other words, a behavioral aesthetic that responds to complex historical adversity. To illustrate his thesis about melancholy as a collective response to an oppressive alien order that has successfully repelled all attempts at reform or rebellion, Lepenies analyzes the aftermath of the aristocracy's failed revolt against its infantilization by the absolute monarchs of seventeenth-century France. In its distinctively belated and self-conscious relation to a failed or forestalled historical action, melancholy distinguishes itself as a "form of resignative behavior which arises out of a surplus of order" (ibid., 47). Starved out of all political relevancy and enfeebled by the luxuriant, though purely symbolic and ceremonial, life at the royal court, the French aristocracy experienced a form of political disillusionment similar to that subsequently experienced by the educated *Bildungsbürgertum* and sectors of the bureaucratic preindustrial petit bourgeoisie in early-nineteenth-century Germany. Having come of age as soldiers and irregulars in Lützow's *Freikorps* between 1813 and 1815, and now established in their various intellectual and professional communities, members of these classes felt, in Immermann's words, "the magnitude of past efforts and the apparently small and impure nature of the results." Given the "consciousness of all things public as inherently incomplete, alienated, and duplicitous, including matters of law and property," those who came of age between 1806 and 1815 "typically reveal more or less developed traits of Hamlet's character" (Immermann, 5: 290–91). Not surprisingly, they initially voiced their keen displeasure with the abrogation of the Prussian reform movement after Waterloo; the intensification of censorship and the organized surveillance of intellectual life at universities, particularly after 1819; the retraction of citizen-status (*Bürgerrecht*) that the Code Napoléon had granted to minorities, notably, Jews; and the temporizing and secretive political strategy of the Deutsche Bund as it had taken shape since the Congress of Vienna. "With the natural progression toward German unity abruptly terminated" (Sengle, 1: 10), the period of *Vormärz* became soon synonymous with the idea of a forestalled development. Threats of insurrection by the extreme nationalists known as *Deutschtümeler* and

Burschenschaftler, were met with a barrage of legislative measures, including the strict surveillance of all university teaching and extensive censorship measures that provided severe penalties for authors, editors, publishers, and booksellers trading in printed matter deemed either to have deceived the censors or to have been smuggled into Germany from adjacent countries.

Overall, the restoration age can legitimately be seen as a period of extended mourning for political and social opportunities that were either being foreclosed or had been altogether missed.[15] Extending his thesis to the bourgeois culture of early- and mid-nineteenth-century France, Lepenies notes that "once the emancipation of the bourgeoisie had reached such heights that the bourgeois [could] emulate the behavioral patterns of the aristocracy . . . there was now no place to left for them to escape to—they could flee only into individuality itself" (Lepenies 1992, 50–51). Most intriguing is Lepenies's view of the strategic fusion of bourgeois melancholy with formal-aesthetic (particularly literary) production such as resonates in the vaunted "aristocracy of mind" that became the veritable signature of German restoration culture. By means of this compensatory aesthetic engagement, "the resignative phenomena of the age . . . lost their collective character," thereby allowing the illusion of melancholy as an authentic affective condition, "supposedly engendered solely in the individual's psyche," to take hold (ibid., 62). At least implicitly, Lepenies argues here against pathologizing conceptions of melancholy. Rather, he suggests, the term encompasses a series of coordinated cultural practices and, associated with these, affective tactics of which the individual may indeed not be conscious. Yet, as such, these practices (or "symptoms") of melancholy display an extremely high degree of formal coherence and purposiveness, so much so as to intimate the profound homology between cultural production and melancholy so eloquently adumbrated in Heine's portrait of Goethe's stony divinities. Hence it would be more accurate to say that melancholy "makes" the individual, rather than to view the latter as simply "suffering" from a condition called melancholy. For individuality itself is the (melancholic) effect of a modernity whose artificial sense of social organization—namely, as communities organized by class, ethnicity, religion, and nationality—invariably entails the creation, ostracizing, and eventual abjection of various others.

The consignment of the French nobility to the salon and, a century later, of Germany's petit bourgeoisie to the transactionalism of *Vereine* and the unique fusion of monastic and genteel elements in the Biedermeier epoch's design of private interiors centered on cultural practices (e.g., reading, *Hausmusik*, private lectures) designed to ennoble and thereby legitimate those spaces.[16] The interior becomes a sanctuary sheltering its subjects from fully recognizing their own political abjection. Rarely acquainted with the technicalities and intricacies of their professed cause, the members of a given association (*Verein*) usually lacked "a clear knowledge of what it is that they promote" (Sengle, 1: 22). As early as 1839, Immermann remarked that "just as the information of journals furnishes but a surrogate for knowledge and truth, so the activity of associations [*Vereine*] offers people merely the surrogate for action proper" (ein Surrogat des eigentlichen Handelns [Immermann, 5: 297]). Striking here is late romanticism's self-recognition as a world filled with simulacra that often stifled or extinguished all resolve for political action. Lepenies's conception of melancholy as the reflex of collective political abjection thus ought to be extended into an analysis of the behavioral aesthetic that mediates this complex mood. Ranging from the conspicuously formulaic quality of melancholic writing as an extended self-conscious citation of literary topoi to the sheltered sophistication of the salon and other interior spaces solely designed for the practice of self-cultivation, melancholy often appears all but synonymous with formalization.[17] In its persistent, if reticent, aesthetic elaboration, melancholy reconstitutes the loss of political opportunity in the modality of ostensibly private grief. Consciously experienced as a supplemental phenomenon, aesthetic form also demotes the period's conception of the human from an expressive and inalienable agency to an epiphenomenon of subtly woven simulacra (Keats's "tapestry empyrean") whose spiritual and moral import remains forever uncertain.

Depending on its specific formal incarnation, such an aesthetic may alternatively disburden the subject of the knowledge of its political irrelevance or allow it to reenact its failed rebellion in the virtual sphere of a stylized interiority. Either way, a strong association between melancholy and cultural production is readily apparent. Indeed, so strong is that association as to suggest that, far from being an ineffable (sublime) pathology, melancholy is wholly bound up with, and effectively perpetuated by, the forms of its cultural expression. Inasmuch as there appears to be no independent verification of melancholy as the "condition" of an individual or a community, the idea of culture as a relatively new form of specialized production may itself be both the manifestation *and* the cause of a melancholy that it purports to express. In other words, there is no such thing or phenomenon as melancholy per se, no supernatural "melancholic fit." Rather, melancholy appears to reflect the subject's acute knowledge of the inherently transactional nature of cultural production; it reflects the subject's full knowledge of the inescapably social and conventional character of its speech—"something universal borne of the utmost individuation," in Adorno's words (1997, 167). Melancholic affect, then, cannot be construed as the lyric's authentic content, however much the poem's grammatical "I" may seek to "create the illusion of nature emerging from alienation" (Adorno 1991, 1: 41). On the contrary, melancholy is the result of subjective insight into the inescapably social determinacy of all forms (literary or otherwise) in which it might seek to embody its supposedly personal, affective constitution. With characteristic irreverence, Heine speaks of a state "where the muse is a cow that has been profitably milked for so long that by now it yields pure water" (wo selbst die Muse eine Milchkuh ist, die so lange für Honorar abgemelkt wird, bis sie reines Wasser gibt [*HSS*, 2: 88]). More than the other affective paradigms that we looked at earlier, melancholy centers on the subject's grasp of romantic expressivity as a myth atrophied by its growing "self-consciousness *as* literary language" (Adorno 1991, 1: 44; emphasis added). Meanwhile, it is just this proximity to critical knowledge that distinguishes melancholic affect per se and renders it intrinsically heteronomous. Now precisely insofar as the heteronomy of affect—its intrinsically self-alienated quality—can be shown to stem from the artwork's distinctive "linguistic quality," we are able to grasp the larger dynamics of historical time *through* concrete acts of interpretation. Similarly, Heine's friend Immermann introduces his autobiographical project, *Memorabilien* (1839) as the telling of "where history made its passage *through* me" (wo die Geschichte Durchzug *durch* mich hielt [emphasis added]). However much popular habit might foreground the role of a few famous historical personalities, historical time ultimately owes "its body . . . at all times to elements and their infinitesimal particulars" [Immermann, 5: 239]). Only in a series of deceptively contingent "reflexes" (*Spiegelungen; Rückspiegelungen*) "through" the individual, that is, can history be grasped as a dynamic and meaningful causality.

At issue here are the cultural politics of restoration Germany (1819–35) and the psychologically complex grounds for their aesthetic stylization or "acculturation" as melancholy. Sengle's thesis that the restoration or Biedermeier age ought to be understood as an era of "deep historical crisis" (1: 8) defined by the condition of melancholy is instructive both on account of its exhaustive documentation and its theoretical contradictions. For in consistently treating his copious literary materials as invariant evidence of a strictly affective problematic (*Seelenproblematik; Seelenbild der Epoche*), Sengle's reading of the period effectively restates analyses already offered by the period's writers themselves. From Lenau to Rückert, Heine, Büchner, Grabbe, and the particularly reflexive Immermann, the statements that Sengle associates with melancholy rarely ever *indulge* in such affect. Rather, they appear to reflect on it with acute critical investment. As the following passage from Immermann's novel *Die Epigonen* shows, melancholy involves recognizing the present as overdetermined, indeed, exhausted by the cultural heritage of the recent past:

> Simply put, we are all epigones [*Epigonen*] and bear the burden borne by every later-born hereditary community. The great movements in the realm of ideas launched by our fathers from their huts and hovels have brought us countless riches, which are now spread out in the cultural marketplace. Even a minor talent can without much effort acquire a basic level of discrimination in art and science. Yet what is true of borrowed money also applies to borrowed ideas: whoever manages the assets of others carelessly will gradually slide into poverty. . . . Even the breeziest conception, the hollowest opinion, and the emptiest of hearts can readily be propped up by rhetoric that is sufficiently ingenious, bountiful, and impassioned. For that reason, good old modest "intuition" has fallen out of favor, and people prefer to prattle on about their various opinions. (Immermann, 3: 136; my translation)

Melancholy here emerges as a literary motif, a highly reflexive, discursive commentary on post-Waterloo and post-Karlsbad (1819) Germany.[18] Given its strong reflexive element, which at times borders on outright narcissism, melancholy is perhaps best thought of as a figurative strategy. Understood as an excess (not a lack) of self-knowledge, rather than as an affective condition that befalls an otherwise intact subject, melancholy revolves around the subject's overwhelming awareness of the determinants and constraints that circumscribe and delimit him or her. Understood as the knowledge of the irremediably pathological character of historical life itself—rather than as unwitting indulgence in the medieval sin of acedia—melancholy can no longer be thought as a simple affective pathology. To understand it, we must approach it through an analysis of its discrete formal and material manifestations, which will yield a more precise understanding of the psychological valences latently in play when writers and critics (then and now) speak of melancholy. As we have seen, Freud himself noted the passive-aggressive element in the melancholic subject's lament, observing that "complaints are accusations" (Klagen sind Anklagen). Precisely this furtive dramaturgy of writing—the excess of emotional theater pruned back to the explosive concision of the lyric—is key if we are to establish a plausible connection between the writing of melancholy and the cultural politics of the restoration age. The unconscious other of melancholy—the term missing from Sengle's otherwise capacious account of the ideological languor of the Biedermeier era—is ressentiment. As we have already observed in Keats, the monotonous serial or montage-like character of melancholic writing also reveals itself as an underhanded insult directed at the exclusionary refinement and delusive transcendence of what Wordsworth called "high Romantic argument."

Throughout Heine's poetry and its remarkably divided (and divisive) reception, melancholy and ressentiment present themselves as wholly inextricable—a structural homology of sorts. In it, melancholy is posited as an affective condition to be rendered back to the public by means of an oddly self-conscious and clichéd technique (the form of the [thematic] content), while ressentiment refers to the toxic effects of such writing itself (the [ideological] content of that form). Heine's melancholic imagery repeatedly encrypts an acute sense of phobia and aggression (*Anklagen*) through the nascent insincerity that shines through the lyric persona's stylized "laments" (*Klagen*)—particularly as regards its supposed betrayal by some generic female. Formalized as a distinctive technique of writing, melancholy partially obscures and partially discloses its origins in a collective and unconscious ressentiment. Not surprisingly, the key trope for such mediation is the dream. Beginning with the *Traumbilder* that open Heine's *Buch der Lieder,* the dream fulfills a dual function: "looked at from a psychological point of view, it serves to unveil previously unknown mental topographies . . . and, from a historical point of view, it functions as an aesthetic camouflage of the contents thus revealed."[19]

The *Buch der Lieder* offers an abundance of examples for this dialectical bond between nostalgic regret and subterranean hostility—between an official screen memory so self-cherishing as to convey to the observer the operation of unconscious resentments. In this world of political repression, rising censorship and surveillance, Christian nationalism, anti-Semitic agitation, political opportunism, and resurgent pauperism, ressentiment flourishes and seeks ever-new outlets. Positioned between quantifiable historical facts and their affective experience as values—between the tacit material and ideological forces of ressentiment and their formal-aesthetic cultivation as melancholy—the concepts in diagram 2 generate virtually the entire conceptual and thematic inventory for this chapter. Needless to say, each concept (or, rather synecdoche) encompasses a great number of discrete material practices and psychological experiences, which vary according to the subject's regional, socioeconomic, ethnic, and religious situation. Yet rather than aiming at an empirical, quantifying account of issues such as censorship, nationalism, anti-Semitism, and so forth, this chapter is concerned with the interpretive refraction of historical experience in acts of aesthetic production and response. Heine's conspicuously interventionist style appears simultaneously committed to certain social effects and solicitous of a type of interpretation aimed at recovering its historical motivation.[20] Not until post-Freudian thought conceived of "sadness [as] the final filter of aggressiveness" (Kristeva, 64), would melancholy and ressentiment again reveal their dialectical kinship in such striking manner and, in so doing, enable the critical reader to articulate the aesthetic's historicity without reducing the forms of such writing to merely allegorical mediations of some putatively "actual" issue. To read Heine is to witness the mutability of affect and the genesis of what Nietzsche would analyze as the culture of ressentiment.

Nietzsche's epoch-making definition of ressentiment in the *Genealogy of Morals* (1886) exhibits all the rhetorical hyperbole and consequent undecidability of his late work. To rely on Nietzsche's concept of ressentiment for purposes of critical writing is problematic, to say the least, and not only because of his sweeping and controversial application of this term to all kinds of ethnic and social groups.[21] He also indicts academic inquiry for its righteous and fetishized ideal of "scientific propriety" (wissenschaftliche Billigkeit). Such ennobling ideals, and the righteous pathos with which they are upheld and enforced, he regards as merely masks for "hatred, envy, malice, suspicion, intrigue, and revenge" (Nietzsche 1996, 54 / 1980, 5: 310). Nietzsche's ressentiment is Freud's unconscious *avant la lettre,* a type of pathos—such as empathy, melancholy, *askesis*—that has substituted itself for a deep-seated impulse of hatred or revenge: a beautiful surface sheltering the subject from recognizing its own "sublime depths."[22] Above all, Nietzsche indicts the entire passion play of Christianity and its recent echo, the romantic cult of feeling, as outgrowths of a pervasive, albeit unconscious, mendacity. However, insofar as affect requires highly evolved and ceaselessly adaptive acts of dissimulation, an intense commitment to formal-aesthetic invention for purposes of expressive self-legitimation as pathos, it is also a highly creative process: "The slave revolt in morals begins when *ressentiment* itself becomes creative and ordains values"

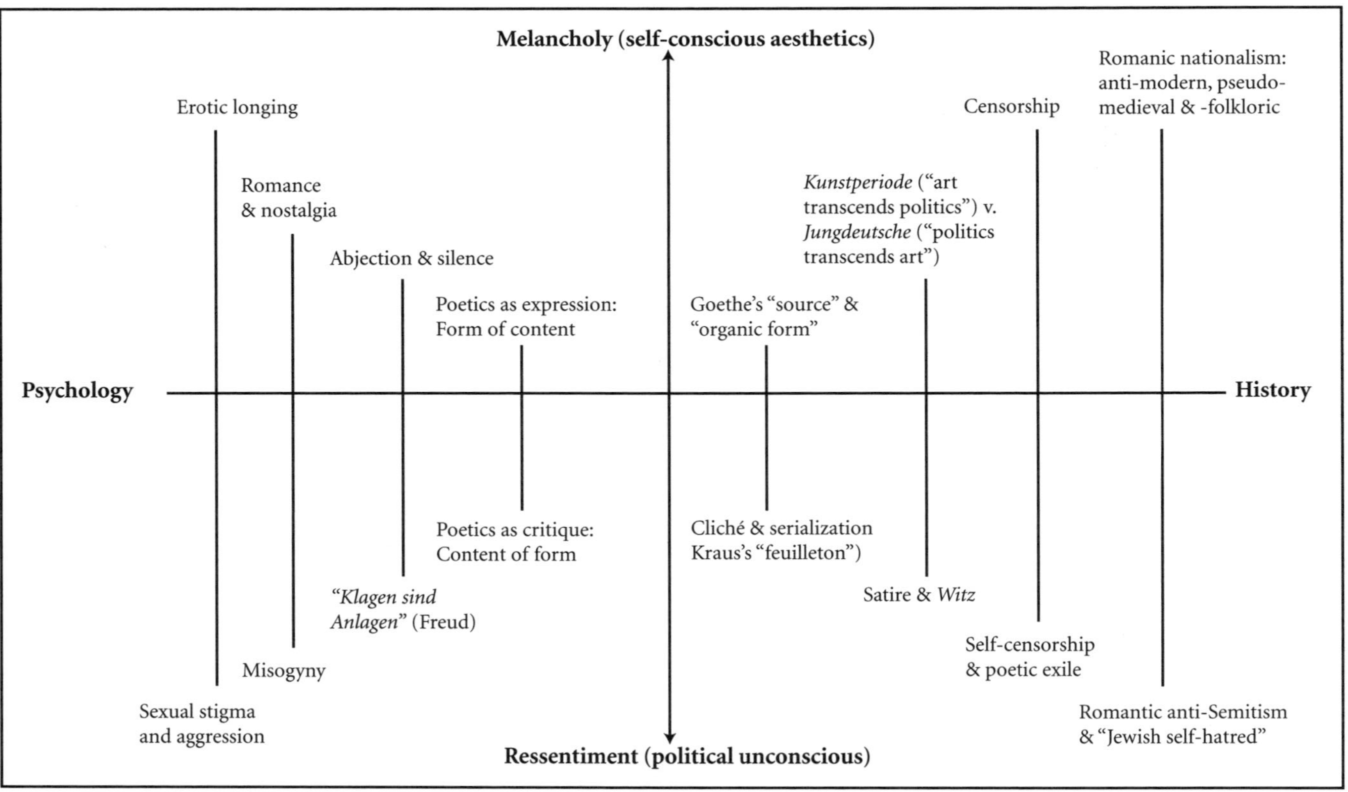

Diagram 2. Psychological and historical connections between melancholy and ressentiment.

(Der Sklavenaufstand in der Moral beginnt damit, daß das Ressentiment selbst schöpferisch wird und Werthe gebiert [Nietzsche 1996, 222 / 1980, 5: 270]). It is this very creativity that, albeit from a profoundly skeptical angle, Nietzsche views as the signature of European culture as a whole: "I am talking, admittedly, of the cultural domains of man, of every kind of 'Europe' which still exists on earth" (Ich rede, wie billig, von den Kulturgebieten des Menschen, von jeder Art "Europa", das es nachgerade auf Erden gibt [Nietzsche 1996, 101 / 1980, 5: 368]).

European culture—particularly in its late-bourgeois phase—is defined by its progressive refinement, indeed, its creation of inwardness as a three-dimensional, supremely differentiated affective spectrum and spectacle. In a sly parenthetical phrase, Nietzsche admits feeling "constrained" to give a "first, preliminary articulation" to his overall "hypothesis." Not surprisingly, it takes the form of a myth, a lucid fable about biologically ill-equipped beings constrained to adapt themselves to "a new, unknown world" where their instincts and drives no longer serve them. Consequently, humans

> were reduced, these unfortunate creatures, to thinking, drawing conclusions, calculating, combining causes and effects, to their "consciousness," their most meagre and unreliable organ! I believe that never on earth had there been such a feeling of misery, such leaden discomfort. Nor did the old instincts all of a sudden cease making their demands! Only it was difficult and seldom possible to obey them: for the most part, they had to seek new and, at the same time, subterranean satisfaction for themselves. Every instinct which does not vent itself externally *turns inwards*—this is what I call the *internalization* [*Verinnerlichung*] of man: it is at this point that what is later called the "soul" first develops in man. The whole inner world, originally stretched thinly as between two membranes, has been extended and expanded, has acquired depth, breadth, and height in proportion as the external venting of human instinct has been *inhibited.* (Nietzsche 1996, 64–65 / 1980, 5: 322)

However vivid and articulate, Nietzsche's fable about the origins of inwardness as the repository of moral and cultural cleverness remains, of course, just that: a fable. Given the pervasive formal and institutional ramifications of this development of "internalization" at the end of the nineteenth century, Nietzsche cannot purport to transcend them but, instead, must seek to capture them in an elliptical account whose synecdoches blatantly disregard the "objectivity" of academic prose. Rather than seeking to "ground" his reflections in principles or axioms, Nietzsche traces the reactive dynamics of ressentiment through its psychosocial symptoms. Consequently, the term "ressentiment" does not so much name a novel form of affect with its own discrete content as expose the unstable and potentially duplicitous nature of theories that explain the modern self as the product of an authentic epigenetic act.[23] Seen as the fusion of moral and aesthetic values into a single "sensibility" or "feeling," the romantic subject, in Nietzsche's account, is simply the apotheosis of a century-old process of adaptation. To unmask it, Nietzsche tells us, will also require an entirely new form of philosophy—namely, philosophy as literature in the strong sense.[24] The unveiling of romantic mood as "symptomatic" stimulates Nietzsche to develop a pugnacious, figurative style aimed, not at some "ultimate ground" (*Letztbegründung*), but at disarticulating any conceivable type of affective or intellectual repose. Thus what Nietzsche calls "interiorization" (*Verinnerlichung*) involves cultivating elaborate forms of self-deception, that is, the work of "culture" in the widest sense. The self's affective core comes into being as a metonymic series comprised of countless discrete acts of "secret self-violation" (heimliche Selbstvergewaltigung). Passing through so many stages of masochistic adaptation and self-deception, the modern individual eventually comes to take a "this artistic cruelty, this desire to give a form to the refractory, resistant, suffering material of one self" (diese Künstler-Grausamkeit, diese Lust, sich selbst als einem schweren widerstrebenden Stoffe eine Form zu geben [Nietzsche 1996, 68 / 1980, 5: 326]). The modern psyche's three-dimensionality appears wholly enmeshed with rhetorical convention, aesthetic form, and indeed with most everything subsumed under the name of "culture."

In a late resumption of his earlier, publicly repudiated *Birth of Tragedy*, Nietzsche conceives of the modern "cultured" individual as a strictly virtual entity, the product of an "ideal and imaginative" epigenesis. For the instincts and drives of a mythical prehistory—such as it is imagined in Nietzsche's self-conscious fable—have undergone a complete reversal of their original thrust. As a result, the "same active force . . . that now builds nations" also serves to establish the virtual empire of the "guilty conscience" with its narcissistic, second-order sense of pleasure and beauty and its brutal undertow of ressentiment:

> This secret self-violation, this artistic cruelty, this desire to give a form to the refractory, resistant, suffering material of oneself, to brand oneself with a will, a

> criticism, a contradiction, a contempt, a No, this sinister labour, both horrific and pleasurable, of a soul voluntarily divided against itself [diese unheimliche und entsetzlich-lustvolle Arbeit einer mit sich selbst willig-zwiespältigen Seele], a soul which makes itself suffer for the pleasure of it, this whole *active* "*bad* conscience," this actual maternal womb of ideal and imaginative events, has ultimately—as will be clear by now—brought to light much that is new and disturbing in the way of beauty and affirmation, and perhaps even first brought to light beauty as *such*. . . . For what would the meaning of "beautiful" be, if contradiction had not first become conscious of itself. (Nietzsche 1996, 68 / 1980, 5: 326)

Beauty here emerges as the vicarious latter-day progeny of a slow adaptive process in which, deprived of all intuitive certitude, the subject takes pleasure in its own figural and narcissistic pathos. Suffering is formally stylized into a psychological depth of sorts. And yet, even as Nietzsche appears to disparage the "recesses, byways, and trap-doors" of ressentiment, he concedes that such adaptive behavior will eventually produce a "smarter" (*klüger*) race, although invariably accompanied by "a faint taste of luxury and refinement" (Nietzsche 1996, 24 / 1980, 5: 273). Thus, the analysis of ressentiment necessarily coincides with that of culture. For it is the very idea of culture as an unconscious agency consumed with the formalization of "affect" and its conspicuous stylization as "sensibility" that constitutes the ultimate target of Nietzsche's polemic. In educating its others, or otherwise exacting their allegiance to cultural forms as embodiments of moral truth—as in Kant's "Beauty as a Symbol of Morality" (Schönheit als Symbol der Sittlichkeit [*Critique of Judgment*, § 59]) or Schiller's *Über Anmut und Würde* (On Grace and Dignity)— late Enlightenment culture effectively falls prey to an illusion of its own making. Wholly absorbed in their own mix of manifest self-denial and covert aggression, such individuals are incapable of transcending the brew of nationalism, anti-Semitism, economic anxiety, Christian righteousness, and romantic reverie from which they distill their affective quintessence. In Nietzsche's sweeping indictment, then, European bourgeois culture marks the end point of a development that has replaced formerly intuitive certitudes—which, in any event, Nietzsche's ultimately discredits as a mythic hypothesis—with intricately self-deceiving affective yearnings. European high culture thus appears calcified and institutional, a museum gathering all the aesthetic forms and social practices that had successively contributed to this attenuation, atrophying, and eventual disestablishment of the instinct:

> Assuming that what is now in any case believed to be the "truth" were true—that is, the meaning *of all culture* to breed a tame and civilized animal, a *domestic animal,* from the predatory animal "man"—then there is no doubt that one would have to consider all the instincts of reaction and ressentiment, with whose help the noble races and their ideals were finally ruined and overcome, as the real *instruments of culture.* Which is not to say that those who possess these instincts are at the same time representatives of culture itself. Rather, the opposite is not only probable—no! today it is *patently obvious!* Those who possess the oppressive and vindictive instincts, the descendants of all European and non-European slavery, of all pre-Aryan population in particular—they represent the *regression* of humanity! These supposed "instruments of culture" are a disgrace to mankind; they arouse suspicion and actually constitute an argument against "culture" as a whole. (Nietzsche 1996, 26–27 / 1980, 5: 276)

The emergence of the modern subject with its unique capacity for displacing ressentiment into dignified and formally subtle expression thus proves inextricable from the inventory of forms, the "tools of culture" that have made this transmutation possible. Yet how is one to contest this conspiratorial phenomenon to which Nietzsche refers, synecdochically, as "Europa" or *Kultur?* How is an adaptive process to be reversed that is said to date back at least as far as the beginnings of Christianity, a process that has by now fundamentally reorganized or reconditioned Western European culture by fashioning its subjects' inwardness as the domain of moral ("passive-aggressive") conquest? How is one to dismantle the subtle, clever passion play of Christian-romantic interiority, with its seemingly inexhaustible capacity for transfiguring the thirst for revenge, domination, and cruelty into such moral icons as mercy, submissiveness, and self-effacement?

The first intimations of the strategic recovery envisioned by Nietzsche can already be found in Keats, who, rather than subscribing to the ethos of preemptive contrition and self-mortification, analyzed ressentiment with acute self-consciousness.[25] Particularly for Heine and Nietzsche, the solution lay in resisting the seductive poses of romantic inwardness and in recognizing their statuesque, marble lifelessness as de facto a citation. Beyond that, it was imperative to move with "negative capability" beyond the positive identification with mere figures toward a genuinely figurative conception of writing. What Keats saw as Byron's inability to envision a strictly figurative state "through the medium of the heart . . . in a world of circumstances" (21 April 1819) helped shape Keats's own reflexive and ironic embrace of writing as aggressively and self-consciously performative. In Keats's words, it had become his "ambition . . . to make as great a revolution in modern dramatic writing as Kean has done in acting" (*LJK*, 2: 139). With its purposely scandalizing rhetoric—and spurning all metaphysical foundations ("the camelion poet . . . who has no identity" [*LJK*, 1: 387])—Keats's later poetry subtly exposes the cult of inwardness and feeling as one of masks, which, above all, delude those who wear them. While Keats's insight into a radically figurative, performative language—and its implicit program of a critique without an Archimedian center—remained unknown to Nietzsche, the latter certainly recognized very similar possibilities to have been opened up by Heine. Among his tributes to Heine, rare in their generosity, the following passage from *Ecce Homo* ranks preeminent:

> The highest concept of the lyrical poet was given to me by *Heinrich Heine.* I seek in vain in all the realms of history for an equally sweet and passionate music. He possessed that divine malice without which I cannot imagine perfection: I estimate the value of men, of races, according to the necessity by which they cannot conceive the god apart from the satyr [den Gott nicht abgetrennt vom Satyr zu verstehen wissen]. And how he handles his German! One day it will be said that Heine and I have been by far the foremost artists of the German language—at an incalculable distance from everything mere Germans have done with it. (1967, 245 / 1980, 6: 286)

At an "incalculable remove" from its mediocre employment at the hand of "mere Germans" (*blosse Deutsche*), Heine's language is that of the genuine artist in that it issues from the profound awareness of an eternal struggle between god and satyr, *eidos* and *physis.* Rather than subordinating the thrust of embodied instincts to putatively higher cerebral and affective notions, Heine's style exposes such ideals as forever infused with "divine malice" (*göttliche Bosheit*). The logic of ressentiment, in other words, cannot be articulated as "pure" thought or as a logical proposition. Rather, it is to be "teased out of thought" by a language that spurns the formalisms of epistemology and aesthetics and the complacency of "native" speech in favor of an unrelentingly inquisitive critical and skeptical practice. For most politically nonconformist romantics (Byron included), Napoleon was the supreme embodiment of Keats's poetic axiom "that which is creative must create itself" (*LJK*, 1: 374).[26] Combining the "revolutionary and counterrevolutionary" principles, Napoleon acted in a "consistently natural" (*beständig naturgemäß*) manner and never succumbed to "local intrigue," the province of "narrow, analytic minds" (*HSS*, 2: 235). His banishment and demise on St. Helena anticipated the figural exile of post-romantic and premodernist writers like Keats, Baudelaire, and Heine, for whom "all of Europe became a St. Helena" (*ganz Europa wurde ein Sankt Helena* [ibid., 664]. Marooned between the apolitical marble deities of Goethe's Weimar and a hopelessly mediocre quotidian model of politically engagé art, these writers can only seek to unmask the fraudulent pretensions of Napoleon's self-appointed successors in the world of restoration culture and politics. Thus Heine appears equally suspicious of middle-class philistinism and of "high romantic" tropes (e.g., medievalism, bardic nationalism). For beneath the calm surface of Jena esotericism and Heidelberg mysticism, Heine senses the fatal undertow of craven bourgeois self-interest, Christian proselytizing, and once-again fashionable anti-Semitism. The rise of the bourgeoisie to socioeconomic preeminence is merely a garish substitute for the loss of political greatness (Napoleon), and the petit-bourgeois idealization of an apolitical "cultural" greatness (Goethe) only conceals a vindictive temper raging beneath its polished aesthetic forms and interior décor. As the following two passages demonstrate, both Heine and Nietzsche understand the writer's task to be that of uncovering precisely this seething and toxic potential of middle-class ressentiment and bourgeois *indifférence.* To articulate the political unconscious of one's own present requires esprit or "gusto" (Hazlitt's word) more than method or theory. The first passage (from Heine's Börne *Denkschrift* of 1840) takes up Börne's implacable loathing of Goethe, a shortcoming that, in Heine's view, cannot simply be ascribed to personal envy or professional animus. Rather, Börne's persistent vituperations of Goethe attest to the unconscious efficacy of ressentiment:

> Just as in his remarks on Goethe, so too in his comments on other writers, Börne reveals his Nazarene limitations. I say "Nazarene" so as to avoid alternative expressions, such as "Jewish" or "Christian," even though I regard these latter concepts as synonymous. For I use them not for the purpose of designating a faith but, rather, a certain kind of sensibility [*Naturell*]. "Jew" and "Christian" strike me as all but synonymous, in contradistinction to "Hellenic," which term, once again, I don't take to denominate a particular people but, rather, a cultural trend and intuitive disposition, themselves at once congenital and acquired. In this regard, then, I should say that all human beings are either Jews or Hellenes, either people of ascetic, iconophobic, and obsessively spiritualizing drives [Menschen

> mit asketischen, bildfeindlichen, vergeistigungssüchtigen Trieben] or those of a life-affirming, proudly capacious, and realistic nature. Thus there are Hellenes among the families of German preachers and Jews perhaps born in Athens or descendants of Theseus. It is fair to say here that the beard no more makes the Jew than the plait [*Zopf:* the pigtail of an eighteenth-century wig] makes the Christian. (*HSS,* 4: 17–18; my translation)

To many of his contemporaries, particularly the German-Jewish community of the 1820s perplexed by the true motives and dismayed by the outrageous conditions stipulated for Jewish cultural assimilation, Heine's statement was little short of a betrayal.[27] Rather than disavowing the Jewish faith, however, Heine's writing effectively redefines Jewishness as a distinctive sensibility (*Naturell*). Yet the latter concept is itself being used in a strictly figural sense. Thus Heine leaves it pointedly undecided as to whether Jewishness constitutes something "congenital or acquired" (*angeboren / angebildet*) by embedding the distinction itself in a "both . . . and" (*sowohl . . . als* [*auch*]) construction. Likewise, the traditionally opposed terms of Judaism and Hellenism are syntactically conjoined, with Heine characterizing each in its own right as both a "cultural trend *and* an intuitive disposition" (Geistesrichtung *und* Anschauungsweise [emphasis added]). To suggest that, for whatever reason, Heine here might have succumbed to the inherited, divisive rhetoric of nationalist, anti-Semitic, or reactionary pamphleteering is to ignore the quick thrust and parry of his figural constructions.

What ultimately invalidates any attempt at reading Heine's passage as a covert or unselfconscious expression of Jewish self-hatred is his wholly reflexive deployment of "Jew" and "Nazarene" representative of an anthropological tendency to strictly reactive behavior, curtailed instincts, and endless prevarication. Only a superficially righteous and self-cherishing reading (itself, perhaps, an expression of such Nazarenism) would repudiate the passage as evidence of a repressive, self-hating individual. If nothing else, Heine's prose itself is far too analytic of just that type of censorious, crudely moralizing approach. If the text conjures up popular anti-Semitic, anti-cosmopolitan, and anti-intellectual prejudices—almost to the point of aligning itself with these—it does so for shrewd tactical purposes. For if Heine's pointedly figural understanding of Jewishness seemed to indulge the age-old and lately revived (Rühs, Fries, Menzel, Pfizer) German proclivity toward anti-Semitism, it only does so only in order to unmask that cultural and affective pattern more effectively. For as gradually becomes clear, the voice of the anti-Semitic cultural and literary critic—with its relentless drumbeat in support of a spiritual and restrained "German-Christian" poetics—oddly resembles its own (vilified) other: the "ascetic, iconoclastic, addictively intellectualized" (asketischen, bildfeindlichen, vergeistigungssüchtigen) Nazarene or Jew. With its unexpected conjunctions and equations, Heine's syntax thus collapses the subject of anti-Semitic prejudice into its declared other. Far from naming some timeless affective essence, "Jewishness" here is recast as a function of contingent interpretation. The word names an indeterminate quality that cannot be parsed along the lines of inborn or acquired intuitive or intellectual traits. Heine's language is neither that of social conformism—the matter of Jewish identity simply looms to large for that—nor one of defiant partisanship on behalf of a determinate Jewish "cause."[28] Ultimately, Heine's text solicits the anti-Semite's festering ressentiment for purposes of its own undoing. As we shall see, it is precisely Heine's uncanny ability to blur boundaries—between the expressive and the merely discursive, poetry and feuilleton, faith and profit, noble esprit and lowly rancor—that makes him the prototype of the modern intellectual.[29]

While bearing a striking resemblance to Heine's idiom, Nietzsche's polemic intensifies its vehemence and broadens the target. As in Heine's passage, the principle of mimesis yields to the logic of the feuilleton.[30] Thus, rather than aiming at the faithful representation of a particular case, the prose figuratively evokes a type:

> a plethora of vindictive men disguised as judges, whose mouths continually secrete the word "justice" like a poisonous saliva, with lips always pursed, ready to spit at anything that looks content and goes its way in good spirits. Among them too there is no shortage of that most revolting species of vain men, the deceitful deformities who are out to play the part of "beautiful souls", and to hawk around their ruined sensuality, dressed up in poetry and other swaddling clothes, as "purity of heart" [etwa ihre verhunzte Sinnlichkeit, in Verse und andere Windeln gewickelt, als "Reinheit des Herzens" auf den Markt bringen: die Spezies der moralischen Onanisten und "Selbstbefriediger"]: the species of moral onanists and those who indulge in "self-satisfaction."[31]

Figuration here no longer serves to express inwardness but, on the contrary, peels back the inauthentic layers of feelings of morality, justice, and a "rundown sensuality." Rather than competing with the philistine's duplicitous sensibility, Nietzsche dismantles the pretensions of those who, in Keats's words, merely "cut a figure" by their excessive use of conventional figuration. In very similar ways, then, Heine and Nietzsche dismantle the putative self-sufficiency of affect by their persistent violation of rhetorical and social etiquette. Far from a lapse of aesthetic or philosophical sobriety, such stylistic dissonance, or *Stilbruch,* emerges as a new literary and social strategy aimed at unmasking ressentiment as the cult of romantic sensibility's unconscious, repressed foundation. The myth of organic form, of aesthetic and psychological values seamlessly and respectably aligned, is here subjected to a figurative and "divine malice" (göttliche Bosheit) unavailable to "mere Germans" (blosse Deutsche). Only in this way can writing open a genuinely critical perspective on the cherished inwardness of the bourgeois philistine and its unconscious other without creating a new myth of intellectual, affective, and formal stability.

Ressentiment, in other words, is neither merely to be indulged nor to be shunned in favor of values such as sobriety, moderation, objectivity, or self-chastisement. Rather, it is to be performed with a deliberate breach of moral-aesthetic etiquette. As Nietzsche so enthusiastically affirmed, reading Heine means following an invitation into the countless alleys and byways of ressentiment—itself the veritable affective signature of nineteenth-century German culture after Waterloo. A short poem from Heine's *Buch der Lieder* (no. 51 in "Lyrisches Intermezzo") articulates the kinship between lyric melancholy and (in this instance, gynophobic) ressentiment in truly programmatic terms:

Vergiftet sind meine Lieder;-
Wie könnt es anders sein?
Du hast mir ja Gift gegossen
Ins blühende Leben hinein.

Vergiftet sind meine Lieder;
Wie könnt es anders sein?
Ich trage im Herzen viel Schlangen,
Und dich, Geliebte mein. (*HSS*, 1: 96)

Envenomed are my songs,
How could it be otherwise, tell?
Since you trickled poison
Into my life's clear well.

Envenomed are my songs,
How could it be otherwise, tell?
My heart holds many serpents,
And you, my love, as well. (HEINE 1995, 24)

It is this motif of inescapable love, precariously generic in its expression and thus forever on the verge of unraveling, that encrypts the writer's experience of political, ethnic, and cultural alienation. The "dream" of a coherent and cherished world is disrupted by "a barren, quotidian reality, passion by a corrosive banality; the idea is distorted in the mirror of the real, and sentiment and mood dissolve into a stale sobriety" (Preisendanz, 16). In repeatedly staging this operation of performative disillusionment in the genre most obviously associated with idealization, Heine's lyrics striking anticipate the Nietzschean theory of ressentiment. The term identifies not so much a distinctive pathos as the ambivalence of any pathos whatsoever. Besides refusing any settled political identity, be it republican radicalism, conservative apostasy, folksy sentimentality, or simply "becoming Catholic out of sheer anger" (aus Ärger katholisch werden [*HSS*, 4: 111]), Heine's writings probe precisely that dilemma of the intellectual caught between these variously inadequate (not to say insincere) ideological positions. Like Keats, whose plea on behalf of his own allegedly incomplete development in his preface to *Endymion* appears to be set forth with rather too much cunning, Heine also proves curiously articulate about the supposed divisions within his own psyche. Keats's "mawkish" in-between is now writ large as an irremediable social rift (*Weltriß*) that reproduces itself in the writer's "disjointed existence" (*Zerrissenheit*):

> Ah! dear reader, rather than complaining about this inner division you should lament that the world itself has been rent in twain. Given that the poet's heart is the center of his world, the state of our present times could not but tear it apart. Whoever claims that their heart has remained intact only confesses that his is merely a prosaic heart, scarcely filling some remote niche. Yet nothing less than a world-historical rift has torn through mine, and it is for just that reason that I know how many years ago the gods favored me above many others and accorded me the honor of a poet's martyrdom. . . . Any imitation of wholeness is but a lie [jede Nachahmung ihrer Ganzheit ist eine Lüge], one that any healthy eye will readily see through, and that scorn won't spare. (*HSS*, 2: 405–6; my translation)

Characteristically perched between melodramatic self-involvement and outright persiflage, "martyrdom" here pertains as much to the act of writing as it does to the writer. For in the postclassical era, the writer must attest to the indelible rift (*Zerrissenheit*) of melancholy at the level of form. To warrant the "favor" and "grace" of the gods, the poet must steadfastly resist all claims to metaphysical totality, no less than to full social integration or "acculturation." At best, *imitatio* (*Nachahmung*) attests to the self-alienated and abject quality of modern existence, while poetry—far from offering redemption—can only expose that predicament by breaking down the defenses of an audience that continues to resist the disconcerting knowledge of its own modernity. This opening sketch of Heine's conception of literary production leaves us with a writer whose moral integrity and aesthetic success depend on the unveiling of an utterly fragmented and historically overdetermined quality in the lyric, the one genre charged more emphatically than any other with reaffirming the affective integrity of the (post-)romantic subject.[32] It is time now to lend greater specificity to these claims by showing how the structural nexus of melancholy and ressentiment is effectively uncovered by the concrete stylistic operations of Heine's poetry.

"Vergiftet sind meine Lieder": Melancholy as Figurative Toxin in Heine's Early Poetry

Heine and his equally shrewd publisher held out little hope for the commercial success of his 1827 *Buch der Lieder.*[33] Moreover, Robert Holub discounts Heine's early poems, reprinted in this collection, as little more than "stock motifs from the romantic arsenal," arguing that few, if any, of them "refer directly to the situation of the Jews," and that Heine's "shift from a disciple to a critic of romanticism" coincides precisely with the end of his early lyric career (Holub 1997, 41, 43).[34] In what follows, I take a substantially different tack. Rather than conceding the power of critique solely to prose and approaching German-Jewish relations from a strictly thematic perspective, I argue that Heine's writings—both prose and verse—constitute an ideologically significant formal insurrection in late romantic writing. Aside from the fact that "stock motifs" can hardly be taken *eo ipso* as evidence of conventional writing, their conspicuous presence in many of Heine's early poems points to a highly innovative aesthetic strategy. Foreshadowing the Dadaist movement that, in Walter Benjamin's lucid description, offered up "a relentless destruction of the aura of their creations, which they branded as reproductions with the very means of reproduction" (Benjamin 1968, 237–38), conventional motifs and oppressively familiar melancholic set pieces are abruptly invoked here, often in a monotonous series, only to be dismantled before the reader's eyes. Uncertain as to whether to embrace what seems the barest scaffolding of sentimental and melancholic effects, or to repudiate it as kitsch, Heine's audience is thus alienated from its own romantic longings and mystifications by an idiom that seems to have elevated *Stilbruch* into an operative principle. Rather than mechanically scanning the text with (necessarily amorphous) expectations of some "Jewish connection" or "Jewish element" (Holub, 53), we ought to connect Heine's relation to Judaism to his overarching preoccupation with unmasking bourgeois philistine ideologies through a critique of their linguistic and aesthetic forms.[35] Written during a period when the social enfranchisement of German Jews was widely understood to pivot on their linguistic assimilation and aesthetic "acculturation," Heine's early poems in the *Buch der Lieder* show romantic sensibility to be a deeply conventional façade supported by "codified stage props of proven efficacy" (Ederer, 33). Behind the complacent formulations of a quintessentially melancholic and estranged interiority, Heine's shrewd strategy of serial *imitatio* uncovers the false and prejudicial paradigm of romanticism as "essentially" Christian, nationalist, and German—that is, as ressentiment. In its irreverent enmeshing of romantic sentimentality with serialization, cliché, and *Witz,* Heine's poetry disrupts the German romanticism's refined obliviousness of its own ideological underpinnings. Well beyond the incidentals of a "Jewish connection," Heine's *Buch der Lieder* disrupts the stylistic homogeneity of romantic lyricism (in such writers as Brentano, Uhland, Fouqué, Kerner, Schlegel, and Lenau) and thereby challenges the cherished axiom of a mythic conformity between romantic aesthetics and a uniquely German type of affect.

If Heine's volume got off to a commercially slow start, the poetry contained in it eventually established a vast audience for itself. People were drawn to Heine's unique fusion of sentimental and critical effects, of affective longings subtly deconstructed as an unwitting rhetorical masquerade of the petit bourgeois unconscious. Moreover, Heine's still persuasive arguments in favor of political convictions that can be realized only in the domain of the aesthetic still challenge his readers. Here, again, we confront the limitations of the new historicist premise that critical insight is a dialectical function of how and what the past agencies of writer and reader (supposedly) could not see, a premise that rests on a further and often unacknowledged assumption that literary form is by definition unfit for the representation of critical insight. Quite the contrary, we shall find Heine's *Buch der Lieder* cunning in its deployment of formal devices, self-conscious about its affective bearings, and foreshadowing the cultural dynamics that would shape its reception for decades to come.[36] Out of the interplay of melancholy and ressentiment, of a deceptively forthright sensibility and its sly dismantling as unwitting aggression (performed both *within* and *as* poetry) a new type of knowledge emerges. It is the knowledge of a modernity that has quietly taken hold of everyone's psyche, rendering affect and topos, feeling and cliché, all but indistinguishable. Here, then, the lines between authentic (self-)expression and mere citation, between a poetry grounded in a bountiful source of inspiration and a serialized, journalistic idiom serving the public's craving for entertainment and scandal appear terminally blurred. For more than a century, Heine continued to be perceived, alternatively, as a pathological instance of this disconcerting modernity or as its diabolical agent. While some readers, Friedrich von Gentz among them, were able to grasp the necessary symbiosis of these two roles, the perception of Heine as the frivolous hireling of a rootless cultural modernity usually prevailed.[37] As Karl Kraus (1874–1936) notoriously declared, Heine had "so loosened the corset of the German language that today any errand boy can fondle her breasts" (der Sprache so sehr das Mieder gelockert hat, daß heute alle Kommis an ihren Brüsten fingern können [193]). Yet Kraus's misogynistic figure of speech noticeably succumbs to the condition of a (supposedly) shiftless style—formally identified by Kraus as the "French disease" of the modern feuilleton—which, he charges, Heine had first imported into the German language.[38] As "the precursor of modern nervous systems" (der Vorläufer moderner Nervensysteme [210]), Heine is a "dangerous mediator between art and life, and a parasite to both" who has "casually" initiated a "dreadful development" (Kraus 189, 191). More than anything, Kraus—to whose (partially self-hating) polemic we shall return later—recoils from the reproducibility of Heine's style, its deliberate enmeshing of sentiment and ressentiment, and "little melancholia's little wisecrack" (den kleinen Witz der kleinen Melancholie [196–97]).

As sketched in diagram 2, it is less the issues or themes that are in doubt in a reading of Heine than the vantage point from which we might legitimately assess their valence. Kraus's vehement response to Heine's fusion of poetry and journalism and to the "mass-appeal [*Massenwirkung*] of his love lyrics" (201) attests to a deeper knowledge of his own, inescapable affiliation with the jaded mass culture of the feuilleton, the best-seller, and the glittering merchandise abounding in the shopwindows of Vienna's Ringstrasse. Similarly, we too cannot eschew the disconcerting truth so inescapably set forth by Heine's poetry. For Kraus, Heine was not a messenger but *the* perpetrator of a modernity in which politics and entertainment, reflection and leisure, authentic passion and its skillfully produced *simulacra* have become inextricable. In his account, the Jewish-born Heine emerges as a peddler and lower-class parvenu eager to profit from the "great feat of verbal forgery rather than verbal creativity" (Der große sprachschwindlerische Trick, der sich in Deutschland viel besser lohnt als die größte sprachschöpferische Leistung [191]). As the Jewish novelist Jakob Wassermann, Kraus's contemporary, noted, this perception of the Jew as incapable of originality and given to counterfeit forms, was widespread, deep-seated, and certainly not confined to the gentile population.[39]

Kraus's highly concentrated litany of prejudices against the Jewish writer / journalist provides an important cue for our assessment of Heine's liminal place between romanticism and modernism, a position he shares above all with Keats and Baudelaire. For Heine's epoch-making volume of lyric poetry, I would argue, marks the beginning of a lifelong concern with dismantling the linguistic and affective underpinnings of the German middle class. However diverse in their economic and educational profiles, the various communities of civil servants, *Bildungsbürger*, merchants, and rising bourgeois industrialists all presented themselves as an ideological phalanx to the Jewish-German subject. Preeminent among the criteria that were being invoked as indispensable attributes of one's "Germanness" was the capacity to "feel deeply"—analogous to Burke's and Wordsworth's self-privileging accounts of Englishness as a matter of "slow and deep" feelings conceived "without immediate external excitement."[40]

In rewriting the language of feeling as a lyric exposé—that is, as a function of technique—Heine may indeed seem but a "skilled technician of pleasure and suffering, the assiduous tailor for any type of mood" (lust- und leidgeübten Techniker, als prompten Bekleider vorhandener Stimmungen [Kraus, 200]). Yet to take that view is to indulge one's own aesthetic misgivings rather than analyzing them, in which case one would also begin to glimpse deeper-seated motives for Heine's practice. As the quintessential Jewish outsider (a matter to which we shall have to return), Heine certainly understood the exclusionary thrust behind the prevailing mystification of German romantic sensibility. A far cry from the Enlightenment's vision of political and religious toleration, the synthesis of bland Christian values with adversarial languages of patriotism and nationalism that emerged after 1815 was to converge in a prescriptive and exclusionary model of linguistic and rhetorical acculturation. To "know" politics, Heine soon understood, required an acute, indeed speculative relationship to tone or (in Roland Barthes's phrase) to "the rustle of language." Traditionally, of course, the purpose of such linguistic proficiency in the vernacular was to advance from the status of a Jewish "subject" to that of a German (or, ideally, German-Jewish) "citizen." As Heine understood all too well, the path of ascendancy was laborious; to be privately "well-spoken" (and "well spoken of") would not suffice. Rather, one's application for membership in the linguistic and aesthetic community of the German *Bürgertum* had to be submitted to the public and "in writing" as it were. For only through one's transferential cultivation of an audience and through its affirmative response could one's bid for social ascendancy and cultural enfranchisement ever succeed. As Heine puts it, "marketability and other aspects of attaining popularity would be my sole concern . . . and this, my principal book would furnish a psychological profile of me" (die Wohlfeilheit und die andern Erfordernisse des Popularwerdens wären meine einzigen Rücksichten . . . und diese Buch würde mein Hauptbuch seyn und ein psychologisches Bild von mir geben [*HB*, 1: 299; my translation]). Exhibiting an astonishing versatility, while also disconcerting its readers by suggesting that such versatility had been achieved far too easily, Heine's *Buch der Lieder* falls into a delicate historical period. The years between 1821 and 1837, spanning from the appearance in print of Heine's first poems to the publication of the hugely popular second edition of the *Buch der Lieder*, witnessed crucial historical and cultural shifts in the German-speaking world. Aside from the complex challenge presented by the *Jungdeutsche* School, discussed earlier, the period witnesses an unprecedented (if not entirely successful) intensification of censorship measures. In addition, we find a resurgence of legislative measures aimed at the economic and civic disenfranchisement of Germany's Jewish minorities, as well as the consolidation of age-old anti-Semitism into a cultural program of sorts, with ancient rhetorical strains now being refined into a divisive cultural strategy.

Again, what connects these macrohistorical issues and the formal specificity of a given poem or group of poems is an underlying "mood." It is only in the volatile and supple design of nonintentional and nonpropositional (i.e., aesthetic) forms that such a dominant "mood" can be traced as the substratum uneasily juggling the topical and explicit realm of quotidian, conscious existence (its countless topics, agendas, and debates, along with so many official memories and competing genealogies), and the realm of the "symptom"—things left inexplicit, elided, or wholly expunged from public perception and memory. For not to do so would cause the conscious order to collapse under the weight of its countless antagonisms and contradictions. The objective of aesthetic form in general and, in the context of late romantic melancholy, of lyric form in particular, thus becomes to mediate these two spheres that are constitutively barred from ever acknowledging one another. In the case of Heine, this means that the lyric objectivates the divided psyche of the late romantic subject *in* and *as* a form at once representative and symptomatic. Through its concise elaboration of a paradigmatic "mood" (*Stimmung*), lyric poetry opens up a partial vista on a certain dissent or ressentiment (*Verstimmung*). Hardly any other form seems as fit to lay bare the peculiar dialectic between affect and rhetoric, between a vision of pure and noncontradictory inwardness and the historical forces at once obstructing its material realization and, thus, urging its continued symbolic reaffirmation. Hence Heine's poems keep obtruding the same set of questions and perplexities: when is a text expressive of a particular affective state (love, grief, fear, loathing, etc.), and when does writing succumb to (or deliberately cite) the social and / or aesthetic grammar regulating expressive behavior? Moreover, how are readers of Heine's poetry to disentangle "use" from "mention" (to borrow John Searle's distinction), expression from citation? Finally, can readers *know* when the border between the expressive and the performative has been crossed and, if so, is it in their interest to acknowledge that fact?[41] Perhaps, the distinction cannot be maintained at all, for as Heine himself remarks, "just as we only form knowledge of things by way of their opposite, so we wouldn't have anything like poetry except by perceiving what is ordinary, vulgar and trivial (alle Dinge sind uns ja nur durch ihren Gegensatz erkennbar, es gäbe für uns gar keine Poesie, wenn wir nicht überall auch das Gemeine und Triviale sehen könnten [*HB*, 1: 83]). It is precisely the lyric's capacity for exhibiting a formalized, settled language to contain its own contrary that also defines Heine's overall understanding of literary practice: "Literature! that's us and our enemies" (Literatur, das sind wir und unsere Feinde [*HB*, 2: 27]). An early poem in the collection reveals the unique enjambment of naïveté and cunning, nostalgia and aggression in Heine's lyrics:

Ich wandelte unter den Bäumen
Mit meinem Gram allein;
Da kam das alte Träumen,
Und schlich mir ins Herz hinein.

Wer hat euch dies Wörtlein gelehret,
Ihr Vöglein in luftiger Höh'?
Schweigt still! wenn mein Herz es höret,
Dann tut es noch einmal so weh.

"Es kam ein Jungfräulein gegangen,
Die sang es immerfort,
Da haben wir Vöglein gefangen
Das hübsche, goldne Wort."

Das sollt ihr mir nicht mehr erzählen,
Ihr Vöglein wunderschlau;
Ihr wollt meinen Kummer mir stehlen,
Ich aber niemanden trau. (*HSS*, 1: 38)

Parading under the trees' green ceiling
Alone with my grief, I wept;
An old, old dream came stealing
And into my heart it crept.

Who taught you that word you sing,
You birds that soar in the air?
Be still! in my heart it is ringing,
It fills me again with despair.

"A maiden came, fair and lonely;
She sang it, and we heard;
And now we birds sing only
That beautiful golden word."

Oh tell me no more, you designing
Deceitful, sly old birds!
You'd steal my sorrow and pining—
But I trust no one's words. (HEINE 1982, 24–25)

Heine's poem offers a fine illustration of what Freud had meant when observing that "the poets have been there before me." From the outset, the speaker's references to his sorrow (*Gram*) appear conspicuously staged. For a person professedly suffering from an as yet unspecified loss, the choice of verb for his absorbed peregrinations (*Ich wandelte*) appears oddly ceremonial and mannered. The stress on *allein* (nicely accented in Schumann's setting of the poem in his 1840 Op. 24 *Song Cycle*) at the close of the second line further heightens our perception of the speaker's relation to his own emotions as narcissistic and ritualized. In what follows, the speaker's acutely self-conscious, indeed, critical, versatility is borne out by the poem's tightly wrought narrative and analytic structure. From the old dreams *(das alte Träumen)* whose covert intrusion into the speaker's psyche is observed almost as a matter of routine to the speaker's concluding defensive affirmation of his sorrow as wholly inalienable, the poem conceives of melancholia as perhaps a miscarriage of self-consciousness but certainly not a lack of it. As Freud puts it, "we see how in this condition one part of the ego sets itself over against the other, judges it critically, and as it were, looks upon it as an object" (Freud 1963b, 168). This critical, reflexive tendency of melancholia manifests itself, above all, in a certain patterning and formalization of speech. Melancholia differs from almost all other neurotic disturbances (with the important exception of paranoia) in that its subject, rather than regressing from speech and symbolization, reveals "the opposite trait of insistent talking about himself and pleasure in the consequent exposure of himself." The melancholic subject exhibits "an impoverishment of his ego on a grand scale" (*eine großartige Ichverarmung* [ibid., 167–68]).

The two middle stanzas of the poem address precisely this threatening possibility that, rather than constituting a private possession, the affect of sorrow might turn out to be a social value of sorts. However, it seems difficult to take the speaker's communion with the birds soaring above as literal or, for that matter, as sincerely figural. The flight of his communion with them appears too overtly ventriloquistic, too precious as to be taken at face value. More plausibly, these stanzas rehearse one of melancholia's intrinsic paradoxes: namely, that what Freud had identified as the melancholiac's "obtrusive communicativeness" (*aufdringliche Mitteilsamkeit*) might furnish evidence of the social determinacy of the subject's inner life. That is, sorrow here is prompted not by the loss of a beloved (who, as remains to be seen, is more likely the target of ressentiment) but, rather, by the speaker's insight into the inescapably social and iterative character of all affective experience as language. "The precious word"—expressly identified as "love" in the handwritten manuscript—of his bereavement turns out to be a commonplace, a cliché whistled from treetops by birds that, in turn, have picked it up from his beloved. Rather than originating in a singular and utterly private moment of loss, melancholy centers on the subject's nascent recognition of its interiority as something inherently social. Not surprisingly, this insight is greeted with resentment no less than with sorrow, for it retroactively threatens to invalidate the subject's presumptive attachment to a cherished other. Only so can we explain the harsh directive at the birds that have purloined, and thus invalidated, the melancholiac's fetishized and supposedly inalienable feeling of pain: "Schweigt still! wenn mein Herz es höret, / Dann tut es noch einmal so weh." The logic of affect undergoes a paradigmatic transformation here, signaled in Schumann's setting by the "pianissimo" (*sotto voce*) instruction during the third stanza's nearly imperceptible shift from G to E♯. For no longer is "sorrow" (*Gram*) occasioned by the loss of the beloved. On the contrary, the sorrow in question is now understood to derive from the fact that it was she herself who had entered the precious word (*das Wörtlein*) and implicitly also herself, into public circulation by singing it over and over again. The betrayal that has given rise to the speaker's melancholy, then, is perpetrated by the otherness of language itself, rather than by another being. Ultimately, it is this indirection of the affective life—indeed, of romantic interiority *tout court*—through language, its inescapably discursive character that lies at the very root of melancholy, even as it also vitiates the speaker's attempts to hold on to it as a strictly inward experience. Hence, beneath the poem's conspicuously mannered expressive veneer, there lurks the toxin of ressentiment. It is here directed at an other who is now accused of having repeatedly (*immerfort*) placed the "precious golden word" of love in the public sphere and thereby having prostituted the supposed integrity of that feeling and indeed herself. Unlike individuals depressed by a genuine and acute sense of inferiority, melancholic subjects, as Freud notes, "are not ashamed and do not hide their heads . . . because everything derogatory that they say of themselves at bottom relates to someone else." It is only that, in the classic sense of what is colloquially known as "passive-aggressive," an "attitude of revolt" is being transformed into one of "melancholic contrition" (Freud 1963b, 169–70). Heine's poem rehearses for us precisely the furtive, second-order creativity of the subject of ressentiment, one whose very soul, in Nietzsche's memorable phrase, is "cross-eyed."[42]

Far from succumbing to the pathology (the "failure to mourn") that delimits Freud's account of melancholia, Heine's lyrics effectively anticipate that very theory as a distinctively shaped readerly response and, in some important respects, move beyond it. Thus, Heine's poem and those that follow it in the *Buch der Lieder,* confront their audience with the self-alienated affective condition of the modern subject, its melancholic estrangement from any intact form of inner experience. Lyric speech is being deployed as an uneasy montage of romantic clichés, colloquialisms, and hackneyed sentiments that seem all but indistinguishable from citations. Form here appears as the ideological content of its historical moment, inasmuch as "the set expression [*Phrase*], the brand name that converts thought into a commodity" reveals the "utterly transformed character of language in the world of high capitalism."[43] In contrast to trauma and paranoia, melancholy expresses the subject's positive knowledge of this transformation as irreversible. Such a mood articulates modernity as a condition of excessive knowledge, including the individual's awareness that the gap between the inner life and social process, the poignancy of subjective affect and the mediated character of historical experience can never be closed. Indeed, Walter Benjamin contends, "melancholy betrays the world for the sake of [that very] knowledge," with the result that in a world thus conceived, we find no longer meanings but only fragments without "any natural, creative relationship to us." No longer functional tools, the things and linguistic forms of the melancholiac's world amount merely to "symptoms of depersonalization" (Benjamin 1998, 157, 140). Benjamin's vision of a thoroughly allegorized world recalls what Immermann and Heine among others refer to as *Epigonentum*—the knowledge of being trapped in a world where every object, every form of speech or writing constitutes part of an essentially outmoded (and partially alien) heritage. Heine's poem presents us with a speaker whose nervous, self-conscious attachment to his own sorrow identifies him as the consummate epigone—"a hybrid of poet and audience" (Greiner, 82). Readers are hard-pressed not to stumble over the repeated instances of narcissistic and mannered self-expression or, for that matter, mounting evidence of covert aggression toward the end of the poem. Beyond all that, however, the lyric also appears to foreshadow the eventual linguistic reorientation of Freudian psychology in the work of Lacan and Kristeva. For the duplicitous character of melancholy in the poem is not the result of some original loss or betrayal but, as we have seen, stems from the recognition that affect of any kind can only endure by giving itself over to language. No matter how much that linguistic form may be fetishized as "that beautiful golden word" (*das hübsche, goldne Wort*), it disarticulates affect as an essentially social form, conspicuously iterative (*Die sang es immerfort*) and hence at risk of being susceptible to public citation—in short, a cliché. It is just this impinging recognition that accounts for the speaker's defensiveness toward the close of the poem. The prospect of subjective affect and its (public) rhetorical form proving inextricable is recast (with overtones of paranoia) as an attempted privation: "You'd steal my sorrow and pining— / But I trust no one's words" (Ihr wollt meinen Kummer mir stehlen, / Ich aber niemandem trau).

In the end, of course, the birds' "marvelously sly" attempt at depriving the speaker of his cherished interiority by circulating the supposed erotic secret between the speaker and the generic female ought to be read figurally. As Adorno puts it, in Heine, "the development of subjectivism is inseparable from a progress of self-reification: the subject becomes the easily accessible, facile content of its own poetry . . . a commodity" (*AGS*, 20, ii: 449). Though Adorno's assessment of Heine warrants substantial qualification (of which more later), the latter's poetry certainly lends a good deal of support to the thesis that here, "as an artistic principle . . . triteness, banality, the hackneyed and the conventionalized" had been "consciously introduced." One only need to consider Heine's (very early) detached characterization of his early lyrics as "honey-coated pain" (in Honig getauchter Schmerz [*HB*, 1: 8]). Such distrust of romantic notions of sensibility and pathos (*Empfindsamkeit*), as well as the casual suggestion that such interior experiences can now be mass-produced, would later be seized upon by nationalist and anti-Semitic critics as evidence of the Jewish writer's supposed incapacity for genuine poetic feeling.[44] Like Freud, whose career was to be materially affected by similar prejudices, Heine's decision to end the lyric with a peremptorily defensive utterance ("Ich aber niemandem trau") may well betray his anticipation a century of tortured, often hostile reactions to his shrewd deconstruction of romantic interiority.

Another poem, no. 50 in "Lyrisches Intermezzo," works with far coarser brushstrokes to viciously satiric effect. Bearing a striking resemblance to the works of Honoré Daumier that were about to appear in Charles Philipon's newly founded satirical magazines *La Caricature* (1830) and *Le Charivari* (1832), Heine here works with the concision and quasi-serial economy of the cartoon.[45] An unidentified, indeed generic "They" opens the poem, incrementally revealed as a random sampling of middle-class men and women—what Karl Gutzkow so succinctly captures as "die pietistisch-bürokratischmilitärische Berliner Welt" (1998, 2: 1936). A couple from the lower gentry whose faded affluence has been exchanged for the ritualized banality of the Bürgertum augments Heine's demographic cross-section. No less generic than this cast of characters, "love" serves as the topic for "much" conversation. Ranging in appearance from the merely vulgar to the physiologically defective, an emaciated mid-level bureaucrat, a wide-mouthed church elder, and a lisping bachelorette combine into a grotesque update on the eighteenth-century conversation piece. All is ennui here, and Heine's purposely flat-footed diction doesn't spare us any part of it:

Sie saßen und tranken am Teetisch,
Und sprachen von Liebe viel.
Die Herren, die waren ästhetisch,
Die Damen von zartem Gefühl.

"Die Liebe muß sein platonisch",
Der dürre Hofrat sprach.
Die Hofrätin lächelt ironisch,
Und dennoch seufzet sie: "Ach!"

Der Domherr öffnet den Mund weit:
"Die Liebe sei nicht zu roh,
Sie schadet sonst der Gesundheit."
Das Fräulein lispelt: "Wieso?"

Die Gräfin spricht wehmütig:
"Die Liebe ist eine Passion!"
Und präsentieret gütig,
Die Tasse dem Herren Baron.

Am Tische war noch ein Plätzchen,
Mein Liebchen, da hast du gefehlt.
Du hättest so hübsch, mein Schätzchen,
Von deiner Liebe erzählt. (*HSS*, 1: 95–96)

They drank tea and waxed theoretic
About love and its sinful allure;
The gentlemen stressed the aesthetic,
The ladies were all for *l'amour.*

Love must be strictly Platonic,
The emaciated Councilor cried.
His spouse smiled slightly ironic,
And murmured, Oh dear me! And sighed.

The Prelate shrieked like a buzzard,
Love must not be rough, don't you know,
Or else it becomes a health hazard!
The little miss whispered How so?

The Countess sighed soulful and tender.
True love is a passion, she trilled,
As with a sweet smile of surrender
The Baron's cup she refilled.

There was still a place at the table,
That should have been yours, my dove;
You'd have been so eager and able
To tell them about your love. (HEINE 1982, 9)

There is no trace of narrative or psychological depth but, on the contrary, mounting and worrisome evidence that the affective lives of late romantic individuals have become utterly atrophied. The gentlemen are merely *ästhetisch*—a word whose utter vacuity Heine emphasizes by rhyming it with and almost anagrammatically deriving it from *Teetisch* (tea table). Here, then, the affective disposition of all the conversationists appears as merely the default of their social setting. And yet, the furtive gestures and monosyllabic expressions sketched with great economy reveal a complex substratum of passion, sensuality, even rage almost effaced by the passage of time or strangled by self-censorship. Thus the bureaucrat's solemn affirmation of platonic love elicits both an "ironic smile" *and* a nostalgic sigh ("Ach!") from his wife. While the smile may betoken an obvious dissent from her husband's clumsy moralizing, the fleeting "Ach!" could be taken as stifled protest or as a wistful recollection of not-so-platonic moments. Likewise, in calling into question the church elder's peculiar rejection of "raw" (rough, physical) "love," the bachelorette's barely lisped "Wieso?" offers a glimpse at heterodox passions seething beneath (and here *visibly* choked off by) the formalisms of polite conversation. Already destabilized by such symptomatic signs and gestures, the poem's basic antithesis between platonic and sexual love, professed sentiments and genuine passions, completely disintegrates in the concluding stanza. For the speaker, who as it turns out has himself been present at the *Teetisch,* now imagines how his own beloved might have "performed" at a scene of such fraudulent sociability. Far from transcending the mannered sentimentality that has defined the entire conversation thus far, the beloved, it is speculated, would merely have added yet another "trite" sententious statement to those already in circulation—thus compromising any assumptions about the superior authenticity of the speaker's inner life.

Rather than indulging in melancholic sentiment, that is, Heine's satiric style critically unveils such affect as a self-imposed delusion and a vainglorious attempt by the late romantic subject to fend off overwhelming evidence that attests to the commodity character of inwardness. The excruciating sociability of the *Teetisch* also shapes the historical condition of *ästhetisch* man, such as the lyric poet holding uneasy communion with Berlin's readers, publishers, booksellers, and critics: "Having been mocked and spat in one's face by the booksellers, one next is to endure the martyrdom of tea and polite conversation, followed by the crown of thorns in the form of inanely conceited praise, and thereafter the crucifixion by literary reviews" (Nach dem buchhändlerischen Verhöhnen und dem Insgesichtgespucktwerden kommt die theegesellschaftliche Geißelung, die Dornenkrönung dummpfiffigen Lobs, die literaturzeitungliche Kreuzigung (*HB,* 1: 55). For Heine, however, the martyrdom depicted here with such wit and hyperbole is neither something to be awaited passively nor merely the prosaic other of his imaginary worlds. On the contrary, poetry itself must assimilate some of the numbing inanity, judgmental arrogance, and brazen self-interest that informs its colloquial other. Woven into the very textures of Heine's lyric-satiric mode, deceit, lies and semblance (*Betrügen, Lüge, Schein*) thus need not be repudiated as the antithesis of true inwardness but, on the contrary, generate a new, peculiarly urbane type of pleasure. The point emerges with full force in the very first line of the following short poem:

In den Küssen welche Lüge!
Welche Wonne in dem Schein!
Ach, wie süß ist das Betrügen,
Süßer das Betrogensein!

Liebchen, wie du dich auch wehrest,
Weiß ich doch, was du erlaubst;

Glauben will ich, was du schwörest,
Schwören will ich, was du glaubst. (*HSS*, 1: 239)

Ah, what lies are told by kisses!
Bliss in false illusions, child!
Sweet are beguiling artifices;
Sweeter yet, to be beguiled!

Your resistance I perceive, dear,
Yet I know what you'll allow.
I'll avow what you believe, dear,
I'll believe what you avow. (Heine 1982, 175)

Besides startling with its harsh affective dissonance, the opening line also produces a textual déja vu effect of sorts, in that it offers a parodic citation of the opening line from Goethe's "Willkommen und Abschied" (In Deinen Küssen, welche Wonne). From here on, all the way to the closing lines' chiasmic precision, this short incidental poem at once asserts and formally exemplifies the homology of affect and illusion, interiority and (self-)manipulation, sentimentality and ressentiment in Heine: "I'll avow what you believe, dear, / I'll believe what you avow." At its most extreme, Heine's style offers a deliberately grotesque amalgam of melodrama, sentimentality, and brazenly satiric indictment—designed, it seems, to sow confusion within an oppressively settled cultural landscape. Time and again, it confounds the declarative with the figural, the referential with the performative, and the vivid illustration of facts with the mocking recitation of sentiment.[46] With its shrewd enjambment of dramatic pathos and analytic interest, Heine's style unsettles just about anyone's political beliefs. As his writings demonstrate in so many ways, grasping the political element in romanticism demands an acute sensitivity to that elusive quality known as "tone."

Like Keats, Heine unsettles with the countless shades and registers of tone: does a given passage express a complex psychological state or insight, or is it but a melancholy or ironic repetition of a specific psychological value bordering on the commonplace? Literature after Goethe often induces in its audience a vertiginous state of self-consciousness, in part because of the aristocratic, larger-than-life presence so scrupulously cultivated by the *Dichterfürst* himself, yet also because the epigone's ironic self-awareness is beyond stabilization. Gone is Goethe's supremely self-assured dramatization of eros, as well as its underlying faith in the text's ability to reclaim the "source" of its inspiration. Contrasting the neurotic self-consciousness of Heine's lyric personae with the statuesque charisma of Goethe's voice in his *Sesenheimer Lieder* (1771) or his *Römische Elegien* (1788) is quite instructive. For both in his letters and in the following short lyric from his *Buch der Lieder* (no. 88 in the section titled "Die Heimkehr" ["The Homecoming"]), Heine himself draws attention to his self-consciously belated and constitutively denatured authorial persona. Where Goethe had prized "above all life, its beautification and continuity, and indeed everything practical" (das Leben, die Verschönerung und Erhaltung desselben, so wie das eigentlich praktische überhaupt" [*HB*, 1: 210]), Heine lyrics present themselves as epitaphs commemorating the demise of Goethe's and early romanticism's aesthetic, erotic, and political confidence:

"Sag, wo ist dein schönes Liebchen,
Das du einst so schön besungen,
Als die zaubermächt'gen Flammen
Wunderbar dein Herz durchdrungen?"

Jene Flammen sind erloschen,
Und mein Herz ist kalt und trübe,
Und dies Büchlein ist die Urne
Mit der Asche meiner Liebe. (*HSS*, 1: 149)

"Tell me, where's the shining love that
Once you sang of, sweet and tragic,
In the days your heart was filled with
Wonder-working flames of magic?"

—Ah, my heart is cold and weary,
And those flames have fled above;
And this book is now the urn with
All the ashes of my love. (HEINE 1982, 110)

The writer here understands himself to be a hybrid—half creator, half journalist—continually looking over his own shoulder toward the aesthetic monuments of Germany's recent past, at once overwhelming and unhelpful.[47] As the repository of an affective plenitude that can only be inferentially claimed a posteriori, the writer's "cold heart" merges figurally with the "book," itself but the "urn" containing the ashes of some irrecoverable (and possibly fantasized) past love. We recall Walter Benjamin's distinction between the vast inquisitiveness of the Renaissance subject and the melancholic bookishness of the baroque: "The Renaissance explores the universe; the baroque explores libraries" (1992, 140). Yet as their dialectical kinship suggests, Goethe's erotic confidence and Heine's stylized despondency both turn out to be poses or, rather, motivic encryptions of a dynamic that pertains less to a particular poem than that it informs the practice of writing overall.[48]

As early as 1823, Heine's friend and fellow member in Berlin's Verein für Kultur und Wissenschaft der Juden, Moses Moser, offered a shrewd Hegelian assessment of the symptomatic (structural rather than thematic) place occupied by love in Heine's lyrics. As Moser puts it,

> The Romantic world, taken in itself, reflects a sensibility that, having abandoned all attempts at a finite presentation of the divine, has withdrawn into interiority; its sphere has already moved beyond art proper as it had been perfected in the ancient world. Consequently, it can no longer present infinity as external appearance but only in mediated form, namely, as the attraction and repulsion of sensibility vis-à-vis the external world, that is, the relation of sensibility toward an Other whom, even in their unity, it confronts as something alien: viz., as *love*. It is in this sense that the pain of love permeates all of [Heine's] lyric compositions.[49]

Moser's analysis is remarkable for the skill with which it applies Hegelian categories to a poetic oeuvre of exact contemporaneity. Unlike most forms of art, which, by Hegel's own account belong strictly to the past and thus affirm the superior cogency of speculative philosophy, Heine's lyrics effectively mirror, even anticipate, the reflexive awareness that resonates in Moser's Hegelian interpretation. The poet's affect of melancholy differs from all other forms of affect in its imminent reflexivity, a fact borne out by the lyrics' persistent enjambment of eros and betrayal, identification and alienation, and by its presentation of eros as a categorically belated experience ("Jene Flammen sind erloschen"). If, in Benjamin's phrase, "melancholy betrays the world for knowledge," the knowledge thus produced will forever bear the mark of that betrayal. Protestations of love, that is, will henceforth appear indistinguishable from the tawdry sentiments of the feuilleton or the invariant motivic catalogue of mournful lilies, nightingales, and some distant beloved's dark eyes. The lyric voice bears witness to its own alienation by exposing—formally and thematically—an irremediable misalignment of affect and discourse ("dies Büchlein ist die Urne / Mit der Asche meiner Liebe"). And yet, however cogent in its deployment of Hegelian thought, Moser's reading of late romantic subjects as melancholically estranged from the Hegelian absolute ultimately obscures the material and psychological motives that prompt the generic codification found throughout Heine's lyric poetry. Given the pointedly secular and eroticized quality of Heine's and also Keats's writings, their lyric forms encrypt a deep alienation from *this* world, rather than some metaphysical longing for abstract (or "absolute") unity (*Einheit*) or infinity (*Unendlichkeit*)—Hegel's and Moser's key words. Two contiguous lyrics, numbers 13 and 14 from "Die Heimkehr" in Heine's *Buch der Lieder,* allow us to trace the precarious nexus between surface and depth, erotic sentiment and social ressentiment (*Stimmung* and *Verstimmung*). I present the poems in their original, contiguous printing so as to accentuate their shared motivic work and to throw into relief the apparently serial character of Heine's lyric production:

Wenn ich an deinem Hause
Des Morgens vorübergeh,
So freut's mich, du liebe Kleine,
Wenn ich dich am Fenster seh.

Mit deinen schwarzbraunen Augen
Siehst du mich forschend an:
"Wer bist du, und was fehlt dir,
Du fremder, kranker Mann?"

"Ich bin ein deutscher Dichter,
Bekannt im deutschen Land;
Nennt man die besten Namen,
So wird auch der meine genannt.

When of a morning early
I happen to pass your place,
I am happy to see you, dear girlie,
Stand at the window case.

Your gazes from dark-brown eyes
Earnestly probe me and scan:
["]Who are you and what ails you,
You strange and suffering man?["]

"And what ails me, little dearie,
Ails many in Germany;
Among those most renowned [translation modified]
They also mention me."

Das Meer erglänzte weit hinaus
Im letzten Abendscheine;
Wir saßen am einsamen Fischerhaus,
Wir saßen stumm und alleine.

Der Nebel stieg, das Wasser schwoll,
Die Möwe flog hin und wider;
Aus deinen Augen, liebevoll,
Fielen die Tränen nieder.

Ich sah sie fallen auf deine Hand,
Und bin aufs Knie gesunken;
Ich hab von deiner weißen Hand
Die Tränen fortgetrunken.

Seit jener Stunde verzehrt sich mein Leib,
Die Seele stirbt vor Sehnen;-
Mich hat das unglücksel'ge Weib
Vergiftet mit ihren Tränen. (*HSS*, 1: 114–15)

The sea was aglitter far and wide
As the last of the sunset shone:
We sat by the lonely cabin's side
Sat silent and alone.

The seagull rode the sky above,
Higher rose mist and swell;
While in your eyes, so full of love,
The teardrops brimmed and fell.

I saw them fall upon your hand
And dropped upon one knee;
And bending over your pallid hand,
I sipped your tears away.

Since then, my flesh has shrunk, sad lust
Tortures my soul and sears;
Alas, the wretched woman must
Have poisoned me with her tears. (HEINE 1995, 53)

Less glaring, and hence more plausibly "romantic" than in other instances (e.g., no. 2 of "Die Heimkehr"), these two lyrics appear to express the speaker's isolated and alienated condition. All the familiar scenic and affective trappings associated with the discursive history of melancholy-as-literary-writing have been deployed with a facility and ease that may disconcert the experienced reader. There is the obligatory "dark-eyed" female, the speaker's pained heart, a mute pair of lovers (or strangers?) found gazing out toward mist-enveloped seas at dusk, involuntary tears shed, and so forth. As so often in Heine, these lyrics "ritually reenact the design . . . and cult-like ceremony of the beautiful world, a beautiful couple in its midst about to merge with a pure, unfettered natural setting, as such embodying a more profound unification of man and nature, and, in further extension, realizing the ultimate purposes of the cosmos" (Matt 1998, 204). This quintessentially Goethean, seemingly effortless transposition of an affective origin into lyric form seems always nearby in Heine's lyrics. Yet while the familiar props of erotic and spiritual inwardness continue to operate within a symbolically congenial setting, their teleological purpose of physical and metaphysical consummation is conspicuously absent.[50]

Precisely this suspension of the lyric's organic and transcendent teleology, however, radically transforms its reading experience. For the opening image of subjective alienation (no. 13) and the natural setting (no. 14) symbolizing the subject's recovery from its predicament, now appear but citations, literary-historical debris washed ashore at the "dusk" ("Im letzten Abendscheine") of the Goethean *Kunstperiode.* While remaining oblique about the particulars of the pain that supposedly afflicts it, the lyric subject proves highly attentive to the formal and social dramaturgy of its melancholic bereavement. Thus the fleeting exchange of glances between a nameless female (conspicuously belittled as "du liebe Kleine") and the ailing poet-stranger (with the speaker ventriloquizing his own appearance as "Du fremder, kranker Mann") is sure to remain an erotic nonevent. As in Keats, melancholy centers on "a recurrent breakdown in the metonymy of pleasure," that is, a visibly forestalled progression from the abstract "erotic thing" to a concrete "Object of desire"

(Kristeva, 14). Likewise, melancholy not only presents itself as an affective indisposition (*Verstimmung*) but also as voice audibly estranged (*verstimmt*) from the myth of the Goethean love lyric as a natural and organic theodicy. It is this discursive or linguistic abjection (whose ethnic and political causes we have yet to address) that prompts Kristeva to characterize "melancholy persons [as] foreigners in their maternal tongue."

This predicament is not so much addressed with analytic clarity as it is enacted through an abrupt shift in tone at the close of each lyric soon recognized as Heine's particular stylistic signature. Thus the speaker's conspicuous absorption in, and display of his oblique "pain" almost certainly compromises any hopes he may have had for an erotic bond with the female figure whose "dark" and "searching" gaze had solicited his narcissistic confessions. In the second lyric, melancholic lament (*Klagen*) yields to outright indictment (*Anklagen*), as female tears of empathy are said to have "poisoned" and thus prolonged the speaker's agony. Again, the last line (*Vergiftet mit ihren Tränen*) disrupts the idyll so carefully assembled from what Peter von Matt calls "the familiar inventory of Romanticism's lyric code" (Matt 1998, 205). Precisely this abrupt flourish of ressentiment at the end of the poem, however, should prompt readers to reexamine the entire poem or, rather, the casual and, as with the speaker, possibly narcissistic set of identifications that they brought to a first reading of it. It is the dialectical nature of Heine's writing that such a revisionary reading can neither be avoided nor anticipated during a first "tour." For at first, Heine's dreamlike images seduce readers into identifying with the melancholic surfaces of his idiom. Only as the reading process advances or, more likely, during a second reading, does the reader begin to grasp the language of *Empfindsamkeit* as one of stylistic artifice and commodity and, by extension, confronts the embarrassment of his or her earlier identification with that idiom. It is this confounding of affective dispositions previously held fundamental and inalienable for all beings—the ideological fantasy of a *humanitas* untrammeled by divisions of class, education, religion, language—that Heine's lyrics fleetingly conjure up and then dismantle. Yet to do so throws into disarray not only an empathetic mode of reading but, by extension, also the aesthetic foundations of these historically specific (romantic) reading practices. Wolfgang Preisendanz rightly points out that the ultimate challenge of Heine's oeuvre involves less a formal accounting for his fracturing of lyric pathos by ironic means. For the more fundamental and pressing question concerns "how it is possible to speak of such an aesthetic borderline phenomena

[*Grenzphänomene des Ästhetischen*] where the claims of aesthetics—as a philosophical and scientific theory of art and the beautiful—have already been shaken or proven irrelevant, along with its self-image as a historical phenomenon." The truly "agonizing" issue concerns the "historicity of aesthetics and its specific kind of competency" (Preisendanz, 68).

What remains is to articulate the historical and ideological critique that is realized by Heine's unique writings. His texts, we have seen, no longer posit feeling as the unimpeachable source for an expressive model of writing. Rather, they treat the very concept of feeling as a spurious imposition, both a formal and an ideological fraud made possible to the extent that a certain aesthetic framework had been unquestionably embraced and perpetuated by both writers and readers, and along with it the paradigm of literature as an authentic and deeply meaningful transposition of affect from the personal into the social realm and its sublation from a merely incidental to a representative, indeed obligatory social meaning. Heine's poetry does not simply contest this paradigm of lyric and affective meaning. Rather, by recasting the lyric as "form in which contradictions could move in a dynamic way," Heine exposes not only the genre's "fictitious and false harmony" (Lukács, 139) but, on a much larger scale, the deep-seated and unwholesome complicity between formal, affective, and social values that, to him, was the very hallmark of romantic culture. Taken as the critique of an entire aesthetic (rather than just one formal variant governed by that aesthetic), Heine's poetry—much like Keats's writings of the previous decade—shows the historical categories of literature and aesthetics acutely distrustful of themselves and on the verge of suspecting their own intrinsic otherness. Through their purposive formal *mésalliance* with the feuilleton, Heine's lyrics reveal the genre's ideological entanglement and thus initiate the self-transcendence of romanticism that was to culminate in the modernist lyrics of Rilke, Trakl, T. S. Eliot, Mallarmé, and Verlaine. Goethe's stony divinities ultimately exemplify the melancholic character intrinsic to all types of art that have unreservedly subscribed to the dream of formal and historical purity. Faced with their spurious triumph—as artifacts consigned to perpetual irrelevance in the lonely halls of a museum or on the musky pages of a lyric almanac—all works dream of becoming their own other, "life," and to that extent find themselves gravitating toward a kind of anti-literature. As with Keats's notion of "the purest English," it is fundamentally language itself that emerges as the focus for this implicit historical critique of romantic aesthetics—a critique that Heine cannily launched, not from some improbable outside vantage point, but from within that aesthetic's most cherished formal progeny: the lyric.

"Gelbveiglein-Hebräisch": Jewish Acculturation and Romantic Language Politics

While initially unwitting participants in the critique of a romantic expressivism ostensibly supported by Heine's early lyrics, readers gradually experienced the cumulative impact of *Das Buch der Lieder* as a provocation to their romanticizing inclinations—a lyric exposé of their own atrophied subjectivity. It is precisely the poetry's formulaic, montage- or citation-like quality that precipitates this recognition. Both at the level of individual lyrics and as a collection of conspicuously serialized character (what Karl Kraus was to label *skandierter Journalismus*), Heine's *Buch der Lieder* thus simultaneously performs a sentimental and a critical gesture. Offering, alternatively, subtle deconstructions and brazen satires of romanticism's dominant poetics—an olio of spurious medievalisms, abstract theorems, petty idylls, and bigoted Christianity—Heine also disables that aesthetic's primary function for its consumers: namely, to shelter them from the de facto modernity of their political and economic existence. In his late "Confessions" (*Geständnisse*), Heine addresses the dialectical character of his writing with a characteristic blend of critical reflection and necessarily ironic exemplification:

> Despite all the murderous campaigns I waged against Romanticism, personally I always remained a Romantic, and more than I ever imagined. I had dealt the taste for romantic poetry the most lethal blows, but then I felt an infinite longing for the "blue flower" in the dreamland of Romanticism steal over me once more. And so I took up the enchanted lute and sang, abandoning myself in that song to all the rapturous excesses, all the moony intoxication, all the blooming nightingale madness of the once beloved melody. I know it was "Romanticism's last free woodland song," and I am its last poet. With me the old lyrical German school comes to an end, while at the same time I inaugurate a new one—the modern German lyric. I have been assigned this double role by German literary historians. (Heine 1981, 21–22 / *HSS*, 6, 1: 447)

Heine's shrewd 1854 assessment of his poetic significance—suspended between the "fatal blows" he had dealt to romantic "nightingale-madness" (*Nachtigallenwahnsinn*) and a lingering susceptibility to that aesthetic "dreamland" professed even in these "Confessions" should be approached with care. For after the early 1830s, Heine's reenacting of his painful split between two incompatible emotive and stylistic positions is so recurrent that it seems self-referential, a kind of commedia dell'arte shtick with the writer as the only protagonist and sole theme. More than anything, the passage amounts to a performance in which the writer-actor struggles to anticipate and control the likely effects of his lyrics on their projected audience. Liberals on the defensive after the repressive legislation pushed through by Metternich at Karlsbad in August 1819 might find their political and social frustrations echoed both in Heine's satiric and melancholy mode. Philistines might initially be taken in by the lyrics' opening veneer of "romantic" sentimentality, only to be confronted with the abrupt tonal shift and persiflage that destroys their underlying notion of reading as "affective emulation" (*Einfühlung*).[51] In their unique amalgamation of nostalgic and critical features—that is, in exhibiting with holographic precision how sentiment and ressentiment are inseparably entwined within one language—Heine's poems ultimately converge on language itself as the true object and objective of all writing.

Not surprisingly, perhaps, his most virulent critics also prove to be the most astute when it comes to identifying the potential effects of his unprecedented violation of the rules of generic autonomy (*Stiltrennungsregel*) and rhetorical decorum. Luciano Zagari and Paolo Chiarini certainly are right to regard "the excessive character of [Heine's] linguistic gesture" and the "shimmering effrontery" (*schillernde Vordergründigkeit*) of his style as "a kind of semiological weapon" (5, 8). The disarticulation of romantic inwardness as a linguistic cliché thus constitutes a gauntlet thrown down by Heine to a generation of writers and readers who identify with romantic and idealizing literary strategies, and it is not surprising to find an entire critical genealogy, dating back to the late 1830s, monotonously repudiating Heine's poetry as a cunning assault on classical ideals of beauty, romantic seriousness, Christian art, and authentic inwardness. Heine's poetry is charged not with perpetrating this assault from an identifiably "other" position, however, but with insidiously emulating and—via serial reproduction—cheapening these values. Time and again we learn of Heine's style as an instance of "linguistic forgery" (*Sprachfälscherei* [Pfizer, 458]); a production exhibiting but a "generic poetic veneer" (*allgemein poetischer Anstrich* [Minckwitz, 338]); "his feuilleton style . . . a sickly mongrel style, neither fish nor flesh" (*sein Feuilletonstil . . . ein krankhafter Zwitterstil, weder Fisch noch Fleisch* (Treitschke, 424); a "virtuoso's ingeniously clever recitation of romanticism's entire tonal scale" (*ein Virtuose . . . der das ganze Register der romantischen Töne raffiniert-geschickt abspielt*" [Bartels, 361]); as "mannered through and through" (Hehn, 179); as "scansioned journalism" (*skandierter Journalismus*) or "artful stage-prop in the shopping window of a pastry shop or a feuilleton writer" (*eine kunstvolle Attrappe im Schaufenster eines Konditors oder eines Feuilletonisten* [Kraus, 202, 200]). Kraus's influential attack on Heine's poetry as a feuilleton style that conceals its prosaic quality behind the barest, technical-prosodic scaffolding seems, perhaps, the most obvious case of a critic swallowing Heine's bait. For Heine begins the Preface to the third edition of *Das Buch der Lieder,* not with a prefatory statement, but by reprinting one of his latest incidental poems (with the mockingly generic title "Love"), which had just appeared in the *Zeitschrift für die elegante Welt* (Journal for Elegant Society [3 September 1839]), and then remarks, "I could have said all that just as well in fine prose" (Das hätte ich alles sehr gut in guter Prosa sagen können [*HSS,* 1: 15]).

While one must certainly not lose sight of the transparently anti-Semitic and anti-liberal overtones of these criticisms, it would be a mistake to seize on the ethnic and anti-Semitic prejudice shared and elaborated over several generations of readers so as to dismiss their critical viewpoint outright. Not in spite of but because the animus of critical responses to Heine from Wolfgang Menzel to the Nazi era is so complex and disconcerting, it warrants an informed and analytic, rather than a preemptive, response. For the very consistency of this vituperation reveals how acutely readers felt Heine's stylistic subversion of romanticism's aesthetic and speculative prescriptions. What Marcel Reich-Ranicki has called Heine's "dismantling of high literary pathos" (*Entpathetisierung* [79]) struck a raw nerve because it was meant to. The shrewd amalgamation of lyricism and feuilleton in Heine's work thus reproduces at the level of style a singularly divisive and adversarial network of politically, religiously, ethnically, and aesthetically charged languages or "ideologemes." In paring down the competing ideological formations of the *Vormärz* period (Old Conservatism, Catholic *Reaktion,* Nationalism, anti-Semitism, Jewish assimilation, Liberalism, Left Hegelianism, etc.) to their artificial rhetorical underpinnings, Heine's writings expose the pathological character of a society where any one community maintains a stubbornly adversarial relation to all the others, while being manifestly self-deceived in its claim to furnish a noncontradictory perspective on modern existence.

Writers of Jewish descent, such as Heine, Börne, or Moritz Saphir, were uniquely positioned to comment on the disingenuous, often purely instrumental relationship between rhetorical form and ideological commitment, between affective claims professed through and the complex ressentiment mediated in the discursive literary forms of the *Vormärz* period. Karl Gutzkow had already surmised, with specific reference to Börne and Heine, how "perhaps a truthful and worthy reaction against our ideology, which was in the process of forging the manacles for a new slavery, could only emerge out of Judaism."[52] As Heine understood well and early in his career, to write German as a Jew meant approaching language from an intrinsically exiled perspective: "We all are in exile" (Wir sind ja im Gohles [*HB,* 1: 63]). Heine's deliberate choice of the Yiddish *Gohles* over the German vernacular *Exil* leaves no doubt how the phrase is to be understood. In a 1968 lecture on Lessing's *Laokoon,* Peter Weiss, who like Heine had to choose exile in order to ensure his survival as a writer, accounts for the modern writer's inherently abject relation to his medium as follows:

> Now that he stood in among all those whose language he had shared in times past, this same language assumed an alien quality. Between the words spoken and his hearing a recollection of some fugitive event interposed itself [Zwischen den ausgesprochenen Wörtern und seinem Gehör lag die Erinnerung an ein Fliehen]. If the words reached him, he heard, emanating from them, something screaming and threatening. When he responded, it was always across a divide. Even though he recognized the language in its minute particulars, he felt as though his struggles to make himself understood in it had to commence all over again. For a long time, he experienced this state as a deficiency. . . . Now, when reaching back to the language that he had formerly spoken, he merely saw in it a tool among many. The lexical roots appeared weatherworn, the words themselves stood detached from their origin, mere husks for which he'd have to devise a content. Just as he had become estranged from this language he also had become estranged from himself. [So wie er sich von dieser Sprache entfernt hatte, hatte er sich von sich selbst entfernt]. (Weiss, 186; my translation)

Analogous to the Cockney Keats, Heine experienced and understood this "linguistic rootlessness" as integral to his German-Jewish identity and to his productivity as a writer. The definitions of literary "propriety" and the criteria for social and cultural enfranchisement—while flexible and subtly evolving—always seem calculated to reinforce the sense of abjection. What, according to Weiss, defines the Jewish writer in exile, is less his geographical or political than his linguistic displacement. From the vantage point of majority, gentile culture whose presumptive "linguistic monopoly masqueraded as a non-linguistic definition of the nation" (Hobsbawm 1990, 97), the literary language of a German-Jewish writer could only ever produce one of two scenarios: recognition of his or her irremediable otherness or the delusion of successful assimilation. Like Keats, Heine also belongs to that first generation of writers who experienced—and whose authorial identity was consequently shaped by—the enforcement of norms pertaining to the aesthetic propriety and social purity of "literary" language. For as an important tool in the service of nation-building, the idea of a normative "grammar" as a reference point for one's inclusion in (or exclusion from) social, ethnic, and aesthetic mainstream culture was intimately entwined with the recent invention of "writing" as a complex and self-policing profession.[53] Like Weiss a century later, Heine first perceived the intrinsically "exiled" character of his ethnically marked voice as a deficit, only to embrace this inalienable condition of "speaking across a distance" as a distinctively modern and enabling condition.

To grasp the larger significance of Heine's strategic disruption of linguistic and aesthetic norms, it is imperative to recall some basic historical facts and problems of German-Jewish cultural relations during the period of romanticism and *Vormärz.* For the long-standing indictment of Heine as a superior linguistic fraud (and the anti-Semitic cultural politics underlying that view) adumbrates the troubled history of Jewish emancipation—specifically linguistic assimilation—as it unfolded roughly between 1780 and 1880. Given that the adult Heine had his most significant encounter with Jewish culture in Berlin around 1823, at the beginning of his career as a poet, a brief review of German-Jewish relations during the period of his life may be limited to Prussia—arguably the dominant political and legal force in nineteenth-century Germany. Following the peace of Westphalia, the newly instituted Elector (*Kurfürst*) Frederick Wilhelm I (1640–1688) sought to modernize and populate the principality of Brandenburg by admitting various groups of refugees, most prominently the Huguenots, who had been forced to leave France after the revocation of the Edict of Nantes in 1685. At the same time, Jewish subjects—who for centuries had been restricted to local money lending and miscellaneous peddling (*Kleinhandel*)—were granted protective and safe-conduct passes (*Schutzbriefe* and *Geleitbriefe*) so as to support the state's long-term objectives of generating economic relations between often insular provinces, instituting modern forms of money- and credit-based trade and exchange, and establishing a stable system of free trade. Predictably, these policies met with fierce resistance from the landed gentry (*Junker*) and, in the cities, from the guilds (*Zünfte*) who had monopolized most trades since the high Middle Ages. In the end, under the succeeding monarchs (Frederick I, 1688–1713, and Frederick Wilhelm I, 1713–1740), attempts to deploy Jewish families in the larger effort of economic modernization succumbed to that resistance.[54] Thus, the latter half of the eighteenth century witnessed the reintroduction of a body tax (*Leibzoll*), protective fees (*Schutzgelder*), obligatory purchases of 500 talers' worth of (usually damaged) china from the state porcelain manufactory for the wedding of every Jewish child, and the especially demeaning principle of the Jews' collective liability (*Sippenhaft*), in force throughout Prussia. In addition, residential prerogatives granted to a Jewish family did not extend to their children after the death of their father, except where assets of 1,000 talers could be demonstrated, in which case one child was eligible to continue residency. Under Frederick II (1740–1786), Jews were further prevented from owning real property and farming (Belke, 34), while at the same time being singled out for the risky and highly unpopular procurement of silver and the minting of increasingly diluted coins to support the state's vast wartime expenditures.[55]

Specifically among the bureaucracy charged with implementing these and many other archaic restrictions, sympathy for the plight of Jews increased. Their misgivings no doubt grew in response to writings by Germany's two most significant Enlightenment figures, Moses Mendelssohn and Gotthold Ephraim Lessing, and to the Bill of Rights published in the American colonies. The milestone publication of the Enlightenment pertaining to the civic condition of Jews in Prussia appeared in 1781. Inspired by Moses Mendelssohn and written by the upper-level administrator Christian Wilhelm Dohm, *Über die bürgerliche Verbesserung der Juden* (On the Civil Improvement of the Jews) analyzed the intolerable condition of Jews at the end of the eighteenth century. For Dohm, the separate corporation of the Jews—routinely assailed as a "state-within-the-state" and hence as a social and political threat—was an "evil wrought by the past erroneous policy" (Mendes-Flohr and Reinharz, 29), now used as a rationale for continuing state-sponsored discrimination. The separate and allegedly "unsociable" character of the Jewish subject was not the cause but the effect of irrational state intervention. The only remedy, in Dohm's sweeping proposal, was to abolish *at once* each and every special law and decree pertaining to the Jews. Like most committed Enlightenment intellectuals, Dohm had little stake in preserving the religious autonomy of *any* group. Indeed, he takes it as axiomatic that "good government and the prosperity all subjects enjoy under such a government [will] weaken the influence of religious principles" (ibid., 28) and identity of the Jewish community. As the ultimate beneficiary of Dohm's reform proposal, the state itself ought "to take charge of the process of reeducation" (Herzig 1997, 147). For it was the state that stood to gain the services of a highly resourceful and talented group whereas—this being the other implication of Dohm's argument—Jews could attain "civil improvement" only at the expense of their religious and cultural identity. Indeed, among those critical of Dohm's proposal, the philologist and theologian Johann David Michaelis (1717–1791) arguably offered the most plausible objections when arguing "that Mosaic law prevented the total integration" (Meyer, 2: 14).

However disingenuous in their motivation, Michaelis's arguments pointed to the fundamental tension between the Enlightenment's secular model of *civitas* and the enduring religious underpinnings of the individual's identity within it.[56] Against Michaelis, Mendelssohn and his student David Friedländer had urged that, on the premise of a thorough separation of state and religion, Jewish ceremonial law would in no way abridge the functioning of the state and thus was fully compatible with it. Baptism, that most conspicuous step toward assimilation—one to which Heine, Börne, and (more seriously) Mendelssohn's own son, Abraham, would submit roughly a generation later—thus appeared superfluous.[57] Even so, a 1787 government review of Dohm's proposals produced virtually no resolutions of benefit to Prussian Jews. By contrast, in a resolution that often copied Dohm's text verbatim, the French National Assembly, urged by Abbé Grégoire and Count Mirabeau, in 1791 granted full civil rights to all Jews. Meanwhile, in Germany, Moses Mendelssohn's untiring efforts at "modernizing" Judaism precipitated a "serious crisis, alienating numerous Jewish intellectuals from their faith and prompting them to convert, particularly in urban communities" (Herzig 1997, 152).[58] At the very least, Mendelssohn's attempt at aligning his project of Jewish emancipation with the efforts of the Prussian state, "which was in the process of freeing itself from traditional corporate structures," caused Judaism "to be redefined as a religious denomination analogous to Christian denominations" (Meyer, 2: 2). As Heine was to muse, "Mendelssohn had toppled the Talmud and overthrown tradition," thereby "demolishing Jewish Catholicism," just as Luther had done with Christian Catholicism. "Having toppled tradition, however, he sought to maintain the mosaic ceremonial law. Had that been an act of cowardice or wisdom?" (*HSS*, 3: 583–84).

The dramatic political and territorial changes wrought by Napoleon effectively prevented a timely debate of that question. Indeed, events between 1798 and 1807 all but foreclosed on the beginning debate between traditional and reform-oriented Jews as to whether Judaism stood for a nation and its holistic "culture" or whether it was simply a confessional term referring strictly to matters of inner faith. Instead, beginning in 1798 and reaching Heine's birthplace, Düsseldorf, in 1800, Napoleon implemented immediate and full civil equality for Jews in Westphalia, the Grand Duchy of Berg, and soon thereafter across the entire newly created Rhenish Federation. However sweeping in its wording, the civil enfranchisement of the Jewish population soon got bogged down in local and regional problems of implementation, and by 1808, it was substantially curtailed by Napoleon's *décret infâme,* which restricted a number of Jewish liberties. In Prussia, meanwhile, the emancipation of the Jews was being explored, rather pragmatically, as part of the intense reform project launched after the state's resounding defeat by Napoleon. At the insistence of the principal reformers, Hardenberg and Humboldt, a law granting civil equality to all Prussian Jews was eventually passed on 11 March 1812.[59] Though its provisions were to be severely undermined almost immediately upon Napoleon's defeat at Waterloo, the law warrants attention in that the conditions stipulated in it throw into relief the disturbing relationship between German romanticism—political and "cultural" in the widest sense—and Jewish identity. Jews had to assume "fixed official family names within six months, use German or another living language [not Yiddish] for their business records, contracts, and legally relevant declarations of intent, and sign their name in Gothic and Latin script" (Meyer, 2: 27). Important for our purposes here is to understand that, where the promise of Jewish civil enfranchisement was extended at all, it was legally predicated on the condition of complete linguistic assimilation.

At that point, due to some canny last-minute revisions of the *Schlußakte* (concluding treaty) of the Vienna congress, all Napoleonic decrees pertaining to the situation of Jews in those parts of Germany previously under his control were ruled null and void. The brief interlude of liberation, always regarded with apprehension by most Jews, had indeed proven a chimera. Moreover, Jews in the new provinces that had been incorporated into a much-strengthened Prussia in 1815 were also excluded from Hardenberg's 1812 reforms. From here on, the process of legislative repression against Prussia's Jewish community is unequivocal and dismaying. Restrictions concerning the acquisition of property (1816), patrimonial jurisdiction, and marriage (Herzig, 156) were reinstated, often in more severe form. Furthermore, Germany's 250,000 Jews were once again excluded from professions requiring state approbation or involving the exercise of public authority (Meyer, 2: 39).[60] They were also barred from working as land surveyors (1820), from holding academic and school positions (1822), from pursuing agriculture, from auction commissions (1827), from holding municipal offices (1831), from joining village councils (1833), from freedom of movement, and so on.[61] At the same time, a "Society for the Promotion of Christianity among Jews" sponsored by the Prussian monarch began its proselytizing work in 1822. Most historians (Meyer, Herzig, Frühwald, and Nipperdey) attribute this vehement backlash to economic anxiety that had taken hold of large segments of the population. Undeniably, the uncertainties of rural populations uprooted by Napoleon's abrupt abolition of serfdom and of tradesmen and artisans distraught over the dissolution of the guild system helped unleash deep-rooted anti-Semitic resentments.[62] Yet economic uncertainty alone does not account for the far more public and organized way in which anti-Jewish opinion was now being expressed—not only in miscellaneous attacks and local rioting, but particularly in a persistent stream of anti-Semitic pamphleteering. Whereas a first surge of this, involving more than sixty publications (including strongly worded responses by Jewish intellectuals) had been stopped by a government decree (Meyer, 2: 22), the publicly waged campaign against Jewish participation in the civil process after 1815 went essentially unchecked by the Prussian government. For the tide of restoration politics had now turned against civic reform and modernization and, consequently, also against the enfranchisement of Prussia's Jews.

During these peak years of restoration and romantic cultural politics, the anti-Semitic movement added the public voices of intellectuals, academics, and writers who, in a number of cases, had already secured a national audience.[63] Under the vocal leadership of philosophers, philologists, poets, and public intellectuals like Fichte, Fries, Rühs, Jacob and Wilhelm Grimm, Ernst Moritz Arndt, Adam Müller, Clemens Brentano, and Achim von Arnim, anti-Semitism now emerged as an integral feature of the divisive conceptions of romanticism as an emphatically Christian culture. Only half-jokingly, Heine (in a letter of 1823) forgoes a longer report about his impressions of Hamburg because, after all, he is "not a German" ("Wär ich ein Deutscher—und ich bin kein Deutscher, siehe Rühs, Fries" [*HB*, 1: 100]). As Heine's reference to the open anti- Semitism of these and other members of the Berlin professorate (e.g., Karl von Savigny) makes clear, the brief interlude of Berlin's famous literary salons, organized by well-known and highly assimilated Jewish women (Rahel Levin [later Varnhagen], Henriette Herz et al.) was finished. It had succumbed to a new type of brazenly anti-Semitic and divisive cultural institutions, such as Karl Friedrich Zelter's Liedertafel and the Christlich-Deutsche Tischgesellschaft. Founded by Brentano and Arnim in 1812, the Tischgesellschaft specifically excluded women, philistines, and Jews, mocking the latter "as flies left over from the Egyptian plagues and now to be found everywhere; among discarded clothes in one's closet, with theater billets and aesthetic gossip at one's tea table, and with promissory notes at the stock exchange."[64] Heine noted, "[A]nti-Semitism first begins with the romantic school . . . a delight in everything medieval, Catholicism, the nobility, intensified by the Germanomaniacs—Rühs—[etc.]."[65] After 1815, partly in consequence of economic reversals, there was a new surge of anti-Semitic pamphlets and caricatures (see figs. 13 and 14), eventually culminating in the so-called Hep-Hep (an acronym for "Hierosolyma est perdita" = "Jerusalem is lost") riots that erupted all over Germany in August 1819. The events prompted Rahel Varnhagen (née Levin), arguably one of the most fascinating letter writers of the entire period, whom Heine called "the most intelligent woman I have ever met" (*HB*, 1: 57), to ponder the evident collapse of the Enlightenment project of emancipation, as well as the implausibility of its romantic successor, "acculturation." To her, the 1819 riots had to be seen as the ghastly progeny of romantic medievalism and its neo-Catholic reactionary politics: "The fanatical renewal of the Christian faith and—may God forgive my sin in saying so—of the Middle Ages, with all their art, poetry, and horrors, incites the people to the one monstrosity to which, recalling ancient license, they remain yet susceptible: anti-Semitic pogroms" (Die Gleißnerische Neuliebe zur Kristlichen Religion[,] Gott verzeihe mir meine Sünde!, zum Mittelalter, mit seiner Kunst, Dichtung und Gräueln, hetzen das Volk zu dem einzigen Gräuel zu dem es sich noch[,] an alte Erlaubniß erinnert[,] aufhezen läßt! Judensturm).[66] Even before these latest riots, Rahel Varnhagen had pondered the irrational and implacable nature of anti-Semitic ressentiment. In her characteristically fitful epistolary style, difficult to render in translation, a letter of 1817 eerily presages future horrors wrought by Germans' mythic fantasy of ethnic, national, and cultural unity and purity. There prevails

> a dark longing to deify something . . . because reason's and perception's grasp of what is actually *at hand* is not sufficiently acute. [It is] the rotten core in this species, the source of all intellectual epidemics, weakness and overheating. . . . Such miserable beings can also turn toward cruelty. . . . During the age of Enlightenment, this entire riffraff of rampant dementia was merely blocked, rendered benign and harmless by ridicule that courageous intellectuals would heap on it. . . . Yet in the end, every great delusion, whose consequences can swell to vast proportions, a nation can only discharge by means of bloodshed. The more people act en masse, the more consequential the weight of *human* thoughts—specifically instinctual ones [*die der Natur*]. Hence my mind forecasts real disasters as long as these madmen continue their work. Oh! poor Novalis, poor Friedrich Schlegel, the latter condemned to witness it all; surely you never expected this to be the fruit of your shallow apostles. Great and benevolent Goethe, read with utter blindness; fiery and honest Lessing and all you great, serene minds: you never thought of that, never *could* have conceived of this extraordinary disaster.[67] (my translation)

At one level, Rahel Varnhagen's letter recalls Heine's characterization of Goethe's stony deities (see the epigraph to this chapter) and the awkward position of the modern writer, perched between the serene and ennobling aesthetic dispensations of the recent past and the foul exhalations of a rising industrial and ideological mass culture. Yet at the same time, her gloomy analysis exhibits none of Heine's stylized melancholy, nor do we find even the slightest trace of irony. Romantic medievalism, neo-Catholic conservatism, Christian anti-Judaism, and radical nationalism all seem bent on emerging as the sole legitimate worldly heir to Goethe's self-sufficient classicism and Novalis's mystical longings. The inchoate landscape of post-Napoleonic cultural politics had transformed the aesthetic dispensations of Weimar and Jena from a complex figurative language into an ideologically serviceable watchword. Brandishing the cultural capital of their former teachers and mentors like swords on a crusade, the "shallow disciples" (among whom Rahel Varnhagen expressly identifies Arnim, Brentano, Rühs, and Fries) had effectively fused the official culture of nostalgia and the subterranean one of hatred—sentiment and ressentiment. The cultural inheritance of Weimar classicism, Jena romanticism, and indeed the invention of a monolithic cultural heritage (*kulturelles Erbe*) as such, are now being mobilized for purposes of a "cultural restoration" of sorts. Yet, given the new disciples' "imperceptiveness to what is *actually there*" (Varnhagen's emphasis) and their irrational longing for an utterly homogeneous culture, the repressive coherence of post-Napoleonic Germany would necessarily be rooted in the majority's deeply irrational hatred of some other group. Romantic melancholy, that "dark longing to deify something," simply cannot exist without the "rotten core" of ressentiment.[68]

And yet, precisely because her voice is one of genuine and wholly lucid abjection, Varnhagen sees no way to extricate herself from the nefarious web of historical determinants. Heine, we know, was no stranger to dark and prescient visions about Germany's nationalist *cum* anti-Semitic tendencies. As the character of Hassan observes in Heine's early tragedy *Almansor:* "where books are burned, there / In the end, people will also be burned" (dort, wo man Bücher / Verbrennt, verbrennt man auch am Ende Menschen (*HSS,* 1: 284–85).

Fig. 13. Anti-Semitic satiric print, (Germany ca. 1819). The text, in a mocking, Yiddish-inflected German, reads: [Students:] "Da liegt der Jude! Lacht ihn aus!" (There lies the Jew! Let's have a laugh at him!) [Jewish pedlar]: "Do ist nichts zum Lachen! Hab ich können in der Luft hängen bleiben?" (There is nothing to laugh at here! Could I have remained suspended in midair?) Courtesy of the Leo Baeck Institute, New York.

Fig. 14. Illustration from Karl Boromaeus Alexander Sessa (1786–1813), *Unser Verkehr; eine Posse in einem Aufzuge* (Our Relations: A Farce in One Act). Text in Yiddish-inflected German: "Gaih! Gaih! Los dich treten von de Leut, los dich werfen aus de Stuben, los dich verklagen bei de Gerichte, los dich hetzen ins Hundeloch, los dich binden mit Strike und Keten, los dich martern halb todt! Aber du must doch werden raich!" (Go on, go on! Let the people kick you; let them throw you out into the street, let them sue you in court; let them hunt you down into the gutter; let yourself be bound in chains; let them torment you until you are half-dead! After all, you want to become rich, don't you?) Courtesy of the Leo Baeck Institute, New York.

Shifting from Golden Age Spain to contemporary Germany, a passage omitted from the third volume of *Reisebilder,* recalls how "at a time when there appeared to be an end to virtually all nationalities . . . just then an obscure sect sprang into existence that conceived the most bizarre dream visions about Germaneness, indigenous culture, and just about devoured oak and acorn [*Ureichelfraßtum*]. They were thorough, critical, historical—capable of accurately determining the degree of one's descent required by the new order of things to have certain people disposed of altogether" (*HSS,* 2: 634; my translation). All that remained to be decided, Heine remarks, was "the method of execution."

Heine's radical wit exposes the grotesque and manic fixations of anti-Semitic nationalists with a wicked new compound noun, *Ureichelfraßtum,* punning on the "acorns" (*Eichel*) figurally devoured by nationalists whose fetishization of the German oak (*Eiche*) has taken an all too literal turn; nose to the ground, they appear bent on sniffing out and ingesting anything primordially (*Ur-*) German. At the very least, such obsession with ethnic purity and authentic lineage confounds figural attributes (i.e., the oak [*Eiche*] as an emblem of Germanness) by literally seeking to devour them. Beyond that, however, Heine's neologism may also pun on romantic nationalism's underlying obsession with discriminating between Jewish and non-Jewish individuals by worrying whether the tip of the male member (fig. *Eichel*) has been circumcised or not. In Heine's view, the stylistic and logical explosions of wit (*Witz*) are best suited to disarticulating the unholy alliance of Christian-romantic mysticism and anti-Semitic nationalism. The modern writer, that is, must unwrite the ominous gravity of romantic sentiment by reproducing it mechanically to the point where expression turns into its own exposé and key concepts inadvertently deteriorate into puns and double entendres.

The critique of a literature predicated on religious and aesthetic purity and homogeneity can be traced back to Heine's earliest writings. Thus in his first published prose piece, a short essay entitled "Die Romantik" (18 August 1820), he is quick to point out how the recent literature so labeled often appears confused in its attempt at an outright repetition or restoration of medieval Christian poetry. Medieval romance sought to give expression to a radically new religious type of affect by "contriving new images and words of precisely the kind that had a secret and sympathetic kinship with these new feelings and, as it were, able to conjure them up all over again" (Heine 1993, 10: 195). By contrast, contemporary romantic writing often appears enslaved to Christianity and medieval knighthood as an inventory to be deployed rather mechanically. The result, Heine contends, is a travestied romanticism, poetry aimlessly rehearsing exhausted motifs and stock images: "an olio of Spanish manners, Scottish mists, and Italian music, confused and shifting images that are being poured, as it were, out of a magic lantern" (ein Gemengsel von spanischem Schmelz, schottischen Nebeln und italienischem Geklinge, verworrene und verschwimmende Bilder, die gleichsam aus einer Zauberlaterne ausgegossen warden [ibid.]). In opposing the narrowly confessional and proselytizing view of Christian romanticism and its anti-classicism, Heine understands the core struggle to be over the boundaries of the German language. Striking a superficially nationalist pose, he extols the liberal and liberating potential of the German language as "our sacred possession, a marker of Germany's borders that no cunning neighbour can shift, a call to freedom which no potentate can stifle" (unser heiligstes Gut, ein Grenzstein Deutschlands, den kein schlauer Nachbar verrücken kann, ein Freiheitswecker, dem kein fremder Gewaltiger die Zunge lähmen kann [ibid., 194]). No doubt, the most immediate target of this early critique is to be found in the aristocratic and repressive authority wielded by Chancellor Metternich, particularly reviled for his uncompromising 1819 crackdown on German nationalism. Moving beyond that apparent political occasion, however, Heine's passage fundamentally grasps the underlying reactionary and socially divisive potential of a rigidly Christian romanticism that has lately appeared on the horizon.

Heine's stylistic development and its rich and controversial impact in German cultural history can be traced back to this early expression of dissent from the aesthetic and religious orthodoxies of an emphatically German and (at least in tendency) reactionary romanticism. By 1823, Heine had expanded this dissent into a highly distinctive stylistic gesture—an idiom of calculated insubordination to the nationalist, religious, and ethnic menace of *Christlich-Deutsch* romanticism. Above all, for friends and foes alike, Heine rehearsed the unsuspected *mobility* of the German word, its quasi-holographic capacity for bringing to the fore both nostalgic and satiric qualities and letting shine through the "rotten core of ressentiment" beneath the visionary glow of Christian-romantic sentiment. In short, the romantic word—that self-proclaimed gold standard of (lately ominous) inspiration and high pathos—is shown to have yielded to a regime of paper currency. Only half jesting in an early letter (May 1823) to his friend Moses Moser, Heine puts it this way:

> Your feelings solid bars of gold, whereas mine are light paper currency. The value of the latter depends on the people's confidence; . . . hasn't this image told you that I am a Jewish poet? No matter, why should I feel embarrassed; after all, we are speaking confidentially here, and I love conjuring up nationalist clichés [*Nationalbilder*]. Some day, when. . . a happier generation than ours blesses its palm branches and chews on unleavened bread on the banks of the Mississippi, and a new Jewish literature flourishes, then our mercantile, stock-jobbing expressions will form part of poetic diction itself [werden unsere jetzigen merkantilistischen Börsenausdrücke zur poetischen Sprache gehören].[69]

Perhaps most significant about Heine's witty improvisation is its explicit conjunction of Judaism and a modernity that is conceived in overtly economic terms. The "new-Jewish" literature here sketched by the young Heine envisions affect as a currency or medium for social exchange. Rather than comprising the inalienable and unique worth of an individual, "feelings" ought to be approached as a strictly figural "paper currency" whose value or purchasing-power is determined by the equally fluctuating longings (or loathings) of readers, rather than by some inflexible set of aesthetic and poetic principles. Moreover, Heine openly embraces the typically hostile association between financial speculation and Jews who, in Brentano's callous satire, were to be found "with theater billets and aesthetic gossip at one's tea table, [and] with promissory notes at the stock exchange."

The modernity and potential success of a new literature thus center around the linguistic and rhetorical versatility with which the (Jewish) writer perceives and articulates continuities between the heretofore separate spheres of culture, religion, and economics. Zagari and Chiarini note that, "like the system of currency exchange (which at that time was becoming emblematic of modern society and culture) the literary word achieved its supreme effect only by a progressive and far-reaching neutralization that pared down individual traits to clichés and commonplaces."[70] Rather than reading passage like the above as "self-torturing" (Prawer, 29)—an argument regrettably universalized by Gilman in his reading of Heine—we ought to read Heine's repeated appropriation of anti-Jewish clichés as instances of "mention," not "use" (to borrow John Searle's distinction). What anti-Semites harbor in the form of furtive, possibly unselfconscious ressentiment is brought out into the open by Heine's strategy of explicit invocation and citation. A case in point can be found in Heine's notorious attack on Count August von Platen in the third volume of his *Reisebilder.* Referring to Platen's attacks on his Jewishness, Heine demurs:

> Yes, dear reader, you aren't mistaken. It is indeed me to whom [Platen] is referring, and in his *Oedipus* you can learn that I am a true-bred Jew who, after having composed love lyrics for a few hours, proceeds to sit down, counting ducats, keep a Sabbath's company with bearded Hymies [*Mauscheln*] singing the Talmud, and how during Easter holiday I'll carve up some hapless Christian minor and, out of sheer malice, always select my victim from among the ranks of unfortunate writers. Indeed, dear reader, I won't lie to you. Such skillfully devised images are nowhere to be found in Platen's *Oedipus,* and precisely their absence is the book's flaw at which I direct my criticism. This Count Platen is occasionally driven by the best of motives, and yet he proves incompetent to put them to effective use. If only he had the least bit of imagination, he would have at the very least depicted me as a pawnbroker; what delightful scenes this would have offered up! It pains my soul to see this poor count miss every opportunity for effective, witty barbs. (*HSS,* 2: 467; my translation)

Heine's brilliant rejoinder highlights both the crude character of anti-Semitic rhetoric, as well as its lazy deployment in Platen's *Oedipus.* Here, as elsewhere, we see Heine move toward a new stylistic ideal of hybridity—with his prose breaking down the heretofore separate spheres of religion, politics, aesthetics through a rapid-fire of cartoon-style sketches, citations of postures and attitudes that can be combined and recombined at will. What Platen lacks, aside from respect for Heine (a point on which the latter could be very sensitive indeed), is rhetorical versatility. Both in his hopelessly mannered lyrics and in his clumsy anti-Jewish polemic, Platen remains mired in the aesthetic formalisms of his manifestly impoverished aristocratic background. Heine's flippant remark in his earlier quoted letter to Moses Moser that some day the "mercantile jargon of the stock exchange" will form part of German literary language thus proves to be more than an ephemeral display of wit. For what ultimately accounts for the uniquely modern character of his literary idiom is its mobility and reflexivity—qualities that Heine's poetry and prose throw into relief by way of their sustained reflection on the problem of language—the German language. What are the constraints and opportunities that define the writer's task at his specific historical moment? How is one to write, as a Jew, in a society given over to ominous yearnings for stylistic, social, and ethnic "purity"? If one resists the ministrations of "corn-cutters" (*Hühneraugenoperateurs* [*HB*, 1: 62]) like David Friedländer, who advocated mass baptism and largely viewed Judaism as a blemish to be surgically removed, how is one to write in a society where virulent prejudice against the supposedly pathological and criminal nature of the Jews' "hidden language" is woven into the vocabulary of countless religious, political, and aesthetic traditions?[71] How is one to write (literary) German without either appearing eager "to escape from Jewishness" (Arendt, 88) or as an unwelcome parvenu in German literature, a highbrow aesthetic dominated by Weimar classicism and romantic medievalism?

Parallel to the uneven development of Jewish political emancipation and social integration, and in curiously inverse relation to the growing respectability of romantic anti-Semitism, another story unfolds. It concerns the often technical and aesthetic quest of German Jews for thoroughgoing linguistic assimilation. Like Keats, whose embrace of Chatterton's "purest English" was prompted by the recognition that only an utterly artificial literary language would be open to skill and "invention" rather than birth, German Jews of the early 1800s also perceived emancipation and acculturation to be bound up with an as yet mysterious conception of "German." While Hebrew had long been colonized as a language of Christian scholarship and, within the ghettos and smaller Jewish enclaves of eighteenth-century Germany, largely functioned as a written language of worship, Jewish linguistic emancipation around 1800 was primarily defined by the tension between Yiddish and High German (*Hochdeutsch*). Widely portrayed as a linguistic miscegenation of German and Hebrew and long vilified as the hidden language whereby Jews sought to conceal their supposed criminality, religious heresy, and blasphemous wit, Yiddish came to be the lightning rod for both, German *and* Jewish Enlightenment intellectuals.[72]

Significantly, the attempt to expunge the Yiddish hybrid correlates with an ongoing and widespread effort after 1750 to define and firmly establish the notion of *Hochdeutsch* as the single and standard language. Thus, the most significant Jewish reformer and intellectual of eighteenth-century Germany, Moses Mendelssohn, drew a delicate and (to many who came after him) fateful line separating good Judaism from bad Jews, good Hebrew from bad (Talmudic) Hebrew and Yiddish. Representative of Mendelssohn's ambitious program of reforms oriented toward "acculturation" (*kulturelle Anpassung*) was his translation of the Pentateuch into German, as well as his publication of numerous essays in *Hochdeutsch,* yet printed, for the benefit of his Jewish readers, in Hebrew characters.[73] Mendelssohn's lifelong advocacy of religious toleration and rational civic dialogue between 1760 and 1786 thus proved inseparable from his commitment to German as the sole public language for Jews and gentiles in Germany. His care for his own people, "mired in spiritual and civic servitude" (Zunz, 104) appears wholly inseparable from a vision of linguistic purity and transparency characteristic of Enlightenment philosophy as a whole: "People may speak pure German or pure Hebrew, depending on the occasion . . . but there shall be no mixing of languages."[74] Similarly, Solomon Maimon—a classic case study of Jewish East-West mobility and of the Enlightenment project of dissolving religious beliefs and communities into a rational and secular conception of culture—understands his quest to pivot on his linguistic emancipation above all. Insisting that Hebrew "must be explained by means of the vernacular," while lamenting how the "vernacular of the Polish Jews is itself full of defects and grammatical inaccuracies" (Mendes-Flohr and Reinharz, 215), Maimon finds German a serendipitous linguistic refuge. For it is only by exiling himself into German linguistic and Enlightenment culture that Maimon feels capable of ascertaining the truth-value of his native Hebrew language and talmudic upbringing. In so embracing his estrangement from Hebrew as a salutary, indeed essential, step in his *Bildung,* Maimon also accepts the impossibility of ever returning from his linguistic exile: "I had received too much education to return to Poland, to spend my life in misery without rational occupation of society, and to sink back into the darkness of superstition and ignorance, from which I had delivered myself with so much labour" (ibid., 216–17).

It is agonizing to watch the generation after Moses Mendelssohn pursue the goal of linguistic assimilation with such single-minded determination. The implementation of Mendelssohn's Enlightenment prescriptions—namely, a wholesale expurgation of the German Jews' linguistic history and identity—soon came to threaten the very foundations and self-definition of Judaism. For Mendelssohn's heirs and successors in the public sphere (among them David Friedländer, Eduard Gans, Saul Ascher, Lazarus Bendavid, Markus Herz, Isaac Bernays, and Leopold Zunz—all acquaintances of Heine's), effacing all traces of Yiddish vocabulary, syntax, and intonation was the most fundamental precondition for Jewish cultural emancipation and social ascendancy.[75] Yet, as Hannah Arendt observes, it was precisely the "trick of obtaining both wealth and culture" that invariably bred a competitive and dissociative ethos within the post-ghetto communities of early-nineteenth-century Jews. Thus, during this "highly tempestuous interval between ghetto and assimilation. . . . [when] the rich were not yet cultured and the cultured not rich," all that remained was "that questionable solidarity . . . among people who all want the same thing: to save themselves as individuals" by "escap[ing] from Jewishness" (Arendt, 87–88). In his 1829 speech commemorating the hundredth anniversary of Moses Mendelssohn's birth, the preeminent scholar of Jewish culture and religious history Leopold Zunz (1794–1886) dwelt primarily on his former teacher's efforts to increase his co-religionists' "general competency in German" and their appreciation for "the euphony of German" (Zunz, 1: 107). Consistent with the ongoing reform movement's objective of conforming the liturgy, music, and indeed the very architectural setting (e.g., the New Synagogue on the Oranienburger Straße in Berlin [fig. 15])[76] of Jewish religious ceremony to the dominant Prussian-Protestant culture, Zunz's speech ends with an apotheosis to the near-complete expurgation of Yiddish linguistic and Jewish village culture:

> The so-called Jewish-German dialect, by now spoken by lower class in Poland and a few regions in Germany, has altogether disappeared from public discourse and from Jewish writings. There is not a single Jewish school in Germany where the Bible has not been recited and rehearsed in High German translation [*die Bibel in hochdeutscher Übersetzung*] for some time. Not just the Pentateuch, but all books of the Bible, even rabbinical commentaries, have been published and exhaustively reprinted in German-language editions. Nowhere will one find rabbis or Jewish preachers giving speeches in any language besides German; all those Yiddish primers, now useless [*die unbrauchbar gewordenen Lesebücher in jüdisch-deutscher Mundart*], have simply vanished. (Zunz, 1: 113; my translation)

Progress here is measured by a community's voluntary expurgation of its own linguistic history, a project in which literary connoisseurship played a crucial role in that "pure, literary German bec[ame] the model for the language spoken by Jews within the Enlightenment tradition" (Gilman, 84). By contrast, speech patterns exhibiting traces of Yiddish, referred to by Jews as *jüdische Mundart* and openly disparaged by non-Jews as *Mauscheln,* are now branded as "useless."[77] Likewise, the traditionally honored books of Jewish learning, including scripture and rabbinic commentaries whose translations contained

Fig. 15. Opening of the New Synagogue in Berlin on 5 September 1866. Courtesy of the Leo Baeck Institute, New York.

traces of linguistic hybridity, have been replaced by a *hochdeutsche Übersetzung*. In Zunz's exuberant sketch, rabbis and Jewish intellectuals alike understand and embrace such a sweeping effacement of the Jews' distinctive linguistic history as a crucial and indispensable step toward complete civic and cultural assimilation. Having initiated this development, Moses Mendelssohn deserves "to be called the benefactor of all German-speaking Jews" (Zunz 13).

More nuanced, if also more technical and ultimately more radical, are the linguistic analyses and prescriptions of the Jewish pedagogue Anton Rée (1815–1891), an influential member of Germany's largest Jewish community in Hamburg.[78] In his 1844 treatise *Über die Sprachverhältnisse der heutigen Juden* (On the Linguistic Situation of Jews Today), Rée offers countless phonetic examples in order to prove that the "Jewish mode of speech" (*die jüdische Mundart* = Yiddish-inflected German) cannot simply be uprooted by a speaker's mere conformity to the phonetic or grammatical laws of High German. "At least traces of [Yiddish] can still be found in the speech patterns of every German Jew today[, which] would be impossible if his idiom were merely the negation of High German and, hence, of merely accidental origin. Yet to take that view is absurd, for nothing that exists can be merely a negation and without its own, necessary origins. Rather, the Jewish idiom must be an organic product of the entire history of those involved in it and continues even now to exercise considerable power over those estranged from traditional lifeforms" (noch immer manche Gewalt selbst über die dem frühern Leben Entfremdeten ausübte [Rée, 12]). Precisely because the postrevolutionary reformers committed either to political emancipation or religious reform had proved so oblivious to the "essential connection between language and the Jews' overall mode of thought and action" (der wesentliche Zusammenhang der Sprache mit unsrer ganzen Denk-und Handlungsweise [ibid., 14]) their efforts could not succeed.

While rejecting the merely practical objectives of emancipation and secularization as simply another expression of liberalism's intrinsic naïveté, Rée's arguments also reflect the emergence of a more "scientific" (and potentially totalitarian) strategy toward Jewish integration. Beneath the religious and political differences that characterize and identify German Jews, albeit with varying degrees depending on locality and region, a more fundamental "social split" continues to be reinforced by the Jews' special linguistic status, Rée observes, and the aim is to abolish it, along with the peculiarities that support it ("Es existiert ein sozialer Zwiespalt, wir wollen ihn vernichten, es existiren auf unsrer Seite Besonderheiten, die ihn unterhalten, wir müssen sie . . . zerstören" [ibid., 26–27]). Above all, the "cultivated Jew of today . . . must feel the rift [*Zerrissenheit*]" between his envisioned membership in the social form of the modern nation-state and his inherited, yet no longer serviceable linguistic identity (ibid., 29). For more than anything, it is language which "offers a pure expression of our interiority, free of all contingency." In order to tear down this "barrier" (*Scheidewand*), Rée intends to pursue across the entire class spectrum the utter expurgation of the Jewish dialect ("so muß er seinen Dialekt vollständig verbannen" [ibid., 39]).

With this prescription, however, Rée also confronts the fundamental implication of his earlier observation that a people's linguistic practices are the living record of its spiritual identity and historical memory. Yet, notwithstanding his express commitment to the Jewish faith— a point on which Rée seems less equivocal than the previous generation of Jewish secular "emancipationists" (Friedländer, Ascher, et al.)—the imperative of linguistic homogenization here prevails. In fact, though the Jewish dialect had, in past years, been intimately woven into the textures of Jewish religious ceremonial, this affiliation merely reflected secular patterns of political discrimination and cultural isolation that, in Rée's view, are no longer valid in 1844. While "the interest in Jewish dialect for religious purposes was well founded in past times," it now seems little more than a fossilized memory ("eine Ruine der Vergangenheit" [45]). The widespread perception of a connection between (Yiddish) linguistic conservatism and a strong religious faith, he argues, proves misleading in that such an association originated only in explicit reaction against the fervor of late-Enlightenment secular reforms previously experienced as a threat to the Jewish faith. By contrast, Rée contends, "the dependency of faith on language is progressively declining, such that today there is no longer an essential relationship between the two." After all, the fundamental objective of Jewish culture "concerns the preservation of the faith, not the segregation of the faithful" (nicht die Absperrung der Gläubigen, sondern die Erhaltung des Glaubens [46–47]).

Rée's argument bears the stamp of classic Hegelian analysis—itself, as the earlier cases of Moses Moser and Eduard Gans prove—a philosophy of great appeal to German Jews who were bent on full incorporation (*Aufhebung*) into the emergent myth of a liberal-bureaucratic Prussian society. The interdependency of thought and expression (*Denken* and *Äusserung*) is expressly acknowledged. At the same time, however, the emergence of the modern, secular nation-state promising political and economic, that is, secular, integration to all its constituencies has effectively removed (*aufgehoben*) the raison d'être for linguistic specificity and, hence, for the preservation of discrete historical traditions. Differences remain, to be sure, yet in the modern bureaucratic nation, they are to be invisible: "Indeed, among the characteristic differences between old and modern times, we find that in times past the particularity of the individual was more overtly expressed. By contrast, notwithstanding differences of character, intelligence, occupation, or circumstances, modern life is dominated by external similarity (*äußerlich Gleichheit* [48]). For Jews no less than for gentiles, the modern nation-state is, in Rée's urgent phrasing, not "merely an accidental habitation but a condition of our spiritual life, an essential part of our selves, our temperament [*Gesinnung*], our thinking" (54). Lest the reservations or misgivings of his Jewish co-religionists revive fears of a "Jewish state within the state," Rée presents the modern secular and bureaucratic state, as well as the anonymity and "external similarity" of its burghers as a fait accompli. For although their folk character (*Volksthümlichkeit*) is inherently venerable, the old structures of familial and religious life are simply no longer viable; precisely because the new fatherland has already struck such deep roots in us, they can only await their "annihilation" (*Vernichtung* [60]).[79]

Aside from their eerily prescient wording, Rée's ominous (or, perhaps, fatalistic) prescriptions raise one key question: what is to be this new language spoken by all members of the Prussian nation? In fact, the gold standard of linguistic propriety and vaunted medium for Jewish acculturation, commonly known as *Hochdeutsch,* turns out to be an abstraction spoken de facto by no one at all. At most, it is a print language (*Schriftsprache*). Jacob Toury has pointed out that Germany's Jewish community assimilated this new linguistic standard with uncanny speed during the early nineteenth century. Consumed by prospects of social and economic mobility, Jews embraced *Hochdeutsch* as a means of shedding any residual ties to village- or small-town culture, and of escaping their inherited dialect culture and its regional and local permutations. The regulative ideal for this urgent linguistic and social mobility, however, was an abstract *Hochsprache* or *Bildungssprache* (Toury, 88) effectively spoken by no one and hence bound to isolate the Jewish minority all over again. Reflecting on Peter Freimark's documentation of "hypercorrect language usage" (260) by the educated Jewish community of early-and mid-nineteenth-century Germany, Jacob Toury points out that

> the most serious charge against the Jews had to be a qualitative one, namely, that they spoke a "normative" language, and hence lacked a vernacular [*also keine Volkssprache*]. Indisputably, these educated [Jews] in large cities . . . availed themselves of a high language [*Hochsprache*], and they did so more consistently and in larger numbers than their educated, non-Jewish counterparts. A German professor could speak Saxon, Berlinese, Swabian, Viennese, or Goethe's Frankfurt dialect. An educated Jew would speak High German. Doing so was both his mark of pride *and* his shortcoming, for by virtue of it he did not belong to the autochthonous language family of his native locale [*seines Wohnsitzes*]. (Toury, 84)

As the most fundamental aspect of "acculturation" (*kulturelle Anpassung*), the linguistic assimilation of German Jews during the first half of the nineteenth century also reflected back to them their alienated status. The price for successful assimilation was to be branded a parvenu and, as Heine more than anyone experienced, a linguistic fraud who had merely "acquired" (*angelernt*) High German. Lacking the organic social identity that most Germans considered to be firmly grounded in the "soil" of organic dialect culture, educated and culturally productive Jews were being identified, as early as the 1820s, as the harbingers of a rootless, dissipated, frivolous culture of cosmopolitan information and gossip.

The Fir or the Palm: Heine's Melancholic Revaluation of German-Jewish Culture

We are now in a position to account for the full scope of melancholy and ressentiment in Heine and late romantic cultural politics. Heine's alienation from Weimar classicism and romantic "nightingale madness" is balanced, we find, by an equally skeptical reaction to Jewish emancipation and, especially, acculturation. Beginning in the early 1820s, Heine's writings (particularly his letters) offer vivid accounts of his being caught between the divergent strands of Christian conservatism, secular Liberalism, and Jewish assimilation. It is their vindictiveness, disingenuousness, or their essentially reactive nature that renders all these positions flawed and often repellent. Indeed, for Heine the unwholesome longing of Germans for one homogeneous, sentimental national community and the utopian and self-destructive longing of many early-nineteenth-century Jews for incorporation into that society converge in the very word "German" (*Deutsch*): "Everything German I find repellent. . . . The

German language violates my ears. My own poems occasionally disgust me when I see that they have been written in German" (Alles was deutsch ist, ist mir zuwider. . . . Die deutsche Sprache zerreißt meine Ohre. Die eignen Gedichte ekeln mich zuweilen an, wenn ich sehe, daß sie auf deutsch geschrieben sind [*HB*, 1: 38]). Only a year later, however, Heine confesses that "that I am a thoroughly German beast; I know only too well that the German language to me is what water is to a fish, and that—to retain the fish-simile—I'll turn into a stockfish if—to retain the watered-down simile—I should ever leap out the Germanic element" (*HB*, 1: 150; my translation).

Almost from the beginning, Heine's career as a writer is shaped by his intuitive (and soon explicit) understanding of "acculturation" as a bankrupt, indeed nefarious, concept and of the duplicitous fiction of *Hochdeutsch* as the linguistic embodiment of Jewish (self-)alienation par excellence. Thus, in his early essay *Über Polen* (On Poland) in which Heine describes those parts of Poland taken over by Prussia after the Congress of Vienna (1814), he draws a sharp, and harshly worded distinction between the autochthonous culture of eastern shtetl Jews and their assimilated co-religionists in the West. Rather than relying, as Sander Gilman has argued, on the cliché of the "bad" eastern Jew, however, Heine's description leaves us in a void between Prussian-Polish Jews genuinely attached to their religious traditions yet lacking their Western counterparts' secular culture and prospects of social mobility. The latter, we are told, are soaked in cosmopolitan esprit and the trophies of high culture; spiritually, however, they are almost wholly dissipated:

> At the very least, however, the Jews always pored over their Hebrew books of learning and religion, for the sake of which they had left their fatherland and their creature comforts behind. They failed, clearly, to keep pace with European civilization, and their spiritual world sank into a morass of unedifying superstition squeezed into a thousand grotesque shapes by a super-subtle scholasticism. And yet, and yet . . . despite the barbarous fur cap that covers his head and the still more barbarous ideas that fill it, I value the Polish Jew much higher than many a German Jew who wears his hat in the latest Simon-Bolivar fashion and has his head filled with quotations from Jean Paul. In rigid seclusion that Polish Jew's character became a homogeneous whole; when breathing a more tolerant air it took on the stamp of liberty. The inner man did not become a composite medley of heterogeneous emotions, nor did it atrophy through being constrained within the walls of the Frankfurt ghetto, ordinances decreed by the

> high, wise, and mighty city fathers, and disabilities charitably decreed by law. I for my part prefer the Polish Jew with his filthy fur, his populated beard, his smell of garlic, and his jabbering jargon, to many another who stands in all the glory of his gilt-edged securities. (trans. in Prawer, 61–62 / *HSS*, 2: 75–77)

Most striking about this well-known passage is, perhaps, its structural equation of affective with religious integrity. In the quick thrust and parry of Heine's prose, both eastern and western European Jews are ultimately simply foils for his struggle with the alienation that he feels, both from the affective sterility of high culture and from the hermetic traditionalism of eastern shtetl Jews. The very suppleness of Heine's prose makes it clear that to partake of the eastern Jew's intact spirituality is impossible for a contemporary Jewish writer whose aesthetic sophistication and urbane professionalism have definitively estranged him from his seemingly timeless, local and modest spiritual existence of his ancestry. Yet Heine's juxtaposition of eastern and western Jews also throws into relief two antithetical forms of affect, that of spiritual subjects embedded in a local community and, on the other hand, the "*quodlibet* composite of heterogeneous emotions" of urban, upwardly mobile Jewish individuals. Behind these topical extremes of local versus cosmopolitan, religious versus secular, and communal versus individual, there once again lurks the deeper conflict between an authentic and a commodified interiority. Thus the spiritual identity of Prussian-Polish Jews has been secured by means of a defiant scriptural traditionalism that Heine finds ultimately disconcerting. On balance, however, that paradigm still seems preferable to the spiritual and emotive limbo of western Jews, whose wholesale embrace of Goethe and Jean Paul has rendered them permanently unable to discriminate between authentic (lived) and contrived (literary) emotions.[80]

Heine's widely acknowledged formal and stylistic brilliance in emulating the tonal and affective scale of German romanticism as a "literary" artifact should be viewed in relation to patterns of linguistic assimilation that dominated the problem of Jewish "emancipation" during in the first half of the nineteenth century.[81] Occurring at the precise moment when the competing nationalist visions of anti-Napoleonic patriots, extreme *Deutschtümeler*, and Prussian and liberal-parliamentary reformers all appeared permanently stifled by Metternich's shrewd, if antiquated, power politics, Heine's radical transformation of German and, indeed, of the idea of literary language proved of tremendous consequence. Not only did it confound the Jena school's paradigm of an autonomous aesthetic, but by enmeshing poetry and prose, expressivity and cliché, pathos and humor (*Witz*), Heine's idiom seemed to expose the German language as no less vulnerable to French corruption (Kraus's *Franzosenkrankheit*) than Prussia's forces had been at Jena and Auerstädt. Rejoicing in his powers of provocation, Heine was to comment (in an 1833 letter written from Paris) that "the destruction of national prejudices and bigoted patriotism" was one of his prime objectives; "for that reason I am cosmopolitanism incarnate"(*HB*, 2: 38). As an artistic monument (*Kunstsprache*), German had to be shown in all its frailty, liable to saccharine lyric miniatures serially reproduced, and thus obvious targets for assimilation by (supposed) non-Germans (i.e., Jews). Precisely the serialized nature of Heine's lyrics, their overtly ex- or interchangeable nature, drew the ire of readers whose investment in an exclusionary paradigm of German nationhood ultimately won out over their aesthetic discernment.[82] The "deliberate falsifying of German literature and poetry at the hands of Jewish esprit" (bewußte Verfälschung deutscher Literatur und Dichtung durch den jüdischen Geist [Bartels, 328]) furnished the leitmotif for several generations of brazenly anti-Semitic readers, from Menzel to Bartels. Even the Jewish convert Karl Kraus, whose essays on Heine may claim pride of place in this unhappy genealogy, echoes the long-standing prejudice against a supposedly lingering Jewish "singing" intonation of the German language.[83]

Wherever (as in the case of Heine) distinctive Yiddish features can no longer be located, criticism switches almost effortlessly to an indictment of his supposedly rootless, cosmopolitan imitation and corruption of the German original. In Heine, Pfizer asserts, "the nimbus of originality vanishes or, rather, having been spread out over an entire race, now merely grants each individual a few meager rays with which to illumine rather than transfigure his deformities" (ein paar fahle Strahlen, welche mehr geeignet sind, Difformitäten zu beleuchten als zu verklären [*HSW*, 6, 2: 453). Pfizer's indictment of Heine's lyrics as mere "natural sounds of corruption" (Naturlaute der Corruption) reverberates in Karl Kraus's vicious attack on Heine's poetry as paltry *Operettenlyrik*, writing bearable only if accompanied by music. Such a statement effectively distinguishes between the good Heine, whom most Germans knew under the name of Robert Schumann, and the bad, brazenly textual Heine who goes unredeemed by Schumann's earnest (and differently innovative) musical rendition of high romantic sentiment. The apotheosis of this line of reasoning can be found in a memorandum from 1936 that takes up the proposal of "replacing those poems by Heine that have become the basis for famous musical compositions with new lyrics by a German pen and a German heart" (reprinted in Wulf, 410).

For Kraus, meanwhile, Heine's poetry had almost single-handedly disrupted the German language's association with an authentic, self-generating affective source of lyric expression and so transformed the supposedly timeless virtues of Weimar classicism into a modern commodity. As he saw it, Heine had commercially trivialized romantic interiority by showing its language to be substantially mediated and reproducible, thus doing it irreparable damage. The damage, of course, had not been inflicted by "bad" poetry—in which case it would have hardly warranted the tirades of Menzel, Pfizer, Minckwitz, Treitschke, Hehn, Bartels, Kraus, and many others. Rather, it was the seductive amalgamation of suspect, even shabby sentimentality with an evocative imagery that effortlessly recreated the stylistic achievements of the European lyric tradition. Thus Heine's *Buch der Lieder* rehearses a vast inventory of long held literary motifs, tones, and forms (Hindu imagery, *Minnesang,* Petrarchanism, romances, Goethean *Naturlyrik*), now laced with much self-consciousness and self-involvement—ranging from profound abjection to melancholia, from narcissism all the way to the colloquial, shabby, and prurient. Kraus in particular understood the paradigmatic shift that had occurred. Heine had effectively imported the prosaic principle of *imitatio* into poetry, thus enmeshing the latter with quotidian discourse. Once woven into the fabric of wholly interested and secular languages, poetry became a function of quick-witted citation and ephemeral daily production, of which the feuilleton was the most representative instance. What Kraus termed Heine's *Operettenlyrik* marked the defeat of content by form, experience by production, value by capital. As Berlioz was to lament in his *Memoirs,* "the wretched feuilletonist, obliged to write on anything and everything within his domain . . . wishes one thing only—to be done with the labor that weighs upon him. More often than not, he has no opinion about the objects on which he is compelled to give an opinion; they stir him to neither anger nor admiration; they do not exist. Yet he has to behave as if he believed in their existence and felt strongly about them" (Berlioz, 374). Notoriously, of course, Heine was to solve this dilemma by simply fabricating some of the music criticism he wrote during the 1840s.[84] Not surprisingly, Heine's most vehement critics are frequently more anxious about formal-linguistic and cultural trends (Pfizer's *Tendenz;* Kraus's *Folgen*) that he supposedly helped set into motion than about his relatively limited output of lyric poetry. "To discuss his effect becomes ever more pressing" (Immer dringlicher wird die Rede von seiner Wirkung), Kraus surmises, clearly apprehensive that the Heine's lyrics will inspire generations of imitators. He elaborates his anxiety with an ingenious appropriation of a specific aspect of Jewish burial ritual: "Every descendant of Heine will lift a small stone out of the mosaic of his oeuvre until none are left. The original fades simply because the garish light of copies opens our eyes."[85]

> One feels ashamed that there should ever have been that slick give-and-take between "hearts" and "smarts" [*Herz und Schmerz* (sorrow)] officially referred to as lyric poetry. Indeed, one is almost ashamed to polemicize against it. Still, by way of experiment, just try to open the *Buch der Lieder* to any given page and read variously on the left and the right page and interchange verses. You won't be disappointed, unless, of course, you can find Heine disappointing. Those who can certainly won't be disappointed now. "Birds gaily caroled in the trees; / They sang love's old sweet melodies" [Heine 1982, 10]. You could find that line on the right or the left page. "Upon my sweetheart's pretty eyes [*Äugelein*]" needn't only rhyme with "my sweetheart's cheek I devise" [*Mündlein klein*], and again, "The deep-blue violets of her eyes [*Äugelein*]" doesn't necessarily have to agree with "Red roses of her little cheek's [*Wängelein*] fair guise," for here or anywhere, Heine could have written his plea: "Lay your hand on my heart so sore, dear love [*Herze mein*]." (Kraus, 200–201; my translation)

Marcel Reich-Ranicki is surely right in observing that Kraus illustrates how "Jewish self-hatred" can be an "extraordinarily productive category" precisely because it combines "Jewish tradition and Jewish ressentiment. For, consciously or not, [Kraus's] intense faith in the word [*Wortgläubigkeit*] was rooted in the world of the Old Testament and, especially, the Talmud" (Reich-Ranicki 1993, 25).

Kraus's critique of Heine is also compromised by his very literal, quasi-legalistic insistence on "propriety" in the realm of manifestly figural literary pursuit. To Heine, one suspects, Kraus would have been just another highly assimilated latter-day Jewish convert whose head was crowned with a stylish *Bolivar* and filled with Jean Paul's recondite witticisms. If Kraus insists on resolving the tension between authentic and lived emotions and, by extension, between expressive writing and literary montage, Heine, the prototypically modern intellectual, refuses to do just that. Indeed, his defiance on this point is explicit and occurs quite early. As early as January 1824, he remarks to a friend (R. Christiani) that "at the very least my literary reputation is to allow me to write as I am inspired, and without having to apprehend a stylistic or grammatical inquisition" (Von meinem Schriftstellerruhm will ich doch wenigstens das haben, daß ich so schreiben darf, wie es mir einfällt, ohne daß ich eine stylistisches oder grammatisches Ketzergericht zu befürchten habe [*HB*, 1: 138]). Heine's provocative reliance on the techniques of serialization, montage, citation, and cliché was very much calculated to unsettle the ideal of a homogeneous linguistic culture by throwing into relief the artificial and intrinsically reproducible nature of "German." His transformation of poetry into an assembly of linguistic props or components (*Versatzstücke*) also enriches the central thesis of this study, because it shows how romantic interiority functions as a dynamic principle whose historical dimensions we can grasp only in dialectical relation to linguistic strategies and literary (lyric) forms.

I shall close with some remarks and readings of Heine's poetry published before he exchanged the figural exile of the melancholic poet for the literal one of the journalist of *haute culture* in Paris. The thematic aspects of Heine's complex and often tortuous relationship to Judaism have been worked through by others—in scrupulous detail by S. S. Prawer and with a more combative edge by Sander Gilman, to name but two important voices. Their strictly thematic approach to Heine, romanticism, anti-Semitism, and Jewish acculturation would rest on very uncertain foundations, however, insofar as it fails to align Heine's intervention in the cultural, civic, and ethnic conflicts of the *Vormärz* with the critique of the German language as it concurrently unfolds in his writings, which specifically target the putative homogeneity of German as affirmed by the literary idioms of Weimar, Jena, and Heidelberg.

Given its fundamental role in German Jewry's uncertain quest for civic and cultural enfranchisement as Germans, language—far more than "descent" or the (usually extorted) concession of "baptism"—also circumscribed the interiority of German Jews in the late romantic era, especially those who were writers.[86] Thus, in his later and overtly combative period of exile, Heine sets the tone for what is arguably an aggressively "political" poem, "Deutschland ein Wintermärchen" ("Germany: A Winter's Tale" [1844]) by merging the memory of what would be his only return to Germany and the opportunity to hear the German language once again: "And hearing the German language I / Felt strange beyond all measure; / It was as if my heart began / To bleed away with pleasure" (Heine 1982, 483) (Und als ich die deutsche Sprache vernahm, / Da ward mir seltsam zumute; / Ich meinte nicht anders, als ob das Herz / Recht angenehm verblute [*HSS*, 4: 577]).

In a way reminiscent of Keats's aggressively synthetic "Chattertonian" conception of a wholly contemporary literary English, Heine perceives German across a cognitive and affective divide that he knows can never be bridged. Yet to Heine, the structural asymmetry between the vernacular dialect culture of the Christian majority in Germany and the emulation of "pure" *Hochdeutsch*—that assimilationist utopia of attaining a linguistic homeland by expurgating all Jewish historical memory and replacing it with gentile literary capital—represents more of an opportunity than an obstacle. Perceiving Jewish acculturation and religious reform as inherently flawed strategies as early as 1822, Heine also foresaw that every successful step toward assimilation would only intensify deep-seated anti-Semitism. If anything, this situation begged the writer to mobilize his gifts of shrewd and effective provocation against the aesthetic conformism of both the mainstream romantic-Christian philistine and the Jew whose "head [was] filled with quotations from Jean Paul" and dreams of total assimilation. Logically, then, Heine's emergent conception of literary writing as a provocation issued to the fetish of a homogeneous "culture" found its primary target in the German language itself. Elsewhere, Heine once again seizes on language scholarship—this time by medieval Christian scholars in pursuit of the historical Hebrew origins of their faith—to lampoon a false romantic longing for origins, as well as the ressentiment and persecutorial fantasies that ensue when such longings produce a discomfiting truth:

> But the knowledge of Hebrew had completely died out in the Christian world. Only the Jews, who kept themselves hidden here and there in some corner or other of the earth, still preserved the traditions of this language. Like a ghost that watches over a treasure once entrusted to it, this massacred people, this ghost of a people [dieses gemordete Volk, dieses Volk-Gespenst], sat in their ghettos and guarded the Hebrew Bible. And into these hiding places of ill repute German scholars could be seen stealthily creeping down to unearth the treasure in order to acquire a knowledge of Hebrew. When the Catholic clergy noticed the danger thus threatening them, that the people might by this bypath arrive at the true Word of God and discover the Romish falsifications, they would have liked to suppress the Jewish tradition as well. They set to work to destroy all Hebrew books, and on the Rhine there began th[e] book-persecution. (Heine 1973, 311–12 / *HSS*, 3: 545)

"Irony," Lukács remarks, "is the highest freedom that can be achieved in a world without God." It is in this deep-structural sense that Heine's prose cultivates irony as a "negative mysticism" (Lukács, 1914, 93; 90) as it conjures up a Jewish isolationism precipitated by the menacing incursions of a preponderantly Christian society. Yet such repression ironically ensures the survival of the repressed—that is, of Judaism's spiritual and linguistic traditions as the "originals" temporarily displaced by the "Roman forgeries" of Christianity but patiently awaiting the day of their return. The irony deepens because a furtive curiosity is said to prompt Christian scholars (e.g., Johannes Reuchlin [1455–1522]) to seek forbidden knowledge of the primordial Hebrew culture of scripture and poetry that will eventually lead to the exposure of their own creed as secondary and etiolated. Heine's reference to the destruction of Jewish books on the banks of the Rhine between 1507 and 1510 also constitutes a pointed allusion to Metternich's censorship and anti-publishing legislation, which had reached its peak in the very year that Heine published this passage in his *On the History of Religion and Philosophy in Germany.*[87] Spurred by Wolfgang Menzel's notorious review of *das junge Deutschland*—pointedly indicted as *das junge Palästina*—Metternich came to regard Heine and Börne as being in effect members of a German government in exile ("Tous ces gens-là sont membres du comité allemand, qui . . . est en realité un centre de Gouvernement").[88] The aristocratic Metternich admired Heine and found the anti-Semitic and francophobic outbursts of Menzel and Pfizer distasteful, but he was enough of a pragmatist to capitalize on the vulgar but effective cultural crusades of the German nationalists. Important, too, is how Heine's exposé connects Menzel's anti-Semitic diatribe against liberal and Jewish intellectuals with Metternich's secret administrative campaign against them. For however fossilized and "murdered," ghettoized and seemingly asleep in the midst of German mainstream culture, the hidden treasures of Jewish religious and linguistic culture retained all their explosive force. Indeed, through its fortuitous recent alliance with a liberal-progressive movement that, in Heine's famous words, had replaced Europe's national boundaries with party allegiances (*HSS*, 2: 376), the subaltern potential of Judaism was able to resurface and unhinge the Viennese government's oppressive and bigoted agenda. Already in an early letter, Heine intimates that he, "the avowed scorner of all positive religions" may yet "adopt the crudest rabbinical method, simply because I regard it as a proper antidote" to the status quo (Ja, ich der Verächter aller positiven Religionen, werde vielleicht einst zum krassesten Rabinismus übergehen, eben weil ich diesen als ein probates Gegengift betrachte [*HB*, 1: 74]).

For Heine, the antidote to the "gangrene" (*Eitermaterie)* and "poisonous exhalations" (*Giftdünste)* (*HB*, 1: 182; 201) of his times is to be found in the opulent imagery of Indian, Persian, and Hebrew myths, many of which had only recently been recovered and translated by philologists like Georg Forster, Franz Bopp, Friedrich Creuzer, Friedrich Schlegel, and Sir William Jones in England. Thus the *Buch der Lieder* commonly deploys images emblematic of distant realms like Persia, India, and Palestine, such as the cedar, cypress, lotus, and palm. While used to richly varied effect, these emblems in one way or another seek to probe the cognitive and emotive tensions between the divisive culture of Restoration Germany and past worlds of rich and seductive imagery. In a tribute to his declared spiritual and poetic precursor, the eleventh-century Sephardic poet and philosopher Jehuda Ben Halevy, Heine revisits the old claim (familiar to English readers from Robert Lowth's *Lectures on the Sacred Poetry of the Hebrews* [1754–87]) of Hebrew as *the* archetypally poetic language. In sharp contrast to the legalistic and disputatious tradition of the Halakah, the Haggadah's inexhaustible treasure of legends, fables, and anecdotes is imagined to have furnished Jehuda Ben Halevy with a figural sanctuary:

Letztre aber, die Hagada,
Will ich einen Garten nennen,
Einen Garten, hochphantastisch
Und vergleichbar jenem andern,

Welcher ebenfalls dem Boden
Babylons entsprossen weiland—
Garten der Semiramis,
Achtes Wunderwerk der Welt.

Königin Semiramis,
. . . .
pflanzte
Einen Garten in der Luft—

Hoch auf kolossalen Säulen
Prangten Palmen und Zypressen,
Goldorangen, Blumenbeete,
Marmorbilder, auch Springbrunnen,

Alles klug und fest verbunden
Durch unzähl'ge Hängebrücken,
Die wie Schlingepflanzen aussahn
Und worauf sich Vögel wiegten—

Große, bunte, ernste Vögel,
Tiefe Denker, die nicht singen, (*HSS*, 6, 1: 132–33)

But the latter, the Haggada,
I would rather call a garden,
A phantasmagoric garden
That is very like another

That once bloomed and sprouted also
From the soil of Babylonia—
Queen Semiramis' great garden,
That eighth wonder of the world.

Queen Semiramis
. . . .
planted
A garden in the air
Rising high on giant pillars
Cypresses and palm trees flourished,
Orange trees and beds of flowers,
Marble statues, even fountains,

All secured with cunning braces
Formed by countless hanging bridges,
Made to look like vines and creepers,
On which birds would swing and teeter—

Big and bright-hued birds, deep thinkers
Much too solemn-faced to warble, (HEINE 1982, 659)

Heine would appear to have slipped back here into the mythology of Brentano, Creuzer and Görres. For the passage seems to offer us an intensely romanticized account of history as a submerged, yet more "authentic," stratum of life waiting to be reclaimed by the figural industry of philologists and poets. Yet it soon becomes apparent that Heine's vision of the young Jehuda is self-consciously figural, a myth presented as fabled artifice. Rather than purporting to *represent* an edenic, sumptuously tropical domain, the Haggadah (as Heine depicts it in his 1851 *Romanzero*) *is* that domain. Himself a refugee from the bureaucratic rigors of a legal career, Heine envisions Jehuda ben Halevy being drawn in by the sheer rhetorical and figural splendors of ancient Hebrew myths and fables.[89] If they stand in stark contrast to the Law (Halakah), their figural structure proves of equal consistency and coherence ("All connected wisely and firmly / By means of countless hanging bridges / That resembled vines and creepers"). What renders the passage obliquely provocative is its implicit claim that the totality of Jewish myths and legends constitutes nothing less than the legitimate origin of what Heine elsewhere refers to as the "Roman forgeries" (Römische Fälschungen [*HSS*, 3: 545]) of Christian culture. What weighs more, Heine's celebration of Jehuda ben Halevy as the archetypal Hebrew poet unfolds in a quintessentially High German and high romantic idiom—opulent in its imagery and transparently evocative (for readers in 1851) of romantic literary convention. The eleventh-century Haggadah appears all but indistinguishable from the self-conscious myth-making of the Heidelberg romantics. Jewish poetics prefigures Brentano's and Creuzer's mythopoiesis with such intensity as to almost coincide with it. Thus, like its figural archetype—the mythical hanging gardens of Semiramis—the Haggadah comprises all the customary motifs and stage props of the romantic writer: "Cypresses and palm trees flourished, / Orange trees and beds of flowers / Marble statues, even fountains."[90] Yet Heine's provocation hardly exhausts itself in such thematic possibilities. Shortly before introducing the Haggadah as the unacknowledged *Urtext* of romantic poetics, his *Hebrew Melodies* map Jehuda's linguistic coordinates by envisioning how his father had initiated the future poet into the study of the Torah:

Diese las er mit dem Sohne
In dem Urtext, dessen schöne,
Hieroglyphisch pittoreske,
Altchaldäische Quadratschrift

Herstammt aus dem Kindesalter
Unsrer Welt, und auch deswegen
Jedem kindlichen Gemüte
So vertraut entgegenlacht.

Diesen echten alten Text
Rezitierte auch der Knabe
In der uralt hergebrachten
Singsangweise, Tropp geheißen—

Und er gurgelte gar lieblich
Jene fetten Gutturalen,
Und er schlug dabei den Triller,
Den Schalscheleth, wie ein Vogel.

Auch den Targum Onkelos,
Der geschrieben ist in jenem
Plattjudäischen Idiom,
Das wir Aramäisch nennen

Und zur Sprache der Propheten
Sich verhalten mag etwa
Wie das Schwäbische zum Deutschen—
Dieses Gelbveiglein-Hebräisch

Lernte gleichfalls früh der Knabe, (*HSS*, 6, 1: 131)

And the youngster read this volume
In the ancient text, whose lovely
Picturesquely hieroglyphic
Old Chaldean squared-off letters

Are derived from the childhood
Of the world, and for this reason
Show familiar, smiling features
To all childlike minds and spirits.

This authentic ancient text
Was recited by the youngster
In the old, original singsong
Known as *Tropp* down through the ages—

And with loving care he gurgled
Those fat gutturals right gladly,
And the quaver, the Shalsheleth,
He trilled like a feathered warbler.

As for Onkelos's Targum,
Which is written in that special
Low-Judaic idiom
That we call the Aramaic

And which bears the same relation
To the language of the prophets
That the Swabian has to German—
In this garlic-sausage Hebrew
Was the boy instructed likewise, (HEINE 1982, 656)

Stressing the near homophony of German and Jewish dialect culture (*Aramäisch / Schwäbisch / Hebräisch*), Heine goes out of his way to confound historical, linguistic, and cultural / ethnic boundaries of all sorts. Jehuda's apprenticeship in the study of the five books of Moses (*Targum Onkelos)*[91] simultaneously marks his initiation into an inherently hybrid culture. Here, of course, the real target of Heine's wit are those self-styled Swabian custodians of German literary purity Gustav Pfizer and Wolfgang Menzel, whose conspicuous dialect (metonymically focused by Heine's regionalism *Gelbveiglein*) actually resembles the linguistic and cultural hybridity of the eleventh-century Sephardic poet.[92] Indeed, in the course of juxtaposing the Greek and Judaeo-Christian (or Nazarene) sensibilities, Heine refers to the confirmed anti-Semite Menzel as "the Jew Menzel" (der Jude Menzel [*HSS,* 4: 47). In the above passage from "Jehuda ben Halevy," Heine also deploys his considerable rhetorical and lexical gifts to transpose the distinctive euphony and opulent imagery of the Pentateuch into German. Yet in stark contrast to Moses Mendelssohn's translation of the Torah into High German—transliterated and printed in classical ("pure") Hebrew characters—Heine's "Hebrew Melodies" stress the phonetic richness of the "low Judaic idiom" (*Plattjudäisch*) of Onkelos's paraphrase of the Pentateuch. With a linguist's technical precision, Heine foregrounds the beauties of precisely that Jewish "ancient tradition of singing speech" (der uralt hergebrachten / Singsangweise, Tropp geheißen) and its rolling trills (*Schalscheleth* [Hebrew 5 chain, necklace]) that cultural assimilationists such as Maimon, Mendelssohn, Friedländer, Zunz, and Rée had been so anxious to expunge.[93] Far from rendering Halevy's language "vaguely comic [and] somewhat degenerate" (Gilman, 181), Heine's imaginative and richly textured depiction of Aramaic affirms its ethnic and spiritual charisma. The point is only reinforced by Heine's sly juxtaposition of Aramaic and Swabian dialect culture. Each idiom appears needlessly self-effacing and bashful in relation to the idea of a normative "pure" language (Hebrew; High German) that may represent an aesthetic ideal for militant nationalists, to be sure, but has never been spoken by any actual person. It is through this imagined and highly specific linguistic kinship with Halevy that Heine at once mimics and mocks the fiction of linguistic and aesthetic purity. Thus a poetry of unimpeachably well crafted and vivid High German—Heine's authorial trademark—celebrates its own other. The German Jew Heine effortlessly simulates *Hochdeutsch,* thereby evincing its serial reproducibility, its modernity as an arbitrary and manipulable semiotic system, while simultaneously unraveling romantic nationalism's mystification of language as strictly autochthonous matter, the quintessence of linguistic and ethnic purity. The point becomes inescapable where Heine's linguistic and rhetorical talents are marshaled for the imitation of Jewish dialect culture and the rich lived existence of which it is an expression. Where Mendelssohn and Rée emphasize the need for flawless High German so as to enable their co-religionists to "forget" their native Yiddish culture, Heine recalls (in perfect German) precisely that imperiled Jewish linguistic past by relating it to the dialect culture of German gentiles (Swabians).

Arguably, the *Romanzero*'s sympathetic portrayal of indigenous Jewish linguistic and cultural practices in a mainstream Christian society reflects Heine's much-discussed "religious turn" after 1848. Yet while the biographical particulars of the aging and sick poet confined to his "mattress-tomb" (*Matrazengruft*) may indeed have intensified a preoccupation with his Jewish identity, the cultural and linguistic paradoxes sketched in the section of *Romanzero* entitled "Hebrew Melodies" can be encountered throughout his entire oeuvre (cf., e.g., his sly critique of German romantic nationalism and its militant Christian underpinnings in his early essay "Die Romantik"). Returning to Heine's *Buch der Lieder,* it is now possible to identify a distinctly political edge in many of his ostensibly conventional lyric set pieces. The well-worn topos of unrequited love frequently encrypts an ethnic and linguistic estrangement between the aspiring Jewish poet and a Christian "mainstream" culture. A short poem from "Lyrisches Intermezzo" pointedly contrasts the recondite expertise of philologists and the writer's rich affective response to the "grammar" of his beloved's countenance; for reasons that will soon become apparent, I juxtapose it with another, even shorter lyric from the same section:

Es stehen unbeweglich
Die Sterne in der Höh'
Viel tausend Jahr', und schauen
Sich an mit Liebesweh.

Sie sprechen eine Sprache,
Die ist so reich, so schön;
Doch keiner der Philologen
Kann diese Sprache verstehn.

Ich aber hab sie gelernet,
Und ich vergesse sie nicht;
Mir diente als Grammatik
Der Herzallerliebsten Gesicht. (*HSS*, 1: 77)

They twinkle in fixed places,
The stars in heaven above;
They gaze at each other for ages,
Yearning and aching with love.

They speak a beautiful language
That is so rich, so grand,
Not one of the learned professors,
Can hope to understand.

And yet my heart has learned it
And will not forget its grace;
The grammar book I studied
Was my belovèds face. (HEINE 1982, 54)

Ein Fichtenbaum steht einsam
Im Norden auf kahler Höh'.
Ihn schläfert; mit weißer Decke
Umhüllen ihn Eis und Schnee.

Er träumt von einer Palme,
Die, fern im Morgenland,
Einsam und schweigend trauert
Auf brennender Felsenwand. (*HSS*, 1: 88)

A single fir stands lonesome
On barren northernly height.
He drowses; frost and snowstorm
Shroud him swathes of white.

He dreams about a palm—she,
In the orient far, alone,
Sorrowing stands and silent
At a blazing scarp of stone. (HEINE 1995, 19)

The opening image of stars immovably fixed in their places and in an impossible longing for one another (echoed by the fir longing for the palm) appears centered around the convention of Petrarchan, idealized eros. At the same time, the temporal frame of "many thousands of years" already hints at the lyric's macrohistorical rather than personal concerns. Eros here does not constitute a thematics, let alone the lyric voice's dominant concern. Rather, it amounts to a *citation* of literary convention, here undertaken for the (figural) purpose of dramatizing an irremediably alienated condition. Rather than attributing this condition to any specific persona, the second stanza further extends the predicament itself by introducing a secondary trope: that of unintelligibility. There is a linguistic barrier here that "learned professors" like Creuzer, Bopp, Zunz, and Rée cannot overcome, and the speaker's claim in the third stanza that he understands the language of the stars because he has learned it from his beloved's face certainly doesn't amount to a translation. This sudden return from the cosmic to the personal, from distant stars to lovers gazing at each other, is no simple conceit for the Aristotelian tension between universal and particular; nor, indeed, does the face of his "most dearly beloved" (*Herzallerliebsten*) affirm the possibility of meaningful community between distinct individuals or cultures. On the contrary, the peculiar eloquence of the beloved's face, its truth, is precisely vested in her persistent aloofness and ultimate unintelligibility. According to Walter Benjamin's "Epistemologico-Critical Prologue" to *The Origin of German Tragic Drama, it may be recalled,* "truth never enters into a relation, and especially not into an intentional one" (die Wahrheit tritt nie in eine Relation, und insbesondere in keine intentionale). Rather, "truth is the death of intention" (der Tod der Intention [Benjamin 1998, 18]). In a similarly stoic sense, Heine's lyric voice understands truth—like the idea of a social and spiritual community—as a subject-object relation forever hovering between the indelible presence of desire and the impossibility of a permanent relation. This view, moreover, applies not only to the affect-based, minimalist paradigm of Petrarchan love but also to the Enlightenment's expansive fantasy of a rational and transparent ideal speech-situation (to borrow Habermas's phrase).[94] Heine's lyric dramatizes this "truth" of community as a fantasy at once irresistible and impossible by stressing the essential random character of erotic longing ("intention") and the inauthenticity of its formal-rhetorical expression. A century later, Adorno was to speak of the processual character of art as a result of its "synthesiz[ing] ununifiable, nonidentical elements that grind away at each other" (1997, 176). Through their thematic and deceptively conventional focus on the beloved's face, Heine's lyrics throw into figural relief the aesthetic lure and social temptation of a hegemonic German language and Gentile culture. Indeed, the negative (though by no means fatalistic) "truth" of personal relations and social community as an impossible, if inescapable, fantasy can be realized only dialectically, namely, as a subjective voice continually betrayed, and hence emotionally and epistemologically chastened by the "face" of his beloved. Hence the voice in Heine's lyric claims, not to have grasped a specific (personally dear) *meaning,* but, through the "grammar" of the beloved's face, to have gained insight into the structural operation of language. The recursive experience of personal, political—and specifically linguistic—disillusionment thus need not be read as a defeat. Rather, inasmuch as eros points up the necessarily and inescapably (self-)deceiving character of personal relations, its formal expression as lyric writing can be said to facilitate (though not compel) audiences to approach poetry as reflection on the dialectical character of language and indeed the reading process itself. Like the Jewish assimilationist's programmatic ("intentional") fantasy of utterly blending into the dominant linguistic and aesthetic patterns of German culture, eros, in its formalization as lyric speech, exposes the dialectical "truth" of such perilous longing through the speaker's recurrent betrayal by an unattainable, haughty beloved.

Perhaps no other lyric in Heine's *Buch der Lieder* attains quite the same hieroglyphic, wintry concision as his short poem "Ein Fichtenbaum" with its improbable depiction of a fir longing for a palm tree. Like the embattled and displaced tree of the first stanza, the poem itself lingers forlorn amid lyrics of a more wittily discursive or opulently imagistic character. Yet this very reticence and compactness takes on a symptomatic quality, particularly if we pause long enough to consider the pointlessness, indeed, the essential absurdity of a fir's supposed erotic longing for a palm. The affect of eros here appears at once contrived and denuded, a literary convention retained only in its barest scaffolding. In its forced application to mute and unrelated trees, this set piece of erotic longing presents lyricism per se as the barest façade of emotionalism, one that urges readers to probe for some recessed experience of loss—not of a gendered other but of self. Heine's poem draws its audience's attention to the transparently figural ways in which longing operates. Specifically, the lyric appears to conceal an unrequited longing on the part of its hypothetical subject—instanced and sustained by the operation of the lyric "voice" itself—for its own proper existence. An analogy seems to prevail between the literary topos of unrequited love and the abjection of a figural voice earnestly striving to imagine its own reality or substantiality. As a strictly metaphoric quality, however, eros also (and more notably) draws attention to the cultural estrangement of the Hebrew poet displaced into the barren and hostile (and Christian) society of northern Europe. Like Jehuda ben Halevy, this subject longs not so much for some idealized feminine other as for his own proper self.

Behind the "libidinous façade" (Veit, 14), the voice's abject and estranged constitution points to a fundamental tension in the lyric subject both as persona and as a formal construct. As a persona, this subject abides in the virtual domain of the symbolic, suspended between a denatured empirical real and the subterranean dreamlife of the imaginary, between the cultural and political ice age of restoration Germany and the longed-for wailing wall (brennende Felsenwand) of "Jeruscholayim."[95] The poem's topical eroticism thinly veils the Jewish writer's intrinsically abject condition. Well beyond "being separated from his spiritual sources" (Veit, 20), however, Heine's lyric persona reveals a fundamental perplexity as to the relevance of such "spiritual sources" in a prosaic and ideologically fragmented modernity. Far from being a naïve melancholic longing for the communal and spiritual plenitude of ancient Hebrews, the abjection in Heine's poem reflects an awareness of that past as fantasy, as outright imaginary. Estranged both from the barren and hostile culture of Christian restoration-age Europe, the lyric voice will only conjure up such longing for Palestine in strictly figural and overtly fantasized, imaginary ways. The homeland exists only as the correlate of sleep and reverie ("Ihn schläfert / Er träumt"). Precisely this self-consciously utopian conception of home as a strictly imaginary value also explains why the poem should mediate this fantasy in such overtly etiolated, conventional form. Finding the Jewish writer's spiritual, cultural, and political abjection embodied in a recognizably conventional Petrarchan rhetoric of erotic longing, readers may either embrace the Petrarchan façade itself or, alternatively, probe for deeper religious, ethnic, and cultural tensions and ambiguities. Yet choosing the latter will place the audience at a reflexive, critical distance vis-à-vis lyric convention from which one does not easily recover. Such a model of reading incrementally places the reader at a dialectical remove vis-à-vis German romanticism's dreamworld of linguistic, cultural, and affective homogeneity and purity. Heine's literary and social provocation as a writer of German involves precisely this reorientation of reading as a cultural practice governed by reflexivity rather than empathy. The result is a style that insistently probes into the romantic subject's historical and social determinacy and, in so doing, lays bare a mood from which the period's merely topical and thematic literarization of subjective feeling constitutes a simultaneously aggressive and regressive escape.

Notes

Introduction

1. Pinch, 19. As Christensen argues, the intractable nature of passion begets a style of "remedial indirection" in Hume, in which "problem follows problem . . . systematically unfolding a discourse that is always intelligible, if never definitive." Hume's reflexively provisional conception of "letters" corresponds to the psychological ideal of "sympathy," a strictly imaginary strategy of containing in the guise of representation what *eo ipso* defies all cognitive mastery (Christensen 1987, 66, 68). See also Pinch, 16–50; E. Schor, 30–40; and, on the "taming of the passions" by deep-structural (economic) interest, Hirschman, 31–66. On sympathy and sensibility in Scottish Enlightenment thought and Augustan literature, see also Mullan, 18–56; Ellison, 23–73; and, specifically focused on the Scottish Enlightenment and the socialization and economic harnessing of self-interest in Adam Smith, Dwyer, esp. 14–53.

2. On this subject, see Guillory's excellent reading of Gray's "Elegy" in the context of language and class politics during the 1760s and 1770s. As he notes, the tandem phenomena of social and psychological mobility precipitated a "linguistic ambivalence [that] takes the form of suspicion toward the classical languages as useless knowledge, and envy of the social distinction they represent" (Guillory, 97).

3. In an essay on "mood" in Heidegger, Stephen Mulhall elaborates the "double sense of thrownness [*Geworfenheit*]" that *Being and Time* expresses. For Heidegger "the relationship between a person's inner life and the vocabulary available to her is an intimate one; and since that vocabulary is itself something the individual inherits from the society and culture within which she happens to find herself, the range of specific feelings or moods into which she may be thrown is itself something into which she is thrown. How things might conceivably matter to her, just as much as how they in fact matter to her at a given moment, is something determined by her society and culture rather than by her own psychic make-up or will-power" (Mulhall, 197). On the question of authenticity of passion, see Austin 1973, 253–71, and Pfau 1995.

4. For different perspectives on the question of romanticism's place within narratives of modernity, see Blumenberg, 37–76; Taylor, 143–58; Pippin, 22–28; Habermas 1994, 1–37; and Giddens who points out that "notions coined in the meta-languages of the social sciences routinely reenter the universe of actions they were initially formulated to describe or account for." As he puts it, "Modernity is itself deeply and intrinsically sociological" (15, 43). See also Pfau 2005a.

5. Kant 1968, 5: 269–70; my trans. In a famous tribute to Kant's epistemological parable, Marcel Proust's *À la récherche du temps perdu* opens with the protagonist awakening to an acute feeling of disorientation in a dark room at night.

6. For some provocative, if less than conclusive speculations on the role of woman in the psycho-social economy of Kantian philosophy, see Edelman, 12–28.

7. In *Being and Time,* Heidegger quotes the same passage from Kant's short essay. See Heidegger 1979, 109. Though reluctant when it comes to philosophical speculation, twentieth-century historicism grapples with Heidegger's *Geworfenheit,* as in Sartre's and Lévi-Strauss's debate about the (im)possibility of a historical knowledge whose methods are not themselves historically conditioned. See James Chandler's fine analysis of the debate, particularly Lévi-Strauss's skeptical view that "whatever sense history has is a sense it has been given. Its sense emerges not by virtue of any 'direction' in its 'movement' but by virtue of the scheme of logical . . . categories to which it is assigned" (Chandler, 71).

8. Lukács, 1971, 72. Adorno sharpens the point, observing that "any order which is self-proclaimed is nothing but a disguise for chaos" (Adorno 2003, xii).

9. Heidegger 1995, 65; trans. modified. Alfonso Lingis remarks on *Dasein*'s persistent eagerness *not* to awaken to its own "mood." "Mood imposes upon us the whole world when we want only to occupy ourselves with the cleared space of a task and its implements" (Lingis, 153).

10. This critical distinction also underwrites much of Adorno's critical work and can be found in many of his works; a relatively early example can be found in his "Introduction" to the *Philosophy of Modern Music* (1948), where Adorno cautions that any positing of art as a direct reflex of its historico-material conditions risks "overlooking and devaluating the individual moment present in this totality of social forces, which is determined by it and, in turn, resolved by it. . . . The dialectical method . . . cannot simply treat the separate phenomena as illustrations or examples of something in the already firmly established social structure and consequently ignore the kinetic force of a concept; in this way dialectic declined to a state religion. It is rather demanded that the force of the general concept be transformed into the self-development of the concrete object and that it resolve the social enigma of this object with the powers of its own individuation" (Adorno 2003, 25–26).

ONE: Romantic Theory

1. See Aristotle, *Nichomachian Ethics* 4.1.

2. Arguably, Nussbaum's distinction between "background and situational" emotions, between the structural and the ephemeral, is hard to sustain, and her discrimination between emotion as a judgment of value and merely contingent feelings "without a rich intentionality or content" (60) that fleetingly surface in everyday life remains problematic. In what follows, I propose to sustain some such distinction, albeit not in the form of mere nomenclature but based on how emotion makes its appearance. Thus it seems legitimate to distinguish between feelings thematized by a speaker or writer (fatigue, agitation, etc.) and a deeper-seated affective charge that only reveals itself to an interpretation that moves independent of a given text's thematic and expressive cues. To anticipate the modernist aesthetic that my study, particularly in its eventual analyses of melancholy, will find lurking within late romanticism, it could be said that the texts on which this study is focused (e.g., writings by Godwin, Wordsworth, Eichendorff, Keats, and Heine) show feeling as a structurally coherent dynamic that often runs counter to a given text's thematic and referential surface operations. Though ultimately more focused on how deep-structural affective disposi-

tions will discharge themselves as conspicuous types of affect, Phillip Fisher does acknowledge that "the passions are not important mainly as momentary situations [but] instead . . . . Legislate what we mean by genre and by form in many of the most profound and culturally important works" (11). See also Redding, 1–8.

3. "For fate (character is nothing else) does not affect the life of innocent plants. Nothing is more foreign to it. On the contrary, fate unfolds inexorably in the culpable life [*im verschuldeten Leben*]. Fate is the nexus of guilt among the living" (Benjamin 1996, 307 / 1980, 75).

4. Again, a more detailed account concerning the sociological and political causes that prompt the aestheticization of emotion and inwardness between 1780 and 1840 will have to wait. There is, in other words, no historical metanarrative that frames my overall argument beforehand. Rather, I derive my line of inquiry and my sense of where to look for admissible evidence from the period's discrete philosophical and literary production. For those anxious to proceed on "solid" historical grounds, some of the following books may offer relief. On the sociological structure of Germany during the pre-1848 revolutionary period known as *Vormärz,* see Hans-Ulrich Wehler, esp. his account of the defensive constitution of the urban middle classes and of the origins of the bourgeoisie, 174–240, and his discussion of the expansion of the sphere of literary production, 520–46. See also Thomas Nipperdey's (1994) survey of social stratification, minorities, 219–270, and of religious and cultural identity formation, 403–593, as well as James Sheehan, 324–87 and 451–587, and Jürgen Kocka's extensive collection of more specialized research on nineteenth-century bourgeois culture, particularly the essay by Koselleck in vol. 2 and those by Kocka and Langewiesche in vol. 4.

5. On the supplementarity of such disciplines, see Rajan 1990, 15–35; and, from a more overtly material perspective, Ziolkowski, esp. 218–308. Pfau 1997, 208–27, takes up this issue in the context of romantic ballad writing.

6. The conception is echoed by Wordsworth in his 1815 "Essay, supplementary to the *Preface,*" where he declares that "to create taste is to call forth and bestow that power, of which knowledge is the effect" (Wordsworth 1989, 656).

7. In rather reductive fashion, Terry Eagleton speaks of the aesthetic in Kant as a "pseudo-knowledge" whereby "we establish ourselves as a community of feeling subjects linked by a quick sense of our shared capacities." Eagleton reads Kant's third *Critique* as "convert[ing] an emotive utterance to the grammatical form of the referential" and, thus, as performatively securing objective authority and social efficacy for essentially irrational, subjective positions. Kant's "sensus communis is ideology purified, universalized, and rendered reflective, ideology raised to the second power . . . to resemble the very ghostly shape of rationality itself" (Eagleton 1990, 75, 95–96). Such a position completely loses sight of the contingency of interpretation and interpretive outcomes actively solicited by the aesthetic, which Eagleton reduces to a conspiracy of socially empowered thought (dissembled as "feeling") against heterodox or subaltern points of view.

8. Angelika Rauch writes of the relation between "sensuality" (*Sinnlichkeit*) and "feeling" (*Gefühl*) in Kant's aesthetic theory: "Because feeling does not have a form, it has to be treated like an inner sensation which can only be understood in terms of the images it triggers. These images do not, however, represent the feeling as such, for they are independently existing representations or fantasies that are merely associated at the moment of pleasure or pain. In the case of the beautiful, it is not the mental representation of a rose that is pleasurable but the images remembered *along with* the subject's

affection by the rose" (Rauch 2000, 79–88). On Kant's aesthetic theory, see Gasché, esp. his discussion of "pleasure" and "voice," 50–53; see also Redding, 71–87.

9. Kramer 1990, 4. See also Carl Dahlhaus's comment on how the concept of "sensation involves the conflation of sensory quality and affect" (Im Begriff der "Empfindung" fließen Sinnesqualität und Gefühl ineinander [1988, 295; my. trans.]), as well as his longer discussion of Kant's aesthetics of music, ibid., 49–55. On the key concept of *Stimmung* as a divide between ancient and modern musical and cosmological order, see Chua on how the equal temperament of modernity, advanced by Vincenzo Galilei, "collapsed music into 'reality' as an audible *fact* divorced from celestial *values.*" Equal temperament "is a method, whereas Pythagorean tuning is an ethos." Chua thus reads the story of the emergent "difference between modern and ancient rationality" as one of disenchantment; "it can be stated as a difference of tuning. Pythagorean tuning harmonises the octave, while equal temperament partitions it equally. Ancient rationality unifies; modernity divides" (Chua, 19–20).

10. Manfred Frank remarks on the proto-articulate status of the aesthetic: "The purposiveness opened up by the judgment of taste is by definition only that of an as if. In the presence of the beautiful our situation resembles that of Siegfried listening to the bird in the forest: 'I feel almost / as if the birds were speaking to me: / I distinctly seem to hear words.' Even so, the 'sweet stammering' refuses (at least for now) to resolve itself into articulate words—into concepts, that is—and thus we are left with the 'as if' of a significant utterance, the conditional anticipation of a purpose whose reality continues to elude us" (Frank 1989a, 77).

11. "Contrary to the beautiful, which at least appears to be all of a piece, the sublime is shot through with dialectical complication" (de Man 1996, 72). Speaking specifically to Kant's formalist account of the aesthetic, and of music in particular, Lawrence Kramer has expressed similar reservations about the restrictive nature of a transcendental knowledge that seems predicated on its incompatibility with linguistic signification (1990, 3–4). Kramer has since pursued this project of rethinking the rigorous formalist premises of much musicological argumentation and analysis to considerable acclaim. Perhaps as a result of his acutely programmatic approach, however, Kramer (among others) does not attend to Kant's broader investment in epistemological and moral cognition. To focus strictly on Kant's explicit references to the subject of music is to miss more subtle and wide-ranging suggestions, scattered throughout the third *Critique,* that all cognition is inherently practical, social, and therefore contingent on the polyvalence of the subject's voice and fundamental attunement (*Stimme/Stimmung*). For a reading more consistent with the interpretation advanced here, see Schutjer, 41–80.

12. Rousseau, 67. Margery Sabin argues that the treatment of "sentiment" in Rousseau's *Reveries* strikingly anticipates the oscillation of Kantian *Gefühl* between a purely formal-transcendental quality and a phenomenal, material one : "The word 'sentiment' . . . implies, as it did in the second *Discours,* both sensation and emotion, emotion reduced to the simplicity of sensation, and sensation as diffuse and pervasive as emotion" (Sabin, 113).

13. Arguing against Paul Frey, for whom this episode opens unmediated access to a past event precisely because the success of its telling allows "language to be forgotten" (Frey, 149), Stanley Corngold cautions that while "the perfect happiness of the *sentiment de l'existence* would appear to be guaranteed by a plenitude that stands above

speech, . . . it is the act of speaking or writing that achieves this bliss" (Corngold 2002, 479–80).

14. See Derrida 1974, 101–64.

15. Kant 1968c, 115; *CrJ* 38. Kant speaks of a "feeling of life, under the name of the feeling of pleasure or pain." For a discussion of Kant's terminology, see Graubner's on Kant's third *Critique,* and Wellbery on "Stimmung" (Mood/Attunement), esp. 703–16.

16. It is precisely this exigency that connects "voice" with "tone" and, ultimately, with music. For different accounts of the implication of music in the broader Kantian preoccupation with the "attunement" of the faculties and socially viable, "communicable" knowledge, see Dahlhaus 1980, 1–39; Chua, 191–234, and Charles Rosen's discussion of "Music and Sound," 1–40.

17. As Eagleton puts it, "the subject seems somehow squeezed out of the very system of which it is the linchpin, at once source and supplement, creator and leftover. It is that which brings the world to presence, but is banished from its own creation and can by no means be deduced from it, other than in the phenomenological sense that there must be something which appearance is an appearance to" (1990, 73). Žižek also remarks on the breakdown of symmetry between the beautiful and the sublime (1993, 47–8).

18. Referring to the asymmetry between infinity and extension in the mathematical sublime, Paul de Man also points to the untenable leap from a crisis predicated on the negative quality of boundlessness and the positive affirmation of the supersensible: "But since the infinite is not comparable to any finite magnitude, the articulation [of perception in a single intuition] cannot occur. It does not, in fact, ever occur and it is the failure of the articulation that becomes the distinguishing characteristic of the sublime: it transposes or elevates the natural to the level of the supernatural, perception to imagination, understanding to reason. This transposition, however, never allows for the condition of totality that is constitutive of the sublime, and it can therefore not supersede the failure by becoming, as in a dialectic, the knowledge of this failure" (de Man 1996, 75).

19. Like Bentham, Kant institutes "fictions" as an indispensable means of affording reality the "discursive-logical consistency" that authenticates it as reality. "Kant's name for these fictions, of course, is "transcendental Ideas. . . . [They] do not simply add themselves to reality, they literally supplement it; our knowledge of objective reality can be made consistent and meaningful only by way of reference to Ideas" (Žižek, 1993, 88). By contrast, Eagleton 1990's characterization of the Kantian aesthetic as mere "pseudo-knowledge" arguably misses the point, for the charge of contrivance and falsehood (*pseudos*) is predicated on the very same rationality of which Kant's formal accord of the faculties of imagination and understanding is the (aesthetic) guarantee.

20. De Man 1996, 76. Similarly, Frances Ferguson observes how Kant's argument "makes the impossibility of sustaining claims for a unified and unitary self seem, paradoxically, to emerge precisely out of their basis in individual experience" (1992, 9). By contrast, my own reading stresses the constructivist, heuristic and self-consciously positional status of aesthetic judgment in Kant's text. On such a reading, subjectivity serves as the virtual linchpin around which an equally virtual, perhaps even utopian, community is to be realized.

21. Terada, 41. Likewise, Rauch reads Kant's critique as a strategic move from nature to culture, with the added proviso that the imaginary network of signs that have sub-

stituted themselves for some affective, if enigmatic, "natural" experience also brings into play history and tradition. "Genius . . . becomes, in the individual's formative process, the mode in which nature is transposed, displaced into representations that we know as culture. . . . Culture merely forms our nature into a sensuality (*Sinnlichkeit*) whose expression causes pleasure both for self and others. As the individual who is in formation learns to negotiate experiences with cultural signs, taste becomes the memory of such a negotiation in terms of what is pleasurable" (Rauch 2000, 110–11).

22. I share this view with Manfred Frank, who notes how "the thesis that the absolute proves inaccessible to reflection throws open the doors for poetry and invites it to accomplish what philosophy had been unable to do: yet this thesis is no mere poeticized thought (*Gedankenpoesie*) but the work of rigorous and focused philosophical speculation" (1989, 248). Similarly, William O'Brien sees Novalis's *Fichte-Studien* as the "decisive point . . . at which Romanticism turns away from Idealistic philosophy, or more precisely, turns back upon it in order to analyze it as language, and ultimately, as a fiction" (78). Walter Benjamin astutely notes that the split in question involves more than "the artist's turning away from the scientific thinker and philosopher," in that "with the Romantics, too, there are philosophical and indeed epistemological motives underpinning this dissociation" (Benjamin 1996, 122).

23. For a nuanced history of German idealism and the emergence of literary theory from the Jena romantics' conception of *Kritik,* see Bowie, 28–103.

24. All quotations are taken from Hans-Joachim Mähl's edition of Novalis's *Werke, Tagebücher und Briefe,* abbreviated as *WTB*. A partial translation of the *Fichte-Studien* can be found in Novalis 1997, 90–112; all other translations of this text are my own.

25. Johann Georg Hamann was a significant precursor of Novalis's linguistic and poetic theories. As early as 1762, in his *Aesthetica in Nuce* (part of his larger *Philological Crusades*), Hamann inaugurated the valorization of image and affect over rational, reflective thought: "The senses and passions speak and form knowledge strictly on the basis of images. The entire repository of human knowledge and happiness consists of nothing but images" (Sinne und Leidenschaften reden und verstehen nichts als Bilder. In Bildern besteht der ganze Schatz menschlicher Erkenntniß und Glückseeligkeit [Hamann, 121–22; my trans.]).

26. Beginning with Walter Benjamin's astonishing dissertation, *The Concept of Criticism in German Romanticism* (1920), the literature on this subject is extensive. See Redding 88–105, my introduction to Schelling 1994, and Pfau 2005a and the secondary literature identified there, esp. Pinkard, 131–71, on the functionalist, performative, and narrative constructions of self-consciousness in Kant, Fichte, and Schelling, and their mutual criticisms and disputes with contemporary philosophy

27. Notwithstanding Fichte's eagerness to escape the aporias of reflection in his quest for autonomous self-constitution free of all presuppositions, "elements of the reflection theory are . . . insinuating themselves into Fichte's counter-proposal. [Thus . . .] we do not yet see how we can use the productive act's encounter with itself to make this knowledge intelligible" (Henrich, 26). See Breazeale 1996, 2002, and Pinkard, 105–30, for more optimistic accounts of Fichte's early philosophy.

28. Characteristically, Novalis would rewrite that Fichtean sentence as "The self must posit itself as actively presenting" (Das Ich muß sich, als darstellend setzen [WTB, 2: 194]), with the emphasis now placed on the temporalized, progressive, and intrinsically aesthetic nature of "positing." For an excellent introduction to Fichte's 1794 *Science of Knowledge,* see Breazeale 2002, esp. 186–92.

29. Notwithstanding his fundamental departure from Fichte's system, Novalis and all early romantics share the epigenetic premise: "How can a person have a sense of something if he does not have the germ of it within himself. What I am to understand must develop organically within me—and what I seem to learn is only nourishment—stimulation of the organism" ("Wie kann ein Mensch Sinn für etwas haben, wenn er nicht den Keim davon in sich hat? Was ich verstehen soll, muß sich in mir organisch entwickeln; und was ich zu lernen scheine, ist nur Nahrung, Inzitament des Organismus" [Novalis 1999, 25 / *WTB,* 2: 233]). Even more clearly, the *Fichte-Studien* comments on the logic of origination: "Origination asserts a self-engendering, a causality that is its own cause" (Entstehen drückt eine Selbsthervorbringung, eine Causalität, die sich selbst Causalität ist . . . aus [*WTB,* 2: 208]).

30. William O'Brien's study offers the most extensive account of Novalis's linguistic theory (77–118), though he appears unaware of the structural affinity between Novalis's semiotic speculations and his critique of idealist models of reflection as *ordo inversus.* The latter concept figures more prominently in Winfried Menninghaus's reading of romantic theories of reflection and representation (74–98).

31. Ulrich Pothast remarks that Fichte's theory "constructs the 'I' as one that knows itself, to be sure, though only at the expense of its internal consistency. The theory succeeds inasmuch as it shows that without the premise of certain paradoxes, i.e., incompatible situations, no 'I' deserving of that name could ever be constructed. Fichte's theory may be characterized as a self-consciously paradoxical one" (44, my trans.).

32. Though he makes no mention of Fichte's "Über Geist und Buchstaben in der Philosophie," a crucial intertext for any discussion of semiotics and linguistic theory relative to the *Wissenschaftslehre,* William O'Brien rightly notes how Fichte, "who took the step [towards semiotics] first, had also recoiled from it" (101).

33. Fichte's insistence on rational and complete self-determination as an epigenetic progression is, as Helmut Müller-Sievers has shown, a necessary assumption, "because all other assumptions come at too high a metaphysical cost. . . . The imposition of epigenesis as a last source, or instance, might well be called an ideological operation. . . . But epigenesis is more: it is the form of a last instance, the sheer possibility of mundane origination, void of all substance—be it biological, linguistic, or even economic—which in the process of appearance could be distorted. Epigenesis generates ideologies by suggesting that their origin be natural" (6). On self-generation, see also Terada, 24–31.

34. For a lucid account of Novalis's theory of semiotics, see Molnar, 39–43. On Novalis's and Schlegel's critical extension of Fichte's early philosophy, see Brown, 80–104, 144–58.

35. "The second reflection as the form of non-Being reinstates the original [preconscious] condition by negating once more what appeared to be its own reality, thereby transcending it toward the original Being" (Frank and Kurz 1977, 79); as the authors go on to show, Novalis is also the first to temporalize this relation between Being and reflection. Being, while the actual basis (*Realgrund*) for all reflection and hence its condition of possibility, can yet be brought into focus only by reflection itself, which thus constitutes the virtual basis (*Idealgrund*) of Being. Being, that is, emerges into philosophical view only by virtue of, according to, and temporally "after" its own effect—namely, reflection. In his discussion of Novalis's romanticism and Freudian psychoanalysis's radicalization of "the Enlightenment's promise of autonomy," Kenneth Calhoon identifies the same paradoxical structure of an effect preceding its

cause: "'Family romance' itself maps a process in which the father is reborn through the reason of his children." On this figure in the context of the 1794 treason trials and Godwin's paranoid model of narrative, see Chapters 1 and 2.

36. I am indebted to Manfred Frank's account of the problem of time in his *Einführung*, 264–70, itself a restatement of Frank's much earlier dissertation on the problem of temporality in German romanticism. As Frank puts it: "Once temporality slides into the innermost core of subjectivity, the reason for the incompatibility of the two components involved in conscious reflection becomes fully intelligible.. . . consciousness can never attain a state of simultaneity with itself, precisely because of the alternation of its abstract parts: as a 'feeling' it has already receded into the past for reflection, and as a tendency toward complementing that lack, it drives towards a future with which once again it can never fully coincide" (1989a, 268; my trans.). On poesy versus the narrower, generic concept of "poetry," see Lacoue-Labarthe and Nancy, 48–49.

37. See *WTB*, 2: 107–8; Frank 1989a, 265–67; and Rauch 2000, 133–50. Marc Redfield notes that inasmuch as "the temporal unfolding of history separates the subject from the Subject . . . the *Bildungsroman* is the pragmatic, humanist rewriting of literature-as-theory" (Redfield, 46–47).

38. Lukács soon afterward insists, like Novalis, however, that "we cannot breathe in a closed world. We have invented the productivity of the spirit: that is why the primaeval images have irrevocably lost their objective self-evidence for us" (Lukács, 33).

39. Terada, 45. Shelley's *Defence of Poetry* offers a strikingly analogous observation: "A child at play by itself will express its delight by its voice and motions, and every inflection of tone and every gesture will bear exact relation to a corresponding antitype in the pleasurable impressions which awakened it. It will be the reflected image of that impression—and as the lyre trembles and sounds after the wind has died away, so the child seeks, by prolonging in its voice and motions the duration of the effect, to prolong also a consciousness of the cause" (Shelley, 482). As language turns into a steadier, more durable, recurrent event, shifting gradually from expression to signification, from mere activity into form, it becomes both "the representation and the medium, the pencil and the picture, the chisel and the statue." Hence grammatical and lexical patterns effectively define the beginning of a consciousness that now oscillates between a Freudian "memory-trace" of a reality antecedent to its linguistic mediation and a lucidity achieved only insofar as that reality has been absorbed into the purely formal and positional play of signifying units. Being itself the effect of such linguistic experimentation, consciousness grasps its constitution as a type of exile precipitated by faltering models of causation. It cannot know its own cause and, consequently, cannot grasp itself—since as "consciousness" it remains forever a heteronomous "effect"—that is, consciousness of language.

40. Novalis's later *Fragmente und Studien* reiterates the point with a stronger emphasis on religion and the oracular dynamics of poetry: "To be attuned to poetry resembles a receptivity for mysticism. It means being cued into idiosyncratic, personal, unknown, and secret matters—yet to be revealed—matters at once necessary and contingent [*das Nothwendig-Zufällige*]. It presents the unpresentable [*Er stellt das Undarstellbare dar]*" (*WTB*, 2: 840).

41. Arguably, Goethe's essays on "Morphology" and on "The Metamorphosis of Plants" are the prime romantic instance of this protoevolutionary model of development. See Goethe 1981, 13: 53–105. For a critical discussion of Goethe's place in pre-Darwinian theory, see Gould, 281–91.

42. "Das entwerfende Sagen ist die Dichtung. . . . Das entwerfende Sagen ist jenes, das in der Bereitung des Sagbaren zugleich das Unsagbare als ein solches zur Welt bringt. . . . Die Kunst ist als das Ins-Werk-Setzen der Wahrheit Dichtung" (Heidegger 1950, 60–61). Heidegger's 1935 essay assigns priority to language as the preservation of the "primordial essence of poesy" (weil die [Sprache] das ursprüngliche Wesen der Dichtung verwahrt).

43. In chapter 2, Heinrich motivates his urgent request for more tales of ancient bards by remarking, "I feel as though I had heard talk of them before, somewhere long ago in the days of my youth" (Mir ist auf einmal, als hätte ich irgendwo schon davon in meiner tiefsten Jugend reden hören [*WTB*, 1: 256]). The harp-playing woman in chapter 4 remarks how the wandering Heinrich appears preternaturally familiar to her (Mein Gedächtniß ist schwach geworden, aber euer Anblick erweckt in mir eine sonderbare Erinnerung aus frohen Zeiten [ibid., 282]). Listening to the old man's song in chapter 5, Heinrich muses on the lyric's distant familiarity (Es dünkte Heinrich, wie der Alte geendigt hatte, als habe er das Lied schon irgend wo gehört [ibid., 297]). The most acute instance of such a déja vu surely involves Heinrich's discovery of his own, as yet incomplete, story written in an unfamiliar language and thus far without title, though faintly recognizable as such by virtue of images depicting him and various of his acquaintances (Eine große Menge Figuren wußte er nicht zu nennen, doch däuchten sie ihm bekannt [ibid., 313]). That the structure of cognition should always take on the formal trappings of a recognition can hardly surprise, given Novalis's embrace of Fichte's epigenetic construction of the individual. At the same time, this recognition significantly remains oddly incomplete, unverifiable, and thus belongs essentially to the order of the déjà vu. The latter, as I have tried to show elsewhere, also operates in Wordsworth's early poetry ("Tintern Abbey" and *The Prelude*); see Pfau 1997, 120–39. For an analysis of déjà vu in the context of romantic art, see Koerner on the insistent motif of the *Rückenfigur* in Friedrich's paintings. By 1815, déja vu has become a romantic convention of sorts in Eichendorff's earlier poetry and prose.

44. Quoting the 1805 *Prelude* ("Of these and other kindred notices / I cannot say what portion is in truth / The naked recollection of that time / And what may rather have been called to life / By after-recollection" [3: lines 644–48]), David Simpson argues that Rousseau's and Wordsworth's poetics confronts us with "the awareness that no description can ever locate the describer in a closed analytical system available as if for third-person inspection, but must always commit him or her to a perpetual and regressive motion through biological, psychological, and historical time" (1993, 140–41). For a reading of Wordsworth's theory of affect, see Pinch's excellent discussion of "female chatter" and "phantom feelings" (72–136).

45. Refocusing critical attention on the phenomenological aspect of representation for nineteenth-century thought, Rajan 1995, 161, remarks how the "linked concerns with process and consciousness ultimately compromise any sense of artworks as finished products identical with themselves in their function as containers of meaning. For not only are the contents of consciousness in excess of the form to which they are reduced, but these 'contents' are already overdetermined by a complex cultural and intellectual context." Rather than treating Hegel's *Aesthetics* strictly as a precursor to the skeptical formalisms of twentieth-century deconstruction, Rajan urges exploration of the "form of content . . . in which even deconstructive forms like allegory are expressions of states of consciousness" (ibid., 158). For a very different reading of Hegel's outlook on emotion, see Redding, 127–44.

46. Adorno 1997, 167, restates Hegel's point in remarking how a "latent I is immanently constituted in the work through the action of the work's language; in relation to the work, the individual who produces it is an element of reality like others. The private person is not even decisive in the factual production of artworks. Implicitly the artwork demands the division of labor, and the individual functions accordingly. By entrusting itself fully to its material, production results in something universal born out of the utmost individuation. The force with which the private I is externalized in the work is the I's collective essence; it constitutes the linguistic quality of works. The labor in the artwork becomes social by way of the individual, though the individual need not be conscious of society; perhaps this is all the more true the less the individual is conscious of society." See also Pfau 1994.

47. On the conjunction of romanticism and high modernism, see esp. Kaufman 2000, 2001.

TWO: Anxious Inspiration

1. See Fredric Jameson's well-known account of a transition from the concept of "the text [as] more or less . . . coinciding with the individual literary work or utterance" to the text as "reconstituted in the form of collective and class discourses of which [it] is little more than an individual parole or utterance." Jameson calls this new object of inquiry an "ideologeme" and defines it as "the smallest intelligible unit of the essentially antagonistic collective discourse of social classes" (Jameson 1981, 76).

2. Paul Smith, 97. The same pattern of retroactivity has been observed in particularly virulent form in the preponderantly Holocaust-centered interpretations of German culture since the 1970s. Michael André Bernstein remarks on the field's tendency to "backshadowing, . . . a kind of retroactive foreshadowing in which the shared knowledge of the outcome of a series of events . . . is used to judge the participants in those events as though they should have known what was to come" (16). Speaking to the field of queer studies in relation to Freudian and Kleinian psychoanalysis, Sedgwick, 3–28, calls into question an axiomatically conspiratorial approach particularly influential in historicist readings of the novel.

3. Logan, 10. See also Barker-Benfield, 3–36, on the emergence of a "new psychoperceptual system" in empiricist writing and novels in the late seventeenth and early eighteenth centuries (e.g., Locke, George Cheyne, Richardson, and MacKenzie), as well as Lawrence 1979 and Mullan, whose closing chapter anticipates some of Logan's concerns and conclusions. The writings of eighteenth-century physicians, Mullan notes, exhibit the "same concentration on the gestural language of feeling" as the novel; moreover, "they also represent a capacity for feeling as ambiguous in similar ways" (Mullan, 201).

4. On this issue, see esp. Kaufman 2000 on Jameson's post-Adornean readings in relation to Kantian aesthetics.

5. See Pfau 1998 and my discussion of "Tintern Abbey" in conjunction with Philip K. Dick's *Blade Runner* in Pfau 1997, 131–37. For discussions of post-romantic anxiety concerning the psychophysiological integrity of the British nation, see Cannon Schmitt 1997 and David Trotter, who links paranoia to the rise of professional classes in part because, like the abstract expertise that constitutes the basis of professional expertise,

paranoia is "inherently anti-mimetic [in that] it puts meaning and value *in place of* the world" (Trotter, 5). For a reading of late Victorian paranoia about the self-estrangement of imperial Britain by its own other, Ireland, see Moses.

6. On the biogenetic revolution wrought in the conception of the "human" and on its representation in contemporary pop culture, see Graham; Hayles; Pyle 2000; Habermas 2002; and Fukuyama 2003.

7. Commentary from British Museum, Dept. of Prints and Drawings, 6: 705: "Dr. Price (r.), seated in an armchair at a small writing-desk, turns in horror towards a vision emerging from clouds (l.): Burke is represented by an enormous spectacled nose which rests on the back of Price's chair and by two gigantic hands, one holding a crown, the other a cross, both of which are surrounded by star-shaped haloes. The spectacles support (between the crown and the cross): *Reflections on the Revolution in France, and On the Proceedings in certain Societies in London, by the Rt honble Edmund Burke.* Price's pen drops from his hand; the paper before him is headed *On the Benefits of Anarchy Regicide Atheism.* The table is lit by a lamp with a naked flame and reflector. Against his chair leans an open book: *Treatise on the ill effects of Order & Government in Society, and on the absurdity of serving God, & honoring the King.* Beside it lies a pamphlet: *Sermon preached Nov 4 1789. by Dr. R. Price, before the Revolution Society.* On the wall above Price's head is a picture: *Death of Charles 1st or, the Glory of Great Britain;* a headsman raises his axe to smite the King whose head is on the block; men with pikes are indicated in the background. After the title is etched: *Vide. A troubled-conscience.*" On conspiratorial narratives of the early 1790s, see also Deane, 4–20; Barrell 2000, 127–41. On satiric prints as a medium of interpretive and ideological instability, see Chapter 3.

8. John Pocock persuasively situates Burke's *Reflections* in the context of the Whigs' increasingly strained efforts at defending the rapidly growing national debt. Not even Burke "was free of the nightmare that multiplying paper credit might end by destroying the value and even the meaning of property, the foundation alike of virtue, manners and the natural relations of society" (Pocock 1986, 197). For Pocock, it is the specter of "revolutionary monied interest grasp[ing] at power in order to carry out a vast expansion of public credit" that prompts Burke to read the "French Revolution as a conspiracy to create a paper-money despotism" (ibid., 200–201).

9. For Steven Blakemore, "Burke's great insight" consisted precisely in the fact "that history, tradition, and reality are essentially linguistic and that the recovery of their presence resides in the recovery of their meaning through inherited documents. . . . Burke sees the new, written 'world' as a falsification of man's experience in time. . . . In fact, the murderous powers of the new language become a kind of linguistic alchemy, a Black Mass where the 'ink' of language is turned into blood, where the spilling of ink on pamphlets and proclamations causes real blood to be spilled and shed" (Blakemore, 93; 95). See also Olivia Smith, 36–40 and Furniss, who observes on Burke's explicit analogy between financial speculation and the deregulated literary marketplace: "Like the new money, [writing] is scandalously loosened from the earth and made radically independent of the proper grounds of landed property, value, and meaning" (Furniss, 1993, 252). Likewise, Clifford Siskin reads "authorship [as] a means of accelerating growth at mid century—and thus ending profitless prosperity—by virtue of its participation in both of the productive processes that characterize Capitalism" (162).

10. Angela Esterhammer reads the Burke-Paine debate in the context of romantic

theories of rhetorical performativity. "Paine takes Burke's own realization that the French Revolution involves a revolution in language and turns it against him by showing that declarative language, as used by the revolutionaries and by Paine himself, is a more potent force than Burke imagined." Ultimately, Paine's linguistic axioms prove more conservative than Burke, in that he purports, "by renaming things, [to] restore their original names" and thus to "claim for his text a paradoxical, pre-linguistic status" (Esterhammer, 52, 57). See also Olivia Smith's reading of the Burke-Paine debate (35–67); and Paul Keen's wide-ranging discussion of the "Republic of Letters" (Keen, 25–75). Most of the over twenty pamphlets published in response to Burke's *Reflections* between 1790 and 1792, see Claeys, vols. 1 and 2.

11. In an analogous argument, Coleridge's 1795 Bristol lecture, *The Plot Discovered*, frames the two bills against "Treasonous and Seditious Practices and Attempts" (introduced in the House of Lords by Greville on 6 November 1795) and against "Seditious Meetings and Assemblies" (introduced in the House of Commons by Pitt on 10 November 1795) as instances where "old Treason Laws are superseded by the exploded commentaries of obsequious Crown lawyers. The commentary has conspired against the text: a vile and useless slave has conspired to dethrone its venerable master." Thus the authors of acts ostensibly introduced to prevent treason are themselves "conspirators against the Constitution" (Coleridge 1971, 288, 286). On the perennial issue of Burke's (crypto-)Catholicism, see Conor Cruise O'Brien, 3–31 and I. Kramnick, 53–57. Perhaps the most lucid critique of Burke's late style, John Thelwall's 1796 pamphlet *The Rights of Nature, against the Usurpations of Establishments*, revives the suspicion of venality in speaking of "the hireling Burke, with the whole clan of pensioned scribblers" (Thelwall, 395).

12. Thomas Jefferson to Benjamin Vaughan, letter of May 1791, in Jefferson, 20: 391. Paine's view of Burke's having corrupted himself late in life, after being a Whig for most of his political career, is echoed in Coleridge's "Sonnet: To Burke." Modeling his opening quatrain on Milton's sonnet "Methought I saw my late espoused Saint," Coleridge sketches a sentimental vision of freedom seeking to embrace Burke ("Great Son of Genius!") and, upon being rebuffed, lamenting how Burke "badst Oppression's hireling crew rejoice / Blasting with wizard's spell my laurell'd fame" (Coleridge 2001, 1: 157).

13. Barruel's *Mémoires pour servir à l'histoire du jacobinisme*, published in four volumes in 1797 and 1798, was quickly translated into English by the Hon. Robert Clifford as *Memoirs Illustrating the History of Jacobinism*. Barruel's publication followed on the heels of John Robinson's *Proofs of a Conspiracy Against all the Governments of Europe, carried on in the secret meetings of Free Masons, Illuminati, and Reading Societies* (London, 1797). On Illuminati, Freemasons, and German metaphysicians as a conspiratorial threat to the culture of British common sense, see Simpson 1993, 84–103.

14. For a particularly vivid example, Burke's notorious account of "stripping the Queen," see Furniss 1993, 138–63.

15. For the young Mackintosh, Burke's style *is* the very embodiment of the ancien régime as conspiracy. "[Burke] can cover the most ignominious retreat by a brilliant allusion. He can parade his arguments with masterly generalship, where they are strong. He can escape from an untenable position into a splendid declamation" (Mackintosh, vii). In what seems at times already more an expression of awe than an indictment of Burke's resourceful oratory—and perhaps foreshadowing his own political and

personal apostasy—Mackintosh remarks on Burke's ability to manipulate the affective state of his readers: "he can advance a groupe of magnificent horrors to make a breach in our hearts, through which the most undisciplined rabble of arguments may enter in triumph" (ibid., vii).

16. See Goldsmith on the significance of "agitation" as the necessary affective state for genuine cognition in Kant and Blake.

17. Adorno and Horkheimer, 12–13, 17–18 / *AGS*, 3: 28–29, 34): "As a system of signs, language is required to resign itself to calculation in order to know nature, and must discard the claim to be like her. As image, it is required to resign itself to mirror-imagery in order to be nature entire, and must discard the claim to know her"

18. Žižek 1989, 19, 21. For a discussion of the relation between female education in Hannah More and Ann Radcliffe, particularly strategies of "internal surveillance" designed to defend an imaginary conception of (female) Englishness against foreign corruption, see Cannon Schmitt, "Paranoia and the Englishwoman: Radcliffe's The Italian," in id., *Alien Nation*, 21–45. On the dynamics of self-surveillance in Wollstonecraft, see my "'Searching Their Hearts': Moral and Aesthetic Pedagogy in Wollstonecraft," in Pfau 1997, 163–79.

19. On this subject, see Hardt and Negri, esp. the discussion of two conceptions of Europe and of empire (69–92) and of the relationship between empire and nation-states (93–113). On the displacement of literary and historical knowledge by the postindustrial global economy, see Liu 2004. "Literature as traditionally understood no longer survives as an autonomous force or, put in the cultural-critical terms of the current academy, as a force positioned by larger forces in the guise of autonomy," Liu observes. "Since the high point of its avowed self-possession (roughly from the eighteenth through the nineteenth centuries), literature has merged with mass-market, media, educational, political, and other institutions that reallocate, repackage, and otherwise 'repurpose' its assets. Such churning of literary capital has only accelerated in the information age as major institutions compete to appropriate that capital under the spotlight of media coverage (e.g., the canon wars pitting political pundits against academics). But all that is done, and we need harbor no false romanticism about the literature that was. Whatever one thinks of cultural criticism, it has been brutally effective in demonstrating that the churning of literary capital has always characterized literature. Literature could not have been part of the life of culture otherwise. What is of interest now is the distinctive form of that churning in relation to the general economic and social churning that Joseph A. Schumpeter (in his classic phrase about capitalism) called 'creative destruction'" (Liu 2004, 1–2).

20. Kaplan, 35. Furniss 1991 stresses Burke as the more immediate and momentous interlocutor for Wollstonecraft's 1792 *Vindication*, and that at least in part "Wollstonecraft . . . ends up endorsing Burke's negative evaluation of the feminine in the very process of placing women in the vanguard of revolutionary action" (93).

21. On Trotter, see Logan, 15–42, and an as yet unpublished essay by Robert Mitchell.

22. Wollstonecraft's indictment of affect as the simulacrum of genuine feeling specifically centers on literature, both the poetry of sensibility and its Burkean amalgamation in a political prose that emulates romance: "In modern poetry the understanding and memory often fabricate the pretended effusions of the heart, and romance destroys all simplicity; which, in works of taste, is but a synonymous word for

truth. This romantic spirit has extended to our prose, . . . or a mixture of verse and prose producing the strangest incongruities." (Wollstonecraft 1960 [1790], 29). Surprisingly, Hannah More offers an equally incisive critique of affect in her 1799 *Strictures on the Modern System of Female Education:* "Another class of co[n]temporary authors turned all the force of their talents to excite *emotions,* to inspire *sentiment,* and to reduce all moral excellence into *sympathy* and *feeling.* These softer qualities were elevated at the expence of principle; and young women were incessantly hearing unqualified sensibility extolled as the perfection of their nature" (More, 146).

23. In strikingly analogous ways, and as early as 1781, Jeremy Bentham also challenges the habit of predicating the authority of one's voice on a purely subjective state. To do so are "but so many contrivances for avoiding the obligation of appealing to any external standard, and for prevailing upon the reader to accept of the author's sentiment or opinion as a reason for itself" (Bentham, 16–17). Bentham's notes (to pp. 16–20) largely illustrate and amplify his arguments against the specious, because self-privileging, character of "moral feelings," "common sense," etc. On Bentham, see also Canuel, 37–44, and Ferguson's 2002 attempt to reclaim a more nuanced and ethically complex position for Bentham.

24. In reading the female body—its purported preoccupation with appearance, materiality, and erotic sensation—as the expression of her culture's political unconscious, Wollstonecraft actually paves the way for Malthus's more insidious arguments in the 1798 and 1803 versions of his *Essay on the Principle of Population.* For Malthus, the female body, in its alleged domination over mind, conspires against the social and economic order. See my reading in Pfau 1997, 341–70.

25. A fully realized exploration of paranoia in Blake's oeuvre would have to address several interconnected plateaus of conspiratorial "vision," among them:

(1) Blake's antinomian view of Anglicanism as an institutional, systemic defrauding of the "human form divine," which pervades most of his early works, particularly *The Marriage of Heaven and Hell, The (first) Book of Urizen,* and numerous poems from *Songs of Innocence and of Experience* (see Thompson, 3–114).

(2) Blake's prophetic critique of a linear, progressive, and uniform conception of historical time fundamentally shared by Whig "laissez-faire" economics, bourgeois secular radicalism and liberalism, and by early utilitarianism (see Balfour, 127–72; Tannenbaum, 55–85, 124–51).

(3) Blake's mystical view, first broached in *America* and *Europe,* and fully developed in *The (first) Book of Urizen,* of finite, corporeal creation as conspiring against the "prolific delight" of "eternity."

(4) The ways in which Blake's oeuvre opposes (or deconstructs) the prevailing model of reading as strictly outcome-oriented, a mere harvesting of "information" or "useful" knowledge (see Makdisi, 2003, 162–175, Goldsmith, and McGann, 1988b, 152–72).

(5) How Blake's alternative conception of reading as endlessly recursive and ruminating—in short, like his illuminated focused on process ("execution") rather than product—dismantles the neoclassical premise of stable and identifiable genres. Not only does the graphic particularity of Blakean design favor the "scroll" over the book, as W. J. T. Mitchell and McGann 1983b have shown, but it does so because it regards the uniformity of commercial print commodities ("copying") as an outright conspiracy against artistic originality and inspiration. Such an approach

would frame the multimedia and mixed-genre approach of *The Marriage of Heaven and Hell*—with its enjambment of narrative, proverbs, parabolic (prophetic) writing, and satire—as counteracting the erosion of spiritual intuition as Blake saw it being perpetrated by the commercialization of British art; see Eaves, esp. his detailed account of varieties of "anti-commercialism" in late-eighteenth-century England (92–96), and McGann 1988b, 32–49.

26. Lowth, 1: 74–102. Originally published in Latin in 1753 and in English translation by Joseph Johnson in 1787, Lowth's treatise was critically extended by Thomas Howes's "Doubts Concerning the Translation and Notes of the Bishop of London to Isaiah, vindicating Ezekiel, Isaiah, and other Jewish Prophets from Disorder in Arrangement" (1883). Like Blake, Howes "seems anxious to deemphasize the predictive nature of prophecy in order to establish its credibility on the basis of its rhetorical or visionary function" (Tannenbaum, 30). On the scholarly debates regarding biblical interpretation and form, specifically as relates to the prophetic books of the Old Testament, see Tannenbaum, 25–54; Balfour, 82–105; and McGann 1988b, particularly the latter's discussion Blake's *Book of Urizen* in conjunction with Alexander Geddes's controversial new translation of (and commentary on) the Bible (152–72). Blake himself speaks of the "Parabolic" style, juxtaposing it with a historicist method that seeks to interpret Scripture on the basis of "evidence" (*CPP*, 618). On the rise in eighteenth-century England and Germany of historicist hermeneutics—the emergence of which Blake deplores—see Frei, 51–85, who observes how in the work of Anthony Collins "an argument over the meaning and interpretation of biblical narratives . . . turned into one over the reference of those narratives" (84).

27. McGann notes how "the idea that 'forms of worship' were fashioned from 'poetic tales' by tyrannizing moralists differs not at all from what [Constantin de] Volney wrote in chapters 22–23 of his *Les Ruines [ou Méditations sur les révolutions des empires]*, a work reviewed in the *Analytical* in 1792" (1988b, 163).

28. W. J. T. Mitchell, 62. See also Jon Mee's discussion of how "Urizen's association with the written law is part of his complex association with the priestly function. Secret writings, designed to keep the truths of religion from the people, were linked with Egyptian priestcraft and the druids in eighteenth-century historiography." Himself mindful of this potentially negative status of writing, "Blake operates with a notion of writing as containing both positive and negative potentialities. He seeks a writing that retains the fluidity of the voice; that seeks the status of 'poetic tales' rather than 'forms of worship'" (105).

29. Adams, 7. See also Dan Miller's "Contrary Revelation," which speaks of "contrariety [as] the relation between an 'outward circumference' and its energetic interior, the relation between the boundary and the inside of a figure—or a body" (497).

30. S. Rosen, 25.

31. Cassirer 1981b, 199. For accounts of the centrality and logical convolutions of the Kantian schematism and its pivotal place in the first *Critique*, see Heidegger 1965, 145–201. For a lucid exposition of the heuristic conception of the Kantian subject—in contrast to the dialectical model (which "arises whenever we try to convert a definite relation, which is valid within experience and for the purpose of uniting its separate members, into an independent substance prior to all experience")—see Cassirer 1981b, 193–211. Johann Gottlieb Herder's *Metakritik zur Kritik der Reinen Vernunft* was the first text to expressly identify the schematism as linguistic in substance, an issue later taken

up by Curtius 1914. For a discussion of Kant's chapter on the "schematism of the pure understanding," see also my introductory essay to Schelling 1994, 8–36. On Kant and post-Kantian Idealism, see Terry Pinkard's excellent *German Philosophy, 1760–1860* and Pfau 2005a.

32. Peter H. Marshall's contention that "for all the emphasis on the subtlety and complexity of the mind, it is true that for Godwin reason remains supreme" (96) not only conflicts with Godwin's persistent attention to irrational elements (dreams, reveries, compulsions, etc.) but also ignores Godwin's express fusion of reason and passion in a conception of the "will" that startlingly foreshadows Schopenhauer's 1819 arguments in *The World as Will and Representation.*

33. Hacking quotes Pierre-Simon Laplace's *Philosophical Essay on Probabilities* (1795) as a landmark document in the sudden collapse of the "doctrine of necessity" and cites Kant's surprising acceptance of statistical probability as a new type of proof in his 1784 "Ideas for a Universal History from a Cosmopolitan Viewpoint" (Hacking 1990, 11–15). Some twenty years after Godwin's *Political Justice,* Coleridge would further challenge the deterministic nexus of agency and outcome by calling into question both the perceptibility of efficient political causes and that of its effects: "So few are the minds that really govern the machine of society, and so incomparably more numerous and more important are the indirect consequences of things than their foreseen and direct effects"(Coleridge 1972, 15).

34. This logical dilemma essentially repeats the circularity of idealist attempts to "ground" the self in a model of self-reflection, already referred to in chapter 1 of this book. For a fuller account of the theoretical problem, see Henrich 1982; Frank 1986, 26–64; and Frank 1889b, esp. lectures 15 and 16 on Husserl. The problem already opens up in the *Critique of Pure Reason,* where one can observe Kant to growing increasingly uneasy with his apparently categorical disjunction of a purely intellectual agency and empirical personality. Kant himself admits that the former—"pure self-consciousness" or "transcendental apperception"—"is known only through the thoughts which are its predicate, and of it, apart from them, we cannot have any concept whatsoever, but can only revolve in a perpetual circle, since any judgment upon it has already made use of its representation. And the reason why this inconvenience is inseparably bound up with it, is that consciousness in itself is not a representation distinguishing a particular object, but a form of representation in general" (Kant 1865, 331 [B 404]). See also ibid., 378 (B 423n), where Kant, in contradiction of his strictly functionalist construction of the subject, appears willing to include actual, empirical "existence" as an implication of his transcendental theory of the *cogito.*

35. *GPJ,* 370. Godwin's epistemology largely recapitulates Hume's, such as in the latter's characterization of "mind [as] a kind of theatre, where several perceptions successively make their appearance; pass, re-pass, glide away, and mingle in an infinite variety of postures and situations" (Hume 2000, 253).

36. This being the case, it is interesting that a translation quickly appeared in France: *Les avantures* [sic] *de Caleb Williams; ou, Les choses comme elles sont* (Paris: H. Agasse, L'an IV de la République [1796]). See also John Bender, who argues that *Caleb Williams* "became a conflictual scene within which Godwin's initial belief in radically individualistic virtue could not maintain itself. . . . Both the old system, based upon honour, and the newer one based upon sympathetic introjection are political in the worst

sense because they personify judgment as an enforcing third person rather than founding it upon the analogous but independent percipience of individuals" (264, 267).

37. For a startlingly precise echo, see the following 1804 Notebook entry by Coleridge: "How opposite to nature & the fact to talk of the one *moment* in Hume; of our whole being an aggregate of successive single sensations. Who ever *felt* a *single* sensation? Is not every one at the same moment conscious that there co-exist a thousand others in a darker shade, or less light" (Coleridge 1991, ♯ 2370)

38. Hays, 61. On the gender-politics of Hays and her contemporaries, see Barker-Benfield, 287–350, and, for a careful parsing of the different levels of cognition within this densely layered novel of narrative and epistolary exchange, see Rajan 1993.

39. Thomas Holcroft's *The Adventures of Hugh Trevor,* published only months before *Caleb Williams,* the scholar Turl offers a critique of the British legal system that relies on exactly the same antithesis of universals and particulars, the law's habitual equation of necessarily unequal things by means of its abstract categories, and the ethical imperative for the minutest discernment of individuals and particulars (251–56).

40. "The historical 'subject' is to be shifted from the collective subject of the emergent nation to the individual agents whose public and private acts connive to produce 'things as they are' " (Klancher 1995, 157).

41. "Hume can only begin when causation is stolen from knowledge," Ian Hacking notes. "That done, his basic skeptical problem is stated succinctly. An expectation that the future will be like the past must either be knowledge or opinion. But all reasoning concerning the future must be based on cause and effect. Reasoning concerning cause and effect is not knowledge. Therefore it must be opinion, or probability. But all probable reasoning is founded on the supposition that the future will resemble the past, so opinion cannot be justified without circularity. Knowledge and probability are exhaustive alternatives. Hence expectation about the future is unjustified" (Hacking 1975, 181). As Godwin's political and fictional oeuvre bears out time and again, the radical visions of the 1790s, secular and religious, all seize on this *merely probabilistic* ideological stability of the present as an opening for political change. "Probability" here is expressly severed from its medieval conjunction with *opinio*—that is, with the superior authority of learned (religious) authority or the "stupendous wisdom" of Burke's "antient constitution." Along with the ascendancy of circumstantial evidence over witness testimony in the area of law, which will be of concern in the next chapter, the rise of statistical frequency as the best evidence for resolving questions of cause and effect spawns a sudden investment in forms of inductive, retroactive reasoning.

42. Dummett, 321. "The motion of each ball, between any two moments at which it strikes the cush or another ball, is one of those processes whose continuance needs no explanation—only its origin and its (uniform) deviation from constant velocity; this would be so whether events occurred in normal or in the reverse order." Indeed, in a revealing extension of his example from a (supposedly immediate, self-evident) *occurrence* to the *representation* of such an occurrence, Dummett later remarks how "it seems conceivable that we should discover a connecting link in some process which begins simultaneously with the quasi-effect and ends simultaneously with the quasi-cause." In other words, the causality at work is the same, regardless of whether we see the cue strike and disperse the billiard balls or "took a film" of that process and played it in reverse. What changes is merely the economy of the explanatory effort. The un-

wieldy character of causal explanations is, of course one of the most salient features in the mechanism of paranoia, as Freud had already observed in his reading of D. P. Schreber's famous autobiography (Freud 1963a, 149, 165).

43. Coleridge's 1795 lecture on "Ministerial Treason" provides a particularly succinct instance of such retroactive causation. Regarding Pitt's and Greville's bills, he notes how "the circumstances stated as causes in this Bill, the same circumstances then existed; but did they appear to produce a similar effect? Were not the higher classes infatuated, were not the multitude maddened with excess of Loyalty? The dispersion therefore of seditious pamphlets was not the cause: *that* was the cause which gave to sedition the colouring of truth, and made disaffection the dictate of hunger, the present unjust, unnecessary and calamitous War. . . . To declare by authority of Parliament that the offenders are so numerous, and the abuse of so spreading and dangerous nature, that the severe penalties already enacted are inadequate to the preventing it, will not this suggest to every unprejudiced man the dread, that enemies so numerous could not have arisen without previous oppression, and that abuse so calculated to spread must have some foundation in truth" (Coleridge 1971, 286–87, 293). In Coleridge's reasoning, the law that claims to be the effect of (and response to) a conspiracy against the constitutional order effectively produces and authenticates its professed cause of past and legitimate discontent, even as it criminalizes that cause in its interventionist and punitive representations.

44. As Pamela Clemit notes, the phrase "things as they are" becomes something of a standing expression in political discourse of the 1790s, making its appearance in Godwin's chapter on "The Aristocratical Character" in the second edition of *Political Justice* (Godwin 1985, 485), as well as in Robert Bage's 1792 novel *Man As He Is,* and Thomas Paine's *Rights of Man* ("I view things as they are, without regard to place or person" [quoted in Clemit, 39]). See also one reviewer's laconic remark that "instead of 'Things as they are,' the novel might, perhaps, as well have been intitled, 'Things as they ever have been'" (*Critical Review,* July 1794, 296).

45. Regrettably Patey does not extend his lucid and highly informed account of probability's rise to prominence in Augustan literature to a discussion of early romantic writing. Still, in his discussion of arguments by Thomas Reid and James Beattie, Patey offers a characterization of the inferential nature of literary reading that disparate romantics such as Wordsworth, Blake, or Godwin were to unfold in a far more radical manner: "From the account of signs to be found in Reid and Beattie emerges a theory of the structure of literary works, and, because all theories of literary structure entail theories about how such structures are properly to be read, an account of interpretation as well" (88).

46. *Monthly Review,* no. 15 (1794): 145, 147.

47. *Critical Review,* July 1794, 291. See also the reviewer for the *Analytical Review,* no. 10 (February 1795), who comments on how "much skill is shown by the author in the movements of intellect and the passions" (171).

48. See Bender 1995 on the question of narrative form and its evidentiary potential for our understanding of the novel's ideological position in late-eighteenth-century life.

49. The central passage where the narrator asserts the (to readers nonetheless undemonstrable) persecutorial gaze of Falkland comes during a surprise meeting with Falkland in, vol. 3, chap. 12, where Falkland supposedly reveals how "I had my eye upon

you in all your wanderings. You have taken no material step through their whole course with which I have not been acquainted" (*GCW,* 291).

50. The protagonist's preoccupation with ensuring the coherence of a plot said to have preceded his narration, as well as with maintaining total control over the narrative form itself, verges on the obsessive. Early on, Caleb usurps the story of Falkland's servant, Collins. Ostensibly "so as to avoid confusion in my narrative, I shall drop the person of Collins, and assume to be myself the historian of our patron" (*GCW,* 11). Late in the novel, Caleb again averts to the vicarious pleasure derived from fashioning an elaborate conspiratorial account: "The writing of these memoirs served me as a source of avocation for several years. For some time I had a melancholy satisfaction in it. I was better pleased to retrace the particulars of calamities that had formerly afflicted me, than to look forward, as at other times I was too apt to do, to those by which I might hereafter be overtaken. I conceived that my story, faithfully digested, would carry in it an impression of truth that few men would be able to resist" (*GCW,* 314).

51. Instructive in the same context proves Caleb's decision to call Falkland as a hostile witness in his own defense (*GCW,* 176). Godwin's move, startlingly foreshadowing Thomas Erskine's decision to depose the duke of Richmond in his defense of Thomas Hardy against charges of high treason later that year (see Chapter 3), appears fundamentally sensible. Yet in so doing, Caleb concedes that accusations of theft lodged against him can only be countered —in a glaringly paranoid inversion of the order of "things as they are"—by accusing Falkland of framing him. In a world solely shaped by the positional power of rhetoric and by the rhetorical nature of social status and charisma, there no longer is any "outside" to which to appeal for confirmation. Tilottama Rajan calls this the shift "from a mimetic to a hermeneutic view of the text" (1990, 169). Analogously, as Alexander Welsh has shown, British law was to experience the rise of circumstantial evidence from its still subordinate position at the beginning of the eighteenth century to a status equal, if not superior to the direct representation of witness testimony during the 1790s. That shift also accounts for the dramatic increase of volume in cases of high treason in 1794. Whereas the trial of David Downie for the same crime only encompassed some 180 pages in Howell's collection of *State Trials,* that of Thomas Hardy (see Chapter 3) took up no fewer than 1,200.

THREE: Paranoia Historicized

1. Siskin's concern is with "*writing* as shorthand for the entire configuration of writing, print, and silent reading" and "writing's capacity to produce change," including "the proliferation of more writing." Like Siskin's argument, my readings in this and subsequent chapters are also premised on a fundamental continuity between "disciplinarity, professionalism, and Literature . . . as *historical* categories" and thus integrate "Literature into a history of writing" (Siskin 1998, 2–6). Indeed, concurrent with Siskin's study, Pfau 1997 examined writing, literary and otherwise, as the predominant medium for configuring anonymous, often competitive middle-class individuals and constituencies into the virtual subject of a nation. The present study, meanwhile, pushes further toward articulating the emotive deep-structure that both accounts for and, in turn, is reinforced by romanticism's diversified, protodisciplinary landscape of professional writing—legal, political, economic, and literary.

2. Freud's work on the Schreber case was notably accompanied by an intense con-

sciousness of his own transferences, particularly those involving Wilhelm Fliess; see Gay 1988, 278–80. Gay does not, however, consider the structural resemblance of the work of projection to that of analysis. For general information about the Schreber case, see Santner 1996 and Allison et al. 1988. Lacan wrote his doctoral dissertation on paranoia in 1932 (Lacan 1975) and mailed a copy to Freud in Vienna (see Trotter, 60n28).

3. The phrase is from Freud's essay on repression: "Psychoanalytic experience of the transference neuroses, moreover, forces us to the conclusion that repression is not a defence-mechanism present from the very beginning, and that it cannot occur until a sharp distinction has been established between what is conscious and what is unconscious: that *the essence of repression lies simply in the function of rejecting and keeping something out of consciousness*" (Freud 1963b, 105). The German original is more categorical, speaking not of "keeping *something* out of consciousness" but rather of the "exclusion and rejection of consciousness" per se: "daß ihr Wesen nur in der Abweisung und Fernhaltung vom Bewußtem besteht" (*FSA*, 3: 108).

4. As Naomi Schor puts it, "if the detail is not seen as referring metonymically back to a whole from which it has become detached, but rather as substituting metaphorically for another detail which it resembles, then we move from the typically Freudian valorization of totalization . . . . to a notion of a detotalized detail, which would make Freud a precursor of modernity, even of the post-modern" (Schor, 72).

5. As Slavoj Žižek remarks, "the symptom can not only be interpreted but is, so to speak, already formed with an eye to its interpretation: it is addressed to the big Other presumed to contain its meaning. In other words, there is no symptom without its addressee . . . without transference, without the position of some subject presumed to know its meaning" (1989, 73).

6. For an interesting conceptual analogue, see Müller-Sievers on epigenetic thought in early German romanticism, esp. 48–64.

7. For an extended discussion of the, by 1794, rather obscure terms "compass and imagine," see Barrell 2000, 1–46. During the 1790s, in part because of Michael Foster's more inclusive assessment of "compass and imagine," it had "become possible to argue that actions could be alleged as overt acts of treason not simply on the basis of their more or less immediate tendency to lead to the king's death, but on the basis also of what might turn out to be their remote consequences, as these might be projected through a long chain of possible intermediate consequences" (ibid., 137).

8. In the wake of World War I, this issue was to vex Oliver Wendell Holmes and his colleagues on the U.S. Supreme Court, specifically in the landmark case of Abrams vs. United States (250 U.S. 616) and in the 1925 action of Gitlow vs. United States (268 U.S. 652).

9. Precisely so as to eschew that post hoc ergo propter hoc fallacy, Thomas Erskine—counsel for the defense in the 1794 treason trials—continually stressed that "the province of the jury over the effect of the evidence, ought not to be so transferred to the judges and converted into matter of law," and that "it is to be submitted to [the jury's] consciences and understandings, whether, even if you believed the overt act, you believe also that it proceeded from a traitorous machination against the life of the king. I am only contending that these two beliefs must coincide to establish a verdict of guilty" (*STT*, 895). See also *STT*, 897–900, and Erskine's precise characterization of this dilemma, viz., "to prevent the possibility of confounding the treason with matter which may be legally charged as relevant *to the proof of it*" (*STT*, 900).

10. In his otherwise trenchant account of the legal rationale for charging high treason, John Barrell does not see Foster wrestle any more sincerely than Blackstone with the question of "constructive" treason. In "Foster's argument . . . the overt acts are not merely evidence . . . [but] also proof of the intention, for the performance of them presupposes the intention" (Barrell 1992, 125). Such a view ignores Foster's repeated concern with avoiding precisely that circular mode of reasoning.

11. A long tradition extending from Coke to Hale, Foster, and Blackstone seems fundamentally in agreement on excluding spoken words from acts that could be construed as evidence of a treasonous intent. See Blackstone 1979, 4, chap. 6: 79–80. Charles James Fox's successful push for legal reform with his 1792 Libel Act, which provided that the jury was no longer restricted to finding fact but also entrusted with determining the relationship between facts and the legal statutes relative to which the former were being invested with evidentiary force ("matters of law") was crucial in this context. For a discussion of this change, see Barrell 1992, 124–29. Fox's Libel Act substantially benefited from Thomas Erskine's eloquent vindication of the rights of juries. See esp. his "Argument in the King's Bench, in support of the Rights of Juries," in Erskine, 1: 264ff.

12. On the transformation of the legal profession and the underlying conception of law in Britain in the late eighteenth century, see Lieberman, 31–55.

13. Quoted in Barrell 2000, 225. Barrell's scrupulous research suggests that members in some chapters of the London Corresponding Society did indeed secretly try to procure arms, though probably without the knowledge or approval of the organization's leaders who now faced indictment for high treason (see ibid., 210–30).

14. On this larger question, see Müller-Sievers; Stanley Rosen, 87–140.

15. As James Eyre was to put it in his "Charge to the Jury," it is but "adding to the crime meditated the deepest dissimulation and treachery." *STT*, 24: 270, 272.

16. On the evidentiary status of words, spoken and written, see Patterson.

17. On Thomas Erskine's brilliant career and approach to the defense of Hardy, Thelwall, and Tooke in particular, see McKillop.

18. Quoted in Goodwin, 329. For the developments of 1793–94, see Goodwin, 307–58; Thompson, 102–85; Barrell 2000, 231–51; and Olivia Smith, 68–109. On the general shape of British intellectual politics during the 1790s, see Simpson 1993, 40–63. A broad outline of legal developments during the 1790s is provided by Emsley.

19. See Thompson, 132–33; Goodwin, 332–37. To a significant extent, however, the evidence produced at the trial was either transparently unconnected with the crime charged or, as in the case of Robert Watt and "Citizen" Groves, had been manufactured by government spies and agents provocateurs. In a development of poignant irony, these latter figures were subsequently called as witnesses by both the prosecution and the defense. For basic documentation of the trial, see Thale.

20. British Museum, Dept. of Prints and Drawings, 7: 435: "The interior of a bare, poverty-stricken room with a raftered roof. Pitt and Dundas, as watchmen, batter down the upper timbers of a door (r.) which has been strongly bolted, locked, and barricaded. Both have long staves, Pitt holds up a lantern. The occupants hide or flee, except Lord Moira, who stands stiffly in profile to the r. on the extreme l., his crisped fingers outspread deprecatingly, dissociating himself from his companions. . . . A heavy but ragged cloth covers a rectangular able in the middle of the room, on which are ink-pot and papers: a *Plan of Invasion* with a map of *France* and *Ireland*. This lies across a paper signed *yours O'Conner*. A dark-lantern stands on the open pages of the

Proceedings of the London Corresponding Society. Prone under the table, their heads and shoulders draped by the cloth, are (l. to r.): Horne Tooke, Nicoll, and Tierny. Fox and Sheridan escape a ladder to a trap-door in the roof. . . . On 27 February 1798 O'Connor, O'Coigley, Binns, and two others were arrested in Margate when about to embark for France to urge (on behalf of the United Irishmen) the prompt dispatch of an invading fleet to Ireland. Binns was a leading member of the London Corresponding Society. The important arrest was due to Pitt's secret service, which had information from Hamburg of the Franco-Irish plans."

21. Gillray's print appears only superficially more sympathetic to the State than his earlier *Smelling out a Rat* of 1790 (fig. 1), in which a bespectacled Edmund Burke gratuitously intrudes on the perfectly civilized and private Richard Price in his study; it bears out Tom Furniss's general observation that "both sets of antagonists make virtually identical assumptions about the relation between imaginative discourse and reality; while each relies on the persuasive power of visionary rhetoric, each condemns the other for doing so" (Furniss 1993, 257).

22. Eyre went so far as to abandon the already questionable practice of retroactively inferring treasonous intent and, in its stead, to reason in rather mechanical fashion from the presumptive consequence of acts back to statutes. Speaking of the London Corresponding Society's plans for calling a national convention, Eyre holds that "the government cannot be said to exist, if the functions of legislation are usurped for a moment; and it then becomes of little consequence indeed, that the original conspirators, perhaps, had only meditated a plan of moderate reform: it is *in the nature of things,* that the power should go out of their hands, and be beyond their control" (*STT,* 208).

23. For a discussion of the recurrence of 1790s modes of paranoid cognition in contemporary criticism, see Paul Smith, 83–99. Since the publication in earlier form of the present chapter, Trotter has pursued a similar line of argument, suggesting that "in the fiction as well as in the symptomatologies and the case-histories, the idea of paranoia made it possible to express concern about the consequences of a profound and far-reaching transformation of English society: the inexorable spread, at all levels, and in all activities, of professional methods and ideals. Paranoia is meritocracy's illness, a psychopathy of expertise" (Trotter, 81–82).

24. Both the epigraph to Chapter 2 from Slavoj Žižek and the analytic writings of the contemporary philosopher Michael Dummett apply here, especially the latter's essay "Can an Effect Precede Its Cause?

25. The bill of indictment, found to be a true one by the grand jury of Middlesex and consequently produced as the government's charge at the trial expressly frames Eyre's metonymic legal argumentation, viz., "to subvert and alter the legislature rule and government now duly and happily established within this kingdom of Great Britain . . . [and] to cause and procure a convention and meeting of divers subjects of our said lord the king to be assembled and held within this kingdom with intent and in order that the persons to be assembled at such convention and meeting should and might wickedly and traitorously without and in defiance of the authority and against the will of the parliament of this kingdom subvert and alter and cause to be subverted and altered the legislature rule" (*STT,* 231–32).

26. Coleridge's "Sonnet: To the Hon. Mr. Erskine," an occasional piece dated November or December 1794, mostly heaps praise on Erskine for pouring out "the

stream divine / Of unmatch'd eloquence" at the "altar" of British freedom (Coleridge 2001, 1: 155–56).

27. *STT,* 276. Olivia Smith points out how sales figures constituted one of the principal criteria of government suspicion. "Price and style were the two means by which the government determined whether or not a work should be prosecuted" (64).

28. As Barbara Herrnstein-Smith puts it, "the extent to which a circular argument is persuasive for some audience seems to depend on, among other things, the extent to which the concepts and conceptual syntax that the argument 'begs'—that is, employs and takes for granted—are also taken for granted by that particular audience" (B. H. Smith, 130).

29. Quoted in Barrell 2000, 329.

30. As Erskine insisted during his otherwise minimal cross-examination, in one of very few direct challenges to the prosecution: "Upon the evidence that is before the Court, every man who has been a member of these Corresponding Societies; who has been a member of this Constitutional Society; every man who has been connected with those acts, if the acts constitute a conspiracy to subvert the government, is liable to be put into the same situation with Mr. Hardy; and any thing that is written by any one person belonging to either of these societies would be equally evidence against him" *(STT,* 472).

31. Quoted in Welsh, 34.

32. Quoted in Welsh, 37.

33. William Godwin, "Cursory Strictures," *Morning Chronicle,* 20 October 1794. Godwin may also have intended to put the defense counsel, Thomas Erskine, on notice. Following the conviction of Thomas Paine for seditious libel on 18 December 1792, Godwin had written a personal letter to Erskine, who had acted as counsel for Paine, upbraiding him for not defending the cause of free speech with sufficient vigor and charging him with having betrayed his client (quoted in Marshall, 91). On Godwin's "Cursory Strictures," see also Barrell 2000, 302–7, who, though mindful of its considerable impact when first published in the *Morning Chronicle* on 2 October 1794, also notes that Godwin's "grasp of the technicalities of the law of treason was at best shaky" (ibid., 302). Barrell credits the anonymous *Observations on the Law of Treason,* published two weeks later, for having had greater impact on the case presented by the defense.

34. Evidently by a mistake of the printer, Howell's *State Trials,* vol. 24, repeats page numbers 219 and 220, albeit with different text columns. The quotation here is from the "first" page 220.

35. Erskine uncompromisingly restricts all forms of criminality to a concept of intention. Consequently, he argues, adjudicating the relationship between the criminal intention alleged and the overt acts adduced in support of that charge is the province of the jury alone. Indeed, Erskine insists that legal authority and technical legal proficiency, however impressive, ought never to be in a position to pronounce on a defendant's guilt, as it were ex officio. See Erskine 1810, 1: 283, 290. In his own defense, reprinted in 1795 as *The Natural and Constitutional Rights of Britons,* John Thelwall succinctly recaptures this most salient point: "Thus then a hypothesis is first assumed, and a fact is afterwards asserted in support of that hypothesis; but before the fact itself can be applied to the subject in debate, it is necessary to take for granted, as already proved, the very conclusion as a foundation for which the fact was itself asserted" (Thelwall, 18).

36. In a broader sense, the patterns of legal argumentation under discussion here are connected to the transformation of causal reasoning by the emergent concept of probability. For two excellent accounts of the role of probabilistic argumentation, see Hacking and Daston. Daston's chapter on "Moralizing Mathematics" is especially pertinent here in that it reviews a fascinating debate between Richard Price and David Hume over how to assess (or calculate) the probability that witness testimony in a given legal case is authentic (Daston, 327–32).

37. Or, as Paul Smith puts it, the task of paranoid narrative is to construct "a fixed and reliable 'subject' who will in a sense endorse or stand behind the fictions as their guarantor. That 'subject' . . . controls the intention and interpretation of the world it has created in such a way as both to protect its own coherence and autonomy and also to fulfill the juridical demands of the symbolic system in which the utterances may be understood" (98).

38. Godwin's recollection that "twelve or fourteen years ago, many of his majesty's present ministers were deeply engaged in a project of this nature [i.e., of constitutional reform]" (*STT,* 221) may offer a significant cue to Erskine's defense strategy at the trial. Not surprisingly, the decision to call the duke of Richmond set off the trial's most intense and hard-fought debate regarding the admissibility of evidence (*STT,* 1048–50). As soon became apparent, this debate was truly paradigmatic in kind, for at issue was the general matter of what constitutes "proper" evidence in a trial where the charge is merely an "unconsummated intention," as Erskine had expressed it. Put differently, the question at issue is the allowable scope of "circumstantiality," and on this count the prosecution was in a weak position. For its strategy had been all along to bury the jury in a blizzard of discrete and, in the view of many observers, unconnected, shreds of letters, pamphlets, and reports of hearsay. Having thus inflated the pool of eligible materials from the outset, it now proved all but impossible to hold the defense to a narrower range of evidence (see *STT,* 1075, 1081).

39. On the association between the grotesque and the unconscious, the etymology of "caricature," and the visual excess of engraved and illuminated satiric prints, with their characteristically imbalanced text/image ratio, see Paulson, 168–211. Following Gombrich, Paulson assesses Gillray's satiric prints as largely remedial, aimed to "provide the viewer-buyer with defenses against anxiety." Byron Jennings's contention that "the formation of fear images is intercepted, at its very onset, by the comic tendency [of the grotesque]" (quoted in Paulson, 187) likewise relies on a strictly thematic or iconic evaluation of Gillray's images by their content. Napoleon and Pitt consuming the world constitute an alarming prospect, yet the two leaders consuming a large pudding shaped like the world supposedly makes "the horrors of contemporary life palatable or at least bearable" (ibid.). My own reading views Gillray's prints as deepening the moral and conceptual undecidability of political, social, and legal conflicts by portraying all sides as driven by equally venal motives, which are concealed, of course, by the obtrusive use of righteous symbolism (e.g., Burke holding scepter and cross as he intrudes into Price's study in Gillray's 1790 print "Smelling out a Rat").

40. British Museum, Dept. of Prints and Drawings, 7: 789: "A hand extends from the l. margin of the design holding the bridge of a pair of spectacles: two ovals in which are bust portraits of Fox (l.) and Sheridan (r.) facing each other in profile, and having (especially Sheridan) the air of sinister conspirators. The rest of the print is supposed to be seen through these spectacles. Fox, dressed partly as Cromwell, raises an axe, the

blade inscribed Rights of Man, to strike the trunk (still intact) of the tree of (?) the Constitution (or the Crown, Church, and nobility). He wears a French cocked hat with a favor inscribed Vive la Nation. The Duke of Portland (l.) sits in profile to the r. astride a cylinder inscribed: Part of the Subscription Whig Pillar of Portland Stone intended to have been erected in Runnimede. He gazes in horror, his hands raised, at a demon of simian appearance, with webbed wings and serpents for hair, wearing a cocked hat like that of Fox; suspended above the hat are the feathers of the Prince of Wales. The demon holds to Portland a picture of a tree growing in a pot inscribed *Republi[ca]nism;* its foliage is inscribed Atheists, Demagogues the Mob; on the ground are a shield inscribed Nobility and a crown. The picture is *A Plan of the new Constitution of France, the Perfection of human Wisdom recommended as a Model for Canada by the Rt [Hon. C. J. Fox].* He sits on two volumes, *Treasonable Seditious Sermons* on which is an open book: *Rights of Man by M P. Paine.* Beside him lies a burning fire-brand. In front of him is a circular aperture in the ground from which rise a skull wearing a wig (and resembling Price) and the two hands of a skeleton, one holding an open book inscribed *Lord now lettest thou thy Servant depart in Peace.*"

41. British Museum, Dept. of Prints and Drawings, 7: 266: "Burke lies back asleep, but scowling, in profile to the l. his arms folded in an arm-chair whose seat is inscribed Otium cum Dignit[ate]. The top of his head is on fire, and the smoke rising from it forms the base of the upper and larger part of the design. Immediately above his head [we read the following somewhat modified quotation from Shakespeare's *King Richard II,* act 2, scene 1]:

This royal Throne of Kings, this sceptred Isle
This Earth of Majesty, this seat of Mars
. . . .
This fortress built by Nature for herself
Against Infection and the hand of War
. . . .
This Nurse, this teming Womb of royal Kings
. . . .
This England that was wont to conquer others
]Will make a shameful Conquest of itself

The British lion stands as if supported on these lines; from his angry mouth issue the words: *I protest against Peace with a Regicide Directory Went: Fitzw.* Their background is a rectangular altar, wreathed with oak leaves which forms a centre to the part of the design. It supports a scroll: Naval Victories East India Conquests &ca &ca Against its base is a scroll headed *Basle* and signed *Wyckham,* the intermediate (illegible) text being scored through. Above the altar flies a dove, an olive-branch in its mouth, clutching a sealed Passport. Behind and above the lion Britannia stands in back view, her discarded spear and shield beside her; she plays a fiddle, intent on a large music score: *A new Opera Il Trattato di Pace Overture Rule Britan* [*nia* scored through and replaced by] *Ca Ira God save ye King* [scored through and replaced by] *The Marsellois Hymn.*"

42. British Museum, Dept. of Prints and Drawings, 7: 267: "French troops march with fixed bayonets up St. James's Street, the houses receding in perspective to the gate of the Palace, which is blazing. In the foreground on the l. and r. are White's and

Brooke's. The former is being raided by French troops; the Opposition is in triumphant possession of the latter. In the center foreground a 'tree of Liberty' has been planted: a pole garlanded with flowers and surmounted by a large cap of Libertas. To this pole Pitt, stripped to the waist, is tied, while Fox (l.) flogs him ferociously, a birchrod in each hand. Between Fox's feet lies a headman's axe, blood-stained; on it stands a perky little chicken with the head of M. A. Taylor. On the r. is an ox, his collar, from which a broken cord dangles, inscribed Great Bedfordshire Ox (the Duke of Bedford); it is tossing Burke, goaded on by Thelwall, who holds its tail, and flourishes a document inscribed Thelwals Lectures. Burke flies in the air, losing his spectacles, and dropping two pamphlets: *Letter to the Duke of Bedford and Reflections upon a Regicide Peace.*"

43. For a short discussion of this print, see Marcus Wood, 60–62.

44. British Museum, Dept. of Prints and Drawings, 7: 275: "Pitt (r.) stands stiffly in profile to the l., holding open a large sack-like wallet inscribed Requisition Budget. He addresses John Bull, the central figure, a stout yokel, who holds out his breeches in his l. hand to Pitt, while he touches his hat. The budget and the breeches pockets are full of guineas. Pitt says: *More Money, John!—more Money! To defend you from the Bloody, the Cannibal French—They're a coming!—why they'l Strip you to the very Skin—more Money. John!—They're a coming—They're a coming.* Dundas, Grenville, and Burke kneel on the r., bending towards the 'Budget', each with his l. hand in an opening in a vertical seam, eagerly grabbing guineas. Behind them is the stone archway of the *Treasury,* with its high spiked gate. Dundas, the most prominent, wears a Highland dress and holds a Scots cap full of coins. . . . John says:-*a coming?—are they?—nay then, take all I've got, at once, Measter Billy! Vor its much better for I to ge ye all I have in the World to save my Bacon,—than to stay & be Strip'd stark naked by Charley, & the plundering French Invasioners, as you say. . . .* Behind (l.) on the shore, stands Fox looking across the water towards the fortress of Brest flying a tricolor flag. He hails it with upraised arms, shouting: What! More Money?—*O the Aristocratic Plunderer!—Vite Citoyens!—vite!—vite! Depechez vous!—or we shall be too late to come in for any Snacks of the l'argant!—vite Citoyens! vite! vite!*"

45. We shall return to the relation between a thoroughly determinate political and social order, one that effectively forecloses on the notion of an "open" future, and an understanding of "melancholy" as a condition affecting entire social groups rather than as the contingent fate of an individual.

46. Although variously attributed to Napoleon and to Marshal François-Joseph Lefebvre (1755–1820), this seems in fact to have been said by General Jean-Andoche Junot (1771–1813). Asked about his ancestry upon receiving the title of duc d'Abrantès, Junot reportedly replied: "Ma foi, je n'en sais rien; moi je suis mon ancêtre !"—"I don't have any idea. I'm my own ancestor!"

FOUR: "Long before the time of which I speak"

1. See Pfau 1997, 208–27, and the texts by Susan Stewart and Robert Mayo quoted there.

2. See Susan Eilenberg's account of the disintegrating collaborative relation between Wordsworth and Coleridge during the spring of 1800 (87–107). On the relationship between broadside and credal ballads and the rhetorical and cognitive logic of Wordsworth's ballads, see Rajan 1990, 136–66.

3. For discussion of new historicism in the context of romantic studies, see Liu 1990, Cole 1995, and Pfau 1998.

4. See readings of "Michael" by Simpson 1987, Levinson 1986, Eilenberg, and Schoenfield. Levinson's account is arguably the most astute and comprehensive in its configuration of the spiritual, economic, and aesthetic dimensions of "Michael." Commenting specifically on the opening of "Michael," Levinson remarks how "this narrator, self-designated a poet, does not merely symbolize or stand in for Luke; he is Luke, reincarnated and sublimated, as it were. The reader is induced to share the narrator's vision of himself as the Son who will perpetuate Michael's line—disseminate the story and finish the sheepfold in finer tone, with language instead of stones" (74). For a critique of Levinson, see Parker.

5. Hobsbawm 1968, 97. See also Thompson 1966, 213–33, "Field Labourers."

6. Hobsbawm 1968, 99; see also Porter, 203–5.

7. Quoted in Thompson 1966, 219.

8. In dramatizing the tension between the illusory time of Michael's lived history and the recognition of that history as an illusion—as merely "empty," chronological time—the poem anticipates a figure of thought that was to be fully articulated in the philosophy of the later Schelling. Unlike Hegel, Schelling conceives of the movement of demystification of past time (and its types of conscious awareness) not as an authentic overcoming but as an unending repetition. "For time is nothing but the reiterated position of eternity." Whereas "eternity is complete at every moment," time is nothing but "semblance" (*die scheinbare Zeit*), mere "succession." "The schema of this very semblance of time is A + A + A . . . , and we ourselves inhabit this mere semblance of time." Such time, Schelling notes, "incessantly repeats itself" and, as such, "it is not authentic time [*keine Wahre Zeit*], but an *epoché,* a stalling and obstruction of authentic time. The latter will only come into being if the semblance of time were to be posited as the past [*als Vergangenheit*]" (Schelling 1969, 160). The recognition of the past as illusory, in other words, involves not merely the subject's repudiation of specific, previously held beliefs; it also compels the notion that the phase of present disillusionment constitutes not a decisive overcoming of the past but only a contingent substitution of one set of illusions for another. Hence, as Freud himself notes, the traumatic recognition of an illusory past is itself continuous with it; it will often enough retraumatize the subject, since he or she recognizes that its cognitive progress is merely an additive process: as Schelling puts it, mere succession and incessant repetition. The same dynamic, so seminal to high modernism, also informs the repeated excursions into the philosophy of inner-time consciousness in Thomas Mann's *Magic Mountain.* See esp. the discussion of Hans Castorp's ancestry in chapter 2 and the protagonist's almost mystical perplexity at experiences of which he can no longer tell whether they are "still" unfolding or "yet again" (Mann 1996, 535).

9. The poem's diction is itself effectively an encryption of the fundamentally ambivalent status of the land; thus Michael tells Luke that he wishes to bequeath his land "free as the wind / That passes over it." For a reading of the multiple ambiguities in these lines, see Levinson 1986, 70.

10. "[T]ruly modern poetry is a poetry that has become aware of the incessant conflict that opposes a self, still engaged in the daylight world of reality, of representation, and of life, to what Yeats calls the soul," Paul de Man writes in "Lyric and Modernity" (de Man 1983, 171). "Translated into terms of poetic diction, this implies

that modern poetry uses an imagery that is both symbol and allegory, that represents objects in nature but is actually taken from purely literary sources."

11. Quoted in Benjamin, "On Some Motifs in Baudelaire" (Benjamin 1968, 158).

12. See Jameson 1981, 11–102, quotation from 35; Althusser, 11–69. It is important, for our purposes, to bear in mind Jameson's (and, previously, Althusser's) claim that the quasi-structural manifestation of that absent cause at a variety of levels (e.g., literary production, various types of theory) renders these levels all isomorphous to one another. This argument evidently runs counter to the Enlightenment notion that it ought to be possible to decode one type of (cultural) production by means of another, ostensibly autonomous, discipline. Hence Jameson speaks of his theory as "a structuralism for which only one structure exists, namely, the mode of production itself, or the synchronic system of social relations as a whole" (Jameson 1981, 36).

13. Similarly, Žižek speaks of the "symptom [as] literally our only substance, the only positive support of our being, the only point that gives consistency to the subject. In other words, symptom is the way we—the subjects—'avoid madness', the way we 'choose something (the symptom-formation) instead of nothing (radical psychotic autism, the destruction of the symbolic universe)' through the binding of our enjoyment to a certain signifying, symbolic formation which assures a minimum of consistency to our being-in-the-world" (1989, 75).

14. See Adam Smith's skeptical account "Of the Agricultural Systems, or of those Systems of Political Economy, which Represent the Produce of Land as either the Sole or the Principal Source of the Revenue and Wealth of Every Country" (Smith 1976, bk. 4, 182–209).

15. Wordsworth 1984, 40–43, letter dated January 14, 1801.

16. Writing in the same period of violent upheaval, Hegel characterizes this type of awakening on the part of consciousness to its own, paradigmatic instability as "reflection" and, significantly, as (figural) "death." As the following, often-quoted passage from the *Phenomenology of Spirit* suggests, the continuities between the Freudian theory of trauma as a dialectic of survival and Hegel's theory of speculative movement are striking: "Death, if that is what we want to call this non-actuality, is of all things the most dreadful, and to hold fast what is dead requires the greatest strength. . . . But the life of the Spirit is not the life that shrinks from death and keeps itself untouched by devastation, but rather the life that endures it and maintains itself in it. It wins its truth only when, in utter dismemberment, it finds itself" (19). I have commented elsewhere on the general debt of Wordsworth's poetic program (and that of Hartman's phenomenological account of that program) to Hegel's theory. See Pfau 1987; 1997, 227–59.

17. Similarly, Levinson argues that "the poem endorses a mode of being which is realized *through* material loss and in the individual's subsequent detachment from 'effort, and expectation, and desire'—or, positively expressed, in his achievement of *apatheia.* Through his failure to preserve his property, Michael is transformed from a man of 'forward-looking thoughts' to one who endures his going hence as a coming hither" (Levinson 1986, 60).

18. See Jakobson, "Linguistics and Poetics" in *Language in Literature.*

19. For a particularly apposite passage, recall the sudden encounter of the poet with the Leech-Gatherer in "Resolution and Independence": "Now, whether it were by peculiar grace, / A leading from above, a something given, / Yet it befell that, in this lonely place, . . . I saw a Man before me unawares" (Wordsworth 1983, 125, lines 50–55).

20. Stewart, 104. See also my own discussion of the ballad form, Pfau 1997, 208–27.

21. Benjamin 1968, 158–59. Not surprisingly, Benjamin extends his reflections on Proust's notion of an "involuntary memory" into a discussion of Freud's theory of trauma (160–63).

22. Quoted in ibid., 158. Lacan's reading of the dream of the burning child, which Freud had first introduced in his *Interpretation of Dreams,* also stresses the accidental nature in which an awakening from a traumatic scene is brought about. See Lacan 1981, 55; Caruth 1996, 100–105. While the present discussion relies on and fundamentally accepts Caruth's model of trauma as a pivotal crisis of representation, her position has not gone unchallenged. For an incisive critique, see esp. Leys, 266–307.

23. Like "The Solitary Reaper," on whose quintessentially Wordsworthian character Coleridge had commented so rhapsodically in his *Biographia,* "Michael" can arguably be regarded as yet another of Wordsworth's most distinctive stylistic achievements. For Benjamin reading Baudelaire, the precarious affinity of a symbolist style with mechanical reproduction is indicative of an advanced "atrophy of experience" and of the poetic object's loss of its aura. Fully conscious of that loss, Baudelaire actually acknowledged what Wordsworth, in writing "Michael," may well have experienced also: that his goal was "the creation of cliché," something he regarded as a stroke of genius. "Créer un poncif, c'est le génie," Baudelaire writes. "Je dois créer un poncif" ("Fusée," XIII, in *Oeuvres complètes,* ed. Claude Pichois, Bibliothèque de la Pléiade [Paris: Gallimard, 1976], 1: 662). As Benjamin, who quotes that statement, goes on to remark: "[Baudelaire] indicated the price for which the sensation of the modern age may be had: the disintegration of the aura in the experience of shock" (1968, 192, 194).

24. See discussion of the 1800 "Preface" in Pfau 1997, 237–59.

25. The question of whether emotions need always assume a conspicuous, manifestly "affective" form is particularly crucial in the case of trauma, a condition whose seemingly stoic, affectless character might even induce some to refuse it the predicate of "emotion" altogether. See Introduction, above, and Redding, 12–14, on "affectless emotions."

26. Coleridge 2001, 1: 698. On Coleridge's poetry, see esp. Rajan 1980, 204–59, and Goodson.

27. Even within the contemporary critical landscape and its often vociferous political disagreements, this basic paradigm of a purely "theoretical" accounting for romanticism, and the consequent reaffirmation of theory as untrammeled by the rough-and-tumble world of material politics holds true. Thus Frank 1989a maintains a strictly text-immanent, exegetical perspective on aesthetic theory. More oddly yet, Gadamer's famous pronouncement regarding the "historicity of all understanding" in the second part of *Truth and Method* confines its own application of that insight to the late-nineteenth-century writers (Dilthey, Yorck, Ranke) who had first formulated it, while leaving previous aesthetic theory (Kant, Schiller, Schlegel) untouched by historical considerations simply because these writers had declared such matter to be incommensurate with aesthetic cognition. See Behler, Lacoue-Labarthe and Nancy, and Seyhan for other instances of preemptive identification with the aesthetic as a purely theoretical, not historical, event.

28. For a discussion of problems intrinsic to contemporary romantic historicism, see Chandler, 3–93; Cole; Liu; and Pfau 1998, 1–37.

29. Eagleton, whose book title *The Ideology of the Aesthetic* I am obviously echoing

here, largely reproduces Adorno's arguments in the context of individual case studies (e.g., Kant, Schiller, Schopenhauer). While I share his opening claim that "the mystery of the aesthetic object is that each of its sensuous parts, while appearing wholly autonomous, incarnates the 'law' of totality," as well as his Manichean view of the aesthetic as locus of both, "emancipatory force" and "internalized repression" (Eagleton 1990, 25, 28), my own readings arrive at a similar position via multilayered interpretation.

30. For a discussion of English folk culture as the product of various literary and philological strategies dedicated to its "recovery," see Trumpener, 67–127, and Hobsbawm and Ranger, specifically the essays by Trevor-Roper and Morgan.

31. The remarks are found in von Arnim's important postscript, entitled "Von Volksliedern," to the most significant gathering of German folk poetry, *Des Knaben Wunderhorn,* which he and Clemens Brentano first published in 1806. Arnim 1975, 6: 407.

32. On the concept of time, see Frank 1990.

33. Benjamin 1998, 47, 36. In "convolute" N of the *Arcades Project,* Benjamin reiterates and sharpens his conception of historical knowledge. For not only does "the historical index of . . . images" locate them in "a particular time; it says, above all, that they attain to legibility only at a particular time." The time of historical knowledge, *Jetztzeit,* is a moment of sheer serendipity: "each 'now' is the now of a particular recognizability. In it, truth is charged to the bursting point with time. (This point of explosion, and nothing else, is the death of *intentio,* which thus coincides with the birth of authentic historical time, the time of truth" (Benjamin 1999a, 463).

34. In England, Wordsworth's sharp discrimination between the "people" and the "public" in his 1800 and 1815 prefaces echoes Burke's earlier antithesis and was taken up by Hazlitt (see "What Is The People?" in *HSW,* 4, 241–60). The absence of firm geopolitical boundaries in Germany, at least until 1815 and, in many ways, until 1871, may account for the, if anything, more urgent symbolic struggle over the idea of a cohesive national polity and its shared cultural endowment. For three excellent accounts of German culture and politics between 1815 and 1840, see Sheehan, Nipperdey, and Wehler.

35. Wellbery 1996, 187–284.

36. On the "strong" hermeneutic role of romantic texts, see Rajan 1990, 15–100; on Schleiermacher's foundational arguments in this regard, see Pfau 1990.

37. See, e.g., Weiskel; Hartman 1986; Nägele 1987.

38. Arnim 1975, 410–11.

39. Stewart, 103. Building on Stewart's thesis, I have argued elsewhere how the redefinition of literature as an unwitting archeology of cultural meanings contributes to the formation of a new type of middle-class readership. The latter views the reading-process as collaboratively extending the romantic paradigm of authorship, namely, as a socially responsible form of remembering; see Pfau 1997, 208–46.

40. In Husserl 1980 (vol. 2, § 22; vol. 5, § 19), the concept of "attentiveness" is introduced as a last resort against the threatening infinite regress of his theory of intentionality.

41. Seidlin notes that the quintessentially "transfixed" (*verzaubert*) disposition of the subject in Eichendorff "ought indeed to be understood in its proper sense: the state of hypnotic fixation on oneself, an immersion in one's own interiority, a dreaming imprisonment and brooding. . . . What Eichendorff's landscape requires . . . is a sudden act

of awakening, a quick rending of the oppressive veil; and precisely that will happen time and again in Eichendorff's work." Seidlin links this feature of rupture (*An-Bruch*) to a preoccupation with time. "Through the medium of a visible landscape, Eichendorff time and again mediates temporal perspectives" (Durch das Medium sichtbarer Landschaft vermittelt Eichendorff immer wieder die Perspektiven der Zeit) (Seidlin, 237–38, 236). Similarly, Rolleston observes how "Eichendorff's images are deliberately unstable, oscillating ceaselessly between an almost naïve claim to contingent immediacy and an erosion of that claim through a skeptical interpretive narrative" (39).

42. Adorno 1981, 1: 57. See also Thum and some of the early, largely dismissive accounts of Eichendorff cited in that essay (Richarda Huch, Gisela Jahn, René Wehrli). A more astute interpretation of the prevalent *literarhistorische Klischeevorstellungen* and *formelhafte Sprachelemente* in Eichendorff's oeuvre can be found in Krabiel 1973, 45–47.

43. Alewyn, 10 (my trans.). A similar, albeit much earlier discussion of this oddly formulaic yet elusive style can be found in a review of Eichendorff's 1835 novel *Dichter und ihre Gesellen* by the contemporary, left-oriented playwright Karl Gutzkow (2: 863–68).

44. See de Man 1979, 3–19.

45. Matt 1989, 53 (my trans.).

46. Indeed, Eichendorff's novel *Dichter und ihre Gesellen* (1834), in which this poem makes its first appearance, extends the vertiginous spiral of reflexive reading. Thus the lyric is introduced just after a female character by the name Fiametta has asked her chambermaid to stand in for her by positioning herself at a window and so inspire a love-struck huntsman to serenade her with his French horn. Accompanying herself on the guitar, Fiametta sings the lyric (*Sehnsucht*) just as the horn serenade has been concluded "and all had fallen silent." Having concluded her song, however, she breaks into tears. The novel continues with her true beloved, Fortunat, trying to reassure her: "'Our travels will take us back there,' Fortunat whispered to her. She raised her head and looked at him with large eyes. 'No,' she said, 'do not deceive me.'" ("Wir reisen wieder hin!" flüsterte ihr Fortunat zu. Da hob sie das Köpfchen und sah ihn groß an. "Nein", sagte sie, "betrüg mich nicht!" [*EW*, 2: 493; my trans.]).

FIVE: *Phantasie*

1. Eichendorff's itinerant life, first as a student during Napoleon's defeat of Prussia and occupation of Germany, then as a volunteer in Lützow's irregular corps of soldiers fighting Napoleon's troops between 1813 and 1815, and eventually as a hapless career bureaucrat, has been painstakingly chronicled by Wolfgang Frühwald (1977), showing how closely the lives of most German intellectuals were enmeshed with the constantly shifting front of Prussia's and Austria's war against Napoleon, which in 1807 was in its final stages (prior to its 1813 resurgence).

2. Quoted in Koch's postscript to *Des Knaben Wunderhorn* (Arnim and Brentano 1995, 899). Elsewhere, Herder remarks on the essential translatability of German and English mid-century poetry: "Still, in its basic constitution, [the] one nation's poetry strongly resembles that of the other, right down to turns of phrase, rhyme, preferred meter and modes of representation. Anyone familiar with chivalric tales, ballads, or fairy tales will know the full extent of this resemblance. The entire tone of this poetry

is so monolithic that one can regularly translate words, phrases, and inversions verbatim. In every country in Europe, the spirit of chivalry knows only *one* dictionary, just as its narrative representation only knows one tone. Likewise, all ballads and romances feature the same cast of principal and subordinate terms, the same declensions and metrical license" (Herder 1877–1913, 1: 323; my trans.).

3. See Willi A. Koch's "Nachwort" to his edition of *Des Knaben Wunderhorn* (Arnim and Brentano 1995, 906–7).

4. Eichendorff's "Wünschelrute" was first published in the *Deutscher Musenalmanach* of 1838, though the manuscript dates from 1834. For a longer reading, see Wellbery 1998, 455–58. Wellbery is right to stress the conditional nature in which insight is being posited in this poem. Indeed, it is precisely this qualification distinguishes Eichendorff's stance from the idealism of Görres, von Arnim, or for that matter, from the logical optimism of Hegel's semiotic account of memory and recollection. For connections between Eichendorff's lyric oeuvre and broader presymbolist tendencies in the German nineteenth-century lyric, see Pfau 2005b.

5. See Rosenkranz, 227–30.

6. Görres's critique of a strictly empirical historiography was undoubtedly inspired by F. Schlegel's critique of that trend, such as in the following aphorism: "The two main principles of the so-called historical criticism are the Postulate of Vulgarity and the Axiom of the Average. The Postulate of Vulgarity: everything great, good, and beautiful is improbable because it is extraordinary and, at the very least, suspicious. The Axiom of the Average: as we and our surroundings are, so it must have always been always and everywhere, because that, after all, is so very natural" (Schlegel 1991, 3 / 1988, 1: 240).

7. Also under way at that time was Friedrich Creuzer's monumental inquiry into ancient religious symbolism. During his long career at the university in Heidelberg as the preeminent authority in classical philology, Creuzer effectively conceived a new discipline, comparative religious studies, whose substance he laid out in his multivolume *Symbolik und Mythologie der alten Völker: besonders der Griechen* (1810–12). For Creuzer, the editorial projects pursued by his colleagues Görres, Brentano, and von Arnim were ultimately rooted in the folk culture of ancient Greece, Persia, India, and Egypt. Thus he refers to the early Greek accounts of creation and progressive civilization as "a comprehensive narrative . . . in images, songs, formulas, customs and myths" (diese Incunabel-Geschichte . . . aber war eine Geschichte in Bildern, in Liedern, Formeln, Bräuchen und in Mythen [1: 159; my trans.]). For a comprehensive discussion of myth and German romanticism, see Williamson's recent monograph, in particular his thorough discussion of Creuzer (121–50).

8. For a witty and irreverent pugnacious account of German romantic mythography, see Heinrich Heine's *On the History of Religion and Philosophy in Germany* (*HSS*, 3, 582).

9. "The Greek word for rustling, or rather whispering—*psithurisma*—is much admired," Leigh Hunt says apropos of Theocritus (*A Jar of Honey from Mount Hybla* [London: Smith, Elder, 1883], p. 98). For a more detailed discussion of early modernist trends in Eichendorff's late lyrics, as well as in the contemporaneous lyric oeuvre of Annette Droste-Hülshoff, see Pfau 2005b.

10. As Nietzsche was to argue, to postulate some continuity between the domain of empirical sensation and that of "literal" representation, between *Empfindung* and

Vorstellung, constitutes a figurative leap: "To begin with, a nerve stimulus is transferred into an image: first metaphor. The image, in turn, is imitated in a sound: second metaphor. And each time there is a complete overleaping of one sphere, right into the middle of an entirely new and different one." Predictably, deconstructionist thought seized Nietzsche's apparent thesis that all intellectual representation involves a conceptual flattening-out of "cases that are never equal and thus altogether unequal" (Jeder Begriff entsteht durch Gleichsetzen des Nicht-Gleichen [Nietzsche 1979, 82]). At the same time, one must guard against converting Nietzsche's supply *figural* critique of philosophical writing into a negative orthodoxy by subsuming the inherently figural notion of "similarity" (at the heart of various poetic figures and tropes, such as metonymy or simile) to a logical and abstract argument about of identity/nonidentity. See, e.g., de Man 1979, 103–18. For an incisive critique of de Man's deconstructive approach, see Staten, 187–216; even before de Man, Sarah Kofman had offered a more flexible and persuasive approach to the problem of metaphor, "not . . . as a transition from one place to another," but as "condens[ation of] several meanings: transfiguration, ecstasy, self-dispossession and metamorphosis" (15).

11. David Wellbery persuasively argues that Eichendorff's lyrics "comes as it were to rest precisely at the border between these two worlds" (Das Gedicht . . . hält gleichsam inne an der Grenze dieser beiden Welten [Wellbery 1998, 458]).

12. For details of Hegel's move from Heidelberg to Berlin and his conspicuous reinvestment in the Prussian state and its institutions, following the period of vocal despair after 1807, see Rosenkranz, 315–28.

13. The lecture is reprinted as an appendix to the *Enzyklopädie* in the *Theorie-Werkausgabe* (Hegel 1970, 10: 400); my trans.

14. Hegel 1978: 3, 167; Hegel's approach was anticipated by Schleiermacher's comments, in his 1808 "Occasional Reflections about Universities of German Character" (*Gelegentliche Gedanken über Universitäten im deutschen Sinne*), an influential document in the lively debate about how to conceive and organize a new university in the Prussian capital. Like Hegel after him, Schleiermacher insists on a central role for philosophy because "in every field the encyclopedic, the general survey of the whole and its connections, is presupposed as the most essential and is made the basis of the entire instruction" (quoted in Ziolkowski, 289).

15. Derrida 1980, 89. This issue is, of course, central also to the progression of Hegel's *Aesthetics.* For a deconstructive reading of Hegel's systematic treatment of art, see Rajan 1995.

16. For a critical discussion of Hegel's semiology, specifically focusing on the interference between Hegel's epistemological claims and their figural quality, see Derrida 1980, 69–108; on the relation between representation and *Bildung* in Hegel's *Phenomenology,* see John Smith, 174–96.

17. For a brilliant analysis of Hegel's subordination of material being to the principle of reflection (and hence to the discourse of logic) of which it is said to constitute but a primitive anticipation, see Frank 1975, 32–66; as Frank notes, Marx's eventual critique of Hegel's strictly ideational relationship to material existence was significantly indebted to the later writings of Schelling, particularly his *Initia Philosophiae Universae* (1820) and his 1841 lectures on the so-called "positive philosophy" at Berlin. For pertinent passages in Schelling, see Frank 1975, 135–68.

18. Robert Schumann's 1840 setting of the lyric requires the interpreter to be atten-

tive to the frequent and abrupt dynamic shifts in this song (op. 39 no. 11). On Schumann's Eichendorff song-cycle, see the excellent monograph by David Ferris (2000), in particular his discussion "Poem and Song," 91–119.

19. As most readers have noted, *rauschen* is a pivotal verb in Eichendorff, often functioning as a trope for the persistence of the unconscious. See Adorno's perhaps slightly mystifying suggestion that "the subject turns itself into *Rauschen,* the rushing, rustling, murmuring sound of nature: into language, living on only in the process of dying away, like language. The act in which the human being becomes language, the flesh becomes word, incorporates the expression of nature into language and transfigures the movement of language so that it becomes life again." Oddly, Adorno invokes the concept of allegory at this juncture, only to retreat from it quickly: "But in Eichendorff's writing the allegorical intention is borne not so much by nature . . . as by his language in its distance from meaning. It imitates *Rauschen* and . . . thereby expresses an estrangement which no thought, only pure sound can bridge." (Adorno 1991, 1: 68–69). Similarly, Hugo Friedrich had observed a tendency in romantic poetry "to sonority rather than meaning. The sonorous material of language attains a suggestive power. Combined with verbal matter that is imbued with associative resonances, such [sonority] opens up a phantasmatic infinity" (erschließt es eine traumhafte Unendlichkeit [Friedrich, 50; my trans.]).

20. Quoted in Sengle, 1: 9.

21. As James Sheehan notes, eastern estates in particular "tended to be consolidated agricultural enterprises rather than scattered farms and open fields. Using the labor of his dependent peasants, the *Gutsherr* worked his land and lived off what he could make by marketing the produce. In contrast to the absentee landlords of the west, therefore, eastern estate owners had a sustained relationship with their property, exercised personal authority over their dependants, and were directly involved in an agricultural market" (131). See also Sheehan's account of the demise of *Herrschaft* as a result of pressures issuing from the increasingly professionalized and self-conscious "non-noble elites" of an academically trained *Bürgertum* (132–43).

22. See also Eichendorff's closely related poem "Der Geist" (*EW,* 1: 143).

23. For Benjamin, sculpted stones are the material reflex of cultural matter as it suffers from the inexorable passage of historical time. As such, however, such stony debris is indicative of an abject (melancholic) rather than traumatized affect; see Benjamin 1998, 150–51.

24. On this issue, see also Rauch 1998.

25. At times, this self-betrayal of the feudal order gives rise to blunt satiric commentary, such as in Eichendorff's portrayal of eighteenth-century aristocratic dress code in *EW,* 1: 899–900.

26. On the *Reichsdeputationshauptschluss* of 1803, see Sheehan, 243–47, and Nipperdey, 1–4.

27. I have rehearsed this claim with greater attention to its theoretical and historical ramifications elsewhere. See Pfau 1997, 3–16, and much of the critical literature cited there.

28. In his seminal memorandum on the reforms, the so-called *Nassauer Denkschrift* of June 1807, Stein expressly refers to the French system of gathering tax revenues as a blueprint for urgently needed fiscal reform in Prussia. (Stein, 114).

29. Nipperdey 1996, 227. For the most detailed survey of the transitional period of

1815–1845 in German social history, see Wehler, who provides also excellent statistical information about the degree to which positions in the Prussian administration were widely coveted (210–19, 301–22).

30. See also Sheehan, 35–36, 252, who rightly emphasizes how the narrow material base of this bureaucracy constrained its members to compromise their ambitions. On Eichendorff's increasingly frustrating career as a member of the *Bildungsbeamtentum*, see the detailed account by Wolfgang Frühwald.

31. Eichendorff 1984, 12: 14, letter to Veit.

32. See Eichendorff's letter to Otto H. von Loeben of 4 August 1814, in which he remarks on the frustration of his military career. Having, in effect, "missed" the momentous departure of Lützow's troops for a front that was itself continually shifting, Eichendorff grew increasingly frustrated by the fact that military "action" continued to elude him. Before long, an armistice was declared and "*in this abyss of inaction and boredom we soon began to ponder and brood over our fate*" (Eichendorff 1984, 12: 28–29; my trans.).

33. Objectively, of course, reading habits expanded in quantity as evidenced, for example, by the exponential increase of new titles at the Leipzig Book Fair: 1,200 by 1764, 1,600 by 1770, and 5,000 by 1800 (Darnton, 144). On reading habits in relation to the concept of *Bildung*, see Sheehan, 157–60; Nipperdey, 35–44.

34. Nolan's English rendition of Nipperdey's text is flawed here. The German original reads: "Je intensiver man sich der 'Kultur' zuwandte, desto eher konnte sie vom allgemeinen Leben abgelöst erscheinen" (Nipperdey 1994, 269).

35. On censorship in romantic and Restoration Germany, including its impact on literary production and circulation, see the bilingual essay collection edited by McCarthy and Ohe, especially the historical survey on censorship between 1789 and 1848 by Siemann and the essay by Koepke on Jean Paul. Another survey of literary censorship during the period in question can be found in Breuer, 145–69. For a thorough treatment of censorship as it affected *das junge Deutschland*, see the collection of essays and documents edited by Hauschild.

36. Indeed, as regarded the conservative (anti-capitalist) dissent from the crudely reactionary and centralist power politics practiced in Vienna and Berlin, leaders like Metternich and Gentz could safely rely on the cultural left to assail writers like Schlegel, Schelling, Eichendorff, and Tieck. For a vivid example of how questions of literary quality became increasingly contingent on a writer's political allegiance, see Arnold Ruge's polemical essay, "Eichendorff and the Secret of a Philosophical Propaganda," in *Hallische Jahrbücher*, 1840, reprinted in Eichendorff 1984, 18: 519–24.

37. On economic change in Eichendorff's native East Prussia and Silesia, see Sheehan, 477; Nipperdey, 35–6. Specifically on the 1,000 years of documented agrarian and feudal management by the Eichendorff family, its decline, and the abrupt financial collapse of its Silesan estates, see Stutzer, esp. 121–27. Stutzer also remarks on the family's uncommonly high private expenses for cultural activities and for the extended and thorough education of its two sons, Joseph and Wilhelm.

38. See Frühwald 1979 and Krüger.

39. See Ritter et al., s.v. "Konservativ, Konservatismus."

40. In a number of poems, Eichendorff lampoons his alienated and unrewarding career as a bureaucrat, while at the same time suggesting that such overtly political

laments can only yield bad or "nonsense" poetry. See "Der Isegrim," "Der Unverbesserliche," or his "Mandelkerngedicht" below:

Zwischen Akten, dunkeln Wänden
Bannt mich, Freiheitbegehrenden,
Nun des Lebens strenge Pflicht,
Und aus Schränken, Aktenschichten
Lachen mir die beleidigten
Musen in das Amtsgesicht.
. . . .
Als der letzte Balkentreter
Steh ich armer Enterbeter
In des Staates Symphonie,
Ach, in diesem Schwall von Tönen
Wo fänd ich da des eigenen
Herzens süße Melodie?
Ein Gedicht soll ich euch spenden:
Nun, so geht mit dem Leidenden
Nicht zu strenge ins Gericht!
Nehmt den Willen für Gewährung,
Kühnen Reim für Begeisterung,
Diesen Unsinn als Gedicht! (*EW*, 1: 91–92)

41. Friedrich von Gentz (1764–1832), chief advisor and political secretary to Metternich, is arguably the most interesting figure in this regard, both for his political style, significantly shaped by Burke (whose *Reflections* he had translated in 1793) and by Adam Smith, and for his close involvement with cultural politics of the restoration era; on Gentz's career, see the accounts by Golo Mann and Paul R. Sweet. On the typology of romantic conservatism, see also Heer.

42. As Karl Mannheim argues, the common assumption that a critique of capitalism only originated with the proletarian socialist movement ought to be revised. "There are many indications that this criticism was initiated by the 'right-wing opposition'" to which such anti-capitalist tendencies were an integral part of its larger "experiential reaction against Enlightenment thinking" (67, 65); see also Riemen and Heer.

43. For a blunt characterization of the ancien régime as a fossilized and moribund society, see *EW*, 1: 898.

44. As Helga Grebing has argued, conservatism is a bourgeois phenomenon, not a feudal one: "Conservatism does not originate as an ahistorical, retrospective form of opposition to bourgeois society. Rather, it emerges from the ideological needs of that society, insofar as it furnishes bourgeois society with a strategy to counteract those emancipatory characteristics that are at once intrinsic to it and appear to imply the bourgeoisie's ongoing transformation in the future. The historical moment for this genesis of conservatism is thus the transition from an old, dissolving mode of production toward a new, capitalist one. As regards both, its mode of origination and its further development, conservatism can thus not be understood as legitimating precapitalist, feudal modes of production per se" (Grebing, 26–27; my trans.).

45. Schleiermacher, 234. Schleiermacher's work is, of course, central to the develop-

ment of any hermeneutics of history. See Manfred Frank's brilliant introduction to his edition of *Hermeneutik und Kritik,* and also my own discussion of Schleiermacher's struggle with the extreme consequences of his radically linguistic grounding of the hermeneutic process, Pfau 1990. Working with broader strokes, Angelika Rauch notes that, "like Lacan, Gadamer oriented himself toward language or signification, developing what could be called a theory of retroaction (*Nachträglichkeit*) in which the meaning of a representation changes as the subject passes through new interpretive horizons of understanding" (Rauch 2000, 112).

46. Burke, 196–97. On Burke's aesthetics, see Furniss 1993, 138–63, and Pfau 1997, 280–88. Like Burke, to whom Müller pays explicit homage as the founding father of modern conservatism (see Müller 1967, 1: 101–2), Müller develops an organic model of culture whose presentation seems metaphorical rather than technical in kind. As such, his writings clearly echo the patriotic fervor of von Arnim and Brentano's recovery of folk culture, yet they also anticipate more abstract definitions by Coleridge and T. S. Eliot of high culture and a "clerisy" entrusted with its guardianship. See the second of Coleridge's *Lay Sermons* and his *On the Constitution of Church and State,* as well as Eliot's essays "Notes Toward a Definition of Culture" and "The Idea of a Christian Society." On Müller's anti-capitalist views, see also Berdahl, 173–75.

47. The notion that the postmodern era is a "*posthistoire*" in which "in terms of intellectual history nothing further is to be expected" is not new. The term already surfaces in the later work of the eminent German anthropologist Arnold Gehlen, regrettably unknown to contemporary theory; see his 1961 essay "Über kulturelle Kristallisation," in Gehlen 1963, 323. And see also the distinction between "historical" and "post-historical" nations in Fukuyama 1992, 276–77.

48. As Carl Schmitt puts it, Müller's "antitheses are rhetorical, . . . oratorical pedants, and with the help of rhythm and the effect of sonority, they can have a suggestive force. . . . [Yet] they always remain mere sounds and chords that blend, contrast, or harmonize in accordance with the oratorical effect in a single case. Müller needs a dramatic image in order to illustrate the relationship between past and future, which for him is also nothing more than an image" (Schmitt, 138).

49. See also Müller's *Lehre vom Gegensatz*—a rather crude attempt at "pure" theory by a writer often regarded as something of an intellectual fraud (see Berdahl, 158–81)—which conceives of social and individual existence as a process of perpetual reorganization and struggle with the adversarial forces of modernity.

50. It bears remembering that Friedrich Schlegel himself emerged as one of the preeminent conservatives of the later romantic period. His conversion to Catholicism and subsequent ascent as a major intellectual presence in Vienna—where he also promoted Eichendorff's literary fortunes—follow a familiar trajectory of conversion and the gradual formulation of an anti-modern metaphysics, notoriously satirized by Heine's *Romantic School* (1833).

51. See also the German text, *AGS,* 2: 197–98. The phrase "Die Kunst ist, einen Genuß hervorzubringen" fuses a definition and a colloquialism: "Art consists in producing an enjoyment" and "The trick is to produce an enjoyment."

52. For Freud's usage of *Nachträglichkeit,* see esp. his 1918 case history of the Wolf-Man (*From the History of an Infantile Neurosis*), in particular, the long footnote where Freud comments how "the patient under analysis, at an age of over twenty-five years,

was lending words to the impressions and impulses of his fourth year which he would never have found at that time." While such delayed eloquence may "seem comic and incredible," Freud defends his patient's substitution of his "present ego into the situation which is so long past" as "legitimate" (*mit Recht*). It is simply a case of "deferred action" (Strachey's translation of *Nachträglichkeit*), as Freud first elaborated in the "Wolf-Man" case ("From the History of an Infantile Neurosis," in Freud 1963a, 230n14). Freud's unusual eagerness to justify a moment of substitution that, in point of fact, eclipses no fewer than "three [intervening] periods of time [*Zeitphasen*]," reflects his professional objective of translating preverbal affect into intelligible propositions. Inasmuch as psychoanalysis renders all preconscious suffering intelligible, the projects of medical "cure" and professional self-legitimation go hand in hand. Not surprisingly, most of Freud's key concepts—such as repression, the unconscious, displacement, and indeed *Nachträglichkeit*—effectively presuppose the entire terminological edifice of psychoanalysis to be already in place. In ways that cannot be taken up in full detail, *Nachträglichkeit* thus not only constitutes a key concept of the unconscious as a "missed" or previously "unclaimed" experience but also reveals that, within the architectonics of Freudian thought, any key concept is by definition always in(tro)duced "retroactively," part of an intellectual economy in which dissent and falsification are preempted by the work of an anterior agency (the unconscious) that can only be caught in its necessarily belated effects, but never *in actu*. Derrida's remark that for Freud "memory . . . is not a psychical property among others; it is the very essence of the psyche" (1978, 201) would, in principle, hold equally true for romantics like Novalis, Eichendorff, and even Hegel. Derrida goes on to observe how "concepts of *Nachträglichkeit* [retroactivity] and *Verspätung* [deferral] . . . govern the whole of Freud's thought and determine all his other concepts" (1978, 203).

53. See Slavoj Žižek who, with perhaps extreme generality, conceives of "the notion of history itself" as the "supreme example of [the] paradoxical coincidence of emergence and loss. . . . On the one hand, pre-capitalist societies allegedly do not yet know history proper; they are 'circular', 'closed', caught in a repetitive movement predetermined by tradition—so history must emerge *afterwards*, with the decay of 'closed' organic societies. On the other hand, the opposite cliché tells us that capitalism itself is no longer historical; it is rootless, with no tradition of its own, and therefore parasitical on previous traditions, a universal order which (like modern science) can thrive everywhere" (Žižek 1997, 13). Here as elsewhere, however, it remains unclear what authority these ostensibly "clichéd" positions hold within Žižek's own argument.

54. Adorno continues: "Like the great philosophy of his time he understood the necessity of the revolution he was terrified of: he embodies something of the critical truth of the consciousness of those who have to pay the price for the advance of the *Weltgeist*. . . . His freedom to see what is irrevocable in the historical process has been completely lost by the conservatism of the late bourgeois phase; the less the precapitalist order is capable of being restored, the more stubbornly ideology clings to the notion that it is ahistorical and absolute" (Adorno 1991, 1: 60–61).

55. Eichendorff 1984, 5, 4: 67. The passage is framed by a reference to the execution of Louis XVI and an imaginary depiction of Versailles as a wasteland where the wind playfully rattles the armorial ensigns of the faded aristocracy: "Der verödete Garten

und Palast von Versailles. Wie der Wind auf den Schilden des Monsieur X klapperned spielt" (ibid., 68).

56. First published in 1833; see also "Vergebener Ärger" and "Rückblick," esp. the second stanza, which ironizes the lyric as a simulacrum of affect.

57. C. D. Friedrich's *Winter Landscape with Church* (1811), *Chasseur in the Forest* (1813–14), *Cloister Cemetery in the Snow* (1817–19), and *Cemetery Entrance* (1824–26) all exhibit poignant similarities with Eichendorff's poetry. Koerner notes how, in these paintings, the artist-traveler, "halted in the landscape, regist[ers] through his presence that what we see is not nature, but the experience of nature belatedly re-imagined." Friedrich's canvases "are finally about [what] is only *almost* visible" (Koerner, 19–20), and this phantasmagorical quality perhaps comes through most obviously in *Cloister Cemetery*, which depicts the fantastic ritual of a procession of monks from a preschismatic historical period through the gate of their ruined cloister chapel in a snow-covered landscape of graves and denuded trees. The painting's aura is one of sterility, of an order without future, which is thus not a plausible object of nostalgia. For a discussion of this picture, and on Friedrich's characteristic use of the *Rückenfigur*, a motionless human figure facing away from the beholder and adjusting our perspective as one of metaphysical perplexity, see Koerner, 133–35, 159–210. Not coincidentally, Friedrich's use of the *Rückenfigur* marks the reappearance of an originally baroque device, a development that echoes Eichendorff's growing deployment of allegorical topoi from the baroque; see also discussion of this motif in Pfau 1997, 131–39.

58. Gillespie briefly cites a poem by Friedrich von Logau (1605–55), the eminent and prolific author of countless epigrammatic, aphoristic, and sententious poems, among them his "Two Hundred Rhymed German Proverbs" (1638) and his 1654 magnum opus, the "Three Thousand German Epigrams" (*Deutscher Sinn-Getichte Drey Tausend).* Logau's "May" ("Der Mai"), centers around the image of the nuptial kiss that weds earth to heaven: "Dieser Monat ist ein Kuß, den der Himmel gibt der Erde, / Daß sie, jetzund seine Braut, künftig eine Mutter werde" (cited in Gillespie, 209). Eichendorff's work nicely corroborates Paul de Man's contention that "truly modern poetry" requires an "imagery that is both symbol and allegory, that represents objects in nature but is actually taken from purely literary sources" (de Man 1983, 171).

59. Echoing Adorno's apprehension of readers complacent enough to construe Eichendorff's allegorical landscape as imbued with metaphysical consolation, de Man cautions against the desire to "understand the relationship between mimesis and allegory as a genetic process, forcing into a pattern of continuity what that which is, by definition, the negation of all continuity" (de Man 1983, 185–86).

60. Walter Killy notes how, in the age of baroque literature, "literary practice transmutes the topical principle of *inventio* for arguments into an inventory of fixed turns of phrase. Cognitive principles are transformed into verbal cues" (In der literarischen Praxis wird aus dem topischen Auffindungsprinzip für Argumente häufig eine Sammlung von feststehenden Redewendungen, allgemeinen Erwägungen, traditionellen Behauptungen, berühmten Aussprüchen usw. Aus dem Denkprinzip wird das Stichwort). Notwithstanding his formidable erudition in medieval and early modern rhetorical convention, Ernst Robert Curtius often appears uncertain as to whether a given topos ought to be approached as a moral commonplace, rhetorical cliché, or the

expression of archetypal, enduring (i.e., substantive) content. See Curtius, 79–105, esp. §§ 2, 3, and 6; also Killy, 14: 436.

SIX: "The Purest English"

1. Hegel 1977, 298 / 1952, 351. For different readings of Hegel's theory of the developmental integration of individual and state (*Bildung*), see Hyppolite, 376–425; Kojève, 51–69; and Pinkard, 229–45.

2. Guarding against possible conflation of lyric and philosophical universality, Hegel's account of the lyric subject in his *Lectures on Fine Art* views the expressivity of lyric poetry as an act of *mediation.* The text reconciles writer and reader to a world riddled with social antagonisms that lyric poetry seeks to comprehend in strictly affective form. The lyric, for Hegel, illustrates the covert intentionality of all feeling, for it shows feeling to be susceptible to, indeed generative of philosophical, reflective thought, even as the lyric itself does not aim to merge with discursive thought itself. For Hegel, lyric poetry enables both poet and audience to displace their antagonistic social and material position, their historical determinacy, by engaging its imagistic textures in seemingly private acts of identification and transference. From Hegel's *systematic* perspective, the lyric constitutes the last phase in the postponement of reflective, analytic, self-alienated *thought,* whose dialectical ascendancy was first narrated in the *Phenomenology.* At the same time, the potential totality contained in "feeling" and, hence, in its condensation as lyric (*Dichtung*) implicitly allows us to glimpse an asystematic dimension in the lyric, one that Hegel's discussion of lyric poetry in the *Lectures on Fine Art* (1123–25 [*Vorlesungen zur Aesthetik,* 3: 430–33]) cannot effectively contain.

3. Abrams, 203. For the somewhat different model of expressive and emotionally complex lyric writing, see Goodson's study of the Coleridgean lyric as formal, critical, and socioeconomic phenomenon, esp. 83–119.

4. Clifford Siskin is right to observe that, beginning with Wordsworth, "the pleasure we now associate with the 'Love of Literature' . . . figured experimentally not only in the reorganization of knowledge which valorized Literature, but also in the reorganization of work which valorized mental labor (Siskin 1998, 151). For a discussion of the moral imperatives behind the Wordsworthian lyric, see my discussion of his 1807 "Ode to Duty" in Pfau 1995.

5. Benjamin 1999a, 473. For a discussion of Benjamin's concept of tradition, see Rauch 2000, 177–217.

6. In his 1489 *De triplice vita,* Marsilio Ficino had proposed a revaluation of the doctrine of the humors, according to which the saturnine, melancholic character had to be understood as a person lapsed from an active and disciplined life of works. The dull and merely inactive disposition of saturnine melancholy was to be viewed as merely a first stage, to be overcome by the intervention of Jupiter, who will reorient melancholy toward genius. Consistent with this humanist revision of melancholy as no longer mere languor or sinfully narcissistic fixation (acedia), Dürer's famous engraving *Melancholia I* depicts a scene of imminent decision. It can be interpreted as the moment just before inspiration. "Everything is task, as yet awaiting a solution." Central to literature is its yearning for, and its simultaneous recognition of, the impossibility of a pure and authentic alignment of inwardness and expression. The melancholiac's ennui

is born of the literary text's dissatisfaction with its own, oppressively overdetermined form. The metonymy between writing, reading, and a deep awareness of mortality is powerfully conveyed in Lorenzo Lotto's 1523 *Portrait of a Young Scholar,* with rose petals standing in for the transience of all study. The otherworldly, almost inaccessible, quality of the young man's countenance further reinforces our sense of learning as "abstraction"—that is, giving rise to an abstracted, distant brooding—or to recall Keats's famous employment of the word in "Ode to a Nightingale" (lines 70–71), "forlorn." For a discussion of Dürer's *Melancholia I,* see Wagner-Egelhaaf, 62–78.

7. Robert Kaufman has offered a provocative discussion of Keatsian formalism as an adumbration of the Frankfurt school and Adorno's work in particular. Perhaps more than his putatively more outspoken political twin, Shelley, Keats in Kaufman's analysis is credited with "formally prepar[ing] the conflicted groundwork, and . . . produc[ing] the structural oppositions, for those later controversies around aesthetic form and aesthetics-and-politics that preoccupy the Frankfurt school" (2001, 362). See also Kaufman's discussion of the political valence of a radical avant-garde formalism (Keats, Valéry, Schoenberg, and Celan, among others) whose meticulously crafted locutions reject any thematic or programmatic accountability for art (ibid., 368n). Similarly, Krystof Ziarek argues that "the truly avant-garde impulse is not reducible to resistance or revolutionary overthrow of particular forms of power and their replacement with new ones." Rather, art effects a disruptive, nonlinear and ateleological caesura—Ziarek invokes Heidegger's *Besinnung*—within thought itself, thus stimulating "a radical rethinking of action apart from the notion of production and control" (95, 97). To what Edward Said (206–7) has called Adorno's "unashamedly Mandarin" and "unwaveringly Eurocentric" critical temper, melancholy reveals itself as constitutive of aesthetic and critical work alike. For the same dialectical struggle with social and economic processes that, in Adorno's view, aesthetic form must perpetually reenact at the level of form (without any hope of resolving it) also burdens a genuinely dialectical model of critical work such as practice by Adorno, a model as distrustful of critical utopias as it is of aesthetic regression. See also Geulen.

8. Heidegger 1962, 175–76 (trans. modified) / 1979, 136–37: "Das zeigt die Verstimmung. In ihr wird das Dasein ihm selbst gegenüber blind, die besorgte Umwelt verschleiert sich, die Umsicht des Besorgens wird mißleitet. Die Befindlichkeit ist so wenig reflektiert, daß sie das Dasein gerade im reflexionslosen Hin-und Ausgegebensein an die besorgte 'Welt' überfällt. Die Stimmung überfällt. Sie kommt weder von 'Außen' noch von 'Innen,' sondern steigt als Weise des In-der-Welt seins aus diesem selbst auf. Damit aber kommen wir über eine negative Abgrenzung der Befindlichkeit gegend das reflektierende Erfassen des 'Innern' zu einer positiven Einsicht in ihren Erschließungscharakter. Die Stimmung hat je schon das In-der-Welt-sein als Ganzes Erschlossen und macht ein Sichrichten auf . . . allererst möglich."

9. Trilling, 432. In an earlier essay, "The Poet as Hero: Keats in His Letters" (1952), Trilling notes how the "pleasure of the senses was for him not merely desirable—it was the very ground of life" and how "the sensory, the sensuous, and the sensual were all one" (Trilling, 232–33). Still, though clearly enthralled by "the wonderful, misspelled immediacy of the letters" (ibid., 229), Trilling does recognize Keats's ambivalent and acutely, almost perversely, self-conscious relation to "pleasure" and "sensation."

10. Coleridge continues to remark on the predictability and exhaustion of writing itself: "Common phrases are, as it were, so stereotyped now by conventional use that it

is really much easier to write on the ordinary politics of the day in the newspaper slang than it is to make a good pair of shoes" (1990, 1: 285). Keats endorses in that assessment, remarking that " Poems are as common as newspapers and I do not see why it is a greater crime in me than in another to let the verses of a half-fledged brain tumble into the reading-rooms and drawing room windows" (*LJK*, 2: 130).

11. Benjamin's image returns in Kristeva, for whom the positive, enabling role of negation ("the intellectual process that leads the repressed to representation on the condition of denying it") stands in sharp contrast to the "denial of negation." In it, the "signs are unable to pick up the intrapsychic primary inscriptions of [a] loss and to dispose of it through that very elaboration; on the contrary, they keep turning it over, helplessly." Such denial of negation, a breakdown in the archetypal Hegelian operation of *Aufhebung*, "devitalizes" representation (Kristeva, 43–45), much the way Benjamin's allegorical text appears to comment on its own speculative futility and nothingness, and nowhere more so than in the emblem of the skull. For other applications of Kristeva's theory to romantic melancholy, see Batten's study of melancholy in Byron, Blake, Shelley, and Wordsworth.

12. Rajan rightly notes how the melancholic text "gestures towards Symbolic structures but refuses to participate in them" (1994, 48). Such accords with the generally ambivalent status of the "symptom" in Freud's own thinking emerge with full force in his 1915 essay on repression, itself an extension of his earlier discussion of repression in paranoia. Thus Freud acknowledges that "substitute-formation" and "repression-proper," far from coinciding are, in fact, "widely divergent, [and] that it is not the repression itself which produces substitute-formations and symptoms, but that these latter constitute indications of a *return of the repressed*" (1963b, 111–12). The functional and essentially intelligent constitution of the symptom strangely conflicts with the placid and ideally "unstimulated" vision of consciousness that gradually emerges in Freud's so-called "meta-psychological" account.

13. See esp. Wagner-Egelhaaf's comprehensive rethinking of melancholy from the perspective of discourse history (*Diskursgeschichte*).

14. Published in the Keatsian year of 1819, Schopenhauer's *World as Will and Representation* thus dismisses the "dull, insipid, optimistic, Protestant-rationalistic . . . view of the world [that] will make the demand for poetic justice and find its satisfaction in that of the demand. The true sense of the tragedy is the deeper insight that what the hero atones for is not his own particular sins, but original sin, in other words, the guilt of existence itself" (nur die platte, optimistische, protestantisch-rationalistische . . . Weltansicht wird die Forderung der poetischen Gerechtigkeit machen und an deren Befriedigung ihre eigene finden. Der wahre Sinn des Trauerspiels ist die tiefere Einsicht, daß was der Held abbüßt nicht seine Partikularsünden sind, sondern die Erbsünde, d.h. die Schuld des Daseyns selbst [Schopenhauer 1969, 1: 254 / 1989, 1: 354)].

15. The implicit dynamic of resentment and covert aggression, to which Freud first drew attention, is a focal point for my discussion of melancholy in both the oeuvre of Keats and, even more so, that of Heinrich Heine. Abraham and Torok helpfully remark on the correlation between the melancholic subjects' overdetermined memory, "cherished as their most precious possession" and its concealing "crypt built with hate and aggression." Sensing its memories—which are also cultural identifications—to be threatened, the subject intensifies its attachment to the "crypt." "Threatened with the imminent loss of its internal support—the kernel of its being—the ego will fuse with

the included object, imagining that the object is bereft of its partner. Consequently, the ego begins the public display of an interminable sadness, his gaping wound, his universal guilt" (Abraham and Torok, 136). Torok's "crypt" is closely related to the formal act of "encryption," and it is the formal-textual and literary-historical dimensions (allegory) of such encryption on which my argument focuses.

16. Kristeva's discussion of the "psychomotor retardation" of melancholic speech startlingly mirrors the rhetorical profile of baroque tragedy as it emerges from Benjamin's interpretation, as well as of Keats's equally symptomatic "early" writings. "Speech delivery is slow, silences are long and frequent, rhythms slacken, intonations become monotonous, and the very syntactic structures . . . are often characterized by nonrecoverable elisions" (Kristeva, 34). On the open-ended temporality of melancholia, see Fisher, 89–92.

17. Nietzsche 2002, 134. Like Jerome Christensen, whose seminal study (1993) avowedly "follow[s] the lead of Nietzsche (himself in Byron's train), who revived a conception of aristocracy as eventful deed rather than as a class united by interest" (xvii), I find the continuities between Byron and Nietzsche compelling.

18. Jerome McGann in Byron 1980, 2: 271. On Byron's ironic mobilization of Augustan poetic forms and the charisma of the eighteenth-century cosmopolitan and aristocratic persona, see Christensen, esp. 185–213 on *Childe Harold,* canto 4. For a fine introduction to Byron's reinvention of his authorial self in *Don Juan,* see McGann 1988a, 255–93. On Byron's equivocal place within a stylistic profile of English literary history, see Manning, 115–44.

19. *LJK,* 2: 67. Byron's comments on Keats, of course, are both more expansive and by and large far more vicious. See William Keach's topical essay, as well as Christopher Ricks's account, 66–114.

20. An early example would be M. R. Ridley's axiom that an early poem like "Isabella" can be read as "a document illustrative of Keats' development, as the stones by which he crossed, not too securely, into the promised land" (Ridley, 18). Morris Dickstein first raised significant questions about "a distinguished group of present or former Harvard scholars who have emphasized Keats' skepticism and moral growth. These writers have little patience with the purely sensuous or incipiently visionary elements . . . especially in the earlier poems." To be sure, Dickstein's avowed intention to read Keats's "major poems . . . in light of Keats' whole development" (xiii–xv)" does not seem to counteract the teleological and redemptive aspiration of the Harvard critics but merely to broaden its evidentiary base.

21. In addition to what has been said already, it bears pointing out that the popular dismissal of Keats's early writings as merely juvenile or immature also falters inasmuch as it measures an individual against a historically invariant, psychodevelopmental standard. To do so is to replace any historical specificity as regards notions such as childhood, youth, anxiety, responsibility, or maturity with colloquial and unreflected notions such as "immaturity," "awkwardness," "embarrassment," "enthusiasm," etc. Indeed, to this day, the one psychological phase most commonly ignored by cultural historiography is "adolescence." Research on the history of childhood and children's literature seems prolific by comparison, to say nothing of the rows of library shelves filled with historical and philosophical accounts of adult careers. Already in his "Preface" to *Endymion* (1817), however, Keats himself suggests that the self-assurance of his surrounding adult culture seemed to rest on the displacement of contradictions that are

arguably experienced most acutely by the adolescent. Students today might benefit from considering Keats's poetry in relation to their own experience with writing, particularly its formal intricacies and its ambivalent social effects. Like Keats in 1817, his college-age readers today seem well positioned to grasp how imaginative constructions of the self *qua* writing help us gauge an interiority that can exist neither independent of writing nor ever be fully contained within it. Hence, rather than opposing his 1817 *Poems* to his later, canonical work, one should approach them as hyperconscious steps toward an idiom whose artificial character is both deliberate and inescapable. Such poetry cultivates a self-consciously and overwrought "literariness" that exposes the censorious and exclusionary logic of taste at work in the age of Regency literary and cultural reviewing and, in so doing, opens a new window onto the abject, melancholy situation of its producer. Beyond that, such a strategy also tends to demystify the high romantic conception of lyricism as organic and deep-individual writing. As time wore on, Keats seems to have grown only more assured of his overarching objective—to conceive of lyricism as the exposé of social and aesthetic abjection by stressing its serial, pointedly artificial character.

22. As happened at the 1996 convention of the North American Society for the Study of Romanticism (NASSR).

23. For a brief recounting of this developmental myth of Keats, also remarked upon by Chandler (396), see Jack Stillinger, "The Story of Keats," in Wolfson 2001.

24. Viswanathan, 6. For the response of romantic literature to the excesses of British imperial rule, see Nigel Leask's study, particularly his reading of Shelley (68–169). Also informative about late-eighteenth-century British imperial ambition, if considerably less readable, is Sara Suleri's *The Rhetoric of English India.* For a particularly lucid account of how "Oriental" culture was domesticated during the Regency years, see Makdisi 1998, esp. 100–22.

25. Quoted in Davie, 15.

26. For some rare exceptions, see Bromwich's and Keach's essays in a 1986 special issue of *Studies in Romanticism,* as well as Jerome McGann's more qualified yet thorough consideration of the politics of Keats's "Cockney style" (1988a, 15–65). Keach's essay on Keats's "Cockney Couplets" also contains some searching observations about McGann (191–92). See also Kaufman's essay connecting the formal tensions of Keats's early verse to the theoretical project of the Frankfurt School (2001, 354–64).

27. Keach, 184. See also Roe, who examines the pathologizing intent behind John Gibson Lockhart's assault on the so-called Cockney school of poetry (published under the pseudonym "Z"). Lockhart himself had revived the term "metromanie" from William Gifford's 1794 *Baviad,* (Roe, 19–20). On the Cockney school and literary politics during the Regency, see Cox, esp. 16–37, 82–122; as well as Roe, esp. 60–71, 202–29.

28. For a rigorous application of historicist method, see Chandler, 425–32. On the conceptual problems of such approaches, see Pfau 1998. My own approach to Keats here partially shares Pyle's declared preference "not to assert a position outside the representations that constitute the text (the strategy of New Historicism) but to *read* for Keats's materialism, to pursue the nature of the poet's (and the critic's) implications in those textual representations" (Pyle 1995, 131).

29. See Lockhart's famous indignation at Keats for invoking Hunt and Wordsworth in the same ("Great Spirits") sonnet: "Wordsworth And Hunt! What a juxta-position! The purest, the loftiest and, we do not fear to say it, the most classical of living English

poets, joined together in the same compliment with the meanest, the filthiest, and the most vulgar of Cockney poetasters" (in Reiman, 7: 91).

30. Adorno 1997, 167. With its exemplary articulation of the intrinsically dialectical status of aesthetic form or work, this passage from Adorno's *Aesthetic Theory* positions his thought in perhaps worrisome proximity to the esoteric conceptions of Viennese modernism and its artistic precursors (the "late" Beethoven, Mahler, Trakl, Schönberg, Berg, Proust, et al.). As a result, dialectical thinking at times appears to have lost sight of its political dimension. Hence, for Edward Said, "Adorno is unthinkable without the majestic beacon provided by Lukács' *History and Class Consciousness,* but also unthinkable without his refusal of the earlier work's triumphalism and implied transcendence" (Said, 203–4). Not until after the emergence of postmodernism as an intellectual formation of some coherence was Fredric Jameson (who had been notably impatient with Adorno's political prevarication and palpable aestheticism in his earlier *Marxism and Form* [1971]) able to reintegrate Adorno's work as offering plausible solutions, notwithstanding its palpably anachronistic political vocabulary (Jameson 1990). For a fine survey of the critical appropriations of Adorno, see Hohendahl, 3–20; Jay, esp. 82–110, and Gibson and Rubin's introduction to *Adorno: A Critical Reader,* 1–26. Adorno's argument implicitly calls into question Pierre Bourdieu's subsequent claim that the social efficacy of cultural production diminishes in proportion to its formal-aesthetic intricacy. Indeed, few historical periods are as likely to challenge Bourdieu's notion of the mutual exclusivity of elite symbolic and economic capital as the first half of the nineteenth century, particularly in Britain.

31. I agree with Marjorie Levinson who, in her well-known comparison of Keats's early writing to masturbation, emphasizes how that process amalgamates the feeling of possession without any loss of reflexive awareness: "Masturbatory pleasure may be conceived as a fantasy of pleasure without . . . the loss of reflexive consciousness *or* the object." Its "defensive virtue" resides in its conversion of a "drive" into a fantasy that, as a "fantasy *of* (in place of / in addition to) sex" guarantees continual self-awareness that, if the drive was "correctly enacted, must obliterate the consciousness which would *own* that pure pleasure" (Levinson 1988, 27).

Peter Dreyer argues, however, that Keats's "Had I a man's fair form . . ." sonnet is actually "a jeu d'esprit deriving from Theocritus and Pope, and the speaker is a bee. Theocritus's lovesick goatherd in Idyll III (who also incidentally fears that he may be funny-looking) says, 'O to be that buzzing bee, and fly into your cave, / Slipping through the ivy and fern you hide behind' (trans. Anthony Verity [New York: Oxford University Press, 2002]). Pope's 'First Pastoral, or Damon' couples Mt. Hybla in Sicily, famous in antiquity for bees and honey, with the Berkshire countryside, and Dr. Johnson, noting Pope's imitation of Theocritus, observes: 'Theocritus makes his lover wish to be a bee, that he might creep among the leaves that form the chaplet of his mistress. Pope's enamoured swain longs to be made the captive bird that sings in his fair one's bower, that she might listen to his songs, and reward him with her kisses' ("Review of an Essay on the Writings and Genius of Pope"). Keats has simply reversed Theocritus's conceit: here, the bee regrets not being a man" (personal communication).

32. For a discussion of Keats's reflexive dissent from his contemporary literary histories, see Rajan's persuasive suggestion that Keats's "nervousness about poetry's place in the contemporary world" would have rendered him skeptical about the value of Campbell's and Southey's literary histories, as well as the more tentative sketches

offered by Wordsworth's "Preface" and "Essay, supplementary" of 1815 and Coleridge's *Biographia.* All of them "were products of a new cultural materialism concerned to defend art against its marginality in a world of capital. They redeemed art and its criticism from uselessness by making them do the work of history or by inscribing them within a substitute history" (1998, 339).

33. *LJK,* 1: 169–70; emphasis added. In a letter of November 1817, Keats once again defines the completion of *Endymion* solely in terms of the number of lines written; "chang[ing] the Scene" to Devonshire shall "give me the spur to wind up my Poem, of which there are wanting 500 Lines" (ibid., 187).

34. *LJK,* 2: 323. The often-quoted line is, of course, from Spenser's *Fairie Queene* (2.7.28, line 5); one must also bear in mind that, in the same letter, Keats disparages his *Endymion* as a "pack of scattered cards."

35. See Benjamin 1968, 232–38. The word "phantasmagoria" only arises at the beginning of the nineteenth century, with early mentions in the 1802 *Gentlemen's Magazine* and in the 1803 *European Magazine.* Though initially coined to describe optical illusions created by magic lanterns that were on display in London beginning in 1802 (*OED*), the term soon emerges as a descriptor for the operation of ideological fantasy. See Schopenhauer's *World as Will and Representation* (1969 [1819]), Hegel's review article of 1828 (*Rezensionen aus den Jahrbüchern für wissenschaftliche Kritik*), and Marx's critique of St. Max [Stirner] in the *German Ideology* (1998 [1845–46]). Marx's argument particularly echoes Hazlitt's analysis of lower-class psychology: "First comes the moral injunction to seek and, moreover, to seek oneself. This is defined in the sense that man should become something that so far is not, namely, an egoist, and this egoist is defined as being an 'all-powerful ego,' in whom the peculiar ability has become resolved from actual ability into the ego, into omnipotence, into the fantastic idea of ability. To seek oneself means, therefore, to become something different from what one is and, indeed, to become an all powerful, i.e., nothing, a non-thing, a phantasmagoria." (Marx 1998, 285). The German text reads: "Zuerst das Moralgebot des Suchens, und zwar des Sich-selbst-Suchens. Dies wird dahin bestimmt, daß man etwas werden soll, was man noch nicht ist, nämlich Egoist, und dieser Egoist wird dahin bestimmt, daß er 'ein allmächtiges Ich' ist, worin das eigentümliche Vermögen aus wirklichem in Ich, in die Allmacht, die Phantasie des Vermögens sich aufgelöst hat. Sich selbst suchen heißt also etwas Andres werden, als man ist, und zwar allmächtig werden, d.h. Nichts, ein Unding, eine Phantasmagorie werden" (Marx 1990, 2: 316–17). In his essay on Wagner, Adorno nicely summarizes the relevant aspects of the term: "Where the dream is at its most exalted, the commodity is closest to hand. The phantasmagoria tends towards dream not merely as deluded wish-fulfilment of would-be buyers, but chiefly to conceal the labour that has gone into making it. It mirrors subjectivity by confronting the subject with the product of its own labour, but in such a way that the labour that has gone into it is no longer identifiable. The dreamer encounters his own image impotently, as if it were a miracle, and is held fast in the inexorable circle of his own labour, as if it would last forever" (Adorno 1981, 91 / *AGS,* 13: 87). Keats also uses the term at least once; see his letter to Fanny Brawne of March 1820: "I rest well and from last night do not remember any thing horrid in my dream, which is a capital symptom, for any organic derangement always occasions a Phantasmagoria" (*LJK,* 2: 277). For a lucid account of phantasmagoria at the beginning of the nineteenth century in London, see Castle, 140–67.

36. For a reading of "Lamia" attentive to its economic logic, see Levinson 1989, 255–99. For interesting, opposed statements in the debate over the reintroduction of the gold standard as it unfolded between 1816 and 1820, see Cobbett and Ricardo. Against Ricardo's contention that "to fix on gold as a standard" is to be deceived by "a commodity obtained under the same contingencies as every other commodity" (Ricardo, 1: 75), Cobbett's "Letter to Henry Hunt, Esq., On the Recent Tricks of the Boroughmongers relative to their Paper-Money" (7 July 1819) offers a searing indictment of the government's logic of perpetual extenuation: "They have been in a state of non-payment for twenty-two years. But, stop! For some one may say, 'if they can go on for twenty-two years, they can *go on for ever;*' but, by the same reasoning, a cancer that does not kill in a year, will *never* kill. A cancer surely kills *at last;* and so does a paper-money not convertible into specie." Cobbett proceeds to lambaste the government's offer to redeem bonds at a lesser rate where payment is asked for in specie and at full value only where the seller is prepared to accept paper money. Such a scheme is patently illegitimate, he contends, since "the paper now in circulation is *owed by,* or *lent by,* the Bank [of England]. The Bank cannot, therefore, obtain gold *with any part of this paper.* It cannot obtain it with the paper it *owes gold for.* It cannot obtain gold for the paper that it has *lent;* because, in order to do that, it must *withdraw its loans,* and *lend no more;* and then prices must fall so greatly as to produce universal ruin." Cobbett's dire portrayal of the Regency political order as a pyramid scheme—"the whole consists of *paper promises to pay*" (Cobbett, 4: 124, 128, 131)—and his prognosis of eventual and complete ruination strikingly mirrors the narrative momentum of "Lamia." For the opposing view, see Ricardo (arguably Cobbett's prime target), esp. chap. 27.

37. "Concocting stories [*fabeln*] about a world 'other' than this one is utterly senseless, unless we have within us a powerful instinct to slander, belittle, cast suspicion on life: in which case we are *avenging* ourselves on life with the phantasmagoria of 'another,' 'better' life" (im letzteren Falle rächen wir uns am Leben mit der Phantasmagorie eines "anderen", eines "besseren" Lebens) (Nietzsche 1998, 19 / 1980, 6: 78).

38. On Wordsworth, see Pfau 1997, 362–82, "'Debasement of the Body or the Mind': Urban Inferno in *the Prelude.*"

39. Adorno 1989, 127 / *AGS,* 2: 181; trans. modified. For Kaufman, the second-generation romantics anticipate and help prepare the way for Adorno's and the Frankfurt School's critical engagement with aesthetic form. In Kaufman's reading, Keats's radically formalist, no less than Shelley's self-deconstructing prophetic, approach to poetry, amounts to "a constructivist *via negativa* to the critical reflection once articulated in relation to aesthetic aura, raised now to the second or third power in the modern experience of that aura's loss" (2001, 383).

40. Doubts remain, however, as to whether the frontispiece of the 1817 volume is meant to depict Spenser or Shakespeare. For a discussion of the matter, see Kandl in Wolfson 2001, 2.

41. Jakobson stresses the mirror-relation of the poetic and the metalingual function by remarking how "in metalanguage the sequence is used to build an equation, whereas in poetry the equation is used to build a sequence" (71). For a critical account, see Anthony Johnson. Jakobson's account of equivalent units in poetry involves the seemingly foundational structure of parallelism, a conception significantly inspired by Gerard Manley Hopkins's *Notebooks.* See Jakobson, 82–83, and, for a much broader analysis of parallelism in aesthetics and theories of self-reflection, Menninghaus, esp.

9–29. See also Garrett Stuart's perceptive account of "Keats and Language" in Wolfson 2001.

42. Larson, 89. She goes on to quote one Thomas Gaisford as saying that "the advantages of classical education are two-fold—it enables us to look down with contempt on those who have not shared its advantages, and also fits us for places of emolument, not only in this world, but in that which is to come."

43. For the textual history of Gray's "Elegy," see Roger Lonsdale's introductory commentary and textual notes in *The Poems of Gray, Collins, and Goldsmith*, 103–41, as well as the discussion in Guillory, 85–133. On Wordsworth's allusive negotiation of Milton and other precursors, see Stein, 19–41.

44. Roe, 61–71. Lockhart's serial review article, which appeared in four installments between October 1817 and August 1818 is reprinted in Reiman, 3, pt. 1: 49–60 and 86–95.

SEVEN: Melancholy into Ressentiment

1. All references to Heine's works refer to his *Sämtliche Schriften* (1997), ed. Klaus Briegleb, cited parenthetically as *HSS*, followed by the volume and page numbers. Chapter 7 epigraph: *HSS*, 3: 395–96.

2. Börne's most explicit repudiation of Goethe, both as a writer and as a political figure, can be found in his *Briefe aus Paris* (1832–34), Börne, 3: 70–71, 286–301.

3. Greiner, 79–80; my trans. And see also Sengle, 1: 93–98.

4. Börne, 2: 1174. Wolfgang Menzel (1798–1873), a member of the Württemberg diet and editor of the influential literary periodical *Cottasches Literaturblatt* between 1826 and 1849, was notorious for his sharply worded and politically divisive critical review essays and for his influential German literary history, *Die deutsche Literatur,* first published in 2 vols. in 1828 and, revised and expanded to 4 vols. in 1836. Menzel's attack on some of the writers who belonged to the movement styled *das junge Deutschland*, particularly Gutzkow and Heine, is widely regarded as having helped precipitate the summary prohibition of all publications (past, present, and future) by members of that group.

5. On this letter and on Christiani's documented worship of Goethe, see the commentary in *HB* 4: 75–6). See also Heine's letters to Christiani (26 May 1825) and to Moses Moser (1 July 1825) in *HB* 1: 210, 216.

6. The Austrian chancellor, Metternich, and his principal policy advisor, Friedrich Gentz (a secret admirer of Heine's works), persistently sought to curtail the impact of liberal literature and journalism, culminating in the December 1835 decree of the federal assembly that outlawed the writings of *das junge Deutschland,* with Heine listed first in a group of several authors. The document broke new ground in that it outlawed all writings, past *and* future, by the authors in question. For the text of the parliamentary decree, see the "Bundesbeschluß vom 10. Dezember 1835" (§ 515), reprinted in Huber, 137. For Heine's response, see *HSS,* 5: 20–21. For a theoretical reflection on how the fact of external censorship blurs the interpretive line between Heine's vivid metaphoric idiom and what may be instances of self-censorship, see Levine, 1–20, and his reading of Heine's novel fragment *Aus den Memoiren des Herrn von Schnabelewopski, HSS,* 1: 503–56 (on which Wagner's *Der fliegende Holländer* was based), 43–70.

7. On Raumer's public act of contrition, see Börne, *Briefe aus Paris*, in *Sämtliche Schriften*, 3: 519. On Menzel, see Sengle, 1: 113, 156–57, 294–95.

8. The comparison is actually reported by Börne himself; see Börne, 3: 503.

9. See Heine's poem "An einen politischen Dichter":

> Du singst, wie einst Tyrtäus sang,
> Von Heldenmut beseelet,
> Doch hast du schlecht dein Publikum
> Und deine Zeit gewählet.
> Beifällig horchen sie dir zwar,
> Und loben, schier begeistert:
> Wie edel dein Gedankenflug,
> Wie du die Form bemeistert.
> Sie pflegen auch beim Glase Wein
> Ein Vivat dir zu bringen
> Und manchen Schlachtgesang von dir
> Lautbrüllend nachzusingen.
> Der Knecht singt gern ein Freiheitslied
> Des Abends in der Schenke:
> Das fördert die Verdauungskraft,
> Und würzet die Getränke. (*HSS*, 4: 485)

10. Habermas 1996, 1126; my trans.

11. As Heine puts it in 1837—likely punning on Börne's name (*borniert*)—"nur gewissen bornierten Geistern konnte die Milderung meiner Rede, oder gar mein erzwungenes Schweigen, als ein Abfall von mir selber erscheinen. Sie mißdeuteten meine Mäßigung, und das war um so liebloser, da ich doch nie ihre Überwut mißdeutet habe" (only certain narrow, opinionated individuals could have interpreted the temperance of my speech or my forcible silence as a case of personal apostasy. They misinterpreted my moderation, and this was all the more heartless as I myself have never misinterpreted their excessive rage) (1837 "Vorrede zum *Buch der Lieder*," *HSS*, 1: 11–12). In this respect, Heine stands much closer to the Left Hegelians. As Friedrich Sengle has shown, the decade leading up to the pre-1848 era known as *Vormärz* was marked by a sharp divide between the didactic proselytizing of the *Jungdeutsche* movement and the young Hegelians (Feuerbach, Vischer, Hebbel, Engels) for whom a politically principled philosophy was by definition an aesthetic one. Accordingly, literature could be political only "in an indirect, dialectical sense," and not in the crudely programmatic sense enforced by the members of *das junge Deutschland* (Sengle, 1: 216). The entire debate is most instructive with regard to the controversy over "political correctness" at universities and in public life in the United States as it has been unfolding since the late 1980s. For the reaction of some of the *Jungdeutsche* to Heine's work and representative quotations from Ruge, Herwegh, and Scherr, see Preisendanz, 21.

12. For the resolution, see Huber, 1: 137. Heine is the first writer in a list of five whose writings, publishers, printers, and distributors are to be prosecuted to the fullest extent of the laws in every state of the German Federation. On the period's literary dynamics, see Sengle, 1: 155–220.

13. Quoted in Sengle, 1: 167. See also the essay by C. P. Magill.

14. Sengle, 1: 9; see also Börne's astute essay on *Hamlet*, 1: 482–99.

15. For a concise summary of Germany's territorial and political reorganization at the Vienna Congress, see Nipperdey 1996, 72–84. On early restoration politics, see also Sheehan, 391–484, and Sengle, 1: 1–82. On the inherently problematic (liberal) idea of Jewish emancipation/assimilation, and on its abrupt termination by resolutions adopted at the Vienna Congress, see Herzig 1997, 146–69; Meyer, 2: 27–37; and Nipperdey 1996, 221–23. On anti-Semitism as an integral feature of German romanticism, see Frühwald 1988, 73–91.

16. On the rapid spread of *Vereine* during the 1820s and 1830s, see Sengle, 1: 20–25, and Sheehan, 533–37. On the reorganization of domestic living space during this period, see Nipperdey 1996, 130–35, and Sheehan, 536–39.

17. See Wagner-Egelhaaf's comprehensive account of melancholy as the condition of a subject consciously embedded in an overdetermined discourse history (*Diskursgeschichte*). More overtly deconstructivist is Anselm Haverkamp who, like Benjamin, Foucault, and de Man before him, premises his readings of Keats and Hölderlin on textuality as the "mortification" of being *qua* representation. As Haverkamp puts it, "reading . . . now means a structural procedure that becomes melancholy in that it mortifies its objects and consequently perceives them as dead texture. Reading is melancholy in its . . . contemplation of the dead letter" (104). Arguably the most canonical statement of this inherently allegorical understanding of literature can be found in Paul de Man's *Allegories of Reading* (1983, 207–8).

18. For a more discursive account of the melancholic dimension intrinsic to literary production—which the author firmly dissociates from an older thematic history of melancholy—see Wagner-Egelhaff, 1–30.

19. Sautermeister, 95; my trans.

20. To be sure, I am not claiming Heine's express or programmatic support for an analysis of his style's historicity. Indeed, an early letter to Immermann (10 June 1823) proclaims the incompatibility of lyric production and historical knowledge, though Heine's objection appears principally to biographical models of explanation (*HB*, 1: 85).

21. An example would be Nietzsche's extravagant claim that Jews *and* anti-Semites are equally informed by the spirit of ressentiment. "Let me first whisper something in the ear of the psychologists, just in case they might for once want to study *ressentiment* at close quarters: this plant now blooms most beautifully among anarchists and anti-Semites, in hidden places, just where it has always flowered, like the violet, although its perfume is admittedly somewhat different. And as like most always proceed from like, so it will come as no surprise to learn that it is from these very same circles that attempts to sanctify *revenge* under the name of *justice* emanate, just as they have so often in the past—compare I, § 14 above—, as if justice were at bottom merely an extension of the feeling of injury—and with revenge to bring all the *reactive* feelings retroactively to a position of honour" (Nietzsche 1996, 54 / 1980, 5: 309–10).

22. See Nietzsche's *Geburt der Tragödie:* "Wherever we encounter the naïve in art, we should recognize that we are in the presence of the highest impact of Apolline culture, which must always overthrow a realm of Titans and monsters, and which must emerge triumphant over a terrible abyss in its contemplation of the world and its most intense capacity for suffering, by resorting to the most powerful and pleasurable illu-

sions" (durch kräftige Wahnvorspiegelungen und lustvolle Illusionen [Nietzsche 1993, 23–24 / 1980, 1: 37]).

23. See Taylor, 368–90. On epigenetic theories of the self, see the discussion of Fichte and Novalis earlier in this volume, as well as secondary literature quoted there.

24. See Nehamas, 13–41, and Staten, 40–68.

25. Consider Keats's acutely self-critical remarks ("when I am among women I have evil thoughts" [*LJK*, 1: 341]) or such character studies in covert aggression as Angela in "The Eve of St. Agnes" and Apollonius in "Lamia."

26. Notably, though, Keats revised his assessment of Napoleon in envisioning his new epic protagonist Apollo, in *Hyperion*, as "not led on, like Buonaparte, by circumstance" but as a truly "fore-seeing God" (23 January 1818) [*LJK*, 1: 207]). For a study of Napoleon's role in the literary imagination of English romanticism, see Bainbridge, esp. 153–82. Heine's most memorable characterization of Napoleon involves a childhood memory of French troops led by Napoleon entering his home town, Düsseldorf; see his account in vol. 2 of *Reisebilder* (*HSS*, 2: 262–83).

27. For a survey of Jewish responses to Heine's work, see Shedletzky 1988.

28. On the contending strategies of Jewish assimilation to the emergent German nation-state or a strictly religious model of separate Jewish incorporation, see Meyer; Belke; Katz; Herzig 1988; and Herzig 1997, 146–72.

29. See Habermas 1996.

30. Wolfgang Preisendanz is right to express misgivings about the opacity of "feuilleton" as a critical category in the interpretation of Heine's oeuvre and its historical significance. See Preisendanz, 28n. Still, the concept was obviously significant in its time, being routinely opposed to some notion of intellectual or literary "sincerity." For a fine contemporary example, see Berlioz, 373–76.

31. Nietzsche 1996, 102 / 1980, 5: 369. See also the following memorable passage from Heine's *Reisebilder,* which strikingly anticipates Nietzsche's imagery: "Aber dieses Geschlecht hat auch Menschen hervorgebracht, in deren Herzen nur faules Wasser sintert und die daher in den Herzen anderer alle Springquellen eines frischen Blutes verstopfen möchten, Menschen von erloschener Genußfähigkeit, die das Leben verleumden und anderen alle Herrlichkeit dieser Welt verleiden wollen, indem sie solche als die Lockspeisen schildern, die der Böse bloß zu unserer Versuchung hingestellt habe, gleichwie eine pfiffige Hausfrau die Zuckerdose mit den gezählten Stückchen Zucker in ihrer Abwesenheit offen stehenläßt, um die Enthaltsamkeit der Magd zu prüfen; und diese Menschen haben einen Tugendpöbel um sich versammelt und predigen ihm das Kreuz gegen den großen Heiden und gegen seine nackten Göttergestalten, die sie gern durch ihre vermummten dummen Teufel ersetzen möchten. Das Vermummen ist so recht ihr höchstes Ziel, das Nackt göttliche ist ihnen fatal, und ein Satyr hat immer seine guten Gründe, wenn er Hosen anzieht und darauf dringt, daß auch Apollo Hosen anziehe. Die Leute nennen ihn dann einen sittlichen Mann und wissen nicht, daß in dem Clauren-Lächeln eines vermummten Satyrs mehr Anstößiges liegt als in der ganzen Nacktheit eines Wolfgang Apollo und daß just in den Zeiten, wo die Menschheit jene Pluderhosen trug, wozu sechzig Ellen Zeug nötig waren, die Sitten nicht anständiger gewesen sind als jetzt" (*HSS*, 2: 218–19).

32. Ralf Schnell has persuasively argued for Heine's conception of a self-consciously historical mode of writing, a radical step beyond Hegel, for whom art by definition

implies a lack of historical self-awareness. Heine "deducts and justifies the existence of poetry precisely by referring to its changing historical significance, its incipient marginalization" (Schnell, 156; my trans.).

33. Heine remarks laconically in a letter of 30 October 1827 that "the *Buch der Lieder* is nothing but a complete edition of my familiar poems. . . . The [book] is beautifully equipped, and as a harmless trade vessel, it is destined to sail peacefully down into the sea of oblivion" (*HB*, 1: 329; my trans.). Heine's faithful and forbearing publisher, Julius Campe, had proposed a printing of only 1,000 copies, as opposed to Heine's initial expectation of 3,000. Recognizing that a collection of (for the most part) previously published poetry would only hold limited appeal, Heine chose not to ask for any royalties from sales of the first edition. After seven years, only 1,200 copies (out of the compromise figure of 2,000) had been sold, as Campe remarked, mostly "to the universities, and to young men and such as have no money" (*HSS*, 1: 631). Still, although the collection got off to a slow commercial start, it gradually established itself as one of the most popular and widely read editions of poetry by a single author. At the time of Heine's death, there had been no fewer than seven editions of the *Buch der Lieder.*

34. By contrast, Marcel Reich-Ranicki argues that "nowhere does the loneliness of the Jew Heine among the Germans emerge more acutely, nowhere is his desperation more apparent than in precisely that part of his oeuvre where the Jews are not a theme at all—in his erotic poetry" (88).

35. See Ederer, 1–115; more convincing than Holub in his later interpretation, Ederer persuasively reads Heine's early lyrics (1820–27) as shrewd articulations of the "manipulability of romantic forms and motifs" (33). See also Heine's very early poem, first written as part of a letter (5 February 1821) to Heinrich Straube:

Wenn der Frühling kommt mit dem Sonnenschein
Dann knospen und blühen die Blümlein auf;
Wenn der Mond beginnt seinen Stralenlauf
Dann schwimmen die Sternlein hintendrein;
Wenn der Sänger zwey süße Aeuglein sieht
Dann quellen ihm Lieder aus tiefem Gemüt;-
Doch Lieder und Sterne und Blümelein
Und Aeuglein und Mondglanz und Sonnenschein,
Wie sehr das Zeug auch gefällt,
So macht's doch noch lang nicht die Welt! (*HB*, 1: 26)

36. It goes without saying that my reading of Heine's *Buch der Lieder* breaks with more conventional views that hold it to be "[self-]evident that Heine employed stock motifs from the romantic arsenal, and that his literary aspirations [until 1286] fell within the mainstream of the German romantic movement" (Holub, 41). Holub's first statement effectively denies the conclusions reached in the second, for Heine invites his readers to witness the perpetual reconfiguration of these inherited literary motifs. Demoted to a stylistic commodity—Klaus Briegleb speaks of *Bildchiffren* (*HSS*, 1: 666–71)—Heine's lyric motifs *visibly* resolve high romantic pathos into trivial, denatured, or possibly nonexistent inner experiences.

37. Remarkable not only for his close involvement with German cultural, especially literary, politics during his years as political secretary to Chancellor Metternich, Gentz

also acknowledged the personal appeal of Heine's poetry during his risqué courtship of the young dancer Fanny Eßler. For Gentz, the "unspeakable magic" of Heine's *Buch der Lieder* "expressed his rather tawdry affair as no poem of Goethe's ever could." Vortriede speaks of Gentz's appreciation for Heine's "new language of the soul with its frivolous-shabby overtones [*die das Liederliche streifende neue Seelensprache*]" (Vortriede, 1: 5–6).

38. Earlier, Kraus had portrayed Heine sympathetically, seeing him as a writer "critical of folk song" (Lensing, 98), a role Kraus envisaged for himself. Indeed, the hostile statement (Heine hat der deutschen Sprache so sehr das Mieder gelockert . . .) is clearly adopted from an essay by Max Kalbeck, praised by Kraus in his periodical *Die Fackel*, which commended Heine's enabling role for any beginning writer of feuilletons, because he had "loosened the corset of language, one fitted all too tightly by the pedants of our schools" (quoted in Lensing, 97n11).

39. "Those for whom I was and remained a Jew wanted me to understand that I could never do enough for them, that is, as a Jew; that, as a Jew, I was incapable of living and partaking of their higher, secret life, touching their soul and sharing their forms of spiritual contact. They did not concede me the colors and imprimatur of a German. Whatever was intuitive [*unbewußt*] and organic [*pflanzenhaft*] about my writing, they dismissed as merely a product of sophistry [*Erklügelung*] Jewish finesse, slyness, and adaptiveness" (Wassermann, 82; my trans.). In a curious echo of Kraus's 1910 essay, Wassermann interpolates several pages (56–58) on Heine in his autobiography in which he applies virtually all these anti-Semitic slurs about counterfeit sentiments, superficial brilliance, and corrupted modernity to Heine's work. On these prejudices, see Gilman, 209–43.

40. Wordsworth, "Preface" to *Lyrical Ballads*" (1802 text [1992a, 753]). Similarly, Burke praises "the cold sluggishness of our national character" and "a sort of native plainness and directness of understanding" (181, 186).

41. On the relation between literary interpretation and theories of the performative, see Austin 1975, esp. 67–82; Derrida 1980, 307–30; Fish 1989, 37–67; Petrey, 22–65; and Pfau 1995.

42. Shortly afterward, Nietzsche resumes his characterization as follows: "The man of *ressentiment* is neither upright nor naïve in his dealings with others, nor is he honest and open with himself. His soul is cross-eyed [*seine Seele schielt*]; his mind loves bolt-holes, secret paths, back doors, he regards all hidden things as *his* world, *his* security, *his* refreshment; he has a perfect understanding of how to keep silent, how not to forget, how to wait, how to make himself provisionally small and submissive" (1996, 24 / 1980, 5: 272).

43. Benjamin 1980, 355; my trans. For a complete translation of the essay on Kraus, see Benjamin 1999b, 433–58.

44. On the anti-Semitic reception of Heine and its consistently ambivalent character, see Peters 1997.

45. On Daumier, Heine, and the relation between nineteenth-century political satire, *Witz*, and aggression, see Gay 1993, 386–401, and Reed.

46. As to the writing of this short lyric, an acquaintance of Heine's, Johann Peter Lyser (1803–70) recalled how, at Heine's request during a meeting in 1830, he had written a short frivolous song. In reading it, Heine remarked that Lyser's closing couplet enjoining the beloved to "Lie brazenly—I'll take my chances / For I am constrained to

love you" (Lüge dreist—ich will's d'rauf wagen, / Weil ich Dich schon lieben muß)—was too reminiscent of Goethe's style and sounded too innocent. In response, Heine then proceeded to write the lyric quoted in the text. Lyser's account is reprinted in Werner, 481–87.

47. As Martin Greiner puts it, the epigone is a "hybrid of poet and audience. Half of him is still the poet who speaks, but the other half is already the addressee, one transformed by the act of reception, not merely shaping language, but also shaped by it" (Greiner 82; my trans.).

48. As David Wellbery puts it, "with the birth of lyric song out of the spirit of idyllic prose, a type of communicative transaction is inaugurated that sends readers, as it were, *into and through the language of the poem in quest of their most intimate subjectivity.* This quest is possible because it has been undertaken in advance by the lyric subject, whose speech emanates from an inner origin toward which, in speaking, it seeks to return" (Wellbery 1997, 18).

49. Moses Moser in *Deutsche Blätter für Poesie, Literatur, Kunst und Theater* (Breslau, 1823), quoted in *HSS*, 1: 640; my trans. On Moser, see Prawer, 184–86.

50. Heine himself appears to offer the best ironic commentary on his set piece of seaside melancholy; see *Reisebilder* (*HSS*, 2: 225–27).

51. Gustav Pfizer's hostile and influential review essay of 1838 clearly understood the wide appeal of Heine's lyrics: "Heine gefiel nämlich wirklich nicht blos den wirklich poetischen Gemüthern durch das wahrhaft Poetische in seinen Gedichten, sondern auch vielen im Grunde nicht oder wenig poetischen Lesern durch sonstige Bestandteile seiner Gedichte. . . . Unter den letztern dagegen fanden sowohl die Sentimentalen manche schöne, frivole Blume unter dem Unkraut, theils machten die Frivolen, die ennuyirten und blasirten Weltleute, an diesen Gedichten einen kostbaren, seltenen Fund, wegen des hineingerührten Witzes, der Ironie, der Bosheit, des Unglaubens, und der Sittenlosigkeit, die sich darin versteckten. Den Halbgebildeten in der Poesie, den Roheren nämlich, erschien er beinahe als Erlöser der von einigen Pedanten gefangen gehaltenen Muse" (*HSS*, 6, 2: 455).

52. Gutzkow 1998, 2: 1168: "Nur aus dem Judenthume konnte vielleicht eine so wahre und dankenswerte Reaktion gegen unsere Ideologie, die sich selbst die Fesseln einer neuen Sklaverei schmiedete, kommen." Gutzkow's position appears to anticipate Thomas Mann's (inherently problematic) statement in support of the Jewish intellectual for offering, "mit seiner Leidenserfahrung, seiner geprüften Geistigkeit und ironischen Vernunft ein heimliches Korrektiv unserer Leidenschaften" ("Zum Problem des Antisemitismus," public address given in Zurich, 1937, in Mann 1986, 859). For a discussion of Mann's complex biographical and literary relationship to Jews and Judaism, see Kurzke, 187–214.

53. On this subject, see Anderson, 32–42; Siskin 1998, 1–26; Olivia Smith, 1–34; and Pfau 1997, 1–16. For a comprehensive account of the emergence of German as a literary language prior to 1775, see Blackall, esp. 482–525.

54. On these early and unsuccessful attempts at Jewish integration in Prussia, see the essay by Belke who, in turn, relies on Selma Stern's landmark study. For a comparison of regional differences concerning Jews in Prussia, as well as different roads toward and against reform elsewhere in Germany, see Meyer, 2: 7–49.

55. A vivid account of this practice can be found in the autobiography of the German-Jewish writer Fanny Lewald (1811–89), 1: 8–10.

56. On reactions to Dohm, see Meyer, 2: 1997, 13–15. Some of the principal texts in this debate—those by Michaelis, Mendelssohn, and Dohm—are translated in Mendes-Flohr and Reinharz, 36–44. For a short introduction to Dohm, see Gilman and Zipes, 75–83, and Katz, 57–71.

57. Notably, a reformer as sympathetic to Jewish emancipation as Wilhelm von Humboldt still considered baptism an essential tool for the "integration" of Jews (4: 95–112).

58. For Meyer and Herzig, this crisis was largely precipitated by Jewish reform efforts, such as those pursued by Isaac Jacobson (1768–1828) in Hamburg. See Herzig 1988, and Herzig 1997, 161–64. For a vivid account of the most crucial steps toward assimilation—changing one's name and, ultimately, accepting baptism—see Lewald, 1: 212–17, 242–44. The best collection of documentary accounts by ordinary German-Jewish subjects is to be found in Richarz. For a detailed account of Jewish assimilation following the Prussian emancipation decree of 1812, see Ismar Freund's two-volume account and the essays by Malino, Simon-Nahum, and Richard Cohen in Brenner, Caron, and Kaufmann.

59. On the emancipation of Prussia's Jews, see Meyer, 2: 19–27, and Herzig 1997, 152–68. See also reference to survey of German-Jewish relations in notes to Sheehan, 269–70, 438–39, 449–50; and Nipperdey, 248–55.

60. For statistical information on the numbers of German Jews, as well as their distribution across the spectrum of professions, regions and cities, and rates of conversion, see Richarz, 28–43.

61. Both Heine and other members of his family were among those affected. Heine's prospects for an academic or legal career were ended by the August 1823 suspension of the Prussian Jewish Emancipation edict of 1812 that had granted civil status to the Jews. Likewise, his brother Gustav, a learned farmer, was now once again barred from practicing agriculture. See *HB*, 4: 47, 66.

62. The term *Antisemitismus* ("anti-Semitism") only emerges in the 1870s, most likely introduced by Wihelm Marr (1819–1904). See Nipperdey and Rürup, esp. 137ff.

63. See Frühwald 1988, 72–91. Examples of anti-Semitic writing in Prussia after 1790 include Fichte 1793; Karl W. F. Grattenauer, *Über die physische und moralische Verfassung der heutigen Juden* (1791), with 13,000 copies, a particularly "successful" book; Christian Ludwig Paalzow, *Wider die Juden* (1799); Karl Borromäus Sessa, *Unser Verkehr* (1815); Friedrich Christian Rühs, *Über die Ansprüche der Juden an das deutsche Bürgerrecht* (1816); Jakob Friedrich Fries, *Über die Gefährdung des Wohlstandes und Charakters der Deutschen durch die Juden* (1816); Ludwig Holst, *Das Judentum in allen dessen Theilen betrachtet* (1821).

64. "Der Philister vor, in und nach der Geschichte," in Brentano 1975, 2: 965–66: "Die Juden, als von welchen noch viele Exemplare in persona vorrätig, die von jeder ihren zwölf Stämmen für die Kreuzigung des Herrn anhängende Schmach Zeugnis geben können, will ich gar nicht berühren, da jeder, der sich ein Kabinett zu sammeln begierig, nicht weit nach ihnen botanisieren braucht; er kann diese von den ägyptischen Plagen übriggebliebenen Fliegen in seiner Kammer mit alten Kleidern, an seinem Teetische mit Theaterzetteln und ästhetischem Geschwätz, auf der Börse mit Pfandbriefen und überall mit Ekel und Humanität und Aufklärung, Hasenpelzen und Weißfischen genugsam einfangen" On the institution of the Tischgesellschaft, see Arendt, 176–80, and Frühwald 1988.

65. *HSS*, 6, 1: 648: "der Judenhaß beginnt erst mit der Romantischen Schule . . . Freude am Mittelalter, Katholizismus, Adel, gesteigert durch die Teutomanen—Rühs—[etc.]."

66. Varnhagen, 9: 583. On the so-called Hep-Hep riots of 1819–20, see also Meyer, 2: 36–38. For the vivid description of the riots, see Rahel Varnhagen's brother's letter from Karlsruhe, 22 August 1819 (Varnhagen, 9: 579–82).

67. Varnhagen, 9: 583: "ein dunkles Bedürfnis etwas zu vergöttern [. . .] weil das Bedürfnis der Vernunft, und der Sinn für das, was da ist, [. . .] nicht scharf genug ist. Der faule Punkt im Geschlecht, woraus sich alle Geistesepidemien, Schwächen und Erhitzungen bilden [. . .]. Solche Elende können auch grausam werden; [. . .] Dieses ganze Gelichter von epidemischen Geisteskrankheiten wurde, in der verschrieenen Aufklärungsepoche, von den braven Aufklärern, heilsam und unschädlich durch Lächerlichmachen gehemmt [. . .]. Jeden großen Irrthum, nämlich der in seinen Folgen groß werden kann, werden Nationen nur durch Blutvergießen los. Jemehr in Massen gehandelt wird und geschieht, je schwerer wirken menschliche Gedanken: alsdann nur immer die der Natur; [. . .] So sieht mein Geist reelles Unglück voraus, wenn die Narren noch länger fortarbeiten [. . .] O! armer Novalis, armer Friedrich Schlegel, der gar noch leben bleiben mußte; das dachtet ihr nicht von euren seichten Jüngern. Großer, lieber, ganz blind gelesener Goethe, feuriger ehrlicher Lessing, und all ihr Großen, Heiteren, das dachtet ihr nicht; konntet ihr nicht denken. Eine schöne Säuerei!" See also Hahn and Isselstein, 17, on this passage.

68. Ludwig Börne's influential *Letters from Paris* often second Rahel Varnhagen's and Heine's analysis of Germany's late romantic culture as barely concealed social ressentiment: "The poor Germans! Living on the first floor, and oppressed by the seven stories of the higher classes, it relieves them of their anxiety to speak of people who live even further down, in the basement. That they are not Jews consoles them for the fact that they are not even court counselors" (Mendes-Flohr and Reinharz, 224). On Börne's often severely critical view of Heine, expressed above all in his letters of the 1830s, see Briegleb, 157–65.

69. *HB*, 1: 79–80; my trans. The metaphoric conflation of writing and paper currency dates back at least to the 1790s, including Edmund Burke's anxious remarks on the subject. Still, Heine and Börne (1977, 1: 669) deploy such images with great frequency, perhaps nowhere more so than in their revealing discussion of Shakespeare's Shylock; see *HSW*, 5: 171–293, and Börne's often quoted essay "On the Jew Shylock in *The Merchant of Venice*" (1977, 1: 499–506); see also Briegleb's discussion of the Shylock-Börne-Heine conjunction, 258–78.

70. Zagari and Chiarini, 10; my trans. See also Heine's 1840 *Denkschrift* on Ludwig Börne, in which the affiliation between the much disparaged Jewish accent (*Mauscheln*) and modern commerce is emphasized and even broadened to include gentile merchants: "Was wir nämlich in Norddeutschland Mauscheln nennen, ist nichts anders als die eigentliche Frankfurter Landessprache, und sie wird von der unbeschnittenen Population ebenso vortrefflich gesprochen wie von der beschnittenen. Börne sprach diesen Jargon sehr schlecht, obgleich er, ebenso wie Goethe, den heimatlichen Dialekt nie ganz verleugnen konnte. Ich habe bemerkt, daß Frankfurter, die sich von allen Handelsinteressen entfernt hielten, am Ende jene Frankfurter Aussprache, die wir, wie gesagt, in Norddeutschland Mauscheln nennen, ganz verlernten" (*HSS*, 4: 24).

71. For Friedländer's cautious proposal of German Jews accepting baptism (under certain conditions), see his 1799 open letter to Probst Teller, reprinted in Mendes-Flohr and Reinharz, 95–100. Coleridge, who was living in Germany at the time that Friedländer's letter was published, summarized it succinctly: "This seems a strange muddle-headed application—neither more nor less than whether the Christian Church will consider and call a Jew a Christian, because instead of believing the Old Testament only he believes neither. This is two negatives make an affirmative with a vengeance" (Coleridge 1980–2000, 2: 796). In 1816, Coleridge published a strong statement in *The Courier* condemning the renewed adoption of laws and ordinances designed to reverse the advance of Germany's Jews toward civic emancipation (Coleridge 1978, 144–45).

72. On the linguistic prejudices against Yiddish, see Gilman, 22–107; Grab, 41–72; Freimark; and Toury.

73. See Gilman, 105–6.

74. "[Man rede] nach Beschaffenheit der Umstände, rein deutsch, oder rein hebräisch . . . Nur keine Vermischung der Sprachen" (quoted in Toury, 77).

75. The case of Eduard Gans, co-founder of the Verein für Wissenschaft und Kultur der Juden in Berlin, which Heine joined in the summer of 1822, is particularly interesting. A committed, if often verbose, Hegelian, Gans eventually was given a position in the law school of the new University of Berlin, though only following many delays, mostly caused by the vehement opposition of Karl von Savigny, the reigning professor in the field of jurisprudence. In order to obtain his position, Gans had to submit to baptism, a step he took shortly after Heine in the summer of 1825. On Gans, see Prawer, 10–43.

76. Begun in May 1859, the New Synagogue was officially dedicated 5 September 1866 and seated 3,000 people. Its modern architecture—distinguished by its innovative lighting and ceiling technology (designed by Eduard Knoblauch)—was widely admired. The dedication ceremonies were attended by Chancellor Otto von Bismarck, thus attesting to the integration of Berlin's Jewish community, already legally incorporated since 1847, into the Prussian State. This synagogue also pioneered special seating for the choir and a large-scale organ, obvious items in Protestant church architecture. Severely damaged by bombing raids in 1943, the synagogue was rebuilt between 1988 and 1995. A related example of the transformation of nineteenth-century Jewish religious culture and its architectural settings by assimilationist objectives can be found in Arno Herzig, who describes the reform school founded by Israel Jacobson (1768–1828) in Brunswick: "Here the Jewish service was celebrated in rites closely modeled on a Protestant model of worship. Thus the temple itself was radically reorganized; the *bima* (lectern) was removed from the center of the room to a corner, while a pulpit was erected for the preacher. The design of the Seesen temple was subsequently copied by the new synagogues in Hamburg and Berlin" (Herzig 1997, 161; my trans.). See also Herzig's account of reforms pertaining to religious chant instituted by the Jewish community in Iserlohn (162–63). As the authors of *Synagogues in Nineteenth-Century Germany* note, "many of the synagogues built between the last quarter of the 19th century and World War I were virtually indistinguishable from contemporary churches. The architects who specialized in synagogue building—most of them Jews—were not perturbed by the stylistic resemblance to Christian churches. . . . The multi-faceted and mystical symbols, derived from the Kabbala—the crown, the leviathan and the Temple

vessels—were replaced by more succinct symbols. The geometric shapes and the obvious harmony of the Star of David and the Tablets of the Law suited the requirements of the time" (39, 37); on this subject, see also Eschwege, 32–42. The work of the most prominent German-Jewish painter of the nineteenth century, Moritz Daniel Oppenheim (1800–1882), often retain a preassimilationist vision of Jewish identity at a time of often rampant acculturation in all aspects of Jewish life and tradition. See Andreas Gotzmann, "Traditional Jewish Life Revivied: Moritz Daniel Oppenheim's Vision of Modern Jewry," in Heuberger and Merk 2000, 232–50.

77. For an account of a Jewish intellectual's westward mobility—away from the talmudic culture of the shtetl and the linguistic olio of Lithuanian-Yiddish, Polish, "pure" Hebrew, and Aramaic dialects, and toward "High German" Enlightenment culture—see Maimon 1995 (1792). An incomplete translation exists (Maimon 1967), but some of the most interesting episodes on Maimon's estrangement from talmudic culture and his characterization of its linguistic deficiencies are curiously omitted. A translation of these portions can be found in Mendes-Flohr and Reinharz, 215–18.

78. For other discussions of Rée, see Gilman, 141–42; Freimark, 251–56; and Hobsbawm 1990, 96–100.

79. Similarly, the constitution for the Israelitische Freischule in Hamburg, which Rée eventually directed, demands in § 3 "the extermination [*Auslöschung*] of all peculiarities concerning custom, language, and manner" and, in § 22, specifies that "for all grades the German language shall be the principal topic . . . so as to spread a distinct and pure vernacular, free of any foreign element" (quoted in Freimark, 252; my trans.). Freimark points out that even Hamburg's more conservative Talmud Torah School, under the leadership of Chacham Isaac Bernays, introduced German-language instruction beginning in 1821 and hired non-Jewish teachers for that purpose. See also Freimark's references to social commentary by the leading Jewish periodical, the *Allgemeine Zeitung des Judentums,* quoted on 249n48.

80. For a reading of this passage, and the paragraphs preceding it, see Prawer, 61–69.

81. See Herzig 1988; Freimark; Toury; and Meyer, 2: 204–7.

82. Even the most rabidly anti-Semitic readers acknowledge their lingering fascination with Heine, though they typically hasten to dismiss it as a youthful indiscretion. On this subject, see Peters.

83. For example, Gerhard Friedrich's generally sympathetic treatise "The Jews and Their Enemies: A Word of Counsel to the Friends of Truth and Against Fanatics" reiterates the notion of a distinctively Jewish "singing intonation that most of the [Jews] can suppress only with much difficulty" (quoted in Freimark, 248). See also Gilman, 16–21.

84. Heine's music reviews were collected in *Lutezia: Berichte über Politik, Kunst und Volksleben,* vols. 2–3 of *Vermischte Schriften von Heinrich Heine* (Hamburg, 1854), trans. as *Lutèce: Lettres sur la vie politique, artistique et sociale de la France,* Bibliothèque contemporaine, 2d ser. (Paris: Michel Lévy Frères, 1855). On Heine's music criticism, see also Susan Bernstein 1998, 10–35.

85. Kraus, 193: "Jeder Nachkomme Heines nimmt aus dem Mosaik dieses Werks ein Steinchen, bis keines mehr übrig bleibt. Das Original verblaßt, weil uns die Grelle der Kopie die Augen öffnet." Lensing reads this passage as a further instance of "Kraus's need to dissociate himself from Heine's Jewishness." Thus "the phrase '*Mosaik des Werks*' . . . acquires a double meaning. It seems to suggest that the 'Mosaic' or Jewish

element in Heine's work produces an *oeuvre* that is fragmentary and construed rather than organic and whole" (Lensing, 110).

86. For a very different position, see Holub. While Holub is right to argue that Heine recognized the "impossibility of a German-Jewish symbiosis early" in his career, his contention that following his "conversion (*Bekehrung*) . . . in 1825 Heine ceased to be a Jew" is little less than bizarre unless, of course, one takes Judaism in the narrowest possible and strictly confessional sense. Heine's famous remark that the baptismal certificate is the ticket of admission to European culture" (Der Taufzettel ist das Entréebillett zur europäischen Kultur [*HSS*, 6, 1: 622]) leaves no doubt about his strictly pragmatic approach to baptism. Far from betokening a "conversion" (Holub's term), the act of submitting to baptism produces a sheet of paper (*Zettel*). Moreover, Heine's alienation from many of his Jewish contemporaries was the result of his opposition to the Jewish reform and emancipation movements, both of which he recognized as declarations of spiritual and cultural bankruptcy. Indeed, Heine himself occasionally suggests that his baptism had the unforeseen effect of strengthening his ties with Jewish culture. "It's ridiculous, but no sooner have I been baptized than I am being denounced as a Jew" (Es ist närrisch, kaum bin ich getauft, so werde ich als Jude verschrieen [*HB*, 1: 251).

87. In his 1507 tract *Der Judenspiegel,* Johannes Pfefferkorn (a converted Jew) demanded that Jews give up the practice of usury, attend Christian sermons, and dispose of all talmudic books. He followed up with several, yet more virulently anti-Semitic treatises—*Wie die blinden Juden ihr Ostern halten* and *Judenbeicht* (both 1508), and *Judenfeind* (1509)—all of which contended that the principal cause of Jewish resistance to conversion lay in their books, whose destruction he strenuously advocated. With the help of recommendations from the Dominican order, Pfefferkorn eventually succeeded in obtaining a decree (19 August 1509) from the emperor Maximilian I ordering the Jews to deliver to Pfefferkorn all books said to oppose the Christian faith; on this history, see Gilman, 27–56.

88. Metternich quoted in *HSS,* 6, 2: 353. Menzel's review of "The New Literature" (*Die junge Literatur*) only appeared in 1836 (in *Literatur-Blatt,* vol. 1–5), yet the main points of his critique had reached their audience through an earlier edition of his literary history, *Die deutsche Literatur.* See also Metternich's closing address delivered on the occasion of final ratification of the *Wiener Schlußakte* (12 June 1834), a landmark resolution adopting censorship and surveillance practices that were to be binding for all the member states of the German Federation. For the text of this resolution, see Huber, 123–35.

89. Heine's principal source for "Jehuda ben Halevy" was published five years before the poem's composition. Michael Sachs, *Die religiöse Poesie der Juden in Spanien* (The Religious Poetry of the Jews in Spain) appeared in Berlin in 1845. A much earlier book, Jacques Basnages *Histoire des juifs, depuis Jesus-christ jusqu'à présent* (The Hague, 1716) was among Heine's favorite readings during his involvement in the "Society for the Culture and Science of Judaism" in Berlin between 1823 and 1824. Also relevant is Markus Jost, *Geschichte der Israeliten seit der Zeit der Maccabäer bis auf unsere Tage, nach den Quellen bearbeitet* (History of the Israelites from the Times of the Maccabeans to the Present, Developed According to Original Sources [Berlin, 1820–28]).

90. For a *locus classicus* for the vicarious identifications of German romanticism with Indian and Persian myths and their rendition, "with hieroglyphic brevity," by the

Hebrew poets, see Friedrich Schlegel's *Lectures on the History of Ancient and Modern Literature* (1812–1814), 4th lecture (1988, 4: 57–63).

91. *Targum* is Aramaic for "translation," and the Greek Scholar Onkelos had rendered the Hebrew Torah into Aramaic, a translation made necessary because in the course of their exile, the Hebrews had begun to adopt Aramaic as their language. As the editors of Heine's *Historisch-kritische Gesamtausgabe* point out, his knowledge of these and other specifics of Jewish religious and linguistic culture is largely informed by Leopold Zunz, *Die gottesdienstlichen Vorträge der Juden* (The Ceremonial Discourse of the Jews [Berlin, 1832]); see Heine 1993, 3, 2: 896–910. For a discussion of Heine's poetic tribute to Jehuda Halevy in his 1851 *Hebrew Melodies*, see Skolnik.

92. In *Deutschland, ein Wintermärchen*, chap. 24, Heine laconically speaks of "Menzel and his Swabians" (*HSS*, 4: 634).

93. As Leopold Zunz explains in his 1832 study of Hebrew ceremonial discourse, *Tropp* identifies a ritualized form of singing recitation, assisted by special marks and punctuation in the text. For general commentary on this poem in *Romanzero,* see the commentary in Heine 1993, 3, 2: 906–8; as well as Cook, 310–17, and Prawer, 561–74. Commenting on Heine's portrayal of Halevy's apprenticeship in Torah studies and pronounciation, Prawer observes how Heine "shows us what must strike the modern non-Jewish European as odd and (at first blush) unappealing; but he tries with all the beauty of sound and rhythm at his command to convey the attraction such an ancient art may still exert" (566).

94. Wolfgang Killy repeatedly stresses Petrarchism's "complexion of stereotypical situations, gestures, forms and metaphors" (ein Komplex von stereotypen Situationen, Gebärden, Formen u. Metaphern [14: 197])

95. Heine's preference for the Hebrew spelling of Jerusalem dates back to his early years as a writer. See his letter to Moses Moser of 9 January 1824, where he paraphrases Psalm 137: "'May my right hand shrivel if I forget thee, Jeruscholayim,' such, more or less, is it said by the writer of Psalms, and such are my words too" ("Verwelke meine Rechte, wenn ich Deiner vergesse, Jeruscholayim," sind ungefähr die Worte des Psalmisten, und es sind auch noch immer meinigen [*HB*, 1: 133]); see also *Atta Troll,* chap. 20 (*HSS,* 4: 444–48). An intriguing restatement of the basic cultural divide between north and south (or, perhaps, west and east), Gentile and Jew, exile and homeland can be found in Fanny Lewald's *Autobiography.* Early on, she remarks on her intuitive preference for the opulent imagery and vividly descriptive, epic scope of oriental fairy tales, as opposed to the "sparse, anecdotal" quality of German fairy tale writing (1: 71).

Works Cited

Abbreviations used in citation follow the year of publication in square brackets.

Abraham, Nicolas, and Torok, Maria. 1994. *The Shell and the Kernel: Renewals of Psychoanalysis.* Translated and edited by Nicholas T. Rand. Chicago: University of Chicago Press. Originally published as *L'Écorce et le noyau* (Paris: Aubier Flammarion, 1978).

Abrams, Meyer H. 1970. "Structure and Style in the Greater Romantic Lyric." In *Romanticism and consciousness.* Edited by Harold Bloom. New York: Norton.

Adams, Hazard. 1983. *Philosophy of the Literary Symbolic.* Tallahassee: University Presses of Florida.

Adorno, Theodor. 1973. *Negative Dialectics.* Translated by E. B. Ashton. New York: Seabury Press. German original 1970.

———. 1974. *Minima Moralia: Reflections from Damaged Life.* Translated by E. F. N. Jephcott. London: New Left Books. German original 1951.

———. 1981. *In Search of Wagner.* New York: Verso.

———. 1989. *Kierkegaard: Construction of the Aesthetic.* Edited and translated by Robert Hullot-Kentor. Minneapolis: University of Minnesota Press.

———. 1991. *Notes to Literature.* Translated by Sherry Weber Nicholsen. 2 vols. New York: Columbia University Press.

———. 1997. *Aesthetic Theory.* Translated and edited by Robert Hulot-Kentor. Minneapolis: University of Minnesota Press.

———. 1998. [*AGS*]. *Gesammelte Schriften.* 20 vols. Darmstadt: Wissenschaftliche Buchgesellschaft.

———. 2003 [1973]. *Philosophy of Modern Music.* Translated by Anne G. Mitchell and Wesley V. Blomster. New York: Continuum.

Adorno, Theodor, and Max Horkheimer. 1972. *Dialectic of Enlightenment.* Translated by John Cumming. New York: Continuum.

Alewyn, Richard. 1966. "Ein Wort über Eichendorff." In *Eichendorff Heute*, ed. Paul Stöcklein. Darmstadt: Wissenschaftliche Buchgesellschaft.

Allison, David B., et al., eds. 1988. *Psychosis and Sexual Identity: Toward a Post-Analytic View of the Schreber Case.* Albany: State University of New York Press.

Althusser, Louis, and Étienne Balibar. 1979. *Reading "Capital."* New York: Verso.

Arendt, Hannah. 1997 [1957]. *Rahel Varnhagen: The Life of a Jewess.* Translated by Richard and Clara Winston. Edited by Liliane Weissberg. Baltimore: Johns Hopkins University Press.

Arnim, Ludwig Achim von. 1975. "Von Volksliedern." In Clemens Brentano, *Werke*, ed. Jürgen Behrens et al., vol. 6. Stuttgart: Kohlhammer.

Arnim, Ludwig Achim von, and Clemens Brentano, eds. 1995 [1806–8]. *Des Knaben Wunderhorn: Alte Deutsche Lieder.* Edited by Willi A. Koch. Darmstadt: Wissenschaftliche Buchgesellschaft.

Auerbach, Erich. 1984. "Figura." In id., *Scenes from the Drama of European Literature.* Minneapolis: University of Minnesota Press.

Austen, Jane. 1987 [1818]. *Persuasion.* Edited by D. W. Harding. Harmondsworth, U.K.: Penguin Books.

Austin, John L. 1973. *Philosophical Papers.* Oxford: Clarendon Press.

———. 1975. *How to Do Things with Words.* Cambridge, Mass.: Harvard University Press.

Baer, Ulrich. 2000. *Remnants of Song: Trauma and the Experience of Modernity in Charles Baudelaire and Paul Celan.* Stanford, Calif.: Stanford University Press.

Bage, Robert. 1792. *Man As He Is.* London: W. Lane.

Bainbridge, Simon. 1995. *Napoleon and English Romanticism.* New York: Cambridge University Press.

Balfour, Ian. 2002. *The Rhetoric of Romantic Prophecy.* Stanford, Calif.: Stanford University Press.

Barker-Benfield, G. J. 1992. *The Culture of Sensibility: Sex and Society in Eighteenth-Century Britain.* Chicago: University of Chicago Press.

Barrell, John. 1992. *The Birth of Pandora and the Division of Knowledge.* Philadelphia: University of Pennsylvania Press.

———. 2000. *Imagining the King's Death: Figurative Treason, Fantasies of Regicide, 1793–1796.* Oxford: Oxford University Press.

Bartels, Adolf. 1924. *Geschichte der Deutschen Literatur.* Leipzig: Haessel.

Barthes, Roland. 1991. *The Responsibility of Forms.* Translated by Richard Howard. Berkeley: University of California Press.

Batten, Guinn. 1998. *The Orphaned Imagination.* Durham, N.C.: Duke University Press.

Bayley, John. 1962. *Keats and Reality.* Proceedings of the British Academy, 48. London: Oxford University Press.

Behler, Ernst. 1993. *German Romantic Literary Theory.* Cambridge: Cambridge University Press.

Belke, Ingrid. 1988. "Zur Emanzipation der Juden in Preußen." In *Conditio Judaica,* ed. Hans Otto Horch and Horst Denkler, 1: 29–46. Tübingen: Niemeyer.

Bender, John. 1995. "Impersonal Violence: The Penetrating Gaze and the Field of Narration in *Caleb Williams.*" In *Vision and Textuality,* ed. Stephen Melville and Bill Readings. Durham, N.C.: Duke University Press.

Benjamin, Walter. 1968. *Illuminations.* Translated by Hannah Arendt. New York: Schocken Books.

———. 1980. *Illuminationen.* Frankfurt a / M: Suhrkamp.

———. 1982. *Ursprung des deutschen Trauerspiels.* Frankfurt a / M: Suhrkamp.

———. 1983. *Das Passagenwerk.* Edited by Rolf Tiedemann. Frankfurt a / M: Suhrkamp.

———. 1996. *Selected Writings, 1913–1926.* Edited by Marcus Bullock and Michael W. Jennings Cambridge, Mass.: Harvard University Press, 1996.

———. 1998. *The Origin of German Tragic Drama.* Translated by John Osborne. New York: Verso.

———. 1999a. *The Arcades Project.* Translated by Howard Eiland and Kevin McLaughlin. Cambridge, Mass.: Harvard University Press.

———. 1999b. *Selected Writings, 1926–1934.* Edited by Marcus Bullock et al. Cambridge, Mass: Harvard University Press.

Bentham, Jeremy. 1827. *Rationale of Judicial Evidence.* London: Hunt & Clarke.

———. 1988 [1789]. *The Principles of Morals and Legislation.* New York: Prometheus Books.

Berdahl, Robert M. 1988. *The Politics of the Prussian Nobility.* Princeton, N.J.: Princeton University Press.

Berlioz, Hector. 1969. *The Memoirs of Hector Berlioz.* Translated by David Cairns. New York: Knopf.

Bernstein, Michael André. 1994. *Foregone Conclusions: Against Apocalyptic History.* Berkeley: University of California Press.

Bernstein, Susan. 1995. "Journalism and German Identity: Communiqués from Heine, Wagner, and Adorno." *New German Critique* 66: 65–93.

———. 1998. *Virtuosity of the Nineteenth Century: Performing Music and Language in Heine, Liszt, Baudelaire.* Stanford, Calif.: Stanford University Press.

Biemel, Walter. 1959. *Die Bedeutung von Kants Begründung der Ästhetik für die Philosophie der Kunst.* Cologne: Kölner-Universitäts-Verlag.

Blackall, Eric A. *The Emergence of German as a Literary Language* (Ithaca, N.Y.: Cornell University Press, 1978)

Blackstone, William. 1979 [1765–69]. *Commentaries on the Laws of England.* Facsimile of the 1st ed. 4 vols. Chicago: University of Chicago Press

Blake, William. 1982 [*CPP*]. *The Complete Poetry and Prose.* Edited by David V. Erdman. New York: Doubleday.

———. 1993. *The Early Illuminated Books.* Edited by Morris Eaves, Robert N. Essick, and Joseph Viscomi. Princeton, N.J.: Princeton University Press.

———. 1995a. *The Continental Prophecies.* Edited by Detlef W. Dörrbecker. Princeton, N.J.: Princeton University Press.

———. 1995b. *The Urizen Books.* Edited by David Worrall. Princeton, N.J.: Princeton University Press, 1995.

Blakemore, Steven. 1988. *Burke and the Fall of Language: The French Revolution as Linguistic Event.* Hanover, N.H.: University Press of New England.

Blumenberg, Hans. 1983. *The Legitimacy of the Modern Age.* Translated by Robert M. Wallace. Cambridge, Mass.: MIT Press.

Börne, Ludwig. 1977. *Sämtliche Schriften.* Edited by Inge and Peter Rippmann. 5 vols. Dreieich: Melzer.

Botstein, Leon. 1994. "History, Rhetoric, and the Self: Robert Schumann and Music-Making in German-Speaking Europe, 1800–1860." In *Schumann and His World,* ed. Larry Todd. Princeton, N.J.: Princeton University Press.

Bourdieu, Pierre. 1984. *Distinction: A Social Critique of the Judgment of Taste.* Translated by Richard Nice. Cambridge, Mass.: Harvard University Press.

Bowie, Andrew. 1997. *From Romanticism to Critical Theory.* New York: Routledge.

Breazeale, Daniel. 1996. "The Theory of Practice and the Practice of Theory: Fichte and the 'Primacy of Practical Reason.'" *International Philosophical Quarterly* 36, 1: 47–64.

———. 2002. "The Spirit of the *Wissenschaftslehre.*" In *The Reception of Kant's Critical*

Philosophy: Fichte, Schelling, and Hegel, ed. Sally Sedgwick. Cambridge: Cambridge University Press.

Brenner, Michael, Vicki Caron, and Uri R. Kaufmann, eds. 2003. *Jewish Emancipation Reconsidered: The French and German Models.* Tübingen: Mohr & Siebeck.

Brentano, Clemens. 1975. *Werke.* Edited by Jürgen Behrens, Wolfgang Frühwald, et al. 38 vols. Stuttgart: Kohlhammer.

Breuer, Dieter. 1982. *Geschichte der literarischen Zensur in Deutschland.* Heidelberg: Quelle & Meyer.

Briegleb, Klaus. 1986. *Opfer Heine? Versuche über Schriftzüge der Revolution.* (Frankfurt a / M: Suhrkamp.

British Museum. Dept. of Prints and Drawings. 1870–54. *Catalogue of Prints and Drawings in the British Museum.* London: Trustees of the British Museum. Vols. 1–4 edited by F. G. Stephens; vols. 5–11, titled *Catalogue of Political and Personal Satires,* edited by M. D. George.

Bromwich, David. 1986. "Keats's Radicalism." *Studies in Romanticism* 25, 2: 197–210.

Brooks, Peter. 1992. *Reading for the Plot: Design and Intention in Narrative.* Cambridge, Mass.: Harvard University Press.

Brown, Marshall. 1979. *The Shape of German Romanticism.* Ithaca, N.Y.: Cornell University Press.

Burke, Edmund. 1986 [1790]. *Reflections on the Revolution in France.* Edited by Conor Cruise O'Brien. Harmondsworth, U.K.: Penguin Books.

Burton, Robert. 1989–94 [1621]. *The Anatomy of Melancholy.* 3 vols. Oxford: Oxford University Press.

Byron, George Gordon, Lord. 1982. *Selected Letters & Journals.* Edited by Leslie Marchand. London: Picador.

———. 1980–93. *The Complete Poetical Works.* Edited by Jerome McGann. 7 vols. Oxford: Oxford University Press

Calhoon, Kenneth. 1991. *Fatherland: Novalis, Freud, and the Discipline of Romance.* Detroit: Wayne State University Press.

Canuel, Mark. 2002. *Religion, Toleration, and British Writing, 1790–1830.* New York: Cambridge University Press.

Caruth, Cathy. 1995. *Trauma: Explorations in Memory.* Baltimore: Johns Hopkins University Press.

———. 1996. *Unclaimed Experience: Trauma, Narrative, and History.* Baltimore: Johns Hopkins University Press.

Cassirer, Ernst. 1981a [1924]. *Idee und Gestalt: Goethe, Schiller, Hölderlin, Kleist.* Darmstadt: Wissenschaftliche Buchgesellschaft.

———. 1981b. *Kant's Life and Thought.* Translated by James Haden. New Haven, Conn.: Yale University Press.

Castle, Terry. 1995. *The Female Thermometer: Eighteenth-Century Culture and the Invention of the Uncanny.* New York: Oxford University Press.

Chandler, James. 1998. *England in 1819: The Politics of Literary Culture and the Case of Romantic Historicism.* Chicago: University of Chicago Press.

Chatterton, Thomas. 1990 [1794]. *The Rowley Poems.* Oxford: Woodstock Books.

Christensen, Jerome. 1987. *Practicing Enlightenment: Hume and the Formation of a Literary Career.* Madison: University of Wisconsin Press.

———. 1993. *Lord Byron's Strength: Romantic Writing and Commercial Society.* Baltimore: Johns Hopkins University Press.

Chua, Daniel K. 1999. *Absolute Music and the Construction of Meaning.* Cambridge: Cambridge University Press.

Claeys, Gregory, ed. 1995. *Political Writings of the 1790s.* 8 vols. London: Pickering & Chatto.

Clemit, Pamela. 1993. *The Godwinian Novel: The Rational Fictions of Godwin, Brockden Brown, Mary Shelley.* Oxford: Clarendon Press.

Cobbett, William. 1998. *Selected Writings.* Edited by James Epstein. 6 vols. London: Pickering & Chatto.

Cole, Steven. 1995. "Evading Politics: The Poverty of Historicizing Romanticism." *Studies in Romanticism* 34, 1: 29–49.

Coleridge, Samuel Taylor. 1971. *Lectures, 1795, on Politics and Religion.* Edited by Lewis Patton and Peter Mann. Vol. 1 of *Collected Works.* Princeton, N.J.: Princeton University Press.

———. 1972. *Lay Sermons.* Edited by R. J. White. Vol. 6 of *Collected Works.* Princeton, N.J.: Princeton University Press.

———. 1978. *Essays on His Times in the Morning Post and The Courier.* Edited by David V. Erdman. Vol. 3 of *Collected Works.* Princeton, N.J.: Princeton University Press.

———. 1980. *The Notebooks of Samuel Taylor Coleridge.* Vol. 2. Edited by Kathleen Coburn. Princeton: Princeton University Press.

———. 1983. *Biographia Literaria.* Edited by James Engell and Walter Jackson Bate. Vol. 7 of *Collected Works.* 2 vols. Princeton, N.J.: Princeton University Press.

———. 1990. *Table Talk.* Edited by Carl Woodring. Vol. 14 of *Collected Works.* 2 vols. Princeton, N.J.: Princeton University Press.

———. 1993. *Aids to Reflection.* Edited by John Beer. Vol. 9 of *Collected Works.* Princeton, N.J.: Princeton University Press.

———. 1995. *Shorter Works and Fragments.* Edited by H. J. Jackson and J. R. de J. Jackson. Vol. 11 of *Collected Works.* 2 vols. Princeton, N.J.: Princeton University Press.

———. 1980–2000. *Marginalia.* Edited by George Whalley and H. J. Jackson. Vol. 12 of *Collected Works.* Princeton, N.J.: Princeton University Press.

———. 2001. *Poetical Works.* Edited by J. C. C. Mays. Vol. 16 of *Collected Works.* 3 vols. Princeton, N.J.: Princeton University Press,

Colley, Linda. 1994. *Britons: Forging the Nation, 1707–1837.* New Haven, Conn.: Yale University Press.

Cook, Roger F. 1998. *By the Rivers of Babylon.* Detroit: Wayne State University Press.

Corngold, Stanley. 1986. *The Fate of the Self.* New York: Columbia University Press.

———. 1998. *Complex Pleasure: Forms of Feeling in German Literature.* Stanford, Calif.: Stanford University Press.

———. 2002. "Implications of Influence: On Hölderlin's Reception of Rousseau." In *Romantic Poetry,* ed. Angela Esterhammer. Amsterdam: John Benjamins.

Cox, Jeffrey. 1998. *Poetry and Politics in the Cockney School : Keats, Shelley, Hunt, and their Circle.* New York: Cambridge University Press.

Creuzer, Georg Friedrich. 1836–43. *Symbolik und Mythologie der alten Völker, besonders der Griechen.* 2d ed. Leipzig.

Cumming, Naomi. 2000. *The Sonic Self: Musical Subjectivity and Signification.* Bloomington: Indiana University Press.

Curtius, Ernst Robert. 1914. "Das Schematismuskapitel in Kants *Kritik der Reinen Vernunft.*" *Kant-Studien* 19: 338–66.

———. 1967. *European Literature and the Latin Middle Ages.* Translated by Willard R. Trask Princeton, N.J.: Princeton University Press.

Dahlhaus, Carl. 1980. *Between Romanticism and Modernism.* Berkeley: University of California Press.

———. 1984. *Die Musiktheorie im 18. und 19. Jahrhundert.* Darmstadt: Wissenschaftliche Buchgesellschaft.

———. 1988. *Klassische und Romantische Musikästhetik.* Laaber, Germany: Laaber Verlag.

———. 1989. *Nineteenth-Century Music.* Translated by J. Bradford Robinson. Berkeley: University of California Press.

Daston, Lorraine. 1988. *Classical Probability in the Enlightenment.* Princeton: Princeton University Press.

Darnton, Robert. 1992. "History of Reading." In *New Perspectives on Historical Writing,* ed. Peter Burke. University Park, Pa.: Pennsylvania University Press

Darwin, Charles. 1979. *Darwin: A Norton Critical Edition.* Edited by Philip Appleman. New York: Norton.

Daverio, John. 1997. *Robert Schumann: Herald of a "New Poetic Age."* Oxford: Oxford University Press.

Davie, Donald. 1967. *Purity of Diction in English Verse.* London: Routledge.

Dawkins, Richard. 1989. *The Selfish Gene.* Oxford: Oxford University Press.

De Man, Paul. 1979. *Allegories of Reading:* Figural Language in Rousseau, Nietzsche, Rilke, and Proust. New Haven, Conn.: Yale University Press.

———. 1983. *Blindness and Insight.* Minneapolis: University of Minnesota Press.

———. 1996. *Aesthetic Ideology.* Minneapolis: University of Minnesota Press.

Deane, Seamus. 1988. *The French Revolution and Enlightenment in England.* Cambridge, Mass.: Harvard University Press.

Derrida, Jacques. 1974. *Of Grammatology.* Translated by Gayatri Chakravorty Spivak. Baltimore: Johns Hopkins University Press.

———. 1978. *Writing and Difference.* Chicago: University of Chicago Press.

———. 1980. *Margins of Philosophy.* Translated by Alan Bass. Chicago: University of Chicago Press.

Dickstein, Morris. 1971. *Keats and His Poetry: A Study in Development.* Chicago: University of Chicago Press.

Dummett, Michael. 1978. "Can an Effect Precede Its Cause?" In id., *Truth and Other Enigmas.* Cambridge, Mass.: Harvard University Press.

Dwyer, John. 1998. *The Age of Passions: An Interpretation of Adam Smith and Scottish Enlightenment Culture.* East Linton, Scotland: Tuckwell Press.

Eagleton, Terry. 1990. *The Ideology of the Aesthetic.* Oxford: Oxford University Press.

———. 1996. *The Illusions of Postmodernism.* Oxford: Blackwell.

Eaves, Morris. 1992. *The Counter-arts Conspiracy: Art and Industry in the Age of Blake.* Ithaca, N.Y.: Cornell University Press.

Edelman, Bernard. 1987. *The House That Kant Built.* Translated by Graeme Hunter. Toronto: Canadian Philosophical Monographs. Originally published as *La Maison de Kant: Conte moral* (Paris: Payot, 1984).

Ederer, Hannelore. 1979. *Die literarische Mimesis entfremdeter Sprache.* Cologne: Pahl-Rugenstein.

Eichendorff, Joseph Freiherr von. 1958. *Neue Gesamtausgabe.* Edited by Gerhart Baumann. 4 vols. Stuttgart: Cotta.

———. 1984. *Sämtliche Werke: Historisch-Kritische Ausgabe.* Edited by Hermann Kunisch and Helmut Koopmann. 15 vols. Tübingen: Max Niemeyer.

———. 1996 [*EW*]. *Werke.* Edited by Jost Perfahl and Ansgar Hillach. 2 vols. Düsseldorf: Artemis & Winkler.

Eilenberg, Susan. 1992. *Strange Power of Speech.* New York: Oxford University Press.

Eliot, George. 1995 [1876]. *Daniel Deronda.* Edited by Terence Cave. Harmondsworth, U.K.: Penguin Books

Eliot, T. S. 1978. *Selected Essays.* New York: Harcourt, Brace & Jovanovich.

Ellison, Julie. 1999. *Cato's Tears: The Making of Anglo-American Emotion.* Chicago: University of Chicago Press.

Emerson, Ralph Waldo. 1987. *The Essays of Ralph Waldo Emerson.* Edited by Alfred R. Ferguson and Jean Ferguson Carr. Cambridge, Mass.: Harvard University Press, Belknap Press.

Emsley, Clive. 1985. "Repression, 'terror' and the Rule of Law in England During the Decade of the French Revolution." *English Historical Review* 100: 801–25.

Epstein, James. 1994. *Radical Expression: Political Language, Ritual, and Symbol in England, 1790–1850.* New York: Oxford University Press.

Erskine, Thomas. 1810. *The Speeches of the Hon. Thomas Erskine.* 3 vols. London: Ridgway.

Eschwege, Helmut. 1980. *Die Synagoge in der deutschen Geschichte.* Wiesbaden: Fourier.

Esterhammer, Angela. 2000. *The Romantic Performative: Language and Action in British and German Romanticism.* Stanford, Calif.: Stanford University Press.

Ferguson, Frances. 1992. *Solitude and the Sublime.* New York: Routledge.

———. 2002. "Envy Rising: The Progress of an Emotion." *English Literary History* 69: 889–905.

Ferris, David. 2000. *Schumann's Eichendorff Liederkreis and the Genre of the Romantic Cycle.* New York: Oxford University Press.

Fichte, Johann Gottlieb. 1973 [1793]. *Beitrag zur Berichtigung der Urtheile des Publikums über die französische Revolution.* Edited by Richard Schottky. Hamburg: Meiner.

———. 1964–95. *Werke.* Edited by Reinhard Lauth and Hans Jacob. Stuttgart: F. Frommann.

———. 1970 [*SK*]. *The Science of Knowledge.* Edited by Peter Heath and John Lachs. New York: Appleton Crofts.

———. 1979 [1794]. *Grundlage der gesamten Wissenschaftslehre.* Edited by Wilhelm G. Jacobs. Hamburg: Meiner.

Fish, Stanley. 1989. *Doing What Comes Naturally.* Durham, N.C.: Duke University Press.

Fisher, Philip. 2002. *The Vehement Passions.* Princeton, N.J.: Princeton University Press.

Flesch, William. 1991. "Quoting Poetry." *Critical Inquiry* 18 (Autumn): 42–63.

Foster, Michael. 1792. *Discourse on Treason* (1783). Reprinted in *Report of Some Proceedings on the Commission for the Trial of the Rebels in the Year 1746, in the County of Surrey; and of other Crown Cases.* 3d ed. London: E. & R. Brooke.

Frank, Manfred. 1969. "Die Philosophie des sogenannten 'magischen Idealismus.'" *Eupherion* 63: 88–116.

———. 1975. *Der unendliche Mangel an Sein.* Frankfurt a / M: Suhrkamp.

———. 1986. *Die Unhintergehbarkeit von Individualität.* Frankfurt a / M: Suhrkamp.

———. 1989a. *Einführung in die frühromantische Ästhetik.* Frankfurt a / M: Suhrkamp.

———. 1989b. *What Is Neostructuralism?* Translated by Sabine Wilke and Richard Gray. Minneapolis: University of Minnesota Press.

Frank, Manfred, and Gerhard Kurz. 1977. "Ordo Inversus: Zu einer Reflexionsfigur bei Novalis, Hölderlin, Kleist und Kafka." In *Geist und Zeichen: Festschrift für Arthur Henkel.* Heidelberg: Winter.

Freedman, Diane P., Olivia Frey, and Frances Murphy Zauhar, eds. 1993. *The Intimate Critique: Autobiographical Literary Criticism.* Durham, N.C.: Duke University Press.

Frei, Hans W. 1974. *The Eclipse of Biblical Narrative: A Study in Eighteenth and Nineteenth Century Hermeneutics.* New Haven, Conn.: Yale University Press.

Freimark, Peter. 1980. "Sprachverhalten und Assimilation: Die Situation der Juden in Norddeutschland in der 1. Hälfte des 19. Jahrhunderts." *Saeculum* 31: 240–61.

Freud, Sigmund. 1955 [1920]. *Beyond the Pleasure Principle.* In vol. 18 of *The Standard Edition of the Complete Psychological Works of Sigmund Freud.* London: Hogarth Press and the Institute of Psycho-Analysis..

———. 1963a [*FCH*]. *Three Case Histories.* Edited by Philip Rieff. New York: Collier Books.

———. 1963b. *General Psychological Theory.* Edited by Philip Rieff. New York: Collier Books, 1963.

———. 1964 [1939]. *Moses and Monotheism.* In vol. 23 of *The Standard Edition of the Complete Psychological Works of Sigmund Freud.* London: Hogarth Press and the Institute of Psycho-Analysis.

———. 1982 [*FSA*]. *Studienausgabe.* Edited by Alexander Mitscherlich. Frankfurt a / M: S. Fischer.

Freund, Ismar. 2004 [1912]. *Die Emanzipation der Juden in Preußen unter besonderer Berücksichtigung des Gesetzes vom 11. März 1812.* 2 vols. Hildesheim: G. Olms.

Frey, Hans-Jost. 1996. *Studies in Poetic Discourse: Mallarmé, Baudelaire, Rimbaud, Hölderlin.* Translated by William Whobrey. Stanford, Calif.: Stanford University Press.

Friedrich, Hugo. 1956. *Die Struktur der Modernen Lyrik.* Hamburg: Rowohlt.

Fries, Jakob Friedrich. 1816. *Über die Gefährdung des Wohlstandes und Charakters der Deutschen durch die Juden.* Heidelberg: Mohr & Winter.

Frühwald, Wolfgang. 1977. *Eichendorff Chronik: Daten zu Leben und Werk.* Munich: Hanser.

———. 1979. "Der Regierungsrat Joseph von Eichendorff." *Internationales-Archiv-für-Sozialgeschichte-der-Deutschen-Literatur,* 4: 37–67.

———. 1988. "Antijudäismus in der Zeit der deutschen Romantik." In *Conditio Judaica,* vol. 2, ed. Hans Otto Horch and Horst Denkler. Tübingen: Niemeyer.

Fukuyama, Francis. 1992. *The End of History and the Last Man.* New York: Free Press.

———. 2003. *Our Posthuman Future: Consequences of the Biotechnology Revolution.* New York: Farrar, Straus & Giroux.

Furniss, Tom. 1991. "Gender in Revolution: Edmund Burke and Mary Wollstonecraft." In *Revolution in Writing,* ed. Kelvin Everest. Philadelphia: Open University Press.

———. 1993. *Edmund Burke's Aesthetic Ideology.* New York: Cambridge University Press.

Gadamer, Hans-Georg. 1960. *Wahrheit und Methode: Grundzüge einer philosophischen Hermeneutik*. Tübingen: J. C. B. Mohr.

———. 1975. *Truth and Method*. Translated by Garrett Barden and John Cumming. New York: Seabury.

Gasché, Rodolphe. 2002. *Idea of Form: Rethinking Kant's Aesthetics*. Stanford, Calif.: Stanford University Press.

Gay, Peter. 1988. *Freud: A Life for Our Time*. New York: Norton.

———. 1993. *The Cultivation of Hatred. Vol. 3 of The Bourgeois Experience, Victoria to Freud*. New York: Norton.

Gehlen, Arnold. 1963. *Studien zur Anthropologie und Soziologie*. Berlin: Luchterhand.

Gelber, Mark H. 1992. *The Jewish Reception of Heinrich Heine*. Tübingen: Niemeyer.

Geulen, Eva. 2000. "Endgames: Reconstructing Adorno's 'End of Art.'" *New German Critique* 81, 3: 153–68.

Gibson, Nigel, and Andrew Rubin, eds. 2002. *Adorno: A Critical Reader*. Oxford: Blackwell.

Giddens, Anthony. 1990. *The Consequences of Modernity*. Stanford, Calif.: Stanford University Press.

Gillespie, Gerald. 1989. "Hieroglyphics of Finality in Eichendorff's Lyrics." *German Life and Letters* 42, 3: 203–18.

Gilman, Sander L., and Jack Zipes. 1997. *The Yale Companion to Jewish Writing and Thought in German Culture, 1096–1996*. New Haven, Conn.: Yale University Press.

Gilman, Sander L. 1986. *Jewish Self-Hatred: Anti-Semitism and the Hidden Language of the Jews*. Baltimore: Johns Hopkins University Press.

Godwin, William. 1797. *The Enquirer: Reflections on Education, Manners and Literature*. London: G. G. Robinson.

———. 1832 [1805]. *Fleetwood, or, The New Man of Feeling*. Standard Novels, No. 22. London: R. Bentley.

———. 1970 [1794] [GCW]. *Caleb Williams*. Edited by David McCracken. London: Oxford University Press.

———. 1985 [1793] [*GPJ*]. *Enquiry Concerning Political Justice*. Edited by Isaac Kramnick. Harmondsworth, U.K.: Penguin Books.

———. 1988 [1794] [*GCW*]. *Things as They Are, or, The Adventures of Caleb Williams*. Edited by Maurice Hindle. Harmondsworth, U.K.: Penguin Books.

Goethe, Johann Wolfgang von. 1981. *Werke*. Edited by Erich Trunz. 14 vols. Munich: C. H. Beck.

Goldsmith, Steven. 1996. "Blake's Agitation." *South Atlantic Quarterly* 95, 3: 753–96.

Goodson, A. C. 1988. *Verbal Imagination: Coleridge and the Language of Modern Criticism*. New York: Oxford University Press.

Goodwin, Albert. 1979. *The Friends of Liberty: The English Democratic Movement in the Age of the French Revolution*. Cambridge, Mass.: Harvard University Press.

Görres, Joseph. 1926 [1807]. *Die teutschen Volksbücher*. In *Gesammelte Schriften*, vol. 3, pt. 1. Cologne: Gilde.

Gössmann, Wilhelm, and Klaus-Hinrich Roth. 1994. *Poetisierung-Politisierung: Deutschlandbilder in der Literatur bis 1848*. Munich: Schöningh.

Gössmann, Wilhelm, and Manfred Windfuhr. 1990. *Heinrich Heine im Spannungsfeld von Literatur und Wissenschaft*. Hagen: Reimar Hobbing.

Gould, Stephen Jay. 2002. *The Structure of Evolutionary Theory.* Cambridge, Mass.: Harvard University Press.

Grab, Walter. 1991. *Der Deutsche Weg der Judenemanzipation, 1789–1938.* Munich: Piper.

Graham, Elaine L. 2002. *Representations of the Post / Human: Monsters, Aliens, and Others in Popular Culture.* New Brunswick, N.J.: Rutgers University Press.

Graubner, Hans. 1977. "'Mitteilbarkeit' und 'Lebensgefühl' in Kants *Kritik der Urteilskraft.* Zur kommunikativen Bedeutung des Ästhetischen." In *Urszenen: Literaturwissenschaft als Diskursanalyse und Diskurskritik,* ed. Friedrich Kittler and Horst Turk. Frankfurt a / M: Suhrkamp.

Grebing, Helga. 1974. *Aktuelle Theorien über Faschismus und Konservatismus: Eine Kritik.* Stuttgart: Kohlhammer.

Greiner, Martin. 1953. *Zwischen Biedermeier und Bourgeoisie; ein Kapitel deutscher Literaturgeschichte.* Göttingen: Vandenhoeck & Ruprecht.

Grimm. See Melchior, Friedrich, baron von Grimm.

Grimminger, Rolf, ed. 1987. *Hansers Sozialgeschichte der deutschen Literatur.* Munich: Carl Hanser.

Grossman, Jeffrey A. 2000. *The Discourse on Yiddish in Germany: From the Enlightenment to the Second Empire.* New York: Camden House.

Guillory, John. 1993. *Cultural Capital: The Problem of Literary Canon Formation.* Chicago: University of Chicago Press.

Gutzkow, Karl Ferdinand. 1998. *Schriften,* 3 vols. Frankfurt a / M: zweitausendeins.

Guyer, Paul. 1979. *Kant and the Claims of Taste.* Cambridge, Mass.: Harvard University Press.

Habermas, Jürgen. 1994. *Structural Transformation of the Public Sphere.* Translated by Thomas Burger. Cambridge, Mass.: MIT Press.

———. 1996. "Heinrich Heine und die Rolle des Intellektuellen in Deutschland." *Merkur* 50, 12: 1122–37.

———. 2002. *Future of Human Nature.* Cambridge: Polity Press.

Hacking, Ian. 1975. *The Emergence of Probability.* Cambridge: Cambridge University Press.

———. 1990. *The Taming of Chance.* Cambridge: Cambridge University Press.

Hahn, Barbara, and Ursula Isselstein, eds. 1987. *Rahel Levin Varnhagen: Die Wiederentdeckung einer Schriftstellerin.* Göttingen: Vandenhoeck & Ruprecht.

Hamann, Johann Georg. 1949. "Aesthetica in Nuce." In *Sturm und Drang: Kritische Schriften,* ed. Erich Loewenthal. Heidelberg: Lambert & Schneider.

Hanslick, Eduard. 1986. *On the Musically Beautiful: A Contribution Towards the Revision of the Aesthetics of Music.* Translated and edited by Geoffrey Payzant. Indianapolis: Hackett Pub. Co.

———. 1991 [1854]. *Vom Musikalisch-Schönen: Ein Beitrag zur Revision der Ästhetik der Tonkunst.* Darmstadt: Wissenschaftliche Buchgesellschaft.

Hardt, Michael, and Antonio Negri, 2000. *Empire. Cambridge, Mass.: Harvard University Press.*

Hartman, Geoffrey H. 1971. *Wordsworth's Poetry, 1787–1814.* Cambridge, Mass.: Harvard University Press.

———. 1980. *Criticism in the Wilderness: The Study of Literature Today.* New Haven, Conn.: Yale University Press.

———. 1986. "The Poetics of Prophecy." In id., *The Unremarkable Wordsworth.* Minneapolis: University of Minnesota Press.

Hauschild, Jan-Christoph, ed. 1985. *Verboten! Das Junge Deutschland 1835.* Düsseldorf: Droste.

Haverkamp, Anselm. 1988. "Kryptische Subjektivität: Archäologie des Lyrisch-Individuellen." In *Individualität,* ed. Manfred Frank and Anselm Haverkamp. Munich: Fink.

———. 1996. *Leaves of Mourning: Hölderlin's Late Work, with an Essay on Keats and Melancholy.* Albany: State University of New York Press.

Hayles, N. Katherine. 1999. *How We Became Posthuman: Virtual Bodies in Cybernetics, Literature, and Informatics.* Chicago: University of Chicago Press.

Hays, Mary. 1996 [1796]. *Memoirs of Emma Courtney.* Edited by Eleanor Ty. New York: Oxford University Press.

Hazlitt, William. 1998. [*HSW*]. *Selected Writings.* Edited by Duncan Wu. 9 vols. London: Pickering & Chatto.

Heer, Friedrich. 1972. "Der Konservative und die Reaktion." *Aurora:-Jahrbuch-der-Eichendorff-Gesellschaft* 32: 30–58.

Hegel, Georg Friedrich Wilhelm. 1828. "Solgers nachgelassene Schriften und Briefwechsel." In *Jahrbücher für wissenschaftliche Kritik.* Stuttgart: Cotta.

———. 1952. *Phänomenologie des Geistes.* Edited by Johannes Hoffmeister. Hamburg: Felix Meiner.

———. 1970. *Enzyklopädie der Philosophischen Wissenschaften.* Edited by Eva Moldenhauer and Karl Markus Michel. Frankfurt a / M: Suhrkamp.

———. 1975. *Aesthetics: Lectures on Fine Art.* Translated by T. M. Knox. Oxford: Clarendon Press.

———. 1977. *Phenomenology of Spirit.* Translated by A. V. Miller. New York: Oxford University Press.

———. 1978. *Hegel's Philosophy of Subjective Spirit.* Part 3 of *Enzyklopädie der philosophischen Wissenschaften im Grundrisse.* Translated and edited by M. J. Petry. Dordrecht, Holland: D. Reidel.

———. 1986. *Vorlesungen über die Ästhetik.* Edited by Eva Moldenhauer and Karl Markus Michel. 3 vols. Frankfurt a / M: Suhrkamp.

———. 1989. *Hegel's Science of Logic.* Translated by A. V. Miller. Atlantic Highlands, N.J.: Humanities Press.

Hehn, Victor. 1909. *Gedanken über Goethe.* Berlin: Borntraeger.

Heidegger, Martin. 1950. *Holzwege.* Frankfurt a / M: Klostermann.

———. 1965. *Kant and the Problem of Metaphysics.* Translated by James Churchill. Bloomington: Indiana University Press.

———. 1962. *Being and Time.* Translated by John MacQuarrie and Edward Robinson. New York: Harper & Row.

———. 1979 [1927]. *Sein und Zeit.* Tübingen: Max Niemeyer.

———. 1983. *Die Grundbegriffe der Metaphysik.* Frankfurt a / M: Klostermann.

———. 1995. *Fundamental Concepts of Metaphysics.* Translated by William McNeill and Nicholas Walker. Bloomington: Indiana University Press.

Heine, Heinrich. 1855. *Lutèce: Lettres sur la vie politique, artistique et sociale de la France.* Bibliothèque contemporaine, 2d ser. Paris: Michel Lévy Frères, 1855.

———. 1950–51 [*HB*]. *Briefe*. Edited by Friedrich Hirth. Mainz: Kupferberg.

———. 1973. *Selected Works*. Translated by Max Knight. Edited by Helen Mustard. New York: Random House.

———. 1981. *Confessions* and *Leo Tolstoy: A Confession*. Translated by Peter Heinegg. N.p.: Joseph Simon.

———. 1982. *Complete Poems*. Translated by Hal Draper. Boston: Suhrkamp/Insel.

———. 1993. *Historisch-kritische Gesamtausgabe*. Edited by Manfred Windfuhr. 16 vols. in 23. Hamburg: Hoffman & Campe.

———. 1995. *Songs of Love & Grief*. Translated by Walter Arndt. Edited by Jeffrey L. Sammons. Evanston, Ill.: Northwestern University Press.

———. 1997 [*HSS*]. *Sämtliche Schriften*. Edited by Klaus Briegleb. [6 vols. in 7. Munich: Carl Hanser Verlag, *1968–76*.] Reprint. Munich: dtv.

Henrich, Dieter. 1982. "Fichte's Original Insight." Translated by David R. Lachterman. *Contemporary German Philosophy* 1 (1982): 15–47.

Herder, Johann Gottlieb. 1877–1913. *Werke*. Edited by B. Suphan. 33 vols. Berlin: Weidman.

Hermand, Jost. 1993. "Der 'deutsche' Jude H. Heine." In *Dichter und Ihre Nation*, ed. Helmut Scheuer. Frankfurt a / M: Suhrkamp.

Herrnstein-Smith, Barbara. 1991. "Belief and Resistance: A Symmetrical Account." *Critical Inquiry* 18: 125–39.

Herzig, Arno. 1988. "Das Assimilationsproblem aus jüdischer Sicht (1780–1880)." In *Conditio Judaica*, ed. Hans Otto Horch and Horst Denkler, 1: 10–28. Tübingen: Niemeyer.

———. 1997. *Jüdische Geschichte in Deutschland*. Munich, C. H. Beck.

Heuberger, Georg, and Anton Merk. 2000. *Moritz Daniel Oppenheim: Jewish Identity in Nineteenth-Century Art*. Frankfurt a.M.: Jüdisches Museum Frankfurt am Main.

High, James L., ed. 1876. *Speeches of Lord Erskine*. 3 vols. Chicago: Callaghan.

Hirschman, Albert O. 1977. *The Passions and the Interests: Political Arguments for Capitalism Before Its Triumph*. Princeton, N.J.: Princeton University Press.

Hobsbawm, Eric. 1968. *Industry and Empire*. Harmondsworth, U.K.: Penguin Books.

———. 1990. *Nations and Nationalism since 1780: Programme, Myth, Reality*. Cambridge: Canto.

Hobsbawm, Eric, and Terence Ranger, eds. 1983. *The Invention of Tradition*. Cambridge: Cambridge University Press.

Hofstaetter, Ulla. 1992. "'Das verschimmelte Philisterland': Philisterkritik bei Brentano, Eichendorff und Heine." In *Romantik im Vormärz*, ed. Burghard Dedner and Ulla Hofstaetter. Marburg: Hitzeroth.

Hohendahl, Peter Uwe. 1989. *Building a National Literature*. Ithaca, N.Y.: Cornell University Press.

———. 1995. *Prismatic Thought: Theodor Adorno*. Lincoln: University of Nebraska Press.

Hohendahl, Peter Uwe, and Sander L. Gilman. 1991. *Heinrich Heine and the Occident*. Lincoln: University of Nebraska Press.

Holcroft, Thomas. 1973. *The Adventures of Hugh Trevor*. Edited by Seamus Deane. London: Oxford University Press.

Hölderlin, Friedrich. 1943–85. *Sämtliche Werke*. Edited by Friedrich Beissner. 15 books in 8 vols. Stuttgart: Kohlhammer & Cotta.

———. 1987. *Essays and Letters on Theory.* Translated and edited by Thomas Pfau. Albany: State University of New York Press.

———. 1994. *Poems and Fragments.* Translated by Michael Hamburger. London: Anvil Press.

Holub, Robert C. 1997. "Personal Roots and German Traditions: The Jewish Element in Heine's Turn Against Romanticism." In *Heinrich Heine und die Romantik—Heinrich Heine and Romanticism,* ed. Markus Winkler. Tübingen: Max Niemeyer.

Howell, Thomas, comp. 1816–28. *A Complete Collection of State Trials and Proceedings for High Treason and Other Crimes and Misdemeanors from the Earliest Period to the Year 1783.* London: T. C. Hansard for Longman, Hurst, Rees, Orme, and Brown [etc.].

Huber, Ernst Rudolf, ed. 1961. *Dokumente zur Deutschen Verfassungsgeschichte,* vol. 1. Stuttgart: Kohlhammer.

Humboldt, Wilhelm von. 1996. *Werke.* 5 vols. Darmstadt: Wissenschaftliche Buchgesellschaft.

Hume, David. 2000 [1740]. *A Treatise of Human Nature.* Edited by David Fate Norton and Mary J. Norton. Oxford: Oxford University Press.

Husserl, Edmund. 1980 [1900]. *Logische Untersuchungen.* Tübingen: Niemeyer. Translated by J. N. Findlay as *Logical Investigations,* edited by Dermot Moran (New York : Routledge, 2001).

Hyppolite, Jean. 1974. *Genesis and Structure of Hegel's Phenomenology of Spirit.* Translated by Samuel Cherniak and John Heckman. Evanston, Ill.: Northwestern University Press.

Immermann, Karl. N.d. *Immermanns Werke.* Edited by Harry Maync. 5 vols. Leipzig: Bibliographisches Institut.

Jakobson, Roman. 1987. *Language in Literature.* Cambridge, Mass.: Harvard University Press.

Jameson, Fredric. 1971. *Marxism and Form.* Princeton, N.J.: Princeton University Press.

———. 1981. *The Political Unconscious: Narrative as a Socially Symbolic Act.* Ithaca, N.Y.: Cornell University Press.

———. 1990. *Late Marxism: Adorno, or, The Persistence of the Dialectic.* London: Verso.

———. 1993. *Postmodernism.* Durham, N.C.: Duke University Press.

Jay, Martin. 1984. *Adorno.* Cambridge, Mass.: Harvard University Press.

Jefferson, Thomas. 1982. *The Papers of Thomas Jefferson.* Edited by Julian P. Boyd. 30 vols. Princeton, N.J.: Princeton University Press.

Johnson, Anthony. 1982. "Jakobsonian Literary Theory and Literary Semiotics: Toward a Generative Typology of the Text." *New Literary History* 14, 1: 33–61.

Johnson, Claudia. 1995. *Equivocal Beings: Politics, Gender, and Sentimentality in the 1790s.* Chicago: University of Chicago Press.

Kant, Immanuel. 1951 [*CrJ*]. *Critique of Judgment.* Translated by J. H. Bernard. New York: Hafner.

———. 1965 [1781]. *Critique of Pure Reason.* Translated by Norman Kemp-Smith. New York: Macmillan.

———. 1968a. *Kritik der Praktischen Vernunft.* Vol. 7 of *Werkausgabe,* ed. Wilhelm Weischedel. Frankfurt a / M: Suhrkamp.

———. 1968b. *Kritik der Reinen Vernunft.* Vols. 3 and 4 of of *Werkausgabe.* Edited by Wilhelm Weischedel. Frankfurt a / M: Suhrkamp.

———. 1968c. *Kritik der Urteilskraft.* Vol. 10 of *Werkausgabe,* ed. Wilhelm Weischedel. Frankfurt a / M: Suhrkamp.

———. 1968d. *Schriften zur Metaphysik und Logik.* Vol. 5 of *Werkausgabe,* ed. Wilhelm Weischedel. Frankfurt a / M: Suhrkamp.

———. 1983. *Perpetual Peace and Other Essays.* Translated by Ted Humphrey. Indianapolis: Hackett.

Kaplan, Cora. 1986. *Sea Changes: Essays on Culture and Feminism.* New York: Verso.

Katz, Jacob. 1998. *Out of the Ghetto: The Social Background of Jewish Emancipation, 1770–1870.* Syracuse, N.Y.: Syracuse University Press.

Kaufman, Robert. 2000. "Red Kant: or The Persistence of the Third *Critique* in Adorno and Jameson." *Critical Inquiry* 26: 682–724.

———. 2001. "Negatively Capable Dialectics: Keats, Vendler, Adorno, and the Theory of the Avantgarde." *Critical Inquiry* 27: 354–84.

Keach, William C. 2001. "Byron Reads Keats." In *The Cambridge Companion to Keats,* ed. Susan Wolfson. New York: Cambridge University Press.

Keats, John. 1958 [*LJK*]. *The Letters of John Keats.* Edited by Hyder E. Rollins. 2 vols. Cambridge, Mass.: Harvard University Press.

———. 1970 [*KCP*]. *The Complete Poems of John Keats.* Edited by Miriam Allott. London: Longman.

Keen, Paul. 1999. *The Crisis of Literature in the 1790s: Print Culture and the Public Sphere.* Cambridge: Cambridge University Press.

Khalip, Jacques. 2004. "Negative Capabilities: Anonymity, Subjectivity, and Romantic Agency." Ph.D. diss., Duke University.

Killy, Walter, ed. 1988. *Literaturlexikon.* 15 vols. Gütersloh: Bertelsmann.

Klancher, Jon. 1995. "Godwin and the Republican Romance: Genre, Politics, and Contingency in Literary History." *MLQ* 56, 2 *(1995)*: 145–65.

Kocka, Jürgen. 1989–94. *Bildungsbürgertum im 19. Jahrhundert.* 4 vols. Stuttgart: Klett-Cotta.

Koerner, Joseph Leo. 1990. *Caspar David Friedrich and the Subject of Landscape.* New Haven, Conn.: Yale University Press.

Kojève, Alexander. 1980. *Introduction to the Reading of Hegel.* Translated by James H. Nichols Ithaca, N.Y.: Cornell University Press.

Kofman, Sarah. 1986. *Melancholie der Kunst.* Translated by Birgit Wagner. Vienna: Passagen. Originally published as *Mélancolie de l'art* (Paris: Éditions Galilée, 1985.)

———. 1993. *Nietzsche and Metaphor.* Translated by Duncan Large. Stanford, Calif.: Stanford University Press .

Koopmann, Helmut. 1977. "Heines 'Millenium' und Eichendorffs 'alte schöne Zeit': Zur Utopie im frühen 19. Jahrhundert." *Aurora:-Jahrbuch-der-Eichendorff-Gesellschaft* 37: 33–50.

Koselleck, Reinhart. 1990. "Zur anthropologischen und semantischen Struktur der Bildung." In *Bildungsbürgertum im 19. Jahrhundert,* vol. 2, ed. Reinhart Koselleck. Stuttgart: Klett-Cotta.

Krabiel, Klaus-Dieter. 1971. *Joseph von Eichendorff: Kommentierte Studienbibliographie.* Frankfurt a / M: Athenaum.

———. 1973. *Tradition und Bewegung: Zum sprachlichen Verfahren Eichendorffs.* Stuttgart: Kohlhammer.

Kramer, Lawrence. 1990. *Music as Cultural Practice, 1800–1900.* Berkeley: University of California Press.

———. 1995. *Classical Music and Postmodern Knowledge.* Berkeley: University of California Press.

Kramnick, Isaac. 1977. *The Rage of Edmund Burke: Portrait of an Ambivalent Conservative.* New York: Basic Books.

Kramnick, Jonathan. 1990. *Republicanism and Bourgeois Radicalism: Political Ideology in Late Eighteenth-Century England and America.* Ithaca, N.Y.: Cornell University Press.

Kraus, Karl. 1960. "Heine und die Folgen." In *Werke,* vol. 8. Munich: Kösel.

Kristeva, Julia. 1991. *Black Sun: Depression and Melancholia.* New York: Columbia University Press.

Krüger, Peter. 1969. *Eichendorffs politisches Denken.* Würzburg : Eichendorff-Stiftung.

Kulenkampff, Jens. 1978. *Kants Logik des Ästhetischen Urteils.* Frankfurt a / M: Klostermann.

Kurz, Gerhard. 1975. *Mittelbarkeit und Vereinigung: Zum Verhältnis von Poesie, Reflexion und Revolution bei Hölderlin.* Stuttgart: Metzler.

Kurzke, Hermann. 2002. *Thomas Mann: Life as a Work of Art.* Translated by Leslie Willson. Princeton, N.J.: Princeton University Press.

Lacan, Jacques. 1968. *Speech and Language in Psychoanalysis.* Translated and edited by Anthony Wilden. Baltimore: Johns Hopkins University Press.

———. 1975 [1932]. *De la psychose paranoïaque dans ses rapport avec la personalité.* Paris: Seuil.

———. 1977. *Écrits: A Selection.* Translated by Alan Sheridan. New York: Norton.

———. 1981. *Four Fundamental Concepts of Psychoanalysis.* Translated by Alan Sheridan. New York: Norton.

Lacoue-Labarthe, Philippe, and Nancy, Jean-Luc. 1988. *The Literary Absolute: The Theory of Literature in German Romanticism.* Translated by Richard and Cheryl Lester. Albany: State University of New York Press.

Langewiesche, Dieter. 1989. "Bildungsbürgertum und Liberalismus im 19. Jahrhundert." In *Bildungsbürgertum im 19. Jahrhundert,* vol. 4, ed. Jürgen Kocka. Stuttgart: Klett-Cotta.

Larson, Magali S. 1977. *The Rise of Professionalism: A Sociological Analysis.* Berkeley: University of California Press.

Lawrence, Christopher. 1979. "The Nervous System and Society in the Scottish Enlightenment." In *Natural Order: Historical Studies of Scientific Culture,* ed. Barry Barnes and Steven Shapin. Beverly Hills, Calif.: Sage Publications.

Leask, Nigel. 1992. *British Romantic Writers and the East: Anxieties of Empire.* New York: Cambridge University Press.

Lensing, Leo A. 1992. "Heine's Body, Heine's Corpus: Sexuality and Jewish Identity in Karl Kraus's Literary Polemics Against Heinrich Heine." In *The Jewish Reception of Heinrich Heine,* ed. Mark H. Gelber. Tübingen: Niemeyer.

Lepenies, Wolf. 1969. *Melancholie und Gesellschaft.* Frankfurt a / M: Suhrkamp.

———. 1992. *Melancholy and Society.* Translated by Jeremy Gaines and Doris Jones. Cambridge, Mass.: Harvard University Press.

Levine, Michael. 1994. *Writing Through Repression: Literature, Censorship, Psychoanalysis.* Baltimore: Johns Hopkins University Press.

Levinson, Marjorie. 1986. *Wordsworth's Great-Period Poems.* Cambridge: Cambridge University Press.

———. 1988. *Keats's Life of Allegory: The Origins of a Style.* London: Basil Blackwell.

Lewald, Fanny. 1988 [1861–62]. *Meine Lebensgeschichte.* 3 vols. Königstein: Helmer.

———. 1992. *An Autobiography.* Translated and edited by Hanna B. Lewis. Albany: State University of New York Press.

Leys, Ruth. 2000. *Trauma: A Genealogy.* Chicago: University of Chicago Press.

Lieberman, David. 1989. *The Province of Legislation Determined.* New York: Cambridge University Press.

Lingis, Alfonso. 1995. "The World as a Whole." *Research in Phenomenology* 25: 142–59.

Liu, Alan. 1989. "The Power of Formalism: The New Historicism." *English Literary History* 56: 721–71.

———. 1990. "Local Transcendence: Cultural Criticism, Postmodernism, and the Romanticism of Detail." *Representations* 32: 75–113.

———. 2004. *The Laws of Cool : Knowledge Work and the Culture of Information.* Chicago: University of Chicago Press.

Logan, Peter M. 1997. *Nerves and Narratives: A Cultural History of Hysteria in Nineteenth-Century British Prose.* Berkeley: University of California Press.

Lowth, Robert. 1969 [1787]. *Lectures on the Sacred Poetry of the Hebrews.* Translated by G. Gregory. 2 vols. Hildesheim: Olms.

Lukács, Georg. 1971. *Theory of the Novel.* Translated by Anna Bostock. Cambridge, Mass.: MIT Press.

———. 1993. *German Realists in the Nineteenth Century.* Translated by Jeremy Gaines and Paul Keast. Edited by Rodney Livingstone. Cambridge, Mass.: MIT Press.

Mackintosh, James. 1989 [1791]. *Vindiciae Gallicae: A Defence of the French Revolution and Its English Admirers Against the Accusations of the Right Hon. Edmund Burke.* Oxford: Woodstock.

Magill, C. P. 1952. "Young Germany: A Revaluation." In *German Studies: Presented to Leonard Ashley Willoughby by Pupils, Colleagues, and Friends on His Retirement.* Oxford: Blackwell.

Maimon, Salomon. 1967. *An Autobiography.* Edited by Moses Hadas. New York: Schocken Books.

———. 1995 [1792]. *Salomon Maimons Lebensgeschichte.* Edited by Karl Philipp Moritz. Frankfurt a / M: Jüdischer Verlag.

Makdisi, Saree. 1998. *Romantic Imperialism.* New York: Cambridge University Press.

———. 2003. *William Blake and the Impossible History of the 1790s.* Chicago: University of Chicago Press.

Mann, Golo. 1994 [1946]. *Friedrich von Gentz: Gegenspieler Napoleons, Vordenker Europas* Frankfurt a / M: Fischer.

Mann, Thomas. 1981 [1924]. *Der Zauberberg.* Edited by Peter de Mendelssohn. Frankfurt a / M: Fischer.

———. 1986. *An die gesittete Welt: Politische Schriften und Reden im Exil.* Edited by Hanno Helbling. Frankfurt a / M: Fischer.

———. 1996 [1924]. *The Magic Mountain.* Translated by John Woods. New York: Vintage Books.

Mannheim, Karl. 1986. *Conservatism: A Contribution to the Sociology of Knowledge.* Translated by David Kettler and Volker Meja. London: Routledge & Kegan Paul.

Manning, Peter. 1990. *Reading Romantics: Texts and Contexts.* New York: Oxford University Press.

Marshall, Peter H. 1984. *William Godwin.* New Haven, Conn.: Yale University Press.

Marx, Karl. 1990. *Werke.* Edited by Hans-Joachim Lieber and Peter Furth. 6 vols. Darmstadt: Wissenschaftliche Buchgesellschaft.

———. 1998 [1845–46]. *The German Ideology.* Amherst, N.Y.: Prometheus Books.

Matt, Peter von. 1989. "Der irrende Leib: Momente des Unwissens in Eichendorffs Lyrik." *Aurora* 49: 47–57.

———. 1998. *Die verdächtige Pracht: Über Dichter und Gedichte.* Munich: Hanser.

McCarthy, John A., and Werner von der Ohe, eds. 1995. *Zensur und Kultur / Censorship and Culture: Zwischen Klassik und Weimarer Republik mit einem Ausblick bis heute / From Weimar Classicism to Weimar Republic and Beyond.* Tübingen: Niemeyer.

McGann, Jerome. 1988a. *The Beauty of Inflections: Literary Investigations in Historical Method and Theory.* Oxford: Clarendon Press.

———. 1988b. *Social Values and Poetic Acts: The Historical Judgment of Literary Work.* Cambridge, Mass.: Harvard University Press.

———. 1996. *The Poetics of Sensibility: A Revolution in Literary Style.* New York: Oxford University Press.

McKillop, Ian. 1991. "Thomas Erskine (1750–1823): Fighting for Liberty in British Courts." In *1789: The Long and the Short of It,* ed. David Williams. Sheffield: Sheffield Academic Press.

Mee, Jon. 1994. *Dangerous Enthusiasm: William Blake and the Culture of Radicalism in the 1790s.* Oxford: Clarendon.

Melchior, Friedrich, baron von Grimm. 1815. *Historical & Literary Memoirs and Anecdotes, Selected from the Correspondence of Baron de Grimm and Diderot with the Duke of Saxe-Gotha, between the years of 1753 and 1790.* London: H. Colburn.

Mendelssohn, Moses. 1983. *Jerusalem: or Religious Power and Judaism.* Translated by Allan Arkush. Hanover, N.H.: University Press of New England.

Mendes-Flohr, Paul R., and Jehuda Reinharz. 1980. *The Jew in the Modern World.* New York: Oxford University Press.

Menninghaus, Winfried. 1987. *Unendliche Verdopplung.* Frankfurt a / M: Suhrkamp.

Menzel, Wolfgang. 1828. *Die deutsche Literatur.* Stuttgart: Gebrüder Franckh.

———. 1858–59. *Deutsche Dichtung* von der ältesten bis auf die neueste Zeit. Stuttgart: A. Krabbe.

Metzner, Ernst E. 1976. "Trakl, die moderne Lyrik und Eichendorff: Zum Thema Traditionsbestimmtheit im Spätwerk Georg Trakls-Im Hinblick auf unerkannte Eichendorff-Anverwandlung." *Aurora:-Jahrbuch-der-Eichendorff-Gesellschaft* 36: 122–50.

Meyer, Michael A., ed. 1996–98. *German-Jewish History in Modern Times.* 4 vols. New York: Columbia University Press.

Miller, Dan. 1985. "Contrary Revelation: *The Marriage of Heaven and Hell.*" *Studies in Romanticism* 24: 491–509.

Minckwitz, Johannes. 1864. *Der illustrierte neuhochdeutsche Parnaß.* Leipzig: Arnold.

Mitchell, Robert. MS. "Chylopoietic Patriotism: Thomas Trotter on Digestion, National Health and Information Gathering in *A View of the Nervous Temperament.*"

Mitchell, W. J. T. 1986. "*Visible Language:* Blake's Wond'rous Art of Writing." In *Romanticism and Contemporary Theory,* ed. Morris Eaves and Michael Fisher. Ithaca, N.Y.: Cornell University Press.

Molnár, Géza von. 1987. *Romantic Vision, Ethical Context: Novalis and Artistic Autonomy.* Minneapolis: University of Minnesota Press.

More, Hannah. 1995. *Selected Writings of Hannah More.* Edited by Robert Hole. London: Pickering & Chatto.

Moses, Michael Valdez. 1997. "The Irish Vampire: *Dracula,* Parnell, and the Troubled Dreams of Nationhood." *Journal X* 2, 1: 66–111.

Mulhall, Stephen. 1996. "Can There Be an Epistemology of Moods?" In *Verstehen and Humane Understanding,* ed. Anthony O'Hear. Cambridge: Cambridge University Press.

Mullan, John. 1988. *Sentiment and Sociability: The Language of Feeling in the Eighteenth Century.* Oxford: Clarendon Press.

Müller, Adam. 1923 [?]. *Schriften zur Staatsphilosophie.* Edited by Rudolf Kohler. Munich: Theatiner Verlag.

———. 1931 [1809]. *Elemente der Staatskunst.* In *Vom Geiste der Gemeinschaft,* ed. Friedrich Bülow. Leipzig: Kröner

———. 1967. *Kritische/ästhetische und philosophische Schriften.* Edited by Walter Schroeder and Werner Siebert. 2 vols. Neuwied: Luchterhand.

Müller-Sievers, Helmut. 1998. *Self-Generation: Biology, Philosophy, and Literature Around 1800.* Stanford, Calif.: Stanford University Press.

Nägele, Rainer. 1985. *Text, Geschichte, und Subjektivität in Hölderlins Dichtung "Uneßbarer Schrift gleich."* Stuttgart: Metzler.

———. 1987. *Reading after Freud : Essays on Goethe, Hölderlin, Habermas, Nietzsche, Brecht, Celan, and Freud.* New York: Columbia University Press.

Nancy, Jean-Luc. 1991. *The Inoperative Community.* Translated by Peter Connor et al. Minneapolis: University of Minnesota Press.

Nehamas, Alexander. 1985. *Nietzsche: Life as Literature.* Cambridge, Mass.: Harvard University Press.

Newmark, Kevin. 1995. "Traumatic Poetry: Charles Baudelaire and the Shock of Laughter." In *Trauma: Explorations in Memory,* ed. Cathy Caruth. Baltimore: Johns Hopkins University Press.

Nietzsche, Friedrich. 1967. *On the Genealogy of Morals & Ecce Homo.* Translated by Walter Kaufman. New York: Vintage Books.

———. 1979. *Philosophy and Truth: Selections from Nietzsche's Notebooks of the Early 1870's.* Translated and edited by Daniel Breazeale. Atlantic Highlands, N.J.: Humanities Press.

———. 1980. *Sämtliche Werke.* Edited by Giorgio Colli and Mazzino Montinari. 15 vols. Munich: dtv.

———. 1993. *The Birth of Tragedy.* Translated by Shaun Whiteside. Harmondsworth, U.K.: Penguin Books.

———. 1996. *On the Genealogy of Morals.* Translated and edited by Douglas Smith. New York: Oxford University Press.

———. 1998. *Twilight of the Idols, or, How to Philosophize with a Hammer.* Translated by Duncan Large. New York: Oxford University Press.

———. 2002. *Beyond Good and Evil.* Edited by Rolf-Peter Horstmann and Judith Norman. Translated by Judith Norman. Cambridge: Cambridge University Press.

Nipperdey, Thomas. 1994. *Deutsche Geschichte, 1800–1866.* Munich: C. H. Beck.

———. 1996. *German History from Napoleon to Bismarck, 1800–1866.* Translated by Michael Nolan. Princeton, N.J.: Princeton University Press.

Nipperdey, Thomas, and Reinhard Rürup. 1974. "Antisemitismus." In *Geschichtliche Grundbegriffe: Historisches Lexikon zur politisch-sozialen Sprache in Deutschland,* ed. Otto Brunner, Werner Conze, and Reinhart Koselleck. Stuttgart: E. Klett, 1972–92.

Novalis [Friedrich von Hardenberg]. 1978 [*WTB*]. *Werke, Tagebücher und Briefe.* Edited by Hans-Joachim Mähl. 3 vols. Munich: Hanser.

———. 1997. *Fichte-Studies.* In *Theory as Practice,* ed. Jochen Schulte-Sasse. Minneapolis: University of Minnesota Press.

———. 1999. *Philosophical Writings.* Translated and edited by Margaret M. Stoljar. Albany: State University of New York Press.

Nussbaum, Martha C. 2001. *Upheavals of Thought: The Intelligence of Emotions.* New York: Cambridge University Press.

O'Brien, Conor Cruise. 1992. *The Great Melody: A Thematic Biography of Edmund Burke.* Chicago: University of Chicago Press.

O'Brien, William A. 1995. *Novalis: Signs of Revolution.* Durham, N.C.: Duke University Press.

Paine, Thomas. 1976 [1795]. *The Age of Reason.* Cutchogue, N.Y.: Buccaneer Books.

———. 1984 [1791–92] [*RM*]. *The Rights of Man.* Edited by Eric Foner. Harmondsworth, U.K.: Penguin Books.

Parker, Reeve. 1987. "Finishing Off 'Michael': Poetic and Critical Enclosures." *diacritics* 17, 4: 53–65.

Patey, Douglas L. 1984. *Probability and Literary Form.* New York: Cambridge University Press.

Patterson, Annabel. 1993. "For Words Only: From Treason Trial to Liberal Legend in Early Modern England." *Yale Journal of Law & Humanities* 5, 2: 389–416.

Paulson, Ronald. 1988. *Representations of Revolution.* New Haven, Conn.: Yale University Press.

Pausch, Holger A., Boehm, Roland, and Riemer, Waldemar. 1992. "Verdacht und Unbehagen: Die Positionen der Sprache Heinrich Heines. Forschungsbericht." *Heine Jahrbuch* 31: 9–56.

Peterfreund, Stuart. 1998. "Wordsworth on Covenants: 'Heart Conditions,' Primogeniture, Remains, and the Ties that Bind in 'Michael' and Elsewhere." *Criticism* 40, 2: 191–216

Peters, Paul. 1994. "Musik als Interpretation: Zu Robert Schumanns 'Dichterliebe.'" *Heine Jahrbuch* 33: 124–44.

———. 1997. "*Ergriffenheit* and *Kritik:* or, Decolonizing Heine." In *Monatshefte für deutschen Unterricht* 83: 285–306.

Petrey, Sandy. 1990. *Speech Acts and Literary Theory.* New York: Routledge.

Pfau, Thomas. 1987. "Rhetoric and the Existential: Romantic Studies and the Question of the Subject." *Studies in Romanticism* 26: 487–512.

———. 1990. "Immediacy and the Text: Friedrich Schleiermacher's Theory of Style and Interpretation." *Journal of the History of Ideas* 51, 1: 51–73.

———. 1994. "The Pragmatics of Genre: Moral Theory and Lyric Authorship in Hegel and Wordsworth." In *Intellectual Property and the Construction of Authorship*, ed. Peter Jaszi and Martha Woodmansee. Durham, N.C.: Duke University Press.

———. 1995. "Immediacy and Dissolution: Notes on the Languages of Moral Agency and Critical Discourse." In *Intersections: Nineteenth-Century Philosophy and Contemporary Theory*, ed. Tilottama Rajan and David L. Clark. Albany: State University of New York Press.

———. 1997. *Wordsworth's Profession: Form, Class, and the Logic of Early Romantic Cultural Production.* Stanford, Calif.: Stanford University Press.

———. 1998. "Reading Beyond Redemption: Historicism, Irony, and the Lessons of Romanticism." In *Lessons of Romanticism*, ed. Thomas Pfau and Robert F. Gleckner. Durham, N.C.: Duke University Press.

———. 2005a. "From Autonomous Subjects to Self-Regulating Structures: Rationality and Development in German Idealism." In *The Blackwell Companion to Romanticism*, ed. Michael Ferber. New York: Blackwell.

———. 2005b. "Between Sentimentality and Phantasmagoria: German Lyric Poetry, 1830–1890." In *German Literature of the Nineteenth Century, 1832–1899*, ed. Clayton Koelb and Eric Downing. Vol. 9 of the Camden House History of German Literature. Rochester, N.Y.: Camden House.

Pfizer, Gustav. 1997. "Heines Schriften und Tendenz." *Deutsche Vierteljahresschrift* (1838), rept. in Heine, *Sämtliche Schriften*, ed. Klaus Briegleb, 6, pt. 2: 452–66. Munich: dtv.

Pinch, Adela. 1997. *Strange Fits of Passion: Epistemologies of Emotion, Hume to Austen.* Stanford, Calif.: Stanford University Press.

Pinkard, Terry. 2002. *German Philosophy, 1760–1860: The Legacy of Idealism.* Cambridge: Cambridge University Press.

Pippin, Robert. 1999. *Modernism as a Philosophical Problem: On the Dissatisfactions of High European Culture.* 2d ed. New York: Blackwell.

Pocock, J. G. A. 1971. *Politics, Language, and Time.* Chicago: University of Chicago Press.

The Poems of Gray, Collins, and Goldsmith. 1969. Edited by Roger Lonsdale. London: Longmans.

Polanyi, Karl. 1957 [1944]. *The Great Transformation: The Political and Economic Origins of Our Time.* Boston: Beacon Press.

Porter, Roy. 1982. *English Society in the Eighteenth Century.* Harmondsworth, U.K.: Penguin Books.

Pothast, Ulrich. 1971. *Über einige Fragen der Selbstbeziehung.* Frankfurt a / M: Klostermann.

Prawer, S. S. 1980. *Heine's Jewish Comedy.* Oxford: Oxford University Press.

Preisendanz, Wolfgang. 1973. *Heinrich Heine: Werkstrukturen und Epochenbezüge.* Munich: Fink.

Pyle, Forest. 1995. *The Ideology of Imagination: Subject and Society in the Discourse of Romanticism.* Stanford, Calif.: Stanford University Press.

———. 2000. "Making Cyborgs, Making Humans: Of Terminators and Blade Runners." In *The Cybercultures Reader*, ed. David Bell and Barbara Kennedy. New York: Routledge.

Raabe, Paul. 1984. *Bücherlust und Lesefreuden.* Stuttgart: Metzler.

Raddatz, Fritz J. 1997. *Taubenherz und Geierschnabel: Heinrich Heine, Eine Biographie.* Berlin: Beltz Quadriga.

Radlik, Ute. 1970. "Heine in der Zensur der Restaurationsepoche." In *Zur Literatur der Restaurationsepoche,* ed. Jost Hermand and Manfred Windfuhr. Stuttgart: Metzler.

Rajan, Tilottama. 1980. *Dark Interpreter: The Discourse of Romanticism.* Ithaca, N.Y.: Cornell University Press.

———. 1990. *The Supplement of Reading.* Ithaca, N.Y.: Cornell University Press.

———. 1994. "Mary Shelley's *Mathilda:* Melancholy and the Political Economy of Romanticism." *Studies in the Novel* 26, 2: 43–65.

———. 1995. "Phenomenology and Romantic Theory: Hegel and the Subversion of Aesthetics." In *Questioning Romanticism,* ed. John Beer. Baltimore: Johns Hopkins University Press.

———. 1998. "Keats, Poetry, and 'The Absence of the Work.'" *Modern Philology* 95, 3: 334–51.

Rauch, Angelika. 1998. "Post-Traumatic Hermeneutics: Melancholia in the Wake of Trauma." *diacritics* (Winter): 111–20.

———. 2000. *The Hieroglyph of Tradition: Freud, Benjamin, Gadamer, Novalis, Kant.* Madison, N.J.: Fairleigh Dickinson University Press.

Raumer, Friedrich von. 1831. *Briefe aus Paris und Frankreich im Jahre 1830.* Leipzig: F. A. Brockhaus.

Redding, Paul. 1999. *The Logic of Affect.* Ithaca, N.Y.: Cornell University Press.

Redfield, Marc. 1998. "Romanticism, *Bildung,* and the Literary Absolute." In *Lessons of Romanticism,* ed. Thomas Pfau and Robert F. Gleckner. Durham, N.C.: Duke University Press.

Rée, Anton. 1844. *Die Sprachverhältnisse der heutigen Juden.* Hamburg: Gobert.

Reed, T. J. 1991. "History in Nutshells: Heine as a Cartoonist." In *Heinrich Heine and the Occident,* ed. Peter Uwe Hohendahl and Sander L. Gilman. Lincoln: University of Nebraska Press.

Reich-Ranicki, Marcel. 1993. *Über Ruhestörer: Juden in der deutschen Literatur.* Munich: dtv.

Reiman, Donald. 1972. *The Romantics Reviewed: Contemporary Reviews of British Romantic Writers.* 3 vols. in 9. New York: Garland.

Ricardo, David. 1817. *On the Principles of Political Economy and Taxation.* London: J. Murray.

Richarz, Monika, ed. 1976. *Jüdisches Leben in Deutschland: Dokumente zur Sozialgeschichte, 1780–1871.* Frankfurt a / M: dva.

Ricks, Christopher. 1984. *Keats and Embarrassment.* Oxford: Clarendon Press.

Ridley, M. R. 1963 [1933]. *Keats' Craftsmanship: A Study in Poetic Development.* Lincoln: University of Nebraska Press.

Riemen, Alfred. 1973. "Die reaktionären Revolutionäre? oder romantischer Antikapitalismus?" *Aurora:-Jahrbuch-der-Eichendorff-Gesellschaft* 33, 77–86.

Ritter, Joachim, et al., eds. 1971– *Historisches Wörterbuch der Philosophie.* 11 vols. to date. Basel: Schwabe.

Roe, Nicholas. 1997. *John Keats and the Culture of Dissent.* Oxford: Clarendon Press.

Rolleston, James. 1987. *Narratives of Ecstasy.* Detroit: Wayne State University Press.

Rosen, Charles. 1995. *The Romantic Generation.* Cambridge, Mass.: Harvard University Press.

Rosen, Stanley. 1987. *Hermeneutics as Politics.* New York: Cambridge University Press.

Rosenkranz, Karl. 1998 [1844]. *Georg Wilhelm Friedrich Hegels Leben.* Darmstadt: Wissenschaftliche Buchgesellschaft.

Rousseau, Jean-Jacques. 1979 [1782]. *The Reveries of the Solitary Walker.* Translated and edited by Charles Butterworth. New York: Harper.

Rühs, Friedrich Christian. 1816. *Über die Ansprüche der Juden an das deutsche Bürgerrecht.* Berlin.

Sabin, Margery. 1976. *English Romanticism and the French Tradition.* Cambridge, Mass.: Harvard University Press.

Said, Edward. 2002. "Adorno as Lateness Itself." In *Adorno: A Critical Reader,* ed. Nigel Gibson and Andrew Rubin. New York: Blackwell.

Sammons, Jeffrey L. 1969. *Heine: The Elusive Poet.* New Haven, Conn.: Yale University Press.

Santner, Eric. 1996. *My Own Private Germany: Daniel Paul Schreber's Secret History of Modernity.* Princeton, N.J.: Princeton University Press.

Sautermeister, Gert. 1997. "Heinrich Heine: Zur Wahrheit entstellt. Drei Traumgebilde Heines." *Cahiers d'Études germaniques* 33: 87–104.

Schelling, F. W. J. 1969. *Initia Philosophiae Universae.* Edited by Horst Fuhrmans. Bonn: Bouvier.

———. 1966–68 [1856–61]. *Ausgewählte Werke.* 10 vols. Darmstadt: Wissenschaftliche Buchgesellschaft. Reprint, 1976–83.

———. 1994. *Idealism and the Endgame of Theory: Three Essays by F. W. J. Schelling,* Translated and edited by Thomas Pfau. Albany: State University of New York Press.

Schiesari, Juliana. 1992. *The Gendering of Melancholia.* Ithaca, N.Y.: Cornell University Press.

Schiller, Friedrich. 1793. *Über Anmut und Würde. An Carl von Dalberg in Erfurth. . . .* Leipzig.

Schlegel, Friedrich. 1988. *Kritische Schriften und Fragmente.* Edited by Ernst Behler. 6 vols. Paderborn: Schöningh.

———. 1991. *Philosophical Fragments.* Translated by Peter Virchow. Minneapolis: University of Minnesota Press.

Schleiermacher, Friedrich. 1977. *Hermeneutik und Kritik.* Edited by Manfred Frank. Frankfurt a / M: Suhrkamp.

Schmid, Ulrich, ed. 1998. *Zwischen Restauration und Revolution, 1815–1848.* Vol. 5 of *Hansers Sozialgeschichte der deutschen Literatur.* Munich: Carl Hanser.

Schmitt, Cannon. 1997. *Alien Nation: Nineteenth-Century Gothic Fictions and English Nationality* Philadelphia: University of Pennsylvania Press.

Schmitt, Carl. 1986 [1919]. *Political Romanticism.* Translated by Guy Oakes. Minneapolis: University of Minnesota Press.

Schnell, Ralf. 1992. "Heines poetische Theodizee." In *Metamorphosen des Dichters: Das Rollenverständnis deutscher Schriftsteller vom Barock bis zur Gegenwart,* ed. Günter E. Grimm. Frankfurt a / M: Fischer.

Schoenfield, Mark. 1996. *The Professional Wordsworth.* Athens: University of Georgia Press.

Schopenhauer, Arthur. 1969 [1819]. *The World as Will and Representation.* Translated by E. F. J. Payne. New York: Dover.
———. 1989 [1819]. *Die Welt als Wille und Vorstellung.* Darmstadt: Wissenschaftliche Buchgesellschaft.
Schor, Esther. 1994. *Bearing the Dead: The British Culture of Mourning from the Enlightenment to Victoria.* Princeton, N.J.: Princeton University Press.
Schor, Naomi. 1987. *Reading in Detail: Aesthetics and the Feminine.* New York: Routledge.
Schulte-Sasse, Jochen, ed. 1997. *Theory as Practice.* Minneapolis: University of Minnesota Press.
Schumannn, Robert. 1971. *Tagebücher.* Edited by Georg Eismann. 4 books in 3 vols. Frankfurt a / M: Roter Stern.
———. 1984–2001. *Clara und Robert Schumann: Briefwechsel.* Edited by Eva Weissweiler. 3 vols. Frankfurt a / M: Stroemfeld / Roter Stern
———. 1985 [1854]. *Gesammelte Schriften über Musik und Musiker.* Wiesbaden: Breitkopf & Härtel.
Schutjer, Karin. 2001. *Narrative Community after Kant: Schiler, Goethe, and Hölderlin.* Detroit: Wayne State University Press.
Schwarz, Egon. 1972. *Joseph von Eichendorff.* New York: Twayne.
Sedgwick, Eve Kosofsky. 19997. "Paranoid Reading and Reparative Reading; or, You're So Paranoid, You Probably Think this Introduction is About You." In *Novel Gazing: Queer Readings in Fiction,* ed. id. Durham, N.C.: Duke University Press.
Seidlin, Oskar. 1966. "Eichendorffs Symbolische Landschaft." In *Eichendorff Heute,* ed. Paul Stöcklein. Darmstadt: Wissenschaftliche Buchgesellschaft.
Sengle, Friedrich. 1971–83. *Biedermeierzeit: Deutsche Literatur im Spannungsfeld zwischen Restauration u. Revolution, 1815–1848.* 3 vols. Stuttgart: Metzler.
Seyhan, Azade. 1992. *Representation and Its Discontents: The Critical Legacy of German Romanticism.* Berkeley: University of California Press.
Shedletzky, Ida. 1988. "Zwischen Stolz und Abneigung: Zur Heine-Rezeption in der deutsch-jüdischen Literaturkritik." In *Conditio Judaica,* ed. Hans Otto Horch and Horst Denkler, 1: 201–13. Tübingen: Niemeyer.
Sheehan, James. 1989. *German History, 1770–1866.* Oxford: Clarendon Press.
Shelley, Percy Bysshe. 1977. *Complete Poetry and Prose.* Edited by Donald Reiman and Sharon B. Powers. New York: Norton.
Siemann, Wolfram. 1987. 'Ideenschmuggel: Probleme der Meinungskontrolle und das Los Deutscher Zensoren im 19. Jahrhundert." *Historische Zeitschrift* 245, 1: 71–106.
Simpson, David. 1987. *Wordsworth's Historical Imagination.* New York: Methuen.
———. 1993. *Romanticism, Nationalism, and the Revolt Against Theory.* Chicago: University of Chicago Press.
———. 1995. *The Academic Postmodern: A Report on Half-Knowledge.* Chicago: University of Chicago Press.
Siskin, Clifford. 1998. *The Work of Writing.* Baltimore: Johns Hopkins University Press.
Skolnik, Jonathan. 2004. "Heine and Haggadah: History, Narration, and Tradition in the Age of *Wissenschaft des Judentums.*" In *Renewing the Past, Reconfiguring Jewish Culture: From Al-Andalus to the Haskalah,* ed. Ross Brann and Adam Sutcliffe. Philadelphia: University of Pennsylvania Press.

Smith, Adam. 1976 [1776]. *An Inquiry into the Nature and Causes of the Wealth of Nations.* Edited by Edwin Cannan. Chicago: University of Chicago Press. Cannan's 1904 edition reissued, with 2 vols. in 1.

———. 1983 [1762–63]. *Lectures on Rhetoric and Belles Lettres.* Edited by J. C. Bryce. New York: Oxford University Press.

———. 1984 [1759]. *The Theory of Moral Sentiments.* Edited by D. D. Raphael and A. L. Macfie. Indianapolis: Liberty Classics.

Smith, Barbara Herrnstein. 1991. "Belief and Resistance: A Symmetrical Account." *Critical Inquiry* 18, 1: 125–39.

Smith, John. 1988. *The Spirit and Its Letter.* Ithaca, N.Y.: Cornell University Press.

Smith, Olivia. 1984. *The Politics of Language, 1791–1819.* Oxford: Oxford University Press.

Smith, Paul. *Discerning the Subject* (Minneapolis: University of Minnesota Press, 1988).

Sperry, Stuart. 1973. *Keats the Poet.* Princeton, N.J.: Princeton University Press.

Staten, Henry. 1990. *Nietzsche's Voice.* Ithaca, N.Y.: Cornell University Press.

Stein, Edwin. 1988. *Wordsworth's Art of Allusion.* University Park, Pa.: Pennsylvania State University Press.

Stein, Karl, Freiherr vom und zum. 1955. *Ausgewählte politische Briefe und Denkschriften.* Edited by Erich Botzenhart and Gunther Ipsen. Stuttgart: W. Kohlhammer.

———. 1957–74. *Briefe und Sämtliche Schriften.* Edited by Erich Botzenhart and Walter Hubatsch. Stuttgart: W. Kohlhammer.

Steinecke, Hartmut. 1988. "Gutzkow, die Juden und das Judentum." In *Conditio Judaica,* ed. Hans Otto Horch and Horst Denkler, 2: 118–29. Tübingen: Niemeyer.

Stendhal. 2002 [1830]. *The Red and the Black.* Translated by Roger Gard. Harmondsworth, U.K.: Penguin Books.

Stern, Selma. 1962–75. *Der Preußische Staat und die Juden.* 7 vols. Tübingen: Niemeyer.

Stewart, Garrett. 2001. "Keats and Language." In *The Cambridge Companion to Keats,* ed. Susan Wolfson. New York: Cambridge University Press.

Stewart, Susan. 1991. *Crimes of Writing.* Durham, N.C.: Duke University Press.

Stöcklein, Paul, ed. 1966. *Eichendorff Heute.* Darmstadt: Wissenschaftliche Buchgesellschaft.

Stutzer, Dietmar. 1974. *Die Güter der Herren in Oberschlesien und Mähren von Eichendorff.* Würzburg: Eichendorff.

Suleri, Sara. 1992. *The Rhetoric of English India.* Chicago: University of Chicago Press.

Sweet, Paul R. 1941. *Friedrich von Gentz: Defender of the Old Order.* Madison: University of Wisconsin Press.

Synagogues in Nineteenth-Century Germany. 1982. Tel Aviv: Beth hatefutsoth.

Szondi, Peter. 1978. *Hölderlin Studien.* In *Schriften,* vol. 1. Frankfurt a / M: Suhrkamp.

Tannenbaum, Leslie. 1982. *Biblical Tradition in Blake's Early Prophecies.* Princeton, N.J.: Princeton University Press.

Taylor, Charles. 1989. *Sources of the Self: The Making of the Modern Identity.* Cambridge, Mass.: Harvard University Press.

Terada, Rei. 2001. *Feeling in Theory: Emotion after the Death of the Subject.* Cambridge, Mass.: Harvard University Press.

Thale, Mary. 1983. *Selections from the Papers of the London Corresponding Society.* Cambridge: Cambridge University Press.

Thelwall, John. 1995. *The Politics of Jacobinism: Writings of John Thelwall.* Edited by Gregory Claeys. University Park, Pa.: Pennsylvania State University Press.

Thielen, Peter Gerrit. 1967. *Karl August von Hardenberg, 1750–1822. Eine Biographie.* Berlin: Grote.

Thompson, E. P. 1966. *The Making of the English Working Class.* New York: Vintage Books.

Thum, Reinhard H. 1983. "Cliché and Stereotype: An Examination of the Lyric Landscape in Eichendorff's Poetry." *Philological Quarterly* 62, 4: 435–57.

Todd, R. Larry, ed. 1994. *Schumann and His World.* Princeton, N.J.: Princeton University Press.

Toury, Jacob. 1982. "Die Sprache als Problem der Jüdischen Einordnung im Deutschen Kulturraum." In *Gegenseitige Einflüsse Deutscher und Jüdischer Kultur,* ed. Walter Grab. Tel Aviv: University of Tel Aviv.

Treitschke, Heinrich von. 1919 [1874–94]. *Deutsche Geschichte im Neunzehnten Jahrhundert.* 7th ed. Leipzig: Hirzel.

Trilling, Lionel. 2000. *The Moral Obligation to Be Intelligent: Selected Essays.* Edited by Leon Wieseltier. New York: Farrar, Straus, Giroux.

Trotter, David. 2001. *Paranoid Modernism: Literary Experiment, Psychosis, and the Professionalization of English Society.* Oxford: Clarendon Press.

Trumpener, Katie. 1997. *Bardic Nationalism: The Romantic Novel and the British Empire.* Princeton: Princeton University Press.

Varnhagen, Rahel (née Levin). 1983. *Rahel-Bibliothek,* ed. Konrad Feilchenfeldt. 10 vols. Munich: Matthes & Seitz.

Veit, Philipp F. 1976. "Fichtenbaum und Palme" *Germanic Review* 51, 1: 13–27.

Vendler, Helen. 1983. *The Odes of John Keats.* Cambridge, Mass.: Harvard University Press.

Viscomi, Joseph.1993. *Blake and the Idea of the Book.* Princeton, N.J.: Princeton University Press.

Viswanathan, Gauri. 1989. *Masks of Conquest: Literary Study and British Rule in India.* New York : Columbia University Press.

Vortriede, Werner, in collaboration with Uwe Schweikert. 1970. *Heine-Kommentar.* Munich: Winkler.

Wagner, Martina. 1983. "'Ein Traum, gar seltsam schauerlich . . . ': Heines Traumbilder als Medium poetischer Selbstreflexion." *Heine Jahrbuch* 22: 179–87.

Wagner-Egelhaaf, Martina. 1991. *Die Melancholie der Literatur.* Stuttgart: Metzler.

Wassermann, Jakob. 1994. *Mein Weg als Deutscher und Jude.* Munich: dtv.

Weber, Max. 1958. *The Protestant Ethic and the Spirit of Capitalism.* Translated by Talcott Parsons. New York: Scribner.

Wehler, Hans-Ulrich. 1996. *Deutsche Gesellschaftsgeschichte, 1815–1845/49.* Munich: C. H. Beck.

Weiskel, Thomas. 1976. *The Romantic Sublime.* Baltimore: Johns Hopkins University Press.

Weiss, Peter. 1968. *Rapporte.* Frankfurt a / M: Suhrkamp.

Wellbery, David E. 1996. *The Specular Moment: Goethe's Early Lyric and the Beginnings of Romanticism.* Stanford, Calif.: Stanford University Press.

———. 1998. "Verzauberung: Das Simulakrum in der romantischen Lyrik." In *Mimesis und Simulation,* ed. Andreas Kablitz and Gerhard Neumann. Freiburg: Rombach.

———. 2003. "Stimmung." In *Ästhetische Grundbegriffe,* vol. 3, ed. Karlheinz Barck, Martin Fontius, Dieter Schlenstedt, Burkhart Steinwachs, and Friedrich Wolfzettel. Stuttgart: Metzler.

Welsh, Alexander. 1992. *Strong Representations: Narrative and Circumstantial Evidence in England.* Baltimore: Johns Hopkins University Press.

Werner, Michael, ed. 1973. *Begegnungen mit Heine: Berichte der Zeitgenossen.* Hamburg: Hoffmann & Campe.

Williams, Raymond. 1977. *Marxism and Literature.* New York: Oxford University Press.

Williamson, George S. 2004. *The Longing for Myth in Germany: Religion and Aesthetic Culture from Romanticism to Nietzsche.* Chicago: University of Chicago Press.

Windfuhr, Manfred. 1970. "Heinrich Heines Modernität." In *Zur Literatur der Restaurationsepoche,* ed. Jost Hermand and Manfred Windfuhr. Stuttgart: Metzler.

Winkler, Markus. 1997. *Heinrich Heine und die Romantik.* Tübingen: Niemeyer.

Wittgenstein, Ludwig. 1997. *Philosophical Investigations.* Translated by G. E. M. Anscombe. Oxford: Blackwell.

Wolfram Siemann. 1995. *Vom Staatenbund zum Nationalstaat: Deutschland, 1806–1871.* Munich: C. H. Beck.

Wolfson, Susan, ed. 2001. *The Cambridge Companion to Keats.* Cambridge: Cambridge University Press.

Wollstonecraft, Mary. 1960 [1790]. *Vindication of the Rights of Men.* Gainesville, Fla.: Scholars Press.

———. *Vindication of the Rights of Woman.* 1992 [1792]. Edited by Miriam Brody. Harmondsworth, U.K.: Penguin Books.

Wood, Gordon S. "Conspiracy and the Paranoid Style: Causality and Deceit in Eighteenth-Century England." 1982. *William & Mary Quarterly* 39: 401–42.

Wood, Marcus. 1994. *Radical Satire and Print Culture, 1790–1822.* Oxford: Clarendon Press.

Wordsworth, William. 1967. *The Letters of William and Dorothy Wordsworth: The Early Years, 1787–1806.* Edited by Ernest De Selincourt and Chester L. Shaver. Oxford: Oxford University Press, 1967.

———. 1983. *Poems in Two Volumes.* Edited by Jared Curtis. Ithaca, N.Y.: Cornell University Press.

———. 1984. *Letters of William Wordsworth.* Edited by Alan G. Hill. Oxford: Clarendon Press.

———. 1989. *Shorter Poems, 1807–1820.* Edited by Karl Ketcham. Ithaca, N.Y.: Cornell University Press.

———. 1992a. *Lyrical Ballads and Other Poems, 1797–1800.* Edited by James Butler and Karen Green. Ithaca, N.Y.: Cornell University Press, 1992.

———. 1992b. *The Thirteen-Book Prelude.* Edited by Mark Reed. 2 vols. Ithaca, N.Y.: Cornell University Press.

Wulf, Josef. 1963. *Literatur und Dichtung im Dritten Reich.* Gütersloh: Mohn.

Youens, Susan. 1996. *Schubert's Poets and the Making of Lieder.* New York: Cambridge University Press.

Young, Arthur. 1798. *An Enquiry into the State of the Public Mind Amongst the Lower Classes and on the Means of Turning It to the Welfare of the State.* Dublin: Milliken.

Zagari, Luciano, and Paolo Chiarini, eds. 1981. *Zu Heinrich Heine.* Stuttgart: Klett.

Ziarek, Krzysztof. 2002. "The Turn of Art: The Avant-Garde and Power." *New Literary History* 33, 1: 89–107.
Zimmermann, Johann Georg. 1784–85. *Über die Einsamkeit.* 4 vols. Leipzig.
Ziolkowski, Theodor. 1990. *German Romanticism and Its Institutions.* Princeton, N.J.: Princeton University Press.
Žižek, Slavoj. 1989. *The Sublime Object of Ideology.* New York: Verso.
———. 1993. *Tarrying with the Negative: Kant, Hegel, and the Critique of Ideology.* Durham, N.C.: Duke University Press .
———. 1997. *The Plague of Fantasies.* New York: Verso.
Zunz, Leopold. 1976 [1875–76]. *Gesammelte Schriften.* 3 vols. Hildesheim: G. Olms.

Index